The Form Book

Borries Schwesinger

The Form Book

Creating Forms for Printed and Online Use

Contents

What’s in a form?

Nur mit Tinte und lesbar ausfüllen!

Zur Zeit ausgeübte Tätigkeit	Serienzeichen und Nummer des DPA (gedruckte Nr.)	Staatsangehörigkeit	Ständige Wohnanschrift und der Ort des besuchsweisen Zwischenaufenthaltes
Dreher	*E 0201000*	*Deutsch*	*Weimar, Stalinstr. 10*
			Zwischenaufenthalt vom 3. 1. 53 – 7. 1. 53, Halle, Luisenstr. 26 bei Schulze
Stenotypistin	*D 0103223*	*Deutsch*	*Halle, Lindenstr. 24*
[illegible]	C 0611199	deutsch	Eichwalde Krs. Teltow, Schillerstr. 2
—	C 0611221	deutsch	Dresden A 52, Königsbrücker Str. 5
[illegible]	C 0611199	deutsch	Eichwalde Krs. Teltow, Schillerstr. 2
[illegible]	HE – 466 / 5982	deutsch	[illegible] Marktstr. [illegible]
Kaufmann	[illegible] 376470	Jugoslawe	Beograd – [illegible]
		India	New Delhi, India, 31, Sunder Nag[illegible]
[illegible]	HE – 466 5982	deutsch	Frankfurt, Hamburger Allee 46
Schlosser	275015	deutsch	Frankfurt, Ederstr. 12
[illegible]	HE – 7/ 375687	deutsch	Frankfurt, Hamburger Allee 46
Angestellter	BW 112 – 15295	deutsch	Frankfurt Ederstr. 12
Kaufmann	4815421	deutsch	[illegible], [illegible] 65
Kaufmann	B 3638034	deutsch	Erkelenz, Krs. Erkelenz
Kr. - [illegible]	B 1795997	deutsch	Markobel/Hanau
Hausfrau	B 1795997	deutsch	Markobel, Hanau
Kaufmann	B 3638034	deutsch	Erkelenz / Krs Erkelenz
Kaufmann	B 3638034	deutsch	Erkelenz Krs Erkelenz

Forms are a kind of silent dialogue. The form asks questions, and the person who completes it answers them.

What can be said is determined by the form, and what remains unsaid is determined by the person providing the answers. The completed form tells a story that has to be deciphered. The task of filling in the gaps is left to the imagination of the reader.

Visitor's book, German Democratic Republic, 1953.
In the former East Germany, all households were obliged to keep an official record of the names, addresses, pass numbers and nationalities of any visitors.

Form 2203

U. S. DEPARTMENT OF LABOR

NATURALIZATION SERVICE

TRIPLICATE
[To be given to the person making the Declaration.]

No. 3763
6452

UNITED STATES OF AMERICA

DECLARATION OF INTENTION

☞ Invalid for all purposes seven years after the date hereof

State of Michigan } ss: In the Circuit Court
County of Saginaw } of Saginaw County, Michigan

I, Carl Schwesinger, aged 22 years, occupation clerk, do declare on oath that my personal description is: Color white, complexion fair, height 5 feet 7 inches, weight 133 pounds, color of hair brown, color of eyes blue other visible distinctive marks none

I was born in Kammerberg, Germany on the 8th day of June, anno Domini 1903; I now reside at 1912 Ames Street, Saginaw, Michigan
(Give number, street, city or town, and State.)

I emigrated to the United States of America from Bremen, Germany on the vessel Columbus
(If the alien arrived otherwise than by vessel, the character of conveyance or name of transportation company should be given)
; my last foreign residence was Germany; I am not married; ~~the name of my wife/husband is ______; she/he was born at ______ and now resides at ______~~

It is my bona fide intention to renounce forever all allegiance and fidelity to any foreign prince, potentate, state, or sovereignty, and particularly to The German Empire, of whom I am now a subject; I arrived at the port of New York, in the State of New York, on or about the 7th day of December, anno Domini 1925; I am not an anarchist; I am not a polygamist nor a believer in the practice of polygamy; and it is my intention in good faith to become a citizen of the United States of America and to permanently reside therein: SO HELP ME GOD.

Carl Schwesinger
(Original signature of declarant)

Subscribed and sworn to before me in the office of the Clerk of said Court this 8th day of May, anno Domini 1926

Edward P. Roeser

Clerk of the Circuit Court.

By Edward P. Roeser, Deputy Clerk.

GOVERNMENT PRINTING OFFICE

14—1170

Forms are true witnesses to their time. Filling in a form changes this commonplace medium into a unique document – proof of a person's existence. The marks that people make in the world can be seen in the forms that they fill in, and their individuality may be revealed through the medium of their handwriting or hidden behind the anonymous letters of the keyboard.

Declaration by an immigrant to the USA, 1925

Todesbescheinigung

– Nicht-vertraulicher Teil–

☒ Zutreffendes ankreuzen!

Personalangaben

Name, ggf. Geburtsname, Vorname	Wird vom Standesamt ausgefüllt	Standesamt
Straße, Hausnummer		Sterbefall beurkundet, Sterbebuch-Nr.:
PLZ, Wohnort, Kreis		Eintragung vorgemerkt, Vormerkliste-Nr.:

Geburtsdatum Tag ☐ Monat ☐ Jahr ☐	Geburtsort
Sterbezeitpunkt, ggf. Datum der Leichenauffindung	Geschlecht: ☐ männlich ☐ weiblich

Identifikation

☐ Aufgrund eigener Kenntnis ☐ Nach Einsicht in den Personalausweis / Reisepaß ☐ Nach Angaben von Angehörigen / Dritten ☐ nicht möglich

Ort und Zeitpunkt des Todes

☐ Sterbeort ☐ Auffindungsort falls nicht Sterbeort	Straße, Hausnummer (Name des Krankenhauses o.ä.) PLZ, Ort, Kreis

Sterbe-zeitpunkt	Tag ☐ Monat ☐ Jahr ☐ Uhrzeit Stunden ☐ Minuten ☐	☐ Nach eigenen Feststellungen ☐ Nach Angaben von Angehörigen/ Dritten
Falls Sterbezeitpunkt unbekannt bzw. tot aufgefunden	Zeitpunkt der Leichenauffindung Tag ☐ Monat ☐ Jahr ☐ Uhrzeit Stunden ☐ Minuten ☐	

Warnhinweise

☐ Herzschrittmacher

☐ Infektionsgefahr (z.B. Meldepflichtige Erkrankung gem. § 3 BSeuchG)

☐ Sonstiges (z.B. Tatbestand gem. § 16 e ChemG)

Anhaltspunkte für einen nicht-natürlichen Tod

☐ Ja, und zwar ☐ Todesart ungeklärt

Zusatzangaben bei Totgeborenen

Totgeborene oder in der Geburt gestorbene Leibesfrüchte von mindestens 1000 g

☐ Als tote Leibesfrucht geboren ☐ In der Geburt verstorben Gewicht der Leibesfrucht ☐ g

Ärztliche Bescheinigung

Aufgrund der von mir sorgfältig und an der unbekleideten Leiche durchgeführten Untersuchungen bescheinige ich hiermit den Tod und die oben genannten Angaben.

Ort, Datum und Zeitpunkt der Leichenschau	Name, Vorname, Anschrift, Unterschrift und Stempel der Ärztin/ des Arztes

Formularsatz 0A 1203 (99)
DRUCKHAUS PANZIG Studentenberg 1a 17489 Greifswald Tel. (0 38 34) 59 52 40 Fax (0 38 34) 59 52 59

Forms are based on the assumption that they are absolutely necessary. It would contradict the whole concept of the form if the same end could be achieved by filling in a different form or even doing without one altogether. There is nothing vague and there are no maybes. Only yes or no, valid or invalid, true or false. And yet many forms appear to be interchangeable and arbitrary both in their design and in the information they request.

Official coroner's form, required for a death certificate, Germany, 1999

35
delsregister BZ
RICEVUTA FISCALE
ZAHLUNGSBELEG

EURO

. 40

3.70

ettivo Pagato / Bezahlt
Non pagato / Nicht bezahlt
trag (IVA inkl.)
cumento ((IVA incl.)
7.10

Tel.0473/233999

41074 /04

Tip. Pieragnolo Guido - 35143 Padova - Via Montericco, 31 - Aut. Min. 365107 Div. XIII del 17-10-79

h the current list of eligible countries.

APITAL LETTERS. USE ENGLISH

lete both the Arrival Record, items 1 tems 14 through 17. The reverse side hildren under the age of fourteen must rdian.

States by land, enter LAND in this ates by ship, enter SEA in this space.

rd

3. Birth Date (day/mo/yr)

5. Sex (male or female)

e and Flight Number

Where you boarded

Insel
KiWi
Knaur
Luchterh
Lübbe
Moewig
Piper
Ravensb. Tabü
Reclam
rororo
romo
ro thr
Rotbuch
rotfuchs
Scherz
Suhrk. Tabü
Suhrk. Wissen
Ullstein
UTB
Wa.T

m:

Name

ร กรุงเทพฯ 10120 เลขประจำตัวผู้เสียภาษีอากร 3 101 08
มทรัพย์ AVINGS
ประจำ FIXED

USÄTZLICHER SERVICE / SERVICES
/ Livraison à domicile
cilio
Telephone notification / Telefonische Benachrichtigur
Avis téléphonique / Avviso telefonico / Aviso telefónic

weis? Yes / Ja No / Nein
'identité valide? Oui / Non
do? Sì / No
Sí / No

If no ID, please provide a test question and answer (maximum 4
Wenn der Empfänger keinen Identitätsnachweis erbringen kann
Si aucune pièce d'identité n'est disponible, veuillez fournir une
Se il destinatario non è in grado di esibire un documento che atte
Si no tiene identificación, sírvase proporcionar una pregunta y
Answer / Antwort
Réponse / Risposta

ERN UNION AND ITS AGENTS ALSO MAKE MONEY FROM THE EXCHANGE OF CURRENCIES. BY SI
TERN UNION UND IHRE AGENTEN AUCH GEWINNE AUS DER UMRECHNUNG FREMDER WÄHRUN
TEN BEDINGUNGEN./ OUTRE LES FRAIS DE TRANSFERT, WESTERN UNION ET SES AGENTS PEUV
ENTIONNÉES AU DOS DE CE FORMULAIRE./ OLTRE ALLE COMMISSIONI DEL TRASFERIMENTO, L
ACCETTO LE CONDIZIONI MENZIONATE SUL RETRO DI QUESTO FORMULARIO./ APARTE DE LOS
ES DE LA CONVERSIÓN DE MONEDAS. FIRMANDO LA PRESENTE DECLARO ACEPTAR LAS COND

FESTSTELLEN DES WIRTSCHAFTLICH BE

zahlungsschein

zahlter Betrag

Landesha
Bezirkska

Euro 8, Cent –
€-Betrag in Buchstaben (ab 1.000 €)

Kapitel 35 11
Titel 11152
Unterkonto

bsender
ostleitzahl

Postanweisung

I II III IV M

Documents
DVD
Calendar

Non-insured
Non-assuré

with ball point pen
CUSTOMER: Before completing read
43-074-172 (04-02)

Gift / Cadeau
Sample / Échantillon
Docum

Signature of Sender
Signature de l'expéditeur

Sender warrants that this item does not contain dangerous goods.
This shipping label is to be used to participating countries only.
See additional Terms and Conditions on reverse side

Customs Declara

Beha
Deuts
Niederla

Deutsche Po
Entreprise de

– AR-Rückschein / Avis de réception / Advice of delivery –

A

915-005-000

POSTO 021
N. RIFERIMENTO
TRENO 114
DATA 2808
CARR. 319
DESTIN
830488460115 VENEZIA-BELLINZ

ich: nein 1 47 ja

Ergebnis
Verd. nicht bestät.
Diagno nicht ab schloss

itales 2 49 | 8 49 | 9 49
2 51 | 8 51 | 9
2 3 4 5 53 | 8 53
10 mm)
10 mm)
2 3 55 | 8 55

Grund:

RIFFRA
19.11.
Wal
resfes
493 235 2
Inkl. 2,4

kons
Warenha
Klement-G
Kassenplatz-Nr.
Abteilung
Menge
Schlüssel-Nr.
Artikel-Bezeichnung

13บาท
2834

เล่มที่ BOOK NO
NON REFUNDABLE
เลขที่ NO
ใบเสร็จรับเงิน
วันที่ DATE
No.
2006

ge für Geschäftslokale

Nr.:
PLZ:

GÜLTIG: 30.05.07
BRIENZ
ZÜRICH HB
VIA BRÜNIG-LUZERN

Many forms are monotonous, their design banal, and their content obscure. But their quantity and ubiquity has led to an impressive variety: not only are there an infinite number of forms, but the same problems – such as the design of checkboxes and text fields – are constantly being resolved in new ways.

A selection of forms, 2007

年　　　　月　　　　日
Y　　　　M　　　　D

おところ
ADDRESS

ふりがな
おなまえ　　　　　　　　　　　　　　　　　　　様
NAME

おでんわ　　　　（　　　　　　　）
TELEPHONE

品名 ITEM	色 COLOUR	数量 QT'Y	金額 AMOUNT
	税込合計金額 TOTAL AMOUNT		
	お預り金額 PAID		
	差引合計 BALANCE		
	代金 PAYMENT		

お渡し予定日 WILL BE READY : 年 Y 月 M 日 D	ご来店・配送 AT SHOP DELIVERY

Minimalism or excess?

Many forms do away with superfluous content and extraneous design features. Their typography is economical, their graphics minimal, and their paper thin. The form is determined by its function and nothing is without a purpose. The content may be stylized, but it is not stylish. Other forms are overflowing with boxes and lines, and awash with graphic patterns and endless lists.

Textile store receipt, Japan, 2007

AOK | LKK | BKK | IKK | VdAK | AEV | Knappschaft

TKK Berlin-City Gst. 996

Name, Vorname des Versicherten

20.09. geb. am

Invaliedenstr. 10
DE 10115 Berlin

Kassen-Nr.	Versicherten-Nr.		Status
0177	2009808	100	9

Vertragsarzt-Nr.	VK gültig bis	Datum
72742	09/10	22.10.05

CHARITÉ UNIVERSITÄTSMEDIZIN BERLIN

Campus CCM ■ KV-Nr. 72 74203
Schumannstr. 20/21, 10117 Berlin
Telefon 45 05-0

Campus CVK ■ KV-Nr. 72 74102
Augustenburger Platz 1, 13353 Berlin
Telefon 45 05-0

Fall-Nr. 301514756-0

Beh. OE MAN-EH

Behandlungstag, -Uhrzeit 22.10.2005 19:27

Angehörige im Warteraum ■ ja ■ nein

TelPat:28099

Erste Hilfe Nr.

Transportart Z ..... Entlasszeit ..... Transportart A

ggf. Hauptversicherter Familienname s.o. Vorname ..... Geburtstag
Wohnort ..... Straße, Nr. ..... Tel.-Nr.

ggf. Kostenträger/Arbeitgeber

AUG	CHIR	DERMA	GYN	HNO	INN	KK-CHIR	KK-INN	MKG	NC	NL	ORTHO	PHYSIO	PSYCH	UNF	URO

Vorgeschichte (bzw. Unfallhergang)

Ohrenschmerz seit 3 Tagen
Flug am 20.10.05; dabei initial
starker Druck & Schmerz li.

Befund

Ø Otorrhoe; Ø Schwindel
I) TF [illegible] opB; Ø SPN [illegible]
II) [illegible]; [illegible] dto; [illegible]
III) [illegible]
V) [illegible]

Letzte Medikamente

RR ■ EKG
Puls ■ Sono
Temp ■ Röntgen

Quick	Hb	CK	BZ
PTT	HK	CKMB	Kreat
Blutgruppe	Leuko	Myo	Hst
Kreuztest	Thromb	Na	GOT
Urinstatus	CRP	K	Lipase
			Troponin

Diagnose (bitte Druckschrift)

Anschoppungs OMA
Tubenkatarrh

Therapie

Abschwellende NT, mehrmals täglich
Valsalva-Manöver (Tubentraining)

Tetanus: ■ ja

10 Euro per Ü.

■ ärztliche Weiterbehandlung empfohlen

Berlin, den 22.10.05 Name des Arztes (in Druckbuchstaben) + Unterschrift [illegible]

■ Frau ■ Herr

Weiterbehandlung durch
HNO - FA

..... zur Kenntnis

Mat.-Nr. 204703

Für den behandelnden Arzt

Unfilled forms are dominated by empty space. They are virginal and at the same time provocative. Only by being filled in can they take on a meaning and come to life. On a completed form, there is a contrast between dynamic handwriting and static print.

First aid treatment record, Germany, 2005

**Ein-
lieferungs-
schein**

Zum Aufkleben des Nummernzettels

Bitte sorgfältig aufbewahren

Absender:

Gebühr (Pf)

Ve…

W…

Wert (in Ziffern) DM

Entrichtete Gebühr Pf

Empfänger:

Gewicht (kg)

(Postleitzahl, Bestimmungsort)

Post…

Gewicht bei Wertpaketen kg g

Postannahme:

........8.64. DIN A6, Kl. XIf

+ P 5, PostO Anl. 12

The concept of a form promises clarity, direction and security. Everything is meant to fit into a rigid hierarchy, regulated by straight lines, and every piece of information should have its own place. There should be no overlaps, no clashes, nothing but straightforward two-dimensionality. In actual fact, however, forms are often hotbeds of chaos and confusion.

Parcel label from the German postal service, 1964

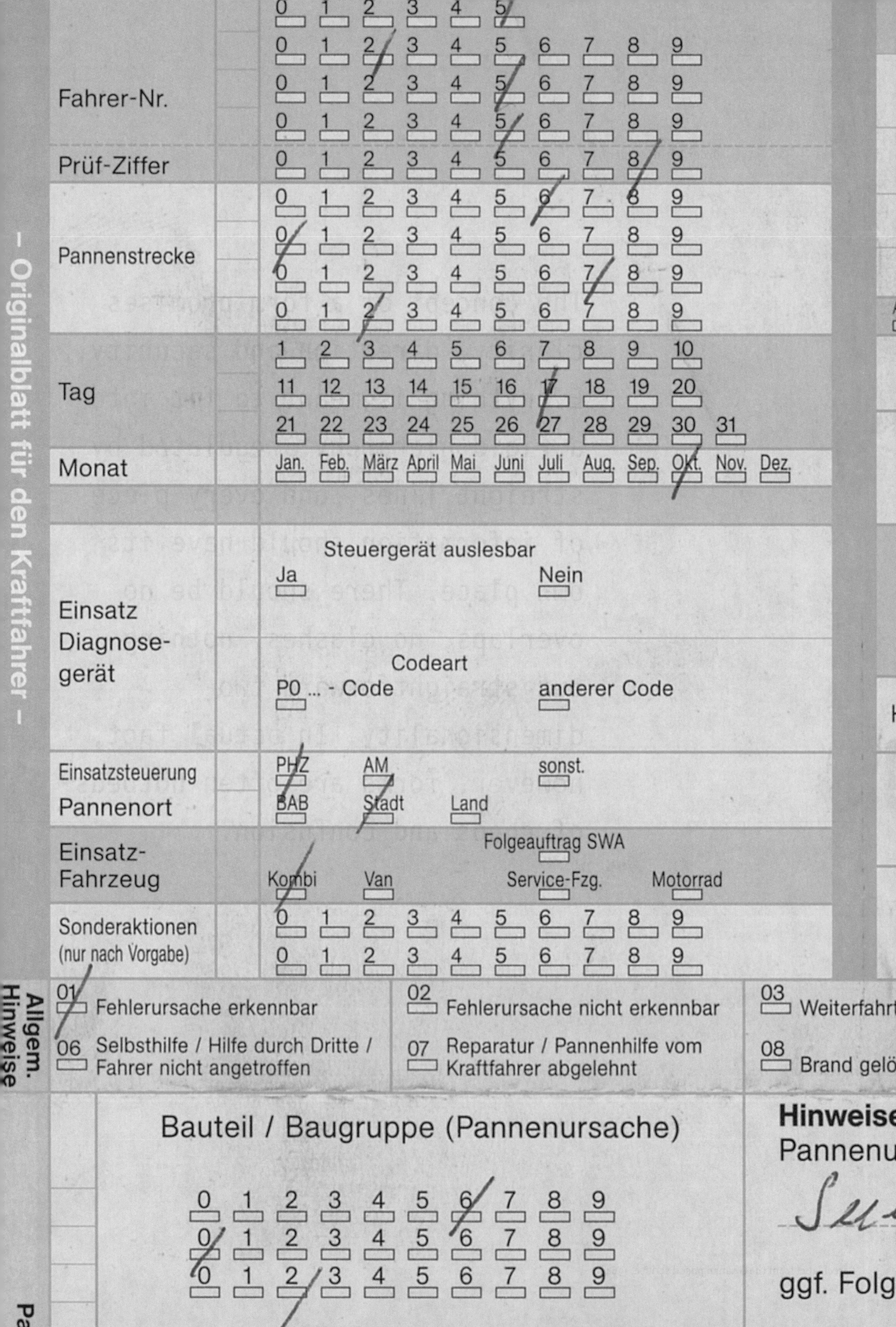

– Originalblatt für den Kraftfahrer –

Fahrer-Nr.	0 1 2 3 4 5 0 1 2 3 4 5 6 7 8 9 0 1 2 3 4 5 6 7 8 9 0 1 2 3 4 5 6 7 8 9
Prüf-Ziffer	0 1 2 3 4 5 6 7 8 9
Pannenstrecke	0 1 2 3 4 5 6 7 8 9 0 1 2 3 4 5 6 7 8 9 0 1 2 3 4 5 6 7 8 9 0 1 2 3 4 5 6 7 8 9
Tag	1 2 3 4 5 6 7 8 9 10 11 12 13 14 15 16 17 18 19 20 21 22 23 24 25 26 27 28 29 30 31
Monat	Jan. Feb. März April Mai Juni Juli Aug. Sep. Okt. Nov. Dez.
Einsatz Diagnose-gerät	Steuergerät auslesbar: Ja / Nein Codeart: P0 ... - Code / anderer Code
Einsatzsteuerung	PHZ AM sonst.
Pannenort	BAB Stadt Land
Einsatz-Fahrzeug	Folgeauftrag SWA Kombi Van Service-Fzg. Motorrad
Sonderaktionen (nur nach Vorgabe)	0 1 2 3 4 5 6 7 8 9 0 1 2 3 4 5 6 7 8 9

Allgem. Hinweise			
	01 Fehlerursache erkennbar	02 Fehlerursache nicht erkennbar	03 Weiterfahrt
	06 Selbsthilfe / Hilfe durch Dritte / Fahrer nicht angetroffen	07 Reparatur / Pannenhilfe vom Kraftfahrer abgelehnt	08 Brand gelö

Bauteil / Baugruppe (Pannenursache)

0 1 2 3 4 5 6 7 8 9
0 1 2 3 4 5 6 7 8 9
0 1 2 3 4 5 6 7 8 9

Hinweise
Pannenu

ggf. Folg

Pa

Forms condense information by encoding data in the form of abbreviations, symbols and numbers. The codes can be deciphered by those who know them, but to everyone else they are incomprehensible signs in a secret language, or else they become a graphic pattern.

Record from a car breakdown service, Germany, 2005

Übermittlungszettel
Feuille de transmission
Foglio di trasmissione
Fegl da transmissiun

Herrn/Frau
Monsieur/Madame
Signor/Signora
Signur/Dunna

☐ zur Kenntnis pour information per informazione per infurmaziun	☐ zur Erledigung pour exécution da risolvere per execuziun	☐ zur Genehmigung pour approbation per approvazione per approvaziun
☐ zu Ihren Akten pour vos dossiers per il vostro incarto per Vossas actas	☐ zur Stellungnahme pour avis per il parere per prender posiziun	☐ bitte Vorakten présenter les documents documentazione p.f. documentaziun p. pl.
☐ auf Ihren Wunsch selon votre demande a vostra richiesta tenor giavisch	☐ bitte besprechen entretien s.v.p. conferire p.f. discutar p. pl.	☐ einverstanden d'accord d'accordo d'accord
☐ gemäss Besprechung suivant l'accord come inteso tenor discussiun	☐ zur Unterschrift/Visum pour la signature/visa per la firma/visto per suttascriver/visar	☐ interessiert Sie vielleicht ça vous intéresse peut-être forse Le interessa forsa As interessa quai
☐ bitte zurückgeben à nous renvoyer s.v.p. da ritornare p.f. returnar p.pl.	☐ Anzahl Kopien je Vorlage Quantité copies par modèle Quantità copie per modello Quantitad copias per model	__________
☐ mit Dank zurück en retour: merci in restituzione: grazie enavos engraziond	☐ bitte anrufen téléphoner s.v.p. telefonare p.f. telefonar p.pl.	☎ __________

bitte weiterleiten an
transmettre à
da spedire a
da transmetter a

Datum/date/
data/data

Mit freundlichen Grüssen
Meilleures salutations
Cordiali saluti
Cordials salids

☐ bitte wenden
tourner s.v.p.
voltare p.f.
volver p.pl.

11.95 40'000 28218

111.904 dfi

Forms set out to cover every eventuality and to fit every individual case. In their constant attempts to bring order to the complexity of the world and in their unlimited desire to embrace every possibility, they reflect the human condition, for their frequent failure to live up to their ambitions often has a tragic inevitability.

Four-language memo sheet, Swiss civil service, 1995

Nine rules for form designers

Learn to love forms

Take forms seriously

Users
All those who use forms – you as a reader, your colleagues, customers and partners.

Get to know your users

Take your users seriously

Providers
All those who issue forms: public services, businesses, institutions, corporations and the self-employed.

Learn how providers think

Think how providers think

Give forms identity and style

Leave nothing to chance

Do not give users one more form – give them one less problem

People go where they want, not always where they ought to go.

Foreword

Forms are a silent dialogue

Wherever we go, forms go with us. Without them, there are no orders, payments, deliveries, marriages, divorces, immigrations, emigrations, tax declarations, arrest warrants or sick notes. They are there from the moment we're born, and we're not even allowed to die without them. They bring order, or at least *form* in the most literal sense, into our lives; they promise clarity and direction, yet so often they cause helplessness, chaos and confusion. A challenge to designers, they are sometimes sadly neglected as they attempt to start a silent dialogue with the people who, frequently put off by the very sight of them, reluctantly have to fill them in.

However, there are ways to improve the relationship between the form that asks the questions and the human being that answers them. There are ways of making it easier to find a path through the jungle of questions. And there are ways to make forms look better and and work more efficiently – of this there is no doubt in Borries Schwesinger's mind. And the first step could be: 'Learn to love forms.'

This is what reading this book will teach you to do. Is that hard to imagine? We thought so too, until Borries Schwesinger turned up, showed us his dissertation, and made us see the magic in something we'd always regarded with a mixture of loathing and apprehension.

With enthusiasm, thoroughness and wit, he takes us into this world of silent interviewers, paper office-workers and printed civil servants. His suggestions prove that interacting with forms can be worthwhile and even fun, if we just follow a few basic rules.

Whether you are a designer or a filler-in of forms, and especially if you are commissioning them, we hope this enthusiasm will rub off on you. If it does, people in the future might actually start to enjoy checking in or checking out, doing tax returns or filing a claim for lost property.

And if you find that this book goes missing, look for it on your colleagues' desks. That can often happen with a really useful book...

Karin and Bertram Schmidt-Friderichs

Preface

> The best form is no form.
> BRUCE LEE

There is scarcely any other medium that costs its user, reader and designer as much time and as much nervous energy as forms do. Whether they're invoices, applications or order forms, they take over offices and businesses every day in their thousands, being filled in, processed, sent off, and eventually filed. And despite all the effort that is taken, much of the time the forms are almost impossible to understand or only half filled in. The work invested in forms is thoroughly disproportionate to their usefulness, and that in itself is a paradox: they cause stress, rejection and widespread abhorrence – and yet they're such a good idea. They're meant to reduce communication to the absolute essentials, and to make it quicker and simpler by standardizing the message.

Successful forms do exist. They work simply and are so well designed that you scarcely realize you're filling in a form. They don't overtax their users but actually help them, and they give the providers the information they really need. There can and should be more examples of forms like this – not because they would make the world a more beautiful place, but so that people could devote their precious energy to something more meaningful, rather than wasting it on badly designed forms.

This book shows what forms can achieve and why it is difficult but not impossible to meet all the demands imposed on them. It offers methodical tips and suggestions for designers, and also acts as an invaluable sourcebook, bringing together a comprehensive collection of great form designs.

It is aimed at designers who want to make complex concepts more simple, those who see form design not as a chore but as a means of communication in the best possible sense. It is also intended for business people and administrators who need forms for their day-to-day work and want a more efficient way of communicating with clients, applicants, partners and colleagues.

Borries Schwesinger

1.1

Forms and their function

What is a form?

Forms determine the choice and order of information

The forms that confront us every day range from simple memo pads, through complex questionnaires and order forms, to invoices and web forms. Even railway information screens and cinema tickets are basically forms. All these types have one thing in common: they are *frameworks* for communication, made up of information which may be fixed or variable. Creating this framework from words and graphic elements is the task of the form designer, who selects the material that is to be included, and decides its positioning and style. The result may be a sheet of paper with checkboxes and text fields, a printed list, or even a computer interface that requests, collates and distributes the information.

Forms give structure to information

On the page opposite are descriptions of the typical features of forms. Among these, the consistent layout of information is a key factor. In this respect, forms are fundamentally different from other modes of communication such as text and the spoken word. The meaning of information is codified not only in the sequence of characters but also through the relationship of that information to the medium itself. The textual content is given a visual structure, so that instead of having to read a completed form in its entirety, a reader can simply see whether there is an entry in a certain field. The text is turned into an image.

Forms are not always recognizable as forms

Sometimes a form cannot easily be recognized as such because its fixed textual and graphic framework is not clearly distinct from the entries. For a long time, this distinction was taken for granted, simply because it was technically unavoidable. Today, however, different approaches are possible, although in the chapters that follow we shall be returning frequently to the fact that the distinction between pre-supplied text and entries that need to be filled in is still an important one.

Definition

Forms are frameworks for communication, comprised of text and graphics, and including fixed and variable pieces of information.

Common features of forms

Forms are a means of communication.

Forms contain blank fields which can be filled with different but specific information.

Forms can be completed or left blank.
When blank, they are only a verbal and visual framework.
When completed, they become a means of communication.

There are multiple copies of every form, and each one will carry different information.

The information requested or communicated by a form is presented in the same way on all copies.

Forms as an interface

Forms are an efficient means of communication for public services, institutions and businesses

As an interface for communication, forms set fixed standards that allow information to be compiled, transferred and processed quickly. They help to finalize business transactions, find out customers' requirements, hold elections, make applications and disseminate information. They do this in a manner which fulfils the provider's need to gather or give out information, the providers being predominantly public authorities, institutions and businesses. All of these use forms to work more efficiently, and indeed it is forms that make their work possible in the first place.

Processes are independent of personnel

There is a specific reason why the need for forms is so great: everything undertaken by an authority, institution or business has to be recorded in writing. This is the only way in which knowledge of contracts, applications, procedures and so on can be made independent of changes in personnel, whose actions can be confirmed and continued regardless of time and distance. As many of these actions are constantly being repeated and are similar to one another, forms offer an excellent method of handling, standardizing and recording them.

In this context, forms play a dual role. On the one hand, they create continuity: everything that forms permit can be understood and depends, at least in theory, on standards that are universally valid. On the other hand, they are the embodiment of bureaucracy – a bureaucracy that has a form for everything and which, although it offers security, is also a means of control.

A place where providers and users meet

Forms are not an end in themselves. To their providers, they are a means of communication with clients, customers, colleagues and partners. As a meeting place for these different groups, however, they create certain problems. For one thing, it is the form providers who determine both the content and the medium of communication in a one-side way. The form users are obliged to act in a prescribed manner, and their only alternative is to refuse. Secondly, providers and users may live in very different worlds. Providers generally represent an institutionalized world with its own specific language and complex procedures, while users will be concerned with the individual experiences, problems and needs of everyday life. One of the most important tasks of forms is to allow the interchange of information between these different worlds, and this task makes great demands in terms of concept and design.

Forms as an interface

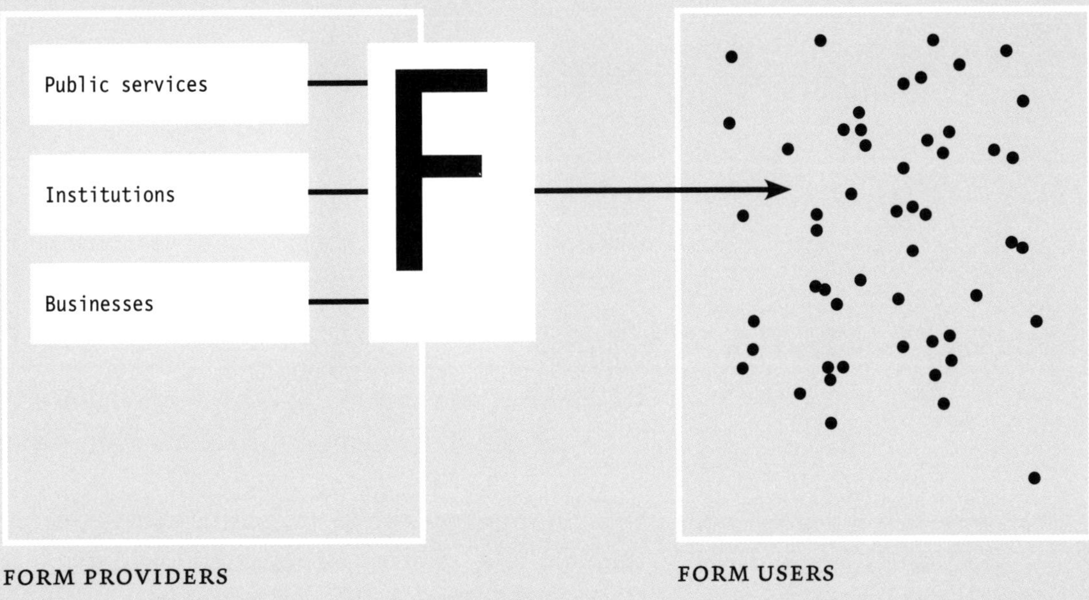

Form providers

Forms are issued by organizations which have some kind of administrative structure that works according to fixed rules: e.g. countries and communities, churches, associations, insurance companies, banks, public and legal institutions, schools and universities, hospitals, unions and businesses of all kinds.

All of these use forms to collect, distribute and store data, both for internal organization and for external communication. These forms are addressed to colleagues, business partners, customers and the general public.

The providers determine the content and layout of the forms, and define what information is to be given.

Form users

Unlike form providers, form users are not organizations but individuals: colleagues, employees, customers or the general public.

The fact that people are all different does not, however, mean that their actions are totally unpredictable. Many people find themselves in similar situations, and have similar experiences, needs and problems. Form providers and designers can make use of this by getting to know their potential users and taking their probable reactions into account when creating the forms.

Interaction and organization

Forms are part of a complex system of interaction and organization

Forms fulfil two functions: externally, they facilitate interaction between the provider and its users, and internally, they create an organizational structure for the provider's work processes. Thus they are simultaneously a means of interaction and organization.

Forms create and guide interaction

Forms create and guide interaction between provider and user. For example, if a public service asks about a householder's income, or a business issues an invoice to a customer, the user recognizes what is being demanded and acts accordingly. A short dialogue has taken place, and the form is a substitute for other modes of interaction such as a personal meeting or a telephone call. This is why it is essential for the form to be comprehensible and to give adequate guidance to its user. Users must not only be able to understand the information conveyed, but they must also be made to respond correctly – i.e. in the manner expected by the provider.

Forms are both instruments and images of internal organization

From the provider's point of view, forms fulfil an organizational function. They guide work procedures, and enable information to be grasped independently of time and space, collected, evaluated and stored. In themselves, however, they are only a means to an end – the end being to rationalize the work involved. Above all, though, they set standards, because the processes they prescribe must be done in that particular way, and cannot be done otherwise.

In order for forms to fulfil their organizational role, their content and design must fit in with the work procedures of the provider. However, this is a two-way process, since procedures may also be influenced by forms, and so herein lies one key to appropriate design: forms are always simultaneously a mirror of internal organization and an instrument that can change and/or optimize that organization.

Designing forms is therefore not just a matter of giving administrative processes a visual form but changing the processes themselves. The two actions cannot take place independently of each other, however. The aim is always to produce forms that will facilitate effective interaction with users and will create the best possible organizational structure for the provider's working practices. But since these are generally established before the forms are created, the conditions required for successful interaction, such as clarity and user-friendliness, are often neglected.

Interaction

The provider of the form is the active agent who elicits a reaction from the user. This may lead to an action by the user, which in turn will elicit a reaction from the provider.

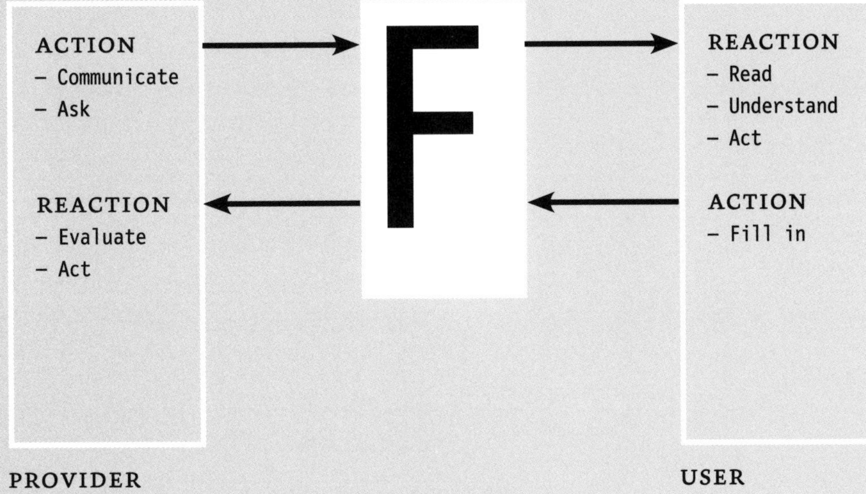

Organization

On the provider's side, a form goes through many stages of processing, and each one makes its own demands with regard to content and design.

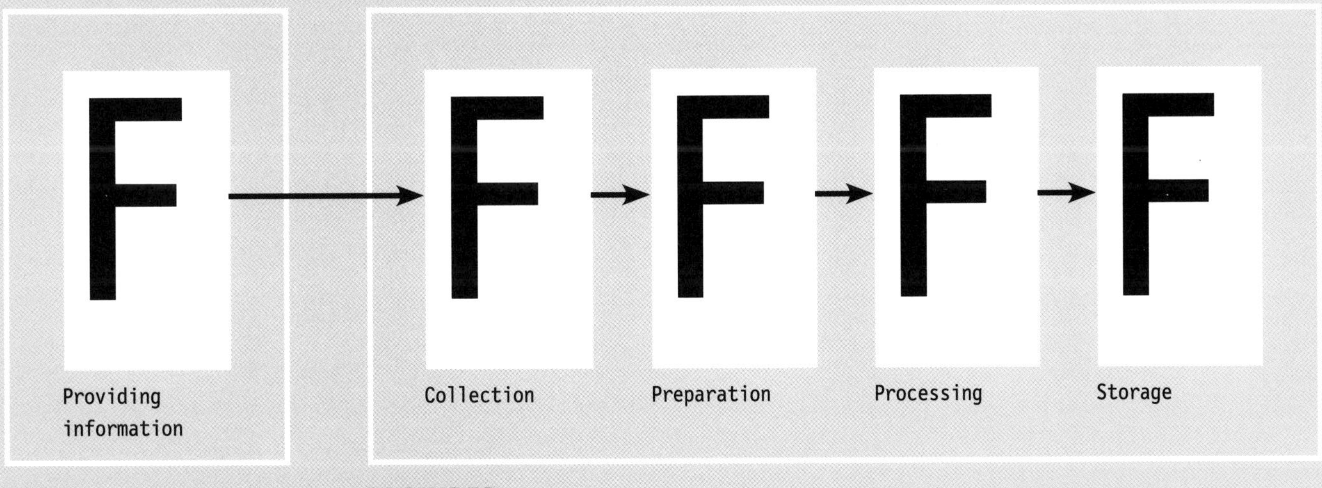

Paper, PDFs and beyond

Forms are part of a media-based process of communication

For a long time, forms were printed papers that had to be filled in by hand or with a typewriter. Now the world of the form has become much more varied. While the typewriter has practically disappeared, digital technology in particular has transformed the way in which forms are produced and distributed. In addition to special types such as electronic scoreboards, forms today can exist as printed paper, digital PDF files, or some other digital on-screen format. They are part of the overall process in which information may pass through a variety of media, and so their design cannot just be confined to a single medium but must be seamlessly integrated into a complex communications network.

Paper forms can be used anywhere

Paper forms are either pre-printed in large quantities, or can be produced on office printers as and when required. They can be filled by hand, with a typewriter, or by computer and overprinted. This can be done either with form-filling software or using an on-screen template. The advantage of paper forms is that they can be read, distributed and stored without the use of technology. The major disadvantage is that once the information has been put down on paper, it requires a great deal of time and trouble to digitize it.

PDF forms combine the advantages of digital and paper forms

PDF forms can either be completed on screen or printed out and filled in by hand. They are easy to produce and distribute, and look exactly the same on screen as they do when printed out. They can be made easier to fill by including interactive functions such as automatic calculators. It is also quite common for forms to be distributed as Word documents rather than PDF files, but this has some disadvantages, because it is hard to prevent these from being modified and presented to different users in multiple variations.

Digital forms are user interfaces

→ For more on digital forms, see pages 206–215

Digital forms are a feature of many websites and software applications. Like menus and buttons, they are part of the user interface, and there are several ways that they can be set up and filled in. The software can check if information has been provided in the correct format, and can restrict input to the type required. Data that has already been provided can be imported from other sources and superfluous questions can be automatically skipped. Since the information is immediately available digitally, it can be saved, compiled and transmitted straight away.

Media types

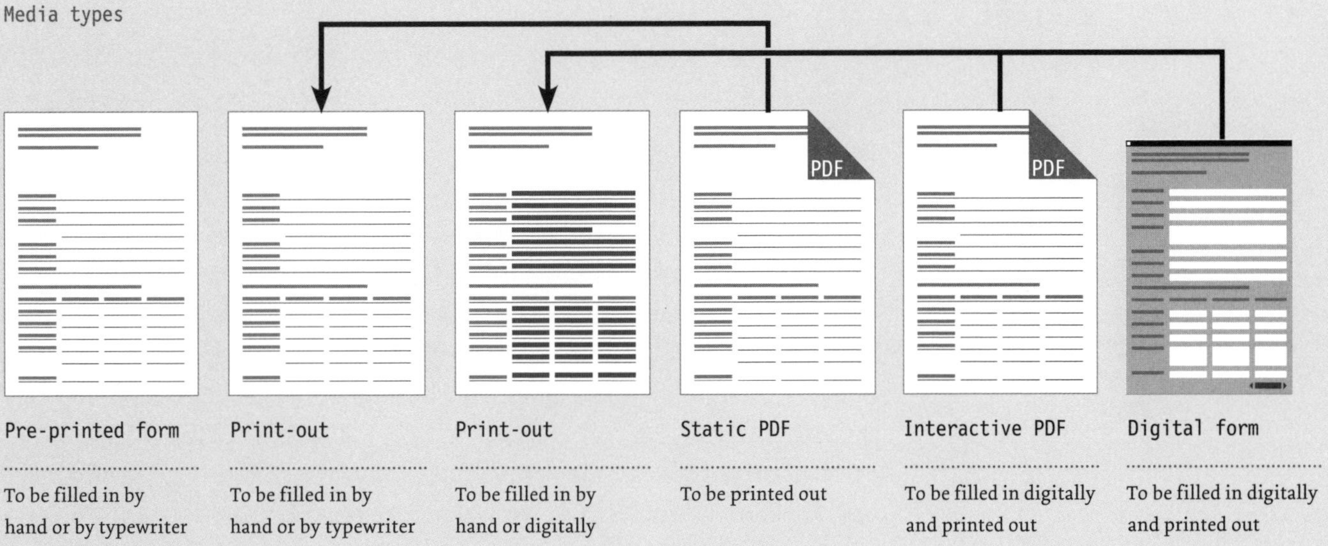

Paper forms

A typical procedure with paper forms: the form is filled in by hand and posted like any other document. If the information then needs to be processed digitally, the contents must be input by hand or by scanner. This time-consuming pause is known as a 'media break', and frequently gives rise to errors.

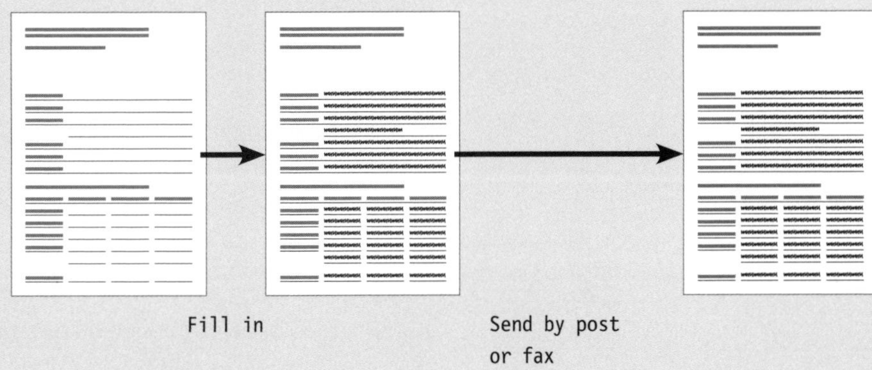

PDF forms

As long as they are designed to be interactive, PDF forms can be filled in directly on the screen, then printed out and sent. If the completed form can also be sent electronically, the need for printing is eliminated.

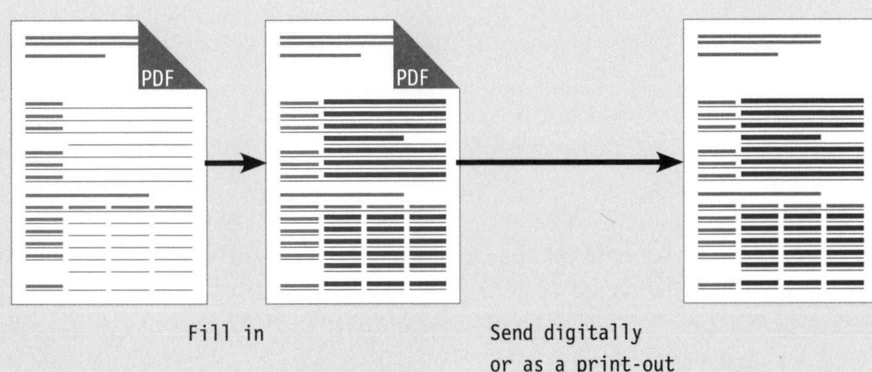

Digital forms

Digital forms are used on webpages, computer software and user interfaces such as touchscreen terminals. The information can be transmitted digitally or printed out on paper.

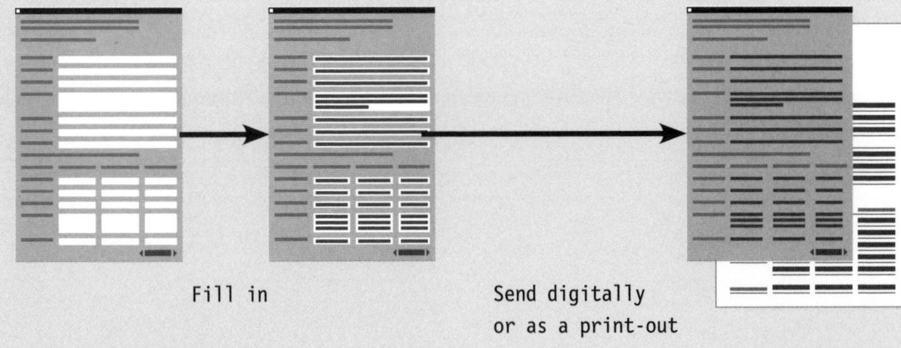

Forms as an obstacle

Forms have an image problem

Forms are meant to lead to efficient communication, and so reduce to a minimum the amount of time required for interaction between the provider and the user. Unfortunately, however, they suffer from an image problem. Although many users see them as a necessity, forms are considered to be a nuisance, time-consuming and difficult to understand. People tend to view them as a tedious mass of paperwork that has to be dealt with but whose point is difficult to fathom. In 1978, at a conference entitled 'Citizens – Forms – Authority', the German professor Siegfried Grosse gave the following pessimistic description: 'Forms are the type of text that is produced by its author (i.e. the person filling it in) with the utmost reluctance.'

Reluctance and lack of understanding lead to communication breakdown

→ For the distinction between dialogue and communication forms, see page 74

This image problem applies predominantly to *dialogue forms*, such as applications. These can only function if most users react in the manner anticipated by the provider and fill in the form completely and correctly. If a user is unable or unwilling to do this, the medium itself becomes an obstacle to communication. Time-consuming queries, expensive misunderstandings, and worst of all, blocked or failed communication are the negative consequences. There may be various causes for this; some are connected with the forms themselves, while others may result from the user's previous experiences of dealing with authorities. Even *communication forms* such as bills and notices may fail to function if they meet with hostility or incomprehension. However, this may not be quite so apparent to the providers, since they do not generally expect any direct response.

Form design can't change everything, but it can make things better

The concept and design of a form need to take account of this image problem. This is quite a challenge, because many of the factors that make forms into an obstacle result from their dual function as a means of organization and interaction. Designers can have little influence on this, and the fact that the content is often unpleasant is also out of their hands. However, the negative image *can* be overcome through consistency and a great deal of careful attention to detail, to ensure that users will not perceive the form as restrictive, condescending or discriminatory. But above all, users must be able to understand the form and see that it serves a purpose. This will not only make it into an efficient means of communication, but can also offer the provider a chance to stand out from the competition.

Six reasons for the negative image of many forms

Forms are:

unpleasant

Filling in forms is seldom an enjoyable activity. It means dealing with things that users would otherwise prefer to avoid, and often implies a negative context: they are short of cash, due to pay their taxes, or in need of permission. The very sight of a form creates negative associations.

bureaucratic

Administrative services have an image problem which transfers itself to their forms. They are regarded as inefficient, authoritarian and remote from the everyday world. This applies not only to public services but also to many departments within the private sector, such as human resources, finance and accounts, which are responsible for issuing a lot of forms.

restrictive

Users can only say what the form allows them to say. The opportunity to give a full description of a particular situation is very limited. Consequently, the information they provide is not necessarily an accurate reflection of their personal reality.

discriminatory

Forms often discriminate. They may use gendered terminology, be written in a single language, be inaccessible to those with literacy issues or visual impairments, or force people into categories that they do not belong to.

condescending

Why certain questions are asked, and what happens to the information, is often unclear to users, and so they cannot foresee the consequences of their own actions. By filling in the form, they are therefore taking a potential risk. They see themselves confronted by a bureaucracy that is a kind of 'black box' system whose workings cannot be seen, and so they feel vulnerable and oppressed.

incomprehensible

Forms can be hard to understand and off-putting in both language and design. Often it is not clear what information is supposed to be supplied and where it should go. Questions are easily misconstrued, terms and explanations can be contradictory and hard to read, and there may be too many pages to take in. Users are left feeling frustrated and disorientated.

Problems with clarity

Clarity means more than legibility

Comprehensible language and clear design are the keys to a good form. While it may sound banal to say so, these are not easy goals to achieve. The page opposite shows a summary of the problems that can affect the language and design of forms. It is obvious that legibility alone is not enough to ensure understanding, because this is a complex process and its success does not depend solely on deciphering words but also on the experiences, expectations and motivations of both the user and the provider.

Clarity must be achieved through language and design

The language of many forms is filled with specialist terms, abbreviations and formal phrasings; it is also often characterized by long sentences and a lack of courtesy. All of these issues play a major role in hindering understanding. Inadequate explanations or instructions and ambiguous or contradictory statements simply serve to confirm the poor image of forms and cause users to reject them.

Bad design causes similar problems: confusion, lack of clear divisions and patterns, poor ergonomics and, not least, a lack of visual appeal all prevent the form from being seen as a simple, useful means of communication.

If, however, the language and design are improved, and every form is made to fit the requirements and expectations of its users, it is possible in the medium term to make communication far more successful and effective.

External influences

For something to be comprehensible, it not only has to be readable, but must also take into account the experiences, expectations and attitudes of users.

Experiences

Frequent negative experiences with incomprehensible forms may lead users to assume that they won't understand right from the start.

Expectations

A comprehensible form relies on both the provider and the user starting out from the basic assumption that each wishes to understand the other. If they expect otherwise, this will affect the chances of success. If a user expects nothing but demands, e.g. from the tax office, any positive offers or benefits are unlikely even to be noticed.

Motivation

The motives of users also influence clarity. Complicated facts and extensive questions are more approachable if the meaning and purpose of the form are clearly laid out and explained to the user, e.g. why certain information is being asked for.

Language issues

There are many reasons why forms may be incomprehensible but none of these is insurmountable.

Specialist language

The language of forms does not match the language of everyday use. Many terms and phrasings stem from legal or bureaucratic contexts, and although they may be correct, they may not be familiar to all readers.

Terminology

Forms often use abstract terminology. This is necessary because it needs to be made as general as possible, but the disadvantage is that the concrete meaning or definition remains unclear. Since there is often a lack of space, abbreviations are common, and this may also affect clarity. Many forms tend to overuse the nominal and passive styles, which can have a bad influence on style and clarity.

Addressing users

The target group is often quite broad, and what may be clear or familiar to some may strike others as alienating and difficult to grasp. The style may not always be suitable for a particular group, and an authoritarian tone is always just as off-putting as clichés of artificial politeness and equally artificial informality.

Point of view

Who is speaking to whom? Is there an 'I' or a 'we' behind the form, or an impersonal organization? Does the form ask its users questions, or are the users simply asked to sign a preformulated declaration? The perspective is often unclear and may cause confusion.

Design issues

This is just a brief overview of basic design issues. Chapter 2 will deal in detail with problems and solutions. → page 120

Structure

The structure of many forms follows the style of a contract or legal text or meets administrative needs. This may be useful for the provider, but doesn't help the user. If user-friendliness is the goal, then clarity, comprehensibility and a consistent structure are all-important.

Guiding the user

All copies of a single form are identical, but its users are not. Since many questions will only affect some users, clear guidance is essential.

Ergonomics

Many forms are difficult to read as well as to write on. They cram as much as possible onto a single page, and forget that a name might be longer than 'Smith', and that not everyone has a magnifying glass to decipher small print. Sometimes the linking of questions, keywords, terms and explanations to text fields or checkboxes is unclear and unsystematic.

Choosing clear language

Forms are a replacement for a personal dialogue. It is therefore all the more important to use language that will not be remote or bureaucratic, but will make a friendly, direct, personal and sympathetic impression. The basic principles set out here can make a form clearer and easier to understand by making its language more accessible.

Clarity

Avoid technical terms

It is best to avoid technical terms, legal or administrative jargon, unfamiliar or out-of-date expressions, longwinded phrases and euphemisms.

instead of emolument → payment
instead of meet your fiscal obligations → pay your tax
instead of punitive measures → a fine
instead of financially disadvantaged → in debt

Try to avoid words which have a colloquial double meaning.

Write abbreviations out in full

Instead of abbreviations and abstract references, write exactly what you mean.

Specialist terms or acronyms should be written out in full when first mentioned, with their abbreviation in brackets. The abbreviated version can be used subsequently, as readers will then understand it.

instead of btw → by the way
instead of DDPP → direct debit payment plan
instead of your acc. no. → your account number

Avoid wordiness

Long strings of nouns make it difficult to address the reader personally. Although they may seem formal and professional, the effect is wooden and abstract. This can be prevented by using shorter verbs, adjectives and adverbs.

instead of Payment without procrastination is obligatory → Please pay now
instead of Notification of our decision will be forwarded → We will let you know
instead of In the event of a refusal → If you refuse
instead of Subsequent to the assessment of your completed application → When we have assessed your application

Clarity

Don't switch terminology

Use the same term for the same subject every time. Clarity matters more than variety for variety's sake.

instead of You can only renew a licence if your previous permit is within a fortnight of its expiry date or if it has already exceeded its validation period.

→ You can only renew a licence if your previous licence is within a fortnight of its expiry date or has already passed its expiry date.

Sentence construction

You should generally try to avoid long sentences. Don't separate nouns and articles, keep subject, verb and object together, and avoid complicated subordinate clauses and parentheses if possible.

instead of The previously notified (though not binding or obligatory) date has been – or will be if, as expected, the government passes the proposed but still pending private member's bill – extended until January 2011.

→ The government is expected to pass a new bill, which will result in the previous date being extended to January 2011.

Friendliness and courtesy

Active language

Passive constructions make the text impersonal and it is harder to understand who should do what. Try to use active verb forms where possible.

instead of Tax is to be paid in full → Please pay your tax in full.

Please and thank you

Very often a simple 'please' or 'thank you' can make a form seem friendlier and more polite.

instead of Pay your tax in full → Please pay your tax in full. Thank you.

Make it personal

Forms are a kind of dialogue. You should therefore address the user directly, as you would in a conversation.

instead of It is important that → Please note that

Customer service

Be concrete

Telephone numbers, addresses, sums of money and dates should always be given precisely and not as vague references. If they are very important, they should be given extra emphasis.

instead of The agreed date → 23 July 2010
instead of The outstanding amount → £3001.25
instead of Further details may be solicited from the department responsible. → For further details, please contact the complaints department.

Identity, image and forms

Forms always communicate something

It goes without saying that forms should not be an obstacle to communication and should at least achieve the purpose for which they were made, i.e. to convey and collect information. However, they can also do much more than that. They play a significant though often undervalued role in the way in which their providers are perceived. They influence the image of public services, institutions and businesses, and they are a major factor in both branding and corporate identity building.

Many providers use forms to communicate with the outside world even if they have never actually devoted much attention to their corporate identity. Indeed, without forms they would scarcely be able to function. Each one not only conveys essential information but also reveals something about the identity of the provider – in other words, whether intentionally or unintentionally, each form influences the public image of the particular company or authority. And it can happen all too easily that the image conveyed is nothing like the image the provider wishes to convey. It is therefore in the interests of all concerned that providers focus more closely on corporate identity issues and include forms as part of this. We are now about to talk exclusively about businesses, but very similar arguments can be put forward for most public bodies and other institutions.

→ For more on corporate identity, see the bibliography on page 318

Just like individual people, every company has an identity which is expressed through its appearance, language and behaviour. This is what the public and the company itself perceive as the *corporate image*, i.e. the way the outside world sees it. Corporate identity means seeking to present a company's values and characteristics in such a way that the external world's view will coincide as closely as possible with its desired self-image.

Three aspects of corporate identity

Corporate identity can be divided into three dimensions, each of which must be made to harmonize with the others: there is *corporate design*, which is omnipresent; *corporate communication*, which is more subtle and not always obvious, and *corporate behaviour*, which is vague and more difficult to control.

Corporate design is the visual unifier, and is far more than just a logo. It defines a system of typefaces, colours, symbols and principles of design, and when used consistently – which means on forms as well – it ensures instant recognition and conveys the company's message visually. Corporate communication comprises all the verbal statements the company makes about itself and its products or actions. The aim is to guide the flow of information about the company so that it remains within the framework of the corporate identity, which is the daily task of PR and marketing departments. Corporate behaviour relates to the conduct of the staff in their dealings with one another and with their customers and partners. This is where the values of the company, such as its policies on management, personnel, customers and products, are put into practice in the real world.

Forms have an influence on all three corporate dimensions, since they reflect aspects of design, communication and behaviour.

Forms are design

Like all visual media, forms are bearers of corporate design in the shape of the company logo, typeface and – if the cost is not too prohibitive – branding colours. On its own, however, this is not enough. Forms must also be considered part of the overall corporate design, because otherwise they will seem arbitrary, without identity, and may even work against the brand image.

Forms are text

Companies use forms to communicate with the outside world, and frequently the outside world responds, which is rarely the case with other methods of corporate communication. Forms therefore play an important role in business communication, but unfortunately they tend not to be covered by common corporate strategies. With the exception of direct mail forms, they are neither advertisements, press releases nor sponsorship activities. Turning them into tools of communication therefore means changing the ways in which the company projects its identity.

Forms are an attitude

Forms are part of the company's everyday relationship with customers, staff and partners. They reflect the company's attitude towards the outside world, which may be customer-focused or authoritarian, egalitarian or condescending, open or secretive, simple or complicated. Internally, however, forms are seldom regarded as an integral part of a company's policies and are generally used as one of many tools of the trade.

Forms make an impression

Don't forget that forms are frequently the only, or the most important, means of communication that a company uses. The first invoice or the first order form will leave a lasting impression on the customer, and it may be difficult to change that impression later. Much subsequent contact will also be through forms, and this can be an advantage: the existence of forms expresses a degree of seriousness and steadfastness on the part of the provider, conveying the fact that the company conducts its business according to fixed standards that apply to all its customers. This advantage, however, can easily be lost if the form itself contradicts that impression.

Forms build trust

Consistency of image and behaviour are the messages that should be conveyed through corporate identity in all its aspects. If forms express this kind of consistency, continuity, competence and seriousness, they will build trust in the company's efficiency. For example, a business trying to sell precision products needs to illustrate its precision in its forms, just as a company offering simple solutions will gain its customer's trust through simple forms.

Forms must convey credibility

It is especially important that contractual forms convey an impression of the utmost reliability. This, after all, is the trickiest moment in any commercial relationship, and a frustrating form can undo all the preceding efforts to build up a user's trust and confidence.

Since forms organize and reflect internal structures, they are a good indication of how credible a company's corporate identity may be. Bad forms can have dire consequences, because they provide tangible evidence that a company's image does not match its reality. To ensure that this image is not merely skin deep, it should be promoted in all aspects of the company's activities, including the design of forms.

Forms need style

Form design should not be limited to avoiding negative consequences. They can also have a positive side, portraying a sense of feeling, a unique style, and an individual message – none of which should detract from their functional efficiency.

Forms are products

Many types of form are not just reflections of the company's image and the quality of its work, but they are products in themselves. The work of many service industries and public authorities has no concrete shape – your insurance policy, bank account or building permit is not an object but simply a *promise*, and its only material expression is a form. Thus the design of policies, statements, certificates and permits is an aspect of product design, and may constitute the company's USP (Unique Selling Point).

Forms within the framework
of corporate identity

Corporate image

How outsiders view the company

Corporate identity

How the company presents itself

CORPORATE DESIGN
Visual image

Elements
- Logo and branding
- Typography
- Colour
- Visual imagery

Areas of application
- Stationery
- Forms
- Publications
- Advertising and publicity
- Websites
- Architecture, trade fairs

**FORMS
AS DESIGN**

CORPORATE COMMUNICATION
Ways of speaking to the world

Instruments
- Corporate language
- Publicity
- Sales promotion
- Public relations
- Sponsorship
- Investor relationship management

**FORMS
AS TEXT**

CORPORATE BEHAVIOUR
Ways of dealing with people

Attitudes and actions
- Towards colleagues
- Towards clients and customers
- Towards partners
- Towards the public

**FORMS
AS AN ATTITUDE**

Aspects of corporate identity that
are communicated through forms

Whether forms are included in an overall corporate identity or not, their design and language still give a great deal of insight into the provider: not only as regards visual image but also into the many features that make up a corporate identity.

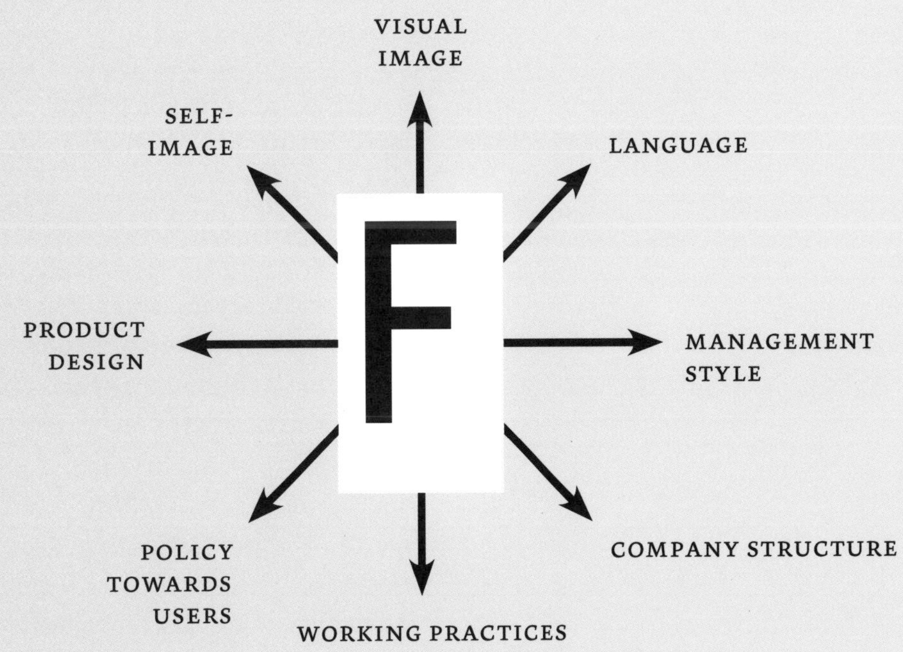

Forms as an opportunity

Functionality can be short and long term

Good forms must meet the demands of functionality. This is short term if they enable effective communication between both parties as speedily as possible and without any misunderstandings. It is long term if the forms establish trust. Both functions can save businesses and public services a great deal of money, make them more successful and open up opportunities to improve brand image.

Forms save money

A systematic and uniform design costs money, but it can be worth the expense, because good forms increase efficiency. The number and size of forms can be reduced by systematization, and work procedures can be simplified by forms that integrate and streamline the actions of all concerned. Communication is made quicker by forms that are simple to fill in, and instances of error or incompleteness are much rarer, while the information itself is more reliable. The better the form, the more the company can leave its clients to compile and convey the data necessary for its growth. All of this saves time and money. Forms that convey something useful attract a higher proportion of responses to direct-mail marketing, and so ultimately increase turnover. They can replace or reinforce personal advice, which takes on a greater degree of reliability, precision and clarity.

Opportunities for companies

It is especially important for companies in competitive markets to distinguish themselves positively from their rivals and establish a trustworthy brand. If customers have no particular preference about which phone company to use, a bad form can alienate them and make them turn to a competitor. Once they have attracted a customer, companies should never neglect an opportunity to make as positive an impression as possible. As customers often engage more intensively with forms than with any other medium, forms are likely to imprint the corporate identity more strongly than other branding media such as ad campaigns.

Opportunities for the public sector

In contrast to businesses, public services have one advantage which at the same time is a handicap: even the most off-putting of forms still has to be filled in. With very few exceptions, no one can opt out of this chore. This monopoly is one of several reasons for the poor image of public sector forms. However, at regular intervals there are demands that bureaucracy must be reduced, and that admin must be made simpler, more efficient and more task-orientated, and so it stands to reason that public services must get to grips with their forms. These institutions represent communities, towns, cities and countries, and as such they are in actual or potential competition for investors, tourists and residents. If they are to compete, a trustworthy image is essential. Communities that want to appear open-minded, modern and attractive to investors invest heavily in promoting their image and facilities, but their forms also need to reflect and communicate the same positive image. This is not just a matter of appearances. It is worth bearing in mind that many businesses spend a substantial proportion of their resources on coping with bureaucracy, and so simplifying this process will provide a concrete economic incentive.

For many people, the existence and influence of public services only become tangible when they are confronted with forms. No democratic society can be indifferent to this impact, for when all is said and done, the bureaucrats are answerable to and legitimized by the government, and are acting on behalf of and for the benefit of everyone.

Design alone is not enough

Good design is not a panacea, and should not be merely cosmetic. Nothing is more disheartening than a harmless, friendly-looking form whose content turns out to be the direct opposite. The fact that tax return forms look so complicated is primarily because the tax system *is* complicated, and paying taxes can't be made more pleasant just by making the forms look good. Hiding things away or sprucing them up will not help, but a clearly laid-out and easy-to-read design may at least soften the blow.

Design for change

In a demanding context, form design has to cope with many obstacles. It always reflects pre-existing structures, and in so doing it often brings to light flaws that can only be rectified by reorganization. But changing existing systems – personal, material or technical – is often very expensive and is liable to meet with strong resistance, so this is one of the greatest challenges to all sides. Companies need to recognize the need for change, and designers must think beyond design for its own sake and attune their minds to the structure of the company and the needs of its customers.

1.2

A brief history of forms

Letter of indulgence (1455)

The predecessor of the printed form was the handwritten document

Long before the first form was printed, the people of the Middle Ages devised ways of simplifying the written work done in monasteries and in the offices of secular and ecclesiastical rulers. Monks, who worked primarily as scribes, would prepare template documents. Along with a seal, these contained the set phrases with which texts began and ended. These templates only had to have names and details added when required, and although this did not reduce the quantity of writing, it was a neat way of saving space and time.

Letters of indulgence were the first forms

A letter of indulgence was a sort of licence issued by the Catholic church, which granted the remission of sins in exchange for a financial donation. Indulgences were often mass produced in manuscript form, so it is not surprising that when Johannes Gutenberg invented the concept of printing with movable type in 1450, the task of producing blank documents such as these was taken over by the printing press. The indulgence illustrated is one of the oldest-known datable documents, and was probably printed in 1455 by Gutenberg himself. This marked the birth of the modern form; from this point on, the standard text that previously had to be written out by hand was pre-printed. For a fee, the commissioner of indulgences simply filled in the gaps with the correct name and date, thus saving the sinner from both penance and purgatory. This amazingly effective idea also saved around 95 per cent of writing time, and soon began to be used for other kinds of document.

Faster, but not yet a new concept of text

This method, however, was only a means of speeding up the production of documents. It did not affect the normal reading process and, like every other text, the document had to be read from start to finish for the content to be understood. As printed type was scarcely any different from handwritten script, these early documents still looked very unlike the forms of today. In a sense, the letter of indulgence is similar to a modern mail-merge letter; these seem to be individual but in fact only differ in the addressee's details.

Letter of indulgence sold to fund 'the battle against the Turks and the defence of Cyprus', 1455

Set in the Donatus-Calendar typeface used for Gutenberg's 36-line Bible, probably printed by Gutenberg himself.

Tax forms (1790)

The layout codifies the information

These French tax forms from around 1790 are not only pleasing to the eye, but they also illustrate a major typographical development. More than 300 years after the first printed letter of indulgence, a new way of compiling, presenting and perceiving information has been developed: it is codified by its layout on the page. The continuous, linear, one-dimensional text has now been changed into a two-dimensional system.

Tax officials discover the concept of the table

This is a vivid illustration of the way that taxes were assessed and recorded – one of the most important tasks of any civil service since time immemorial. Until the 14th century, officials simply recorded names and amounts, one after the other. Later they separated the amounts to make them easier to add up. Then, from the 15th century onwards, the information began to be divided into columns, although these were created with hand-drawn lines. This stringing together of information became a standard system of notation, in which the meaning of an entry was determined by its position on the page. A figure in the 'Credit' column meant something quite different to an identical figure in the 'Debit' column. Even an absent entry – i.e. a blank space – was a piece of information in itself. Thus was born the concept of the table, one of the principles on which modern forms are based.

Typography as a means of organizing information

After the development of typesetting and printing technology, it became possible to print ready-made tables. From then on, design features such as horizontal and vertical rules in varying weights, horizontally set curly brackets and typefaces of different styles and sizes all contributed to the development of the form.

Forms record the world around us

The ingenious concept of the table revolutionized more than the field of tax collection. The 18th century was an age of statistics: populations were counted, land was measured, the possessions of subjects or soon-to-be free citizens were recorded. It was not only the governing authorities that used this information – the knowledge of these facts represented a rational spirit that favoured the Enlightenment and the new middle-class way of life.

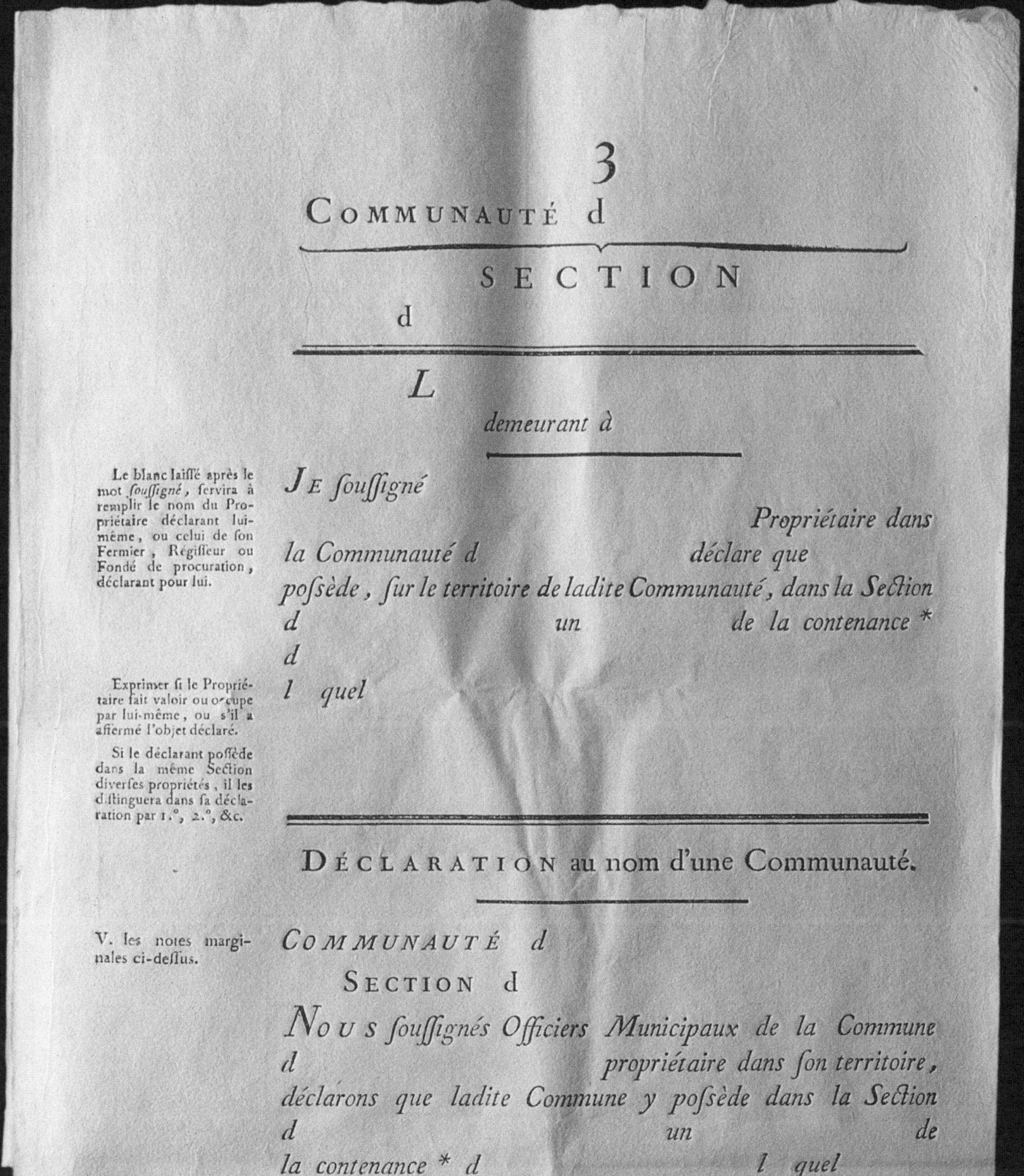

3

COMMUNAUTÉ d

SECTION

d

L

demeurant à

Le blanc laissé après le mot *soussigné*, servira à remplir le nom du Propriétaire déclarant lui-même, ou celui de son Fermier, Régisseur ou Fondé de procuration, déclarant pour lui.

JE soussigné

*Propriétaire dans la Communauté d déclare que possède, sur le territoire de ladite Communauté, dans la Section d un de la contenance * d*

l quel

Exprimer si le Propriétaire fait valoir ou occupe par lui-même, ou s'il a affermé l'objet déclaré.

Si le déclarant possède dans la même Section diverses propriétés, il les distinguera dans sa déclaration par 1.°, 2.°, &c.

DÉCLARATION au nom d'une Communauté.

V. les notes marginales ci-dessus.

COMMUNAUTÉ d

SECTION d

*NOUS soussignés Officiers Municipaux de la Commune d propriétaire dans son territoire, déclarons que ladite Commune y possède dans la Section d un de la contenance * d l quel*

* La déclaration de la contenan
locales, quels que soient leur étendue
L'on ne sera obligé de se servir
devront jouir des exceptions détaill

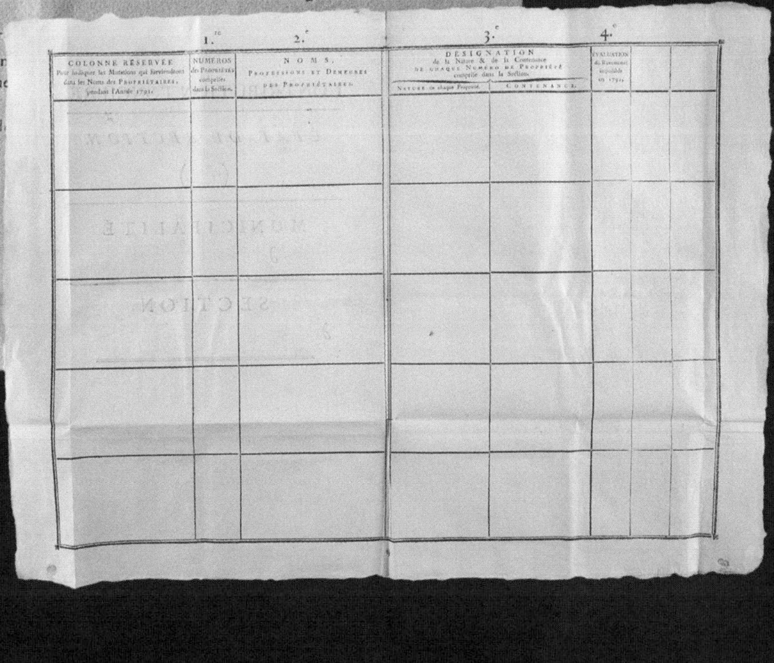

	1.re	2.e	3.e		4.e		
COLONNE RÉSERVÉE Pour indiquer les Mutations qui surviendront dans les Noms des Propriétaires, pendant l'Année 1791.	NUMÉROS des Propriétés comprises dans la Section.	NOMS, Professions et Demeures des Propriétaires.	DÉSIGNATION de la Nature & de la Contenance de chaque Numéro de Propriété comprise dans la Section. Nature de chaque Propriété	Contenance.	ÉVALUATION du Revenu imposable en 1791.		

The text has simple blank spaces that need to be filled. However, it has been embellished with dividing lines, different styles of type and even explanatory notes in the margin.

Forms for collecting land tax in France, 1790–91

Passenger list (1892)

FRIEDRICH SCHILLER
'On the Aesthetic Education of Man, a series of letters', Sixth Letter, 1795

'Everlastingly chained to a single little fragment of the Whole, man himself develops into nothing but a fragment; everlastingly in his ear the monotonous sound of the wheel that he turns, he never develops the harmony of his being, and instead of putting the stamp of humanity upon his own nature, he becomes nothing more than the imprint of his occupation or of his specialized knowledge. But even that meagre, fragmentary participation, by which individual members of the State are still linked to the Whole, does not depend upon forms which they spontaneously prescribe for themselves...; it is dictated to them with meticulous exactitude by means of a formula which inhibits all freedom of thought. The dead letter takes the place of living understanding.'

Forms divide humanity

The quote above shows the eminent German writer Schiller criticizing the conditions of his time, but also making an observation that is as true now as it was then: modern mankind is no longer an indivisible, harmonious whole, but must always be separated into categories. Since the beginning of the modern age, the workings of the state and its administrators have not been confined to protecting the unity of the land but have increasingly intruded upon the everyday lives of ordinary people. Education, public security, health and safety, even waste disposal all became part of the public sector, and so more and more information had to be collected and processed at ever greater speeds, and for all of this, forms were soon required. In the late 18th century, administration became a central principle of state affairs, and the state itself became a rational, functional industry. The aristocracy gave way to the bureaucracy, and the rule of the upper classes gave way to the circulation of paperwork. Even omnipotent monarchs no longer imbued their states with their own personality, but delegated their powers in matters of law, finance, order and security to dedicated departments.

Bureaucracy is the price of modernity

This was not necessarily a loss, but eventually the public sector took over more and more services and oversaw (and still oversees) the workings of the ever expanding towns and cities of our modern age. The price has been the bureaucratization of everyday life. People now no longer live in social communities but in bureaucratic systems.

The passenger manifest of an ocean liner, delivered on its arrival at the port of New York in 1892, illustrates precisely what Friedrich Schiller pointed out a hundred years earlier. Humans are recorded only as fragments, as names registered on a form. Even the New World – refuge of the poor and oppressed, the land of endless opportunity – painstakingly registered on a form everyone lucky enough to reach it.

(18) PASSENGERS' LIST.
"The Passenger Act, 1882."

District of the City of New York, Port of New York.

I, [illegible], Master of the S. S. "Nevada" do solemnly, sincerely and truly declare that the following List or Manifest, subscribed by me, and now delivered by me to the Collector of the Customs of the Collection District of the City of New York, is a full and perfect list of all the passengers taken on board the said vessel at Liverpool & Queenstown from which port said vessel has now arrived; and that on said list is truly designated the age, the sex, and the calling of each of said passengers, the location of the compartment or space occupied by each during the passage, the country of citizenship of each, and also the destination or location intended by each; and that said List or Manifest truly sets forth the number of said passengers who have died on said voyage, and the dates and causes of death, and the names and ages of those who died; also of the pieces of baggage of each; also a true statement, so far as it can be ascertained, with reference to the intention of each alien passenger as to a protracted sojourn in this country. So help me God.

and I further declare that the Master is ill on board & not able to be present

Sworn to this 2 January 1892, before me. [illegible signature]

[illegible signatures]

List or Manifest OF ALL THE PASSENGERS taken on board the S. S. Nevada whereof John A. P. Cushing is Master, from L'pool & Q'town burthen 2351 tons

No.	NAMES.	AGE. Years.	AGE. Mths.	SEX.	CALLING.	The country of which they are citizens.	Intended destination or location.			Date and cause of death.	Location of compartment or space occupied.	Number of pieces of baggage.	Transient, or in transit, or intending protracted sojourn.
	Embarked at Queenstown												
1	Ellen King	21		F	Spinster	Ireland	Nebraska	yes	yes		After Steerage Stern	1	Pro. [illegible]
2	Annie Moore	13		"	"	"	New York	"	"		" " "		"
3	Anthony "	11		M	Child	"	"	"	"		" " "	1	"
4	Phillip "	7		"	"	"	"	"	"		" " "		"
5	John Ryan	24		"	Labourer	"	Minnesota	"	"	4–3	Forward "		"
6	Mary "	30		F	Wife	"	"	"	"		" "	2	"
7	Michael Connell	20		M	Labourer	"	Connecticut	No	No		After " Port	1	"
	Embarked at Liverpool												
8	[illegible] Knop	50		M	Smith	Russia	New York	yes	yes		After Steerage Port	1	Pro. [illegible]
9	Morris [illegible]	20		"	Machinist	England	"	"	"		" " "	1	"
10	Charles Kelly	45		"	Tailor	U. States	Trenton N. J.	"	"	1–0	" " "	1	"
1	Israel [illegible]	22		"	[illegible]	Russia	New York	"	"		" " "	1	"
2	Yankel [illegible]	31		"	"	"	"	"	"		" " "	1	"
3	Esther [illegible]	32		F	Wife	"	"	No	No		" " Stern		"
4	[illegible] "	11		M	Child	"	"	Yes	Yes		" " "		"
5	Isaac "	7		"	"	"	"	No	No		" " "	2	"
6	Golde "	4		F	"	"	"	"	"		" " "		"
7	[illegible] "	—	5	"	Infant	"	"	"	"		" " "		"
8	Mrs. G. Spence	24		"	Wife	England	Pittsburg Pa.	Yes	Yes		" " "		"
9	Annie "	4		"	Child	"	"	No	No		" " "		"
20	Nellie "	2		"	"	"	"	"	"	2–3	" " "	2	"
1	Leonard "	—	5	M	Infant	"	"	"	"		" " "		"
2	David [illegible]	21		"	Farmer	Russia	Phil^a Pa	Yes	Yes		" " Port	1	"
3	[illegible]	20		"	Farmer	"	New York	"	"		" " "	1	"
4	Abraham [illegible]	40		"	Labourer	"	"	"	"		" " "	1	"
5	N. S. [illegible]	19		F	Spinster	"	"	"	"		" " Stern	1	"
6	[illegible]	36		"	Wife	"	"	No	No		" " "		"
7	[illegible] "	4		M	Child	"	"	"	"	12–8	" " "	1	"
8	Rochel [illegible]	30		F	Wife	"	"	"	"		" " "		"
9	[illegible] "	7		M	Child	"	"	"	"		" " "		"
30	Moses "	6		"	"	"	"	"	"		" " "	4	"
1	Israel "	4		"	"	"	"	"	"		" " "		"
2	[illegible]	26		F	Wife	"	"	Yes	Yes		" " "	1	"
33	Lea [illegible]	30		"	Spinster	"	"	No	No		" " "	1	"

19 — 14 — 33

senger list of the ocean liner Nevada

ued on the arrival of the S.S. *Nevada* at the port of New York

January 1892. The Irishwoman Annie Moor is listed on the

Typographically this form is scarcely distinguishable from the

tax form of a hundred years earlier illustrated on the previous page.

Business forms (1900s)

Forms enable the growth of industry

Forms were used not only by state administrators but also by private individuals and businesses. In the industrial age of the 19th century, there was an enormous need for efficient organization to accompany the construction of railways, mines, steelworks and factories, not to mention the banks that were founded to finance this era of invention. Small businesses now became limited companies and more and more cheques had to be issued, invoices written, incomes taxed, and the wages of a rapidly growing workforce calculated to the nearest penny.

At this time, two new developments changed the appearance and function of the forms used by businesses in increasing numbers: lithography and the typewriter.

Lithography allows decoration

Lithography was invented in 1796, and for the first time it enabled illustrations to be mass-produced, even in colour. In letterpress printing, which had previously been the dominant technique, all graphic elements such as rules and vignette images were very expensive to produce and had to be built into the relief printing plate. With lithography, however, the design could be drawn directly on the plate (originally a flat piece of limestone) with special ink or chalk. Illustrations, trademarks, crosshatching and other motifs became relatively simple to reproduce. As shown by the examples opposite, industrialists and bankers were keen to make use of this new technique, which was widespread well into the 1930s. A detailed image of a firm's factory with smoking chimney stacks, elaborate decorations and ornate typefaces could all be used to proclaim the prosperity of a business or bank.

Typewriters increase efficiency

The typewriter, meanwhile, invented in the 19th century and an essential piece of office equipment for many decades, did not make forms more decorative, but it did make them more efficient. With just a little practice, it became possible to write much faster and much more legibly. The uniform characters and line spacing allowed figures to be placed precisely beneath one another and at regular distances apart, making it easier to do calculations. Forms now had to match these standard distances, and so from now on their designs were determined by measurements.

Note: the phrase 'carbon copy' led to the abbreviation 'cc', which is still used in emails

The biggest advantage of the typewriter, however, lay in the fact that it was possible to create an immediate copy of any typewritten document with the aid of carbon paper.

Invoice issued by the Ernst Plange metalware factory This invoice was typewritten in 1924, but typographically it is still typical of business forms used at the turn of the century.

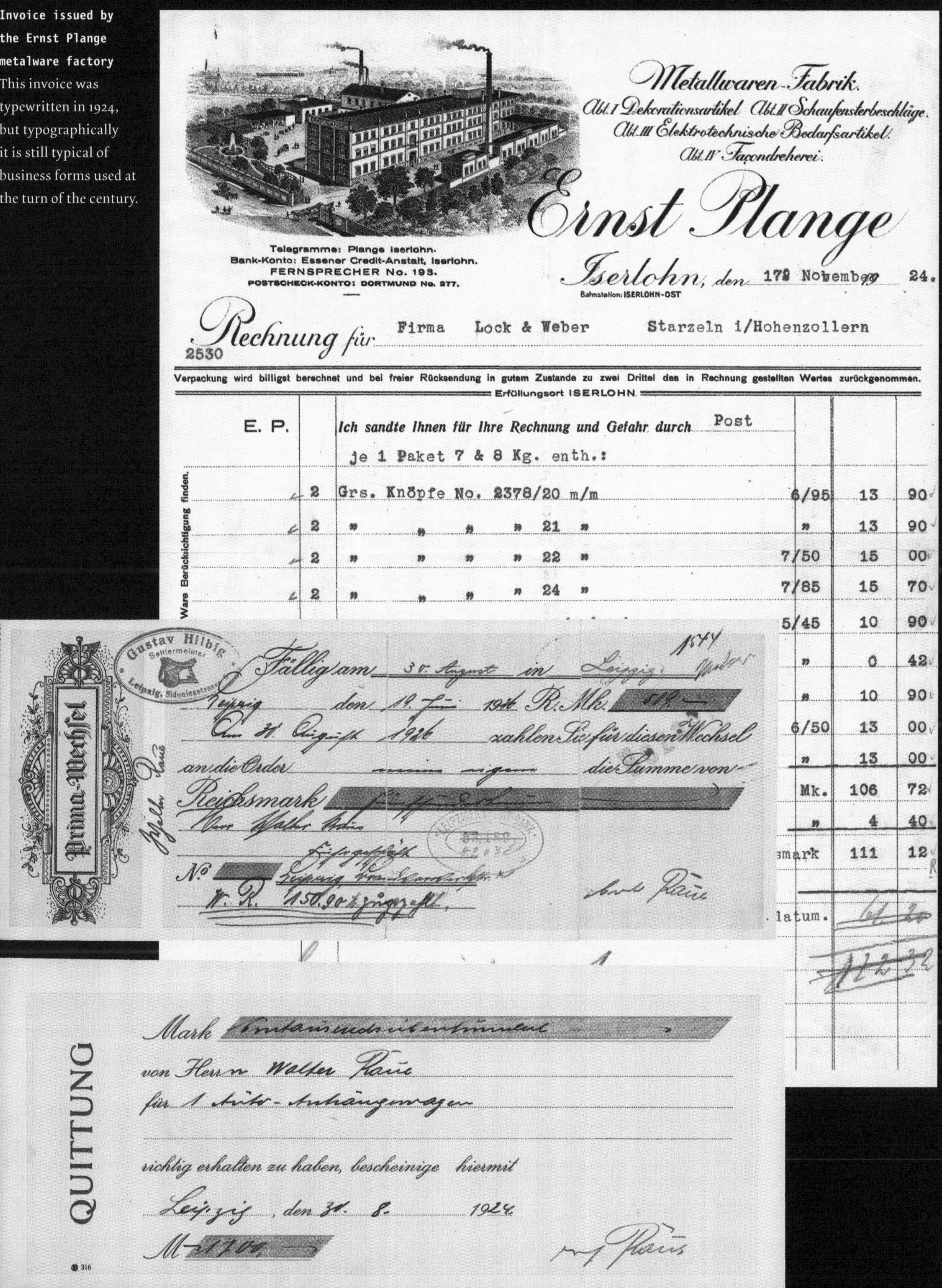

Metallwaren-Fabrik.
Abt. I Dekorationsartikel Abt. II Schaufensterbeschläge.
Abt. III Elektrotechnische Bedarfsartikel.
Abt. IV Façondreherei.

Ernst Plange

Telegramme: Plange Iserlohn.
Bank-Konto: Essener Credit-Anstalt, Iserlohn.
FERNSPRECHER No. 193.
POSTSCHECK-KONTO: DORTMUND No. 277.

Iserlohn, den 17. November 1924.
Bahnstation: ISERLOHN-OST

Rechnung für Firma Lock & Weber Starzeln i/Hohenzollern
2530

Verpackung wird billigst berechnet und bei freier Rücksendung in gutem Zustande zu zwei Drittel des in Rechnung gestellten Wertes zurückgenommen.
Erfüllungsort ISERLOHN.

... Ware Berücksichtigung finden.

E. P.		Ich sandte Ihnen für Ihre Rechnung und Gefahr durch Post			
		je 1 Paket 7 & 8 Kg. enth.:			
	2	Grs. Knöpfe No. 2378/20 m/m	6/95	13	90
	2	" " " " 21 "	"	13	90
	2	" " " " 22 "	7/50	15	00
	2	" " " " 24 "	7/85	15	70
			5/45	10	90
			"	0	42
			"	10	90
			6/50	13	00
			"	13	00
			Mk.	106	72
			"	4	40
		...smark		111	12
		...latum.			

Gustav Hilbig
Sattlermeister
Leipzig, Sidonienstrasse

Prima-Wechsel

Fällig am 30. August in Leipzig

Leipzig den 19. Juni 1924 R.Mk. 500.—

Am 30. August 1924 zahlen Sie für diesen Wechsel

an die Order meine eigene die Summe von

Reichsmark fünfhundert

No

Leipziger Credit-Bank

QUITTUNG

Mark

von Herrn

für 1 Auto-Anhängewagen

richtig erhalten zu haben, bescheinige hiermit

Leipzig, den 30. 8. 1924

M 1700.—

316

Bill of exchange and receipt issued in the 1920s

Modernist forms (1929)

Functionalism finds its ideal expression in forms

Instead of old-fashioned embellishments and typographical flourishes, these German administrative forms make use of the modernist style known as the New Typography. It was no longer just the technological possibilities that determined how printed matter was laid out, but ideology also played its part. In the wake of the Werkbund, the Bauhaus and De Stijl, typography was renewed and modernized, and designers such as Jan Tschichold, Kurt Schwitters and Paul Renner promoted a radical change from conventional type design under the umbrella title of the New or Elementary Typography: on the one hand they wanted experimentation, and on the other practical functionality. It was this functionalism that found its ideal domain in forms.

These forms, designed by Kurt Schwitters, were completely in tune with the new concepts. They feature a strict layout of horizontal and vertical lines, have clear divisions, and use a straightforward sans serif typeface. This approach was a much better fit with the rational, technical nature of the new trades and industries, and it was not confined to letterheads and invoices. Architects such as Peter Behrens began to design whole companies, from factory buildings through to products and even the logo, thus laying the foundations for what we now call corporate design.

It is interesting, however, that Schwitters's intention was not to impose the same design scheme on every written document, poster and printed paper issued by the city of Hanover. Instead, his aim was to make identical things as identical as possible, different things as different as possible, and similar things merely similar.

Sans serifs and severity are no guarantee of a good form

The ideals of the New Typography underwent further development in Switzerland, resulting in the International Typographic Style (also known as the Swiss Style), which is still influential today. This has led to both good results, regarding issues such as order and systematization which are important in the field of forms, and to misunderstandings, such as a short-sighted insistence on sans serif type and the confusion of severity and minimalism with functionality. The use of straight lines and Helvetica in itself is simply not enough to create a properly functioning form.

STÄDT. TUBERKULOSEKRANKENHAUS HANNOVER
HEILSTÄTTE HEIDEHAUS

VERNEHMUNG eine__ Hilfsbedürftigen, d__ am ______ öffentl. Armenfürsorge beansprucht hat.

Verhandelt **HANNOVER,** den 19

1. Vollständiger Vor- und Zuname: (Der Rufname ist zu unterstreichen.)
2. Geburtsort (Kreis u. Regierungsbezirk):
3. Datum der Geburt:
4. Stand oder Gewerbe:
5. Staatszugehörigkeit:
6. Religion:
7. Wohnung:

		Namen	Beruf	Wohnort	Todestag
8. **Eltern:**	Vater:				
	Mutter:				
9. **Gatten:**	Ehemann:				
	Ehefrau:				

10. **Kinder:** Namen	Geburtstag	Geburtsort	Beruf	Wohnort, Arbeitsstelle, Verdienst

11. Wo hat d. Hilfsbedürftige sich während des letzten Jahres aufgehalten?

12. Aufenthaltsort (Gemeinde, Kreis, Regierungsbezirk.)	Dauer des Aufenthalts vom bis	Wohnung und Arbeitsstelle

13. Wo, von wann bis wann und bei wem stand d. Hilfsbedürftige (bei Frauen und Kindern: der Mann bzw. Vater) zuletzt gegen Lohn oder Gehalt in einem Dienst- oder Arbeitsverhältnis? — Bei Frauen u. Kindern unter 16 Jahren ist anzugeben, ob sie sich bei Eintritt ihrer Hilfsbedürftigkeit beim Familienoberhaupte befunden haben?
14. Welcher Krankenkasse gehörte er / sie infolge dieser Beschäftigung an oder aus welchem Grunde unterlag er / sie nicht dem Versicherungszwange?
15. Hat der Hilfsbedürftige in den letzten 3 Wochen vor seiner Erkrankung wegen Erwerbslosigkeit seine Arbeit aufgegeben, so ist anzugeben, ob und wo er in den vorangegangenen 12 Monaten mindestens 26 Wochen oder unmittelbar vorher mindestens 6 Wochen — in beiden Fällen gerechnet vom Eintritt der Erwerbslosigkeit ab — in versicherungspflichtiger Beschäftigung gestanden und welcher Krankenkasse er angehört hat.
16. Ist d. Hilfsbedürftige freiwilliges Mitglied einer Kranken- und Sterbekasse, ev. welcher und seit wann?
17. Renten- und Pensionsbezüge? aus welcher Kasse? — monatl. ____ RM. vierteljährl. ____ RM.
18. Ausstehende Forderungen (Lohn usw.)? gegen wen? — wie hoch?

H. 29. 1000.

MAGISTRAT HANNOVER
STEUERAMT / BIERSTEUER-ABTEILUNG

Die Steuererklärung über die in einem Kalendermonat steuerpflichtig gewordenen Getränke ist bis zum 15. des folgenden Monats dem Steueramt, Rathaus, Zimmer 68, Schalter 1, zugleich mit der Berechnung der Steuer einzureichen. Die Steuer ist spätestens bis zu demselben Tage bei der Steuerkasse, Rathaus, Zimmer 76, unter Vorlage der vom Steueramt abgefertigten Empfangsbescheinigung einzuzahlen. Wird die Steuer auf Postscheckkonto Hannover 17 der Städtischen Steuerkasse unter der Angabe Biersteuer eingezahlt, ist dieses hierunter zu vermerken.

BIERSTEUER-ERKLÄRUNG

über die von der Firma ________________________________

____

als Einbringer — Empfänger — in der Zeit vom __________ bis __________ 19___
in die Stadt Hannover **eingeführten** Biere.

a) **Es sind eingeführt worden:**

		Steuersatz	Steuerbetrag
1. Hannoversche Biere und Bier der Brauerei Scheele, Anderten	____ hl ____ l	2.— RM.	= ______ RM.
2. Andere auswärtige Biere	____ hl ____ l	2.25 RM.	= ______ RM.
3. Starkbier	____ hl ____ l	3.— RM.	= ______ RM.

zusammen ______ RM.
hiervon ab zu vergütende Steuer (s. unten) . . . . . . ______ RM.
bleiben zu zahlen . . . . . ______ RM.

b) **Es sind zu erstatten:** für nach Einführung und Versteuerung wieder ausgeführtes Bier.

		Steuersatz	Steuerbetrag
1. Bier der Brauerei Scheele, Anderten	____ hl ____ l	2.— RM.	= ______ RM.
2. Auswärtige Biere	____ hl ____ l	2.25 RM.	= ______ RM.
3. Starkbier	____ hl ____ l	3.— RM.	= ______ RM.

Gesamtbetrag der zu vergütenden Steuer . . . . . . = ______ RM.

Die Richtigkeit und Vollständigkeit dieser Steuererklärung sowie die Übereinstimmung mit den Geschäftsbüchern versichere ich — versichern wir — hiermit ausdrücklich.

HANNOVER, den __________ 19___

____
(Unterschrift des Steuerpflichtigen)

Rechnerisch geprüft und festgestellt auf

RM. ________________________

Hebebuch Nr. ________________________

HANNOVER, den __________ 19___

____

h. 671 29 1000.

MAGISTRAT DER STADT HANNOVER

EINÄSCHERUNGS-URKUNDE

Die Leiche d____ am ____ ten __________________ 19____ verstorbenen

____

ist am ______ ten ______________ 19____ in der Feuerbestattungs-

anlage der Stadt Hannover eingeäschert worden.

Nr. ________ des Einäscherungsregisters 19______ Aschenkapsel Nr. ________

HANNOVER, den ______ ten ______________ 19____

Die Verwaltung des Stadtfriedhofes an der Seelhorst

h. 589. 29. 1000.

Forms issued by Hanover City Council, 1929
Above left: Hospital examination form
Above right: Tax declaration for imported beer
Below right: Certificate of cremation

Kurt Schwitters was responsible for the design of all the city of Hanover's printed matter from 1929 to 1934. In the top right corner of every form is Schwitters's reworking of the city's emblem: a triangular clover leaf

Forms in Nazi Germany (1933–45)

Forms as an expression of arbitrary power

Forms are not always rational and neutral – they can also be instruments of arbitrary power, cruelty and terror. This is particularly evident in the forms used during the Third Reich.

Selection by means of forms

Aside from the swastika stamp, the documents illustrated appear to be perfectly ordinary administrative forms. Their shocking and horrific nature lies not in their design but in the questions, information and procedures they record. They announce the withdrawal of all civic rights, the confiscation of property, and deportation, and even give decisions on whether someone is to live or die. In those days, a suspicious-sounding name or the 'wrong' entry on someone's identification papers could determine that person's fate, and this was not a matter of chance but was part of a meticulously planned system. It started out from the insane concept of recording the family background of vast swathes of the population, and used this to divide them up into lives 'worth living' and 'not worth living' by means of forms containing information about religion, political allegiance and health.

Forms and responsibility

The fact that a bureaucracy could become an administrative weapon of mass destruction was perhaps connected to the functional image that all bureaucracies have. They adhere rigidly to the procedures laid down for them, and questioning the basis of their own actions is not on the agenda. Nazi officials were not supposed to concern themselves with issues of conscience or of personal responsibility, for they were only doing their duty. With the use of forms and the associated reduction of people and relationships to abstract objects, even the most appalling decisions no longer seemed arbitrary but appeared to follow a logical, legitimate course with inevitable consequences. The form did not permit any alternative, and this bureaucratic power made it easier to ignore individual responsibility.

These events certainly came to embody the dark side of bureaucracy, and forms and stamps were no longer commonplace tools of the trade but for many people represented the concepts of surveillance, injustice and helplessness.

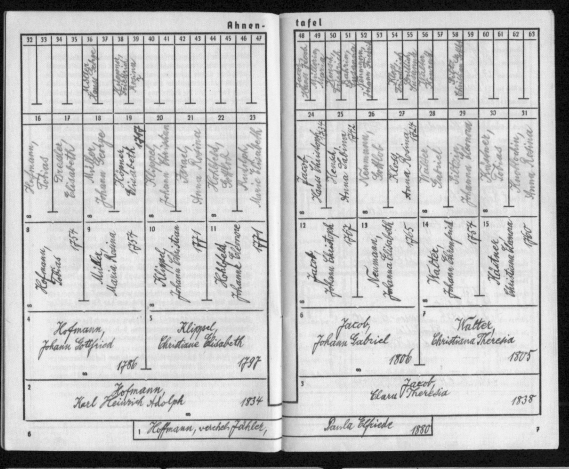

Above: Double page of a pass showing proof of ancestry
Below left: Certificate of exclusion from the Wehrmacht
Below right: Certificate of expatriation
While the other two forms are almost exclusively in blackletter type, in keeping with the characteristic style of the Nazis, the especially cruel expatriation certificate uses Paul Renner's modernist sans serif Futura. The expression *Alterstransport* ['transport of the elderly'] is a euphemism for deportation to an extermination camp.

Electronic data processing (c. 1983)

Forms remain consistent

Forms are not a medium that tends to embrace new design trends quickly. On the contrary, form design is always characterized by pragmatic consistency. This saves money, and many forms barely change at all for decades on end. The new printing and typesetting techniques of the 20th century, such as phototypesetting and offset printing, certainly allowed for greater freedom of design than the old hot-metal typesetting, but this did not necessarily lead to improvements. After this point, the print could be reduced, compressed and distorted at will, with as many items as possible squeezed onto the page, often at the cost of readability and ergonomics.

IT has changed the role, use and appearance of forms

A much more far-reaching change which has continued into the present is illustrated by the form shown opposite, which is designed for electronic data processing (EDP). Since the 1970s, digital data processing systems have made conventional forms largely redundant, or have changed them radically. Companies and public services have gained enormously from digitalization: customer information, and business and payment procedures can now be centrally stored, linked together, copied and retrieved from anywhere. Processing times have been shortened, thus at least theoretically saving on working hours and staff. On the other hand, ways and means had to be found to transfer the information from paper to computer, and then from computer back to paper. In the example opposite, the form structures the data in a manner suitable for computer input, but it first has to be filled in by hand. It was also in the 1970s that the first document readers were introduced. These automatically read the handwritten entries so that they did not need to be transcribed manually. Paper forms were no longer the only processing and storage medium, and became a kind of halfway house between human and machine.

Forms and their users, however, are still dependent on technology, and since the software can only accept a specific number of characters, and the document reader can only recognize individual characters, responses can no longer be written in any old fashion. Character dividers and boxes compel users to split words and numbers into letters and digits and to stick rigidly to the text fields provided.

Legibility suffers and the form threatens to disappear

Even the provision of information was initially a problem. The legibility of new invoices, instructions and statements suffered because of poor text quality and the limited capabilities of early dot matrix and laser printers. It was, however, possible to issue statements quickly and in large quantities without requiring a pre-printed form, and this meant the end of many kinds of form that had been used down through the centuries.

British Telecommunications
Prestel (UK)
APPLICATION FORM

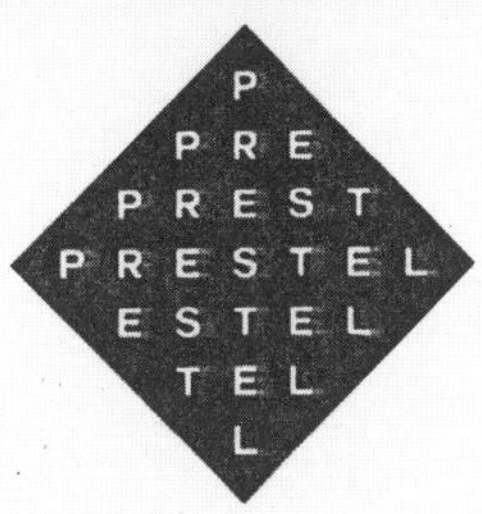

29815

Please use a ballpoint pen and print clearly in block capitals

All applicants please complete details below

Name (for use in correspondence)
1

Address (at which service is required)
3
Postcode

Contact name (if different from 1)
5
Daytime telephone number | extension no.

Business description or occupation
6

Telephone No. service is to be used on (incl. dialing code)
7 | extension no.

Please state the type of Prestel Equipment you will be plugging into the telephone line.

8	Manufacturer PRISM		
	Model Name/Number VTX5000		
	Modem ✓	Adaptor	Prestel set

Name (for bills, if different from 1)
2

Address (to which bill should be sent if different from 3)
4
Postcode

Please tick appropriate boxes below

44	Y / N	I do not wish my telephone number, as given in box 7, to appear on the screen.
45	R	I am a residential user
	B	I am a business user
46	Y / N	I request that a PST jack socket be ordered on my behalf.
47	Y / N	My telephone line is a shared line. NB: If you have a shared line it will need to be de-shared before you can link to Prestel. You will need to contact British Telecom to arrange this.

I apply for Prestel Service to be provided as described in this application. I have read the Notice to Customers and the Special Terms and Conditions (Existing Customers should not sign here) I am over 18 years of age.

9 Signature

on behalf of (company name)

Position in company

Partnership applications should be signed by a partner in the firm 'For self and partners'. Applications by limited companies should be signed by an authorised person on behalf of the company.

Date

FOR OFFICIAL USE ONLY

New line 10 Y/N | 11 PST JACK REQUIRED Y/N | PST JACK ORDERED Y/N | Terminal telephone number 12 | Extension number | Ex directory 13 Y/N

Tariff 14 B/R/S | Area 15 | 16 Issued by | Duty ref | Date

Account number 17 | Bill day 18 6 9 | Tariff type 19 M | Rebate 20 | Null CUG 21 | IRCs 22 Dryden, Kipling, Derwent, Enterprise, Dickens, Keats

Customer identity 23 | Password 24 | Welcome frame Main Index 38 3 | Stats 'A' 25 1 M Orig. | Tabs code 26

Registration date (& tariff date) 27 | Off date | Terminal type 28 | Stats 'B' 29 S S micro | II 30

VAT 33 Y/N | Additional information 35

36 Prepared by | Date | Keyed by | Date | PAF number 37 M

Prestel application form, c. 1983

Prestel was an early interactive videotext service run by British Telecom. So that the information can be correctly entered into the data processing system, the user must keep strictly within the character boxes provided. Note the unusual numbering of

E-government (present day)

E-government is meant to make public services more user-friendly, flexible, accessible and also cheaper

The years of the New Economy included the advent of two new concepts: *e-commerce* and *e-government*. Since then, e-commerce has become part of everyday life, as exemplified by Amazon, eBay and online banking. E-government, on the other hand, has remained more of a ideal, which claims to make public services more user-friendly, more flexible and easier to deal with, while reducing processing costs and staff levels. However, while internal communications are already paperless to a large degree, interaction with clients has proved to be a fundamental problem. There are to date no simple, unified methods in general use to establish beyond doubt the identity of clients over the Internet. And so in most communities, e-government has remained limited to the use of PDF forms that can be printed out.

E-government is not always practical

Nevertheless, some aspects of public service interaction can now be implemented almost entirely by means of online forms. Each one solves the identity problem in a different way, by chip-and-PIN cards, registration and passwords, or with the conventional printout and signature. But compared to online banking, in matters of user-friendliness, readability and design, these are often less practical and even inferior to their paper predecessors. Instead of exploiting the potential for interaction and making it easier to fill in the blanks, they are confusing, and often suffer from incomprehensible jargon, compounded by equally incomprehensible menus and symbols. There can also be major problems when the form is displayed in different browsers, and layout designs can range from non-existent to overly fussy.

Forms still have a future

We shall end this potted history of forms with a question: what is the future role of forms? Are standardized methods of communication even feasible in a time of increasing personalization? On the one hand, of course, there is a great need for individually tailored products, and these require personal advice rather than a form. In countries where the state has withdrawn from areas of public welfare, there is also a need to replace *formalized* approaches with *individualized* solutions. On the other hand, however, an increasing number of private and public services are becoming automated, and are now implemented without any personal contact. Both now and in the future, these services need to be based on well-designed forms that will be of real help to companies, services and clients, whether on paper or online.

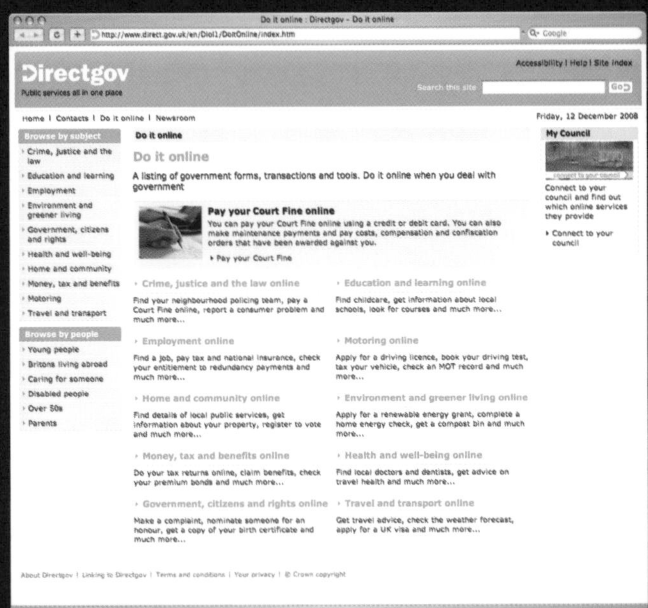

Directgov public services web portal, UK
The Directgov website brings together all official information and practical advice from the UK government and public services. Payments, applications and other transactions can all be made online.

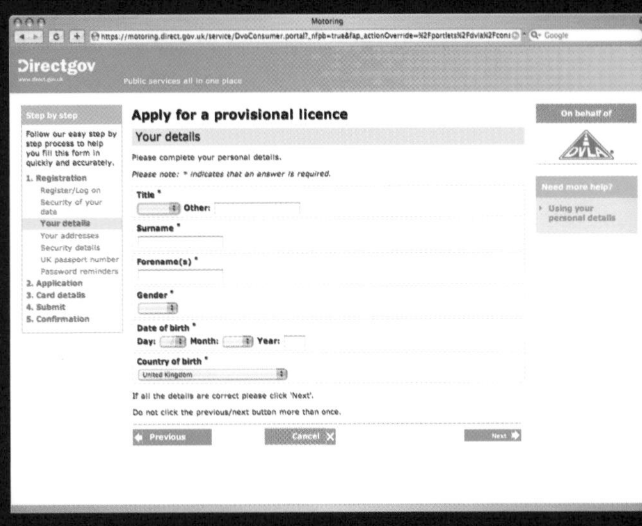

Directgov driving licence application, UK
An example of an online application form. Instructions are given in plain English and are easy to understand, but the visual presentation seems rather unfinished. The use of the colour red (usually used to attract attention or highlight errors) for the 'Previous' and 'Next' buttons is potentially misleading.

Australian Electoral Commission website, Australia
Online forms for public services often include long stretches of unstructured text with many cross-references, which require a lot of clicking before the goal is reached. It is rare to find one that takes a quick-start approach.

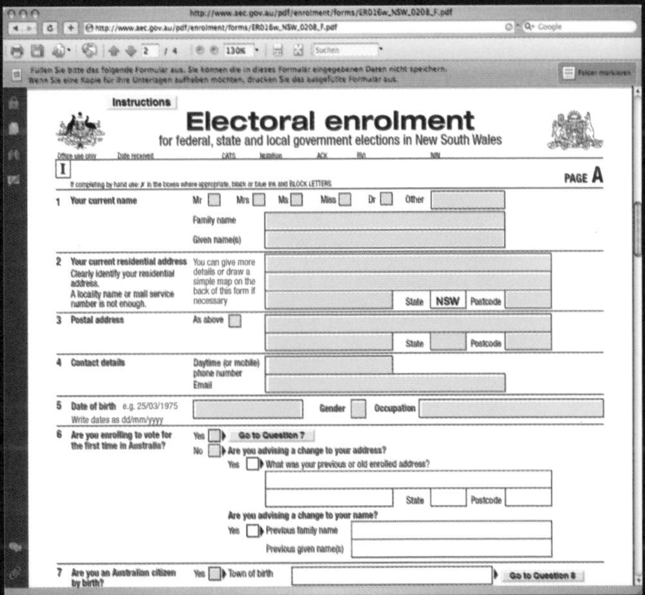

PDF electoral enrolment form, Australia
E-government users often find themselves filling in PDF forms such as this one. It can be completed on screen, but it's really just a digital version of a paper form and must be printed out and sent by normal mail.

Four examples of e-government forms, from the UK and Australia

1.3

Types of form

Communication forms and dialogue forms

Forms for communication, forms for dialogue

The variety of forms in circulation seems to be endless, with forms for practically every aspect of bureaucracy. Since form design always begins by looking at existing form types and the purposes they serve, we shall now try to offer a quick overview.

Forms can basically be divided into two groups, depending on the direction in which the information flows: *communication forms* and *dialogue forms*. Each of these includes several subgroups, and these will be shown on the following pages. Another distinguishing feature is the target group, which may be internal (colleagues) or external (clients, partners, the public).

Communication forms convey information

Communication forms serve to send information in one direction only: from the provider to the user. The provider creates the form, fills it with information, and passes it on to the user, who reads the content and acts accordingly. Examples are invoices, receipts, notices, statements and records.

Dialogue forms gather information

Dialogue forms go a step further. The provider creates a form with blank spaces which is passed on to the user. This too is a kind of information, since it is a request for the form to be filled in, the object being to obtain information from the user in the manner specified by the form. The user inserts the information, and returns it to the provider for evaluation, thereby reversing the roles: the user becomes the sender, and the provider becomes the receiver. Thus the form initiates a dialogue. Examples of this type of form include applications, order forms and questionnaires.

Internal forms organize, external forms interact

Internal forms include such items as time sheets, expenses forms and sick notes. Their main function is organizational and they reflect internal divisions of labour. *External forms* include applications, contracts and invoices. They permit interaction and exchanges of information between provider and user, and as well as being efficient tools of the trade, they are also a means for providers to present themselves to the outside world.

Communication forms

- Invoices, bills and receipts
- Notices and statements
- Records and checklists
- Certificates and passes
- Tickets, cheques and shares

The provider uses the form to give out information and does not expect a response from the user.

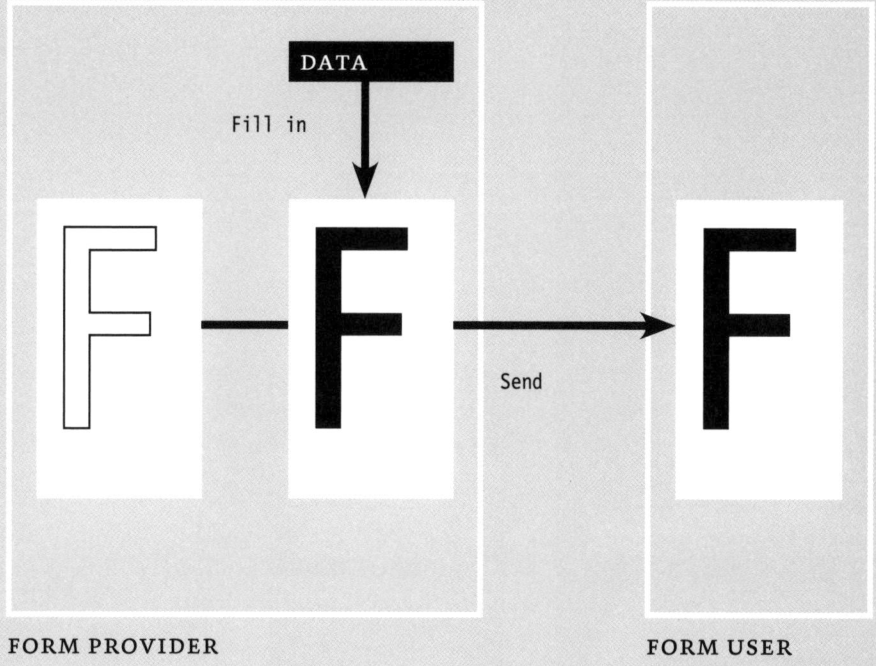

Dialogue forms

- Application forms
- Registration forms
- Declarations
- Orders and contracts
- Questionnaires

The provider sends out the form; the user fills in the form. Data is passed forwards and backwards, and the form enables interaction between provider and user.

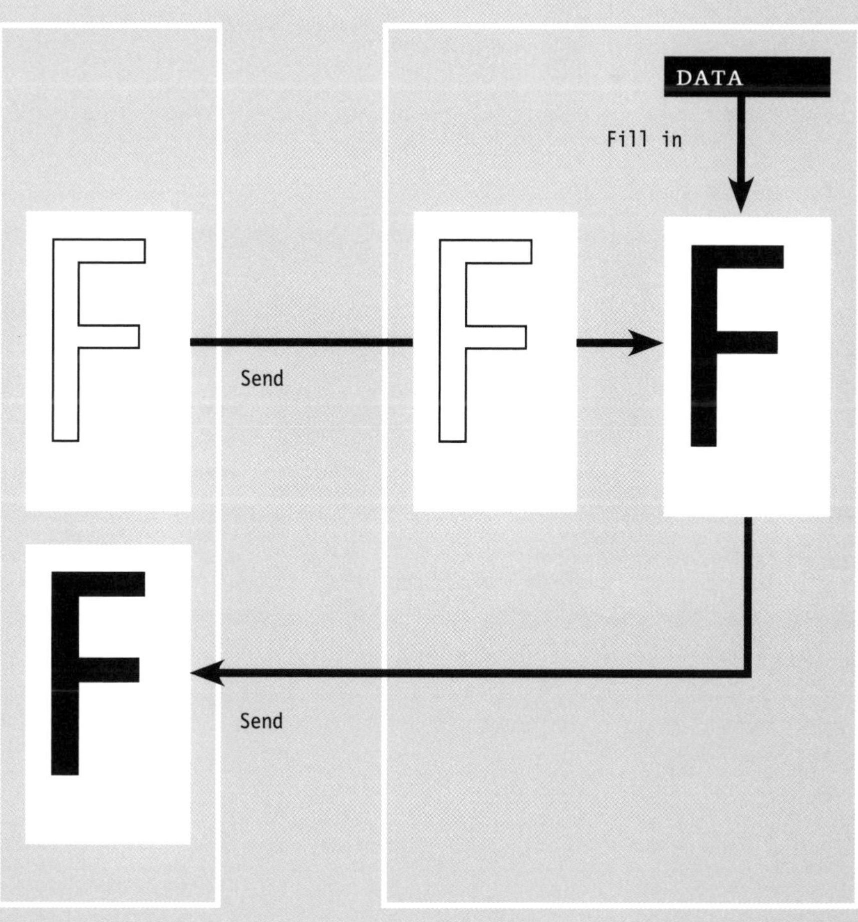

Application forms

Application forms express claims and requirements

The purpose of application forms is to ask public services to meet demands or requirements relating to money, services or permission. Some businesses in the private sector, such as insurance or credit companies, also issue application forms.

These forms are designed to communicate the applicant's request and to provide the organization or company with the information needed to reach a decision.

Application forms collect sensitive information

Applications, in contrast to order forms, almost always involve some kind of justification. Applicants must put their reasons into writing, and the form determines the way these will be presented. Quite often, however, the justification means supplying personal information about an applicant, and this requires trust on one side and sensitivity on the other. Application forms therefore serve their purpose better if they are not felt to be a bureaucratic and even unnecessary intrusion into the private domain, but can be regarded simply as an effective way of obtaining what the law allows. They should not appear to be an off-putting obstacle, but should be an accessible, clear and uncomplicated means of communication.

Turning applications into order forms

With application forms that serve a contractual purpose – e.g. opening an account or applying for credit – it is always worth considering whether they could be designed as order forms. Potential users may well find it easier and more pleasant to fill in a form that is an order rather than an application, particularly when they are the ones who will end up having to pay.

Provider

The logo represents the provider of the form.

→ page 161

Return address

The completed form needs to be sent here. The pre-printed address is positioned so that it will appear in the window of the return envelope.

→ page 164

Applicant

Requested details usually include name, date of birth, address and phone number.

Contact details

These should be complete and placed somewhere easy to find, as they are essential if problems or queries arise.

→ page 162

Basis for decision

This is information that the providers will use to judge whether or not the application is valid.

NEWFORT CITY COUNCIL

Housing Benefits Claim

→ Please fill in this form and return it to:

Newfort City Council
Benefits Service
PO Box 10
1 Haymarket Square
Newfort NF1 8HL

Benefits Service
phone 01456 23 23 10
fax 01456 23 23 11
e-mail benefits@newfort.gov.uk

Benefits office
Town Hall
1 Haymarket Square

Office hours
Monday to Friday 10 am to 6 pm

1 ABOUT YOU

Title: ☑ Mr ☐ Mrs ☐ Miss ☐ Ms ☐ Other
Last name: WILLIAMS
First name(s): DAVID JAMES
Address: 92 VICTORIA LANE
SOUTH GARDENS
NEWFORT Postcode NF4 7JP
Date of birth: 23.01.1968
Daytime phone number: 01456 279610

2 ABOUT YOUR EARNINGS

Annual salary: £ 11645.00
Money is paid every: ☐ week ☐ fortnight ☐ 4 weeks ☑ month

3 ABOUT YOUR RENT

Rent: £ 845.00
Rent is due every: ☐ week ☐ fortnight ☐ 4 weeks ☑ month
Rent includes: ☐ Gas ☑ Water charges ☐ Electricity ☐ None of the above

4 HOW YOU WANT TO BE PAID

Housing Benefit should be paid: ☐ by cheque
Please go straight to 5.
☑ into a bank or building society account
Please give us your account details below.

Name of bank or building society: NFB BANK
Account holder: D. J. WILLIAMS
Account number: 9747 9742
Sort code: 66 22 02

5 DECLARATION

I declare that the information I have given on this form is correct.

Signature: D. Willi—
Date of signature: 08.11.2010

Official use only
Verified by
Checked by
Date stamp

Declaration

A dated signature confirms the information given and makes the form a legally binding document.

→ page 177

Official use only

Sections that the applicant does not need to fill can be obtrusive. If they must be included, they should be clearly separated from the rest.

→ page 199

ANTRAG AUF LEISTUNGEN ZUR SICHERUNG DES LEBENSUNTERHALTS NACH DEM ZWEITEN BUCH SOZIALGESETZBUCH (SGB II)

- ARBEITSLOSENGELD II / SOZIALGELD -

Ihre Angaben werden aufgrund der §§ 60 - 65 Erstes Buch Sozialgesetzbuch (SGB I) und der §§ 67a, b, c Zehntes Buch Sozialgesetzbuch (SGB X) für die Leistungen nach dem SGB II erhoben. Die Daten unterliegen dem Sozialgeheimnis (vgl. auch S. 57 f des Merkblattes).

Ausfüllhinweise sind bei den örtlich zuständigen Stellen erhältlich oder im Internet unter http://arbeitslosengeld2.arbeitsagentur.de **abrufbar.**

Bitte den Antragsvordruck in Druckbuchstaben ausfüllen!

Dienststelle

Nr. der Bedarfsgemeinschaft

Org.Einheit

- nur ausfüllen, wenn die Angaben bekannt sind -

Tag der Antragstellung

EINGANGSSTEMPEL

- nicht vom Antragsteller auszufüllen -

Antrag angenommen am:

Der Antragsteller/Die Antragstellerin hat sich ausgewiesen durch:

☐ Bundespersonalausweis
☐ Pass
☐ Sonstige Ausweispapiere (Hz. Datum)

I. Allgemeine Daten des Antragstellers/der Antragstellerin

Familienname

Vorname

Straße, Haus-Nr. - ggf. bei wem -

PLZ, Wohnort

☎ Telefonnummer (mit Vorwahl) und/oder E-Mail-Adresse für mögliche Rückfragen

Bankverbindung (bitte angeben, weil die Leistungen bargeldlos überwiesen werden)
Bankleitzahl (BLZ) Konto-Nr.

bei Bank/Postbank/Sparkasse, sonstigem Kreditinstitut

Name des Kontoinhabers

Die Übermittlung der Leistungen an den Wohnort ist in der Regel kostenpflichtig.
Ausnahme: Sie können ohne eigenes Verschulden kein Girokonto eröffnen (bitte Nachweis beifügen).

Hinweise für die Sachbearbeitung
(wird von der zuständigen Stelle eingetragen)

Personen ☐① ☐② ☐③ ☐④ ☐⑤

Arbeitsaufnahme am

Erste Lohn-/Gehaltszahlung am

Arbeitsunfähig ab

Stat. Erfassung

(Hz.Dat./Org.E)

Haben Sie in den letzten drei Monaten vor dem Tag der Antragstellung (Datum siehe oben) mindestens einen Tag Arbeitslosengeld II bezogen und sind seitdem nicht umgezogen? ☐ ja ☐ nein
Wenn die Frage mit „**ja**" zu beantworten ist, wird Ihnen das Ausfüllen dieses Antragsvordrucks erleichtert.
Sie können dann in den **Abschnitten II bis X** das Feld „**keine Änderung**" ankreuzen, wenn gegenüber den Angaben im vorherigen Antrag tatsächlich **keine Änderungen** eingetreten sind.

II. Persönliche Verhältnisse der zur Bedarfsgemeinschaft gehörenden Person/en — **Keine Änderung** ☐

	Antragsteller / Antragstellerin Ich bin ☐ allein stehend ☐ allein erziehende(r) Mutter/Vater Die Kinder sind in Abschnitt III einzutragen.	Ich lebe zusammen mit: ☐ nicht dauernd getrennt lebendem Ehegatten ☐ nicht dauernd getrennt lebendem/r eingetragenen/r Lebenspartner/in ☐ Partner in Verantwortungs- und Einstehensgemeinschaft *) ☐ sonstiger Person (kein/e Verwandte/r) bitte nur Zusatzblatt 5 ausfüllen
	①	②
Name (ggf. Geburtsname)		
Vorname		
Geschlecht	☐ weiblich ☐ männlich	☐ weiblich ☐ männlich
Geburtsdatum/Geburtsort		

*) Nähere Erläuterungen zum Begriff „Partner/in in Verantwortungs- und Einstehensgemeinschaft" siehe Ausfüllhinweise

BA Alg II - A1 - 2007.01 1

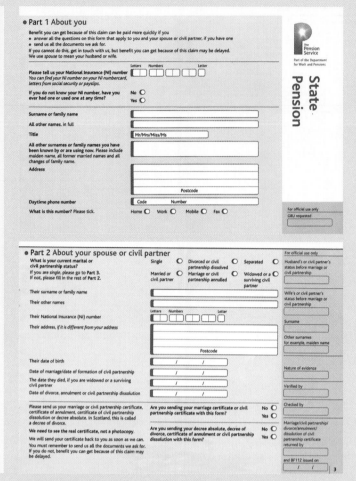

Unemployment benefit form, Germany

This is a familiar benefit form in Germany. The German unemployment benefit system was recently reformed at a cost of billions, but evidently there was neither time nor money available to create more readable and ergonomically designed forms.

• Part 1 About you

Benefit you can get because of this claim can be paid more quickly if you
- answer all the questions on this form that apply to you and your spouse or civil partner, if you have one
- send us all the documents we ask for.

If you cannot do this, get in touch with us, but benefit you can get because of this claim may be delayed.
We use *spouse* to mean your husband or wife.

Please tell us your National Insurance (NI) number Letters Numbers Letter
You can find your NI number on your NI numbercard, letters from social security or payslips.

If you do not know your NI number, have you ever had one or used one at any time? No ○ Yes ○

Surname or family name

All other names, in full

Title Mr/Mrs/Miss/Ms

All other surnames or family names you have been known by or are using now. Please include maiden name, all former married names and all changes of family name.

Address

Postcode

Daytime phone number Code Number

What is this number? Please tick. Home ○ Work ○ Mobile ○ Fax ○

The Pension Service
Part of the Department for Work and Pensions

State Pension

For official use only
GBU requested

• Part 2 About your spouse or civil partner

What is your current marital or civil partnership status?
If you are *single*, please go to **Part 3**.
If not, please fill in the rest of **Part 2**.

Single ○ Divorced or civil partnership dissolved ○ Separated ○
Married or civil partner ○ Marriage or civil partnership annulled ○ Widowed or a surviving civil partner ○

Their surname or family name

Their other names

Their National Insurance (NI) number Letters Numbers Letter

Their address, *if it is different from your address*

Postcode

Their date of birth / /

Date of marriage/date of formation of civil partnership / /

The date they died, if you are widowed or a surviving civil partner / /

Date of divorce, annulment or civil partnership dissolution / /

Please send us your marriage or civil partnership certificate, certificate of annulment, certificate of civil partnership dissolution or decree absolute. In Scotland, this is called a decree of divorce.

We need to see the real certificate, not a photocopy.

We will send your certificate back to you as soon as we can.
You must remember to send us all the documents we ask for. If you do not, benefit you can get because of this claim may be delayed.

Are you sending your marriage certificate or civil partnership certificate with this form? No ○ Yes ○

Are you sending your decree absolute, decree of divorce, certificate of annulment or civil partnership dissolution with this form? No ○ Yes ○

For official use only
Husband's or civil partner's status before marriage or civil partnership
Wife's or civil partner's status before marriage or civil partnership
Surname
Other surnames for example, maiden name
Nature of evidence
Verified by
Checked by
Marriage/civil partnership/divorce/annulment/dissolution of civil partnership certificate returned by
and BF112 issued on / /

3

State pension claim, UK

Unlike the German application form for unemployment benefit, this British pension claim looks neat and well structured. British forms often include a substantial amount of text. Questions are generally written out in full, and are accompanied directly by explanatory notes. The downside of this is the large number of pages.

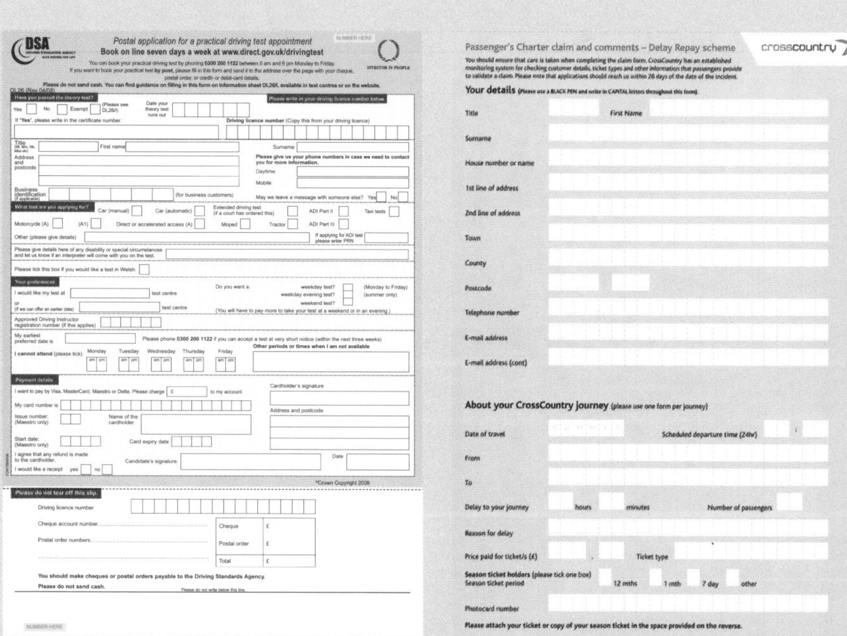

Postal application for a practical driving test appointment
Book on line seven days a week at www.direct.gov.uk/drivingtest

Passenger's Charter claim and comments – Delay Repay scheme

Please complete all white sections in BLOCK CAPITALS using blue or black ink.
Applicants must be 18 or over.

apply today

Driving test application, train fare compensation claim, credit card application, UK

A selection of everyday application forms. It is curious that the credit application form looks just as confusing and off-putting as a claim to an official public body, given that a credit card is first and foremost a product for sale.

Freie und Hansestadt Hamburg
Behörde für Inneres
Einwohner-Zentralamt

Den ________

Gz. E 5 - ________

Es erschein/t/en ________

wohnhaft in ____ Hamburg ________ ☎ ____
ausgewiesen durch ________
und erklär/t/en ____: Ich/Wir stelle(n) hiermit einen

Einbürgerungsantrag

für ________

Anschrift ________

A Personalien | **Ehegatte**

1. Familienname
2. Vornamen
3. geb. am ____ in ____ Krs./Bez. ____ Land ____ | geb. am ____ in ____ Krs./Bez. ____ Land
4. Staatsangehörigkeit (auch frühere)

nachgewiesen durch

5. Volkstumszugehörigkeit
6. Militärdienst: im Heimatlande / in Deutschland
7. Mit einzubürgernde Kinder

Namen	Geburtstag	Geburtsort	Rechtsstellung

8. Familienstand ☐ ledig ☐ verheiratet ☐ verwitwet ☐ geschieden.
   8.1. letzte Eheschließung am ____ in ____
   Standesamt/Kirche ____ Reg. Nr. ____
   Tod des Ehegatten/Scheidung am ____ in ____
   Standesamt/Kirche/Landgericht ____ Reg. Nr. ____
   getrennt lebend seit ____
   8.2. Angaben über frühere Ehen (Eheschließungsort und Zeitpunkt, Personalien des früheren Ehegatten, Staatsangehörigkeit, Auflösungsgrund):

Ehegatte

Hinweis: Der Formantrag besteht aus 4 Seiten!

Naturalization form, Hamburg, Germany

Filling in this form ought to be the crowning moment for foreigners living in Germany, as they take the final step towards integration. Unfortunately, this application does not make any such impression, but it is certainly typical of German bureaucracy.

You must read the guidance notes on the reverse of this form
Please:
- do not write in this area or in the Official Use area
- write clearly in BLACK INK using CAPITAL LETTERS
- provide all the details below
- provide details of any changes to your vehicle, if applicable

1

1 Vehicle Details
Registration mark 2
Make of vehicle (e.g. Ford, Vauxhall, etc)
Model / type of vehicle (e.g. Focus, Vectra etc)
Colour or colours of vehicle
Taxation class of vehicle (e.g. Private/Light Goods, Petrol Car, HGV, Bicycle etc)
Chassis, Frame or VIN number (usually shown on a plate near the engine)

2 Name and Address of Vehicle Keeper
(Please tick box or give title below) Mr 1 Mrs 2 Miss 3
† Unincorporated bodies: If registration is in business or association name, please give full name of person responsible for vehicle
Other title or † Business Name
Forename(s) (in full) 9
Surname 10
Address — Address must be in England, Scotland or Wales 11
Post town 12
Postcode — Your certificate may be delayed if the postcode is not quoted 13
Date of birth 31 (You are not required by law to provide your date of birth.)
Daytime telephone number
You do not have to provide a telephone number but doing so may help us to quickly resolve any problems with your application.

3 Acquisition Details
Have you had a Registration Document/Certificate for this vehicle in YOUR name?
Please tick the appropriate box Yes ☐ No ☐
If NO write the date you acquired the vehicle in this box — Day Month Year 14

4 Declaration *£25 fee payable
I declare that the Registration Certificate: (Please tick one box)
❑ was signed by me to notify acquisition but I have not received a replacement
❑ was not given to me by the previous keeper of this vehicle
❑ has been lost, stolen or damaged whilst in my possession
❑ cannot be produced for other reasons
I undertake to return the Registration Certificate if it is found, or given to me by the previous keeper, to DVLA, Swansea, SA99 1AR.
I declare that I have checked the information given on this application and that to the best of my knowledge it is correct and that the vehicle is licensed or is to be licensed in accordance with the tax class shown above.
(Making a false declaration is a criminal offence for which you could be fined and imprisoned).
* I enclose/do not enclose the payment of £____ (£25 at the time of printing).
The fee does not need to be paid if you can meet the criteria below. For further information see note D overleaf.
❑ I am the new keeper and have the new keeper's supplement (V5/2 or V5C/2) from the Registration Certificate. (This MUST be attached to this application form.)
❑ The last Registration Certificate was destroyed by the insurance company because the vehicle is categorised as "C" salvage.

Signature ____ Date ____
See section J for where to send this form.
Mileage (to last complete mile) (You are not required by law to provide the present mileage.) 28

Official Use Only V62
2/07

VC 3
MKE 4
MDL 5
CLR 6
TC 7
V10/V85/V70 Proc L
Independent Ø 8
DVLA Date Stamp
DOE
CD 15 FI 16
ISC 17
UW 18
DOW 19
SC 20
EN 21
CC 22
W/BT 23 F 24
AM 25
RW 26
DOP 27
SP 29
PWR 30
ID N A
DUP V5

Vehicle registration application, UK

There are two major problems with this form: first, the inconsistent and confusing design of the main left-hand column, which looks uneven and messy; second, the right-hand column, which is much too dominant and consists almost entirely of incomprehensible codes. Even though they are for 'official use only', they make the form seem unnecessarily complicated.

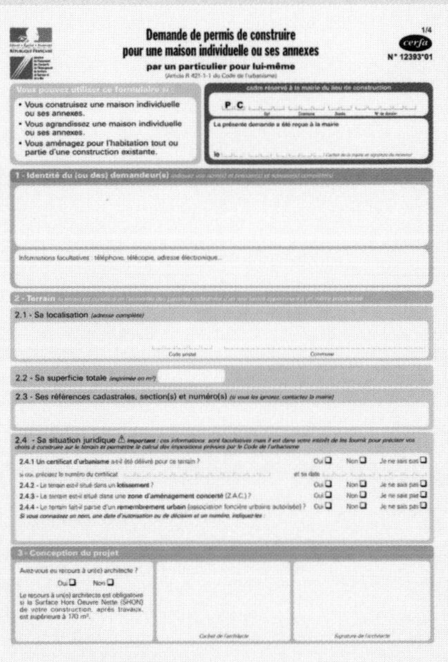

Demande de permis de construire pour une maison individuelle ou ses annexes
par un particulier pour lui-même
N° 12393*01

1 - Identité du (ou des) demandeur(s)
2 - Terrain
2.1 - Sa localisation
2.2 - Sa superficie totale
2.3 - Ses références cadastrales, section(s) et numéro(s)
2.4 - Sa situation juridique
3 - Conception du projet

Aanvraag **bouwvergunning**

1 Gegevens van de aanvrager
1a Naam en voorletters
1b Vertegenwoordiger rechtspersoon
1c Correspondentieadres in Nederland
1d Postcode en plaats
1e Telefoon overdag
1f Faxnummer
1g E-mailadres
1h Bent u ☐ eigenaar ☐ huurder ☐ anders, namelijk

2 Uw bouwvergunning
2a Welke bouwvergunning vraagt u aan?
☐ Lichte bouwvergunning
☐ Reguliere bouwvergunning
☐ Reguliere bouwvergunning fase 1
☐ Reguliere bouwvergunning fase 2
2b Heeft u voor deze bouwwerkzaamheden al eerder een bouwvergunning aangevraagd?
☐ Ja, ga naar 2c ☐ Nee, ga naar 3
2c Op welke datum is de eerdere bouwvergunning verleend/geweigerd? DD-MM-JJJJ
2d Wat is het (registratie)nummer van de eerdere aanvraag om bouwvergunning?

3 Lokale en kadastrale aanduiding van het bouwwerk/perceel en eigendomssituatie
3a Straat en huisnummer
Postcode en plaats
3b Kadastrale aanduiding
Gemeente
Sectie en nummer
3c Eigendomssituatie perceel/kavel
☐ Eigen grond ☐ Erfpacht ☐ Huur

1

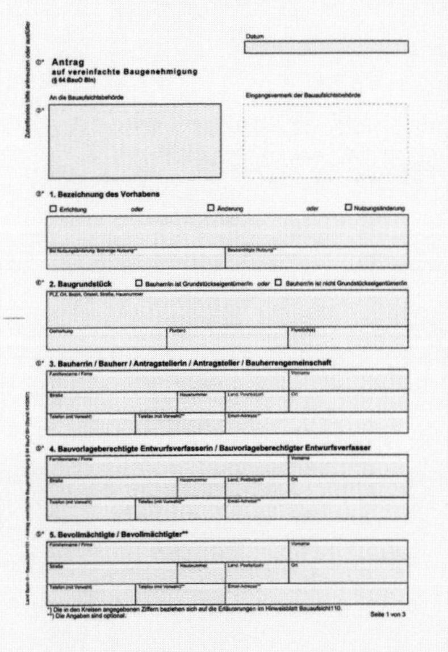

Antrag auf vereinfachte Baugenehmigung
1. Bezeichnung des Vorhabens
2. Baugrundstück
3. Bauherrin / Bauherr / Antragstellerin / Antragsteller / Bauherrengemeinschaft
4. Bauvorlageberechtigte Entwurfsverfasserin / Bauvorlageberechtigter Entwurfsverfasser
5. Bevollmächtigte / Bevollmächtigter
Seite 1 von 3

Applications for planning and building permission, France, Netherlands and Germany

Filling in application forms for a building permit generally presupposes a degree of expert knowledge. The difficulty here lies in the fact that the same form is used whether the proposed building is a garage or a car factory. Comparison between the forms reveals certain national characteristics of design: the French prefer rounded corners, the Dutch like marginal columns, and the Germans opt for cells.

Registration forms

Registration forms give access

Registration forms declare a desire to take part in something or to continue to take part. This declaration may be compulsory, for instance when buying a motor vehicle or starting a business. Generally, however, registration is voluntary but it is nonetheless required before you can gain access to services, join associations, get married, take up a place at an educational institution, or even get a key to a hotel room.

There are no standard ways of asking for personal information

Registration forms are designed to provide information about those who are registering, and are among the many forms that ask for names and addresses. There is no standard sequence or order for providing details such as first name, surname, house number, street and postcode. However, the forms issued by any one provider should attempt to be consistent, preferably by using a template or style sheet for this information.

The purpose should be made clear

Registration forms that have to be filled in but are of no direct benefit to the user are generally regarded as a nuisance. It is essential that the purpose be explained, as well as what use – even if only indirect – is to be made of the information. In this context, questions not related to the specific purpose should be avoided.

A registration can also be a contract

Registration is often a form of contract. Both sides undertake certain obligations, and so it should always be clear whether registration is binding or not, what the consequences of this are, and how the agreement can be cancelled.

Provider

→ page 161

Heading

→ page 160

Return address

The completed form should be sent here.

→ page 164

Information field

The people or things being registered by the form are recorded here.

Contact details

→ page 162

Signature

→ page 177

NEWFORT CITY COUNCIL

Voter Registration

→ Please fill in this form and return it to:

Newfort City Council
Electoral Services
PO Box 10
1 Haymarket Square
Newfort NF1 8HL

Electoral Services
phone 01456 23 23 20
fax 01456 23 23 21
e-mail elections@newfort.gov.uk

1 **ABOUT YOU**

Address: 47 GRAY STREET / WEST PARK GROVE / NEWFORT

Postcode: NF2 3TK

Daytime phone number: 01456 239233

2 **PEOPLE LIVING AT YOUR ADDRESS**

A Please enter the names of anyone living at your address on 15 October 2010, who is **18 years old or over**.

Last name	First name(s)	Nationality
GABRIEL	ANDREW	BRITISH
GABRIEL	SANDRA	BRITISH

→ **Age:** You are entitled to register to vote if you are 16 or older. However, you must be 18 to vote.

→ **Nationality:** You are entitled to register to vote if you are a:
- British Citizen
- Citizen of the Irish Republic
- EU Citizen
- Commonwealth Citizen

B Please enter the names of anyone living at your address on 15 October 2010, who is **16 or 17 years old**.

Last name	First name(s)	Nationality	Date of Birth
GABRIEL	ELLA	BRITISH	24-11-1993
			DD-MM-YYYY
			DD-MM-YYYY

3 **DECLARATION**

I declare that as far as I know, the information I have given on this form is correct.

Name: ANDREW GABRIEL

Signature: Andrew Gabriel

Date of signature: 07-10-2010

Explanations

Any concepts or terms that users may not understand must be explained. These explanations have been placed in a marginal column close to the terms to which they refer, so they are easy to find.

→ page 200

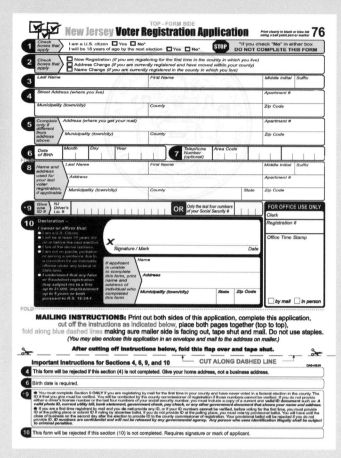

Register of Electors form, UK

Unlike many other countries, the UK and the US do not have compulsory electoral registration, and so anyone who wants to vote must register to do so. Unfortunately, the content of this form is very hard to understand. Although an effort has been made to divide it into different coloured areas, there is no clear hierarchy. Everything looks equally prominent, so users have no idea where they should start filling it in.

Voter registration application, US

This registration form also includes far too many competing elements. The overall effect is a messy combination of text fields, icons, captions and explanations. Especially intrusive are the boxed notes at the foot of the page. These look like text fields, but in fact hold additional explanatory notes for the questions asked above.

Business registration, TV licence registration, library registration, Germany

These three registration forms give the impression of having registered the fact that nobody wants to fill them in.

OXFORDSHIRE COUNTY COUNCIL www.oxfordshire.gov.uk

Oxfordshire Adult Learning Enrolment Form 2008/2009

Learner ref no: (Office use only) | Unique learner no:

Please complete this WHOLE FORM in BLOCK CAPITALS and tick all appropriate boxes. (This information is essential to secure funding for your course.) **Please remember to sign this form.**

Personal Information

Forename | Family Name (Surname)

☐ Male ☐ Female | Title: ☐ Mr ☐ Mrs ☐ Ms ☐ Miss ☐ Other | Date of birth

Address

Postcode

Preferred phone number for contact (e.g. cancelled class)

Email | Alternative contact number

Telephone number for emergency contact during a class (next of kin)

Course(s) you wish to join

Course title	Course code	Venue	Start date	Amount payable

Possible Support Needs – Disability

Disability
☐ No disability ☐ Visual impairment ☐ Hearing impairment ☐ Disability affecting mobility ☐ Other physical disability ☐ Other medical condition ☐ Emotional/behavioural ☐ Mental health difficulty ☐ Temporary disability after illness/accident ☐ Profound/complex disabilities ☐ Multiple disabilities ☐ Aspergers syndrome ☐ Not known/information not provided ☐ Other

Learning difficulty
☐ No learning difficulty ☐ Moderate learning difficulties ☐ Severe learning difficulties ☐ Dyslexia ☐ Dyscalculia ☐ Other specific learning difficulty ☐ Multiple learning difficulties ☐ Autism spectrum disorder ☐ Other ☐ Not known/information not provided

☐ I would like to discuss my support needs (for disability and/or learning difficulty)

Ethnic origin

Which of these do you consider describes your ethnic origin?
☐ Asian or Asian British - Bangladeshi ☐ Asian or Asian British - Indian ☐ Asian or Asian British - Pakistani ☐ Asian or Asian British - any other Asian background ☐ Black or Black British - African ☐ Black or Black British - Caribbean ☐ Black or Black British - any other Black background ☐ Chinese ☐ Not known/not provided ☐ Mixed - White and Asian ☐ Mixed - White and Black African ☐ Mixed - White and Black Caribbean ☐ Mixed - any other mixed background ☐ White - British ☐ White - Irish ☐ White - any other White background ☐ Any other

If not permanently resident in the UK for the last 3 years, in which country have you lived?

Adult Learning enrolment form, UK

A typical registration form which is relatively easy to read and understand, and is well laid out. One problem area is 'Possible Support Needs', since it does not begin by asking whether the applicant has special needs, but only lists various disabilities. This could give the impression that only those with a disability are eligible to enrol.

SOUTHERN ELECTRIC ENERGY TRANSFER REQUEST / REGISTRATION FORM

FINDERS KEEPERS PARKEND | Letting agent ref: 50122 | Hallmark id FKPA1

NEW REGISTRATION / CHANGE OF TENANCY

INCOMING TENANT / LANDLORD DETAILS (Delete as applicable) Date moving in:

Tenant Title/Forename/Surname: Borries Schwesinger
Supply address including postcode
Correspondence address if different from above
Daytime phone: 01865 Evening phone

OUTGOING TENANT / LANDLORD DETAILS (Delete as applicable) Date moving out:

Tenant Title/Forename/Surname: mr G
Forwarding address including postcode: c/o finders Keepers
Daytime phone: 01865 297 999 Evening phone

ENERGY PAYMENT OPTIONS

ELECTRICITY Southern Electric — General domestic or E7 day reading 68356 — E7 night reading — S
Tick one box: General domestic NSC ☐ Economy 7 NSC ☐
Tick one box: Quarterly payment ☐ Monthly direct debit ☒ Prepayment meter ☐
Current supplier — Meter serial number

GAS — Meter reading 2880 — Meter point reference 3 9 9 9 8 1 0
Tick one box: General domestic NSC ☐
Tick one box: Quarterly payment ☐ Monthly direct debit ☒ Prepayment meter ☐
Current supplier: Southern Electric Gas — Meter serial number

THIS SECTION ONLY TO BE COMPLETED IF PAYING BY DIRECT DEBIT

Bank name and address: Barclays Bank PLC
Account name
Branch sort code — Account number
Payment date (1st-28th) Electricity 01 Gas 01 Monthly payment Electricity 20 Gas 20

Signature(s) Date 14/11/2007

Signed Date 14/11/2007

Energy transfer request, Southern Electric, UK

This form is for new tenants applying to change their energy supplier. Sadly, this is difficult to do without making mistakes. The different fields are spread out higgledy-piggledy over the page, which makes it easy to overlook something, and some of them are far too small. The many obscure abbreviations turn completing the form into a guessing game. This is not a way to inspire confidence in the company.

Anmeldung der Eheschließung

Familienname | Verlobter | Verlobte

Marriage registration, Germany

This marriage registration form is very severe and certainly does not reflect the happiness of the event that it records.

Join now

Member £45
Concessionary Member £40
Student Member £25
Family Member £70
Concessionary Family Member £65
Pay by Direct Debit and save £5 on the above
Voluntary donation £
Subtotal (Gift Aidable) £
Add a guest for a year add £10
Contributing Member £250
Total: £

Gift Aid it

Member details (block capitals please)

Membership No. (office use only) — Title — Forename — Surname — Address — Postcode — Telephone — Email

Gift Membership

Title — Forename — Surname — Address — Postcode — Telephone — Email — Message

V&A Membership method of payment

I would like to pay by annual Direct Debit and have completed the form below

Name of your bank or building society — Address of your bank or building society — Postcode — Name of account holder(s) — Account number — Sort code — V&A reference number — Signature(s) — Date

I would like to pay by cheque. I enclose a cheque payable to 'The Friends of the V&A'

I would like to pay by debit or credit card — Amex — Visa — Mastercard — Maestro — Card number — Issue number — Valid from — Expiry — Security number

I would like to pay by cash

Thank you for supporting the V&A

V&A Museum membership form, UK

A fairly straightforward registration form. The long lines with very little space between them are unnecessarily hard to read. The fields are also too squashed for comfort.

Declarations

Declaration forms help to obtain required information

Declaration forms are used to provide public services and administrative bodies with information that they require: on income for the tax authorities, imported goods for customs and excise, or power of attorney for banks. The forms therefore usually consist of set phrases and content fields.

Declarations should win the user's trust

Many declarations are made with some reluctance, and users are either obliged to fill them in or need to be convinced by good arguments. Often users are unsure what the consequences are going to be, so if they need to supply clear and complete information, they must first be told why the declaration is necessary. Secondly it's important to formulate the questions in such a way that all respondents are able to fit their personal details into the overall scheme. It must be borne in mind that the more complicated a subject is, the more potential answers there are, and so the more extensive the forms will need to be. This is evident in the case of tax forms, with multiple sections that not only provide an impressive indication of how complex the tax system is, but also show how many different ways there are of earning money and of spending it.

Nearly all forms contain a declaration

In order to avoid confusion, it should be pointed out that virtually every form serves as a declaration of some kind. An application form declares a request, a registration form is a declaration of participation, and an invoice declares a debt. In all these cases, however, the main focus is on a concrete demand, not on the declaration itself.

Provider

Declarations reveal a problem common to many forms: who is the sender and who is the receiver? The declaration is addressed *to* the building society, but the logo indicates that in fact it comes *from* the building society.

→ page 161

The same issue occurs in the examples on pages 77, 81 and 89.

User

Details of the person making the declaration.

Contact details

→ page 162

Content

The information being declared. It is important to state the details in terms as concrete as possible.

Signature

→ page 177

DECLARATION
OF INCOME

Newfort City Branch
18 Queen Street
Newfort NF1 8HL
T 01456 725 578 **F** 01456 725 579
E city@building-newfort.com

NEWFORT BUILDING SOCIETY

	APPLICANT 1	APPLICANT 2
1 ABOUT ME/US		
First name(s)	CLEO	
Last name	JOHNSON	
Address	4 BENNET ROAD	
	NORTH DRIVE	
	NEWFORT	
	Postcode NF6 1QP	Postcode
Date of birth	11-03-1965	DD-MM-YYYY
National Insurance Number	PS 334720J	
2 MY/OUR OCCUPATION		
Occupation	CIVIL SERVANT	
Self-employed	☑ no ☐ yes	☐ no ☐ yes
Claiming benefits	☑ no ☐ yes → **If yes** please provide a copy of your approval letter or bank statement showing the credited payment.	☐ no ☐ yes → **If yes** please provide a copy of your approval letter or bank statement showing the credited payment.

3 MY/OUR INCOME	Source	Gross Monthly Income	Source	Gross Monthly Income
Source 1 *(please specify)*	SALARY	£2645.00		£
Source 2 *(please specify)*		£ —		£
Source 3 *(please specify)*		£ —		£
Total *(Source 1 + 2 + 3)*		£2645.00		£
Combined Gross Monthly Income		£2645.00		

I/We certify that all the above information is both current and correct. Given the income declared above, I/we am/are financially able to meet the monthly payments on my/our proposed mortgage together with the payments on all other existing financial commitments (including household expenses).

4 CONFIRMATION		
Signature	C. Johnson	
Date	19.10.2010	

Instructions

It is not always enough simply to make a declaration. Evidence must also be supplied for certain statements. It is helpful if the user can see at a glance what proofs are required.

→ page 200

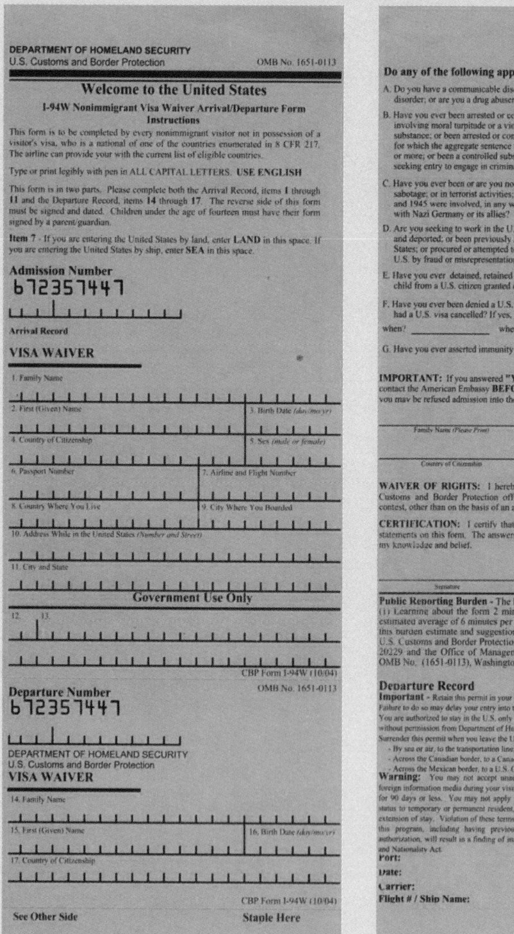

DEPARTMENT OF HOMELAND SECURITY
U.S. Customs and Border Protection — OMB No. 1651-0113

Welcome to the United States

I-94W Nonimmigrant Visa Waiver Arrival/Departure Form

Instructions

This form is to be completed by every nonimmigrant visitor not in possession of a visitor's visa, who is a national of one of the countries enumerated in 8 CFR 217. The airline can provide you with the current list of eligible countries.

Type or print legibly with pen in ALL CAPITAL LETTERS. USE ENGLISH

This form is in two parts. Please complete both the Arrival Record, items 1 through 11 and the Departure Record, items 14 through 17. The reverse side of this form must be signed and dated. Children under the age of fourteen must have their form signed by a parent/guardian.

Item 7 - If you are entering the United States by land, enter **LAND** in this space. If you are entering the United States by ship, enter **SEA** in this space.

Admission Number
672357447

Arrival Record

VISA WAIVER

1. Family Name
2. First (Given) Name
3. Birth Date (day/mo/yr)
4. Country of Citizenship
5. Sex (male or female)
6. Passport Number
7. Airline and Flight Number
8. Country Where You Live
9. City Where You Boarded
10. Address While in the United States (Number and Street)
11. City and State

Government Use Only

12. 13.

CBP Form I-94W (10/04)

OMB No. 1651-0113

Departure Number
672357447

DEPARTMENT OF HOMELAND SECURITY
U.S. Customs and Border Protection
VISA WAIVER

14. Family Name
15. First (Given) Name
16. Birth Date (day/mo/yr)
17. Country of Citizenship

CBP Form I-94W (10/04)

See Other Side — Staple Here

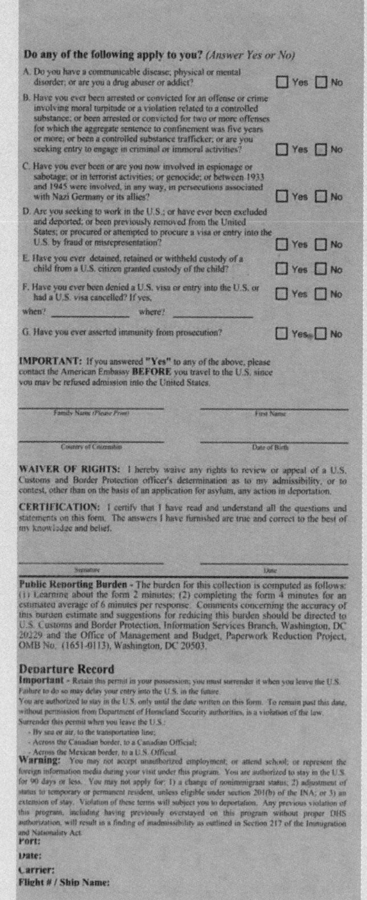

Do any of the following apply to you? *(Answer Yes or No)*

A. Do you have a communicable disease; physical or mental disorder; or are you a drug abuser or addict? ☐ Yes ☐ No

B. Have you ever been arrested or convicted for an offense or crime involving moral turpitude or a violation related to a controlled substance; or been arrested or convicted for two or more offenses for which the aggregate sentence to confinement was five years or more; or been a controlled substance trafficker; or are you seeking entry to engage in criminal or immoral activities? ☐ Yes ☐ No

C. Have you ever been or are you now involved in espionage or sabotage; or in terrorist activities; or genocide; or between 1933 and 1945 were involved, in any way, in persecutions associated with Nazi Germany or its allies? ☐ Yes ☐ No

D. Are you seeking to work in the U.S.; or have ever been excluded and deported; or been previously removed from the United States; or procured or attempted to procure a visa or entry into the U.S. by fraud or misrepresentation? ☐ Yes ☐ No

E. Have you ever detained, retained or withheld custody of a child from a U.S. citizen granted custody of the child? ☐ Yes ☐ No

F. Have you ever been denied a U.S. visa or entry into the U.S. or had a U.S. visa cancelled? If yes, when? where? ☐ Yes ☐ No

G. Have you ever asserted immunity from prosecution? ☐ Yes ☐ No

IMPORTANT: If you answered **"Yes"** to any of the above, please contact the American Embassy **BEFORE** you travel to the U.S. since you may be refused admission into the United States.

Family Name (Please Print) — First Name
Country of Citizenship — Date of Birth

WAIVER OF RIGHTS: I hereby waive any rights to review or appeal of a U.S. Customs and Border Protection officer's determination as to my admissibility, or to contest, other than on the basis of an application for asylum, any action in deportation.

CERTIFICATION: I certify that I have read and understand all the questions and statements on this form. The answers I have furnished are true and correct to the best of my knowledge and belief.

Signature — Date

Public Reporting Burden - The burden for this collection is computed as follows: (1) Learning about the form 2 minutes; (2) completing the form 4 minutes for an estimated average of 6 minutes per response. Comments concerning the accuracy of this burden estimate and suggestions for reducing this burden should be directed to U.S. Customs and Border Protection, Information Services Branch, Washington, DC 20229 and the Office of Management and Budget, Paperwork Reduction Project, OMB No. (1651-0113), Washington, DC 20503.

Departure Record

Important - Retain this permit in your possession; you must surrender it when you leave the U.S. Failure to do so may delay your entry into the U.S. in the future.

You are authorized to stay in the U.S. only until the date written on this form. To remain past this date, without permission from Department of Homeland Security authorities, is a violation of the law.

Surrender this permit when you leave the U.S.:
- By sea or air, to the transportation line;
- Across the Canadian border, to a Canadian Official;
- Across the Mexican border, to a U.S. Official.

Warning: You may not accept unauthorized employment; or attend school; or represent the foreign information media during your visit under this program. You are authorized to stay in the U.S. for 90 days or less. You may not apply for: 1) a change of nonimmigrant status; 2) adjustment of status to temporary or permanent resident, unless eligible under section 201(b) of the INA; or 3) an extension of stay. Violation of these terms will subject you to deportation. Any previous violation of this program, including having previously overstayed on this program without proper DHS authorization, will result in a finding of inadmissibility as outlined in Section 217 of the Immigration and Nationality Act.

Port:
Date:
Carrier:
Flight # / Ship Name:

Home Office
UK Border Agency
LANDING CARD
Immigration Act 1971

Please complete clearly in English and BLOCK CAPITALS
à remplir en anglais et en LETTRES MAJUSCULES, s.v.p.
Bitte in Englisch und DRUCKBUCHSTABEN ausfüllen

Family name Nom de famille / Familienname

First name(s) Prénom (s) / Vorname (n)

Sex Sexe / Geschlecht ☐ M ☐ F

Date of birth Date de naissance / Geburtsdatum D D M M Y Y Y Y

Town and country of birth Lieu et pays de naissance / Geburtsort und Land

Nationality Nationalitié / Staatsangehörigkeit **Occupation** Profession / Beruf

Contact address in the UK (in full) Adresse en Royaume-Uni / Kontakt Adresse in das VK (in worten)

Passport no. Passport nr. / Pass Nr. **Place of issue** Délivre à / Ausstellungsort

Length of stay in the UK Duré du séjour en Royaume-Uni / Dauer des Aufenthalts in VK

Port of last departure Port du dernier départ / Letzter Abflugsort

Arrival flight/train number/ship name Vol d'arrivée / Nr. du train / nom du bateau Ankunfts Flugnummer / Zugnummer / Schiffsname

Signature Firma / Unterschrift

IF YOU BREAK UK LAWS YOU COULD FACE IMPRISONMENT AND REMOVAL
Si vous enfreignez les lois du Royaume-Uni pourrait faire face à vous emprisonnement et d'enlèvement
Wenn Sie UK Gesetze brechen sie könnten zu Haftstrafen verurteilt und Umzugsbeihilfen

CAT	-16	CODE	NAT	POL

For official use Reservé usage officiel / Nur für den Dienstgebrauch

Visa waiver form, US

The questions in the notorious visa waiver for entry into the US are so close to the answer field of the previous question that many passengers may mix up the fields when they're filling in the form. It's interesting to see that on the back there is an official estimate of the time needed to fill it in, plus information about who to turn to if you have suggestions for improvements.

UK Border Agency landing card

The British equivalent includes fewer questions, but it suffers from the same problem of how to lay out the questions and text fields. There is also a translation mistake: in the last section, which warns against giving false information, the word 'removal' (i.e. from the country) has been wrongly translated into German as *Umzugsbeihilfe* (financial help with the costs of moving).

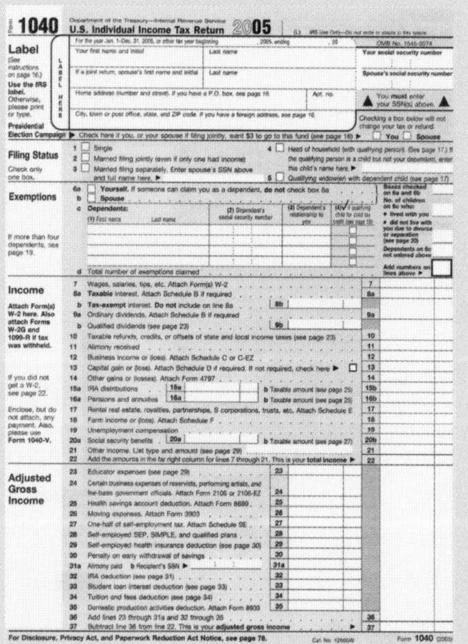

Tax return forms, US, UK and Canada

Tax forms are a typical source of frustration for many people. They are generally badly structured, ask complicated and often incomprehensible questions, provide too little space for the answers, and are overloaded with text. Comparison between different countries shows that there are only a few positive exceptions, such as the UK and the Netherlands (see page 228).

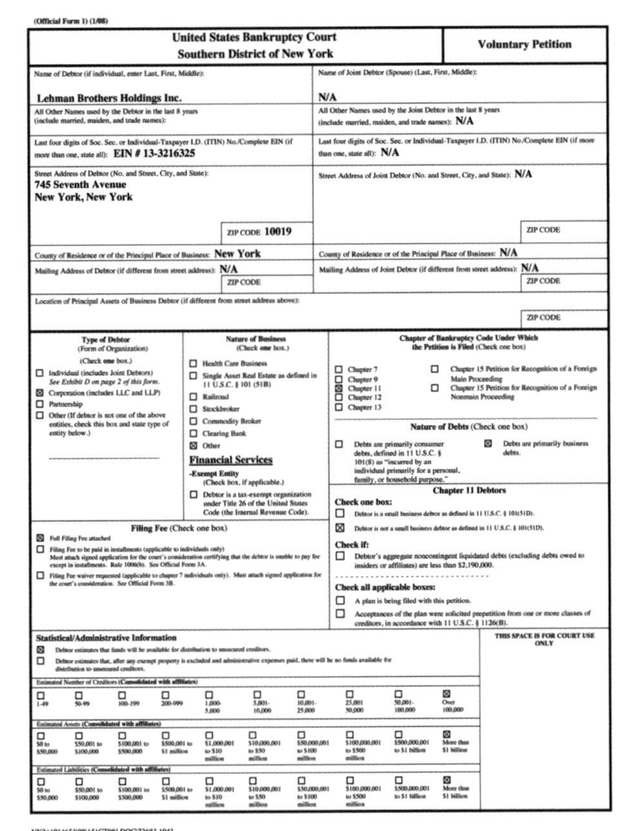

(Official Form 1) (1/08)

United States Bankruptcy Court
Southern District of New York

Voluntary Petition

Name of Debtor (if individual, enter Last, First, Middle): **Lehman Brothers Holdings Inc.**	Name of Joint Debtor (Spouse) (Last, First, Middle): **N/A**
All Other Names used by the Debtor in the last 8 years (include married, maiden, and trade names):	All Other Names used by the Joint Debtor in the last 8 years (include married, maiden, and trade names): **N/A**
Last four digits of Soc. Sec. or Individual-Taxpayer I.D. (ITIN) No./Complete EIN (if more than one, state all): **EIN # 13-3216325**	Last four digits of Soc. Sec. or Individual-Taxpayer I.D. (ITIN) No./Complete EIN (if more than one, state all): **N/A**
Street Address of Debtor (No. and Street, City, and State): **745 Seventh Avenue New York, New York** ZIP CODE **10019**	Street Address of Joint Debtor (No. and Street, City, and State): **N/A** ZIP CODE
County of Residence or of the Principal Place of Business: **New York**	County of Residence or of the Principal Place of Business: **N/A**
Mailing Address of Debtor (if different from street address): **N/A** ZIP CODE	Mailing Address of Joint Debtor (if different from street address): **N/A** ZIP CODE
Location of Principal Assets of Business Debtor (if different from street address above): ZIP CODE	

Type of Debtor (Form of Organization) (Check **one** box.)
- ☐ Individual (includes Joint Debtors) *See Exhibit D on page 2 of this form.*
- ☒ Corporation (includes LLC and LLP)
- ☐ Partnership
- ☐ Other (If debtor is not one of the above entities, check this box and state type of entity below.)

Nature of Business (Check **one** box.)
- ☐ Health Care Business
- ☐ Single Asset Real Estate as defined in 11 U.S.C. § 101 (51B)
- ☐ Railroad
- ☐ Stockbroker
- ☐ Commodity Broker
- ☐ Clearing Bank
- ☒ Other

Financial Services

-Exempt Entity (Check box, if applicable.)
- ☐ Debtor is a tax-exempt organization under Title 26 of the United States Code (the Internal Revenue Code).

Chapter of Bankruptcy Code Under Which the Petition is Filed (Check one box)
- ☐ Chapter 7
- ☐ Chapter 9
- ☒ Chapter 11
- ☐ Chapter 12
- ☐ Chapter 13
- ☐ Chapter 15 Petition for Recognition of a Foreign Main Proceeding
- ☐ Chapter 15 Petition for Recognition of a Foreign Nonmain Proceeding

Nature of Debts (Check one box)
- ☐ Debts are primarily consumer debts, defined in 11 U.S.C. § 101(8) as "incurred by an individual primarily for a personal, family, or household purpose."
- ☒ Debts are primarily business debts.

Filing Fee (Check one box)
- ☒ Full Filing Fee attached
- ☐ Filing Fee to be paid in installments (applicable to individuals only) Must attach signed application for the court's consideration certifying that the debtor is unable to pay fee except in installments. Rule 1006(b). See Official Form 3A.
- ☐ Filing Fee waiver requested (applicable to chapter 7 individuals only). Must attach signed application for the court's consideration. See Official Form 3B.

Chapter 11 Debtors

Check one box:
- ☐ Debtor is a small business debtor as defined in 11 U.S.C. § 101(51D).
- ☒ Debtor is not a small business debtor as defined in 11 U.S.C. § 101(51D).

Check if:
- ☐ Debtor's aggregate noncontingent liquidated debts (excluding debts owed to insiders or affiliates) are less than $2,190,000.

Check all applicable boxes:
- ☐ A plan is being filed with this petition.
- ☐ Acceptances of the plan were solicited prepetition from one or more classes of creditors, in accordance with 11 U.S.C. § 1126(B).

Statistical/Administrative Information
- ☒ Debtor estimates that funds will be available for distribution to unsecured creditors.
- ☐ Debtor estimates that, after any exempt property is excluded and administrative expenses paid, there will be no funds available for distribution to unsecured creditors.

THIS SPACE IS FOR COURT USE ONLY

Estimated Number of Creditors (**Consolidated with affiliates**)

☐	☐	☐	☐	☐	☐	☐	☐	☐	☒
1-49	50-99	100-199	200-999	1,000-5,000	5,001-10,000	10,001-25,000	25,001 50,000	50,001-100,000	Over 100,000

Estimated Assets (**Consolidated with affiliates**)

☐	☐	☐	☐	☐	☐	☐	☐	☐	☒
$0 to $50,000	$50,001 to $100,000	$100,001 to $500,000	$500,001 to $1 million	$1,000,001 to $10 million	$10,000,001 to $50 million	$50,000,001 to $100 million	$100,000,001 to $500 million	$500,000,001 to $1 billion	More than $1 billion

Estimated Liabilities (**Consolidated with affiliates**)

☐	☐	☐	☐	☐	☐	☐	☐	☐	☒
$0 to $50,000	$50,001 to $100,000	$100,001 to $500,000	$500,001 to $1 million	$1,000,001 to $10 million	$10,000,001 to $50 million	$50,000,001 to $100 million	$100,000,001 to $500 million	$500,000,001 to $1 billion	More than $1 billion

NY2:\1914653\08\151CT08!.DOC\73683.1043

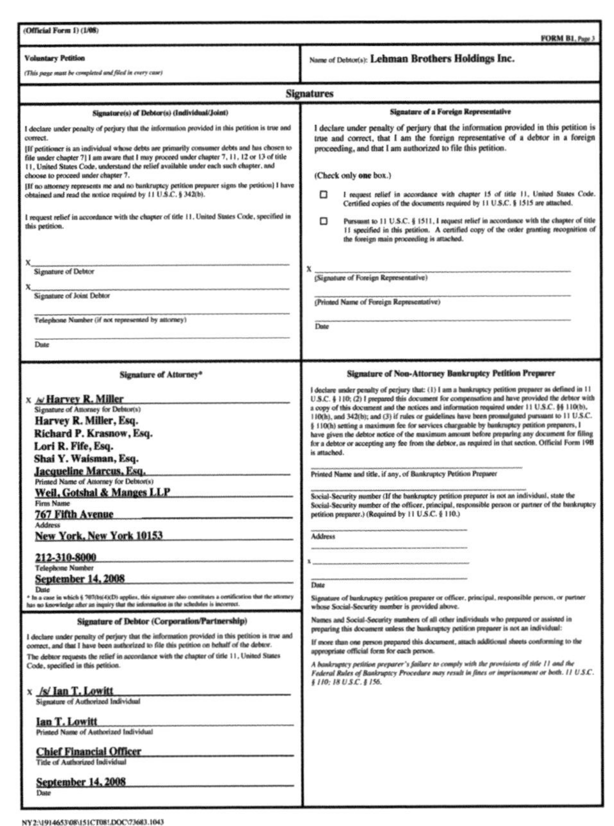

(Official Form 1) (1/08) FORM B1, Page 3

Voluntary Petition
(This page must be completed and filed in every case)

Name of Debtor(s): **Lehman Brothers Holdings Inc.**

Signatures

Signature(s) of Debtor(s) (Individual/Joint)

I declare under penalty of perjury that the information provided in this petition is true and correct.

[If petitioner is an individual whose debts are primarily consumer debts and has chosen to file under chapter 7] I am aware that I may proceed under chapter 7, 11, 12 or 13 of title 11, United States Code, understand the relief available under each such chapter, and choose to proceed under chapter 7.

[If no attorney represents me and no bankruptcy petition preparer signs the petition] I have obtained and read the notice required by 11 U.S.C. § 342(b).

I request relief in accordance with the chapter of title 11, United States Code, specified in this petition.

X__________ Signature of Debtor

X__________ Signature of Joint Debtor

Telephone Number (if not represented by attorney)

Date

Signature of a Foreign Representative

I declare under penalty of perjury that the information provided in this petition is true and correct, that I am the foreign representative of a debtor in a foreign proceeding, and that I am authorized to file this petition.

(Check only **one** box.)
- ☐ I request relief in accordance with chapter 15 of title 11, United States Code. Certified copies of the documents required by 11 U.S.C. § 1515 are attached.
- ☐ Pursuant to 11 U.S.C. § 1511, I request relief in accordance with the chapter of title 11 specified in this petition. A certified copy of the order granting recognition of the foreign main proceeding is attached.

X__________ (Signature of Foreign Representative)

(Printed Name of Foreign Representative)

Date

Signature of Attorney*

X **/s/ Harvey R. Miller**
Signature of Attorney for Debtor(s)
Harvey R. Miller, Esq.
Richard P. Krasnow, Esq.
Lori R. Fife, Esq.
Shai Y. Waisman, Esq.
Jacqueline Marcus, Esq.
Printed Name of Attorney for Debtor(s)
Weil, Gotshal & Manges LLP
Firm Name
767 Fifth Avenue
Address
New York, New York 10153

212-310-8000
Telephone Number
September 14, 2008
Date

* In a case in which § 707(b)(4)(D) applies, this signature also constitutes a certification that the attorney has no knowledge after an inquiry that the information in the schedules is incorrect.

Signature of Non-Attorney Bankruptcy Petition Preparer

I declare under penalty of perjury that: (1) I am a bankruptcy petition preparer as defined in 11 U.S.C. § 110; (2) I prepared this document for compensation and have provided the debtor with a copy of this document and the notices and information required under 11 U.S.C. §§ 110(b), 110(h), and 342(b); and (3) if rules or guidelines have been promulgated pursuant to 11 U.S.C. § 110(h) setting a maximum fee for services chargeable by bankruptcy petition preparers, I have given the debtor notice of the maximum amount before preparing any document for filing for a debtor or accepting any fee from the debtor, as required in that section. Official Form 19B is attached.

Printed Name and title, if any, of Bankruptcy Petition Preparer

Social-Security number (If the bankruptcy petition preparer is not an individual, state the Social-Security number of the officer, principal, responsible person or partner of the bankruptcy petition preparer.) (Required by 11 U.S.C. § 110.)

Address

x__________

Date

Signature of bankruptcy petition preparer or officer, principal, responsible person, or partner whose Social-Security number is provided above.

Names and Social-Security numbers of all other individuals who prepared or assisted in preparing this document unless the bankruptcy petition preparer is not an individual:

If more than one person prepared this document, attach additional sheets conforming to the appropriate official form for each person.

A bankruptcy petition preparer's failure to comply with the provisions of title 11 and the Federal Rules of Bankruptcy Procedure may result in fines or imprisonment or both. 11 U.S.C. § 110; 18 U.S.C. § 156.

Signature of Debtor (Corporation/Partnership)

I declare under penalty of perjury that the information provided in this petition is true and correct, and that I have been authorized to file this petition on behalf of the debtor.

The debtor requests the relief in accordance with the chapter of title 11, United States Code, specified in this petition.

X **/s/ Ian T. Lowitt**
Signature of Authorized Individual
Ian T. Lowitt
Printed Name of Authorized Individual
Chief Financial Officer
Title of Authorized Individual
September 14, 2008
Date

NY2:\1914653\08\151CT08!.DOC\73683.1043

Bankruptcy petition, Lehman Brothers, USA

Just a few bare facts declare the bankruptcy of a large investment bank. And yet this was a key event in the financial crisis of 2008, and it had worldwide repercussions. The fact that this crash involved a huge amount of money is clear from the three checkboxes at the bottom of the first page, which record the number of creditors and the size of the liabilities and assets. Note that the last option in each row is an open category: 'More than $1 billion'.

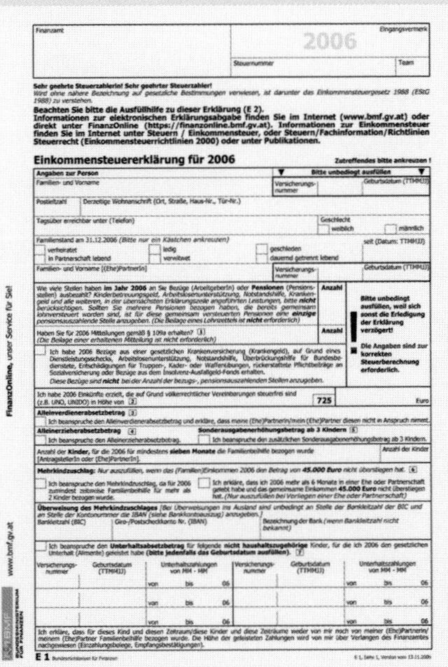

Einkommensteuererklärung für 2006

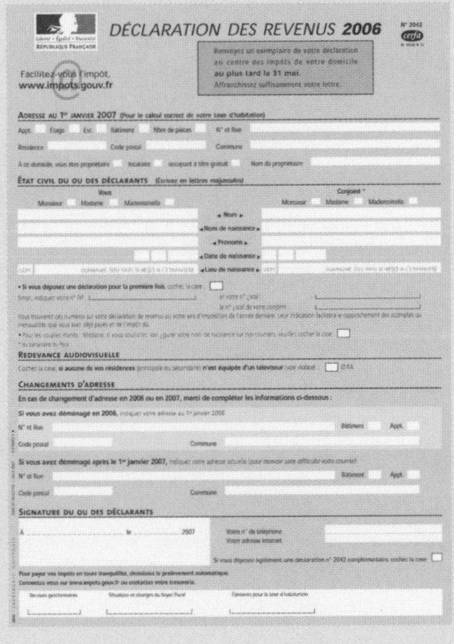

DÉCLARATION DES REVENUS 2006

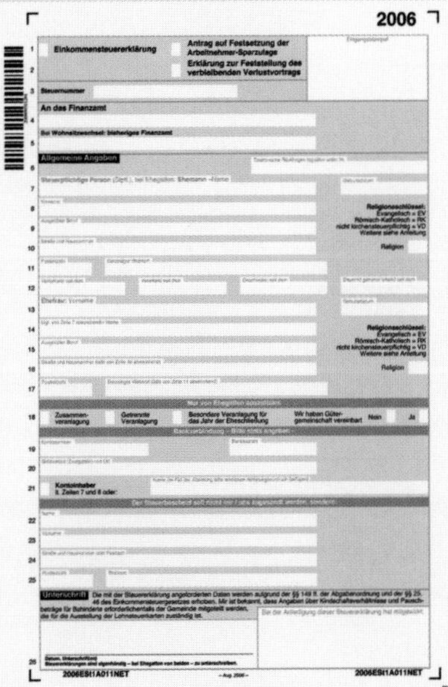

2006

Einkommensteuererklärung

Tax return forms from Austria, France and Germany

Icons, coloured areas and frames can be used to give tax forms a more friendly and efficient appearance, but these versions look cluttered and unhelpful.

Orders and contracts

Orders and contracts are standardized agreements

Forms for orders and contracts are standardized agreements, used to purchase goods from a catalogue, commission services, or fix rents or working conditions in writing.

The form defines the content

A feature of many orders and contracts is that the content is largely predefined by the form, and it is only the specifics that need to be chosen or specified. The contractor or at least one of the signatories to the agreement, is already prescribed – generally, it is the form provider, who also sets out the conditions of the agreement. One exception to this is the type of blank agreement sold ready-printed in stationery shops, which is left for the different parties to fill in. Once the form is signed, it becomes a binding document that specifies rights and obligations for both parties.

Orders must look serious and professional

Building and maintaining trust is particularly important with this kind of form, since placing the order is in itself an advance token of the user's confidence in the provider.

It cannot be taken for granted that the transaction will actually take place in the manner expected, and so every effort must be made to establish and maintain trust. Design, language and content should ensure that potential customers do not begin to doubt their decision. The content of the contract should be totally clear, and the form must reflect the seriousness and professionalism of the provider. It is, after all, the last and decisive link in the chain to attract new clients.

Heading

The fact that this is an order form must be stated clearly and unequivocally.

→ page 160

Provider

The person or firm being contracted to provide the goods or service is the receiver of the order.

User details

Order details

An itemized table of the products or services being ordered.

→ page 184

Signature

The signature confirms the contract and acknowledges the conditions.

→ page 177

Order form

THE VENDORS LIMITED

25 Vendors Lane
Newfort Business Park
Newfort NF9 1BA

T 01456 689 689
F 01456 689 688

E order@the-vendors.com
W www.the-vendors.com

MY DETAILS

Title	☑ Mr ☐ Mrs ☐ Miss ☐ Ms
Full Name	MARC L. FUSCONI
Company	RISTORANTE BOCCA DI LUPO
Address	87 GEORGE STREET
	NEWFORT
	Postcode NF3 1XL
Telephone	01456 277799
e-Mail	marc@lupofood.net

MY ORDER

Quantity	Code	Description	Unit price £	Total price £
12	342108	CAST IRON FRYING PAN 23CM	23·00	276·00
1	344502	CAST IRON FRYING PAN 28CM	30·50	30·50
2	297638	MINCER PRO	42·00	84·00
Total price of all items (including VAT, Standard Delivery and packing)				390·50

DELIVERY AND PAYMENT OPTIONS

Delivery	☑ Standard (2–3 days, no charge)	☐ Next Day (additional £ 8.00)
Payment	☑ after invoice receipt	☐ Cash-on-delivery

CONFIRM ORDER

I hereby state that I have the authority to place orders for the above mentioned company and accept and understand the **Terms & Conditions** (see overleaf) of THE VENDORS LIMITED.

Signature	M. Fusconi
Date	25·2·2010

TDC Switzerland AG
Sales & Info
Hagenholzstrasse 20/22
CH-8050 Zürich

Nur für internen Gebrauch
PROMO-97042

➔ **Vor dem Ausfüllen bitte unbedingt Telefonnummer auf ADSL-Verfügbarkeit prüfen: www.sunrise.ch/ADSL**

Spezialangebot für sunrise ADSL und sunrise select (Privatkunden)

Gültig bis 31.01.2006 (Datum Poststempel)

Frau
Höppner Corina
Burstwiesenstrasse 80
8055 Zürich

Adressänderung
Vorname / Name
Strasse / Nr.
PLZ / Ort

Formular bitte mit schwarzem Stift in GROSSBUCHSTABEN ausfüllen, unterschreiben und an oben stehende Adresse retournieren.

Erreichbarkeit tagsüber zwischen Uhr und Uhr unter /
Korrespondenzsprache Deutsch Französisch Italienisch Englisch
Sperrung von Mehrwertdienste-Nummern 090x xxx xxx 0906 xxx xxx

Mein Telefonanschluss Vorwahl Nummer ISDN
Auf folgender Telefonnummer soll ADSL aufgeschaltet werden /
sunrise select wird für Sie auf dieser Telefonnummer automatisch installiert, falls dies noch nicht der Fall ist.
Ich bin bereits sunrise select Kunde
Folgende Telefonnummern – nur eigene – möchte ich ebenfalls für sunrise select anmelden (falls zutreffend). /

Mein heutiger ADSL-Provider (falls zutreffend)

ADSL-Abonnement (techn. Angaben siehe Produktbeschreibung)
sunrise ADSL 150 flex* (CHF 9.90/Monat) – gratis Aufschaltgebühr (Wert CHF 49.–) – gratis 5 x Monatsgebühr (Wert CHF 49.50) – Qualitätsmodem (Wert CHF 175.–) – unentbehrliche Sicherheits CD-Rom
sunrise ADSL 600 (CHF 49.–/Monat) – gratis 2 x Monatsgebühr (Wert CHF 98.–) – Qualitätsmodem (Wert CHF 175.–) – unentbehrliche Sicherheits CD-Rom

ADSL-Starterkit (alle inkl. Sicherheits-Paket) **Analog-Anschluss** **ISDN-Anschluss**
ADSL-Starterkit Spezialangebot (Zyxel 623ME, mit USB- & Ethernet) gratis gratis
ADSL-Starterkit LAN (Zyxel 660H inkl. 4-Port-Ethernet-Switch, Firewall) CHF 199.– CHF 209.–
ADSL-Starterkit WLAN (Zyxel 660HW inkl. 4-Port-Switch, Firewall) CHF 229.– CHF 239.–
Nur Sicherheits-Paket (gratis) Anzahl Filter à CHF 28.– (nur analog)

In den Starterkits für analoge Anschlüsse ist jeweils ein Filter enthalten. Pro Telefon, Faxgerät oder Anrufbeantworter muss jeweils ein Filter installiert sein. Sie können hier zusätzliche Filter bestellen oder diese direkt im Fachhandel beziehen.

* Preis inkl. Volumen von 20 MByte. Zusätzliches Volumen wird mit CHF 0.19 pro MByte verrechnet.

Der/Die Unterzeichnende ist
Inhaber des Swisscom-Telefonanschlusses **oder**
Ehepartner/in (Vor-/Nachname)

Ort, Datum Unterschrift***

** Die erwähnten Dokumente finden Sie auf http://www.sunrise.ch/agb.htm. bzw. auf http://www.sunrise.ch/abonnementsbestimmungen_adsl2.pdf.
*** Rechtsgültige Unterschrift. Bei Minderjährigen oder Bevormundeten müssen die Eltern bzw. der Vormund unterschreiben.

Bitte nur Original senden

sunrise is a brand of TDC Switzerland AG

154325

POA. Res. KOM. 150flexpromo. V2. D. 1005

Customer order for a broadband service, Switzerland

A machine-readable order form, which looks rather cluttered, mixes up different points of view ('my' changes to 'the undersigned'), and also has the heading 'Special Offer' instead of 'Order'.

Order Form Send your order to: The Organic Gardening Catalogue, Riverdene Business Park, Molesey Road, Hersham, Surrey, KT12 4RG

Code	Item Description	Qty	Price £
	Sub Total		£
	Garden Organic Members deduct 10%		-£
	P & P delete if over £25.00		+ £1.50
	Order Total		£

Order Line 0845 130 1304
Fax Line 01932 252707
www.OrganicCatalogue.com

Your details *only fill in if different from overleaf*
Name
Address
Postcode
Garden Organic Member Number
You don't need to be member to order, but check our website for the benefits!
Daytime phone
email

Payment
I enclose a cheque for £
OR Please charge my Credit/Debit card Account
Expiry Start Issue
Signed

Any special instructions *if different from overleaf*
No substitutes

Returns and queries

If you have any questions regarding your order or if an item is faulty, damaged, incorrect or not satisfactory, please call us on 0845 130 1304 between 9 am and 5 pm Monday to Friday, or email to enquiries@chaseorganics.co.uk

Please quote your Customer Number or Order Number, both shown overleaf.

Our customer services advisors will be happy to help.

Catalogue order form, UK

This order form is printed on the back of the invoice for the previous order. This will only work if the order is faxed rather than sent by post. Unfortunately, the careless design – no visual divisions and far too little space to write in – does not exactly encourage the customer to order anything else.

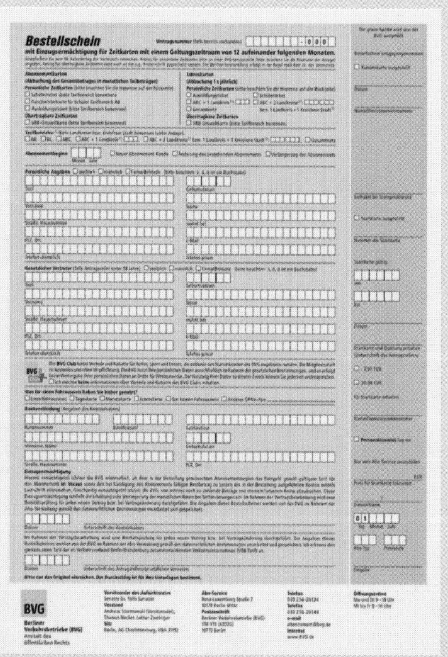
Bestellschein

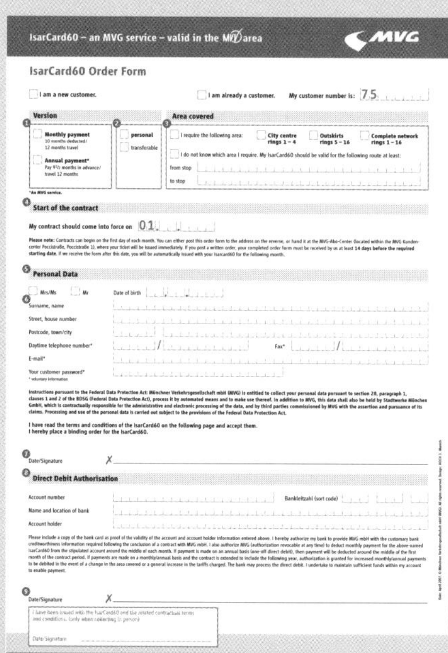
IsarCard60 – an MVG service – valid in the MVV area

IsarCard60 Order Form

Ticket Application

Order forms for travel passes, Germany and Australia

All three are forms that are meant to sell or order products – i.e. travel passes. The two German forms could be more user-friendly, and require a lot of information to be entered letter by letter. The Australian form is much more colourful and attractive.

Royal Mail delivery certificates, UK

The postal service has a long and distinguished tradition of forms. Over time, the mail in many countries has shifted from a state-run organization to a service industry. This is also reflected in the design and content of its forms, which have become increasingly user-friendly.

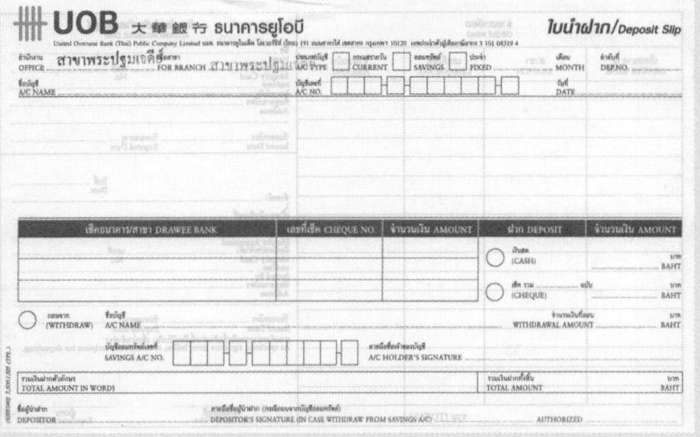
UOB 大華銀行 ธนาคารยูโอบี

ใบนำฝาก/Deposit Slip

OFFICE | FOR BRANCH | A/C TYPE: CURRENT / SAVINGS / FIXED | MONTH | DEP.NO.

A/C NAME | A/C NO. | DATE

DRAWEE BANK	CHEQUE NO.	AMOUNT	DEPOSIT	AMOUNT
			(CASH)	BAHT
			(CHEQUE)	BAHT

(WITHDRAW) A/C NAME | WITHDRAWAL AMOUNT BAHT

SAVINGS A/C NO. | A/C HOLDER'S SIGNATURE

TOTAL AMOUNT IN WORDS | TOTAL AMOUNT BAHT

DEPOSITOR | DEPOSITOR'S SIGNATURE (IN CASE WITHDRAW FROM SAVINGS A/C) | AUTHORIZED

Lottery ticket, Switzerland

There are many forms whose completion is linked to hopes for a better life, ranging from visas to building applications. However, none are completed by so many people as a lottery ticket, even though the result of the draw is totally independent of any entry form.

Paying-in slip, Thailand

A form for depositing cheques. The English translation is only of use to someone who has already filled in the form at least once.

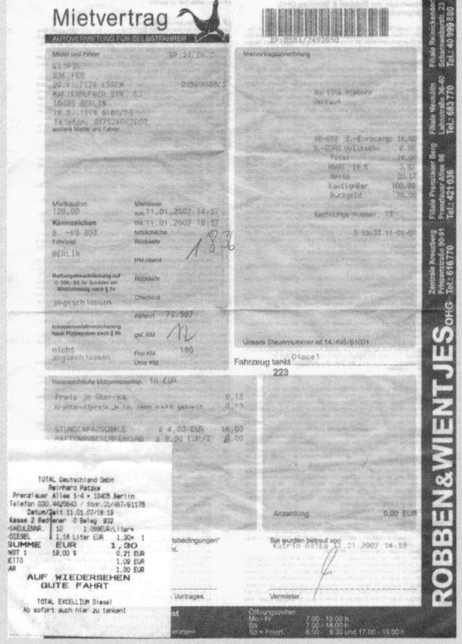
Mietvertrag

AUTOVERMIETUNG FÜR SELBSTFAHRER

Fahrzeug tankt Diesel

AUF WIEDERSEHEN GUTE FAHRT

ROBBEN&WIENTJES OHG

Barclays Wellwoman insurance form, UK

This is an acceptance form for a specific insurance service. Once again, however, the text fields are all extremely small.

Opening a company bank account, Germany

The main point of this bank form is completely lost in a sea of explanatory text.

Contract for car rental, Germany

Division into two columns can be a helpful device, but why does the column width change partway down? And why is the fact that the car uses diesel directly below the licence number?

Invoices, bills and receipts

No bills without forms

As soon as money is involved, forms play a major role. There are forms for invoices, bills, receipts, bank statements, payslips, and more. Once they are filled in, they become documents that determine a particular payment procedure, because as any accountant will tell you: *No payment without proof, and no proof without a form.*

Invoices and receipts are external communications

While some payment slips are only important for internal accounting, some of the most widely used forms – invoices, bills and receipts – are also aimed at external users. They denote the successful completion of a transaction, and are the last opportunity to make a positive impression on the customer.

Invoices must be paid

Bills and invoices constitute a demand for money and list the goods delivered or the services rendered. The sole purpose of a bill is to get itself paid, and so it is in the interests of the provider to make it as simple as possible for the debtor. This can be done through friendly wording, readability and clarity, and by giving prominence to important information such as the invoice number and the amount to be paid.

Receipts prove the safe arrival of money or other forms of payment

A receipt shows that money or some other form of payment has been received, and it provides documentary evidence that a demand – such as an invoice, for example – has been met. Unlike bills and invoices, receipts should be signed.

Forms have advantages

It is relatively rare nowadays for invoices, bills and receipts to be handwritten – they are generally printed out – so pre-printed invoices have become increasingly unnecessary, but this does not mean that invoices should not be proper forms. They are much more comprehensible if the information is always presented in the same order and if they make a distinction between standard elements and variable contents. Pre-printed invoices and bills also allow for a greater use of colour and embellishment.

Heading

The fact that this is an invoice and not a delivery note or order confirmation needs to be obvious at a glance.

→ page 160

Receiver of the invoice

→ page 164

Invoice number

The number and amount of the invoice are two of the most important items of information and must be easy to find.

Provider

Invoice

Mr Marc L. Fusconi
Ristorante Bocca di Lupo
87 George Street
Newfort
NF3 1XL

THE VENDORS LIMITED

25 Vendors Lane
Newfort Business Park
Newfort NF9 1BA

T 01456 689 689
F 01456 689 688

E order@the-vendors.com
W www.the-vendors.com

Registered
in England and Wales
Number 213265457898

VAT Number GB 12345678

Date	27 Feb 2010
Invoice No.	16779-01
Order No.	14500
Order date	25 Feb 2010
Shipment date	27 Feb 2010

Quantity	Code	Description	Unit price	Total price
12	342108	Frying pan (cast iron) ø 23 cm	£23.00	£276.00
1	344502	Frying pan (cast iron) ø 28 cm	£30.50	£30.50
2	297638	Mincer Pro	£42.00	£84.00

Shipping	£0.00
Sub-Total	£390.50
VAT Total	£68.33
Total	£458.83
Please pay by	13 Mar 2010

We accept payment by bank transfer or cheque.
Bank transfer: Please state the invoice number.
Cheques: Please make payable to THE VENDORS LIMITED.

Account information
Bank of Newfort plc
1 St. Giles, Newfort NF1 1AA
Sort Code 10-20-30
Account No. 1234567890

Invoiced items

The list of goods and services that must be paid for. Additional costs such as shipping or delivery charges are added at the bottom.

Total

The total payment required is broken down into a sub-total for the goods and the VAT or other tax required.

Payment deadline

An important piece of information that should be impossible to miss.

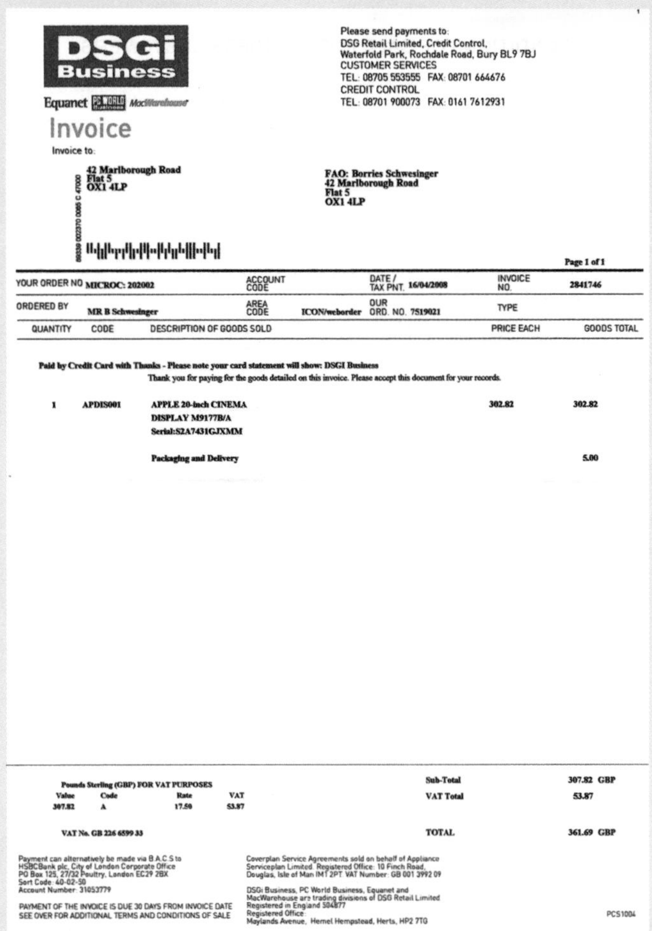

DSGi Business

Equanet PC WORLD Business MacWarehouse

Please send payments to:
DSG Retail Limited, Credit Control,
Waterfold Park, Rochdale Road, Bury BL9 7BJ
CUSTOMER SERVICES
TEL: 08705 553555 FAX: 08701 664676
CREDIT CONTROL
TEL: 08701 900073 FAX: 0161 7612931

Invoice

Invoice to:

42 Marlborough Road
Flat 5
OX1 4LP

FAO: Borries Schwesinger
42 Marlborough Road
Flat 5
OX1 4LP

Page 1 of 1

YOUR ORDER NO MICROC: 202002 | ACCOUNT CODE | DATE / TAX PNT. 16/04/2008 | INVOICE NO. 2841746

ORDERED BY MR B Schwesinger | AREA CODE ICON/weborder | OUR ORD. NO. 7519021 | TYPE

QUANTITY	CODE	DESCRIPTION OF GOODS SOLD	PRICE EACH	GOODS TOTAL
1	APDIS001	APPLE 20-inch CINEMA DISPLAY M9177B/A Serial:S2A7431GJXMM	302.82	302.82
		Packaging and Delivery		5.00

Paid by Credit Card with Thanks - Please note your card statement will show: DSGI Business
Thank you for paying for the goods detailed on this invoice. Please accept this document for your records.

Pounds Sterling (GBP) FOR VAT PURPOSES

Value	Code	Rate	VAT
307.82	A	17.50	53.87

VAT No. GB 226 6599 33

Sub-Total 307.82 GBP
VAT Total 53.87
TOTAL 361.69 GBP

Payment can alternatively be made via B.A.C.S to HSBCBank plc, City of London Corporate Office PO Box 125, 27/32 Poultry, London EC29 2BX Sort Code: 40-02-50 Account Number: 31053779

PAYMENT OF THE INVOICE IS DUE 30 DAYS FROM INVOICE DATE
SEE OVER FOR ADDITIONAL TERMS AND CONDITIONS OF SALE

Coverplan Service Agreements sold on behalf of Appliance Serviceplan Limited. Registered Office: 10 Finch Road, Douglas, Isle of Man IM1 2PT. VAT Number: GB 001 3992 09

DSGi Business, PC World Business, Equanet and MacWarehouse are trading divisions of DSG Retail Limited Registered in England 504877 Registered Office: Maylands Avenue, Hemel Hempstead, Herts, HP2 7TG

PCS1004

Business invoice, UK

A typical example of a modern invoice. It's no longer necessary for them to be pre-printed, but everything can be printed out on demand, even the different colours. Unfortunately, the use of colours and different type styles and sizes does not always improve clarity or readability. The most important item of information, the final total, takes a long time to find.

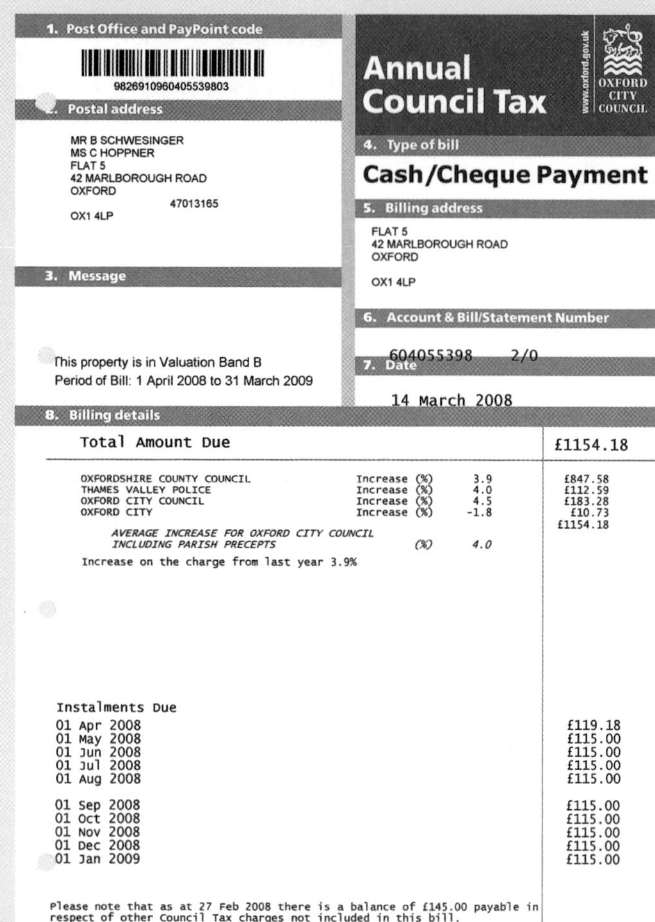

1. Post Office and PayPoint code
9826910960405539803

2. Postal address
MR B SCHWESINGER
MS C HOPPNER
FLAT 5
42 MARLBOROUGH ROAD
OXFORD 47013165
OX1 4LP

Annual Council Tax
www.oxford.gov.uk
OXFORD CITY COUNCIL

4. Type of bill
Cash/Cheque Payment

5. Billing address
FLAT 5
42 MARLBOROUGH ROAD
OXFORD
OX1 4LP

3. Message
This property is in Valuation Band B
Period of Bill: 1 April 2008 to 31 March 2009

6. Account & Bill/Statement Number
604055398 2/0

7. Date
14 March 2008

8. Billing details

Total Amount Due £1154.18

OXFORDSHIRE COUNTY COUNCIL	Increase (%)	3.9	£847.58
THAMES VALLEY POLICE	Increase (%)	4.0	£112.59
OXFORD CITY COUNCIL	Increase (%)	4.5	£183.28
OXFORD CITY	Increase (%)	-1.8	£10.73
			£1154.18

AVERAGE INCREASE FOR OXFORD CITY COUNCIL INCLUDING PARISH PRECEPTS (%) 4.0

Increase on the charge from last year 3.9%

Instalments Due

01 Apr 2008	£119.18
01 May 2008	£115.00
01 Jun 2008	£115.00
01 Jul 2008	£115.00
01 Aug 2008	£115.00
01 Sep 2008	£115.00
01 Oct 2008	£115.00
01 Nov 2008	£115.00
01 Dec 2008	£115.00
01 Jan 2009	£115.00

Please note that as at 27 Feb 2008 there is a balance of £145.00 payable in respect of other Council Tax charges not included in this bill.

Council tax bill, UK

The two-column structure of the heading and the different type sizes make this tax bill seem difficult to understand at first. The reader's eye is not guided, and so has to shift constantly between the different items of information.

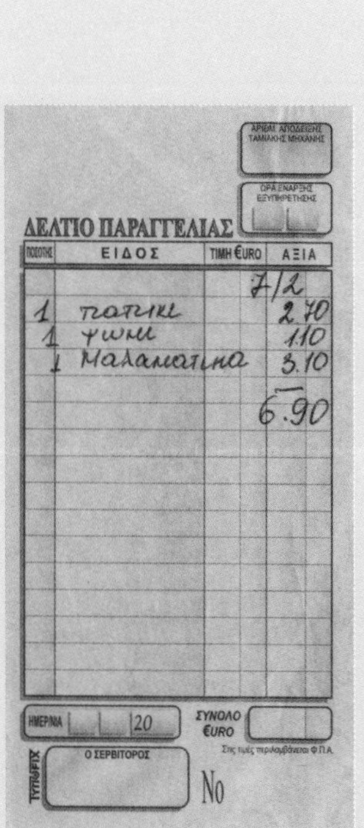

ΔΕΛΤΙΟ ΠΑΡΑΓΓΕΛΙΑΣ

ΕΙΔΟΣ	ΤΙΜΗ €URO	ΑΞΙΑ
		7/12
1 παπικι		2.70
1 ψωμι		1.10
1 Μαλαματινα		3.10
		6.90

ΗΜΕΡΑ 20 ΣΥΝΟΛΟ €URO

Ο ΣΕΡΒΙΤΟΡΟΣ

No

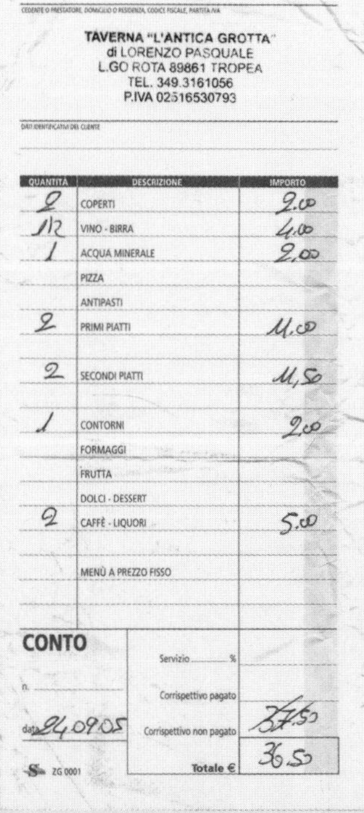

TAVERNA "L'ANTICA GROTTA"
di LORENZO PASQUALE
L.GO ROTA 89861 TROPEA
TEL. 349.3161056
P.IVA 02516530793

QUANTITÀ	DESCRIZIONE	IMPORTO
2	COPERTI	2.00
1/2	VINO - BIRRA	4.00
1	ACQUA MINERALE	2.00
	PIZZA	
	ANTIPASTI	
2	PRIMI PIATTI	11.00
2	SECONDI PIATTI	11,50
1	CONTORNI	2.00
	FORMAGGI	
	FRUTTA	
	DOLCI - DESSERT	
2	CAFFÈ - LIQUORI	5.00
	MENÙ A PREZZO FISSO	

CONTO

Servizio %
Corrispettivo pagato
data 24.09.05 Corrispettivo non pagato 37.50
Totale € 36.50

เล่มที่ BOOK NO
เลขที่ NO
ใบเสร็จรับเงิน 27 JUL 2006
วันที่ DATE
RECEIPT
ได้รับเงินจาก RECEIVED FROM
Room No. 20
ชำระค่า IN PAYMENT OF
Room Rental For 27/7
เป็นจำนวนเงิน TOTAL
บาท BAHT 500
ผู้รับเงิน COLLECTOR

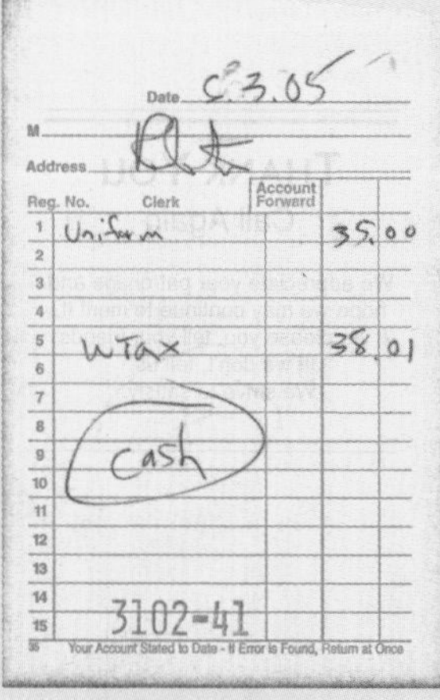

Date 6-3-05
M
Address

Reg. No.	Clerk	Account Forward	
1	Uniform		35.00
2			
3			
4			
5	w Tax		38.01
6			
7			
8			
9	Cash		
10			
11			
12			
13			
14			
15	3102-41		

Your Account Stated to Date – If Error is Found, Return at Once

Receipts and restaurant bills from Greece, Italy, Thailand and the US

Restaurant bills and receipts are similar all over the world. Only the Thai example is somewhat different. This generally long and narrow form is an endangered species thanks to the triumph of the electronic cash register.

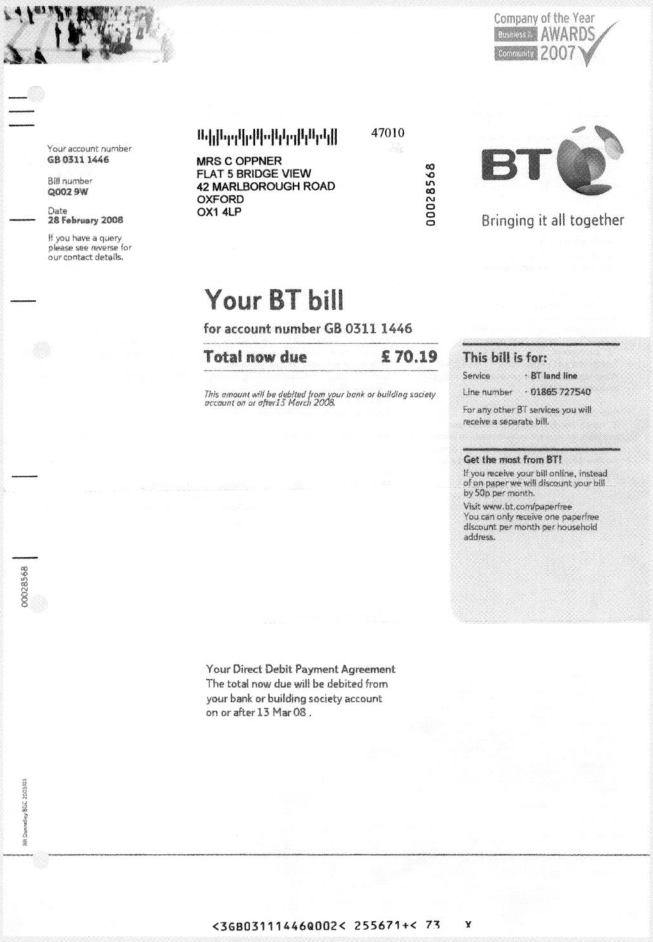

Company of the Year
Business in the Community AWARDS 2007

Your account number
GB 0311 1446

Bill number
Q002 9W

Date
28 February 2008

If you have a query please see reverse for our contact details.

47010

MRS C OPPNER
FLAT 5 BRIDGE VIEW
42 MARLBOROUGH ROAD
OXFORD
OX1 4LP

00028568

BT

Bringing it all together

Your BT bill

for account number GB 0311 1446

Total now due	**£ 70.19**

This amount will be debited from your bank or building society account on or after13 March 2008.

This bill is for:

Service · **BT land line**
Line number · **01865 727540**

For any other BT services you will receive a separate bill.

Get the most from BT!

If you receive your bill online, instead of on paper we will discount your bill by 50p per month.

Visit www.bt.com/paperfree
You can only receive one paperfree discount per month per household address.

Your Direct Debit Payment Agreement
The total now due will be debited from your bank or building society account on or after 13 Mar 08 .

<3GB031114460002< 255671+< 73 Y

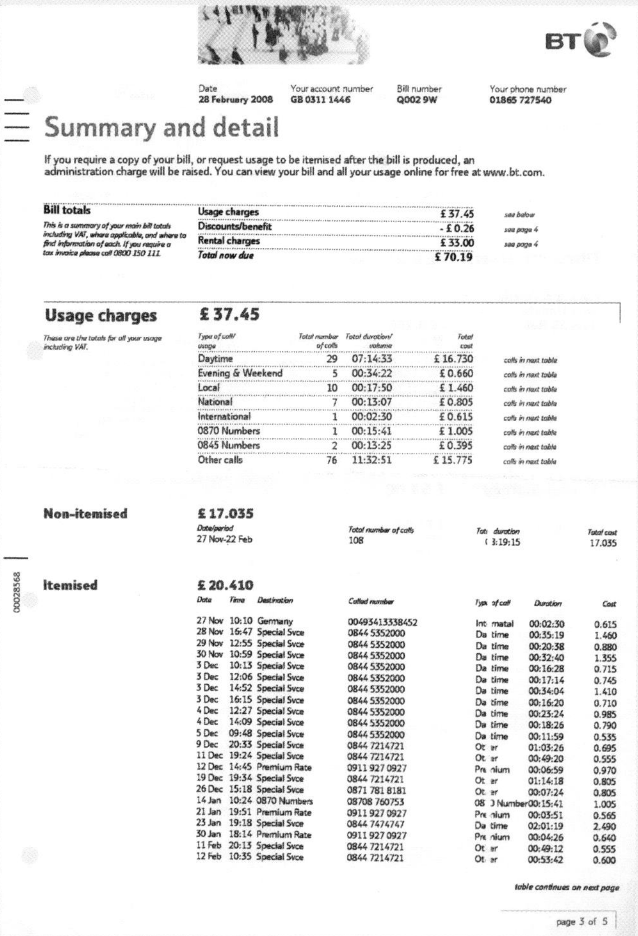

BT

Date	Your account number	Bill number	Your phone number
28 February 2008	**GB 0311 1446**	**Q002 9W**	**01865 727540**

Summary and detail

If you require a copy of your bill, or request usage to be itemised after the bill is produced, an administration charge will be raised. You can view your bill and all your usage online for free at www.bt.com.

Bill totals

This is a summary of your main bill totals including VAT, where applicable, and where to find information of each. If you require a tax invoice please call 0800 150 111.

Usage charges	£ 37.45	*see below*
Discounts/benefit	- £ 0.26	*see page 4*
Rental charges	£ 33.00	*see page 4*
Total now due	**£ 70.19**	

Usage charges **£ 37.45**

These are the totals for all your usage including VAT.

Type of call/ usage	*Total number of calls*	*Total duration/ volume*	*Total cost*	
Daytime	29	07:14:33	£ 16.730	*calls in next table*
Evening & Weekend	5	00:34:22	£ 0.660	*calls in next table*
Local	10	00:17:50	£ 1.460	*calls in next table*
National	7	00:13:07	£ 0.805	*calls in next table*
International	1	00:02:30	£ 0.615	*calls in next table*
0870 Numbers	1	00:15:41	£ 1.005	*calls in next table*
0845 Numbers	2	00:13:25	£ 0.395	*calls in next table*
Other calls	76	11:32:51	£ 15.775	*calls in next table*

Non-itemised **£ 17.035**

Date/period	*Total number of calls*	*Total duration*	*Total cost*
27 Nov-22 Feb	108	(3:19:15	17.035

Itemised **£ 20.410**

Date	*Time*	*Destination*	*Called number*	*Type of call*	*Duration*	*Cost*
27 Nov	10:10	Germany	00493413338452	Int matal	00:02:30	0.615
28 Nov	16:47	Special Svce	0844 5352000	Da time	00:35:19	1.460
29 Nov	12:55	Special Svce	0844 5352000	Da time	00:20:38	0.880
30 Nov	10:59	Special Svce	0844 5352000	Da time	00:32:40	1.355
3 Dec	10:13	Special Svce	0844 5352000	Da time	00:16:28	0.715
3 Dec	12:06	Special Svce	0844 5352000	Da time	00:17:14	0.745
3 Dec	14:52	Special Svce	0844 5352000	Da time	00:34:04	1.410
3 Dec	16:15	Special Svce	0844 5352000	Da time	00:16:20	0.710
4 Dec	12:27	Special Svce	0844 5352000	Da time	00:23:24	0.985
4 Dec	14:09	Special Svce	0844 5352000	Da time	00:18:26	0.790
5 Dec	09:48	Special Svce	0844 5352000	Da time	00:11:59	0.535
9 Dec	20:33	Special Svce	0844 7214721	Ot er	01:03:26	0.695
11 Dec	19:24	Special Svce	0844 7214721	Ot er	00:49:20	0.555
12 Dec	14:45	Premium Rate	0911 927 0927	Pre nium	00:06:59	0.970
19 Dec	19:34	Special Svce	0844 7214721	Ot er	01:14:18	0.805
26 Dec	15:18	Special Svce	0871 781 8181	Ot er	00:07:24	0.805
14 Jan	10:24	0870 Numbers	08708 760753	08) Number	00:15:41	1.005
21 Jan	19:51	Premium Rate	0911 927 0927	Pre nium	00:03:51	0.565
23 Jan	19:18	Special Svce	0844 7474747	Da time	02:01:19	2.490
30 Jan	18:14	Premium Rate	0911 927 0927	Pre nium	00:04:26	0.640
11 Feb	20:13	Special Svce	0844 7214721	Ot er	00:49:12	0.555
12 Feb	10:35	Special Svce	0844 7214721	Ot er	00:53:42	0.600

table continues on next page

page 3 of 5

Phone bill, UK

In recent years, there has been a tendency for the energy and telecoms industries to restructure the bills that they send to customers at regular intervals. The first page no longer begins with an itemized list, but with a brief and easily understood summary, often in the form of a short text. Only on the subsequent pages is there a detailed itemization of units used, etc. This makes it easier for the customer to skim-read and pick out the most relevant information.

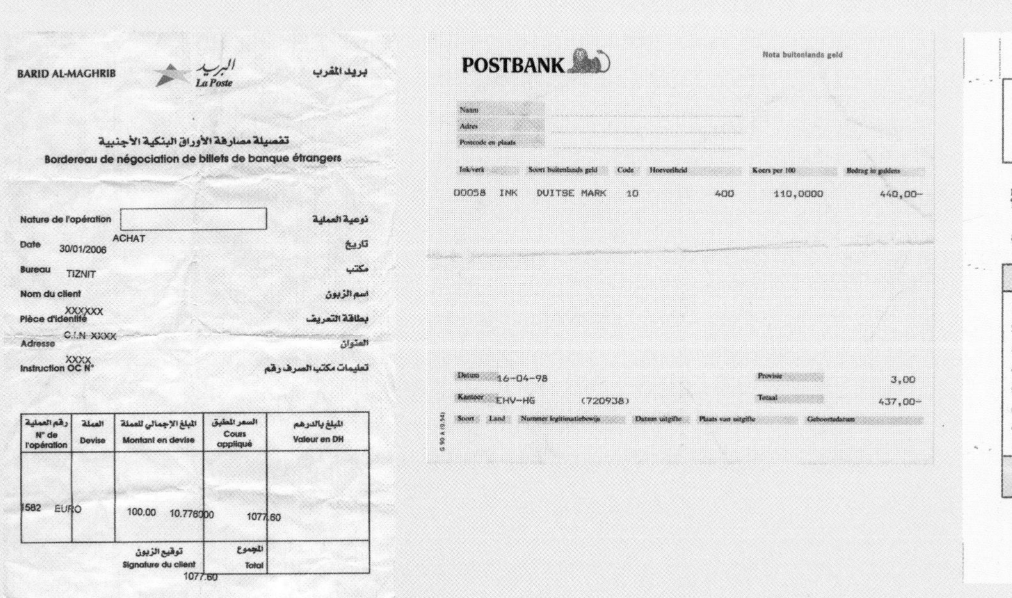

BARID AL-MAGHRIB البريد La Poste بريد المغرب

تفصيلة مصارفة الأوراق البنكية الأجنبية
Bordereau de négociation de billets de banque étrangers

Nature de l'opération ACHAT نوعية العملية
Date 30/01/2006 تاريخ
Bureau TIZNIT مكتب
Nom du client اسم الزبون
Pièce d'identité XXXXXX بطاقة التعريف
Adresse C.I.N XXXX العنوان
Instruction OC N° XXXX تعليمات مكتب الصرف رقم

رقم العملية N° de l'opération	العملة Devise	المبلغ الإجمالي للعملة Montant en devise	السعر المطبق Cours appliqué	المبلغ بالدرهم Valeur en DH
1582	EURO	100.00	10.776000	1077.60
		توقيع الزبون Signature du client 1077.60	المجموع Total	

POSTBANK

Nota buitenlands geld

Naam
Adres
Postcode en plaats

Ink/verk	Soort buitenlands geld	Code	Hoeveelheid	Koers per 100	Bedrag in guldens
00058 INK	DUITSE MARK	10	400	110,0000	440,00-

Datum 16-04-98 Provisie 3,00
Kantoor EHV-HG (720938) Totaal 437,00-

Soort Land Nummer legitimatiebewijs Datum uitgifte Plaats van uitgifte Geboortedatum

G 90 A (9.94)

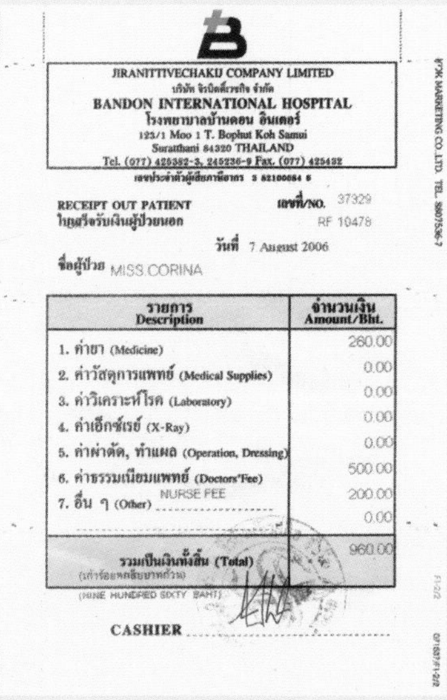

JIRANITTIVECHAKIJ COMPANY LIMITED
BANDON INTERNATIONAL HOSPITAL
โรงพยาบาลบ้านดอน อินเตอร์
123/1 Moo 1 T. Bophut Koh Samui
Suratthani 84320 THAILAND
Tel. (077) 425382-3, 245236-9 Fax. (077) 425432

RECEIPT OUT PATIENT เลขที่/NO. 37329
ใบเสร็จรับเงินผู้ป่วยนอก RF 10478

วันที่ 7 August 2006

ชื่อผู้ป่วย MISS.CORINA

รายการ Description	จำนวนเงิน Amount/Bht.
1. ค่ายา (Medicine)	260.00
2. ค่าวัสดุการแพทย์ (Medical Supplies)	0.00
3. ค่าวิเคราะห์โรค (Laboratory)	0.00
4. ค่าเอ็กซ์เรย์ (X-Ray)	0.00
5. ค่าผ่าตัด, ทำแผล (Operation, Dressing)	0.00
6. ค่าธรรมเนียมแพทย์ (Doctors'Fee)	500.00
7. อื่น ๆ (Other) NURSE FEE	200.00
	0.00
รวมเป็นเงินทั้งสิ้น (Total)	960.00

(NINE HUNDRED SIXTY BAHT)

CASHIER

Receipts from Morocco, the Netherlands and Thailand

The design of the Moroccan receipt is sturdy enough to withstand the fact that the entries are crooked, the Dutch one is as spacious and well structured as many other Dutch forms, and the warm pink of the Thai receipt has a friendly look.

Notices and statements

Notices and statements provide information

Notices and statements are pre-formulated communications addressed to one or more receivers, providing information about a specific subject. A tax statement tells taxpayers what they owes, and a notice from the local council tells the residents of a particular street that the water is going to be turned off on a particular day.

A standard way of communicating

The aim of this type of form is to send a message in which the content has been unified, making it easier to produce and to read. It could include anything from a standardized invitation to a sick note, but some notices are official and must comply with certain legal standards.

Public notices

Some notices from public services and government bodies have legal weight. They convey administrative decisions which are not always welcomed by those who receive them. For instance, they may demand the payment of taxes, or explain that a service has been withdrawn. It is therefore all the more important that these notices are not only accurate but are also comprehensible to readers without specialist knowledge. Only if it is clear which decision has been taken, and on what grounds, will it be possible for members of the public to complain, respond or appeal in a timely and correct fashion.

Provider

→ page 161

Receiver of the statement

→ page 164

Demands

Fixed demands for action should not be vague but must be formulated in a concrete way.

Main items of information

Statements contain a lot of information, including calculations and explanations. It is therefore important to highlight or emphasize the most relevant items.

→ page 132

NEWFORT ELECTRIC

Ms Jane Ragson
10 Cobden Crescent
Newfort
NF7 3MN

Your Account Number

168887045

Call us with any enquiries

0800 123 123

Your **electricity** statement

Period	1 Jan 2010 until 31 Mar 2010
Balance	**You owe £3.19**
	We will carry forward this balance.

Date	27 March 2010
Page	1/2

Your electricity statement explained

YOUR ELECTRICITY USAGE

Meter No.	S75C35165
Reading last time	68781
Reading this time	69378
Units	597

YOUR ELECTRICITY BILL

Your tariff	General Domestic

Period	Energy Charge	Standing Charge	Total
1 Jan – 28 Feb 2010	415 units at 9.32p	59 days at 15.00p	£47.52
1 Mar – 31 Mar 2010	182 units at 13.22p	31 days at 13.00p	£28.09
	Total charges before VAT		**£75.61**
	VAT		£3.78
	Total charges this bill including VAT		**£79.39**
	Total from previous bill		£13.80
Payments received	20 Jan 2010	£30.00	
	20 Feb 2010	£30.00	
	20 Mar 2010	£30.00	
	Less your payments		-£90.00
	Total this bill		**£3.19**

Newfort Electric Limited
14a Malvern Road
Townsend
Newfortshire
NT8 1CC

Registered in England and Wales
Number 87894489992

Page numbering

If the statement extends across several sheets, the pages should be individually numbered.

→ page 167

VI
Kreiswehrersatzamt

, den 10.03.97

WICHTIG! Bitte genau beachten!

Personenkennziffer

Personenkennziffer bei Anfragen und Eingaben bitte angeben.

Bei Reisen in oder durch Gebiete außerhalb der Bundesrepublik Deutschland darf dieser Bescheid nicht mitgenommen werden. Dieser Bescheid ist sorgfältig aufzubewahren!

Herrn

Die Sie betreffenden Feststellungen sind angekreuzt! Bitte Hinweise auf der Rückseite beachten!

☒ **MUSTERUNGSBESCHEID** ☐ **BESCHEID**

Sehr geehrter Herr!

Aufgrund ☒ des Ergebnisses Ihrer Musterung am 10.03.97
☐ Ihres Antrags vom ___ und vom ___
☐ Ihres Widerspruchs vom ___
☐ Ihrer nochmaligen ärztlichen Untersuchung am ___
☐ vorliegender Unterlagen

ergeht folgende

Entscheidung

☐ Sie sind von der Pflicht zur persönlichen Vorstellung nach ☐ §3 Abs. 1 Nr. ___ der Musterungsverordnung ☐ §43 Abs. 2 Satz 1 WPflG befreit.

☒ **Tauglichkeitsgrad**
Aufgrund ☒ des Ergebnisses der ärztlichen Untersuchung ☐ der vorliegenden Unterlagen
wird festgesetzt, daß Sie gem. § 8a Abs. 1 Satz 1 WPflG
☐ wehrdienstfähig und nach Maßgabe des ärztlichen Urteils gem. § 8a Abs. 2 WPflG
☐ voll verwendungsfähig sind.
☐ verwendungsfähig mit Einschränkung für bestimmte Tätigkeiten sind.
☐ verwendungsfähig mit Einschränkung in der Grundausbildung und für bestimmte Tätigkeiten sind.
☐ verwendungsfähig für bestimmte Tätigkeiten des Grundwehrdienstes unter Freistellung von der Grundausbildung sind.
☐ vorübergehend nicht wehrdienstfähig sind.
☒ nicht wehrdienstfähig sind.
☒ Eine Durchschrift des ärztlichen Untersuchungsergebnisses / Verwendungsausweises ist beigefügt.

☒ **Wehrdienstunfähigkeit**
Sie werden gem. § 9 WPflG nicht zum Wehrdienst herangezogen.

☐ **Ausschluß vom Wehrdienst**
Sie sind gem. § 10 Abs. 1 Nr. ___ WPflG vom Wehrdienst ☐ dauernd ☐ bis einschließlich ___ ausgeschlossen.

☐ **Befreiung vom Wehrdienst**
Sie sind gem. § 11 Abs. ___ Nr. ___ WPflG vom Wehrdienst befreit.

Notice of exemption from military service, Germany

A notice with information that is important for the receiver – namely, that he has been exempted from military service. This notice is a typical embodiment of German bureaucracy.

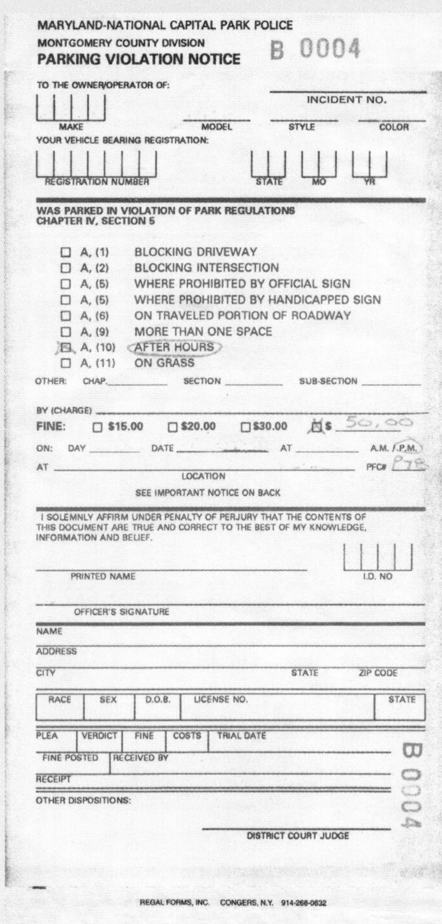

MARYLAND-NATIONAL CAPITAL PARK POLICE
MONTGOMERY COUNTY DIVISION
PARKING VIOLATION NOTICE B 0004

TO THE OWNER/OPERATOR OF:
INCIDENT NO.
MAKE / MODEL / STYLE / COLOR
YOUR VEHICLE BEARING REGISTRATION:
REGISTRATION NUMBER / STATE / MO / YR

WAS PARKED IN VIOLATION OF PARK REGULATIONS
CHAPTER IV, SECTION 5

☐ A, (1) BLOCKING DRIVEWAY
☐ A, (2) BLOCKING INTERSECTION
☐ A, (5) WHERE PROHIBITED BY OFFICIAL SIGN
☐ A, (5) WHERE PROHIBITED BY HANDICAPPED SIGN
☐ A, (6) ON TRAVELED PORTION OF ROADWAY
☐ A, (9) MORE THAN ONE SPACE
☒ A, (10) AFTER HOURS
☐ A, (11) ON GRASS

OTHER: CHAP. ___ SECTION ___ SUB-SECTION ___
BY (CHARGE) ___
FINE: ☐ $15.00 ☐ $20.00 ☐ $30.00 ☒ $ 50.00
ON: DAY ___ DATE ___ AT ___ A.M. / P.M.
AT ___ PFC# ___
LOCATION
SEE IMPORTANT NOTICE ON BACK

I SOLEMNLY AFFIRM UNDER PENALTY OF PERJURY THAT THE CONTENTS OF THIS DOCUMENT ARE TRUE AND CORRECT TO THE BEST OF MY KNOWLEDGE, INFORMATION AND BELIEF.

PRINTED NAME / I.D. NO
OFFICER'S SIGNATURE
NAME
ADDRESS
CITY / STATE / ZIP CODE
RACE / SEX / D.O.B. / LICENSE NO. / STATE
PLEA / VERDICT / FINE / COSTS / TRIAL DATE
FINE POSTED / RECEIVED BY
RECEIPT
OTHER DISPOSITIONS:
DISTRICT COURT JUDGE
B 0004

REGAL FORMS, INC. CONGERS, N.Y. 914-268-0832

Parking ticket, US

The parking ticket is one of the most common forms of communication between local government and the ordinary citizen. This makes it a costly and unwelcome official visiting card.

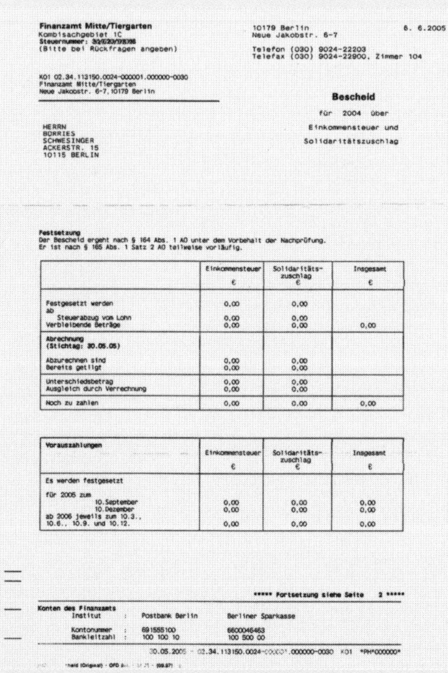

Finanzamt Mitte/Tiergarten

Bescheid
für 2004 über
Einkommensteuer und
Solidaritätszuschlag

REPRINTED BILL

PHIL FRANEY - KCTTC

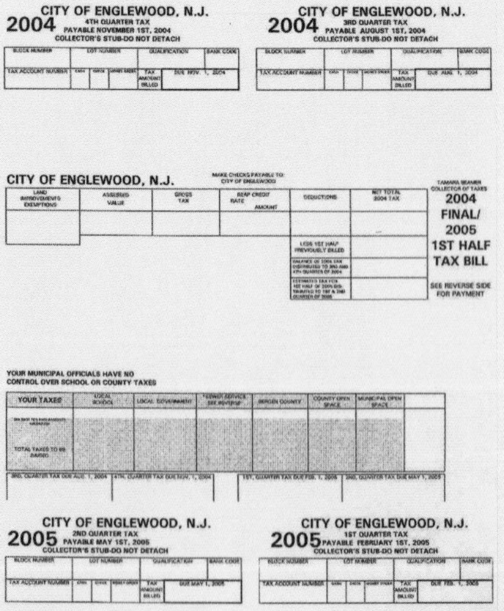

CITY OF ENGLEWOOD, N.J.

2004 FINAL/ 2005 1ST HALF TAX BILL

Tax demands from Germany and the US

These notices are clearer than the tax declaration forms, though still far from perfect. The attempts to divide up the information are weak, and the form in the centre uses a distracting selection of colours.

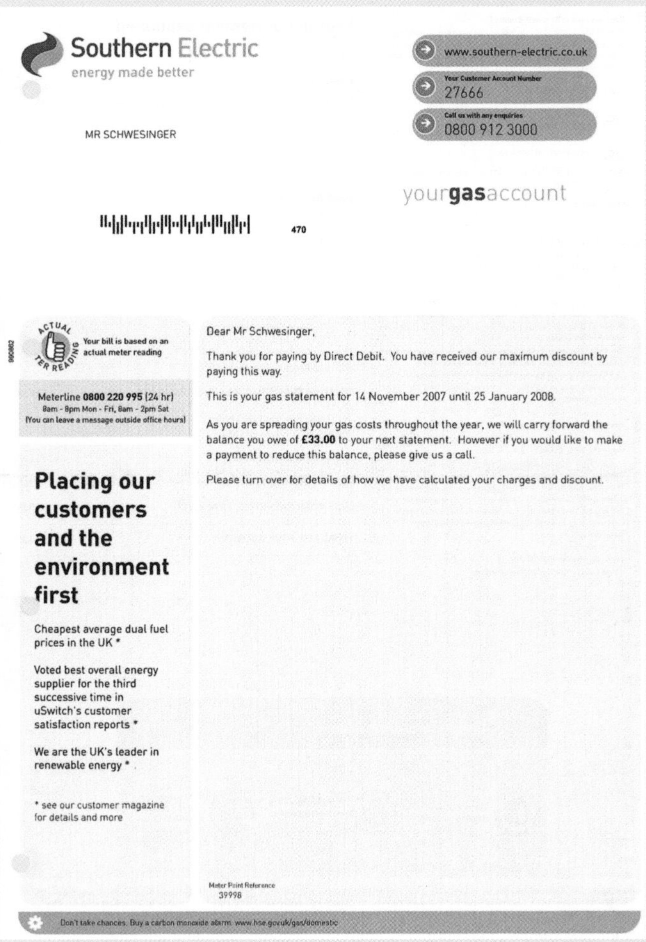

Southern Electric
energy made better

www.southern-electric.co.uk

Your Customer Account Number
27666

Call us with any enquiries
0800 912 3000

MR SCHWESINGER

yourgasaccount

470

Your bill is based on an actual meter reading

Meterline **0800 220 995** (24 hr)
8am - 8pm Mon - Fri, 8am - 2pm Sat
(You can leave a message outside office hours)

Placing our customers and the environment first

Cheapest average dual fuel prices in the UK *

Voted best overall energy supplier for the third successive time in uSwitch's customer satisfaction reports *

We are the UK's leader in renewable energy *

* see our customer magazine for details and more

Dear Mr Schwesinger,

Thank you for paying by Direct Debit. You have received our maximum discount by paying this way.

This is your gas statement for 14 November 2007 until 25 January 2008.

As you are spreading your gas costs throughout the year, we will carry forward the balance you owe of **£33.00** to your next statement. However if you would like to make a payment to reduce this balance, please give us a call.

Please turn over for details of how we have calculated your charges and discount.

Meter Point Reference
39998

Don't take chances. Buy a carbon monoxide alarm. www.hse.gov.uk/gas/domestic

Have a question or moving home?
It's quicker and easier for us to answer your questions straightaway if you call us on the number below. Or if you are moving home please call us on the same number with your final meter reading and new address details. Thank you.

0800 912 3000

Customer Service, Southern Electric, PO Box 7506, Perth PH1 3QR

www.southern-electric.co.uk

Please note: to help us improve our service further, we may record customer phone calls from time to time.

Emergencies
Smell gas? Call 0800 111 999 immediately (open 24 hours).

Our commitment to you
If you would like to know more about the service standards we promise to all our customers, visit our website for details of our Domestic Energy Customer Charter or call us.

If we have let you down in any way, please call us. If our adviser can't help, please ask for a manager. If you remain unhappy, write to our Director of Customer Service at Inveralmond House, 200 Dunkeld Road, Perth PH1 3AQ or send an email to directorofcustomerservice@southern-electric.co.uk. If you are still not satisfied, you can contact the Energy Supply Ombudsman on 0845 055 0760 or www.energy-ombudsman.org.uk or Energywatch, the industry watchdog, on 0845 906 0708, typetalk: 18001 0845 906 0708 or www.energywatch.org.uk

Your gas transporter
For details of your gas transporter, call us. Lines are open 8am to 8pm Monday to Friday and 8am to 2pm Saturday.

Calculating your gas
To work out your gas bill we convert units used to kilowatt hours in the following way: gas units used x imperial to metric conversion factor of 2.83 (you don't need to do this if you already have a metric meter) x correction factor x calorific value, divided by the kilowatt hour conversion factor of 3.6.

VAT registration number 553 7696 03
Bill date and tax point date 31 January 2008

Your gas statement explained

This bill is for the period 14 Nov 2007 to 25 Jan 2008

YOUR GAS USAGE

	Reading last time	Reading this time	Units
Meter: G4K0247			
Gas Unrestricted kWh	2880	3085	205
Correction factor 1.02264		Calorific value 38.7863	
Total metric units used		209.64 cu mtrs	
Units converted to kilowatt hours		2258.65 kWh	

YOUR GAS BILL
Your Tariff is General Saver

Standard energy		
2258.65 kWh at 2.210p each	£49.91	
Standing charge at 11.400p for 73 day(s)	£8.32	
Less your Monthly Direct Debit Discount	-£2.99	
Total charges before VAT	£55.24	
VAT at 5.00% on charges of £55.24	£2.76	
TOTAL CHARGES THIS BILL INCLUDING VAT		**£58.00**
Gas Adj to A/C Standard Rate	-£4.77	
VAT at 5.00% on credit of £4.77	-£0.23	
ACCOUNT ADJUSTMENTS		**-£5.00**
Payment received 20 January 2008	-£20.00	
LESS YOUR PAYMENTS, THANK YOU		**-£20.00**
TOTAL FOR YOUR ACCOUNT		**£33.00**

Thumbs up to great value →

Your bill is based on an actual meter reading

Thank you for paying by monthly direct debit.

Don't miss out on your energyplus reward. Call us to find out more.

Southern Electric and Southern Electric Gas are trading names of the Scottish and Southern Energy Group of which SSE Energy Supply Limited Registered in England & Wales No. 3757502 and Southern Electric Gas Limited Registered in England and Wales No. 2716495 are members with their Registered Offices at 55 Vastern Road Reading RG1 8BU
southern-electric.co.uk

Gas statement, UK

Statements tell customers how much energy they have used over a particular period of time, or let them know the current status of their account. Rather like the phone bill on page 95, the content and design no longer have much in common with the classic type of form. The information is divided into two – a personalized text on the first page, and an itemized table on the back. The statement is still a form, however, because of the formulaic layout of information and the coloured boxes on the first page, which separate the text areas from one another.

Card No: 8 7 4 3 9 9

DPD

Sorry we missed you

We'll automatically attempt delivery a second time on the next business day. If this is acceptable you do not need to contact us.
Or choose 1, 2 or 3
Your parcel will be returned to the sender if you have not contacted us within 3 days of the 1st attempted delivery

1 Upgrade delivery
Choose a morning or afternoon slot or a Saturday morning for an additional charge (charges overleaf)
Call 0844 824 05 05

2 Change delivery day
Reschedule online
Visit www.dpd.co.uk/redelivery
or
Call 0844 824 05 05

3 Leave in a safe place
Simply sign the box below leave this card for us to collect
Our driver must be able to collect this card at the point of delivery

For DPD Driver to complete
Receiver's name: B. SCHWEISINGER
Parcel No: 0 9 1 2 1 3 5 3 5 7 4
Date: 17/4/08 Time: 4 25
Route: 406

Please leave my parcel at (indicate a safe place at your address): ______
I agree to accept full responsibility for any goods that are left
Name: ______ Signature: ______

Royal Mail

Sorry, you were out

Time 12.30	Today's date 5.12
Name Boris Sch	
Address 42 Marlborough	
Postcode	

You were out and your ☐ Letter ☑ Special Delivery
☐ Recorded Signed For ☐ Packet ☐ Perishable item
☐ Royal Mail Tracked ☐ Catalogue ☐ Large item
could not be delivered to you ☐ International item

because
☑ A signature is required
☐ It's too big for your letterbox

Please see overleaf for information on where your item is now.

Item number
Photo ID card serial number
ZV 7921 7317 6GB

www.royalmail.com/redelivery

Delivery notes, UK

These are two everyday communications that get stuck on doors or through letterboxes. The colours of the Royal Mail notice are instantly recognizable, offering the customer more detailed information in a more accessible manner.

Questionnaires

Questionnaires collate information for comparative evaluation

Questionnaires collect personal data, attitudes and opinions through polls, surveys and ballots. They are often components of applications and advertising campaigns, and their purpose is to collate a quantity of standardized and therefore comparable information.

Questionnaires hold a dialogue

A questionnaire takes the form of a written, structured interview with standardized ways of answering. The provider asks questions, and the user responds. While the identity of the provider is or ought to be obvious, the user may well remain totally anonymous. This distinguishes questionnaires from many other types of form. In elections, ballots and most other kinds of poll, the guarantee of anonymity is in fact a precondition for the success and authenticity of the exercise.

Questionnaires must motivate

It is important to distinguish between questionnaires that are to be filled in independently and those for which an interviewer writes down the answers supplied, i.e. during a telephone interview or face to face. The latter simply give the interviewer guidance about the information that needs to be collected, but questionnaires designed to be filled in independently must first motivate the users to participate. With the exception of exams and ballot papers, forms do not generally offer any personal benefit to those who fill them in, so goodwill is required. This can be attained in several ways: through convincing arguments, through the offer of a reward or prize, and also through good design. Questionnaires must therefore be easy to understand, clear, and as concise as possible if they are not to end up in the recycling bin.

Questionnaires often contain rank order scales

A designer of questionnaires often has to find good ways of presenting complex scales in order to gauge people's attitudes and opinions.

Questionnaires must not build barriers

To reach as wide an audience as possible, questionnaires must sometimes be presented in several languages. With some, such as ballot papers, it may even be necessary to make them comprehensible to illiterate users: this can be done by including elements such as pictograms and illustrations.

Provider

→ page 161

Introduction

Time limit for return

Personal contact

No one likes to be interrogated by an impersonal institution, so it is reassuring to be able to contact a specific person.

Questions

A questionnaire is a written interview. The questions are on the left, and the answers on the right. This clear structure prevents confusion.

FACTINFORM
Research Consultancy

CLIENT QUESTIONNAIRE

We aren't satisfied until you're satisfied!

Dear client

Your opinions are valuable to us. Please help us to improve our future services by completing this questionnaire and returning it to us by post or fax before 23 October 2010.
All completed questionnaires will be entered into a prize draw to win one of ten £50 gift vouchers.
We can assure you that all data supplied will be considered confidential and will not be shared with third parties.

If you have any queries or comments about this questionnaire, please contact
Miriam Fraser on 01632 420 111 or at m.fraser@factinform.com

- **How satisfied were you with the following?**

	extremely satisfied				extremely unsatisfied
FACTINFORM's range of services?	○	○	○	○	○
FACTINFORM's customer service?	○	○	○	○	○
FACTINFORM's prices?	○	○	○	○	○

- **On how many occasions have you used FACTINFORM services in the last 12 months?**

○ not at all ○ 1 ○ 2–3 ○ 4–6 ○ more than 6

- **Which FACTINFORM services have you used in the last 12 months?**

○ None
○ Customer surveys
○ Brand name creation
○ Individual profiling
○ Other *(please state)* ....

- **Please rate the following statements:**

	strongly agree				strongly disagree
FACTINFORM is a young and modern company.	○	○	○	○	○
The services offered by FACTINFORM are unique.	○	○	○	○	○
The FACTINFORM staff are helpful and able to answer all queries.	○	○	○	○	○

- **Personal details**

Sex ○ male ○ female
Age ○ under 30 ○ 30 to 39 ○ 40 to 49 ○ 50 to 59 ○ 60 or over
Annual income ○ under £20,000 ○ £20,000 to £39,999
○ £40,000 to £59,999 ○ £60,000 or over

Answers

The answers are in multiple choice format or make use of rating scales.

→ pages 170, 178, 182

Personal details

The amount of detail requested will depend on the type of questionnaire and on the user's need for anonymity. Instead of specific figures, number categories are often sufficient.

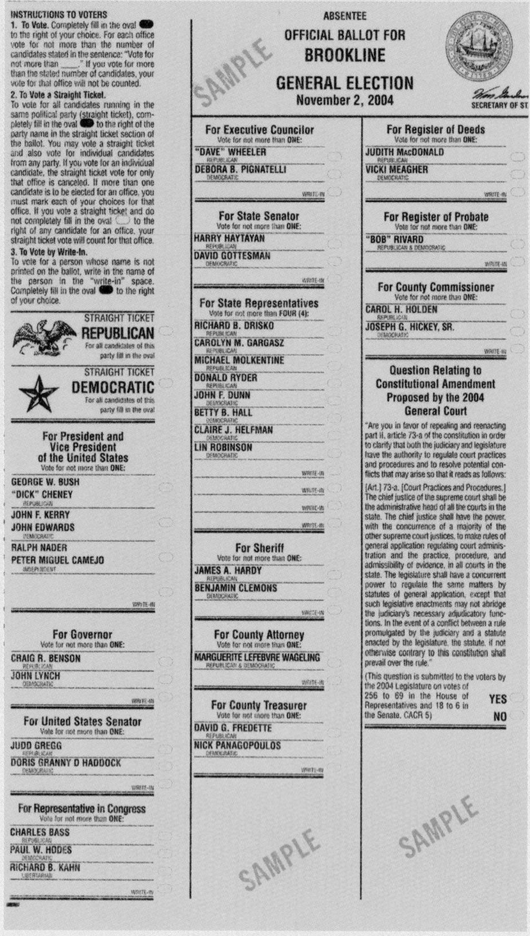

INSTRUCTIONS TO VOTERS
1. To Vote. Completely fill in the oval to the right of your choice. For each office vote for not more than the number of candidates stated in the sentence: "Vote for not more than ___." If you vote for more than the stated number of candidates, your vote for that office will not be counted.
2. To Vote a Straight Ticket. To vote for all candidates running in the same political party (straight ticket), completely fill in the oval to the right of the party name in the straight ticket section of the ballot. You may vote a straight ticket and also vote for individual candidates from any party. If you vote for an individual candidate, the straight ticket vote for only that office is canceled. If more than one candidate is to be elected for an office, you must mark each of your choices for that office. If you vote a straight ticket and do not completely fill in the oval to the right of any candidate for an office, your straight ticket vote will count for that office.
3. To Vote by Write-In. To vote for a person whose name is not printed on the ballot, write in the name of the person in the "write-in" space. Completely fill in the oval to the right of your choice.

STRAIGHT TICKET REPUBLICAN
For all candidates of this party fill in the oval

STRAIGHT TICKET DEMOCRATIC
For all candidates of this party fill in the oval

For President and Vice President of the United States
Vote for not more than ONE:
GEORGE W. BUSH
"DICK" CHENEY
JOHN F. KERRY
JOHN EDWARDS
RALPH NADER
PETER MIGUEL CAMEJO

For Governor
Vote for not more than ONE:
CRAIG R. BENSON
JOHN LYNCH

For United States Senator
Vote for not more than ONE:
JUDD GREGG
DORIS GRANNY D HADDOCK

For Representative in Congress
Vote for not more than ONE:
CHARLES BASS
PAUL W. HODES
RICHARD B. KAHN

ABSENTEE
OFFICIAL BALLOT FOR BROOKLINE
GENERAL ELECTION
November 2, 2004
SECRETARY OF ST

SAMPLE

For Executive Councilor
Vote for not more than ONE:
"DAVE" WHEELER
DEBORA B. PIGNATELLI

For State Senator
Vote for not more than ONE:
HARRY HAYTAYAN
DAVID GOTTESMAN

For State Representatives
Vote for not more than FOUR (4):
RICHARD B. DRISKO
CAROLYN M. GARGASZ
MICHAEL MOLKENTINE
DONALD RYDER
JOHN F. DUNN
BETTY B. HALL
CLAIRE J. HELFMAN
LIN ROBINSON

For Sheriff
Vote for not more than ONE:
JAMES A. HARDY
BENJAMIN CLEMONS

For County Attorney
Vote for not more than ONE:
MARGUERITE LEFEBVRE WAGELING

For County Treasurer
Vote for not more than ONE:
DAVID G. FREDETTE
NICK PANAGOPOULOS

For Register of Deeds
Vote for not more than ONE:
JUDITH MacDONALD
VICKI MEAGHER

For Register of Probate
Vote for not more than ONE:
"BOB" RIVARD

For County Commissioner
Vote for not more than ONE:
CAROL H. HOLDEN
JOSEPH G. HICKEY, SR.

Question Relating to Constitutional Amendment Proposed by the 2004 General Court

"Are you in favor of repealing and reenacting part II, article 73-a of the constitution in order to clarify that both the judiciary and legislature have the authority to regulate court practices and procedures and to resolve potential conflicts that may arise so that it reads as follows:
[Art.] 73-a. [Court Practices and Procedures.] The chief justice of the supreme court shall be the administrative head of all the courts in the state. The chief justice shall have the power, with the concurrence of a majority of the other supreme court justices, to make rules of general application regarding court administration and the practice, procedure, and admissibility of evidence, in all courts in the state. The legislature shall have a concurrent power to regulate the same matters by statutes of general application, except that such legislative enactments may not abridge the judiciary's necessary adjudicatory functions. In the event of a conflict between a rule promulgated by the judiciary and a statute enacted by the legislature, the statute, if not otherwise contrary to this constitution shall prevail over the rule."
(This question is submitted to the voters by the 2004 Legislature on votes of 256 to 69 in the House of Representatives and 18 to 6 in the Senate. CACR 5)
YES
NO

SAMPLE SAMPLE

RSA 1994

AFRICAN CONGRESS OF AZANIA — PAC
SPORTS ORGANISATION FOR COLLECTIVE CONTRIBUTIONS AND EQUAL RIGHTS — SOCCER
THE KEEP IT STRAIGHT AND SIMPLE PARTY — KISS
VRYHEIDSFRONT - FREEDOM FRONT — VF-FF
WOMEN'S RIGHTS PEACE PARTY — WRPP
WORKERS' LIST PARTY — WLP
XIMOKO PROGRESSIVE PARTY — XPP
AFRICA MUSLIM PARTY — AMP
AFRICAN CHRISTIAN DEMOCRATIC PARTY — ACDP
AFRICAN DEMOCRATIC MOVEMENT — ADM
AFRICAN MODERATES CONGRESS PARTY — AMCP
AFRICAN NATIONAL CONGRESS — ANC
DEMOCRATIC PARTY - DEMOKRATIESE PARTY — DP
DIKWANKWETLA PARTY OF SOUTH AFRICA — DPSA
FEDERAL PARTY — FP
LUSO - SOUTH AFRICAN PARTY — LUSAP
MINORITY FRONT — MF
NATIONAL PARTY - NASIONALE PARTY — NP
INKATHA FREEDOM PARTY - IQEMBU LENKATHA YENKULULEKO — IFP

Stimmzettel
für die Wahl zum Deutschen Bundestag im Wahlkreis 222 München-West/Mitte am 18. September 2005

Sie haben 2 Stimmen

hier 1 Stimme für die Wahl eines/einer Wahlkreis-abgeordneten
Erststimme

hier 1 Stimme für die Wahl einer Landesliste (Partei) – maßgebende Stimme für die Verteilung der Sitze insgesamt auf die einzelnen Parteien –
Zweitstimme

	Erststimme	Zweitstimme	
1	Dr. Uhl, Hans-Peter — CSU Christlich-Soziale Union in Bayern e.V.	CSU	1
2	Jung, Stephanie Friederike Dorothee — SPD Sozialdemokratische Partei Deutschlands	SPD	2
3	Janecek, Dieter Gerald — GRÜNE BÜNDNIS 90/DIE GRÜNEN	GRÜNE	3
4	Dunskus, Adrian Walter Erich — FDP Freie Demokratische Partei	FDP	4
		REP	5
6	Schreer, Klaus — Die Linke. Die Linkspartei.PDS	Die Linke.	6
7	Werner, Stefan Ludwig — NPD Nationaldemokratische Partei Deutschlands	NPD	7
		PBC	8
		BP	9
		DIE FRAUEN	10
		GRAUE	11
12	Zuse, Werner — BüSo Bürgerrechtsbewegung Solidarität	BüSo	12
13	Dr. Wächter, Anton Edmund — FAMILIE FAMILIEN-PARTEI DEUTSCHLANDS	FAMILIE	13
		MLPD	14
15	Holl, Matthias-Johannes — HP Humanistische Partei		

Ballot papers from the US, South Africa and Germany

In ballot papers, votes must clearly be marked for one candidate or one party. The German ballot gives a list of candidate names, whereas the South African ballot takes lower rates of literacy into account and includes party logos and candidate portraits as well. In the USA, the complicated voting process demands a fairly lengthy explanatory text.

refresh us

www.oxford.gov.uk

OXFORD CITY COUNCIL

We actively encourage and welcome your feedback on the services we provide. Your views are vital as we constantly strive to improve our standards for your benefit.

Location visited:
Date: Time:
Activity/sport undertaken:

Please tick the picture that best represents your feelings!

	Delighted	Happy	Satisfied	Unhappy	Dissatisfied
Service at reception					
Cleanliness of changing rooms					
Helpfulness of staff					
Café/vending facilities					
Quality of centre information available					
Overall satisfaction of visit					

Customer feedback form, UK

A pleasingly brief feedback form. The bright orange colour and the smiley faces – as opposed to the usual graduated rating scale – make the whole thing lively and light-hearted.

BARCLAYS
Financial Planning

Please answer the following questions.

	Yes	No	Don't know
Investments Are you getting the return you expect from your savings and investments?			
Life Cover Will your family be financially secure if you die?			
Sick Pay Will you receive a monthly income until you can return to work?			
Inheritance Tax Is your house plus other assets worth less than £285,000?			
Pensions Do you have a pension?			
If you do, are you certain your current arrangements will be enough?			
Have you reviewed your existing arrangements in the last 12 months?			

If you have answered No or Don't Know to any of the questions you should consider meeting with a Barclays Financial Planning Manager who can help.

Personal details
First name(s)
Surname
Contact Number
Mobile Number
Account Number
Sort Code
Signature
Date

Financial planning questionnaire, UK

A short questionnaire which is not for statistical purposes, but is designed to encourage customers to make an appointment for a sales talk with their bank manager.

QUESTIONNAIRE

You are kindly requested to complete this form to facilitate our quarantine procedures.

Name in Full ______ First Name / s ______ Last Name
Nationality ______ Passport No. ______
Sex ☐ Male ☐ Female Age ______ Arrival Date ______ (Y / M / D)
Flight No. or Ship's Name ______ Seat No. ______
Contact Address in Japan ______
Tel ______

Please list the names of countries / territories where you have stayed for the past 4 weeks before coming to Japan.

Please check any of the following symptoms for the past 4 weeks before arrival. (If you have any health problem listed below or something else, please report it to the quarantine officer.)

diarrhoea	☐ no	☐ yes	abdominal pain	☐ no	☐ yes
vomiting	☐ no	☐ yes	headache	☐ no	☐ yes
sore throat	☐ no	☐ yes	rash	☐ no	☐ yes
jaundice	☐ no	☐ yes	convulsion	☐ no	☐ yes
severe cough	☐ no	☐ yes	difficulty in breathing	☐ no	☐ yes
fever	☐ no	☐ yes	abnormal bleeding	☐ no	☐ yes
others	☐ no	☐ yes			

Any person who knowingly give false information or who refuse to answer a question may be punished by regulation of the Quarantine Law.

Quarantine Station, JAPAN

Quarantine questionnaire, Japan

All visitors to Japan must fill in this form. Here too, the answers are less for statistical purposes than to establish whether the visitor might present a health risk or not.

LEJRN

RENAISSANCE®
HOTELS & RESORTS

RENAISSANCE LEIPZIG HOTEL

Thank you for choosing *Renaissance Hotels* for your recent trip. It is our goal to completely satisfy our guests on every stay. We value your opinion and invite you to take a few minutes to share your feedback about your experience. By completing this survey, you may be contacted by the hotel so that they may understand your experiences to help improve the quality of services provided. We sincerely thank you for sharing your opinions as we continue to do our best to provide you with the ultimate hotel experience.

Name: ____

Address: ____

Country: ____ **Phone:** ____

Email: ____ **Guest Room Number:** ____

Please use pen. **Arrival Date:** ____ **Departure Date:** ____

1. We are interested in how satisfied you were with your experience at the Renaissance Hotel listed above. **Overall**, how would you rate your experience? — Excellent 10 9 8 7 6 5 4 3 2 1 Poor
2. If in this area again, how likely would you be to stay at **this Renaissance** rather than other hotels in this area? — Definitely Will / Probably Will / May or May Not / Probably Will Not / Definitely Will Not / Not Returning to Area
3. Compared to other similarly priced hotels that you have stayed at during the past six months within the same general area, would you say that: — Much Better / Better / About the Same / Worse / Much Worse / Not Applicable
   a. this Renaissance **overall** is
   b. the **physical condition** of this Renaissance is
   c. the **overall staff service** at this Renaissance is
4. How will your experience at **this Renaissance** influence your likelihood to stay at **other Renaissance** Hotels in the future? — Much More Likely / Somewhat More Likely / No Effect / Somewhat Less Likely / Much Less Likely
5. How will your experience at **this Renaissance** influence your likelihood to **recommend this Renaissance** to others? — Much More Likely / Somewhat More Likely / No Effect / Somewhat Less Likely / Much Less Likely
6. How would you rate the overall value of **this hotel**? — Excellent 10 9 8 7 6 5 4 3 2 1 Poor
7. The hotel offered a distinctive and enjoyable experience — Strongly Agree 10 9 8 7 6 5 4 3 2 1 Strongly Disagree
8. Thinking of your experience at **this Renaissance**, please rate the following: — Excellent 10 9 8 7 6 5 4 3 2 1 Poor N/A
   a. **Staff service** overall
   b. Your **room** overall
   c. **Maintenance and upkeep** of the hotel
   d. **Check-in experience**
   e. Feeling of **security**
   f. Overall **breakfast** experience (excluding in-room)
   g. Overall **lunch** experience (excluding in-room)
   h. Overall **dinner** experience (excluding in-room)
   i. Overall **restaurant dining** experience
   j. Overall **in-room dining** experience
9. Please indicate your level of agreement or disagreement with each of the following statements about your experiences at **this hotel**: — Strongly Agree 10 9 8 7 6 5 4 3 2 1 Strongly Disagree N/A
   a. The **staff** made me feel **welcome** throughout my stay
   b. The **room** was completely **clean**
   c. The hotel was **stylish**
   d. The hotel had a **warm and inviting** environment
   e. Everything in the **room** was in **working order**

Schulz Printing

please continue ▶

201

9. (continued) Please indicate your level of agreement or disagreement with each of the following statements about your experiences at **this hotel**: — Strongly Agree 10 9 8 7 6 5 4 3 2 1 Strongly Disagree N/A
   f. The **staff** treated me with **respect**
   g. I felt **special** and **well looked after**
   h. The **bed** was **comfortable**
   i. The **room** enabled me to get a **good night's rest**
   j. The **hotel** enabled me to **relax and enjoy** my stay
   k. The **restaurant** was like those I would choose to eat in *outside* of **hotels**
   l. The **meeting/event rooms** were **comfortable**
   m. The **fitness center or exercise facility** met my needs
   n. The in-room **technology** met my needs
   o. The **hotel** enabled me to be **productive**
10. Did you receive your **preferred room type** (e.g., bed type, non-smoking)? — Yes / No / Don't Recall
11. Did you experience any problems with the hotel **during your stay**? — Yes / No (*please skip to Question 12*)
   a. **If yes**, would you describe that problem as minor, moderate, or severe? — Minor / Moderate / Severe
   b. Please describe this problem. *Please select all that apply.*
      Hotel Related: Pre-arrival requests not met; Arrival experience; Departure experience; Condition of hotel; Smoking/non-smoking issues
      Staff Related: Professionalism of associate; Took too long to respond
      Dining/Food Related: Restaurant service; Restaurant food quality; In-room dining experience
      Guest Room Related: Guest room assignment; Guest room cleanliness; Cleanliness of linens; Noise level; In-room mini-bar/snack bar; Something was not working →
      Other: ____
   c. Clock; Clothes iron; Coffee/tea maker; Telephone; TV/remote control; Heating/cooling; Condition of furniture; Bathroom drains; Toilet; Water temperature; High speed internet access; Room odors; Light bulbs; Room safe; Smoking/non-smoking
   d. Did you report the problem to anyone? — Yes / No
   e. **If yes**, overall how satisfied are you with the resolution of the problem(s)? — Very Satisfied / Somewhat Satisfied / Neither / Somewhat Dissatisfied / Very Dissatisfied
   f. If you are ***Not Satisfied*** with the resolution, what causes you to feel that way? *Please select all that apply.* — Took too long to acknowledge problem; Took too long to resolve problem; Received no response to problem; Problem could not be resolved; Attitude/professionalism of associate; Staff did not understand problem
12. Are you currently a member of the **Marriott Rewards Programme?** — Yes / No / Don't Recall
   a. Did you receive the service you have come to expect as a Marriott Rewards Member? — Yes / No / Don't Recall
13. What was the purpose of your trip? *Please select only one.* — Convention/Meeting at Hotel / Business Travel / Relocation / Leisure/Personal / Combination Business/Personal
14. Did you personally select the hotel for this stay? — Yes / No
15. Is this hotel in the country in which you currently reside? — Yes / No
16. How many **nights** did you spend in a hotel in the last twelve months? — 1-9 / 10-24 / 25-49 / 50-74 / 75+
17. Are you male or female? — Male / Female
18. What is your age? — 18-24 / 25-44 / 45-64 / 65 or over
19. In what month were you born? — Jan / Feb / Mar / Apr / May / Jun / Jul / Aug / Sep / Oct / Nov / Dec

Additional Comments: ____

Thank You for your participation!

Please return this questionnaire in the enclosed business reply envelope as soon as possible. Meeting the needs and expectations of our customers has always been our highest priority and that includes protecting your privacy. The sole purpose of this survey is to allow us to measure and monitor guest satisfaction at our hotels. Responses to this survey are forwarded to our headquarters office in the United States for analysis and follow-up. You are not required to provide any personal information such as your name and address when completing the survey. If you choose to provide personal information, it may only be used for follow-up contact regarding your survey responses. If you have any concerns about the privacy of your personal information, please contact us at privacy@Renaissance.com.

Hotel questionnaire, Germany

Guests at this hotel, which is part of an international chain, are asked to answer two pages of questions about their stay. It must be a pretty boring stay if the guest has time to fill in such a badly designed questionnaire. You can tell at a glance that it's going to take a lot of time and effort, and there isn't even the inducement of a reward at the end of it.

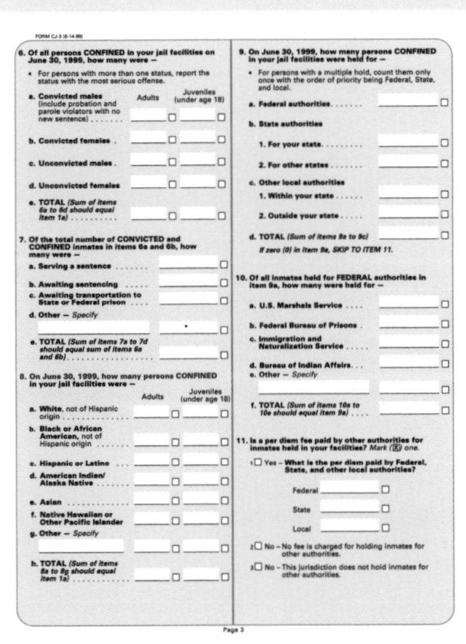

FORM CJ-3 (6-14-99)

6. Of all persons CONFINED in your jail facilities on June 30, 1999, how many were –
- For persons with more than one status, report the status with the most serious offense.

(Adults / Juveniles (under age 18))

a. **Convicted males** (include probation and parole violators with no new sentence)
b. **Convicted females**
c. **Unconvicted males**
d. **Unconvicted females**
e. **TOTAL** *(Sum of items 6a to 6d should equal item 1a)*

7. Of the total number of CONVICTED and CONFINED inmates in items 6a and 6b, how many were –

a. **Serving a sentence**
b. **Awaiting sentencing**
c. **Awaiting transportation to State or Federal prison**
d. **Other** – *Specify*
e. **TOTAL** *(Sum of items 7a to 7d should equal sum of items 6a and 6b)*

8. On June 30, 1999, how many persons CONFINED in your jail facilities were –

(Adults / Juveniles (under age 18))

a. **White**, not of Hispanic origin
b. **Black or African American**, not of Hispanic origin
c. **Hispanic or Latino**
d. **American Indian/ Alaska Native**
e. **Asian**
f. **Native Hawaiian or Other Pacific Islander**
g. **Other** – *Specify*
h. **TOTAL** *(Sum of items 8a to 8g should equal item 1a)*

9. On June 30, 1999, how many persons CONFINED in your jail facilities were held for –
- For persons with a multiple hold, count them only once with the order of priority being Federal, State, and local.

a. **Federal authorities**
b. **State authorities**
   1. **For your state**
   2. **For other states**
c. **Other local authorities**
   1. **Within your state**
   2. **Outside your state**
d. **TOTAL** *(Sum of items 9a to 9c)*
   If zero (0) in item 9a, SKIP TO ITEM 11.

10. Of all inmates held for FEDERAL authorities in item 9a, how many were held for –

a. **U.S. Marshals Service**
b. **Federal Bureau of Prisons**
c. **Immigration and Naturalization Service**
d. **Bureau of Indian Affairs**
e. **Other** – *Specify*
f. **TOTAL** *(Sum of items 10a to 10e should equal item 9a)*

11. Is a per diem fee paid by other authorities for inmates held in your facilities? *Mark (X) one.*

1 ☐ Yes – **What is the per diem paid by Federal, State, and other local authorities?**
   Federal ____ State ____ Local ____
2 ☐ No – No fee is charged for holding inmates for other authorities.
3 ☐ No – This jurisdiction does not hold inmates for other authorities.

Page 3

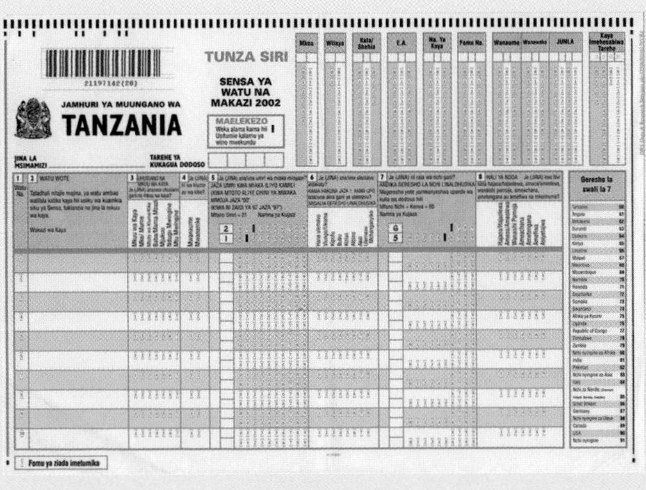

21197142(28)

JAMHURI YA MUUNGANO WA
TANZANIA

TUNZA SIRI

SENSA YA WATU NA MAKAZI 2002

MAELEKEZO

JINA LA MSIMAMIZI

TAREHE YA KUKAGUA DODOSO

Mkoa | Wilaya | Kata/ Shehia | E.A. | Na. Ya Kaya | Fomu Na. | Wanaume | Wanawake | JUMLA | Kaya Imehesabiwa Tarehe

1 | 2 WATU WOTE

Geresho la swali la 7

Fomu ya ziada imetumika

Census forms, US and Tanzania

Censuses are regular questionnaires that collect statistics about whole nations or specific sections of the population. The US example is for prison inmates only. The Tanzanian census covers the whole nation and looks extremely complex. It is therefore only to be filled in by trained interviewers.

Certificates and passes

Certificates mark events

Certificates are the epitome of administrative documents, for what they announce is demonstrably true. This may be the foundation of a city, the nomination of a Pope, or the birth of a child.

Certificates make statements about people, situations and rights

Certificates and passes are forms that link a person, situation or right with a statement. Someone called Smith was born on such and such a date, this plot of land belongs to Jones, and only the firm of Smith and Jones is allowed to manufacture product XYZ. Such forms include birth and death certificates, certificates of ownership, letters patent, and passes of all kinds. One feature common to such documents is that they are issued by an official authority and can therefore be used as proof of identity.

Certificates stand for values

The primary task of a certificate is to present a statement in a prescribed way. With most other categories of form, the main focus is on their practical use in improving efficiency. This generally leads to a thoroughly restrained approach, whereas certificates can be rather more expressive, for they not only make statements but also represent value of some kind. This can be abstract, like grades on a report, or very concrete, like shares in a company. Very frequently, certificates mark a special achievement or an outstanding talent. They should give adequate expression to the value of the achievement without using clichés such as centred type or fancy paper. There are plenty of typographical options available, as well as printed embellishments such as stamps, seals and gloss.

Heading

It should be immediately apparent that the document is a certificate.

→ page 160

Provider

The name of the organization that issued the certificate is what gives it value.

Receiver

The person who has been given the award.

Main content

Signature

→ page 177

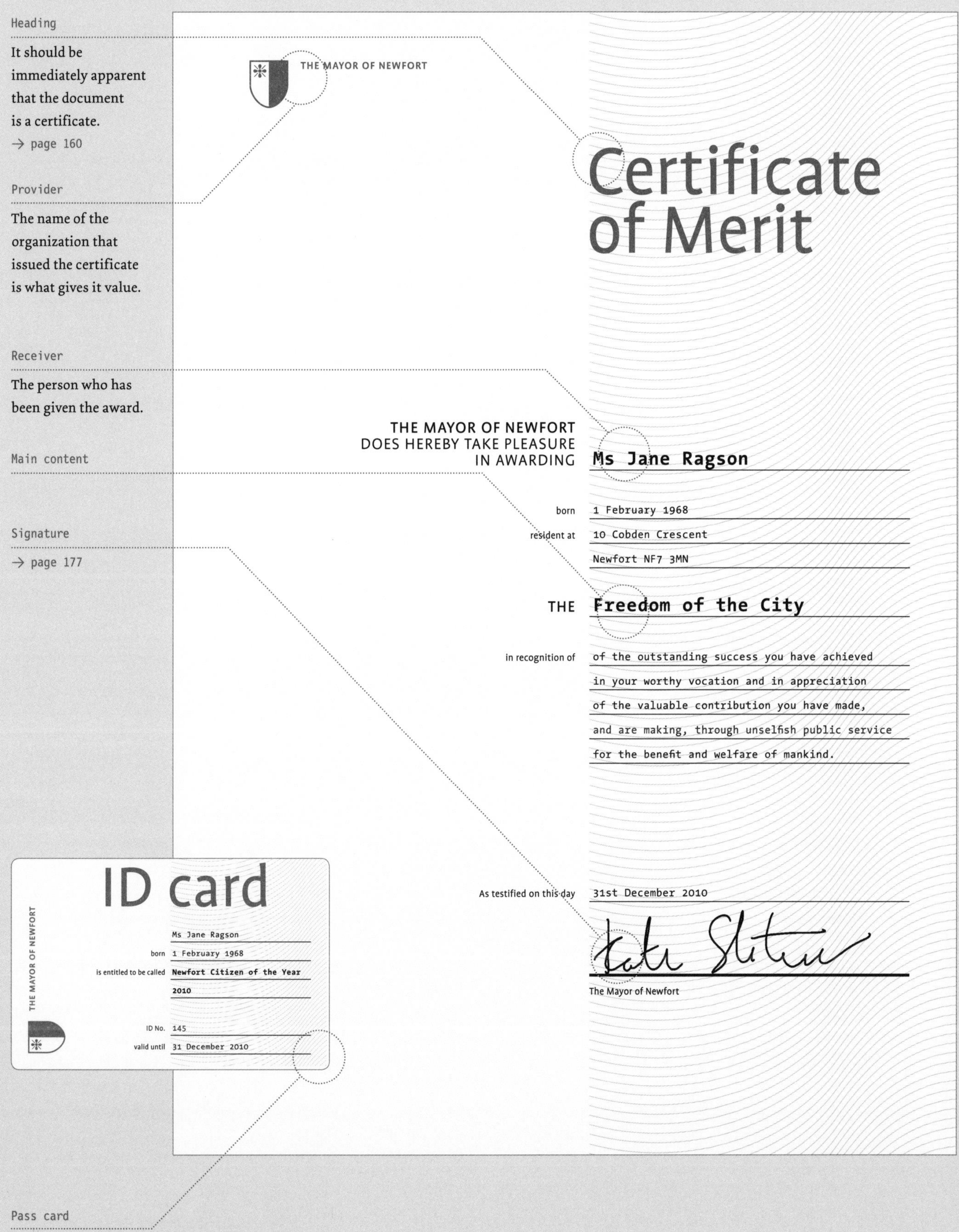

THE MAYOR OF NEWFORT
Certificate of Merit
THE MAYOR OF NEWFORT DOES HEREBY TAKE PLEASURE IN AWARDING
Ms Jane Ragson
born
1 February 1968
resident at
10 Cobden Crescent
Newfort NF7 3MN
THE
Freedom of the City
in recognition of
of the outstanding success you have achieved in your worthy vocation and in appreciation of the valuable contribution you have made, and are making, through unselfish public service for the benefit and welfare of mankind.
As testified on this day
31st December 2010
The Mayor of Newfort
ID card
THE MAYOR OF NEWFORT
Ms Jane Ragson
born
1 February 1968
is entitled to be called
Newfort Citizen of the Year 2010
ID No.
145
valid until
31 December 2010

Pass card

The most important information on a pass card is the name of the person, what the pass is for, and its period of validity.

No fee is chargeable for this certificate.

GZ 854

1 & 2 ELIZ. 2 CH. 20

CERTIFICATE OF BIRTH

Name and Surname SUSAN RAGSON

Sex Female

Date of Birth Sixth February 2009

Place of Birth — Registration District Newfort

Sub-district Newfort

I, Ryan Morton Registrar of Births and Deaths for the sub-district of Newfort in the Registration District of Newfort do hereby certify that the above particulars have been compiled from an entry in a register in my custody.

Date 13/02/2009

Registrar of Births and Deaths

CAUTION: THERE ARE OFFENCES RELATING TO FALSIFYING OR ALTERING A CERTIFICATE AND USING OR POSSESSING A FALSE CERTIFICATE. ©CROWN COPYRIGHT

WARNING: A CERTIFICATE IS NOT EVIDENCE OF IDENTITY.

STATE OF WASHINGTON
DEPARTMENT OF HEALTH

Local File Number — Washington State Certificate of Death — State File Number

1. Legal Name: Walter Robert Ragson
2. Death Date: Feb. 15, 2008
3. Sex: M
4a. Age – Last Birthday: 87
5. Social Security Number: 123-45-6780
6. County of Death: Western Ross
7. Birthdate: April 9, 1921
8a. Birthplace (City, Town, or County): Newfort
8b. (State or Foreign Country): England
9. Decedent's Education: Elementary
10. Was Decedent of Hispanic Origin?: No
11. Decedent's Race(s): White
12. Was Decedent ever in U.S. Armed Forces? No
13a. Residence Number and Street: 624 SE 5th St.
13b. City or Town: Saginaw
13c. Residence County: Western Ross
13d. Tribal Reservation Name (if applicable)
13e. State or Foreign Country: Washington
13f. Zip Code + 4: 98884
13g. Inside City Limits? ☒ Yes ☐ No ☐ Unk
14. Estimated length of time at residence: 25 Years
15. Marital Status at Time of Death: Widowed
16. Surviving Spouse's Name (Give name prior to first marriage)
17. Usual Occupation: Salesman
18. Kind of Business/Industry: Business Machine Trade
19. Father's Name: Thomas Ragson
20. Mother's Name Before First Marriage: Joan Richards
21. Informant's Name: Jane Ragson
22. Relationship to Decedent: Daughter
23. Mailing Address: 10 Cobden Crescent, Newfort NF7 3MN, United Kingdom
24. Place of Death, if Death Occurred in a Hospital / Place of Death if Death Occurred Somewhere Other than a Hospital: Home
25. Facility Name (If not a facility, give number & street or location): 624 SE 5th St.
26a. City, Town, or Location of Death: Saginaw
26b. State: WA
27. Zip Code: 98884
28. Method of Disposition: Cremation
29. Place of Final Disposition: Saginaw Cremation Center
30. Location-City/Town, and State: Saginaw, WA
31. Name and Complete Address of Funeral Facility: Acadia Gardens, 248 State Street, Saginaw, WA 98884
32. Date of Disposition: Feb. 21, 2008
33. Funeral Director Signature X

Cause of Death (See instructions and examples)

34. Enter the chain of events – diseases, injuries, or complications – that directly caused the death. DO NOT enter terminal events such as cardiac arrest, respiratory arrest, or ventricular fibrillation without showing the etiology. DO NOT ABBREVIATE. Add additional lines if necessary

		Interval between Onset & Death
IMMEDIATE CAUSE (Final disease or condition resulting in death)	a. Rupture of myocardium	Minutes
Sequentially list conditions, if any, leading to the cause listed on line a. Enter the UNDERLYING CAUSE (disease or injury that initiated the events resulting in death) LAST	b. Acute myocardial infarction	6 days
	c. Coronary artery thrombosis	5 years
	d. Atherosclerotic coronary artery disease	7 years

35. Other significant conditions contributing to death but not resulting in the underlying cause given above
36. Autopsy? ☐ Yes ☒ No
37. Were autopsy findings available to complete the Cause of Death? ☐ Yes ☐ No
38. Manner of Death: ☒ Natural ☐ Homicide ☐ Accident ☐ Undetermined ☐ Suicide ☐ Pending
39. If female: ☐ Not pregnant within past year ☐ Pregnant at time of death ☐ Not pregnant, but pregnant within 42 days before death ☐ Not pregnant, but pregnant 43 days to 1 year before death ☐ Unknown if pregnant within the past year
40. Did tobacco use contribute to death? ☐ Yes ☒ Probably ☐ No ☐ Unknown
41. Date of Injury
42. Hour of Injury (24hrs)
43. Place of Injury (e.g. Decedent's home, construction site, restaurant, wooded area)
44. Injury at Work? ☐ Yes ☐ No ☐ Unk
45. Location of Injury: Number & Street, Apt No., City or Town, County, State, Zip Code+4
46. Describe how injury occurred
47. If transportation injury, specify: ☐ Driver/Operator ☐ Pedestrian ☐ Passenger ☐ Other (Specify)
48a. Certifying Physician X
48b. Medical Examiner/Coroner X
49. Name and Address of Certifier – Physician, Medical Examiner or Coroner (Type or Print)
50. Hour of Death (24hrs)
51. Name and Title of Attending Physician if other than Certifier (Type or Print)
52. Date Signed
53. Title of Certifier
54. License Number
55. ME/Coroner File Number
56. Was case referred to ME/Coroner? ☐ Yes ☒ No
57. Registrar Signature X
58. Date Received
59. Amendments

DOH/CHS 003 Rev 2/06/2004

Birth certificate, UK, and death certificate, US

Forms follow people from the cradle to the grave – an oft-quoted aphorism that happens to be true. We are often asked to produce our birth certificates in order to prove that we officially exist, whereas other people need our death certificate in order to prove the opposite.

By authority of the Board of Trustees of the

UNIVERSITY OF ILLINOIS

and upon recommendation of the Senate at Chicago

Rupert F. Fusconi

has been admitted to the Degree of

Master of Urban Planning and Policy

and is entitled to all rights and honors thereto appertaining. Witness the Seal of the University and the Signatures of its Officers this eleventh day of May, two thousand and eight.

Urkunde

Fachhochschule Potsdam
Fachbereich Design

Frau Sybille Musterstudentin

geboren am 31. März 1977 in Braunschweig
hat die Abschlussprüfung im

Masterstudiengang Design

in der Studienrichtung Kommunikationsdesign
mit sehr gutem Erfolg abgelegt.

Thema des Masterprojekts
»Gestaltungsstrategien für konvergente Medien«

Die Fachhochschule Potsdam
verleiht Frau Sybille Musterstudentin den akademischen Grad

Master of Arts

Der Dekan
Prof. Walter Hardt

Die Rektorin
Prof. Dr. Helene Kleine

Potsdam, den 23. Mai 2005

FHP:-) FHP:-) FHP:-) FHP:-) FHP:-) FHP:-) FHP:-) FHP:-) FHP

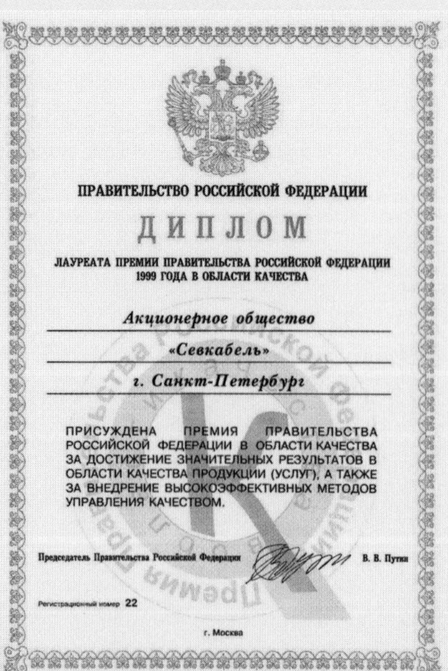

ПРАВИТЕЛЬСТВО РОССИЙСКОЙ ФЕДЕРАЦИИ

ДИПЛОМ

ЛАУРЕАТА ПРЕМИИ ПРАВИТЕЛЬСТВА РОССИЙСКОЙ ФЕДЕРАЦИИ
1999 ГОДА В ОБЛАСТИ КАЧЕСТВА

Акционерное общество

«Севкабель»

г. Санкт-Петербург

ПРИСУЖДЕНА ПРЕМИЯ ПРАВИТЕЛЬСТВА РОССИЙСКОЙ ФЕДЕРАЦИИ В ОБЛАСТИ КАЧЕСТВА ЗА ДОСТИЖЕНИЕ ЗНАЧИТЕЛЬНЫХ РЕЗУЛЬТАТОВ В ОБЛАСТИ КАЧЕСТВА ПРОДУКЦИИ (УСЛУГ), А ТАКЖЕ ЗА ВНЕДРЕНИЕ ВЫСОКОЭФФЕКТИВНЫХ МЕТОДОВ УПРАВЛЕНИЯ КАЧЕСТВОМ.

Председатель Правительства Российской Федерации В. В. Путин

Регистрационный номер 22

г. Москва

University certificates, US, Germany and Ukraine

Here are three very different approaches to the design of certificates. The US version is decorative and conservative; the German one is austere and official; and the Ukrainian one is stately and ornamental.

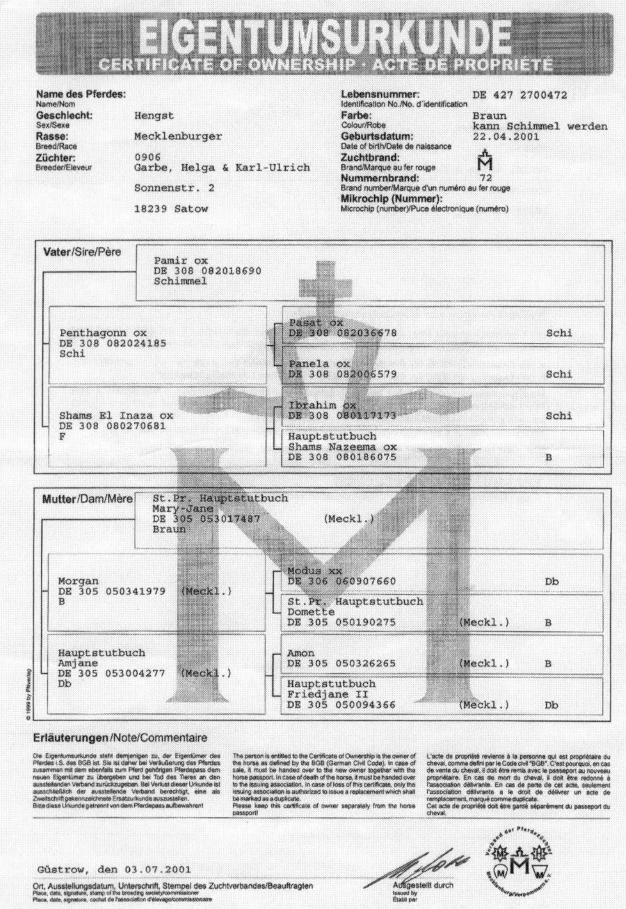

EIGENTUMSURKUNDE
CERTIFICATE OF OWNERSHIP · ACTE DE PROPRIÉTÉ

Name des Pferdes: Name/Nom		Lebensnummer: Identification No./No. d'identification	DE 427 2700472
Geschlecht: Sex/Sexe	Hengst	Farbe: Colour/Robe	Braun kann Schimmel werden
Rasse: Breed/Race	Mecklenburger	Geburtsdatum: Date of birth/Date de naissance	22.04.2001
Züchter: Breeder/Eleveur	0906 Garbe, Helga & Karl-Ulrich Sonnenstr. 2 18239 Satow	Zuchtbrand: Brand/Marque au fer rouge	
		Nummernbrand: Brand number/Marque d'un numéro au fer rouge	72
		Mikrochip (Nummer): Microchip (number)/Puce électronique (numéro)	

Vater/Sire/Père
Pamir ox DE 308 082018690 Schimmel
Penthagonn ox DE 308 082024185 Schi
Pasat ox DE 308 082036678 Schi
Panela ox DE 308 082006579 Schi
Shams El Inaza ox DE 308 080270681 F
Ibrahim ox DE 308 080117173 Schi
Hauptstutbuch Shams Nazeema ox DE 308 080186075 B

Mutter/Dam/Mère
St.Pr. Hauptstutbuch Mary-Jane DE 305 053017487 (Meckl.) Braun
Morgan DE 305 050341979 (Meckl.) B
Modus xx DE 306 060907660 Db
St.Pr. Hauptstutbuch Domette DE 305 050190275 (Meckl.) B
Hauptstutbuch Amjane DE 305 053004277 (Meckl.) Db
Amon DE 305 050326265 (Meckl.) B
Hauptstutbuch Friedjane II DE 305 050094366 (Meckl.) Db

Erläuterungen/Note/Commentaire

Güstrow, den 03.07.2001
Ort, Ausstellungsdatum, Unterschrift, Stempel des Zuchtverbandes/Beauftragten
Ausgestellt durch

Certificate of horse ownership, Germany

This certificate denotes the ownership of a horse, and includes its family tree. It's a shame that this rather aristocratic form does not have a very aristocratic appearance.

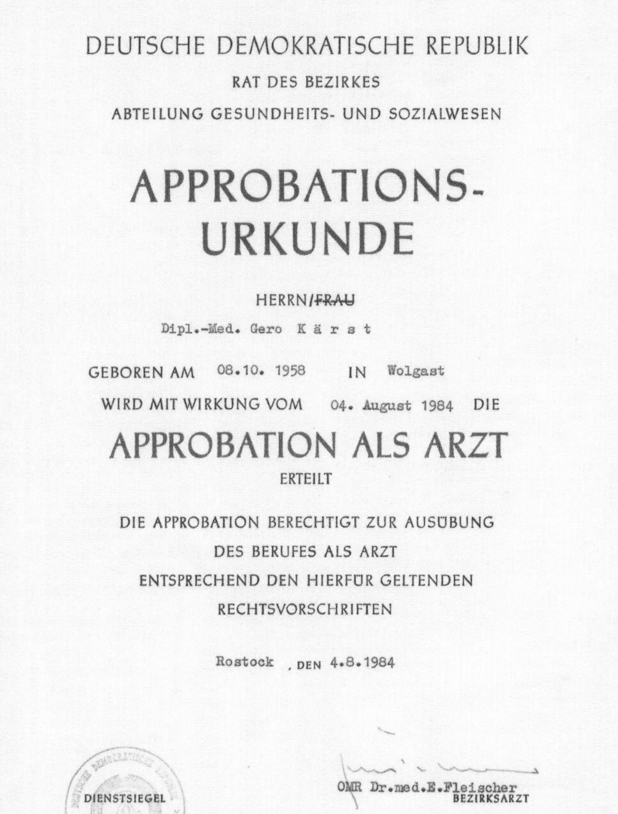

DEUTSCHE DEMOKRATISCHE REPUBLIK
RAT DES BEZIRKES
ABTEILUNG GESUNDHEITS- UND SOZIALWESEN

APPROBATIONS-URKUNDE

HERRN/~~FRAU~~
Dipl.-Med. Gero K ä r s t

GEBOREN AM 08.10. 1958 IN Wolgast
WIRD MIT WIRKUNG VOM 04. August 1984 DIE

APPROBATION ALS ARZT

ERTEILT

DIE APPROBATION BERECHTIGT ZUR AUSÜBUNG DES BERUFES ALS ARZT ENTSPRECHEND DEN HIERFÜR GELTENDEN RECHTSVORSCHRIFTEN

Rostock , DEN 4.8.1984

DIENSTSIEGEL

OMR Dr.med.E.Fleischer
BEZIRKSARZT

Reg.-Nr. 77/84

Doctor's registration certificate, Germany

A certificate that could be hung with pride in any consulting room: centred text, classically styled typography, decorative and yet unfussy.

A
csce
№ 01600
Conference on Security and Cooperation in Europe Helsinki 1975
ISSUED BY
NAME
H.E. Erich Honecker
TITLE
Chairman of the Delegation
COUNTRY
German Democratic Republic

Security pass

A pass belonging to a prominent participant at a major conference during the Cold War.

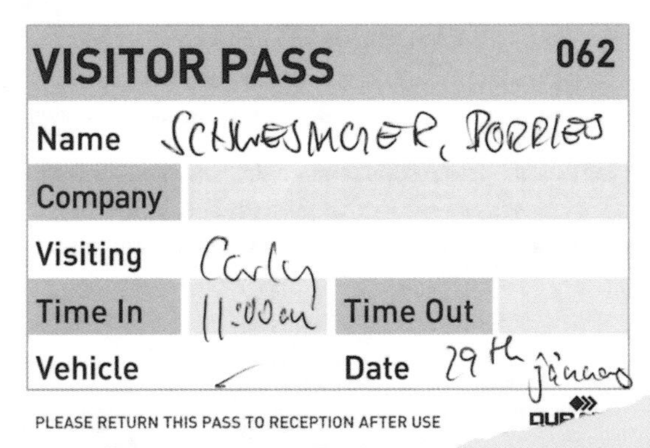

VISITOR PASS 062
Name Schwesinger, Robbie
Company
Visiting Carly
Time In 11:00am Time Out
Vehicle Date 29th January
PLEASE RETURN THIS PASS TO RECEPTION AFTER USE

1993 MICHIGAN DAILY FISH STAMP HOLDER
No.W 178562
Name of Licensee (Print) Gabriele
Address (No. and Street or Route) West End St. 7
City or Town Berlin State GR. Zip Sex F Date of Birth
Agent Acct. No. 40122 Agent City or Town Koscommon Date & Time Issued 0713 1993 AM PM
THIS IS NOT A LICENSE
ONE STAMP IS ONE DAY. STAMPS MUST BE PLACED ON THIS HOLDER.
Signature of Licensee X
PR 1374 (9-92) STAMP PURCHASER COPY
ISSUING AGENT
Daily Fish Stamp is for Residents or Non-Residents and covers all species of fish including Trout, Splake and Salmon. One stamp is one day and is good until midnight of the date written on the stamp. Stamps must be placed on the back of this holder. There is no limit to the number of stamps that may be purchased.
DATES TO BE USED 07-13-93

Visitor permit, UK and fishing permit, US

Many passes and other forms of identity card are only used very briefly and are then thrown away. These include boarding cards, visitor passes, and also items such as a one-day fishing permit.

Tickets, cheques and shares

Tickets and cheques convey rights

Tickets, cheques and shares are all documents with a certain value, which bestow certain rights on their possessors.

Strictly speaking, vouchers and banknotes are not exactly documents as such, but they fit into the same category, since their possession also conveys rights. While shares nowadays are almost exclusively virtual, and at best have a representative function, bus, rail and entrance tickets, cheques and vouchers still tend to be mainly on paper.

Forms with a set value

All such documents bear information about their value as well as about who issued them, who now owns them, and what rights they have as a result. They also inform their purchasers that the trust they placed in the seller will not be betrayed, and that the document is worth what it says it is worth.

Security issues

It is vital that particularly valuable or widely distributed documents of this nature should be security protected. Although elaborate fine-line graphics can make forgery more difficult, better protection is offered by devices such as built-in holograms, watermarks and security threads.

Newfort Bus & Tram Company
Annual season ticket
travelzone 1+2
valid 01/01/2010–31/12/2010
price £895.00
no. 02577898-1
2010

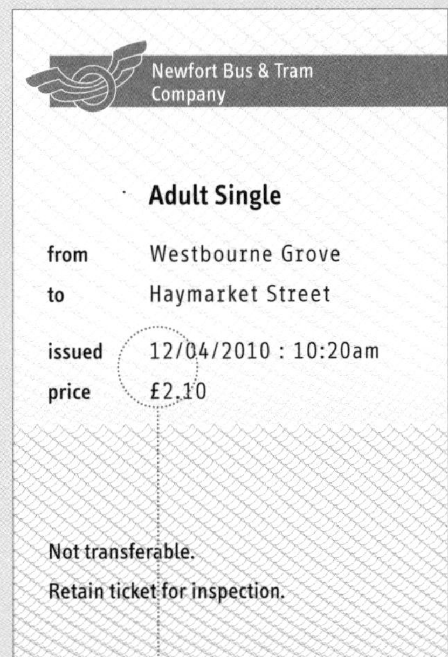

Newfort Bus & Tram Company
Adult Single
from Westbourne Grove
to Haymarket Street
issued 12/04/2010 : 10:20am
price £2.10
Not transferable.
Retain ticket for inspection.

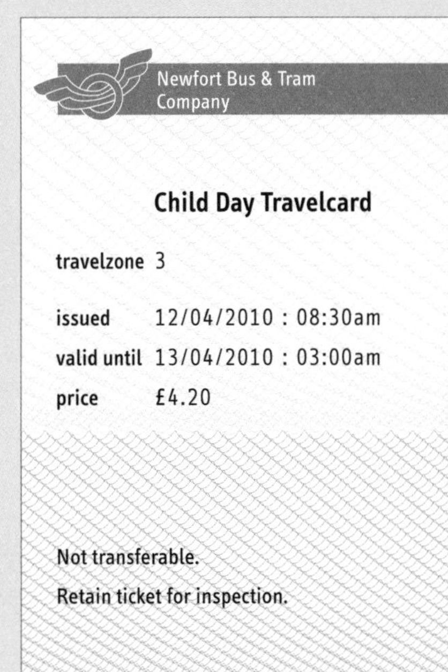

Newfort Bus & Tram Company
Child Day Travelcard
travelzone 3
issued 12/04/2010 : 08:30am
valid until 13/04/2010 : 03:00am
price £4.20
Not transferable.
Retain ticket for inspection.

Fine-line patterns

These not only provide forgery protection, but also show that the tickets are documents with a value.

Information

Facts about the cost and validity of the ticket, and any restrictions that apply.

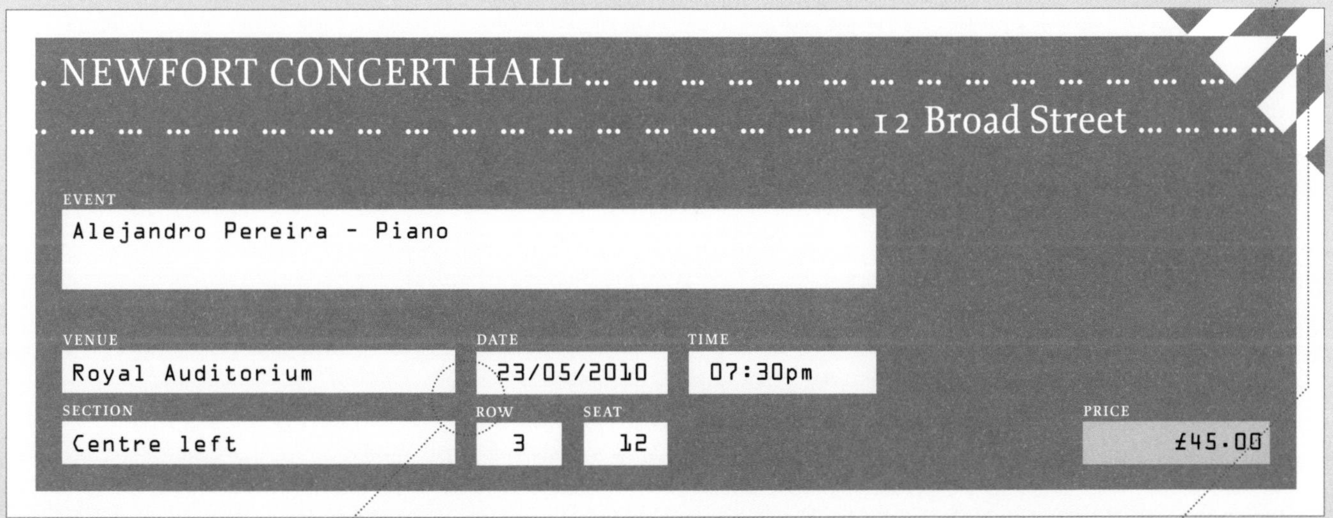

NEWFORT CONCERT HALL
12 Broad Street
EVENT
Alejandro Pereira - Piano
VENUE
Royal Auditorium
DATE
23/05/2010
TIME
07:30pm
SECTION
Centre left
ROW
3
SEAT
12
PRICE
£45.00

Information

This entrance ticket is printed with various items of information, not all of which are of the same importance at the same time. That is why the form separates the information very clearly. First comes the name of the event, then the time and place, and finally the exact location of the seat. After purchase, the price is no longer of any interest.

Cancellation

After the user has entered the venue, the ticket is cancelled by the tried and trusted method of tearing off the corner.

Train and bus tickets from Italy, the US, Thailand, Switzerland and Greece

Travel tickets function in much the same way as shares. They bestow certain rights on their owners – in this case, the right to be transported from one place to another. At the same time, they serve as physical souvenirs of a journey, and are often kept and even collected. A typical design feature is the fact that the data printed on them often overruns the fields provided.

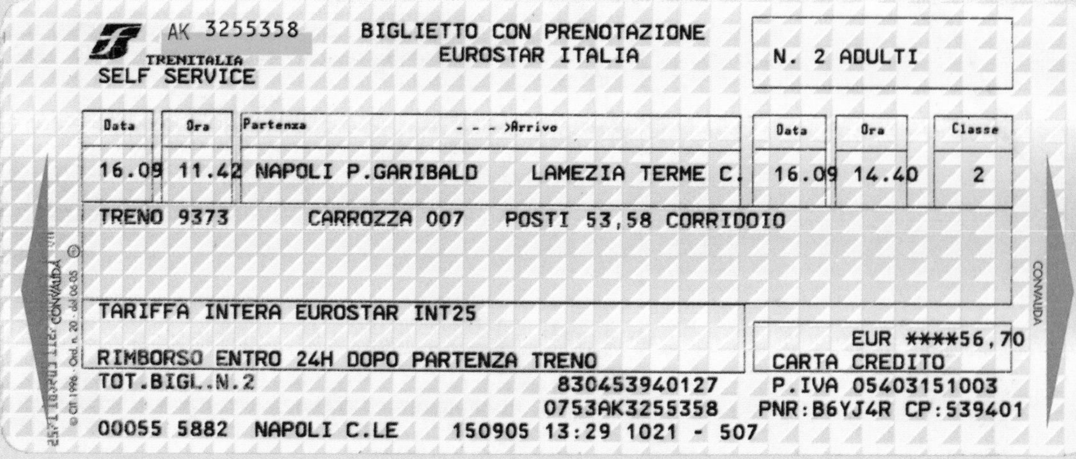

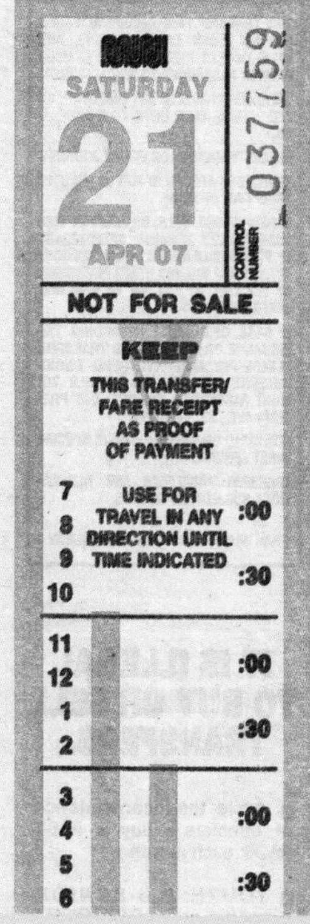

№ 255

ชื่อ Name SCHWESINER	ที่อยู่ Address	โทรศัพท์ Tel.	ป
บัตรโดยสาร Passenger Ticket	จาก From มส		ถึง To กทม
วันออกบัตร Date of Issuer	วันเดินทาง Dep.Date 1/8/49	เที่ยวไป Forth Trip	เวลา Time 21:30
	วันเดินทาง Dep.Date	เที่ยวกลับ Back Trip	เวลา Time
หมายเลขรถ Bus Number	เลขที่นั่ง Seat No. A B 1		สำรอง Reserve
ราคา Fare	412 X 2 = 824		ผู้ออกบัตร Issuer 2

RENUM
Aktiengesellschaft

Bonn

45.077 Namensaktien
über je einen (1) Euro

ProBonnum GmbH

Bonn, im Oktober 2004
RENUM AG

Der Aufsichtsrat
Jörg Kempenich (Vorsitzender)

Der Vorstand
Wilfried Wöhler

Nur zur Verrechnung

Deutsche Bank
Aktiengesellschaft

Bankleitzahl
100 700 00
Berlin

Bewag AG

EUR
EUR

Betrag
*********2,75

Zahlen Sie gegen diesen Scheck
an

Kundenkonto 210004308336

Herrn/Frau/Firma
Schwesinger
Borries
RA und Notar
Pettenkoferstr. 32
10247 Berlin

oder Überbringer
Berlin, 16.01.2004
Ausstellungsort, Datum

Unterschrift der Ausstellers
Der vorgedruckte Text darf nicht geändert oder gestrichen werden. Die Angabe einer Zahlungsfrist auf dem Scheck gilt als nicht geschrieben.

Scheck-Nr. | X | Konto-Nr. | X | Betrag | X | Bankleitzahl | X | Text

3200401160550⑈ 0017760001⑆ 2,75 ⑇ 100700000⑈ 01⑆

Bitte dieses Feld nicht beschriften und nicht bestempeln

VORSTELLUNG
F.U.C.K.

Uraufführung

ORT
Neues Theater
So, 22.04.2007, 19:00 Uhr

Hochparkett Links Reihe Platz
10 31

Dienstkarte

0157790312100353

hansottotheaterpotsdam

Beim Verlassen der Vorstellung verliert die Eintrittskarte ihre Gültigkeit.

Share certificate and cheque, Germany

Cheques are documents that indicate payment. In practical terms, they are handled just like other valuable documents, but instead of looking valuable, their appearance is dictated by the requirements of machine reading. Shares are generally given a more elaborate design, as their representative function is very much in the foreground.

Theatre ticket, Germany

An entrance ticket is also a form. The electronic booking system has printed all the information, and the typography is fairly restricted. However, the pre-printed background gives the ticket a degree of quality and a clear identity of its own.

Die Bahn DB

OnlineTicket

ICE Fahrkarte

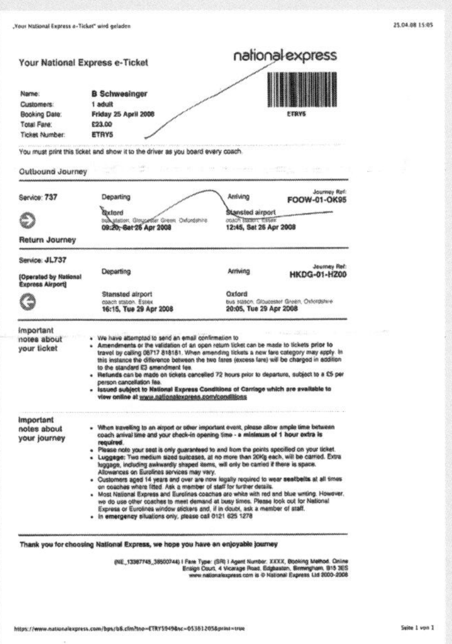

Your National Express e-Ticket

national express

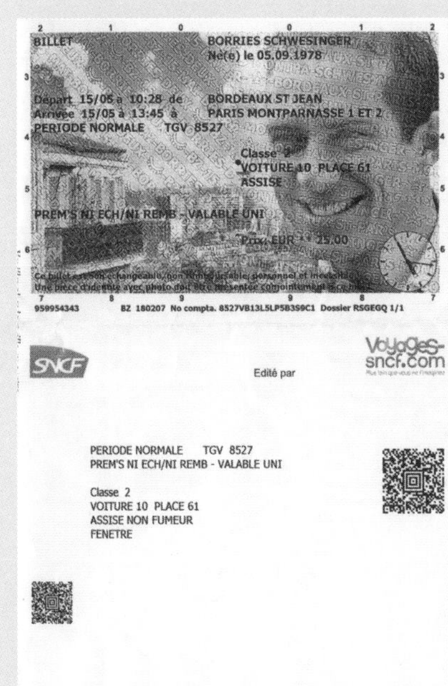

BILLET

BORRIES SCHWESINGER
Né(e) le 05.09.1978

Départ 15/05 à 10:28 de BORDEAUX ST JEAN
Arrivée 15/05 à 13:45 à PARIS MONTPARNASSE 1 ET 2
PERIODE NORMALE TGV 8527

Classe 2
VOITURE 10 PLACE 61
ASSISE

PREM'S NI ECH/NI REMB - VALABLE UNI

Prix EUR **25.00

SNCF

Edité par

Voyages-sncf.com

PERIODE NORMALE TGV 8527
PREM'S NI ECH/NI REMB - VALABLE UNI

Classe 2
VOITURE 10 PLACE 61
ASSISE NON FUMEUR
FENETRE

Online travel tickets from Germany, the UK and France

These mark the end of printed tickets and thus of passenger anonymity. Online tickets are often valid only with proof of ID, and they have little appeal to collectors. There are few technical limitations on their design, but they are often badly structured and hard to read. The UK specimen stands out for its clarity.

Records and checklists

Procedures are written down, stored and passed on

Records, reports, minutes and checklists compile and store information about events, procedures and situations. They are put together after meetings, telephone conversations and the completion of particular tasks. The recorded information helps the form user, as well as others, to pass on, archive, refer to and if necessary justify what has taken place.

Maintaining standards and making records comparable to one another

Records and checklists can be produced without the aid of forms, but forms speed up the process and will, above all, ensure that all the important information is noted down. They also ensure that the record will comply with fixed standards, which will make it comparable to other records.

Forms of this type often record specialized information, and the person who completes one will generally be familiar with the terminology used. But the same is not always true of people who will read the record later and need to understand it. The need for clarity and legibility is therefore just as great in this context as it is in others.

Filling in forms under difficult conditions

It must be assumed that record-keeping is generally viewed as a chore – a task to be put off, a load of paper-shuffling and never the most interesting part of a job. The motivation of the user is liable to be low, and this should not be further reduced by a list of incomprehensible demands. Records are not always written down at a desk in a quiet office – they often have to be compiled in the open air, on building sites, scribbled on notepads or clipboards, and time is also a factor.

Provider and heading

→ page 160

Date and time

Content

In addition to lists and spaces for comments, diagrams are a quick and clear way of recording information.

→ page 177

Signature

Space for not one but two signatures. The customer's signature confirms the details given by the technician, providing a double guarantee since one signature is worthless without the other.

→ page 177

FIXMACHINE LTD

Service Record

Record no. 000012

Date [MM/DD/YYYY] 12·10·2010

Start time 8.45 End time 10.20

Client

Customer no. 42660/B

Client name CLAIRE SANDERS

Company name CUPCAKE BAKERY

Address 491 GRAY STREET NEWFORT NF2 3TN

Appliance diagram

Serial no. CCB 9731120-F

Side view
Please mark affected parts

Top view
Please mark affected parts

Work carried out

- [x] Maintenance
- [x] Diagnostic
- [x] Repair
- [ ] Installation
- [ ] Deinstallation
- [ ] Custom configuration
- [ ]
- [ ]
- [ ]

Disposal of waste

- [ ] Oil
- [ ] Batteries
- [x] Fixative
- [ ]

Parts supplied

Quantity	Description
3	CIRCULAR WASHER C29
1	FIXING BOLT FB16
2	DRIVE SCREWS DS73

Notes

—

I hereby confirm that the works detailed above have been carried out.

Signature of installer

Signature of client

Pannenbericht
ADAC-Straßenwacht

01/2005

Wichtiger Hinweis: Den Pannenbericht bitte nicht als Reparaturauftrag verwenden.
Die Fehlerdiagnose auf der Straße kann nicht mit absoluter Sicherheit erfolgen.
Durch die Fehlersuche kann der Fehlerspeicher des Steuergerätes unkorrekte Daten liefern.
Bitte unterrichten Sie vor der Erteilung eines Reparaturauftrages den Werkstattmeister.

ADAC

ADAC-DATEN

Fahrer-Nr. 0 1 2 3 4 5 6 7 8 9

Prüf-Ziffer 0 1 2 3 4 5 6 7 8 9

Pannenstrecke 0 1 2 3 4 5 6 7 8 9

Tag 1 2 3 4 5 6 7 8 9 10 11 12 13 14 15 16 17 18 19 20 21 22 23 24 25 26 27 28 29 30 31

Monat Jan. Feb. März April Mai Juni Juli Aug. Sep. Okt. Nov. Dez.

Einsatz Diagnose-gerät: Steuergerät auslesbar Ja Nein; Codeart P0 - Code, anderer Code

Einsatzsteuerung: PHZ AM sonst.

Pannenort: BAB Stadt Land

Einsatz-Fahrzeug: Kombi Van Service-Pkw Motorrad (Folgeauftrag SWA)

Sonderaktionen (nur nach Vorgabe) 0 1 2 3 4 5 6 7 8 9

– Originalblatt für den Kraftfahrer –

DATEN DES HILFESUCHENDEN

Name: Brendel Vorname: Hr.

ADAC-Mgl.-Nr. 24 12 03 Kfz-Kennzeichen B-0055

Bitte vollständige Anschrift bei ausländischem Kennzeichen mit AIT-Schutzbrief, kein Mitglied oder Mgl.-Karte nicht dabei.

Straße:

PLZ: Ort:

Schutzbrief-Nr. (nur bei AIT-Mgl.):

Mitglied im: AA ANWB TCB RAC TCS ÖAMTC ACI NAF ACP RACE ELPA AMZS HAK AMK FDM M ACL AMSJ sonst.

Länderkennzeichen (nur bei ausländ. Kennzeichen): A B CH CZ DK E F GB GR H HR I IRL L MC N NL P PL RO S SK SLO sonst.

Fahrzeug-Typ-Nr.: sonstige Benziner Diesel Turbo 0 1 2 3 4 5 6 7 8 9 neues Modell

Hubraum bis: Liter 0 1 2 3 4 5 6,0 und mehr Liter; 0,1 Liter 0,0 0,1 0,2 0,3 0,4 0,5 0,6 0,7 0,8 0,9

km-Stand (in tausend) 0 1 2 3 4 5 6 7 8 9

Erst-zulassung: Monat 01 02 03 04 05 06 07 08 09 10 11 12; Jahr 0 1 2 3 4 5 6 7 8 9

DATEN DES HILFESUCHENDEN

Allgem. Hinweise: 01 Fehlerursache erkennbar; 02 Fehlerursache nicht erkennbar; 03 Weiterfahrt möglich; 04 Weiterfahrt beschränkt möglich; 05 Weiterfahrt nicht möglich; 06 Selbsthilfe / Hilfe durch Dritte / Fahrer nicht angetroffen; 07 Reparatur / Pannenhilfe vom Kraftfahrer abgelehnt; 08 Brand gelöscht; 09 Unfallhilfe / Absichern / Erste Hilfe geleistet; 10 Bedienungsfehler

Panne: Bauteil / Baugruppe (Pannenursache) 0 1 2 3 4 5 6 7 8 9

Hinweise zu Pannenursache: K-Seil gerissen Seil ungezogen

ggf. Folgeschaden:

24 kein Detail; 25 Schraube, Stehbolzen; 26 Mutter; 27 Befestigung; 28 Seegerring, Sprengring, Splint, Befestigungsclip, etc.; 29 Schlauchbinder; 35 Dichtung; 36 Wellendichtring; 40 Unterdruckleitung, -schlauch; 41 Antriebsriemen (nicht Zahnriemen); 42 Spannvorrichtung, Spannrolle; 51 Glühlampe, Glühbirne; 52 Plusversorgung, Plusanschluss; 53 Masseanschluss; 54 Kabel; 55 Sicherung; 56 Schalter; 57 Relais; 58 Stecker, Steckverbindung; 59 Magnetventil; 60 Stellmotor; 70 Steuergerät; 75 Fernbedienung allg., Fernbedienung-Batterie

Maßnahmen: 81 Starthilfe / angeschleppt; 82 Ausfahrt/Parkpl./sonst. geschleppt; 83 zur Werkstatt / nach Hause geschleppt; 84 Abschleppen veranlasst; 85 Kraftstoff abgegeben; 86 aufgefüllt, ergänzt; 87 abgelassen, entfernt; 88 Bauteil überbrückt; 89 eingestellt; 90 vorhandenes Ersatzteil eingebaut; 91 Ersatzteil beschafft und eingebaut; 92 Fahrzeug öffnen; 93 Notdienst des FZ-Herst. verständigt; 94 Rep. in WST veranlasst

Fahrgestell-Nr.: (nur nach Aufforderung)

Bemerkungen zur Pannenhilfe:

Kraftfahrerin / Kraftfahrer wurde an nächste Werkstatt verwiesen

auf nebenstehendes Beschädigungs- bzw. Folgerisiko aufmerksam gemacht

Unterschrift der Kraftfahrerin / des Kraftfahrers

Fragen oder Hinweise zu dieser Panne? 0 89 / 76 76 50 50

Pannenhilfe rund um die Uhr: 0180 2 22 22 22 (0,06 € pro Anruf)
Mobiltelefon: 22 22 22 (ohne Vorwahl)
An Autobahn-Notrufsäulen bitte ausdrücklich den ADAC verlangen

Record of car repairs, Germany

This record is handed to the customer whose car has broken down, but it is virtually indecipherable.

BOMB THREAT CALL PROCEDURES

Most bomb threats are received by phone. Bomb threats are serious until proven otherwise. Act quickly, but remain calm and obtain information with the checklist on the reverse of this card.

If a bomb threat is received by phone:

1. Remain calm. Keep the caller on the line for as long as possible. DO NOT HANG UP, even if the caller does.
2. Listen carefully. Be polite and show interest.
3. Try to keep the caller talking to learn more information.
4. If possible, write a note to a colleague to call the authorities or, as soon as the caller hangs up, immediately notify them yourself.
5. If your phone has a display, copy the number and/or letters on the window display.
6. Complete the Bomb Threat Checklist (reverse side) immediately. Write down as much detail as you can remember. Try to get exact words.
7. Immediately upon termination of the call, do not hang up, but from a different phone, contact FPS immediately with information and await instructions.

If a bomb threat is received by handwritten note:

- Call ____________________
- Handle note as minimally as possible.

If a bomb threat is received by e-mail:

- Call ____________________
- Do not delete the message.

Signs of a suspicious package:

- No return address
- Excessive postage
- Stains
- Strange odor
- Strange sounds
- Unexpected Delivery
- Poorly handwritten
- Misspelled Words
- Incorrect Titles
- Foreign Postage
- Restrictive Notes

DO NOT:

- Use two-way radios or cellular phone; radio signals have the potential to detonate a bomb.
- Evacuate the building until police arrive and evaluate the threat.
- Activate the fire alarm.
- Touch or move a suspicious package.

WHO TO CONTACT (select one)

- Follow your local guidelines
- Federal Protective Service (FPS) Police 1-877-4-FPS-411 (1-877-437-7411)
- 911

BOMB THREAT CHECKLIST

Date: ______ **Time:** ______

Time Caller Hung Up: ______ **Phone Number where Call Received:** ______

Ask Caller:

- Where is the bomb located? (Building, Floor, Room, etc.)
- When will it go off?
- What does it look like?
- What kind of bomb is it?
- What will make it explode?
- Did you place the bomb? Yes No
- Why?
- What is your name?

Exact Words of Threat:

Information About Caller:

- Where is the caller located? (Background and level of noise)
- Estimated age:
- Is voice familiar? If so, who does it sound like?
- Other points:

Caller's Voice	Background Sounds:	Threat Language:
❑ Accent	❑ Animal Noises	❑ Incoherent
❑ Angry	❑ House Noises	❑ Message read
❑ Calm	❑ Kitchen Noises	❑ Taped
❑ Clearing throat	❑ Street Noises	❑ Irrational
❑ Coughing	❑ Booth	❑ Profane
❑ Cracking voice	❑ PA system	❑ Well-spoken
❑ Crying	❑ Conversation	
❑ Deep	❑ Music	
❑ Deep breathing	❑ Motor	
❑ Disguised	❑ Clear	
❑ Distinct	❑ Static	
❑ Excited	❑ Office machinery	
❑ **Female**	❑ Factory machinery	
❑ Laughter	❑ Local	
❑ Lisp	❑ Long distance	
❑ Loud		
❑ **Male**	**Other Information:**	
❑ Nasal		
❑ Normal		
❑ Ragged		
❑ Rapid		
❑ Raspy		
❑ Slow		
❑ Slurred		
❑ Soft		
❑ Stutter		

Homeland Security

Bomb threat checklist, US

This standardized list provides guidelines for dealing with telephone threats. It is meant to assist in recording accurate and useful information about potential terrorist risks as quickly as possible.

Landlord's Gas Safety Record

This inspection is for gas safety purposes only in accordance with the Gas Safety (Installation and Use) Regulations 1994. Flues were inspected visually and checked for satisfactory evacuation of products of combustion. A detailed internal inspection of the Flue integrity, construction and lining has not been carried out.

CORGI Registration Number 1929

Installer Details
Name: RK Signed: RR
Address: Eastfield Rd. Bucks Tel: 01844

TENANT DETAILS
Name
Address Marlborough Rd Oxford. OX1
Tel:

LANDLORD DETAILS
Name Bricks + Mortar
Address 226 Banbury Rd. Summertown Oxford.
Tel: 01865

	LOCATION	TYPE	MAKE	MODEL	FLUE TYPE OF or RS	Operating Pressure mbar	Safety Device Correct Operation Yes/No	Ventilation Adequate Yes/No	Flue Flow Test Pass/Fail	Spillage Test Pass/Fail	Termination Satisfactory Yes/No	Visual Condition Pass/Fail	Appliance Safe to use Yes/No	Requested To Test
1	Kitchen	Boiler	Potterton	Gold HE	RS	6.8mb	YES	YES	PASS	NA	YES	PASS	YES	
2	Kitchen	HOB	Bosch	–	FV	20.5mb	NA	YES	NA	NA	NA	NA	✓	
3														
4														
5														

(APPLIANCE DETAILS: LOCATION–FLUE TYPE; INSPECTION DETAILS: Operating Pressure–Visual Condition; FLUE PERFORMANCE CHECK: Flue Flow Test–Visual Condition)

	DETAILS OF ANY FAULTS AND RECTIFICATION WORK NEEDED	LABEL AND WARNING NOTICE ISSUED YES/NO	GAS INSTALLATION SOUNDNESS TEST PASS	FAIL
1			✓	
2				
3				
4				
5				

This Safety record is issued by. Signed RR Print name R Date 18/12/08
Number of Appliances Tested
Received on behalf of the Landlord. Signed .... Tenant/Agent/Landlord

NEXT SERVICE CHECK DUE WITHIN 12 MONTHS

Key: White Copy - Landlord/Agent, Green Copy - Tenant, Gold Copy - Installer   TO REORDER QUOTE REF: CP12

Gas safety record, UK

The problem with this record is that although it records that gas appliances have been safety checked, it doesn't say who the information is for: landlord or tenant. It is also unclear what should be done if a problem is found.

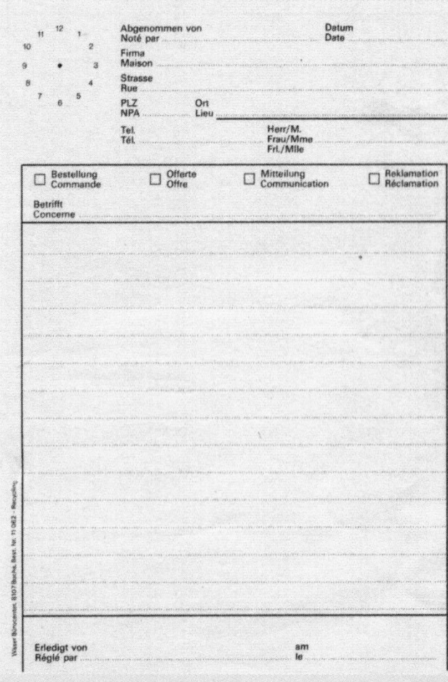
12 11 1 10 2 9 3 8 4 7 5 6

Abgenommen von
Noté par .... Datum
Date ....
Firma
Maison ....
Strasse
Rue ....
PLZ Ort
NPA .... Lieu ....
Tel.
Tél. .... Herr/M.
Frau/Mme
Frl./Mlle

☐ Bestellung Commande ☐ Offerte Offre ☐ Mitteilung Communication ☐ Reklamation Réclamation

Betrifft
Concerne ....

Erledigt von
Réglé par .... am
le ....

Office memo, Switzerland

The epitome of the type of humble form that inspired this book.

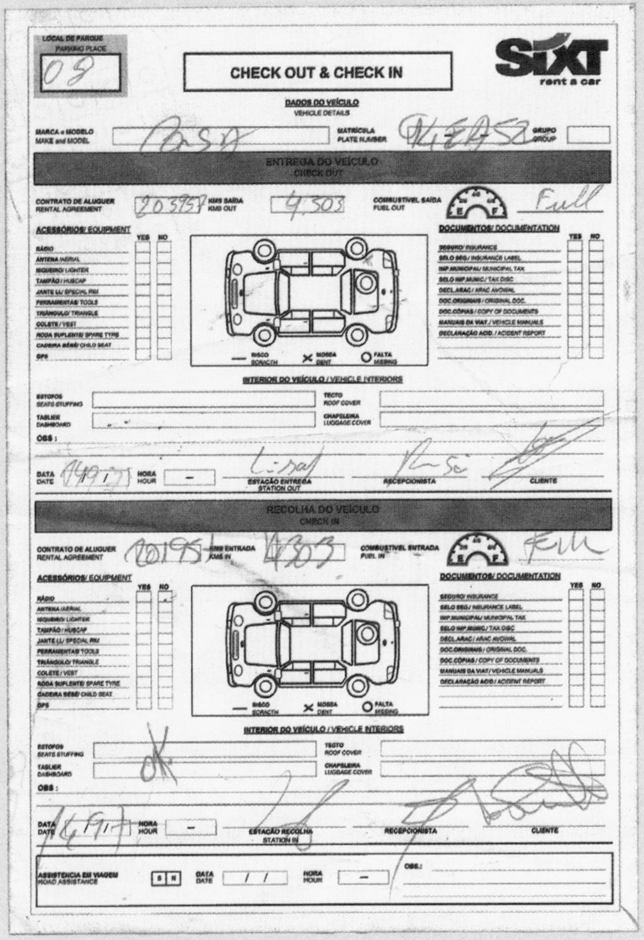

LOCAL DE PARQUE
PARKING PLACE
09

CHECK OUT & CHECK IN

SIXT rent a car

DADOS DO VEÍCULO
VEHICLE DETAILS

MARCA e MODELO / MAKE and MODEL | MATRÍCULA / PLATE NUMBER | GRUPO / GROUP

ENTREGA DO VEÍCULO
CHECK OUT

CONTRATO DE ALUGUER / RENTAL AGREEMENT 205951 | KMS SAÍDA / KMS OUT 9.503 | COMBUSTÍVEL SAÍDA / FUEL OUT Full

ACESSÓRIOS/ EQUIPMENT (YES / NO): RÁDIO; ANTENA /AERIAL; ISQUEIRO/ LIGHTER; TAMPÃO / HUBCAP; JANTE LL/ SPECIAL RIM; FERRAMENTAS/ TOOLS; TRIÂNGULO/ TRIANGLE; COLETE / VEST; RODA SUPLENTE/ SPARE TYRE; CADEIRA BÉBÉ/ CHILD SEAT; GPS

RISCO / SCRATCH — MOSSA / DENT — FALTA / MISSING

DOCUMENTOS/ DOCUMENTATION (YES / NO): SEGURO/ INSURANCE; SELO SEG./ INSURANCE LABEL; IMP MUNICIPAL/ MUNICIPAL TAX; SELO IMP MUNIC./ TAX DISC; DECL.ARAC / ARAC AVOWAL; DOC.ORIGINAIS / ORIGINAL DOC.; DOC.CÓPIAS / COPY OF DOCUMENTS; MANUAIS DA VIAT. / VEHICLE MANUALS; DECLARAÇÃO ACID. / ACIDENT REPORT

INTERIOR DO VEÍCULO / VEHICLE INTERIORS
ESTOFOS / SEATS STUFFING | TECTO / ROOF COVER
TABLIER / DASHBOARD | CHAPELEIRA / LUGGAGE COVER
OBS :

DATA / DATE | HORA / HOUR | ESTAÇÃO ENTREGA / STATION OUT | RECEPCIONISTA | CLIENTE

RECOLHA DO VEÍCULO
CHECK IN

CONTRATO DE ALUGUER / RENTAL AGREEMENT | KMS ENTRADA / KMS IN | COMBUSTÍVEL ENTRADA / FUEL IN

ACESSÓRIOS/ EQUIPMENT | DOCUMENTOS/ DOCUMENTATION

INTERIOR DO VEÍCULO / VEHICLE INTERIORS
ESTOFOS / SEATS STUFFING | TECTO / ROOF COVER
TABLIER / DASHBOARD | CHAPELEIRA / LUGGAGE COVER
OBS : ok

DATA / DATE | HORA / HOUR | ESTAÇÃO RECOLHA / STATION IN | RECEPCIONISTA | CLIENTE

ASSISTÊNCIA EM VIAGEM / ROAD ASSISTANCE | DATA / DATE | HORA / HOUR | OBS.:

Car rental checklist, Portugal

A noticeable feature of this check-out, check-in car rental record is just how easy it is to go racing away beyond the text fields. Nevertheless, the form fulfils its purpose.

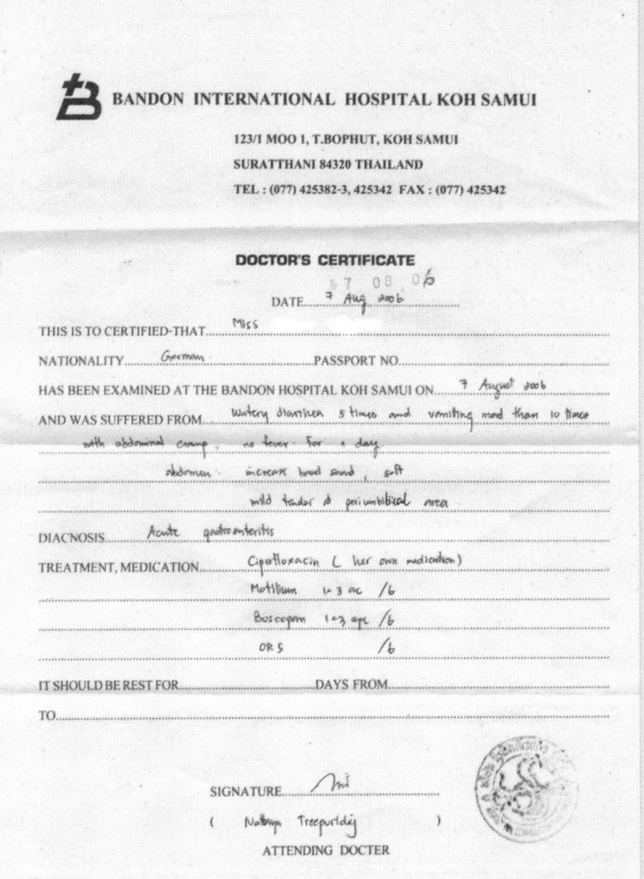

BANDON INTERNATIONAL HOSPITAL KOH SAMUI

123/1 MOO 1, T.BOPHUT, KOH SAMUI
SURATTHANI 84320 THAILAND
TEL : (077) 425382-3, 425342 FAX : (077) 425342

DOCTOR'S CERTIFICATE

DATE 7 Aug 2006

THIS IS TO CERTIFIED-THAT Miss

NATIONALITY German PASSPORT NO.

HAS BEEN EXAMINED AT THE BANDON HOSPITAL KOH SAMUI ON 7 August 2006

AND WAS SUFFERED FROM watery diarrhea 5 times and vomiting more than 10 times with abdominal cramp, no fever for 1 day

DIAGNOSIS Acute gastroenteritis

TREATMENT, MEDICATION Ciprofloxacin (her own medication)
Motilium /6
Buscopan /6
ORS /6

IT SHOULD BE REST FOR ...... DAYS FROM ......

TO ......

SIGNATURE

ATTENDING DOCTER

Doctor's certificate, Thailand

Thanks to their often indecipherable handwritten entries, doctors' certificates are similar the world over. This serves to keep their content discreet, if little else.

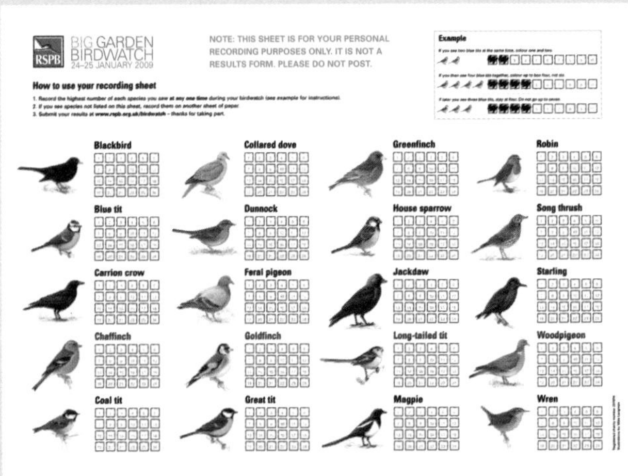

RSPB BIG GARDEN BIRDWATCH 24–25 JANUARY 2009

NOTE: THIS SHEET IS FOR YOUR PERSONAL RECORDING PURPOSES ONLY. IT IS NOT A RESULTS FORM. PLEASE DO NOT POST.

How to use your recording sheet

1. Record the highest number of each species you saw at any one time during your birdwatch (see example for instructions).
2. If you see species not listed on this sheet, record them on another sheet of paper.
3. Submit your results at www.rspb.org.uk/birdwatch – thanks for taking part.

Example

Blackbird · Collared dove · Greenfinch · Robin
Blue tit · Dunnock · House sparrow · Song thrush
Carrion crow · Feral pigeon · Jackdaw · Starling
Chaffinch · Goldfinch · Long-tailed tit · Woodpigeon
Coal tit · Great tit · Magpie · Wren

Bird survey recording sheet, UK

Nature-lovers use this form to record the birds they have seen in their gardens over a fixed period of time. Every year a large number of volunteers from all over Britain take part in this survey.

Driving Test Report DL25A

Form Ref. DL25

Driving test report, UK

This report is basically a list of potential errors. Every mistake made by the candidate is noted down, and reaching a certain number means failing the test.

Direct mail

Direct mail demands a response

Forms play an important part in advertising too, particularly as part of *direct response marketing* campaigns or print ads with cut-out coupons. Although most reply forms of this type are limited to name and address, direct mail often features semi-completed agreements for purchase or credit.

The task of direct mail is to attract customers: drawing the attention of a particular target group and eliciting a reaction in the form of a response. The form is therefore presented as a request for information or a commitment, e.g. to take out a magazine subscription or accept some other offer.

The role of reply forms

By comparison with the actual message of an advertisement, reply coupons are very limited in content and design. Often they are little more than a necessary appendage, and compared to other types of form their design is extremely simple. However, they deserve just as much care and attention as the overall concept of the ad itself. In fact, the problem with a lot of direct mail is that instead of being seen as a welcome offer, it is often viewed as an intrusion or an unappealing chore.

The task of a reply coupon is to follow up the loud and often obtrusive approach of the ad by creating a dialogue of trust with customers, who need to be convinced of the concrete benefits that the offer will bring them. Above all, they must feel that the company is investing just as much care in the dialogue as in its attempts to attract customer attention in the first place.

Advertisement

The success of direct mail stands or falls by its message. This needs an idea that will impress the target group. Be easily understood, and give a clear answer to the question: *'What do I gain from this?'*

Dividing line

Reply coupons, if they are not already separate, must be detachable from the rest of the mail. Keeping things simple is better.

Yes, I will

The yes box is a typical feature of direct mail. Its use is questionable, however, because potential customers do not feel like they are making their own decisions.

Name and address

This is the most important information that direct mail can collect. There is often very little room for it in most advertisements, but it's essential that there should be space for the user to fill it in properly.

SHOOT 'N' COOK

SEND BACK TO THE RANCH
OR VISIT WWW.SHOOT-N-COOK.COM

1

Yes, please send me these free guides:

How to cook like Billy the Kid

How to cook like Lucky Luke

How to cook like Butch Cassidy

How to cook like Wild Bill Hickok

PETE BRIDGES
Name

279 CARVER LANE
Address line 1

EASTLEIGH
Address line 2

NEWFORT — NF9 2RP
Town/City — Postcode

01456 202133
Telephone

Freepost 1234-1234-1234

Newfort Culinary School
41 Turf Street
Newfort
NF1 3LP

Return address

Remember that different countries have different standards for formatting the elements of an address, such as the position of the postcode.

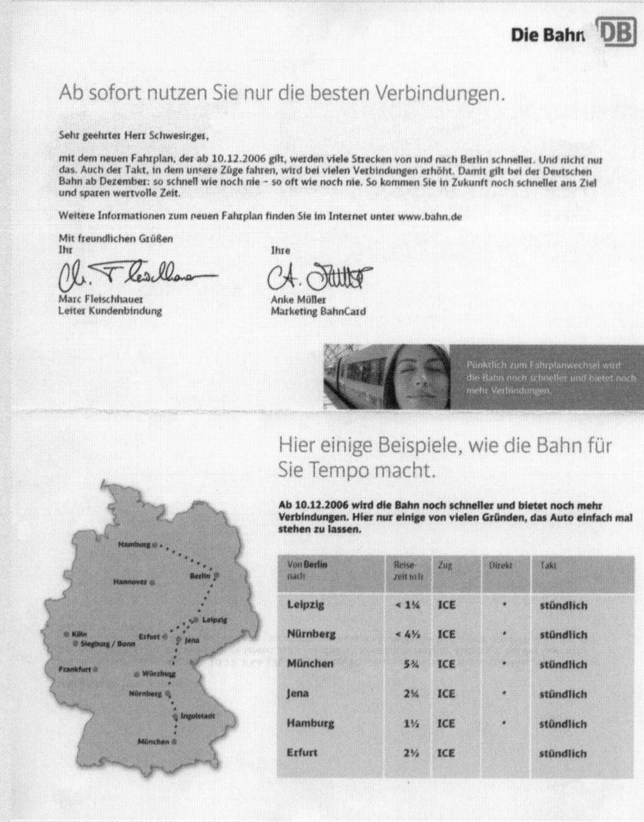

Von Berlin nach	Reisezeit in h	Zug	Direkt	Takt
Leipzig	< 1¼	ICE	•	stündlich
Nürnberg	< 4½	ICE	•	stündlich
München	5¾	ICE	•	stündlich
Jena	2¾	ICE	•	stündlich
Hamburg	1½	ICE	•	stündlich
Erfurt	2½	ICE		stündlich

Water Aid charity appeal, UK

The goals of this charity organization are worthy and their arguments are persuasive. However, as is often the case with direct mail, the process of filling the form has not been made easy for those who wish to donate. The text fields are tiny and barely large enough for average-sized handwriting.

Customer information about rail services, Germany

A direct mail that gives information but does not require a reply. One interesting point is that the rail routes overprinted on the map of Germany have been customized to match the receiver's home address.

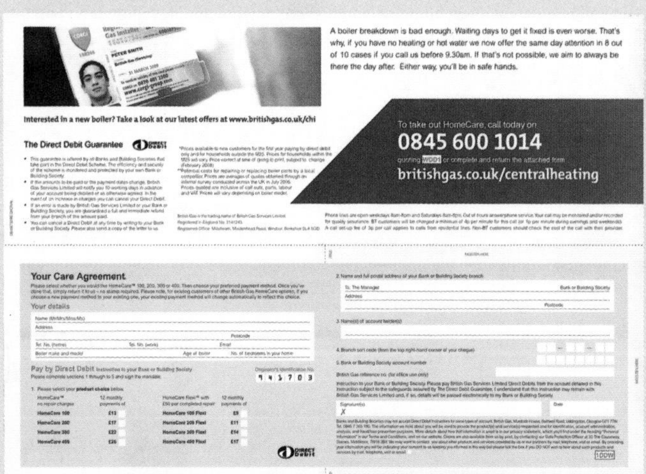

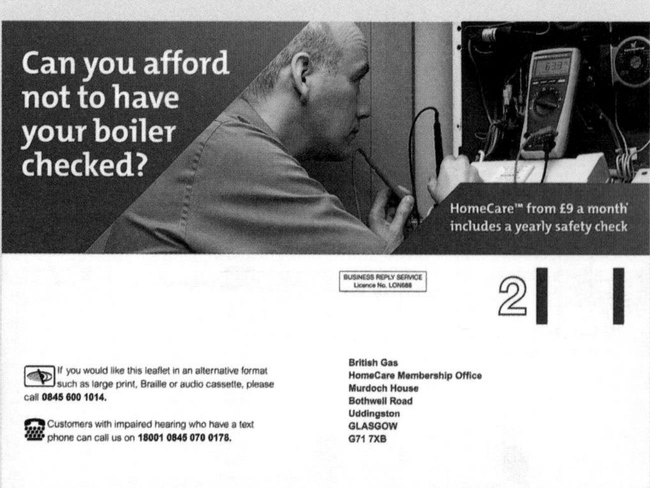

Direct mail for British Gas care plans, UK

This direct mail is designed to persuade householders to take out a care plan for their heating systems. For this purpose, the mail includes a ready-made contract which can be folded and posted back without an envelope. Unfortunately, the text fields are very small.

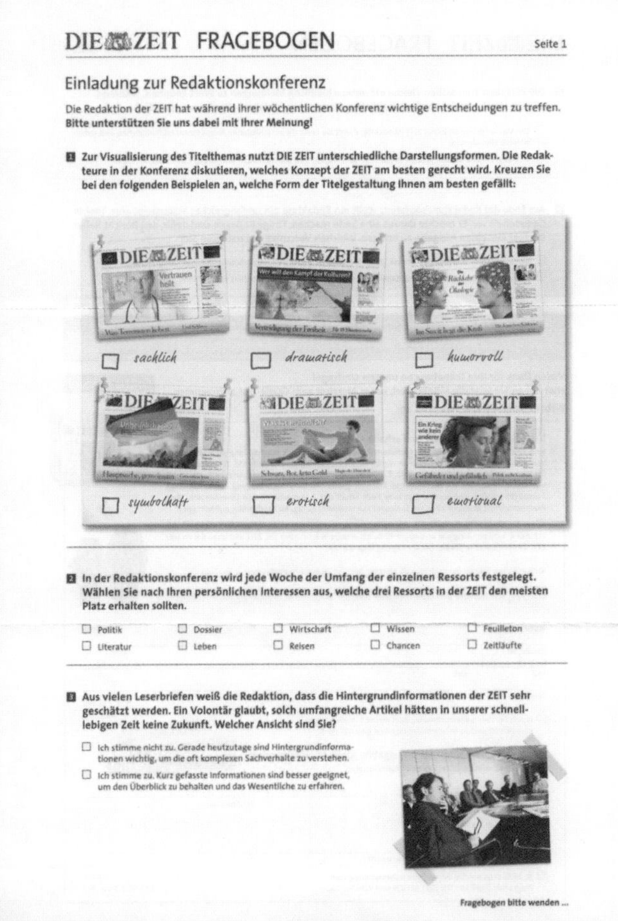

DIE ZEIT FRAGEBOGEN Seite 1

Einladung zur Redaktionskonferenz

Die Redaktion der ZEIT hat während ihrer wöchentlichen Konferenz wichtige Entscheidungen zu treffen. **Bitte unterstützen Sie uns dabei mit Ihrer Meinung!**

1 Zur Visualisierung des Titelthemas nutzt DIE ZEIT unterschiedliche Darstellungsformen. Die Redakteure in der Konferenz diskutieren, welches Konzept der ZEIT am besten gerecht wird. Kreuzen Sie bei den folgenden Beispielen an, welche Form der Titelgestaltung Ihnen am besten gefällt:

☐ sachlich ☐ dramatisch ☐ humorvoll

☐ symbolhaft ☐ erotisch ☐ emotional

2 In der Redaktionskonferenz wird jede Woche der Umfang der einzelnen Ressorts festgelegt. Wählen Sie nach Ihren persönlichen Interessen aus, welche drei Ressorts in der ZEIT den meisten Platz erhalten sollten.

☐ Politik ☐ Dossier ☐ Wirtschaft ☐ Wissen ☐ Feuilleton

☐ Literatur ☐ Leben ☐ Reisen ☐ Chancen ☐ Zeitläufte

3 Aus vielen Leserbriefen weiß die Redaktion, dass die Hintergrundinformationen der ZEIT sehr geschätzt werden. Ein Volontär glaubt, solch umfangreiche Artikel hätten in unserer schnelllebigen Zeit keine Zukunft. Welcher Ansicht sind Sie?

☐ Ich stimme nicht zu. Gerade heutzutage sind Hintergrundinformationen wichtig, um die oft komplexen Sachverhalte zu verstehen.

☐ Ich stimme zu. Kurz gefasste Informationen sind besser geeignet, um den Überblick zu behalten und das Wesentliche zu erfahren.

Fragebogen bitte wenden ...

DIE ZEIT FRAGEBOGEN Seite 2

4 DIE ZEIT lässt zum selben Thema oft unterschiedliche Meinungen zu Wort kommen, während andere Medien meist einen einheitlichen Standpunkt beziehen. Was bevorzugen Sie?

☐ Die Meinungsvielfalt in der ZEIT ist wichtig, damit die Leser die verschiedenen Perspektiven nachvollziehen und selbst entscheiden können.

☐ Eine einheitliche Meinung in der Redaktion wäre besser, weil die Leser sich dann besser orientieren könnten.

5 Am Ende der Redaktionskonferenz stellt ein Redakteur ein umfangreiches Manuskript zum Thema Gesundheit vor. Er möchte daraus eine Serie machen. Einige Kollegen sind dafür, den Bericht lieber in einer einzelnen Ausgabe zu bringen. Welchen Vorschlag unterstützen Sie?

☐ Als Serie veröffentlichen. Das Thema Gesundheit hat viele Facetten, damit beschäftigt man sich gern länger.

☐ In einer Ausgabe veröffentlichen, damit das Thema übersichtlicher präsentiert werden kann.

Fragebogen bitte ausfüllen und in beiliegendem Kuvert zurücksenden.
Oder faxen Sie an **0180/525 29 08** (14 Cent/Min. aus dem deutschen Festnetz).
Die Erfassung der Ergebnisse erfolgt ohne Personenzuordnung. Eine Weitergabe der Daten an Dritte erfolgt nicht.

Vielen Dank für Ihre Teilnahme an unserer Umfrage!
Hier haben Sie jetzt die Möglichkeit, unser Angebot zum Gratis-Test anzunehmen.
Bitte kreuzen Sie Ihre Wünsche an:

Gratis für Sie!

☐ Ja, **ich teste DIE ZEIT und erhalte sie** 3 Wochen gratis!
Schicken Sie mir DIE ZEIT von der nächsterreichbaren Ausgabe an **3 Wochen lang gratis frei Haus.** Wenn mir DIE ZEIT gefällt, brauche ich nichts weiter zu tun. Ich erhalte dann DIE ZEIT wöchentlich für zzt. nur € 2,88 pro Ausgabe statt € 3,20 im Einzelkauf frei Haus und spare 10%. Wenn ich weiterlese, bekomme ich die elegante ZEIT-Uhr gratis (Versand nach Eingang der 1. Zahlung). Ansonsten genügt eine kurze Mitteilung nach Erhalt der 2. Ausgabe an den Leser-Service. Mein Abonnement ist jederzeit kündbar. (Angebot nur im Inland gültig. Auslandspreise auf Anfrage.)

☐ Ich bin Student und erhalte DIE ZEIT in Kombination mit ZEIT CAMPUS. Nach dem Test zahle ich zzt. nur € 1,90 pro Ausgabe und spare 40%. Ich erhalte wöchentlich DIE ZEIT und dazu 6x im Jahr ZEIT CAMPUS. Meine Studienbescheinigung füge ich bei.

Bitte schicken Sie mir die exklusive ☐ Herren- oder ☐ Damenuhr gratis! (Bitte nur ein Kreuz.)

☐ Ja, **ich nehme am Gewinnspiel teil.** Die Teilnahme ist unabhängig von einer Bestellung.

Name, Vorname

Straße, Nr.

PLZ Ort

Telefon E-Mail

518 956 N3
518 957 Stud. N3

☐ Ja, ich bin damit einverstanden, dass meine E-Mail-Adresse gespeichert und zu Informationszwecken genutzt wird.

Extra-Vorteil: 2 weitere ZEIT-Ausgaben gratis bei Bankeinzug!
☐ Ich zahle einfach und bequem per Bankeinzug.

Kontonummer BLZ Geldinstitut

☐ Ich zahle per Rechnung.

Datum Unterschrift

☐ Ja, bitte schicken Sie mir weitere Informationen zum Programm 2007 von DIE ZEIT REISEN und WINDROSE.

518 958 N5
518 959 Stud. N5

+ 2 x gratis!

Reader questionnaire from the newspaper Die Zeit, Germany

Readers like to think that their newspapers take them seriously and keep them informed. This questionnaire for readers is actually trying to sell an annual subscription to the paper, and so is not especially credible.

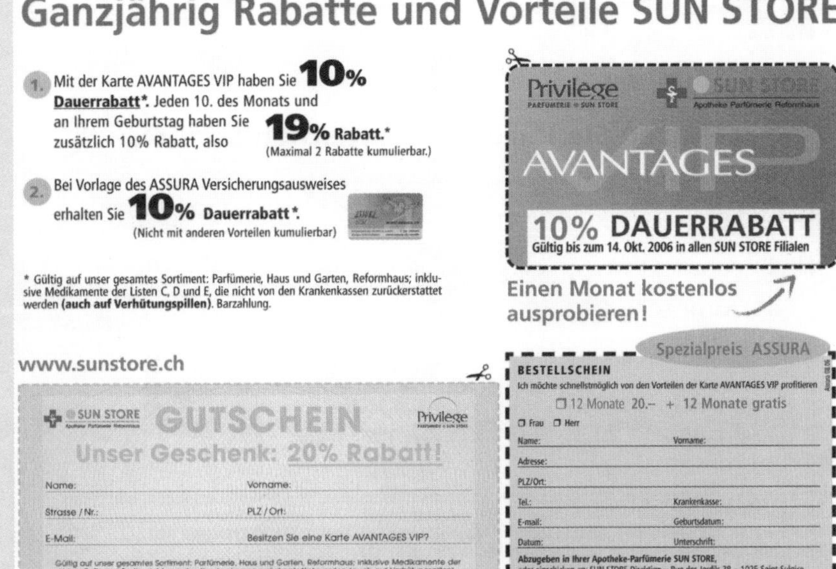

Discount coupons, Switzerland

This direct mail for a chain of drugstores looks so cheap that its claims simply have to be believed. But with so much visual clutter, it's almost impossible to work out which coupon gives which discount.

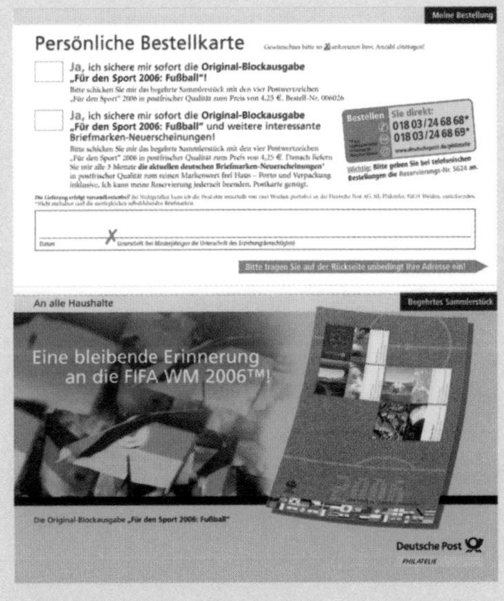

Ad for collectible postage stamps, Germany

The order form is marked 'personal', but how can it be if it's delivered to every household in the country? And why are the checkboxes so large?

2.1

Macro-level design

The design process

Designing forms means designing a way of communicating

Designing a form means far more than just arranging the content on a page. It also entails designing a means of communication. The first question is therefore not: what should the form look like? It's: what is the form meant to do? And is the form the right medium for the task?

Analysing and optimizing communication structures

The design process, especially for a complex system, generally begins by looking at existing forms and the communication structures associated with them. Who uses which forms? How are they produced and distributed? What work is involved?

The following stage involves streamlining this data with a view to cutting out everything that is unnecessary, duplicated or inconsistent. You need to know precisely who actually needs what information. It may be that a good deal of it has already been gathered, or that it isn't all needed immediately, or from all clients.

The next phase is to categorize the types of content and layout required, and as far as possible to divide these into modules. Recurring elements such as names and addresses can be presented in the same format. In this way, you can create a library of modules for use on all forms, either as they are or adapted if necessary.

Design decisions apply to macro and micro levels

The subsequent visual design of the form takes place on two different levels: on the macro or higher level are basic decisions regarding production, layout and typography. The micro or detailed level, on the other hand, concerns the smaller design elements such as questions, text fields and checkboxes.

Forms must be tested and continually adjusted

An element of form design that should never be neglected is comprehensive testing and continual adjustment of prototypes. In this way, you can eventually build up a system that can be implemented in the form of templates, style libraries and design manuals. To make sure that the chosen system has as long a lifespan as possible, it should also be reviewed regularly after the initial guidelines have been determined, and then adapted to fit any circumstances that may have changed.

The ten steps of the design process

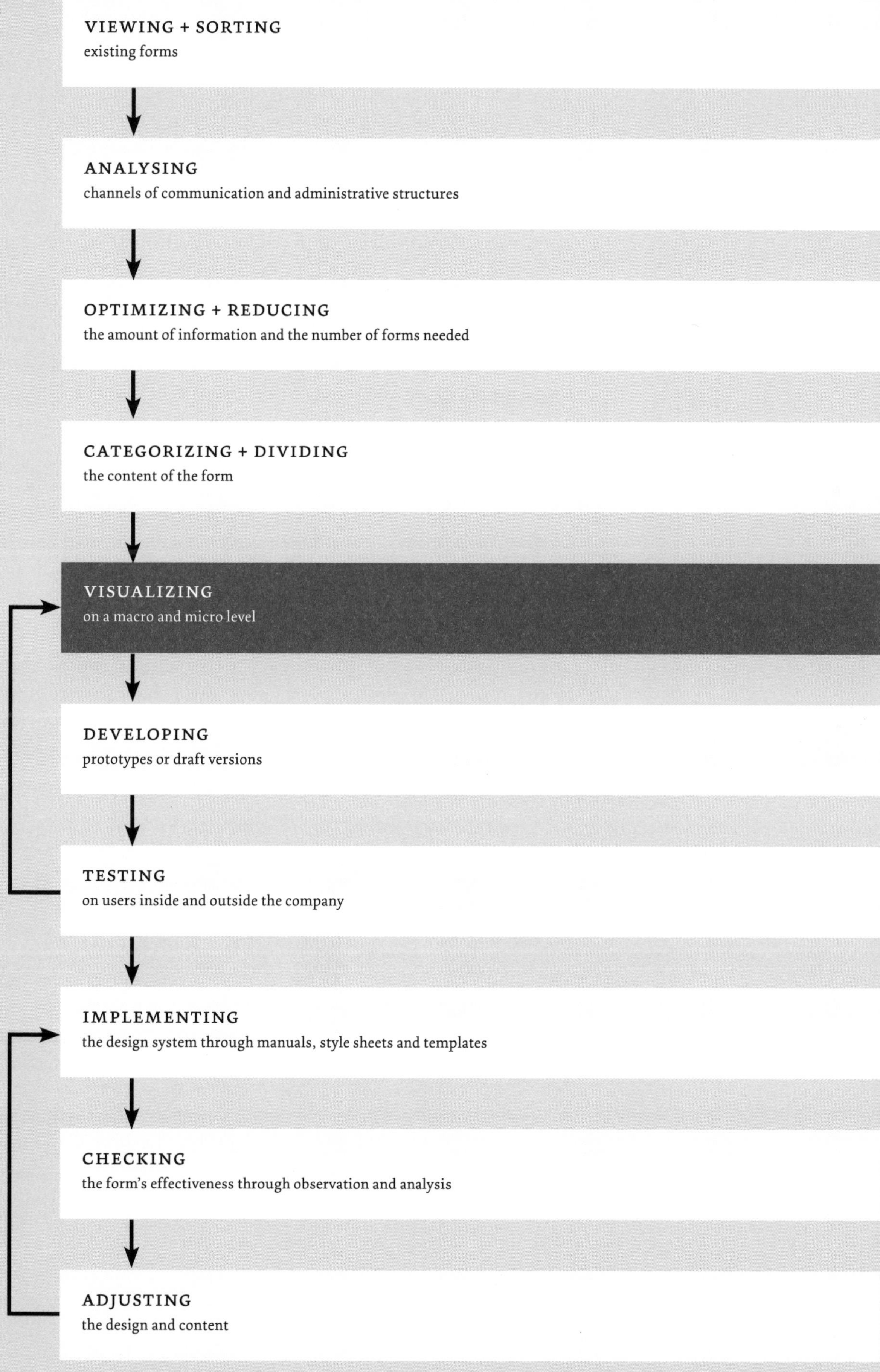
VIEWING + SORTING
existing forms
ANALYSING
channels of communication and administrative structures
OPTIMIZING + REDUCING
the amount of information and the number of forms needed
CATEGORIZING + DIVIDING
the content of the form
VISUALIZING
on a macro and micro level
DEVELOPING
prototypes or draft versions
TESTING
on users inside and outside the company
IMPLEMENTING
the design system through manuals, style sheets and templates
CHECKING
the form's effectiveness through observation and analysis
ADJUSTING
the design and content

Keeping it relevant

Avoiding irrelevance helps users to understand the form

Forms are complex visual structures consisting of many different signs. There are graphic elements like spaces, lines, symbols and pictograms, and typographical elements such as letters, numbers and punctuation marks. Each element of a form conveys information, and the more complicated, dense and varied the form is, the more stressful it is for a user to read, understand and fill in the blanks. One strategy that can help to make forms simpler is to get rid of as many unnecessary and irrelevant items of information as possible.

Human perception is based partly on coordinating the impressions we receive from our senses with the stored templates and patterns in our minds. We can perceive things more quickly if they conform to our expectations and if familiar items are repeated. Using the *Gestalt rules of design* (see page 126) is one way to cut out irrelevance, and although designers often make use of these principles unconsciously, it is well worth the effort to give them some deliberate consideration.

Establish connections

The Gestalt rules of design, such as proximity, similarity and unity, help to make connections clear and give structure to a form. They show how elements that belong together can be visually characterized by position, shape or colour.

Prioritize information

Techniques such as dividing the content according to its importance, laying emphasis on the most significant items, giving less visual prominence to less important elements, and leaving out unnecessary items can all help users to find their way and absorb the relevant information. The rules of *intensity* and *contrast* (see page 127) show ways in which a reader's attention can be influenced.

Use principles consistently

Once your principles of layout, division and emphasis have been established, stick with them, both for individual forms and in the overall system. In this way, users' expectations will be met and they will find it easier to use the form.

Graphic variables

Semiology of graphics

This overview is based on Jacques Bertin's *Semiology of Graphics*. Bertin's principles were originally applied to cartographic symbols, but the issues are very similar to those posed by form design: how can the meanings of elements and the connections between them be represented in visual terms?

Forms are two-dimensional surfaces on which dots, lines, spaces and typographical signs are arranged. Each of these graphic elements can have a number of *variables* applied to it. By altering these variables you can establish simple connections and hierarchies between the individual elements, and codify their meanings. The graphic variables can be used in different ways: they may denote only interconnections, only a hierarchy, or both of these.

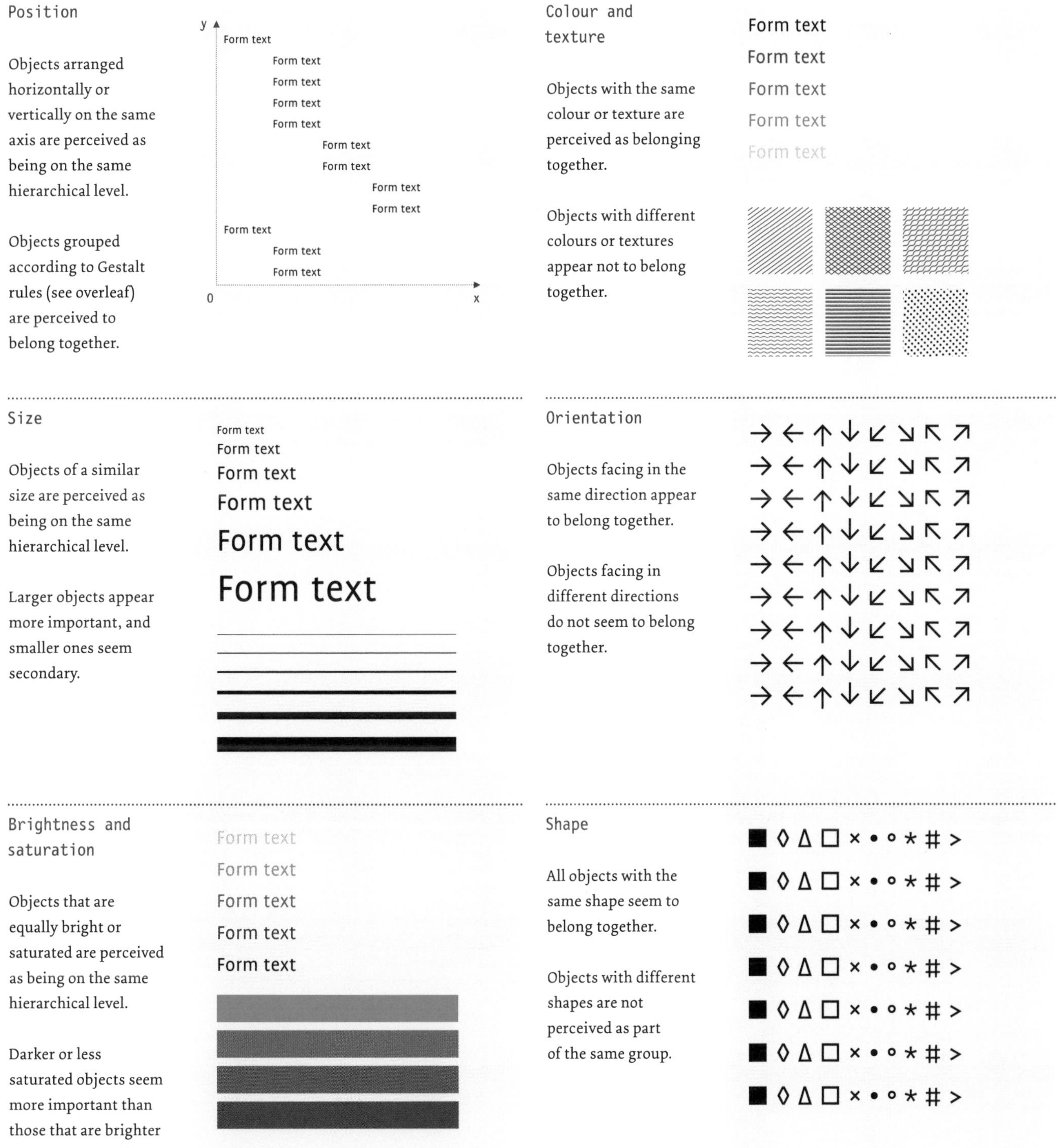

Position

Objects arranged horizontally or vertically on the same axis are perceived as being on the same hierarchical level.

Objects grouped according to Gestalt rules (see overleaf) are perceived to belong together.

Colour and texture

Objects with the same colour or texture are perceived as belonging together.

Objects with different colours or textures appear not to belong together.

Size

Objects of a similar size are perceived as being on the same hierarchical level.

Larger objects appear more important, and smaller ones seem secondary.

Orientation

Objects facing in the same direction appear to belong together.

Objects facing in different directions do not seem to belong together.

Brightness and saturation

Objects that are equally bright or saturated are perceived as being on the same hierarchical level.

Darker or less saturated objects seem more important than those that are brighter or more saturated.

Shape

All objects with the same shape seem to belong together.

Objects with different shapes are not perceived as part of the same group.

Gestalt rules of design

One way to avoid irrelevance is to observe the Gestalt rules of design. *Gestalt* is a term taken from the psychology of perception, and refers to the idea that any whole is made up of individual elements that are perceived to interact in specific ways. The Gestalt rules can be applied to graphic design and typography by altering the variables described on the previous page.

Rule of proximity

Elements that are close together are perceived as being related, whereas those that are separate are seen as individual.

In this example, the three groups of questions are distinguished only by the gaps between them. Following the same principle, the checkboxes clearly relate to one of three possible responses.

Question

Question

Question

Question

Question

Question ☐ yes ☐ no ☐ don't know

Rules of similarity

Elements that share common features are perceived as belonging together.

In this example, texts with the same kind of content (e.g. explanations) are denoted by using the same type style.

Question

Question

Texts that look alike (in this case through the use of italics) are always perceived as having the same level of content, even if their lengths and alignments are different.

Question

Similar design – same function as the text above.

Question

Rule of closure

Elements that are arranged to enclose a single space are perceived as a coherent shape. Elements that are enclosed or separated from one another by a single shape are perceived as a group.

In this example, dotted lines produce unified shapes, so the elements within them appear connected. This principle comes into play when, because of increased complexity, the rules of proximity and similarity are no longer enough to create a division or distinction.

Question

Question

Question

Question

Question

Question

Question

Question

This text seems to belong together with the one below, whether this is intended or not.

This text belongs with the one above, whether this is intended or not. Free will simply doesn't enter into the equation.

The hierarchical division of the text, the emphasis of important elements, and the accentuation of entry points all give guidance to readers. The rules of *intensity* and *contrast* can be used to influence their powers of attention.

Rule of intensity

According to this rule, a reader's attention depends on the strength of variables such as position, brightness, saturation, colour and size. The larger something is, the more attention it will grab.

As not everything can be equally attention-grabbing, the content must first be considered carefully, in order to differentiate between degrees of dominance.

In this example, the importance of different sections of the text is expressed solely by the changing type size.

However, you should not rely exclusively on the principle that if something is particularly large, it will also be read with a corresponding degree of attentiveness. In particular, any information that readers already think they know will tend to be ignored. If you want to present readers with new information, you must therefore go against their expectations and present this information so that it comes as a surprise.

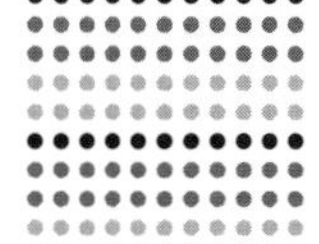

In case of emergency, call:

0808 157 0555

Reading text: The quick, brown fox jumps over a lazy dog. Junk MTV quiz graced by fox whelps. Bawds jog, flick quartz, vex nymphs. Waltz, bad nymph, for quick jigs vex. Fox nymphs grab quick-jived waltz. Brick quiz whangs jumpy veldt fox. Bright vixens jump; dozy fowl quack. Quick wafting zephyrs vex bold Jim. Quick zephyrs blow, vexing daft Jim. Sex-charged fop blew my junk TV quiz. How quickly daft jumping zebras vex. Two driven jocks help fax my big quiz. Quick, Baz, get my woven flax jodhpurs! Five quacking zephyrs jolt my wax bed. A very bad quack might jinx zippy fowls. Few quips galvanized the mock jury box. Quick brown dogs jump over the lazy fox. The jay, pig, fox, zebra, and my wolves quack. Blowzy red vixens fight for a quick jump.

Small print: The quick, brown fox jumps over a lazy dog. Junk MTV quiz graced by fox whelps. Bawds jog, flick quartz, vex nymphs. Waltz, bad nymph, for quick jigs vex. Fox nymphs grab quick-jived waltz. Brick quiz whangs jumpy veldt fox. Bright vixens jump; dozy fowl quack. Quick wafting zephyrs vex bold Jim. Quick zephyrs blow, vexing daft Jim. Sex-charged fop blew my junk TV quiz. How quickly daft jumping zebras vex. Two driven jocks help fax my big quiz. Quick, Baz, get my woven flax jodhpurs! Five quacking zephyrs jolt my wax bed. A very bad quack might jinx zippy fowls. Few quips galvanized the mock jury box. Quick brown dogs jump over the lazy fox. The jay, pig, fox, zebra, and my wolves quack. Blowzy red vixens fight for a quick jump.

Rule of contrast

According to the rule of contrast, anything that is designed to be different from its surroundings will be particularly striking. Any of the graphic variables may serve this purpose, especially shape and colour.

By this means, information can be made to stand out, independent of the hierarchy.

Question A __________

Question B __________

Question C __________

Question D __________

Question E __________

Question F __________

→ Question F __________

Question G __________

Question H __________

Design layers

Form design takes place on two levels

As already mentioned, the visual design of forms takes place on two levels. Macro-level or high-level design involves basic decisions regarding production, layout and typography, while micro-level design relates to the details of the text itself, the fields, checkboxes and other elements.

In this chapter we shall be dealing initially with macro-level design, introducing the main elements before we take a close-up view in the next chapter.

The graphics on the opposite page show the kind of decisions that are part of macro-level design. These include selecting a grid and module system, determining the layout, and choosing typefaces and colours – all of which apply to each individual form as well as to a whole system. A uniform but flexible macro-level design for all forms will make them easier to produce and to use, and will also ensure brand recognition for the provider.

Digital forms include interactive information levels

With interactive digital forms, there is a further level of design: paper forms can only show what has already been printed, whereas digital forms can add or remove items of information as and when needed. This is useful for instructions, explanations or questions that do not always have to be displayed.

Follow, extend or escape from corporate design

The way in which an existing corporate design is to be integrated into a form is a macro-level decision. Typefaces and colours as well as logos and branding are often given factors, but typefaces in particular are not always practical for use on forms. Colours, visual frameworks and grids may also prove to be unsuitable, so pre-existing elements like these may have to be adapted or changed completely. Issues that are specific to form design, such as text fields, are rarely specified by corporate design manuals, so solutions must be found that will fit with the existing corporate style. If, for instance, the provider uses specific brand colours, these could be used on the forms as well, with the text fields presented as white spaces within the colour field.

Apart from the demands of corporate design, there may also be technical and organizational factors at work which limit the choice of paper, the method of printing or the arrangement of certain elements.

Grids

A vertical column grid and a horizontal baseline grid provide the basic layout of the form.

→ page 146

Layout choices

For all forms, the layout determines where and how the elements or modules are to be arranged.

→ page 150

Modules

Recurring elements are linked together in the form of modules, which fit into the grid like building blocks.

→ page 149

Typography

Typography is the most important element of form design. The choice of typeface and how it is handled is one of the most important macro-level design decisions.

→ page 130

Visual frameworks

These determine the overall appearance of the form, and may be based on cells, frames, shaded areas or lines.

→ page 152

Colour

Colour can help to guide the user and may also make the form and its provider more easily identifiable.

→ page 138

Paper, format and printing

The choice of paper, format and printing technique determine the physical feel of the form.

→ page 140

Typefaces and typography

→ For more on typography, see the bibliography on page 318

Typography is the most powerful tool for designing forms. Good typography is a prerequisite for optimal legibility and demands a particular and considered approach to text. From the choice of type style and weight, tracking and kerning, leading and column width, to the choice of justified or ranged type, there are many factors that influence the user-friendliness of a form. Here are some general tips on selecting type for forms, along with an overview of the basics of typography.

The choice of typeface is often dictated by corporate style guidelines, but this is not always an advantage. Sometimes a corporate style will specify a face that is not very well suited to forms, or you will be asked to use the typefaces that come installed as standard on every PC. Ideally, form design should be a component of a complete corporate identity. Any corporate typefaces should be carefully chosen and licensed so that they are available for all co-workers to use.

Forms contain a high density of information. In most cases, a lot of material must be fitted onto a single page. These factors make demands on the typefaces that are used. They need to be legible at small point sizes, yet at the same time robust enough to withstand photocopying and faxing. The best faces are those in which the individual letterforms can easily be distinguished from one another, rather than blending together, while at the same time creating a calm and balanced look. Because of the lack of space on many forms, relatively narrow faces are better than broader ones. In order to differentiate between different sorts of information and emphasize particular elements or areas, type should be available in a range of weights. The choice of typeface alone, however, is not the only factor: just as important is the way in which it is used. This is what makes a form readable or not.

While functionality is a prerequisite in the design of forms, the choice of typeface plays a major role in giving every form its own style. Of course, every typeface has a personality of its own too. Type can be austere or accessible, straight or rounded, emotive or exaggerated.

The following pages explain some general rules that are useful when considering typography for forms

Typeface categories

Here is a simplified overview of different varieties of typeface. The main distinction is whether or not the characters have serifs, and what form the serifs take. Fancy, script or blackletter faces are not included, since these don't usually play a role in form design. More sample typefaces are shown on pages 136–137.

Handgloves 123

Sans serif face (Univers)

Handgloves 123

Serif face (Minion)

Handgloves 123

Semi-serif face (The Mix)

Handgloves 123

Slab serif face (Egyptian)

In proportional faces, the characters have different widths. In monospace faces, each character has the same width, giving a classic typewritten look.

Handgloves 123
Berlyxjeri 456

Proportional face (Profile)

Handgloves 123
Berlyxjeri 456

Monospace face (Thesis Mono)

Type families and styles

A set of different styles of the same typeface is called a type family. These have been designed to combine well together and create a harmonious overall design.

Many software applications can create forced italics by tilting the roman version of the face to one side, and forced small caps by shrinking down the face's full-size capital letters. These should not be used: true italics and small caps have their own specially designed letterforms.

Handgloves 123

Roman type (Profile)

Handgloves 123

Italic (or oblique)

Handgloves 123

Forced italic

HANDGLOVES 123

Small caps

HANDGLOVES 123

Forced small caps

Typefaces also come in a range of bold and broad (or extended) variants. As well as those shown here, many other variations are possible.

Handgloves 123

Light,
in this case Univers 45

Handgloves 123

Bold,
here Univers 65

Handgloves

Extended,
here Univers 53

Handgloves 123

Condensed,
here Univers 57

Figures

Numbers can be set with lining figures, which are all the same height and sit above the baseline, or with old-style or non-lining figures, which vary in height and cross the baseline. Figures also come in proportional and tabular styles. Tabular figures are all of the same width, so that they always fall exactly below each other when used in a table.

Within running text, proportional figures are better. While lining figures stand out in the text like capital letters, old-style figures fit better within the overall image of the text.

12345678.90
09876543.21

Proportional lining figures

12345678.90
09876543.21

Tabular lining figures

12345678.90
09876543.21

Proportional old-style figures

12345678.90
09876543.21

Tabular old-style figures

The sample typeface is Myriad Pro, which features all these figure styles.

Emphasis

Adding emphasis to text means that different sorts of information can be distinguished and and highlighted.

There are two ways of doing this: integrated and active emphasis.

Integrated emphasis

This type of emphasis is only noticed when the text is read, because it fits into the overall text unobtrusively. It is most often employed to distinguish items such as names or long quotations. Italics and small caps are the most commonly used styles for this.

The quick, brown fox jumps over a lazy dog. Bawds jog, flick quartz, vex nymphs. Waltz, bad nymph, for quick jigs vex. Fox nymphs grab quick-jived waltz. Brick quiz whangs jumpy veldt fox. Bright vixens jump; dozy fowl quack. Quick wafting zephyrs vex bold Jim. Quick zephyrs blow, vexing daft Jim. Sex-charged fop blew my junk TV quiz. How quickly daft jumping zebras vex. Zachary said: '*Two driven jocks help fax my big quiz. Quick, Baz, get my woven flax jodhpurs.*' Five quacking zephyrs jolt my wax bed. A very bad quack might jinx zippy fowls. Few quips galvanized the mock jury box. Quick brown dogs jump over the lazy fox. The jay, pig, fox, zebra, and my wolves quack.

Integrated italics used to highlight a quotation

The quick, brown fox jumps over a lazy dog. Bawds jog, flick quartz, vex nymphs. Waltz, bad nymph, for quick jigs vex. Fox nymphs grab quick-jived waltz. Brick quiz whangs jumpy veldt fox. Bright vixens jump; dozy fowl quack. Quick wafting zephyrs vex bold JIM. Quick zephyrs blow, vexing JIM, DAPHNE, FLORENCE and QUENTIN. How quickly daft jumping zebras vex. Two driven jocks help fax my big quiz. Quick, BAZ, get my woven flax jodhpurs. Five quacking zephyrs jolt my wax bed. A very bad quack might jinx zippy fowls. Few quips galvanized the mock jury box. Quick brown dogs jump over the lazy fox. The jay, pig, fox, zebra, and my wolves quack.

Integrated small caps used to highlight names

Active emphasis

Using active emphasis means that readers will notice the emphasized features of the text or page right away.

Within text, it can be used to differentiate or emphasize certain pieces of information.
→ left-hand column

Emphasizing keywords, headings and subheads will help readers to orientate themselves and move through the text efficiently.
→ right-hand column

The method of emphasis that is chosen depends on how noticeable those elements need to be. Because not everything can be marked as of equal importance, emphasis needs to be used with care and consideration, to avoid excessive clutter.

Lorem ipsum dolor sit amet, consectetur adipiscing elit. Sed vitae aliquam mauris. Pellentesque imperdiet enim vel tellus blandit a **tempus** nisi **dapibus**. Sed non porttitor metus. Morbi pharetra.

Bold text for emphasis

Subhead
Lorem ipsum dolor sit amet, consectetur adipiscing elit. Vestibulum ligula leo, venenatis at adipiscing ut, pretium non nisi. Maecenas lacinia viverra eros nec.

Bold text for headings

Lorem ipsum dolor sit amet, consectetur adipiscing elit. Vestibulum ligula leo, venenatis at adipiscing ut, pretium non nisi. Maecenas lacinia viverra eros nec faucibus. Vivamus pretium aliquam.

Underlining for emphasis

Subhead
Lorem ipsum dolor sit amet, consectetur adipiscing elit. Vestibulum ligula leo, venenatis at adipiscing ut, pretium non nisi. Maecenas lacinia viverra eros.

Underlined text for headings

Lorem ipsum dolor sit amet, consectetur adipiscing elit. Vestibulum ligula leo, venenatis at adipiscing ut, pretium non nisi. Maecenas lacinia viverra eros nec faucibus. Vivamus pretium aliquam.

Coloured type for emphasis

Subhead
Lorem ipsum dolor sit amet, consectetur adipiscing elit. Vestibulum ligula leo, venenatis at adipiscing ut, pretium non nisi. Maecenas lacinia viverra eros nec faucibus.

Coloured type for headings

Lorem ipsum dolor sit amet, consectetur adipiscing elit. Nullam non dui eget mauris egestas volutpat ut sit amet tellus. Aenean condimentum placerat luctus. Nunc eget.

Larger type size for emphasis

Subhead
Lorem ipsum dolor sit amet, consectetur adipiscing elit. Nullam non dui eget mauris egestas volutpat ut sit amet tellus. Aenean condimentum placerat luctus. Nunc eget.

Larger type size for headings

Lorem ipsum dolor sit amet, consectetur adipiscing elit. Fusce diam dui, mollis quis rutrum id, rutrum ac erat. **Nunc molestie** rhoncus libero **tincidunt porttitor**. Donec congue neque id nunc tempus viverra.

Different typeface for emphasis

Subhead
Lorem ipsum dolor sit amet, consectetur adipiscing elit. Fusce diam dui, mollis quis rutrum id, rutrum ac erat. Nunc molestie rhoncus libero tincidunt porttitor.

Different typeface for headings

Letterspacing and kerning

Kerning, tracking and word spacing are all different ways of influencing the legibility of a piece of text.

Every character in a typeface is a set width with a fixed amount of space on either side. A typeface with bad letterspacing leads to text with an uneven, messy look.

Lore m ipsum d olor sit amet, co nsectetur adipiscing elit. Aliquam ut tortor at massa tristique viverra id facilisis augue. Ut eget sapien n eque, id malesuada metus. S ed eget lacinia le o. Sed fer mentum, velit ul trices faucibus posuere, eni m odio egestas el it, vel vulputa te nisi magna in tort or.

Poor letterspacing

Lorem ipsum dolor sit amet, consectetur adipiscing elit. Aliquam ut tortor at massa tristique viverra id facilisis augue. Ut eget sapien neque, id malesuada metus. Sed eget lacinia leo. Sed fermentum, velit ultrices faucibus posuere, enim odio egestas elit, vel vulputate nisi magna in tortor.

Good letterspacing, but without kerning

Kerning controls the distances between individual pairs of letters, e.g. between a capital V and a lower-case o. Good kerning improves the overall look of the text and makes it easier to read. Most typefaces include standard settings for kerning, but sometimes these need to be adjusted by hand to get the best result.

Voyage Airways

Without kerning

Voyage Airways

With automatic kerning

Voyage Airways

With optimum kerning

Lorem ipsum dolor sit amet, consectetur adipiscing elit. Aliquam ut tortor at massa tristique viverra id facilisis augue. Ut eget sapien neque, id malesuada metus. Sed eget lacinia leo. Sed fermentum, velit ultrices faucibus posuere, enim odio egestas elit, vel vulputate nisi magna in tortor.

Good letterspacing with additional kerning

Tracking

Tracking controls the overall letterspacing of a block of text. The standard setting is zero.

For small type sizes, the tracking usually needs to be looser, and for large type sizes, tighter.

When the tracking is too tight, the letters are squashed together, giving a cramped and unattractive appearance.

When the tracking is too loose, the words lose their cohesion. Readers stop perceiving the words or word groups as a whole, and instead notice the individual letterforms.

Lorem ipsum dolor sit amet, consectetur adipiscing elit. Etiam ut blandit ipsum. Curabitur posuere nisl vel nibh fringilla tempor. Integer nisi elit, pharetra hendrerit pellentesque vel.

8.5 pt, standard tracking

Voyage Airways

30 pt, standard tracking

Lorem ipsum dolor sit amet, consectetur adipiscing elit. Etiam ut blandit ipsum. Curabitur posuere nisl vel nibh fringilla tempor. Integer nisi elit, pharetra hendrerit pellentesque vel.

8.5 pt, looser tracking, better

Voyage Airways

30 pt, tighter tracking, better

Lorem ipsum dolor sit amet, consectetur adipiscing elit. Etiam ut blandit ipsum. Curabitur posuere nisl vel nibh fringilla tempor. Integer nisi elit, pharetra hendrerit pellentesque.

8.5 pt, very loose tracking, not good

Voyage Airways

30 pt, very tight tracking, not good

Word spacing

Spaces between words should be judged in relation to the chosen line spacing. Each word needs to be clearly divided from the next, but overly large gaps need to be avoided, because these make the eye 'fall' into the spaces.

A good rule of thumb is: the space between words must be smaller than the space between lines.

Lorem ipsum dolor sit amet, consectetur adipiscing elit. Etiam ut blandit ipsum. Curabitur posuere nisl vel nibh fringilla tempor. Integer nisi elit, pharetra hendrerit pellentesque vel, venenatis a velit. Donec neque turpis.

8.5 pt, tight word spacing, acceptable

Lorem ipsum dolor sit amet, consectetur adipiscing elit. Etiam ut blandit ipsum. Curabitur posuere nisl vel nibh fringilla tempor. Integer nisi elit, pharetra hendrerit pellentesque vel, venenatis a velit. Donec neque turpis.

8.5 pt, regular word spacing, good

Lorem ipsum dolor sit amet, consectetur adipiscing elit. Etiam ut blandit ipsum. Curabitur posuere nisl vel nibh fringilla tempor. Integer nisi elit, pharetra hendrerit pellentesque vel, venenatis a velit. Donec neque turpis.

8.5 pt, loose word spacing, not good

Leading and column width

If a text is to be easy to read, it needs leading (or line spacing) that matches the column width and the shape and size of the type. In simple terms, the longer the lines, the larger the leading needs to be. The shorter the lines, the smaller the leading can be.

With leading that is too tight, the lines lose their horizontal clarity, so the eye can easily reach the end of a line and skip back to the wrong one.

With leading that is too large, the text loses its cohesion and the lines seem to float in space.

The examples shown here all use the same type size but the leading and column widths have been changed.

Lorem ipsum dolor sit amet, consectetur adipiscing elit. Duis non tellus a mi tincidunt varius. Aenean augue libero, vehicula vel faucibus condimentum, feugiat a ipsum. Nullam porttitor pretium magna, in fermentum nisl.

Leading 9.5 pt, acceptable

Lorem ipsum dolor sit amet, consectetur adipiscing elit. Duis non tellus a mi tincidunt varius. Aenean augue libero, vehicula vel faucibus condimentum, feugiat a ipsum. Nullam porttitor pretium magna, in fermentum nisl.

Leading 11 pt, better

Lorem ipsum dolor sit amet, consectetur adipiscing elit. Duis non tellus a mi tincidunt varius. Aenean augue libero, vehicula vel faucibus condimentum, feugiat a ipsum. Nullam porttitor pretium magna, in fermentum nisl.

Leading 13 pt, too big

Lorem ipsum dolor sit amet, consectetur adipiscing elit. Duis non tellus a mi tincidunt varius. Aenean augue libero, vehicula vel faucibus condimentum, feugiat a ipsum. Nullam porttitor pretium magna, in fermentum nisl bibendum a. Quisque sem purus, vestibulum et varius ac, varius quis mauris.

Leading 9.5 pt, too tight

Lorem ipsum dolor sit amet, consectetur adipiscing elit. Duis non tellus a mi tincidunt varius. Aenean augue libero, vehicula vel faucibus condimentum, feugiat a ipsum. Nullam porttitor pretium magna, in fermentum nisl bibendum a. Quisque sem purus, vestibulum et varius ac, varius quis mauris.

Leading 11 pt, good

Lorem ipsum dolor sit amet, consectetur adipiscing elit. Duis non tellus a mi tincidunt varius. Aenean augue libero, vehicula vel faucibus condimentum, feugiat a ipsum. Nullam porttitor pretium magna, in fermentum nisl bibendum a.

Leading 13 pt, also good

Lorem ipsum dolor sit amet, consectetur adipiscing elit. Duis non tellus a mi tincidunt varius. Aenean augue libero, vehicula vel faucibus condimentum, feugiat a ipsum. Nullam porttitor pretium magna, in fermentum nisl bibendum a. Quisque sem purus, vestibulum et varius ac, varius quis mauris.

Leading 9.5 pt, much too tight

Lorem ipsum dolor sit amet, consectetur adipiscing elit. Duis non tellus a mi tincidunt varius. Aenean augue libero, vehicula vel faucibus condimentum, feugiat a ipsum. Nullam porttitor pretium magna, in fermentum nisl bibendum a. Quisque sem purus, vestibulum et varius ac, varius quis mauris.

Leading 11 pt, good

Lorem ipsum dolor sit amet, consectetur adipiscing elit. Duis non tellus a mi tincidunt varius. Aenean augue libero, vehicula vel faucibus condimentum, feugiat a ipsum. Nullam porttitor pretium magna, in fermentum nisl bibendum a. Quisque sem purus, vestibulum et varius ac, varius quis mauris.

Leading 13 pt, better

Very small type

At very small point sizes, it is sometimes better not to change the leading in relation to the type size, but to do the opposite and choose a smaller type size with larger leading.

Lorem ipsum dolor sit amet, consectetur adipiscing elit. Duis non tellus a mi tincidunt varius. Aenean augue libero, vehicula vel faucibus condimentum, feugiat a ipsum. Nullam porttitor pretium magna, in fermentum nisl bibendum a. Quisque sem purus, vestibulum et varius ac, varius quis mauris. Curabitur nisl urna, euismod vitae sollicitudin.

Type size 6.5 pt / Leading 6.5 pt

Lorem ipsum dolor sit amet, consectetur adipiscing elit. Duis non tellus a mi tincidunt varius. Aenean augue libero, vehicula vel faucibus condimentum, feugiat a ipsum. Nullam porttitor pretium magna, in fermentum nisl bibendum a. Quisque sem purus, vestibulum et varius ac, varius quis mauris. Curabitur nisl urna, euismod vitae sollicitudin.

Type size 6.0 pt / Leading 7.5 pt

Justified type

Justification creates a column of text with straight edges on both sides. This has a neat appearance, but if the justification causes too many gaps and stretched lines, the text can become difficult to read.

Most word processing and DTP software can justify text automatically by changing the word spacing. It is important to find the right balance between squashed or gappy lines and the number of hyphens used.

It is not a good idea to justify text by altering the line tracking, because this gives an uneven and messy look.

With narrow column widths, neat type is very hard to achieve. With lines of fewer than 45 characters, gaps and rivers are created. For readability, an optimum line length is around 60 characters.

Lorem ipsum dolor sit amet, consectetur adipiscing elit. Duis non tellus a mi tincidunt varius. Aenean augue libero, vehicula vel faucibus condimentum, feugiat a ipsum. Nullam porttitor pretium magna, in fermentum nisl.

Justified type with increased word spaces c. 25 characters wide

Lorem ipsum dolor sit amet, consectetur adipiscing elit. Duis non tellus a mi tincidunt varius. Aenean augue libero, vehicula vel faucibus condimentum, feugiat a ipsum. Nullam porttitor pretium magna, in fermentum nisl.

For comparison: justified type with adjusted tracking

Lorem ipsum dolor sit amet, consectetur adipiscing elit. Duis non tellus a mi tincidunt varius. Aenean augue libero, vehicula vel faucibus condimentum, feugiat a ipsum. Nullam porttitor pretium magna, in fermentum nisl bibendum a.

c. 45 characters wide

Lorem ipsum dolor sit amet, consectetur adipiscing elit. Duis non tellus a mi tincidunt varius. Aenean augue libero, vehicula vel faucibus condimentum, feugiat a ipsum. Nullam porttitor pretium magna, in fermentum nisl bibendum a. Quisque sem purus, vestibulum et varius ac, varius quis mauris.

c. 60 characters wide

Unjustified type

Unjustified type with a ragged right edge gives a relaxed look. However, without additional work, ugly step-like line endings can be created. At its best, ragged right text should have a balanced series of lines of different lengths, but it takes time to achieve this.

Duis non nibh ut velit sodales tempor eu interdum mi. Vivamus non cursus urna. Nulla varius nulla nec purus sodales lobortis. Morbi neque justo, rhoncus ut blandit a, dictum a orci. Sed ultrices adipiscing risus, nec malesuada nunc faucibus ac.

Ragged right with messy right edge

Duis non nibh ut velit sodales tempor eu interdum mi. Vivamus non cursus urna. Nulla varius nulla nec purus sodales lobortis. Morbi neque justo, rhoncus ut blandit a, dictum a orci. Sed ultrices adipiscing risus, nec malesuada nunc faucibus ac.

Ragged right with neatened edge

Column spacing

If the text is set in columns and the paragraphs have space between them, the gutter between columns should be larger than the space between paragraphs. This will prevent the risk of the eye skipping across the gutter when reading, instead of moving down the column.

Lorem ipsum dolor sit amet, consectetur adipiscing elit. Aenean lorem ante, feugiat at porta sit amet, consequat vitae leo. Fusce adipiscing dictum arcu eu mollis. Nam a risus sit amet elit lacinia adipiscing. Aliquam quis blandit eros. Sed ac tellus mi, eu pellentesque nunc. Praesent et placerat orci. Integer justo purus, lobortis eget ullamcorper ut, vulputate eget tortor.

Etiam volutpat consequat nibh, nec sollicitudin elit hendrerit eu. Lorem ipsum dolor sit amet, consectetur adipiscing elit. Aenean dapibus est non elit dictum sed ornare lacus vehicula. Quisque viverra elementum sem eu rhoncus. Phasellus consectetur ornare nulla, quis bibendum urna tempor vitae.

Nullam hendrerit laoreet sollicitudin. Mauris commodo facilisis tellus et placerat. Phasellus placerat enim vitae orci vestibulum id aliquam ligula interdum.

Indents

Indents help the reader to see where one paragraph ends and another starts. The size of the indent must be chosen to match the selected type size and leading.

The first line of a new section, especially if it starts below a heading or subhead, should not be indented.

Lorem ipsum dolor sit amet, consectetur adipiscing elit. Sed malesuada ultrices ligula, sit amet vestibulum nisl tristique vitae. In quis dui lectus.

Quisque malesuada mattis massa vitae sagittis. Duis non nibh ut velit sodales tempor eu interdum mi. Vivamus non cursus urna. Nulla varius nulla nec purus sodales lobortis. Morbi neque justo, rhoncus ut blandit a, dictum a orci. Vestibulum fermentum convallis accumsan. Curabitur id elit augue, at ullamcorper tortor. Sed ultrices adipiscing risus, nec malesuada nunc faucibus ac.

Subhead
Nullam ipsum est, luctus consectetur malesuada in, scelerisque at neque. Integer felis orci, placerat ut sodales ac, aliquam id erat. Pellentesque habitant morbi tristique senectus et netus.

Sans serif typefaces

These two pages showcase just a small selection of sans serif and serif typefaces along with some monospace faces. All of them are well suited to forms, being predominantly quite narrow and also legible at small point sizes. In addition, most of them are well constructed and include a range of styles and weights, allowing a great deal of typographic variation.

FF Info

A narrow typeface that was designed to be used for a signage system. In its InfoText variant, it also works well at small point sizes.

InfoText Book
InfoText Normal
InfoText Medium
InfoText Semibold
InfoText Bold

Lorem ipsum dolor sit amet, consectetur adipiscing elit. Mauris sollicitudin, velit eu varius vulputate, lorem ipsum sollicitudin arcu, a fringilla arcu ipsum nec lectus. Curabitur porta tortor sed mi vehicula eu tempor tortor tempor. Maecenas quam lectus, pulvinar a blandit nec, malesuada ut erat. Etiam id ipsum in nulla consequat ornare ut at felis. Nunc sed tortor ipsum, a vehicula.

Normal 7.5/10 pt

FF Profile

A well-constructed, lively sans serif, which includes tabular, proportional and old-style figures.

Profile Light — SMALL CAPS
Profile Regular — SMALL CAPS
Profile Medium — SMALL CAPS
Profile Bold — **SMALL CAPS**
Profile Black — **SMALL CAPS**

Lorem ipsum dolor sit amet, consectetur dipiscing elit. Mauris sollicitudin, velit eu varius vulputate, lorem ipsum sollicitudin arcu, a fringilla arcu ipsum nec lectus. Curabitur porta tortor sed mi vehicula eu tempor tortor tempor. Maecenas quam lectus, pulvinar a blandit nec, malesuada ut erat. Etiam id ipsum in nulla consequat ornare ut at felis. Nunc sed tortor ipsum, a vehicula.

Regular 7.5/10 pt

Bell Centennial

This typeface's notches and large counter spaces mean that small type is legible, even after low-quality printing. It can be problematic, however, at larger point sizes.

Bell Centennial Address
Bell Centennial Name & Number
Bell Centennial Sub Caption
BELL CENTENNIAL BOLD LISTING

Lorem ipsum dolor sit amet, consectetur adipiscing elit. Mauris sollicitudin, velit eu varius vulputate, lorem ipsum sollicitudin arcu, a fringilla arcu ipsum nec lectus. Curabitur porta tortor sed mi vehicula eu tempor tortor tempor. Maecenas quam lectus, pulvinar a blandit nec, malesuada ut erat. Etiam id ipsum in nulla consequat ornare ut at felis. Nunc sed tortor ipsum, a vehicula.

Karowsky

Address 7.5/10 pt and 21 pt

Vectora

Developed for use on railway timetables, this typeface has a tall x-height (the height of the lower-case x), so it can be read easily at small point sizes.

Vectora 45 Light — *46 Italic*
Vectora 55 Roman — *56 Italic*
Vectora 75 Bold — ***76 Italic***
Vectora 95 Black — ***96 Italic***

Lorem ipsum dolor sit amet, consectetur adipiscing elit. Mauris sollicitudin, velit eu varius vulputate, lorem ipsum sollicitudin arcu, a fringilla arcu ipsum nec lectus. Curabitur porta tortor sed mi vehicula eu tempor tortor tempor. Maecenas quam ut erat. Etiam id ipsum in nulla consequat ornare ut at felis. Nunc sed tortor ipsum, a vehicula.

55 Roman 7.5/10 pt

Formata

The special feature of this sans serif is its subtly curved strokes. It has a dynamic look and is well constructed.

Formata Light — *Italic*
Formata Regular — *Italic*
Formata Medium — ***Italic***
Formata Bold — ***Italic***
Formata Condensed — *Italic*

Lorem ipsum dolor sit amet, consectetur adipiscing elit. Mauris sollicitudin, velit eu varius vulputate, lorem ipsum sollicitudin arcu, a fringilla arcu ipsum nec lectus. Curabitur porta tortor sed mi vehicula eu tempor tortor tempor. Maecenas quam lectus, pulvinar a blandit nec, malesuada ut erat. Etiam id ipsum in nulla consequat ornare ut at felis. Nunc sed tortor ipsum, a vehicula.

Regular 7.5/10 pt

FF Meta

First developed for the German Post Office but never used, this has nonetheless become a popular typeface. Here are the basic weights from this now very extensive type family.

Meta Normal — *Italic*
META CAPITALS — *ITALIC*
Meta Bold
META BOLD CAPITALS

Lorem ipsum dolor sit amet, consectetur adipiscing elit. Mauris sollicitudin, velit eu varius vulputate, lorem ipsum sollicitudin arcu, a fringilla arcu ipsum nec lectus. Curabitur porta tortor sed mi vehicula eu tempor tortor tempor. Maecenas quam lectus, pulvinar a blandit nec, malesuada ut erat. Etiam id ipsum in nulla consequat ornare ut at felis. Nunc sed tortor ipsum, a vehicula.

Normal 7.5/10 pt

Serif typefaces

For use on forms, sans serif typefaces often tend to be chosen because they are more legible at smaller point sizes and their austerity makes them suitable for forms. But this generalization isn't always correct. These two serif faces, for example, also work well at small sizes.

Proforma

This serif face was specially developed for forms. It is compact and very legible, and available in a range of finely graduated weights, including small caps.

Proforma UltraLight *Italic*
Proforma Light *Italic*
Proforma Book *Italic*
Proforma Medium *Italic*
Proforma SemiBold ***Italic***
Proforma Bold ***Italic***

Lorem ipsum dolor sit amet, consectetur adipiscing elit. Mauris sollicitudin, velit eu varius vulputate, lorem ipsum sollicitudin arcu, a fringilla arcu ipsum nec lectus. Curabitur porta tortor sed mi vehicula eu tempor tortor tempor. Maecenas quam lectus, pulvinar a blandit nec, malesuada ut erat. Etiam id ipsum in nulla consequat ornare ut at felis. Nunc sed tortor ipsum, a vehicula.

Book 7.5/10 pt

Proforma UltraLight SC
Proforma Light SC
Proforma Book SC
Proforma Medium SC
Proforma SemiBold SC
Proforma Bold SC

Lorem ipsum dolor sit amet, consectetur adipiscing elit. Mauris sollicitudin, velit eu varius vulputate, lorem ipsum sollicitudin arcu, a fringilla arcu ipsum nec lectus. Curabitur porta tortor sed mi vehicula eu tempor tortor tempor. Maecenas quam lectus, pulvinar a blandit nec, malesuada ut erat. Etiam id ipsum in nulla consequat ornare ut at felis. Nunc sed tortor ipsum, a vehicula.

Book Italic 7.5/10 pt

Arnhem

A multipurpose serif face, which remains legible even on coarse-textured paper.

Arnhem Blond *Italic*
Arnhem Normal *Italic*
Arnhem Bold ***Italic***
Arnhem Black ***Italic***

Lorem ipsum dolor sit amet, consectetur adipiscing elit. Mauris sollicitudin, velit eu varius vulputate. Curabitur porta tortor sed mi vehicula eu tempor tortor tempor. Maecenas quam lectus, pulvinar a blandit nec, malesuada ut erat. Etiam id ipsum in nulla consequat ornare ut at felis. Nunc sed tortor ipsum, a vehicula.

Normal 7.5/10 pt

Monospace typefaces

Monospace typefaces have a typewritten look. They are particularly well suited to printing personal information and covering letters. The content looks less pre-printed and therefore more individual than is the case with proportional faces.

They are also easier to work with than proportional type because there are fewer typographical details that need to be adjusted.

As well as the timeless Courier, plenty of classic and modern alternatives are available.

The Sans Mono

Part of the extensive Thesis type family.

The Sans Mono Plain
The Sans Mono Italic
The Sans Mono Bold
The Sans Mono Bold

Lorem ipsum dolor sit amet, consectetur adipiscing elit. Mauris sollicitudin, velit eu varius vulputate, lorem ipsum tempor tortor tempor. Maecenas nec, malesuada ut erat. Etiam id ipsum in nulla consequat ornare ut at felis. Nunc sed tortor ipsum, a vehicula.

Plain 7.5/10 pt

Quadraat Sans Mono

Part of the Quadraat family, this typeface is comparatively narrow with distinctive shapes.

Quadraat Sans Mono Regular
Quadraat Sans Mono Italic
Quadraat Sans Mono Bold
Quadraat Sans Mono Bold Italic

Lorem ipsum dolor sit amet, consectetur adipiscing elit. Mauris sollicitudin, velit eu varius vulputate, lorem ipsum sollicitudin arcu, a fringilla arcu ipsum nec lectus. Curabitur porta tortor sed mi vehicula eu tempor tortor tempor. Maecenas quam lectus, pulvinar a blandit nec, malesuada ut erat. Etiam id ipsum in nulla consequat ornare ut at felis. Nunc sed tortor ipsum, a vehicula.

Regular 7.5/10 pt

Prestige Elite

Classic typewriter faces like this one often look thin. With a real typewriter, the characters look bolder due to the pressure with which they are applied to the paper.

Prestige Elite Regular
Prestige Elite Slanted
Prestige Elite Bold
Prestige Elite Bold Slanted

Lorem ipsum dolor sit amet, consectetur adipiscing elit. Mauris sollicitudin, velit eu sollicitudin arcu, a fringilla nec, malesuada ut erat. Etiam id ipsum in nulla consequat ornare ut at felis. Nunc sed tortor ipsum, a vehicula.

Bold 7.5/10 pt

Colour and type

As a basic principle, coloured forms must also work in black and white, because they usually need to be photocopied, faxed or printed out. Nevertheless, colour can still be an important and practical element of form design.

Colour can help users to read, understand and complete a form by emphasizing important elements, downplaying longer areas of text, and colour-coding labels or instructions. Colour is also a key part of brand recognition for a form provider. The simplest way of making a form part of a corporate identity, aside from including a logo, is to carry over the colour scheme. Optical scanning also requires the use of special drop-out colours that the scanner will not pick up (see p. 145 for more on this topic).

Colour should always be used on forms in a purposeful way. However, this does not mean that forms cannot be brightly coloured if this would make them appear friendlier, for example.

CMYK and RGB colour systems

The most common method of colour printing on paper is the four-colour process (also known as CMYK or process colour). Overprinting cyan *(C)*, magenta *(M)* and yellow *(Y)* inks together theoretically creates black, but the resulting colour is fairly weak, so a fourth layer of pure black *(K = Key)* is added. These colours are combined by using the halftone process, which turns the inks into tiny dots of colour, to produce a full range of shades.

On a computer display screen, colours are made from combinations of red, green and blue light *(RGB)*. All three colours together produce white.

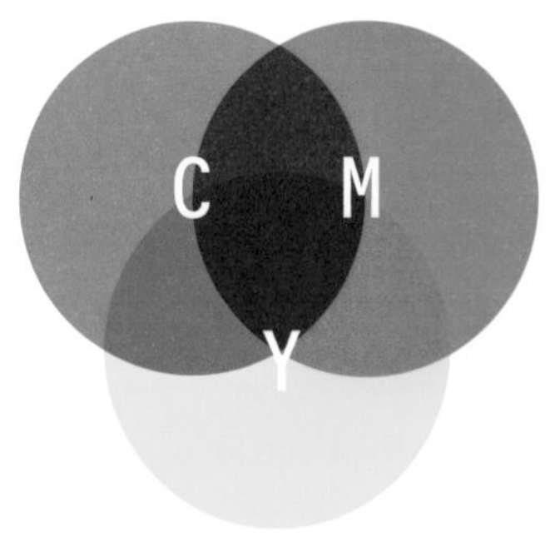

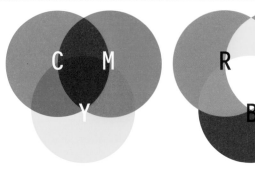

CMY *(subtractive colour mixing)*

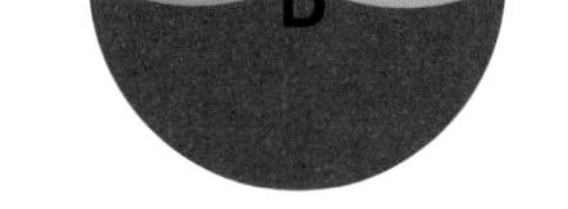

RGB *(additive colour mixing)*

Spot colours

CMYK is not the only method of colour printing: it is also possible to use spot colours. Among the most widely used spot colour systems are Pantone and HKS. For coloured text and solid blocks of colour, spot colours are better because they are not made up of halftone dots in the way that process colours are.

The top row shows the spot colour used in this book, Pantone 5757U, in several tints. The bottom row shows the same shades rendered in CMYK. The halftone dots of the CMYK version have an adverse effect on the sharpness of the text in particular.

Text

Pantone 5757U, 100%

Text

Pantone 5757U, 75%

Text

Pantone 5757U, 50%

Text

Pantone 5757U, 25%

Text

CMYK 10/0/70/60, 100%

Text

CMYK 10/0/70/60, 75%

Text

CMYK 10/0/70/60, 50%

Text

CMYK 10/0/70/60, 25%

Coloured text and fills

Coloured text appears lighter than a box filled with the same colour.

Pure cyan, which looks bright when used as a fill, makes text seem thin and hard to read. With the addition of 10% magenta, the text becomes more legible, but still rather weak. With 50% magenta both the text and the fill look fairly strong. Darker colours show up when used as fill, but text in the same shade looks almost black.

Lorem ipsum dolor sit amet, consectetur adipiscing elit. Nunc non bibendum ante. Etiam malesuada ullamcorper sem, eget accumsan orci congue ultrices. Nunc eu nunc eu justo.

CMYK 100/0/0/0

Lorem ipsum dolor sit amet, consectetur adipiscing elit. Nunc non bibendum ante. Etiam malesuada ullamcorper sem, eget accumsan orci congue ultrices. Nunc eu nunc eu justo.

CMYK 100/10/0/0

Lorem ipsum dolor sit amet, consectetur adipiscing elit. Nunc non bibendum ante. Etiam malesuada ullamcorper sem, eget accumsan orci congue ultrices. Nunc eu nunc eu justo.

CMYK 100/50/0/0

Lorem ipsum dolor sit amet, consectetur adipiscing elit. Nunc non bibendum ante. Etiam malesuada ullamcorper sem, eget accumsan orci congue ultrices. Nunc eu nunc eu justo.

CMYK 100/60/0/60

Halftone type

Halftone text is always problematic because the halftone dots make the edges of the type appear hazy or rough. The smaller the type, the more noticeable this effect is. At large point sizes, four-colour halftone type looks better than single-colour halftone. At small point sizes, both are poor. The red type is legible, mainly because the magenta layer is not halftone, but at 100%. The green type on the far right includes a 100% yellow layer, but it is so pale that the halftone dots of the other colour layers affect the type.

This effect is aggravated by the fact that forms are often printed on low-quality paper, on which a low screen ruling is usually employed.

Qual

Questions

Lorem ipsum dolor sit amet, consectetur adipiscing elit. Nunc non bibendum ante. Etiam malesuada ullamcorper sem, eget accumsan orci congue ultrices. Nunc eu nunc eu justo.

CMYK 0/0/0/45

Qual

Questions

Lorem ipsum dolor sit amet, consectetur adipiscing elit. Nunc non bibendum ante. Etiam malesuada ullamcorper sem, eget accumsan orci congue ultrices. Nunc eu nunc eu justo.

CMYK 40/30/30/0

Qual

Questions

Lorem ipsum dolor sit amet, consectetur adipiscing elit. Nunc non bibendum ante. Etiam malesuada ullamcorper sem, eget accumsan orci congue ultrices. Nunc eu nunc eu justo.

CMYK 0/100/40/0

Qual

Questions

Lorem ipsum dolor sit amet, consectetur adipiscing elit. Nunc non bibendum ante. Etiam malesuada ullamcorper sem, eget accumsan orci congue ultrices. Nunc eu nunc eu justo.

CMYK 30/20/100/0

White text on a coloured ground

White text works well against a spot colour ground. On a halftone ground, white text in a small point size becomes hard to read.

Black or dark-coloured text is generally better for forms. If the background colour is pale enough, it will still be legible after black and white photocopying.

Lorem ipsum dolor sit amet, consectetur elit. Nunc non bibendum ante. Etiam malesuad.

Fill
CMYK 100/10/0/0

Lorem ipsum dolor sit amet, consectetur elit. Nunc non bibendum ante. Etiam malesuad.

Fill
CMYK 60/6/0/0

Lorem ipsum dolor sit amet, consectetur elit. Nunc non bibendum ante. Etiam malesuad.

Fill
CMYK 30/20/100/0

Lorem ipsum dolor sit amet, consectetur elit. Nunc non bibendum ante. Etiam malesuad.

Fill
CMYK 30/20/100/0

Colour combinations

Colour combinations should be selected so that there is sufficient contrast between the shades of the text and the background.

Blue text on a dark blue ground may make a document difficult to copy, but also makes it difficult to read. Harsh contrasts such as red text on a blue or green ground create a dazzle effect that makes them very hard to read.

Lorem ipsum dolor sit amet, consectetur elit. Nunc non bibendum ante. Etiam malesuad.

Fill
CMYK 20/2/0/0

Type
CMYK 100/0/0/0

Lorem ipsum dolor sit amet, consectetur elit. Nunc non bibendum ante. Etiam malesuad.

Fill
CMYK 100/70/0/0

Type
CMYK 100/0/0/0

Lorem ipsum dolor sit amet, consectetur elit. Nunc non bibendum ante. Etiam malesuad.

Fill
CMYK 100/30/0/0

Type
CMYK 0/100/0/0

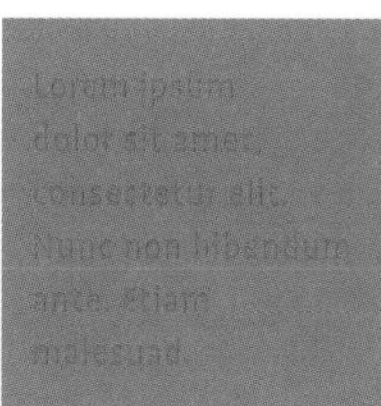

Lorem ipsum
dolor sit amet,
consectetur elit.
Nunc non bibendum
ante. Etiam
malesuad.

Fill
CMYK 75/5/100/0

Type
CMYK 100/0/0/0

Paper, format and printing

Paper forms are a two-dimensional medium with material properties. As for any other printed product, decisions must be made regarding the paper, format, printing method and processing. All of these affect the tactile and functional quality of the form and are an important part of the overall design.

The choice of paper, its structure, weight and surface, can give a form particular tactile qualities – it is a simple and elegant way to embody a particular style and perhaps even stir the emotions. In addition, paper used for forms sometimes needs to meet certain technical criteria, which can restrict the choice available.

As paper is to a printed form, the screen is to a digital form. The screen resolution, size, frame frequency and colour calibration are the physical properties that influence the display quality of digital forms. Unlike printed forms, however, these factors are far harder to control.

Paper permanence

Many forms are important documents that must be stored for long periods of time. There are two standards that regulate which types of paper can be described as permanent or age-resistant. The German DIN 6738 standard divides wood-free, wood-pulp and recycled papers into a range of lifespan categories, ranging from 'at least fifty years' to 'permanent'. The more rigorous ISO 9706 standard may only be applied to permanent paper made exclusively from cellulose. Wood-pulp or recycled papers are not eligible for this standard.

International standard for permanent paper: **ISO 9706**

International standard for age-resistant paper: **DIN 6738**

Selected paper types

The paper used for a form should be suitable for use with any type of writing instrument and, in most cases, suitable for use with inkjet and laser printers. Countless types of paper are available, both for standard use and for special purposes [→ Carbonless paper]. *Uncoated paper* has a natural feel and is easy to write on. At low weights it is relatively transparent. *Coated paper* has been coated with a substance to alter its weight, gloss, smoothness or opacity. Paper with a matt coating is particularly suitable for forms. *Bank paper* is high-quality uncoated paper, often watermarked, which has a prestigious look. *Bible paper* is lightweight but relatively opaque.

OCR use

If forms need to be optically scanned [→ Machine-readable forms: p. 144], the paper must meet special standards (DIN 6723/6724) of smoothness, uniformity and weight (80–120 g/m²).

Standard for paper suitable for OCR use: **DIN 6723/6724**

Carbonless paper

Carbonless copy paper makes it possible to write on several sheets at the same time. It is also known as *NCR paper (No Carbon Required)* or *non-carbon copy paper*. Its surface is coated with micro-encapsulated dye or ink (the donor layer) or with reactive clay (the receptor layer), which records the marks made on it. Form sets are made of multiple layers of pre-printed carbonless paper, and are designed to produce one or more copies of a completed form. For the top sheet of the form, plain uncoated paper can also be used.

Carbonless layers and typical weights

CB *coated back* *54–95 g/m^2*	Top sheet Donor layer on the reverse.
CFB *coated front and back* *45–60 g/m^2*	Middle sheet Receptor layer on the front, donor layer on the back.
CF *coated front* *51–170 g/m^2*	Under sheet Receptor layer on the front.
SC *self-contained* *53 g/m^2*	Under sheet For form sets with an uncoated top sheet: both donor and receptor layers on front.
SC CB *self-contained coated back* *58 g/m^2*	Middle sheet For form sets with an uncoated top sheet: both donor and receptor layers on front, donor layer on back.

Multi-part carbonless form sets

Top sheet CB
Middle sheet CFB
Under sheet CF

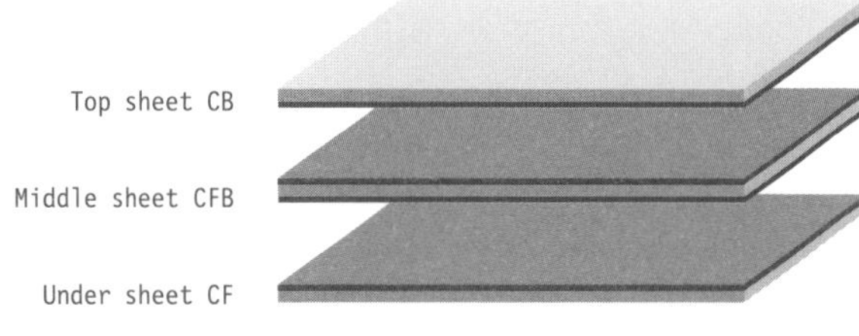

3-part form set

Top sheet
Under sheet SC

2-part form set
with uncoated top sheet

Top sheet
Middle sheet SC CB
Middle sheet CFB
Under sheet CF

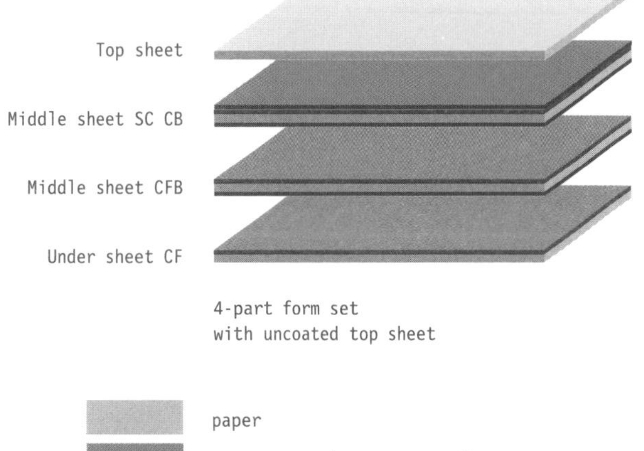

4-part form set
with uncoated top sheet

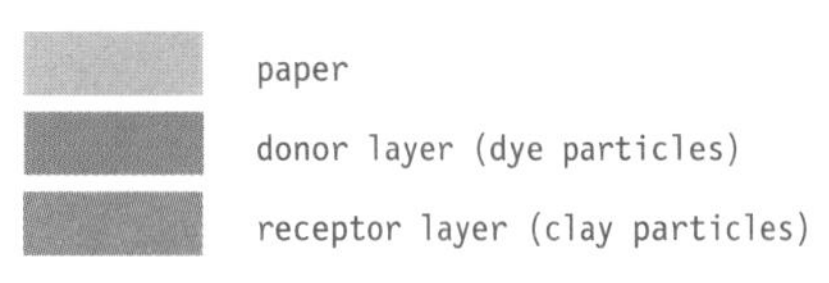

paper
donor layer (dye particles)
receptor layer (clay particles)

Coloured paper

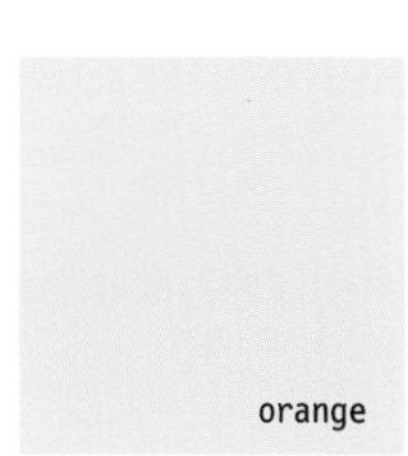

Carbonless copy paper is available in white and a small range of standard colours. These provide a simple way to differentiate between forms and copies for the purposes of distribution and filing. At the same time, these colours are often seen as an embodiment of bureaucracy and so should be used with care.

Paper formats

The ISO A series is the recognized standard format for paper in the UK and much of the rest of the world. A4 paper is the most familiar size. All office stationery, envelopes, files, printers, etc. are designed around it.

Beginning with A0 as the largest, each format in the A series is determined by dividing the preceding size in two along its longest side. All the A formats are based on the same aspect ratio of the square root of 2.

In the US and Canada, standard paper sizes traditionally include letter, legal, ledger and tabloid. Letter is the standard for office use.

If office use is not a priority, other more unusual formats may be used to give the form a distinctive look.

Continuous form paper has its own special formats, which are usually measured in inches.

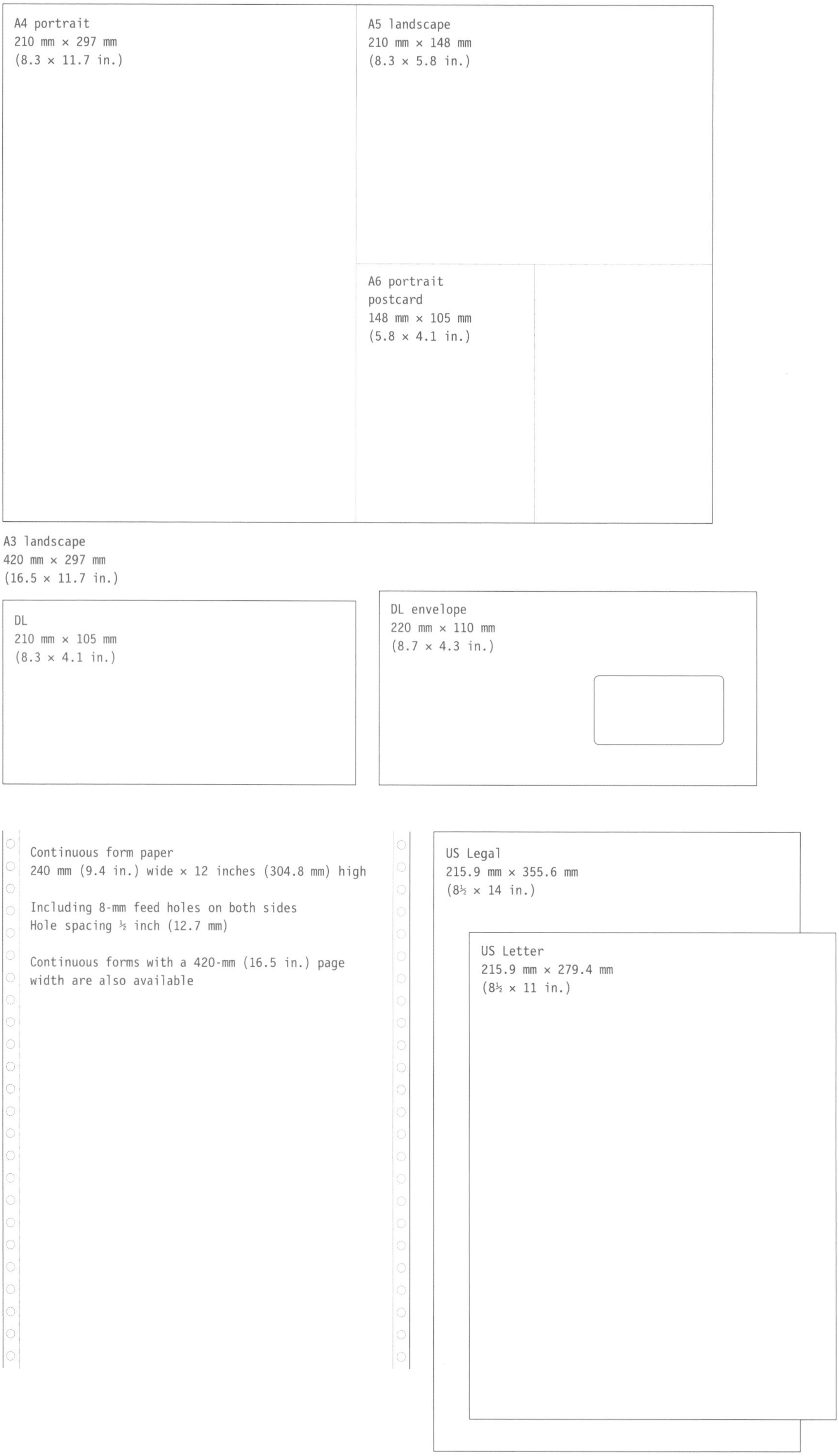

A4 portrait
210 mm × 297 mm
(8.3 × 11.7 in.)

A5 landscape
210 mm × 148 mm
(8.3 × 5.8 in.)

A6 portrait
postcard
148 mm × 105 mm
(5.8 × 4.1 in.)

A3 landscape
420 mm × 297 mm
(16.5 × 11.7 in.)

DL
210 mm × 105 mm
(8.3 × 4.1 in.)

DL envelope
220 mm × 110 mm
(8.7 × 4.3 in.)

Continuous form paper
240 mm (9.4 in.) wide × 12 inches (304.8 mm) high

Including 8-mm feed holes on both sides
Hole spacing ½ inch (12.7 mm)

Continuous forms with a 420-mm (16.5 in.) page width are also available

US Legal
215.9 mm × 355.6 mm
(8½ × 14 in.)

US Letter
215.9 mm × 279.4 mm
(8½ × 11 in.)

Printing

When it comes to forms, 'printing' can mean quite different things, so it is important to distinguish clearly between these.

Pre-printing	The printing of a form in large quantities to be filled in later. Usually done with offset printing.
Print-out	Copy of an individual form, either completed on screen or uncompleted, produced with a laser or inkjet printer.
Overprinting	Using a laser, inkjet or dot matrix printer to print responses onto a pre-printed form.

Printing methods

The choice of printing method depends on the quantity and quality required. Other important issues are where the form is to be printed and how it is to be filled out.

For pre-printed forms, it's important to consider whether any large areas of colour or special coatings on the paper could cause problems when photocopying or laser printing. In such cases, the choice of paper and printing method should be tested first.

Offset printing	Commercial lithographic printing that produces high-quality results on most paper types, in monochrome or colour. Fast and convenient for high print runs. Sheet-fed offset uses individual sheets of paper. Web-fed offset uses paper in a long roll called a web. This is only worthwhile for very high print quantities, e.g. when pre-printing continuous forms.
Laser printing	Suitable for single-colour printing of small quantities or individual forms. Good quality and moderate speed. Flexible and available in most offices.
Digital printing	A similar process to laser printing, but faster and better suited to both colour printing and high print runs. Not usually possible in offices, but available at specialist print shops.
Inkjet printing	Relatively slow and expensive. For high-quality printing, special paper is required. Very widely available and used for occasional print-outs by private users.
Dot matrix printing	Noisy, slow and poor quality. Nonetheless, still common for overprinting forms, because carbonless paper can easily be used with this printer type.

Other processes

Once printed, forms can be subjected to additional processes including scoring, folding, glueing, perforating or punching.

Form pads	A pad of individual forms, which can be torn off one by one. Often available with pre-punched holes.
Form sets	Form sets consist of two or more stacked layers of carbonless paper glued together at the edge, so several sheets can be filled in at once.
Continuous forms	Continuous forms are designed for EDP use (electronic data processing). After printing, the long strip of paper is punched with feed holes, perforated along the edges and across, and fanfolded (in a zig-zag fashion). Continuous forms can also be produced as multi-part sets.
Numbering and personalization	With automatic numbering, every copy of a form can be marked with a sequential serial number. This can be done during printing or as a separate stage. As part of the laser printing process, individual forms can also be personalized with the user's name, address and any other information that is already available.

Machine-readable forms

The demands of digitization are the Achilles heel of modern paper forms. Because so many working processes are now entirely computerized, the data gathered by forms must also be converted into digital format. Inputting information by hand is laborious, time-consuming, expensive and can create errors, although it is often necessary for individual forms and cannot be avoided. For forms that are filled in very large quantities, several types of scanning technology are available. Items such as questionnaires, banking forms and lottery tickets are scanned by machine using readers of different kinds.

Unfortunately, the design of forms and the way they are filled must fit the requirements of reading equipment. The most widely used machine-reading techniques and the demands that these make on the form design are discussed on the page opposite. The methods differ in the way in which they convert characters that humans can read into digital data, and in the kinds of data they can understand. It must be established at an early stage if a form needs to be machine-readable, because adapting it later is expensive.

Overview of machine reading

Electromagnetic reading is the oldest technique, and was developed by banks for processing cheques. The equipment recognizes characters by their magnetic signal. These are printed in magnetic ink or toner in a special typeface that can also be read by human eyes.

In optical reading, a scanner reads the marks and recognizes their position, sequence or shape. OMR and OCR are most commonly used for forms, and the data they scan can also be manually input.

Electromagnetic reading

MICR *(Magnetic Ink Character Recognition)*

This recognizes a hidden sequence of magnetic impulses in the text.

1234567890

Optical reading

Barcode reader

Numbers and letters are encoded into a horizontal series of lines or a two-dimensional area of dots which can be scanned by a barcode reader.

OMR *(Optical Mark Recognition)*

These scanners recognize the positions of marks.

Enlarged image

OCR *(Optical Character Recognition)*

These scanners recognize printed and handwritten characters by their shape.

100 300 43 00 Abc

0 1 2 3 4 5 6 7 8 9

OMR – Optical mark reading

OMR scanners are used to read forms in which information is presented as marks in different positions, such as lottery tickets, ballot papers or questionnaires. They can scan at speeds of up to 7,000 sheets per hour and the error rate is very low.

So that only the marked responses are registered, the form is printed in what are known as drop-out colours, which the scanner will not pick up.

The type of OMR scanner also determines the shape of the response boxes, which may be squares, circles or ovals, and how the answers should be marked. The form should specify whether the boxes should be completely filled in or simply struck through with a horizontal or vertical line.

Question A 1 2 3 4 5 6
Question B 1 2 3 4 5 6

Question A 2 3 4 5 6
Question B 1 2 3 5 6

Question A 1 2 3 4 5 6
Question B 1 2 3 4 5 6

For OMR scanners that use an infrared reading head, the marks must made with a pencil or a black pen. Any shade can be used as a drop-out colour, with the exception of black.

Enlarged image

For OMR scanners that use a red-light reading head, marks can be made in any colour except red. This restricts the list of possible drop-out colours to red, orange and yellow.

Enlarged image

OCR – Optical character recognition

These scanners recognize letters and figures by their shapes. Early versions could only recognize special OCR typefaces. Today they can recognize almost all typefaces, as well as handwritten letters and figures.

OCR scanners may be single-font, multi-font (able to read a specified range of type) or omni-font (able to read almost any typeface).

In this case too, drop-out colours must be used for text fields, explanatory text and backgrounds. Due to the high sensitivity of the scanner, pale drop-out colours are required, and these need to meet high demands in terms of purity and evenness.

In any case, the guidelines for the scanner should be followed, and it should always be controlled with the aid of special testing equipment that is suitable for the chosen printing method.

ABCDEFGHIJKLMNOPQRSTUVWXYZ
abcdefghijklmnopqrstuvwxyz
124567890

OCR-A typeface

ABCDEFGHIJKLMNOPQRSTUVWXYZ
abcdefghijklmnopqrstuvwxyz
124567890

OCR-B typeface

ABCDEFGHIJKLMNOPQRSTUVWXYZ
abcdefghijklmnopqrstuvwxyz
124567890

Normal sans serif typeface

ABCDEFGHIJKLMNOPQRSTUVWXYZ
abcdefghijklmnopqrstuvwxyz
124567890

Normal serif typeface

Because people do not usually write in individual letters, but in whole words, they must be made to do so on the form. Character dividers create small boxes to keep each letter separate, allowing the scanner to register them correctly. The dividers are usually accompanied by a written instruction, such as 'Please write in the boxes provided.'

Alternatively, text fields can be scanned as images and displayed on a screen.

0123456789
abcdefghijklmnopqrst
ABCDEFGHIJKLMNOPQRST

Grids and modules

There are two reasons why forms should be designed around grids, columns and modules.

Firstly, forms can be designed more uniformly, systematically and easily with columns and baseline grids than without them. Repeated structures of this kind also give the forms a recognizable look and help to prevent irrelevance. Defining the text area is the first step to defining the basic grid, and this in turn provides the basis for all other measurements, including column width and line spacing.

Secondly, a baseline grid pattern ensures equal distances between all the text fields, which is necessary if the form is to be filled in by typewriter or matrix printer.

Text area

The text area defines the printing space and the margins of the form. In book design, the text area is always designed as facing pages, and every effort is made to ensure a balanced or evocative relationship between the printed and the unprinted areas.

Forms, on the other hand, are usually single pages, and so the text area has no mirror image. The margins are mainly determined by practical considerations such as the minimum measurements for filing, copying or printing, as well as the optimum use of space.

It is not necessarily the case that the text area should be as big as possible, but a well-defined and generous text area can certainly be an advantage to a form.

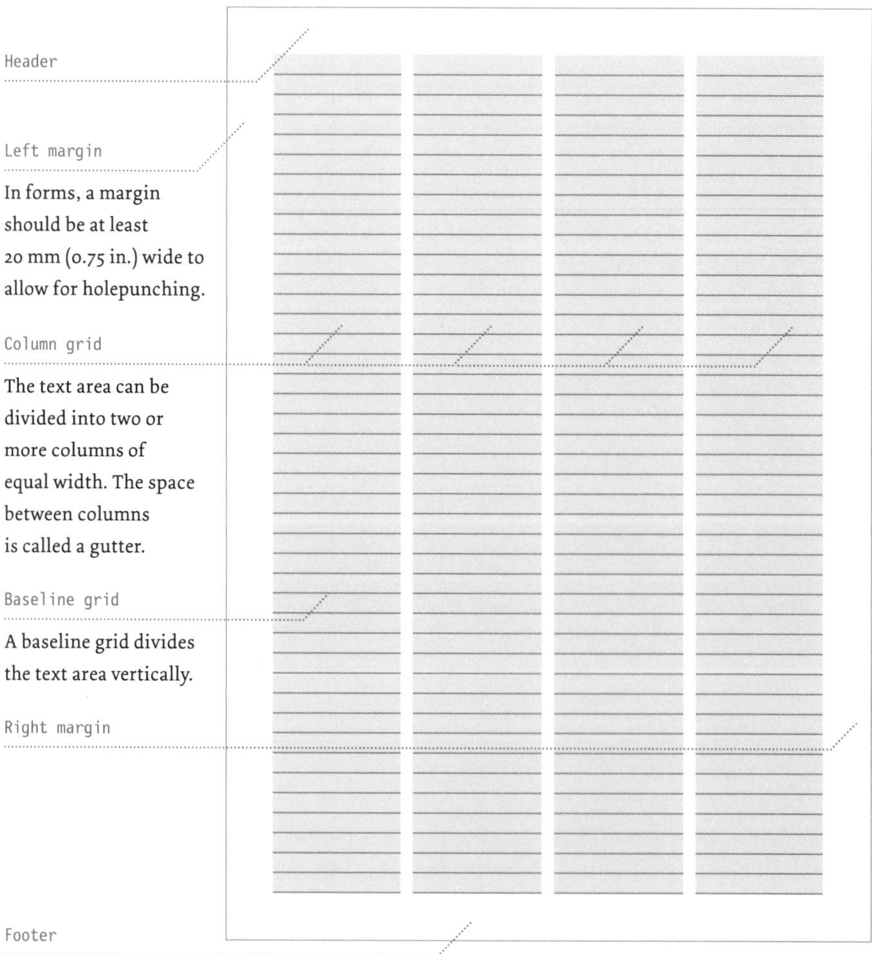

Header
Left margin
In forms, a margin should be at least 20 mm (0.75 in.) wide to allow for holepunching.
Column grid
The text area can be divided into two or more columns of equal width. The space between columns is called a gutter.
Baseline grid
A baseline grid divides the text area vertically.
Right margin
Footer

Baseline grids

The baseline grid creates a uniform gap between all the lines in a text. Each line on the grid is a baseline.

In books, the grid ensures that when pages are printed on both sides, the text on one side does not show through and interrupt the text on the other.

In forms, the baseline grid ensures that the lines of type are evenly spaced. This makes it easier to fill the form in with a typewriter or keyboard, and also makes it easy to design and produce template documents, e.g. in Word or other software.

The baseline grid determines the height of the text fields.

For text that runs over several lines, especially if it is in a smaller point size than the main text, a standard baseline grid tends to be too wide. The solution is either to not align small type to the baseline grid, or to divide the chosen baseline grid into smaller units, based on the size of the overall document grid. The examples illustrated show three ways of doing this with an 18-point baseline grid.

Single baseline grid

The text fields are set with a leading of 18 points, but this baseline grid is too wide for the text above. The text in the marginal column is therefore aligned only with the first line on the grid.

Heading

Double-line spacing works well for the text fields below, but is rather too wide for running text. The lines are too far apart and lose their cohesion. Either this text should not be aligned to the baseline grid, or a narrower grid should be chosen.

First name

Surname

House no., street

Text in marginal columns is often in smaller type. The baseline grid is far too wide for type of this size, so this text is not aligned with the grid.

Grid divided by two

Here the main grid is halved, so the running text is on a 9-point grid (green lines). It looks better, but the text is a little cramped.

Heading

The spacing for the text fields below is good, but for the running text, this line spacing is too tight and the type has no room to breathe. Either this text should not be aligned with the baseline grid, or a wider grid should be chosen.

First name

Surname

House no., street

Text in marginal columns is often in smaller type. Dividing by two produces an ideal grid for this text.

Grid divided by three

Division into three gives more flexibility. The text in the marginal column and the main text are set on every second line, while the text fields are determined by every third line.

Heading

The spacing for the text fields below is good, and for the running text this spacing is ideal. The running text is easy to read, and the text fields are wide enough.

First name

Surname

House no., street

Text in marginal columns is often in smaller type. This line spacing is adequate.

Typewriter settings

Even though forms nowadays are rarely filled in by typewriter, it is advisable to arrange the baseline grid according to the same standard line spacings, which are also used by Word. The 1.5-line spacing is the most practical of these options.

First name John
Surname Smith
House no., street 20 High Street

Single-line spacing 12 pt = 4.23 mm

First name John

Surname Smith

House no., street 20 High Street

One-and-a-half line spacing 18 pt = 6.35 mm

First name John

Surname Smith

House no., street 20 High Street

Double-line spacing 24 pt = 8.46 mm

Column grids

Many elements have to be arranged on a form. If you need to design more than one type of form, it is easier to keep the layout uniform and systematic if the grid is divided into two or more columns. The more columns there are, the more flexible the layout will be. Depending on the number of columns, the form may be symmetrical or asymmetrical.

Layout elements such as blocks of text, questions and text fields can be extended across one or more columns. For example, an introductory text may cover three columns, questions just one, text fields two, and there can also be a marginal column for explanations and instructions.

There are therefore endless ways of dividing up a form. These illustrations show sample grids with one, two, three, four and five columns. Of course, you could design a form with even more, but the advisability of this depends on the complexity of the content and the overall size of the page.

The decision on how many columns to use will also depend on the connection between questions and text fields. If they are above or below one another, as in examples 1 and 2, fewer columns are needed. But if questions and text fields are alongside one another, as in the remaining examples, the divisions need to be smaller so that questions and text fields can be allotted columns of different widths.

Another feature of the layout is the gutters between columns, as these too influence the effectiveness of the form. A wide gutter makes each column seem independent, whereas a smaller one suggests more cohesion. At the same time, the gutter needs to be wide enough to separate the blocks of text clearly.

Example 6 takes us a step further. In addition to the vertical gutters, this form is also divided horizontally into a number of separate fields. The horizontal gutter between the fields is equal to a single line space. This allows for even more possible layouts with strictly defined spaces for the individual elements.

1: Single-column grid

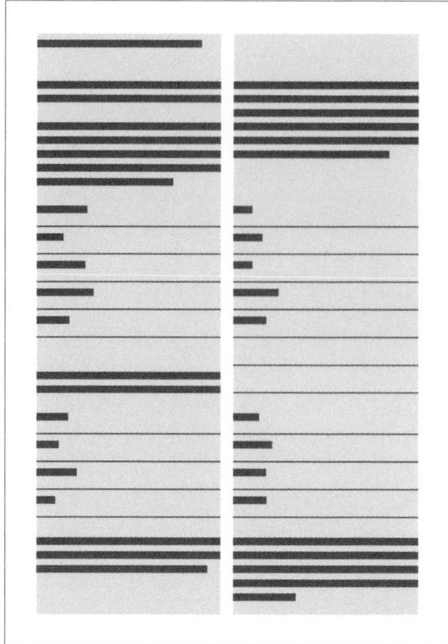

2: Two-column grid

3: Three-column grid

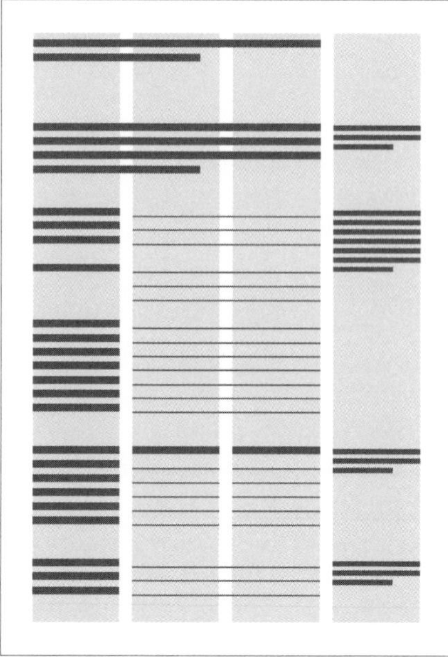

4: Four-column grid

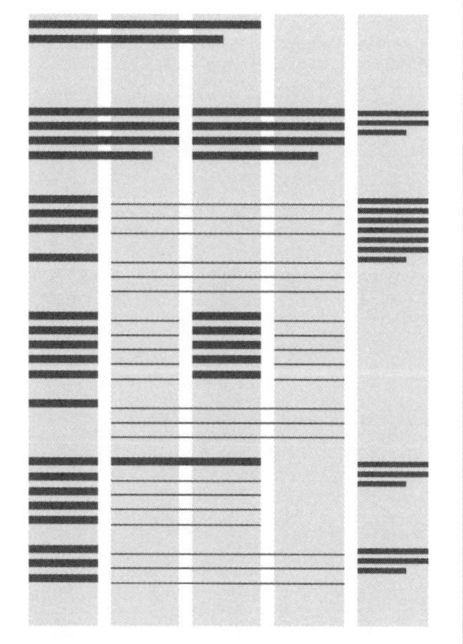

5: Five-column grid

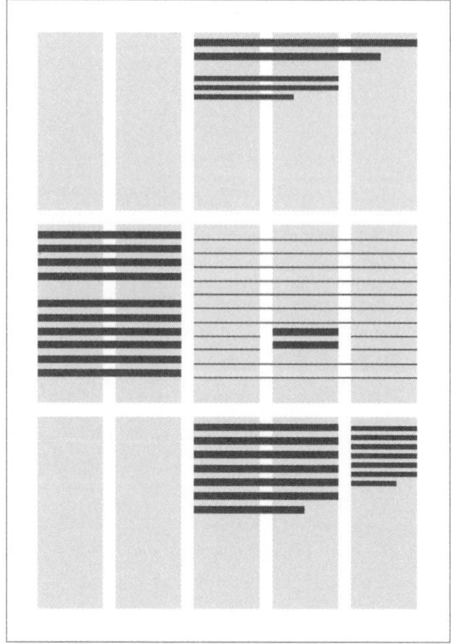

6: Five-column grid with fifteen fields

This is an example of how to design modules to accommodate individual elements and repeated sections such as personal details, account number and signature. These fit like building blocks into the columns of the grid.

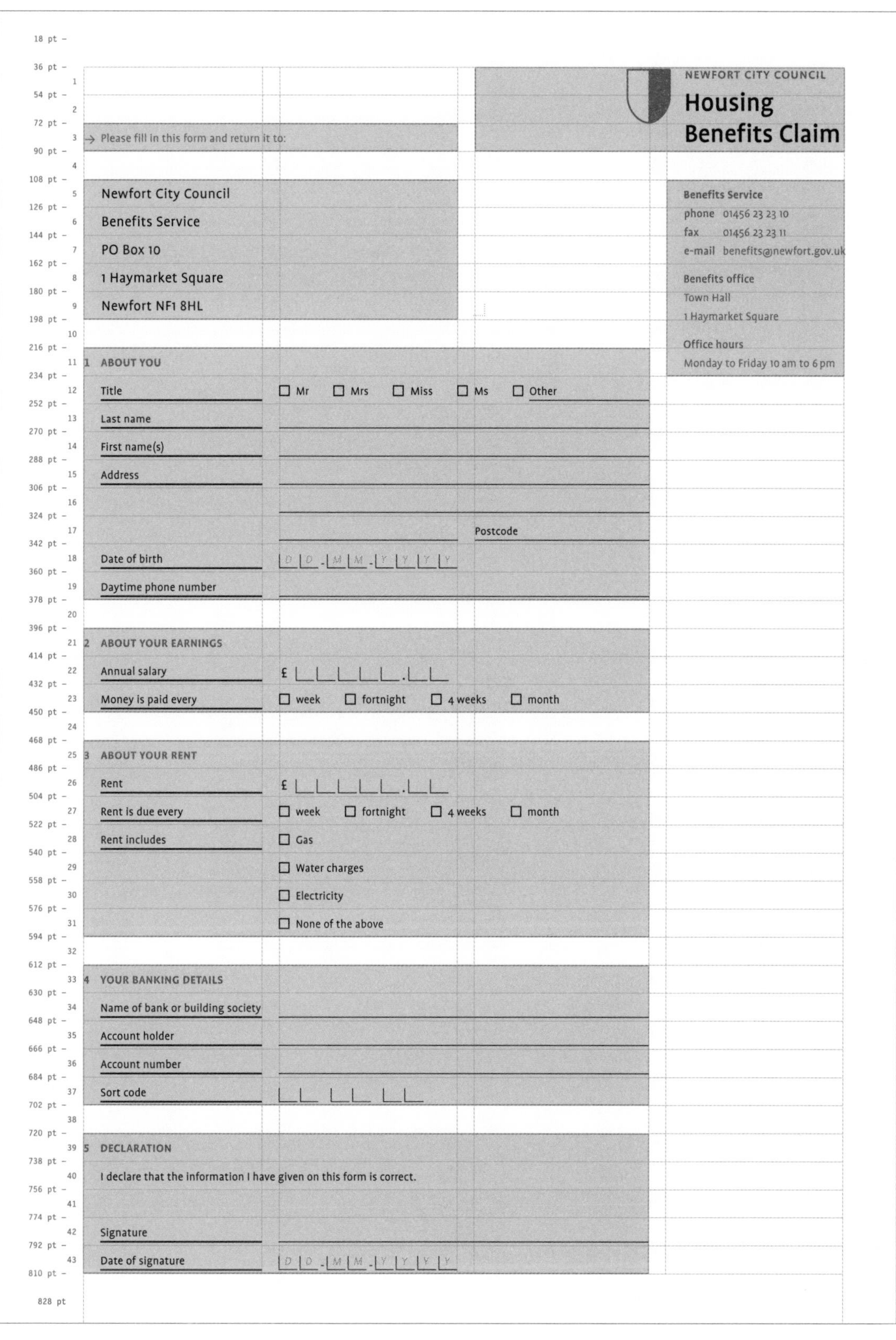

NEWFORT CITY COUNCIL

Housing Benefits Claim

→ Please fill in this form and return it to:

Newfort City Council
Benefits Service
PO Box 10
1 Haymarket Square
Newfort NF1 8HL

Benefits Service
phone 01456 23 23 10
fax 01456 23 23 11
e-mail benefits@newfort.gov.uk

Benefits office
Town Hall
1 Haymarket Square

Office hours
Monday to Friday 10 am to 6 pm

1 ABOUT YOU

Title ☐ Mr ☐ Mrs ☐ Miss ☐ Ms ☐ Other

Last name

First name(s)

Address

Postcode

Date of birth D D - M M - Y Y Y Y

Daytime phone number

2 ABOUT YOUR EARNINGS

Annual salary £ _ _ _ _ _ . _ _

Money is paid every ☐ week ☐ fortnight ☐ 4 weeks ☐ month

3 ABOUT YOUR RENT

Rent £ _ _ _ _ _ . _ _

Rent is due every ☐ week ☐ fortnight ☐ 4 weeks ☐ month

Rent includes ☐ Gas
☐ Water charges
☐ Electricity
☐ None of the above

4 YOUR BANKING DETAILS

Name of bank or building society

Account holder

Account number

Sort code

5 DECLARATION

I declare that the information I have given on this form is correct.

Signature

Date of signature D D - M M - Y Y Y Y

Layout choices

Starting with your chosen grid, you can begin to lay out the basic elements and modules in a design. This can then be used for all forms for the same provider, ensuring instant recognizability and making the forms easier to use. Almost every form can be divided into three areas: information for the user, interaction (i.e. the fields that need to be filled) and administrative information about the form itself.

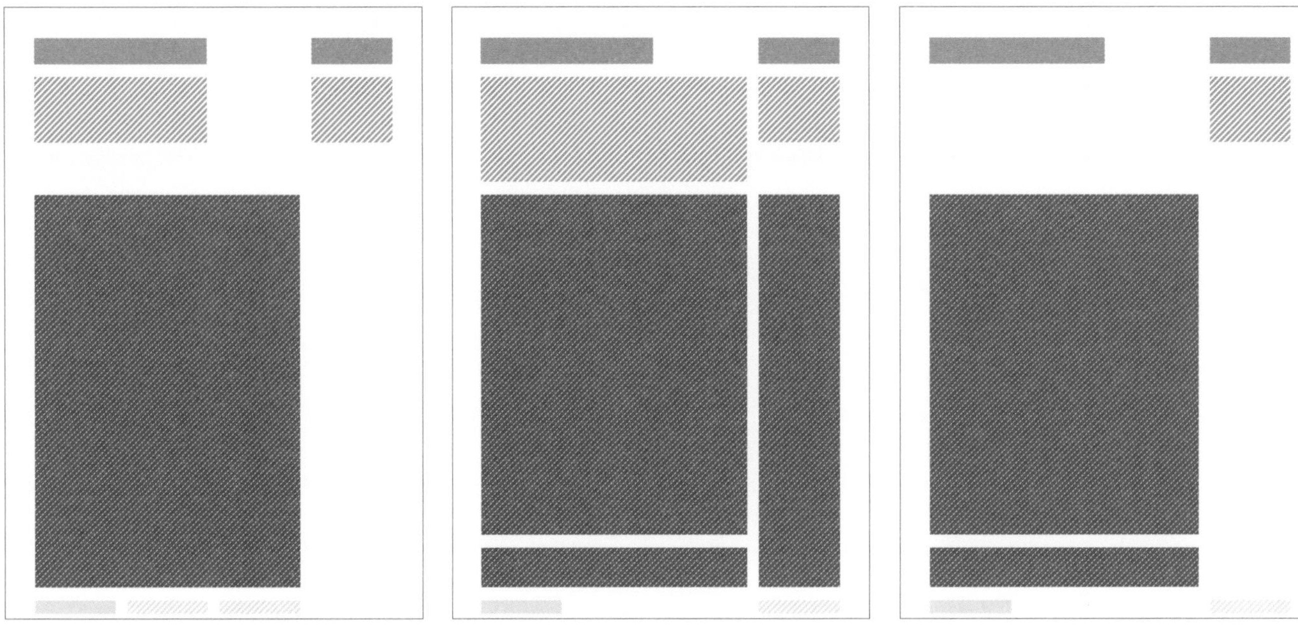

Basic layouts

The illustrations above and below each show three variations on the same layout. The aim is not to give every form exactly the same structure – that is virtually impossible since each form serves a different purpose and has different content – but the basic layout needs to be the same. This can be achieved by using a system of fixed and variable fields.

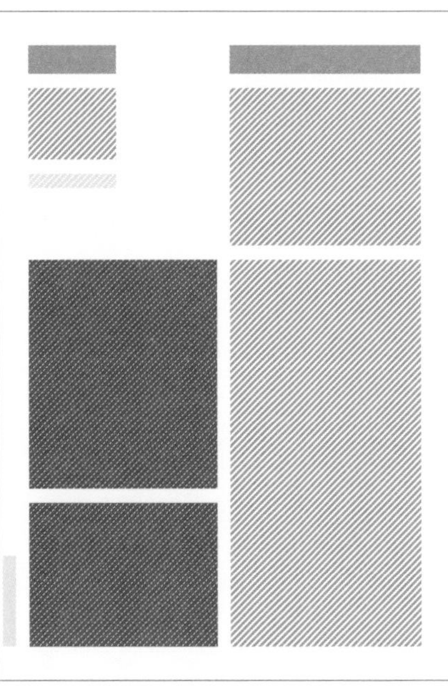

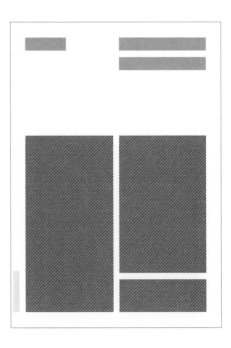

Layout options

Here is a sample layout that includes clearly defined fields for different elements.

Information

Elements that convey information: heading, address, contact details and general notes.

Interaction

This is where interaction between the user and the provider takes place.

It makes sense to subdivide this field into general questions that are repeated on most forms, questions that are specific to this particular form, and instructions and/or explanations.

Administration

These are the less important elements aimed at the form providers (form label, serial number, etc.).

Hierarchy

In order to keep the layout flexible, you need to distinguish between elements that feature on every form and those that are optional. It is also important to decide whether their position and size are to be fixed or flexible.

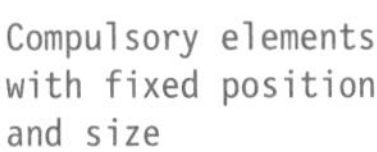

Compulsory elements with fixed position and size

Optional elements with fixed position and size

Optional elements with flexible position and size

Visual frameworks

The visual framework gives the form its overall look. There are only four basic ways of constructing this graphic framework: using cells, frames, colour fields, and horizontal lines. These four basic approaches are illustrated here and show the varied range of styles that are possible, even when the contents are similar.

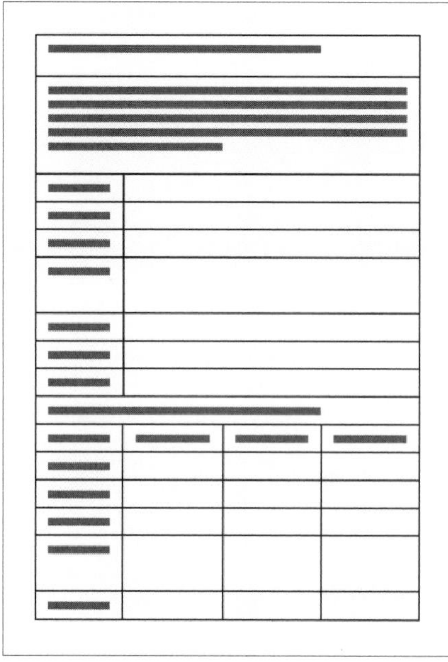

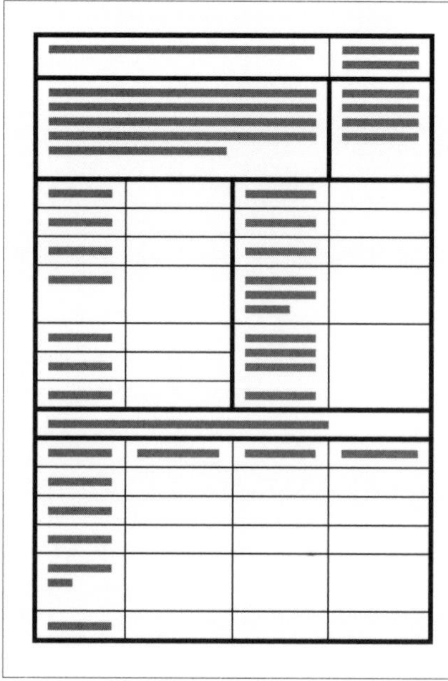

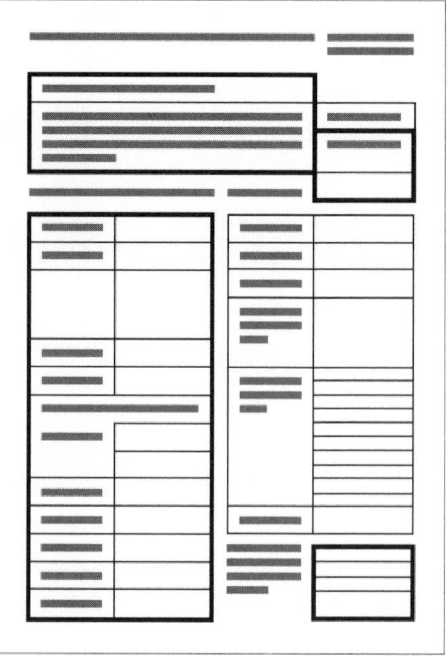

Cells

These forms are based on cellular tables, with the empty cells constituting the text fields. The form can be divided up by changing the weight of the cell borders and by subdividing it into individual tables. The effect is very neat, and also very unified. A lot of information can be fitted in here, because even if the cells are full and the gaps are small, the separation remains very clear.

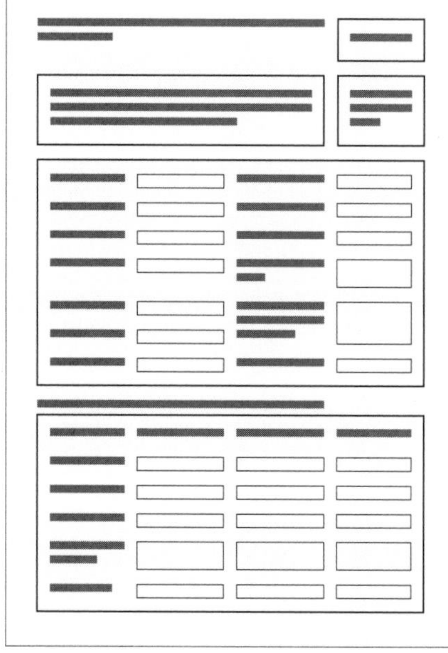

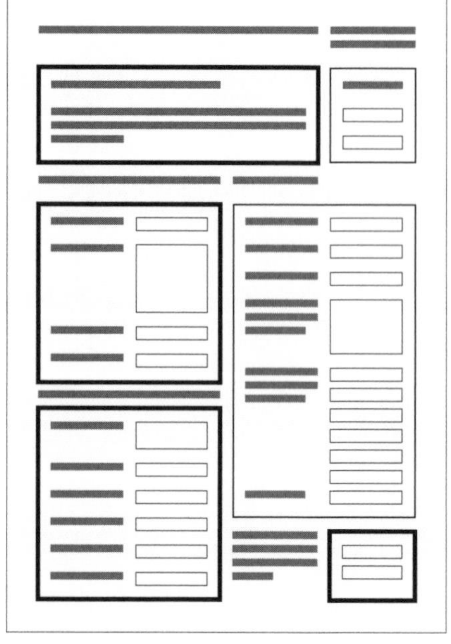

Frames

These examples consist of multiple frames which themselves constitute the text fields. The form can be divided up by using frames of different line weights, but a relatively large amount of space is required because every frame needs its own space around it. The individual fields can also look a little bit lost and insecure on the page.

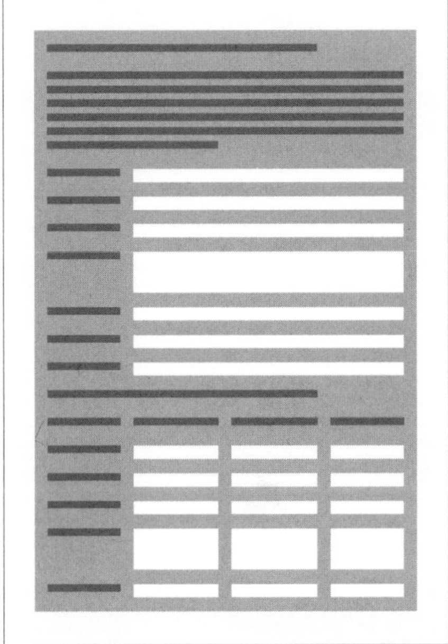
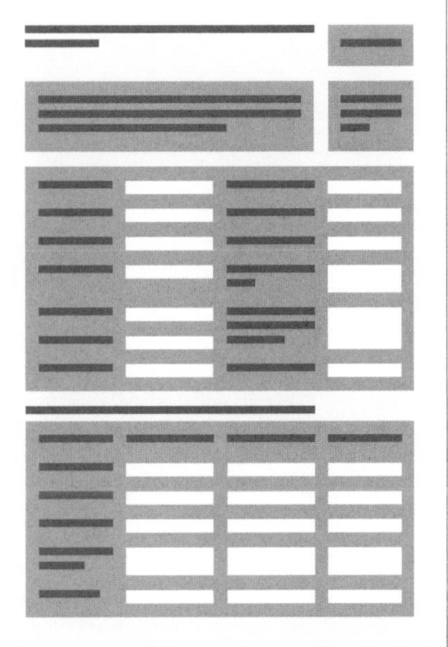
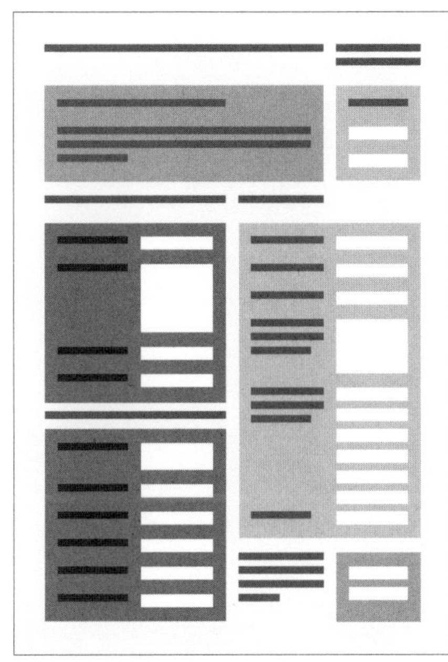

Colour fields

In these coloured boxes, the text fields are gaps in the shading. Division into several distinct areas gives the form structure, and the areas themselves are given differently tinted backgrounds. The text fields stand out because they are in stark contrast to the filled areas that surround them, but legibility is often affected by the background colour.

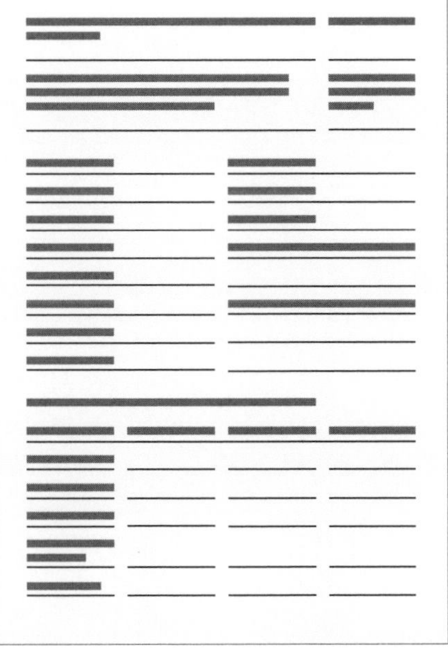

Lines

This style of form is based on horizontal lines. Different weights of line are used to define the text fields and divide the form into different areas. The user's eye is thus guided line by line, and all the emphasis is on horizontality, which creates a light and open effect. However, this rigid ordering also requires a particularly clear structuring of the content.

2.2

Micro-level design

Style and punctuation rules

→ See also the style guides in the bibliography on page 319

The following four pages give a brief overview of style and punctuation rules that can be applied not only to forms but to texts of any kind. While many points can be endlessly debated, the most important thing is to ensure that the text reads smoothly and the meaning is clear. Consistency is often the key. Style and punctuation rules vary between English-speaking countries, so consult a style guide if necessary.

Word spaces

As well as the standard word space, narrower spaces are also available in most proportional typefaces.

Standard word space

This is produced by hitting the space bar.

Normal spaces between words look like this.

Thin space

This narrow space can be used where a normal space would create too wide a gap, or to prevent punctuation marks from touching.

((for keeping punctuation marks separate))

25° C

Hyphens and dashes

Three types of dashes are commonly used:
- *hyphen*
– *en dash*
— *em dash*

A hyphen should not be used where an en dash would be more appropriate. The em dash is used less frequently than the other two, particularly in UK style.

Hyphen

This is the shortest form of dash and is used in compound words and to create word breaks at the end of lines.

21st-century art, a thirty-year-old woman, stainless-steel plating

Word-processing and DTP software can automatically create hyphen-ation at the end of lines.

It also appears in website URLs, but should not be confused with the underscore (_) or tilde (~).

www.the-form-book.com/~borries/style_rules.html

En dash

This is longer than a hyphen and shorter than an em dash. It is used as follows:

- hyphen
– en dash
— em dash

– to separate a parenthetical phrase.

The en dash – named after the standard width of the letter n – is commonly used to separate parenthetical phrases like the one above in UK-style text. In this context it is set with a space on each side.

The em dash—named after the standard width of the letter m—is used to separate parenthetical phrases in US-style text. It is set without spaces.

– to link two words of equal importance, with the meaning 'to' or 'and'. It is set without spaces.

a north–south axis
the US–Mexico border
The London–Paris service runs from 6 a.m. to 11 p.m. every day.

– to link the elements of an inclusive range of dates, numbers or alphabetically ordered items. In this case, too, it is set without spaces.

2005–2012	*but* from 1990 to 2000	*not* from 1990–2000
129–131 Palace Road		pages 12–17 inclusive
Aardvark–Zebra		23. 9. 2010–1. 11. 2011

– to introduce items in a list, as an alternative to a bullet point (•). In this case, it is usually followed by one or two spaces.

Please include copies of the following documents:
– driving licence
– birth certificate
– full UK passport

– as a minus symbol (although some typefaces include a separate minus symbol). Note the different spacing in the two examples.

1000 – 9 = 991
The average winter temperature was –5° C.

Term	Usage	Examples
Slash Also known as the stroke or solidus, this symbol is used for joining or dividing names, numbers and terms.	It is often used to divide pairs or lists of alternatives. In these cases, it takes the place of the word 'or'.	either/or his/her London/New York/Sydney I can/cannot attend this meeting (delete as applicable).
	When used with years, it indicates the last part of one year and the first part of another.	the 1998/99 tax year Winter 2010/11
	It is also used in numerical dates, especially in US style.	06/08/99 04/24/10
Quotation marks Also referred to as 'quotes', these are used in many contexts. Be sure to use curved (or 'smart') quotation marks, rather than the straight variety.	Right Single quotation marks are most commonly used in UK-style text. Double quotation marks are more common in the US.	'Single quotation marks' "Double quotation marks"
	For quotes within quotes, use double quotation marks within single quotation marks, and vice versa.	'Single quotes with "double quotes" used inside' "Double quotes with 'single quotes' used inside"
	Wrong The following should not be used. Check your software preference settings if need be.	"Vertical double quotes" 'Vertical single quotes' \`Accents´ «French-style guillemets» ”Quote marks that curve the wrong way“
Apostrophe Take care: this is often used incorrectly.	Apostrophes are used to indicate contractions.	You don't, she can't, he wouldn't, they shouldn't
	They are also used to indicate possession.	Susan's car The company's recruitment policy The managers' bonuses
	They are not used to indicate plurals (the so-called 'greengrocer's apostrophe').	
	Do not use the straight or vertical apostrophe if a curved (or 'smart') apostrophe is available.	Don't use a vertical apostrophe like this one.
Full stop (period), question mark, exclamation mark, comma, colon, semicolon	All of these should be followed by a single space. (It is a common error to use two spaces at the end of a sentence.) There should never be a space before them.	Use a space after a full stop. What about after question marks? Yes, and exclamation marks too! The same rule applies to other punctuation marks: commas are also followed by a single space; colons and semicolons likewise.
Units of measurement	Leave a space between the figure and the unit. In UK style, most units are written without a full stop, with the exception of 'in.' for inches.	27 cm 4 km 25 kg 11 lb 9 in. 150 ft
	In US style, full stops (periods) are generally used.	11 lb. 150 ft.
Titles	In UK style, personal titles have no full stop.	Mr Mrs Ms Dr
	In US style, a full stop (period) is always used.	Mr. Mrs. Ms. Dr.
Brackets	Use brackets (properly called parentheses) with caution, because they can make text look cluttered. Square brackets are used for two main purposes: (1) where you need a set of brackets within another set, and (2) where explanatory text is needed within a quotation.	Too many brackets can (in my opinion) make text hard to read (they interrupt it [the flow of the text] too much).

Special symbols

Percentage symbol (%)

Do not add a space between the numeral and the symbol.

62% of forms were completed correctly and returned; 27% were completed incorrectly; 11% were not returned.

Currency symbols

These precede the sum that they refer to. Do not add a space between the symbol and the numeral.

Sums over £100 and under £500
$345.00
€1,455.00

Hash symbol (#)

Also known as the number sign or pound sign (US only), this is not used in UK style. In US usage it can be used in place of the abbreviation 'no.'.

Issue #3 in a series of 12

Multiplication symbol

A specially designed multiplication symbol should be used, not a lower-case x.

Don't use an x in place of the × sign.

Punctuation of numbers

A comma is used to separate thousands. Years have no comma, however.

1,303
45,233,288
in the year 2018

Decimals are indicated with a full stop. Many European languages use a comma in place of a decimal point so be aware of this issue with multilingual forms.

0.126
Jackpot prize £1,501,274.82

Telephone numbers

These are easier to read if the figures are separated into groups.

In UK style, phone numbers are generally separated into groups with word spaces. Area codes or country codes may be placed in brackets.

with area code	*with international code*
01456 798 579	+44 (0)1456 798 579
(01456) 798 579	(+44) (0)1456 798 579

In US style, phone numbers are generally written with hyphens between the groups of figures.

with area code	*with international code*
800-555-1234	1-800-555-1234
(800) 555-1234	(1-800) 555-1234

Postal codes

UK postcodes have between five and seven characters, divided by a word space. They are always placed last in an address. Letters should be in caps, and figures should be lining. If only non-lining figures are available, small caps may look neater.

NF3 4ZT
WC1V 7QX

In the US, ZIP codes have five digits and are preceded by a two-letter state abbreviation. Extended ZIP codes have five digits, a hyphen, and an additional four digits.

CA 97123
NY 14593-2912

Dates

In the UK and most other English-speaking countries, dates are generally given in the order day–month–year. Numerical dates are separated by full stops.

5 November 2010
5.11.10

In the US, dates are given in the order month–day–year (note the use of the comma). Numerical dates are separated by slashes. To avoid confusion, it may be better to write out the month, either in full or in abbreviated form.

November 5, 2010
11/5/10

Times

In UK style, hours and minutes are usually divided with a full stop.

4.30 p.m.

In US style, a colon is used.

4:30 p.m.

Monospace type

In monospace typefaces, all characters are the same width and there is only one available size of space, which makes text styling more straightforward. Monospace typefaces are therefore excellent for the variable entries on forms. However, for longer texts they take up too much space and are less comfortable to read.

Size

A type size between 8 and 11 points creates a typewritten look.

Handgloves 123 — 8 pt
Handgloves 123 — 9 pt
Handgloves 123 — 10 pt
Handgloves 123 — 11 pt

Word spaces

Unlike proportional typefaces, monospace faces only include one size of space. No thin spaces are available.

14°C at 11.15 p.m.
Dr Eve Morgan, tel. 01456 584 499
CREDIT $2,355.00

Text alignment

Only ragged right setting can be used, because justified text would create uneven word spacing and the characters would not align.

The quick, brown fox jumps over a lazy dog. Quick wafting zephyrs vex bold Jim. The jay, pig, fox, zebra and my wolves quack. How quickly daft jumping zebras vex.

Hyphens and dashes

Monospace faces do differentiate between hyphens and en dashes, so these should be used where appropriate.

Both the hyphen and the en dash exist in mono-space typefaces, so use them – okay?

23 – 56 = -33

Quotation marks

Some monospace faces do not contain curved quotation marks. If they are not available in your chosen type, straight ones may be used instead.

‘single quotes’ “double quotes”

'single quotes' "double quotes"

Tables

The space bar should not be used to make tables using proportional faces, because the characters will not align neatly in columns. With monospace type, however, it is easy to align hundreds, tens and units correctly.

Item······Price······Delivery
Brush····£2.25······3·weeks
Sack·······£8.15·······1·week
Nail········£0.05······4·days

Item···Price···Delivery
Brush··£2.25···3·weeks
Sack···£8.15···1·week
Nail···£0.05···4·days

Headings

A good heading should sum up the type of form and its purpose at first glance. Ideally, these two categories are the same, but many forms are so complicated that their precise nature can't be reduced to a single concrete term or phrase. In such cases, it is better to keep the heading simple and include a more exact description as a subhead.

Size and position

The size and position of the heading can either be large and obvious or small and discreet. For a form that needs to make an impact on users, it is best to use a dominant heading. For a compulsory form that is guaranteed attention – such as a tax return – a more discreet heading is enough.

Elements of a heading

The word *form* can often be left out – it is usually obvious that the form is a form.

Application ~~form~~

Application

The heading should clearly state what the form is for, and express the relationship between user and provider.

Is the user an applicant, a customer or a respondent?

Application for Housing Benefit

Home Delivery Order

Declaration of Income

Customer Questionnaire

Abbreviations or acronyms are best avoided unless their meaning is obvious to users, but making them bold and visible can help users to navigate between different forms. Important and less important elements of the title can be distinguished typographically.

~~Inc. Tax Dec. Form A6~~

Income Tax Declaration **A6**

To keep the main heading concise, subheads can be used to convey essential information such as the legal status of an application.

Application for Child Benefit

Awarded in accordance with section 39, paragraph VII

The subhead can also be presented like a small form.

Application

- ☐ For changes to a driving licence
- ☐ For an international driving licence
- ☐ For a replacement driving licence in case of loss or theft

Logos and branding

Adding a logo in the top right-hand corner of a form is not enough to make it part of a corporate design. However, it does at least tell the user who the provider is. Whether and how branding of this kind is used will also depend on the function that the form is meant to fulfil.

Size and position

Logos and other forms of branding are often placed in a prominent position and ensure that the provider is recognized. This approach is suitable for any sort of notification, bill, invoice or certificate.

With forms that are intended to pass information from the user back to the provider, the positioning of the logo can be less prominent, since it is the user and not the provider who is sending off the completed form.

Heraldic symbols

Heraldic symbols such as coats-of-arms and seals indicate authority. These can be prominently placed because they guarantee attention. This does not, however, mean that the whole form should create an authoritarian impression – relevance is the important thing.

Reproducibility

Forms generally need to be copied, faxed and printed out. Logos that use gradients or are positioned in the bleed may need to be reworked in solid colours to accommodate this.

Contact details

Contact details are necessary on almost every form. They establish a practical connection with the provider, indicating who sent the form, where it should be returned, who is the contact person and how he or she can be reached. This information is especially important in the event of questions or problems, i.e. in situations that require urgent communication. Contact details should therefore not be hidden away, but must be clear and complete.

Position

Where possible, contact details should be positioned where users will expect to find them. In most cases, that means the top right-hand corner. Connecting them with the logo is useful but not essential. The most important thing, however, is to keep the same layout on all forms for the same provider.

One useful detail that can be added is to repeat the fax number on the reverse side of the form. This will be helpful to users when the form has been placed face down in the fax machine but the number has not yet been dialled.

Content and personalization

Contact details may range from name and address of the company, telephone number, and email address to tax, licence and bank account numbers. It is important that different elements should be clearly and logically separated into categories, e.g. postal address, phone numbers and web addresses.

In many forms, such as notifications and invoices, the information has to be personalized and, if necessary, supplemented by changing the date, customer number and so on. In the example on the far right, variable information is printed in a monospace typeface, so that it is clearly distinguishable from the details that are fixed. This makes for quicker reading.

Smith and Smythe Ltd
1 Bickingham Road
Woodhaven
Newfort NF8 9RD

Tel. 01456 567 890
Fax 01456 567 890

info@smithsmythe.com
www.smithsmythe.com

Managing directors:
John Smith, Jane Smythe

Newfort City Council
HRB 7889
Tax no.: 9125/116/00299
Reg. no.: UK 78990201

Bank details:
Account no. 9747 9742
NFB Bank
Sort code 66 22 02

Newfort Create
119 Peel Street
Newfort NF1 2BC

Sales adviser	Eve Morgan
Department	Customer Services
Phone	01456 029 222
Fax	01456 029 029
Email	e.morgan@nfcreate.net
Office hours	Mon-Fri 9 am-6 pm
Your billing number	**223577-01**
Date	23.08.2011

Document numbers and other details

On some forms it is necessary to include information that functions like a publisher's imprint. This enables them to be identified and classified more precisely than through the heading alone. The information may include details such as publication dates, document numbers or copyright restrictions, and although it will generally only be of importance to the provider, it may also be read by the user. It should therefore be just as open, friendly and accessible as the rest of the form.

Positioning

As this information is not relevant to most users and is secondary to the rest of the form, it can be in very small print and positioned outside of the main text area.

Content

The exact information given will naturally depend on the provider's administrative requirements. Common elements include repeating the heading, giving the form an individual number or identification code, and adding facts about the date of publication, provider, printer and copyright. The same format should then be used for all forms.

This information can be in very small print, but it should still be legible. Just how small it can be depends on the typeface and the print quality, and the leading should also be taken into account. These are sample settings for InDesign.

DOI/MA/172191_42015 | Newfort Building Society | 02/2010 | Registered in England

SR 019-A · Fixmachine Ltd, Newfort · Printed in the UK at Fortprint Studios

Donation request 471092 (07.09.10) – GBJP Third Edition – Registered charity no. 3013B – All rights reserved

4 pt, tracking 68

DOI/MA/172191_42015 | Newfort Building Society | 02/2010 | Registered in England

SR 019-A · Fixmachine Ltd, Newfort · Printed in the UK at Fortprint Studios

Donation request 471092 (07.09.10) – GBJP Third Edition – Registered charity no. 3013B – All rights reserved

5 pt, tracking 50

DOI/MA/172191_42015 | Newfort Building Society | 02/2010 | Registered in England

SR 019-A · Fixmachine Ltd, Newfort · Printed in the UK at Fortprint Studios

Donation request 471092 (07.09.10) – GBJP Third Edition – Registered charity no. 3013B – All rights reserved

6 pt, tracking 38

DOI/MA/172191_42015 | Newfort Building Society | 02/2010 | Registered in England

SR 019-A · Fixmachine Ltd, Newfort · Printed in the UK at Fortprint Studios

Donation request 471092 (07.09.10) – GBJP Third Edition – Registered charity no. 3013B – All rights reserved

6.5 pt, tracking 34

Addresses and letterheads

For more on point of view, see page 168

In most cases, forms need to be addressed to someone. If you want to avoid writing the address by hand or putting it on the envelope, it should be printed straight onto the form itself. However, the address that is written there will depend on the point of view: basically, whenever possible, the address of the receiver should be pre-printed in the right place, which makes life easier for the sender.

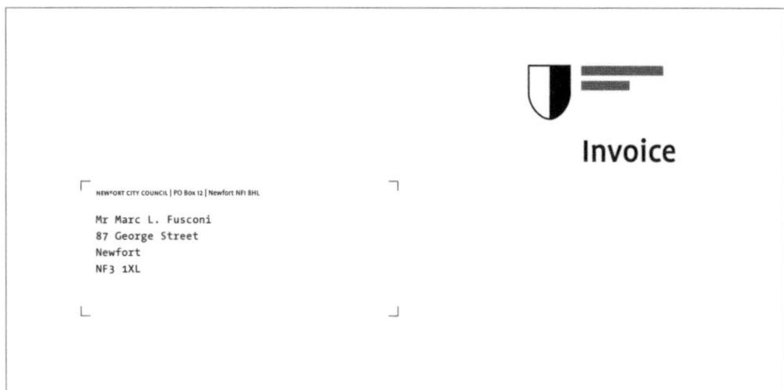

Application

Newfort City Council
Benefits Service
PO Box 10
1 Haymarket Square
Newfort NF1 8HL

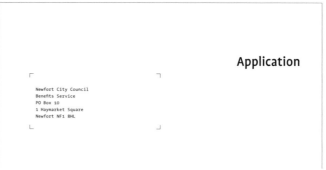

The address needs to be positioned on the paper in a way that will ensure that it appears in the window of the envelope. With communication forms, the receiver's (i.e. the user's) address obviously needs to be printed on the form (above left), while dialogue forms that need to be returned to sender should have the provider's address on them, of course (above right).

Declaration

Newfort NF2 7JH

If the return address is not known – for example, if it could be one of several administrative departments – the address field has to be left blank for the user to fill in.

An elegant but space-consuming method is to put two addresses on the form. Either of these can then be placed in the window of the envelope, depending on the way the form is folded. This is particularly useful for customer questionnaires that are sent out by post and need to be returned.

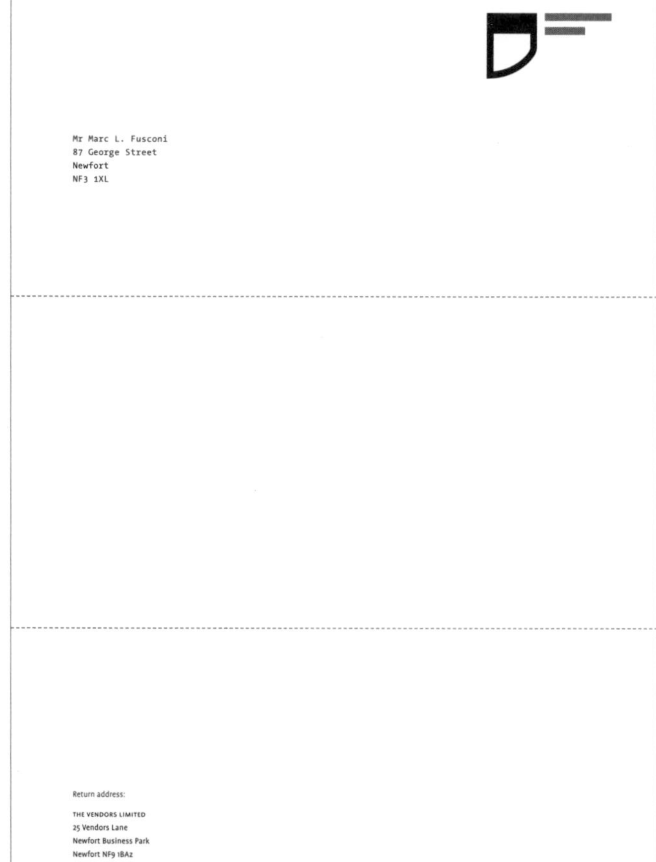

Standard grids for A4 business letters

These two grids for the positioning of addresses and fold marks on A4 paper will ensure that the address appears in the window of the envelope. If necessary, you can easily create similar grids for other paper formats and non-standard envelopes.

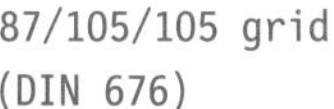

87/105/105 grid (DIN 676)

This provides more space for the content, because the address field is higher up.

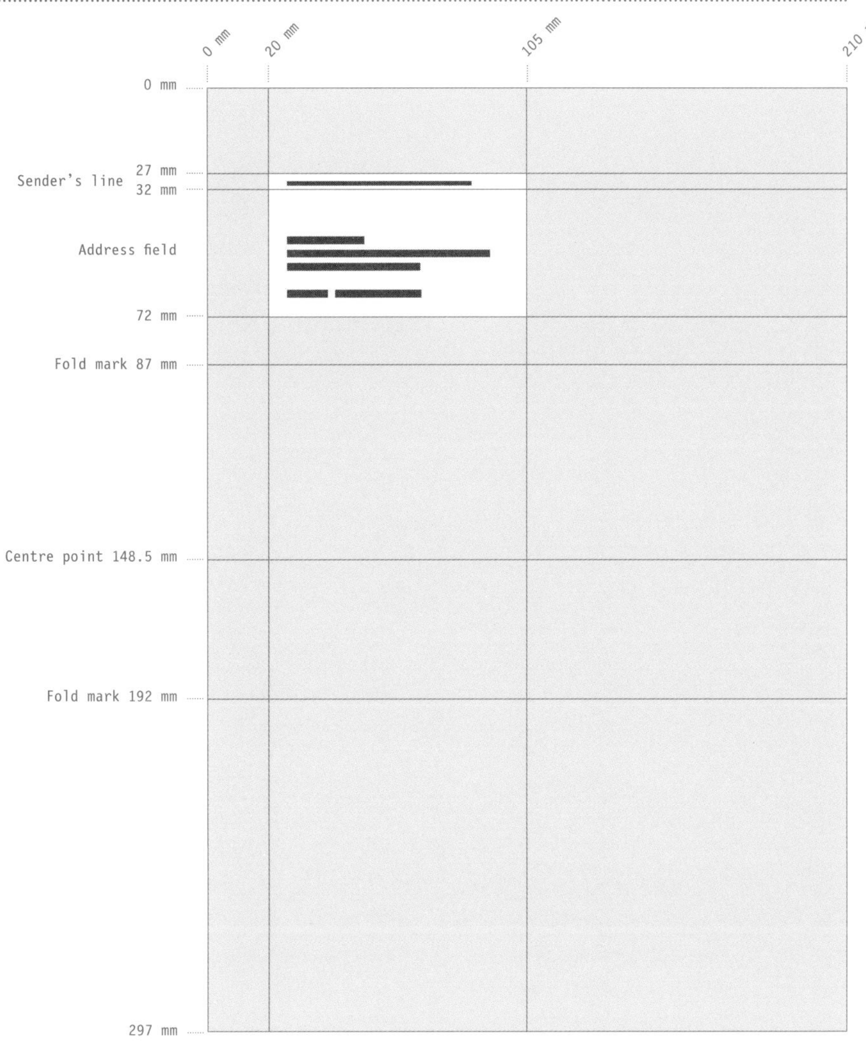

105/105/87 grid

This variant allows more space for the letterhead.

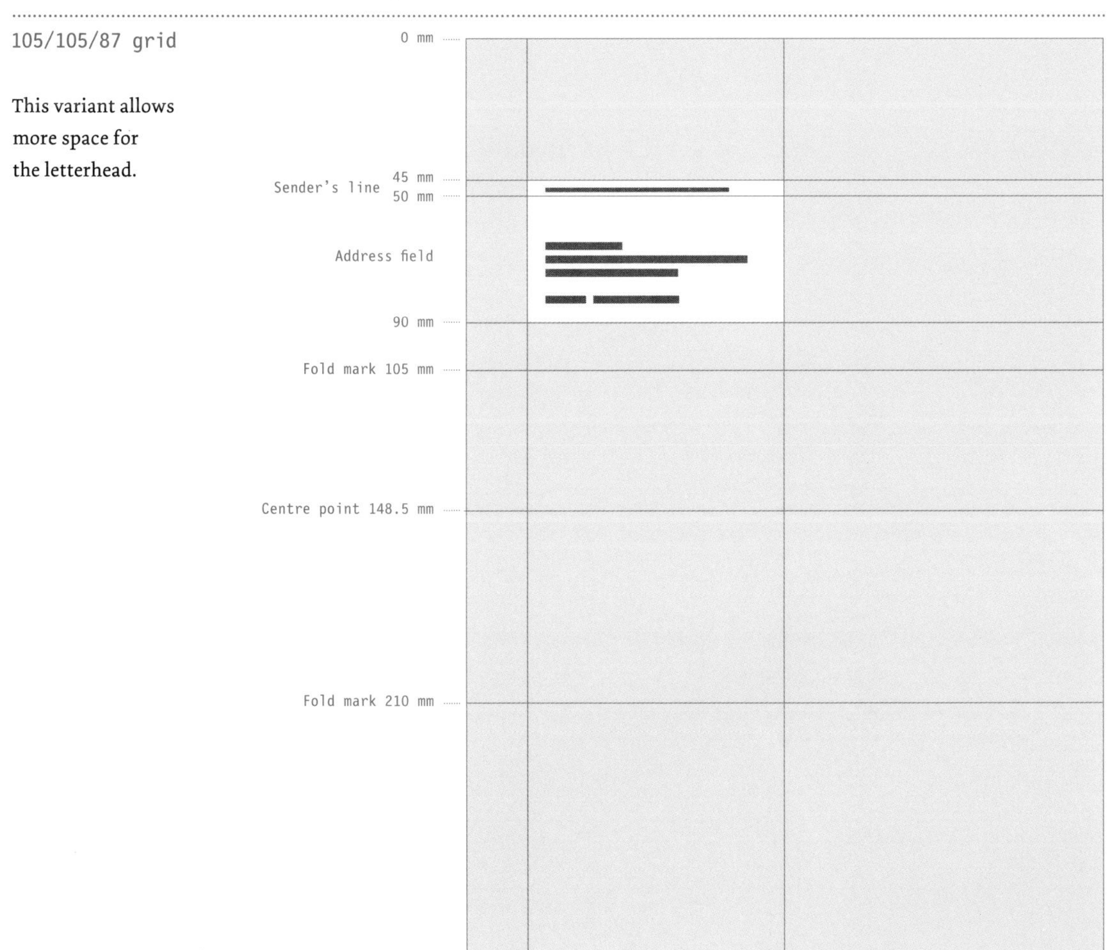

Serial numbers

If the distribution of each individual form needs to be recorded and controlled, continuous serial numbers can be used. For pre-printed forms, this is generally done by machine at the printing house. However, special software is also available to add automatic numbering to forms that have to be printed out.

It's not usually possible to choose the typeface of the serial number, as this is normally built into the numbering machine.

Consecutive numbers are usually set without spaces. The word 'number' can be omitted or abbreviated to 'no.' or 'N°', or replaced with a hash symbol (#).

7180984 A

no. 18987

#0000056889

№ 56

Copy distribution

Pre-printed form sets consist of several copies of the same form stuck together. The destination of the different copies – in essence, who receives which version – needs to be clearly indicated.

One way of doing this is to include a distribution plan on the form itself. Using different colours for each copy is a common device, but since colour coding is seldom self-explanatory, the categories need to be indicated.

white → personnel department
red → switchboard
yellow → supervisor
green → employee

Direct instructions on each copy are easier to understand. These are best phrased as active sentences and should be positioned where they are easy to see.

Please return this page to us

Your customer adviser will keep this page

For your files

Page numbering

When a form consists of multiple pages, it is essential to number them. This helps to guide users through the form and makes it easy for them to see its organization and extent.

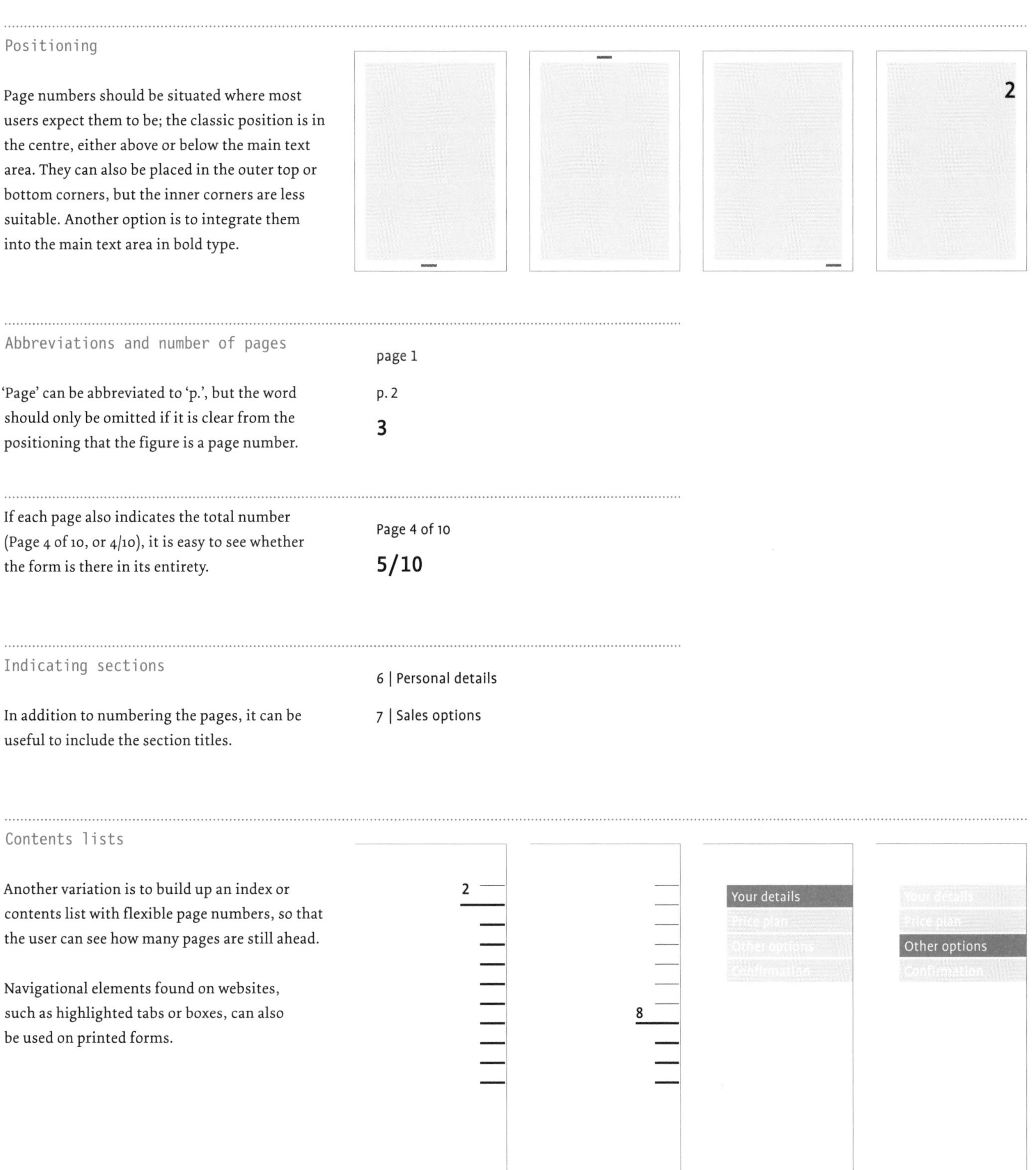

Positioning

Page numbers should be situated where most users expect them to be; the classic position is in the centre, either above or below the main text area. They can also be placed in the outer top or bottom corners, but the inner corners are less suitable. Another option is to integrate them into the main text area in bold type.

Abbreviations and number of pages

'Page' can be abbreviated to 'p.', but the word should only be omitted if it is clear from the positioning that the figure is a page number.

If each page also indicates the total number (Page 4 of 10, or 4/10), it is easy to see whether the form is there in its entirety.

Indicating sections

In addition to numbering the pages, it can be useful to include the section titles.

Contents lists

Another variation is to build up an index or contents list with flexible page numbers, so that the user can see how many pages are still ahead.

Navigational elements found on websites, such as highlighted tabs or boxes, can also be used on printed forms.

Choosing a point of view

Every form involves a kind of dialogue, and this can take place from three different viewpoints: as a set of questions to the user, a declaration to the provider, or from a neutral perspective. It is important to settle on one of these and maintain it throughout.

Question and answer

If a question-and-answer perspective is chosen, the form becomes the direct transcription of a dialogue. The form asks questions, and the user answers them.

What is your name?
John Smith
What is your date of birth?
1 February 1968
What is your name? JOHN SMITH
What is your date of birth? 1 FEBRUARY 1968

Explanatory perspective

As a declaration, the form is the result of preformulated statements by the user. The form provides statements. The user completes them.

My name is John Smith, and my date of birth is 1 February 1968
My name JOHN SMITH
My date of birth 1 FEBRUARY 1968

This type of form also involves a dialogue, but it is one that users conduct with themselves. It is generally done unconsciously, but hidden behind the preformulated statements are the questions that are being asked of the user.

My name
What did I say my name was? Oh yes, John Smith
My name JOHN SMITH

Neutral perspective

Instead of formulating questions or statements, both of these can be shortened to the relevant keywords. The point of view is then unclear: these could be questions to the user or declarations by the user. This is a practical but impersonal approach.

The neutral nouns could, however, also be combined with one of the other two viewpoints, especially if a statement or response consists of several elements, as in this example.

Question types

It is the interplay between questions and answers that makes a form interactive. According to the type of information being gathered, several types of question may be used, and each of them has a different visual format and needs its own design. The primary distinction is between free response and multiple choice questions.

Free response or open questions

With open questions, no preformulated answers are provided but only a blank field in which the answer is to be written. This allows for all kinds of responses.

By stipulating measurements or units, however, you can restrict the range of possible answers.

Profession: CAKE DECORATOR
Annual income in £: 21,000
Tax reference no.: F P 2 3 4 7 6 3 8 7 X
Workplace: BAKERY
Directions: HEAD SOUTH ON MAIN ROAD, TURN LEFT INTO PARK DRIVE AND STOP AT FRONT GATE

Multiple choice questions

Multiple choice questions offer a limited number of answers. They form categories, from which the user may choose one or more.

The advantage of these over open questions is that they can be filled in more quickly and all the answers are standardized.

Profession: ☐ mattress tester ☐ banker ☒ burglar
Annual income in £: ☐ under 20,000 ☒ 20,000–50,000 ☐ over 50,000
Workplace: ☐ home ☐ office ☒ other people's houses
Field of expertise: ☐ leisure ☐ gambling ☒ lock picking

An extreme example of multiple choice questions is the either/or variety – questions which can only be answered with a yes or no, or statements which must be accepted or rejected.

Are you law-abiding? ☐ Yes ☒ No

☒ I hereby confirm that all information provided is accurate, to the best of my knowledge.

Extended multiple choice

It is also possible to combine both types of question, by supplying likely responses but also including a blank field where other answers can be added.

Profession: ☐ mattress tester ☐ banker ☒ COWBOY

Free response questions

There are two issues associated with free response questions: 1) how to position them in relation to the text fields, and 2) how to design the text fields themselves. Questions can be placed next to, above, or below the text fields, and all of these options have advantages and disadvantages. The text fields can be represented by means of lines, frames, cells or shaded areas, and this choice will determine the overall appearance of the form.

Principle

The principle underlying free response questions is that of a text with spaces to be filled, but such forms are rarely seen nowadays.

The sentence is .... years, eligible for parole after .... years, with the earliest date of release .... The parole officer in charge of the case is ....

Instead, the text is divided into questions and text fields.

Total sentence ______ years

Eligible for parole after ______ years

Earliest release date ______

Parole officer's name ______

Lines or boxes?

The form of the text field determines how the user will write. Open text fields are always preferable to individual letter spaces or boxes, as they do not hinder the flow of writing.

Boxes or character dividers should only be used if they are absolutely necessary. This may be the case if the number of characters needs to be limited in some way, if the form is to be machine-read, or if you wish to oblige users to write more legibly.

The divisions between characters need to be clear and obvious, so that users will take them seriously.

It is much easier to write figures inside character dividers than letters.

It's easy to write on a line like this.

This is also easy, but you may go over the edges.

Should I write one letter for each dash?

THIS IS CLEAR AND NEAT

SO IS THIS

AND SO IS THIS

0123456789

0123456789

0123456789

0123456789

Height of the text field

The height of the text field depends on whether the form is to be filled in by hand or with a typewriter or computer.

For handwritten use, leading of between 15 and 21 points is most suitable. If forms are to be filled in by machine, the leading can be tighter. Leading below 12 points with 9-point type will create legibility problems.

handwritten / ABC ghi 123	typed / ABC ghi 123	Leading 9 pt / 3.175 mm
handwritten / ABC ghi 123	typed / ABC ghi 123	Leading 12 pt / 4.233 mm
handwritten / ABC ghi 123	typed / ABC ghi 123	Leading 15 pt / 5.292 mm
handwritten / ABC ghi 123	typed / ABC ghi 123	Leading 18 pt / 6.35 mm
handwritten / ABC ghi 123	typed / ABC ghi 123	Leading 21 pt / 7.408 mm
handwritten / ABC ghi 123	typed / ABC ghi 123	Leading 24 pt / 8.467 mm

Width of the text field

The text field should be as wide as possible, as names, telephone numbers and addresses can be longer than expected.

If the user leaves something out, or writes something illegible because there is not enough space, the result will be errors which will waste time, money and energy.

Fields for information of predictable length, such as postcodes, dates or sums of money should not be unnecessarily long but tailored to the expected figures.

Contact	Alexandra Huntingdon-Featherstone
Street address	749 Queen Elizabeth Street North
Town or city	Newfort
Postcode	NF7 8TT
Daytime telephone	01456 553388
Date	4.2.2010
Annual income in £	37,000.00
Years in current job	4

Questions alongside the text field

This principle is well suited to handwritten answers, and matches the convention of reading from left to right. It establishes a clear link between question and text field, and allows the questions to be in type that is large enough for easy reading. Longer questions, however, can often create space issues.

For left-handed users, this solution is unfortunately not ideal, as their pen or hand tends to cover the question.

Question Answer

First name
Surname
Date of birth

left-handed

First name
Surname
Date of birth

right-handed

Alignment and positioning

Questions may be right-aligned or left-aligned.

This means that either the questions or the beginning of the text field will be ragged. The latter does not look attractive.

First name
Surname
Date of birth Place of birth

First name
Surname
Date of birth Place of birth

It is better to align the start of the text fields, even if this makes the questions and text fields seem a little disconnected.

First name
Surname
Date of birth Place of birth

If the question stands within the text field, the user may be uncertain where to start writing.

First name
Surname
Date of birth Place of birth

The best solution is one that will simultaneously separate and connect the questions and the text fields that follow.

First name
Surname
Date of birth Place of birth

Using lines

Using different line weights and textures, you can create a clear distinction between questions and text fields.

First name
Surname
Date of birth
Place of birth

First name
Surname
Date of birth
Place of birth

Vertical lines at the start of each line give the fields more definition.

First name
Surname
Date of birth
Place of birth

Using shading

Here the text fields are blank white spaces within an area of coloured fill.

First name
Surname
Date of birth
Place of birth

If you combine shaded areas with lines, the linear aspect of the form is emphasized.

First name
Surname
Date of birth
Place of birth

Using frames

Instead of simple frames, you can also use more open and interesting variations.

First name
Surname
Date of birth
Place of birth

First name
Surname
Date of birth
Place of birth

These right-angled lines are good because they show the user exactly where to start writing.

First name
Surname
Date of birth
Place of birth

Using cells

Cell-based text fields have more impact and look better when divided by different weights of line.

First name			
Surname			
Date of birth		Place of birth	

First name			
Surname			
Date of birth		Place of birth	

Top-aligned questions

This is also known as the TLC (top left corner) position. If the form is filled in with a typewriter, the user can still see the question. Questions must be set small because they encroach on the text field and reduce the available writing space.

Question

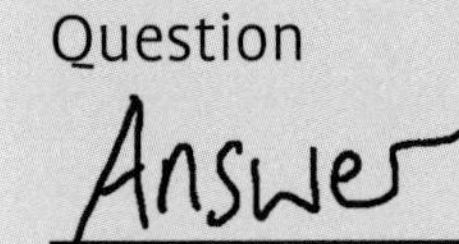

Layout

This layout is clear when there is only one question, but when there are several, it can lead to confusion. By the third line down, the user is no longer sure whether to write above or below the lines.

Customer number

First name

Surname

Date of birth | Place of birth

House number, street

Using lines

To create a clearer layout, the questions must be visually enclosed in some way. If they lie within the text field itself, they reduce the space for writing. It is also unclear whether users should begin writing below the question, next to it, or even over it. Therefore you should be sure to leave enough space, or else position the question outside the text field.

First name

Surname

Date of birth | Place of birth

First name

Surname

Date of birth | Place of birth

First name

Surname

Date of birth | Place of birth

Using shading

If the boxed questions are of equal width, it suggests that users should start writing after them, rather than below them.

First name

Surname

Date of birth | Place of birth

Using frames

First name

Surname

Date of birth | Place of birth

Using cells

First name

Surname

Date of birth | Place of birth

Bottom-aligned questions

This principle goes against the logical sequence of 'question first, then answer'. However, it can be used if each line is simply marked with keywords rather than full questions. Once again the questions need to be in small type.

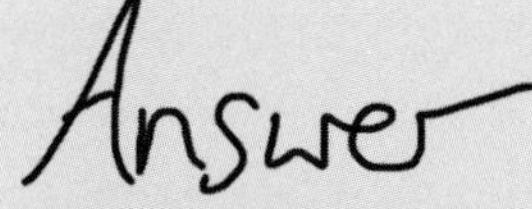

Question

Layout

The same issue arises as with TLC positioning (see opposite). Lines alone do not make for a clear layout, unless there is a wide gap between the questions.

Customer number

First name

Surname

Date of birth

Place of birth

House number, street

Using lines

There are several different ways to use simple right-angled lines to define the text field and connect it to the question. Here too, the gap between questions needs to be relatively large, so that there is sufficient space for writing.

First name

Surname

Date of birth

Place of birth

First name

Surname

Date of birth

Place of birth

First name

Surname

Date of birth

Place of birth

Using shading

If the questions are positioned close enough to a clearly defined text field, this approach also works well.

First name

Surname

Date of birth

Place of birth

Using frames

First name

Surname

Date of birth

Place of birth

Using cells

First name

Surname

Date of birth

Place of birth

Special questions

Some questions require specially designed text fields.

Date and time

A simple text field can be used for this.

Date

Time

However, if the answer needs to be in a specific format, this should be indicated to the user by providing appropriate spaces.

Date . .

Month / Year /

Period Year to year

Time :

Delivery time hours minutes

Quantities and measures

These can be placed before or after the text field, so long as the layout is consistent.

Amount owed £ | Amount owed £

Weight kg | Weight kg

Contents parts | Contents parts

Size mm wide

mm high

Decimal points

These can be fixed within the writing spaces, but if you want users to give an answer in whole numbers, it's best to provide the figures that follow the decimal point.

Energy used . kWh

Gross revenue .00

Children . –

Money

Large sums of money can be indicated with micro-print lines to protect them against subsequent alteration.

Receipt amount £

Value

Sums

No one who has to fill in a form wants to do complicated calculations as well. Sometimes, however, this is unavoidable. Proper alignment of the digits will make it easier to do the arithmetic.

Room rate £ .

Minibar + £ .

Subtotal = £ .

Gift vouchers – £ .

Subtotal = £ .

Tax × 1.175

Total £ .

Signature

Signature fields are often accompanied by a line on which users can print their name and add the date. Remember to leave enough space for the signature: double or triple the regular line spacing. The signature field is also sometimes marked with a cross, which may be in colour.

Print name ______ Date ______

Signature ✗ ______

Comment boxes

Comment boxes are different from ordinary text fields, as users can write more freely and in more detail. This can be shown by marking the field in a different way, e.g. with dotted lines.

Title ______

Description ------

Diagrams and drawings

It can sometimes be helpful to allow users draw on forms as well as write on them. A grid or readymade diagram can be provided for this.

Sketch of vehicle

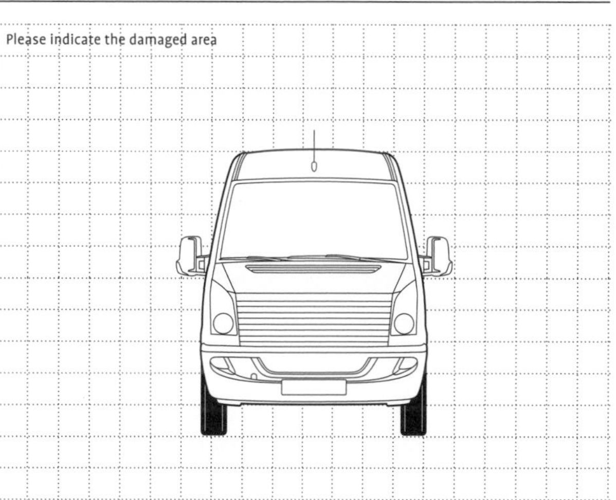

Please indicate the damaged area

Passport photos and stamp

Some forms require passport photos to be provided, and some have to be stamped too. In both cases, enough space should be allotted.

Size requirements for passport photos vary from country to country. In the UK, the EU and Australia, the standard size is 45 × 35 mm (1.75 × 1.3 in.). In the US, it is 2 × 2 in. (51 × 51 mm), and in Canada, 70 × 50 mm (2.75 × 2 in.).

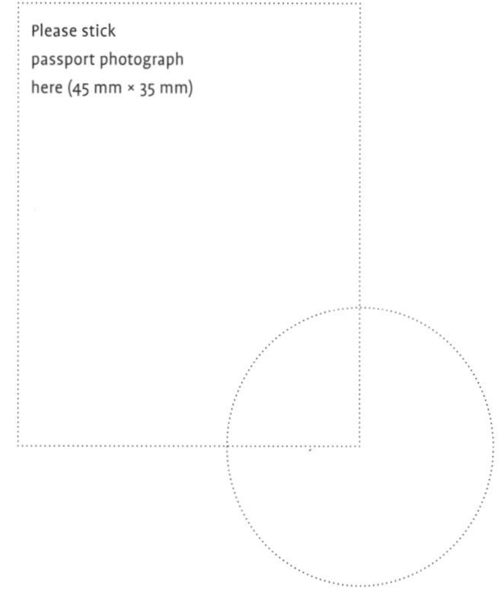

Please stick
passport photograph
here (45 mm × 35 mm)

Multiple choice questions

The design of multiple choice questions always involves the use of checkboxes of some sort. You need to establish the range of answers that will give you the information you require. Unclear or illogical answers will lead to confusion, false information or gaps.

Basic principle

Before checkboxes became commonplace, the chosen answer had to be underlined, and the rest crossed out. The resulting text is hard to read and awkward to fill in.

The application is herewith – ~~rejected~~ – accepted – ~~deferred~~.

This decision may – not – be appealed under subsection 12.

In the modern style, the text is divided into questions and a selection of possible answers with checkboxes. This is clearer and much simpler to fill in.

Application ☒ accepted ☐ rejected ☐ deferred

Appeal in accordance with subsection 12 ☐ allowed ☒ not allowed

Single and multiple choice

Each question must make it clear whether it is possible or permitted to give more than one answer. If this is not apparent from the question itself, instructions must be given.

One way of distinguishing is through a horizontal sequence of responses which are mutually exclusive. If several boxes can be marked, these should be listed below one another. But this principle needs to be made clear to the user.

Age ☐ < 18 years ☐ 18–26 years ☐ 27–67 years ☐ > 67 years

Language skills
☐ Finnish
☐ Japanese
☐ Chinese
☐ Hindi
☐ Somali

Another variation is to give a precise explanation of each possible answer.

Please mark only one box

Family status
☐ unmarried
☐ married ☐ living with a partner
☐ divorced ☐ separated from a partner
☐ widowed ☐ partner deceased

Extended multiple choice

Extended multiple choice combines a range of suggested responses with an empty text field in which additional answers can be noted.

You may mark more than one box

Assets ☐ Shares ☐ Property ☐ Jewelry
☐ Art ☐ Racehorses ☐ Sports cars
☐ Other ______________

Marking responses

In most cases, other than with some machine readable forms, it doesn't matter how the box is marked. Any mark will mean 'this is the answer'. However, omitting checkboxes completely can lead to confusion unless instructions are given.

☒ Yes ☐ No

☑ Yes ☐ No

■ Yes ☐ No

Yes (No)

The marks can also be coded, as shown by the example illustrated. However, this type of coding is not widely familiar, and is certainly not intuitive – it has to be learned, and so an explanatory key must be provided.

☒ law-abiding → means true

☐ law-abiding → means partly true

☐ law-abiding → means not true

This variation has a little more logic behind it. In order to say no, you put a diagonal stroke downwards through the box. As with any prohibition sign, a rectangle or circle with a diagonal line through it symbolizes NO.

☐ law-abiding → means no

☐ = ⊘ = NO

Either/or questions

These allow only one of two answers. If yes is not marked, it means no, and vice versa, so in fact only one box is needed.

However, for the sake of clarity, it is often better to give the alternatives of yes and no.

If the 'no' alternative is omitted, firstly the answer can be changed later, and secondly if it is not marked, the meaning could be 'don't know' or 'don't wish to answer'.

If the alternatives of yes and no are offered, a clear answer has to be given, and it is immediately evident if a question has been overlooked or left out.

Convicted of forgery ☐ Yes ☐ No

☐ Convicted of forgery

Convictions for: ☐ Forgery

☐ Burglary

☐ Minor driving offences

Convictions for:

Forgery	☐ Yes	☐ No
Burglary	☐ Yes	☐ No
Minor driving offences	☐ Yes	☐ No

Statements

Statements must be used carefully, since it is not clear whether they also have to be marked to show that they are valid. They are simply there. It is especially tricky when not marking them or overlooking them could mean agreement, or marking them with a cross could mean a kind of double negative. It is better to offer a genuine choice.

☐ I have read and understood the small print

☐ I do not want my details to be passed on to third parties → when unmarked, this creates a confusing double negative

I have read and understood the small print	☐ Yes	☐ No
My details may be passed on to third parties	☐ Agree	☐ Disagree

Printing the tick in advance as if the user has only one option is unnecessary and even questionable.

☑ Yes, I wish to receive information from other carefully selected companies.

Sequence

The checkbox should always stand before the response. Placing it after the response is unusual and may make it difficult to connect the question and the answer. It only works if the gaps between answers are very wide.

☐ Beef ☐ Pork ☐ Lamb ☐ Kangaroo

Camembert ☐ Brie ☐ Pecorino ☐ Cheddar ☐

Gaps between checkbox and answer

The gap should not be too small. A double letterspace is a good rule of thumb. If the gap is too wide, the checkboxes and responses start to seem disconnected.

☐kangaroo

☐kangaroo

☐ kangaroo

☐ kangaroo

☐ kangaroo

Gaps between answers

This gap must be substantially wider and never smaller than the gap between box and answer. It's better to be too generous than to cause confusion.

☐ cat ☒ dog ☐ kangaroo ☐ crocodile → gap far too small, dog becomes cat

☐ cat ☒ dog ☐ kangaroo ☐ crocodile → still too small, dog could also be cat

☐ cat ☒ dog ☐ kangaroo ☐ crocodile → better, dog remains dog

☐ cat ☒ dog ☐ kangaroo ☐ crocodile → safer

☐ cat ☒ dog ☐ kangaroo ☐ crocodile → eliminates any doubt

However, exaggerated gaps should also be avoided, because then the answers are disconnected from each other.

☐ full price ☐ 50% reduction

It looks tidier if the checkboxes are always evenly spaced. Answers of different lengths, however, create an unbalanced look.

☐ cat ☐ sabre-toothed tiger ☐ eel

☐ crocodile ☐ hippopotamus ☐ dog

In these cases, it is better to keep the gaps between the answers consistent.

☐ cat ☐ sabre-toothed tiger ☐ eel ☐ crocodile ☐ hippopotamus

☐ sparrow ☐ macaw ☐ chicken ☐ goose ☐ Tasmanian devil

Line weight and size of checkboxes

The line weight of the checkboxes can be matched with the weight of the type.

To create a contrast with the type, you can combine a roman typeface with bold checkboxes.

Checkboxes with thin, pale lines may not be sufficiently prominent.

The optimum size is usually a square between 2.5 and 3.5 mm across.

Size	Line weight 0.25 pt	0.5 pt	0.75 pt	1.25 pt
1.5 mm	☐ Experiment	☐ Experiment	☐ Experiment	☐ Experiment
2.0 mm	☐ Experiment	☐ Experiment	☐ Experiment	☐ Experiment
2.5 mm	☐ Experiment	☐ Experiment	☐ Experiment	☐ Experiment
3.0 mm	☐ Experiment	☐ Experiment	☐ Experiment	☐ Experiment
3.5 mm	☐ Experiment	☐ Experiment	☐ Experiment	☐ Experiment
4.0 mm	☐ Experiment	☐ Experiment	☐ Experiment	☐ Experiment

Other options

Square checkboxes are not the only option, however. Using different shapes can help to give a form individuality.

By comparison with a closed checkbox, an open-sided rectangle can seem much lighter.

Boxes that are open in the bottom right-hand corner are the easiest to mark, because the right angle shows where to put the pen initially, and then the cross can go straight into the empty space.

Arne Bach Chopin Dvořák Elgar Fauré Grieg
Handel Ives Janáček Kodály Liszt Mozart Nielsen

Arne Bach Chopin Dvořák Elgar Fauré Grieg
Handel Ives Janáček Kodály Liszt Mozart Nielsen

Arne Bach Chopin Dvořák Elgar Fauré Grieg
Handel Ives Janáček Kodály Liszt Mozart Nielsen

Arne Bach Chopin Dvořák Elgar Fauré Grieg
Handel Ives Janáček Kodály Liszt Mozart Nielsen

Arne Bach Chopin Dvořák Elgar Fauré Grieg
Handel Ives Janáček Kodály Liszt Mozart Nielsen

Arne Bach Chopin Dvořák Elgar Fauré Grieg
Handel Ives Janáček Kodály Liszt Mozart Nielsen

Arne Bach Chopin Dvořák Elgar Fauré Grieg
Handel Ives Janáček Kodály Liszt Mozart Nielsen

[ ] Arne [ ] Bach [ ] Chopin [ ] Dvořák [ ] Elgar [ ] Fauré [ ] Grieg
[ ] Handel [ ] Ives [ ] Janáček [ ] Kodály [ ] Liszt [X] Mozart [ ] Nielsen

Arne Bach Chopin Dvořák Elgar Fauré Grieg
Handel Ives Janáček Kodály Liszt Mozart Nielsen

Arne Bach Chopin Dvořák Elgar Fauré Grieg
Handel Ives Janáček Kodály Liszt Mozart Nielsen

Arne Bach Chopin Dvořák Elgar Fauré Grieg
Handel Ives Janáček Kodály Liszt Mozart Nielsen

Arne Bach Chopin Dvořák Elgar Fauré Grieg
Handel Ives Janáček Kodály Liszt Mozart Nielsen

Avoid very small shapes with a coloured fill. These look too much like bullet points.

Arne Bach Chopin Dvořák Elgar Fauré Grieg
Handel Ives Janáček Kodály Liszt Mozart Nielsen

Not good at all, though frequently encountered, are tabular checkboxes made up of cells or lines. The boxes lose their visual independence.

	Orff	X	Puccini
	Quilter		Ravel

	Orff		Puccini
X	Quilter		Ravel

Rank order scales

Questionnaires use scales in order to collate facts and opinions, or to ascertain degrees of knowledge. The given categories for each scale must be organized in such a way that answers are not unconsciously prioritized or classifications confused.

Types of scale

Here is an overview of the different scales that may be used. The chosen scale will be determined by the type of data that needs to be gathered.

Nominal scales

These are for information that cannot be ranked in any order. They record only equality and difference, i.e. quality not quantity.

Your profession

☐ bus driver ☐ politician ☐ journalist ☐ novelist

Your favourite ice cream flavour

☐ vanilla ☐ chocolate ☐ strawberry ☐ tutti frutti

Ordinal scales

These are for responses that can be prioritized or ranked from minor to major.

Your position in the company

☐ junior ☐ assistant ☐ manager ☐ director

Your company car

☐ subcompact ☐ compact ☐ mid-size ☐ luxury

Interval scales

With interval scales it is important that all the checkboxes are evenly spaced.

These are for data with prioritization and equal distance between categories. This makes it possible to calculate sums, differences and averages. The zero point on these scales has no mathematical significance, and so 20° C is not twice as warm as 10° C.

Average grades at school

☐ excellent ☐ good ☐ fair ☐ poor ☐ awful ☐ ran away

Today's maximum temperature in the shade

☐ < 5° C ☐ 5–9° C ☐ 10–14° C ☐ 15–19° C ☐ 20–24° C ☐ > 24° C

How do you react to a tax demand?

delighted ☐ ☐ ☐ ☐ ☐ ☐ *depressed*

Ratio scales

Ratio scales require equal gaps and a real zero point. This makes it possible to draw conclusions from the relative values of the data.

How many bars of chocolate did you buy last week?

☐ 0 ☐ 1 ☐ 2 ☐ 3 ☐ 4 ☐ 5 or more

What percentage of your income is spent on chocolate?

☐ 0–5% ☐ 6–10% ☐ 11–15% ☐ 16–20% ☐ > 20%

How high is your cholesterol level?

☐ < 210 ☐ 210–219 ☐ 220–229 ☐ 230–239 ☐ > 240

Rating scales

Rating scales produce judgments based on intervals. These ratings are used in opinion polls and in the evaluation of achievements or abilities.

There are often five or seven grades, with each step on the scale being roughly equal. If there is no 'golden mean' and the user is forced to lean one way or another, the number of grades will be even – generally six.

Here are several examples of the rating scales used on questionnaires.

Likert scale

A rating scale to evaluate a series of statements.

Please give your views on the following statements:

	strongly agree	*agree*	*neither agree nor disagree*	*disagree*	*strongly disagree*
Forms are a pleasure	☐	☐	☐	☐	☐
Forms are practical	☐	☐	☐	☐	☐

Semantic differential scale

A rating scale which requires users to choose a position between pairs of opposing concepts.

What do you think of most political speeches?

Please mark the appropriate box between each pair of descriptions.

necessary	☐	☐	☐	☐	☐	unnecessary
exciting	☐	☐	☐	☐	☐	depressing
fascinating	☐	☐	☐	☐	☐	boring
factual	☐	☐	☐	☐	☐	fictional

Stapel scale

This rating scale uses numbers instead of verbal descriptions. The advantage is that there is no need to come up with descriptive terms for each grade.

Please evaluate the following statements:

Those who do not honour the form are not worthy of support

☐ -5 ☐ -4 ☐ -3 ☐ -2 ☐ -1 | ☐ +1 ☐ +2 ☐ +3 ☐ +4 ☐ +5

Every form has a right to be beautiful

☐ -5 ☐ -4 ☐ -3 ☐ -2 ☐ -1 | ☐ +1 ☐ +2 ☐ +3 ☐ +4 ☐ +5

Visual analogue scale

If you prefer not to stipulate categories but want to leave the user as much freedom as possible, you can use scales without grades, but these are harder to assess.

What do you think of your boss?

Please mark the line between each pair of judgments in the appropriate place

A dream |————————————| A nightmare

A great leader |————————————| A terrible leader

Totally selfless |————————————| Totally selfish

Symbol scales

If you want to do without words, you can use pictograms, icons or images, but this type of scale is limited to less complex questions.

How do you feel about your boss?

☐ ☐ ☐ ☐ ☐

Don't know

The category 'don't know' or 'not applicable' should be clearly separated from the rest of the scale, because it does not fit within the ranked responses.

How fair do you consider Paragraph 69, Subsection 42 of the Council's Revised Regulations concerning the regulation of regulations?

very fair				very unfair	don't know
☐	☐	☐	☐	☐	☐

Tables and matrix charts

Tables and matrix charts are used on many forms. They avoid the need to repeat the same questions, and they give a clear overview of connected information. Basically, every table – even one without blank spaces to be filled – is a form, because the information it contains is given meaning through its presentation.

Tables

Tables consist of a header, which includes the column names, and a number of columns that are subdivided into rows and cells.

The column headers contain the questions, and the cells are for the answers. One special feature is that all the answers in a row are linked together without the need for this to be indicated.

Header
Column heading
Row
Cell
Column

Name of elephant	Date of birth	Weight

Matrix charts

Matrix charts contain questions or categories both in column headers and in the first column. The content of each cell therefore refers to two questions or categories at the same time.

	Husband 1	Husband 2	Husband 3
First name			
Surname			
Date of birth			
Place of birth			
Occupation			
Length of marriage			
Reasons for divorce			

This is another possible format. The repetition of the questions in each cell, however, is unnecessary.

Husband 1	Husband 2	Husband 3
First name	First name	First name
Surname	Surname	Surname
Date of birth	Date of birth	Date of birth
Place of birth	Place of birth	Place of birth
Occupation	Occupation	Occupation

Alignment and line weight

Because handwriting is ranged left, the column titles should also be ranged left.

Variations in line weight add interest to the table, emphasize the columns and lines, and direct the user's gaze.

Diagnosis	Medication	Result	Full recovery?
			☐ Yes ☐ No
			☐ Yes ☐ No

Diagnosis	Medication	Result	Full recovery?
			☐ Yes ☐ No
			☐ Yes ☐ No

Two-part headers

Table headers can be subdivided into upper and lower rows.

To prevent the headers from becoming overcrowded, the hierarchy should be made clear through different line and type weights.

Time		Repairs			Problem resolved?
Start	End	Description	Parts	Fee	
					☐ Yes ☐ No
					☐ Yes ☐ No
					☐ Yes ☐ No

Closed header

Time		**Repairs**			**Problem resolved?**
Start	End	Description	Parts	Fee	
					☐ Yes ☐ No
					☐ Yes ☐ No
					☐ Yes ☐ No

Open header, better

Long column headers

Column titles can often be longer than the width of the text fields.

It is not a good idea to squash them up or reduce the size of the print. It's better to set them on several lines or, as here, write them diagonally.

Applicant number	Tasks assigned for assessment	**Performance**	excellent	good	average	below average	hopeless
			☐	☐	☐	☐	☐
			☐	☐	☐	☐	☐
			☐	☐	☐	☐	☐

You can also use more elaborate constructions in order to accommodate longer titles.

Some design or space issues can be resolved by positioning questions in the first column instead of the table header.

Grade	brilliant at all subjects	good at some subjects	generally average	usually mediocre	indescribably bad	Name
	☐	☐	☐	☐	☐	
	☐	☐	☐	☐	☐	
	☐	☐	☐	☐	☐	

Sample tables

Tables do not have to be made up of cells.

To create a sense of unity, they should be built from the same framework elements as the rest of a form.

Lines

The right angle at the beginning of each line is optional, but it helps to give the table a more defined shape.

Quantity	Item number	Description	Price per item

Shading

Areas of shaded fill are a good way to distinguish between lines. They also help to visually unite the fields on each row.

Quantity	Item number	Description	Price per item

Frames

The vertical lines emphasize the columns.

Quantity	Item number	Description	Price per item

Cells

Cell-based tables hold information neatly, but they look best with some variation in line weight, so that either the horizontals or the verticals are slightly heavier.

Quantity	Item number	Description	Price per item

Filter questions

Forms often include one or more questions that do not apply to everyone. Unnecessary questions are a source of irritation to users, so you need to create a filter that leads them to the questions that are relevant to them.

Filtering by adding a condition

This is the simplest way of building a filter directly into the question.

Customer number
if available

Annual salary
if below £100,000

Filtering by explanation

You can also begin with an explanation, but it must be clear which question this refers to.

Please answer these questions only if your parents earn less than £15,000 p.a.

Name of university

Subject of studies

Total course fees in £

Filtering by questions

If/then questions filter users and allow them to move ahead to more relevant questions.

Assets ☐ No ☐ Yes, as follows:

☐ clothes
☐ books
☐ furniture

Assets ☐ No

☐ Yes, as follows:

clothes £

books £

furniture £

If you prefer not to connect the responses and follow-up questions through the layout, you need to build in a less elegant 'if so' construction.

Assets ☐ Yes ☐ No

If yes:

clothes £

books £

furniture £

Visual filters

Filtering can also be accomplished by using graphic elements. A practical example of this approach is the AssTech questionnaire [→ pages 244–245].

Were you born on or before 1 January 1992?

☐ No ☐ Yes

Political affiliation

Donation to party

Will you vote for me?

☐ No ☐ Yes

Cross references

If the questions or sections are numbered, you can tell the user to skip to the next relevant section after an if-then question.

1 Do you own a cow? ☐ Yes → *Go to question 2*

☐ No → *Go to question 4*

2 Name of cow

3 Milk yield per day ☐ does not produce milk

4 Size of your garden m²

Flow charts

Attractive to look at, clear and almost like a game, this kind of form guides the user along by using yes/no questions.

Dutch tax forms [→ page 229] are a good example of the way that this approach can make complicated connections look clear.

It's important to highlight the first question in some way, so that the user knows where to begin.

Do you own a cow? ☐ Yes → Name of cow / Milk yield per day

☐ No ↓

Do you plan to acquire a cow? ☐ Yes → Size of your garden m²

☐ No ↓

What is your general opinion of cows?

I love cows ☐ ☐ ☐ ☐ ☐ ☐ *I hate cows*

Do you know anyone who might be interested in acquiring a cow? ☐ Yes → Name / Telephone number

☐ No

Creating structure with graphic elements

There are various ways in which you can structure the sequence of elements such as questions, instructions and text fields. The more complex the form, the more important it is to create a clear and comprehensible structure.

In many cases a simple, sequential division is enough, i.e. all connected elements are grouped together to form units of meaning. If some elements are more important than others, the structure should be hierarchical, so that the items on different levels are visually distinct from each other.

The following examples are just a few of the possibilities, and can also be combined or expanded.

Structure through spacing

The spaces are smaller between connected questions and larger between those that are not connected. This is fine for sequential structures, but is generally not succinct enough to denote a hierarchy.

Structure through enclosure

Connected questions are enclosed within a frame or given a shaded background. This is a very compact method and is also suitable for hierarchical structures.

Structure through similarity

Connected questions are given shared attributes, and those on the same hierarchical level share the same format. This principle works well in combination with other structuring techniques.

Spaced structuring

Four examples of how spacing can be used to structure a sequence of questions. Hierarchical divisions are difficult to convey using spacing alone, so they are not illustrated on this page.

Using lines

This solution requires larger gaps so that the divisions are clear.

First name
Surname
House number, street
Town, postcode

Position
Department

Car make and model
Daily mileage ☐ 5 miles ☐ 50 miles ☐ 150 miles
Rental period ☐ 6 months ☐ 12 months ☐ 18 months

Using shading

The shaded areas make the underlying structure clear.

First name
Surname
House number, street
Town, postcode

Position
Department

Car make and model
Daily mileage ☐ 5 miles ☐ 50 miles ☐ 150 miles
Rental period ☐ 6 months ☐ 12 months ☐ 18 months

Using frames

Frames are not as clear as shading, because the gaps look similar to the text fields.

First name
Surname
House number, street
Town, postcode

Position
Department

Car make and model
Daily mileage ☐ 5 miles ☐ 50 miles ☐ 150 miles
Rental period ☐ 6 months ☐ 12 months ☐ 18 months

Using cells

Table cells make the divisions very clear, as the linked fields are joined directly together.

First name	
Surname	
House number, street	
Town, postcode	

Position	
Department	

Car make and model			
Daily mileage	☐ 5 miles	☐ 50 miles	☐ 150 miles
Rental period	☐ 6 months	☐ 12 months	☐ 18 months

Structuring through enclosure

Connected fields are enclosed or shaded. This column illustrates sequential divisions.

This column illustrates hierarchical structures.

Using lines

The sections are formed using linear outlines alone.

First name
Surname
House number, street
Town, postcode

Position
Department

Car make and model
Daily mileage ☐ 5 miles ☐ 50 miles ☐ 150 miles
Rental period ☐ 6 months ☐ 12 months ☐ 18 months

Using cells

The heavy borderlines create internal divisions that structure the form.

First name			
Surname			
House number, street			
Town, postcode			
Position			
Department			
Car make and model			
Daily mileage	☐ 5 miles	☐ 50 miles	☐ 150 miles
Rental period	☐ 6 months	☐ 12 months	☐ 18 months

Using shading

The areas with the darker fill belong to the top level of the hierarchy.

Name of creditor
Subject of dispute
Amount in dispute
Account number
Sort code

Name of debtor
House number, street
Town, postcode
Date of birth
Place of birth

Using frames

The heavier lines indicate the top level of the hierarchy.

Name of creditor
Subject of dispute
Amount in dispute
Account number
Sort code

Name of debtor
House number, street
Town, postcode
Date of birth
Place of birth

Structuring through similarity

This column shows how a hierarchy can be depicted by using similar attributes.

In this column the hierarchy of the questions is shown by similar formatting.

Using lines

The black rectangles are used to mark the top-level questions.

Name of creditor

Subject of dispute

Amount in dispute

Account number

Sort code

Name of debtor

House number, street

Town, postcode

Date of birth

Place of birth

Using shading

Subsidiary questions are indented, and connected questions are closely grouped.

Name of creditor

Subject of dispute

Amount in dispute

Account number

Sort code

Name of debtor

House number, street

Town, postcode

Date of birth

Place of birth

Using colours and shading

Colours separate different types of content, while shading conveys the hierarchy.

Name of creditor

Subject in dispute

Amount in dispute

Account number

Sort code

Name of debtor

House number, street

Town, postcode

Date of birth

Place of birth

Using lines

Indenting often creates a problem, in that it reduces the space available for either the questions or the answers.

Name of creditor

Subject in dispute

Amount in dispute

Account number

Sort code

Name of debtor

House number, street

Town, postcode

Date of birth

Place of birth

Creating structure with section headings

Graphic elements alone are not enough to give structure to a form. Section headings are a natural and important component of all layout designs, and they must be carefully positioned and given sufficient emphasis.

Highlighting section headings

There are various typographical means of giving emphasis to section headings, such as changing the type style, size or weight.

Type styles

Bold headings create clear divisions, while italics are more discreet and may be overlooked, although that is not an issue in this case.

Personal details

Customer

First name

Surname

Address

House number, street

Town, postcode

Pet

Do you own a pet? ☐ Yes ☐ No

If yes: Species

Name

Product selected

Model ☐ Globokleen ☐ Maxokleen

Service agreement ☐ Basic (9 to 5) ☐ Deluxe (24 hour)

Reversed out

This is even clearer, with the black boxes also adding graphic structure.

Customer

First name

Surname

Address

House number, street

Town, postcode

Pet

Do you own a pet? ☐ Yes ☐ No

If yes: Species

Name

Model ☐ Globokleen ☐ Maxokleen

Service agreement ☐ Basic (9 to 5) ☐ Deluxe (24 hour)

Positioning section headings

To make the structure clear, it's often not enough simply to highlight the section headings. By separating them from the questions you can create an asymmetric effect that looks neat but also interesting.

Indented

Here the questions are placed in a marginal column.

PERSONAL DETAILS

Customer

First name

Surname

Address

House number, street

Town, postcode

Pet

Do you own a pet? ☐ Yes ☐ No

If yes: Species

Name

PRODUCT SELECTED

Model ☐ Globokleen ☐ Maxokleen

Service agreement ☐ Basic (9 to 5) ☐ Deluxe (24 hour)

Aligned

The section headings become focal points that guide the user's eye.

PERSONAL DETAILS

Customer First name

Surname

Address House number, street

Town, postcode

Pet Do you own a pet? ☐ Yes ☐ No

If yes: Species

Name

PRODUCT

Selected item Model ☐ Globokleen ☐ Maxokleen

Service agreement ☐ Basic (9 to 5) ☐ Deluxe (24 hour)

Hanging subheads

These subheads act as anchors which the eye can use for orientation.

PERSONAL DETAILS

Customer

First name

Surname

Address

House number, street

Town, postcode

Pet

Do you own a pet? ☐ Yes ☐ No

If yes: Species

Name

PRODUCT

Selected item

Model ☐ Globokleen ☐ Maxokleen

Delivery ☐ Basic (9 to 5) ☐ Deluxe (24 hour)

Arrows or symbols

Not a structuring principle in the strictest sense, but a simple and effective way to give emphasis to headings.

→ **Personal details**

→ *Customer*

First name

Surname

→ *Address*

House number, street

Town, postcode

→ *Pet*

Do you own a pet? ☐ Yes ☐ No

If yes: Species

Name

→ **Product selected**

Model ☐ Globokleen ☐ Maxokleen

Service agreement ☐ Basic (9 to 5) ☐ Deluxe (24 hour)

Creating structure with numbers and letters

Creating a numbering scheme for section headings and questions is another way of giving a form structure. You can choose to either deliberately draw attention to the numbers and letters, or keep them discreetly in the background in order to minimize their impact.

Numbering section headings

By numbering only the section headings, you can clearly convey a hierarchy. Single numbers do not refer to individual questions, but only to sections.

Roman numerals

These give a clearly defined order, but many people find Roman numerals above III more difficult to read than Arabic numerals.

I Personal data

I.I *Customer*

First name

Surname

I.II *Address*

House number, street

Town, postcode

I.III *Pets*

Do you own a pet? ☐ Yes ☐ No

If yes: Species

Name

II.I Product selected

Model ☐ Globokleen ☐ Maxokleen

Service agreement ☐ Basic (9 to 5) ☐ Deluxe (24 hour)

Arabic numerals

These are more familiar and easier to read. There is no full stop after the last digit.

1 Personal data

1.1 *Customer*

First name

Surname

1.2 *Address*

House number, street

Town, postcode

1.3 *Pets*

Do you own a pet? ☐ Yes ☐ No

If yes: Species

Name

2 Product selected

Model ☐ Globokleen ☐ Maxokleen

Service agreement ☐ Basic (9 to 5) ☐ Deluxe (24 hour)

Numbering questions

If the questions are numbered, it is easy to cross-reference them elsewhere. It is also possible to number both the questions and the section headings, either separately or using the same scheme.

Consecutive numbering

A method designed to make the numbers as discreet as possible.

	Personal data		
	Customer		
1	First name		
2	Surname		
	Address		
3	House number, street		
4	Town, postcode		
	Pets		
5	Do you own a pet?	☐ Yes	☐ No
5a	*If yes:* Species		
5b	Name		
	Product selected		
6	Model	☐ Globokleen	☐ Maxokleen
7	Service agreement	☐ Basic (9 to 5)	☐ Deluxe (24 hour)

Outline numbering

Questions and headings are numbered according to their place in the hierarchy. This can seem technical and may be off-putting to users.

1	**Personal data**		
1.1	*Customer*		
1.1.1	First name		
1.1.1	Surname		
1.2	**Address**		
1.2.1	House number, street		
1.2.2	Town, postcode		
1.3	**Pets**		
1.3.1	Do you own a pet?	☐ Yes	☐ No
1.3.2	*If yes:* Species		
1.3.3	Name		
2	**Product selected**		
2.1	Model	☐ Globokleen	☐ Maxokleen
2.2	Service agreement	☐ Basic (9 to 5)	☐ Deluxe (24 hour)

Numbering and lettering combined

The section headings are marked with letters, while the questions are numbered consecutively within each section.

A	**Personal data**		
	Customer		
1	First name		
2	Surname		
	Address		
3	House number, street		
4	Town, postcode		
	Pet		
5	Do you own a pet?	☐ Yes	☐ No
5a	*If yes:* Species		
5b	Name		
B	**Product selected**		
1	Model	☐ Globokleen	☐ Maxokleen
2	Service agreement	☐ Basic (9 to 5)	☐ Deluxe (24 hour)

Line numbering

Here every line of text is numbered consecutively. This means that any element, whether it is a heading or a question, can be cross-referenced.

1	**Personal data**		
2	*Customer*		
3	First name		
5	Surname		
6	*Address*		
7	House number, street		
8	Town, postcode		
9	*Pet*		
10	Do you own a pet?	☐ Yes	☐ No
11	*If yes:* Species		
12	Name		
13	**Product selected**		
14	Model	☐ Globokleen	☐ Maxokleen
15	Service agreement	☐ Basic (9 to 5)	☐ Deluxe (24 hour)

Highlighting a field

A good structure creates order and makes references visually clear. However, anything especially important, unusual or new on a form needs to be highlighted independently if it is to be noticed. Best suited to this purpose are graphic and typographical forms of emphasis, as these will stand out from their surroundings.

Framed and reversed out — This gives emphasis to the highlighted question.

First name
Surname
House number, street
Town, postcode

Position
Department

Car make and model
Daily mileage ☐ 5 miles ☐ 50 miles ☐ 150 miles
Rental period ☐ 6 months ☐ 12 months ☐ 18 months

Using colour — Red signals the fact that this is or should be something important.

First name
Surname
House number, street
Town, postcode

Position
Department

Car make and model
Daily mileage ☐ 5 miles ☐ 50 miles ☐ 150 miles
Rental period ☐ 6 months ☐ 12 months ☐ 18 months

Shaded fill — A more discreet means of emphasis.

First name
Surname
House number, street
Town, postcode

Position
Department

Car make and model
Daily mileage 5 miles 50 miles 150 miles
Rental period 6 months 12 months 18 months

Size — A purely typographical form of emphasis that looks good.

First name
Surname
House number, street
Town, postcode

Position

Department
Car make and model
Daily mileage ☐ 5 miles ☐ 50 miles ☐ 150 miles
Rental period ☐ 6 months ☐ 12 months ☐ 18 months

Blocking off a field

Many sections of a form are not meant to be filled in by the user but should be left blank for the provider's additions and comments at a later stage. These areas must be clearly marked off in a way that 'blocks' them to the user.

Faded out

Lightweight lines make the relevant questions fade into the background.

First name			
Surname			
House number, street			
Town, postcode			

Position	
Department	

Please do not fill in this section

Car make and model			
Daily mileage	☐ 5 miles	☐ 50 miles	☐ 150 miles
Rental period	☐ 6 months	☐ 12 months	☐ 18 months

Stripes

The striped area indicates: 'Warning! No entry!'

First name
Surname
House number, street
Town, postcode

Position
Department

↘ Please do not fill in this section

Car make and model			
Daily mileage	5 miles	50 miles	150 miles
Rental period	6 months	12 months	18 months

Dotted line

A clearly defined border makes the separation obvious, but its purpose should still be explained somewhere.

First name
Surname
House number, street
Town, postcode

Position
Department

Car make and model			
Daily mileage	5 miles	50 miles	150 miles
Rental period	6 months	12 months	18 months

Textured fill

The same idea as above, but an explanation is needed here too.

First name
Surname
House number, street
Town, postcode

Position
Department

Car make and model			
Daily mileage	☐ 5 miles	☐ 50 miles	☐ 150 miles
Rental period	☐ 6 months	☐ 12 months	☐ 18 months

Instructions and notes

Ideally, users should be able to fill in a form intuitively, but sometimes it is necessary to provide general instructions for the whole form or specific explanations for individual questions. Too many explanations, however, will make the form seem over-complicated. What's more, users don't often read explanatory texts in their entirety anyway. Instead, they scan the form and target the information they are looking for. You can make use of this tendency by giving the text a clear structure, e.g. by highlighting keywords or phrases.

General instructions

These should be logical and clearly structured, providing the following information:

→ purpose and function of the form
→ deadline for its return
→ where to send it
→ documents to be enclosed
→ instructions for completing the questions
→ explanation of symbols

As always, instructions should be friendly and easy to understand.

Highlighting key phrases typographically makes it easier for users to grasp the most important facts.

Dear Mr Brown,

In order to process **your application of 1 April 2010** for the **erection of a cowshed in your garden**, we need some information from you.

Please fill in this form as comprehensively as possible and send it back to us by **30 April 2011**. If you have any questions, our advisers will be only too pleased to assist you.

Thank you for your attention.

Yours sincerely,

A tried and trusted approach is to supply answers to *frequently asked questions (FAQ)*.

Who can apply for membership of your political party?
Anyone who is genuinely concerned about social problems, the economy, education and the environment. In practice, membership depends on your willingness to obey the demands of our Glorious Leader, so please fill in this form as comprehensively as possible.

How much will it cost to join your political party?
Membership is absolutely free, apart from an affiliation fee of £1000 and an annual subscription of £500.

If documents need to be supplied along with the completed form, users often have to hunt for these. A clear list of exactly what is required is therefore very helpful.

Please enclose the following documents with your application:

→ building society passbook (original)
→ bank statement (photocopy acceptable) and ten blank cheques (signed by yourself)
→ credit card complete with PIN number

Pictograms and icons can also be very helpful. It should not, however, be assumed that these are self-explanatory: they should always be accompanied by an explanatory key.

Complete the form as follows:

Please mark boxes with a cross
Please enclose originals of documents
Please enclose copies of documents
ABC abc — Please write in block capitals
0 1 2 3 4 — Please write in the boxes
Please leave blank

Positioning of general instructions

General instructions are best placed at the beginning of the form.

If lengthy explanations are required, these can be listed on a separate sheet or on the back of the form.

Positioning of notes

Notes referring to individual questions or sections should ideally be placed alongside the text in question.

Notes can be positioned in a marginal column, between the questions, or as a hanging indent.

If the notes are very long, another possibility is to add reference numbers and treat them as footnotes.

The best option depends on the layout, the available space, the length of the notes and, not least, how important they are. Should they be consulted only if in doubt, or are they obligatory reading?

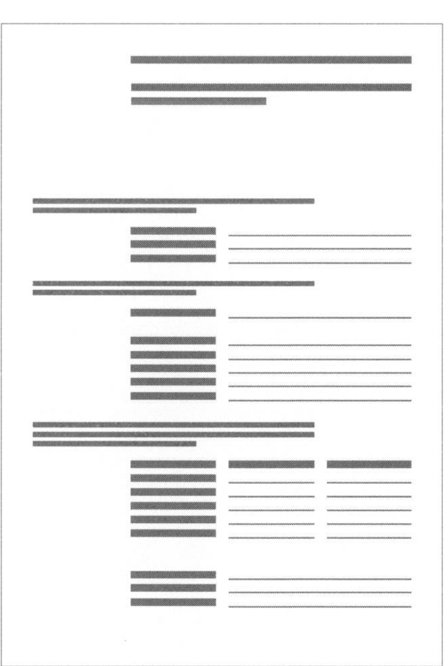

Notes in a marginal column

If the notes are positioned in a left or right-hand marginal column, users can decide for themselves whether or not to read them.

This information is for statistical purposes only and will not affect your human or statutory rights

First name ____________________

Surname ____________________

Pet crocodile ☐ Yes ☐ No

First name only → Crocodile's name ____________________

Length in metres ____________________

Favourite foods ____________________

____

____

If you are in any doubt → *please telephone Veterinary Services on 0808 157 0444*

Place of birth ☐ Zoo ☐ Elsewhere

Valid licence ☐ Yes → ☐ No

House-trained ☐ Yes ☐ No

☐ Training still in progress

Notes between the questions

Here the user is obliged to read the notes or deliberately to skip them.

This information is for statistical purposes only and will not affect your human or statutory rights.

First name ____________________

Surname ____________________

Pet crocodile ☐ Yes ☐ No

Crocodile's name ____________________

(first name only)

Length in metres ____________________

Favourite foods ____________________

____

____

If you are in any doubt, please call Veterinary Services on 0808 157 0444.

Place of birth ☐ Zoo ☐ Elsewhere

Valid licence ☐ Yes → ☐ No

House-trained ☐ Yes ☐ No

☐ Training still in progress

Notes in a hanging indent

A flexible and clear way of positioning instructions.

This information is for statistical purposes only and will not affect your human or statutory rights.

First name ______

Surname ______

Pet crocodile ☐ Yes ☐ No

Give first name only → Crocodile's name ______

Length in metres ______

Favourite foods ______

If you are in any doubt, please call our Veterinary Services department on 0808 157 0444.

Place of birth ☐ Zoo ☐ Elsewhere

Valid licence ☐ Yes → ☐ No

House-trained ☐ Yes ☐ No

☐ Training still in progress

Notes as footnotes

If space is tight or notes are very extensive, reference numbers can be used. The explanations can then be placed at the foot of the page or on a separate page.

The reference numbers beside each question should be discreet, so that they do not seem obtrusive.

The reference numbers alongside the explanations need to be more prominent, so that users can find them easily.

→ 1 First name ______

Surname ______

Pet crocodile ☐ Yes ☐ No

→ 2 Crocodile's name ______

Length in metres ______

→ 3 Favourite foods ______

Place of birth ☐ Zoo ☐ Elsewhere

→ 4 Valid licence ☐ Yes → ☐ No

Notes

1 *This information is required for statistical purposes and does not affect your rights.*

2 *Under paragraph 42, subsection 68 of the Exotic Housepet Act, crocodiles must be wholly identifiable by first name only. We cannot be responsible for cases of mistaken identity.*

3 *Please make a note of any special dietary requirements.*

4 *Even if your crocodile is house-trained, you will need a special permit if you wish to use the same bathroom.*

Multilingual forms

Designing multilingual forms is not always easy but is often necessary. Many official forms need to include more than one language, as do forms for the tourist industry. The main problems are space and the translation of specialist terms. The design must take into account the relative importance of each language – is there one principal language plus one or more translations, or do all the languages have the same status?

Layout

If all the languages are equally important, they should be styled in the same manner.

If one language has precedence, it can be distinguished by using a different size or weight of type, for instance.

If there are only two languages, one can be in roman and the other in italics.

Equal importance

Separating the languages with slashes is acceptable but can be hard to read.

First name / Prénom / Vorname / Nombre de pila

Surname / Nom de famille / Nachname / Apellido

House number, street / No., rue / Hausnummer, Straße /Número, calle

Sex / Sexe / Geschlecht / Sexo

☐ male / masculin / männlich / masculino ☐ female / féminin / weiblich / feminino

An en dash flanked by letterspaces gives the words more prominence and makes it easier for readers to find their own language.

First name – Prénom – Vorname – Nombre de pila

Surname – Nom de famille – Nachname – Apellido

House number, street – No., rue – Hausnummer, Straße – Número, calle

Sex – Sexe – Geschlecht – Sexo

☐ male – masculin – männlich – masculino ☐ female – féminin – weiblich – feminino

This style of layout needs a lot more space but the results are very clear to read.

First name
Prénom
Vorname
Nombre de pila

Sex
Sexe
Geschlecht
Sexo

☐ male
masculin
männlich
masculino

☐ female
féminin
weiblich
feminino

Differentiated

One language can be given precedence over the others by being printed in bold.

First name | Prénom | Vorname | Nombre de pila

Surname | Nom de famille | Nachname | Apellido

House number, street | No., rue | Hausnummer, Straße | Número, calle

A different type size makes the distinction even clearer.

First name
Prénom, Vorname, Nombre de pila

Sex
Sexe, Geschlecht, Sexo

☐ male
masculin, männlich, masculino

☐ female
féminin, weiblich, feminino

The italic text seems slightly less dominant than the roman type.

First name
Nombre de pila

Sex
Sexo

☐ male
masculino

☐ female
feminino

Glossary of common phrases

Here is a list of terms commonly found on forms, translated into some widely spoken languages.

The translations correspond to the way the terms are used in English-speaking countries (e.g. house number is followed by street name), which does not necessarily correspond to the order in which the same information would appear in other countries.

English	French	German	Italian	Spanish
Name	Nom	Name	Nome	Nombre
First name	*Prénom*	*Vorname*	*Nome*	*Nombre de pila*
Surname	*Nom de famille*	*Nachname*	*Cognome*	*Apellido*
Address	Adresse	Anschrift	Indirizzo	Dirección
House number, street	*Nº, rue*	*Hausnummer, Straße*	*Numero, via*	*Número, calle*
Town / city	*Commune*	*Ort*	*Località*	*Localidad / ciudad*
Postcode / ZIP code	*Code postal*	*Postleitzahl*	*CAP*	*Código postal*
Country	*Pays*	*Land*	*Paese*	*País*
Phone	Téléphone	Telefonnummer	Telefono	Teléfono
Fax	Téléfax	Telefaxnummer	Fax	Fax
E-mail	E-mail	E-Mail-Adresse	E-mail	E-mail
Date of birth	Date de naissance	Geburtsdatum	Data di nascita	Fecha de nacimiento
Place of birth	Lieu de naissance	Geburtsort	Luogo di nascita	Lugar de nacimiento
Marital status	État civil	Familienstand	Stato civile	Estado civil
single	*célibataire*	*ledig*	*celibe / nubile*	*soltero / a*
married	*marié (e)*	*verheiratet*	*sposato / a*	*casado / a*
husband	*époux*	*Ehemann*	*marito*	*esposo*
wife	*épouse*	*Ehefrau*	*moglie*	*esposa*
Nationality	Nationalité	Staatsangehörigkeit	Nazionalità	Nacionalidad
Sex	Sexe	Geschlecht	Sesso	Sexo
male	*masculin*	*männlich*	*maschile*	*masculino*
female	*féminin*	*weiblich*	*femminile*	*feminino*
Date, place	Date, lieu	Datum, Ort	Data, luogo	Fecha, lugar
Signature	Signature	Unterschrift	Firma	Firma

English	Portuguese	Polish	Turkish	Russian
Name	Apelido	Nazwisko	Isim	имя
First name	*Nome próprio*	*Imię*	*Ad*	*имя*
Surname	*Apelido*	*Nazwisko*	*Soyad*	*фамилия*
Address	Endereço	Adres	Adres	адрес
House number, street	*Nùmero, rua*	*Nr domu,ulica*	*Ev no., sokak*	*улица, номер дома*
Town / city	*Localidade*	*Miejscowość*	*Yer*	*город*
Postcode / ZIP code	*Código postal*	*Kod pocztowy*	*Posta kodu*	*почтовый индекс*
Country	*País*	*Kraj*	*Ülke*	*страна*
Phone	Telefone	Nr telefonu	Telefonnumarasi	номер телефона
Fax	Fax	Fax	Faxnumarasi	факс
E-mail	E-mail	Adres e-mail	E-mail-adresi	эмаль
Date of birth	Data de nascimento	Data urodzenia	Doğumtarihi	дата рождения
Place of birth	Local de nascimento	Miejsce urodzenia	Doğumyeri	место рождения
Marital status	Estado civil	Stan cywilny	Medeni hali	семейное положение
single	*solteiro / a*	*wolny*	*bekâr*	*холостой*
married	*casado / a*	*żonaty / zamężna*	*evli*	*женатый*
husband	*esposo*	*małżonek*	*koca*	*супруг*
wife	*esposa*	*małżonka*	*kari*	*супруга*
Nationality	Nacionalidade	Obywatelswo	Uyruk	гражданство
Sex	Sexo	Płec	Cinsiyet	пол
male	*masculino*	*męska*	*erkek*	*мужской*
female	*feminino*	*żeńska*	*disi*	*женский*
Date, place	Data, lugar	Data, miejscowość	Tarih, yer	дата, город
Signature	Assinatura	Podpis	Imza	подпись

2.3

Digital forms

Digital or analogue

Paper forms are now generally thought to be a rather outdated and old-fashioned concept. Aside from this, they also suffer from an increasingly serious problem: slow response times. One issue is that, on paper, it is hard to control how users handle a form, and what information they supply and how. Another is that the forms cannot be altered by their users, adapting to their needs and capabilities. Digital or paperless forms, particularly those in HTML or PDF format, therefore offer several advantages over paper alternatives.

Digital forms are nonlinear

Embedded links within digital forms make it possible for a user to switch quickly between different sections and questions, but with paper forms, the same thing occurs in a faster and more intuitive way when users turn pages. But the outstanding advantage of digital forms is that they only need to display the sections and questions that are relevant. Depending on the responses given to particular filter questions, additional questions can be included or omitted, and entire sections can be skipped. This nonlinearity also gives more freedom to users, who don't have to deal with questions that don't apply to them.

Digital forms can check input

On paper, users who have made mistakes or omissions can easily send off a wrongly completed form. To prevent this, digital forms can oblige users to answer important questions and allow only certain types of information to be submitted. For example, some fields may only permit input in figures, or may specify a particular number of digits that have to be included. The advantage is that only correct and complete data can be submitted, preventing the need for additional requests for information or clarification. The disadvantage is that if the number of error messages is high, due to incorrect or missing information, and if the form has no tolerance for errors, many users may give up. In the worst cases, clients may be lost who would not have been alienated by a paper form. Ultimately, an incomplete form is usually more useful to its providers than no information at all.

Digital forms can help users to fill them

If required, explanations and tips can be dynamically built into a digital form. There is no need to turn to the back of the page or additional sheets to look things up. It is also easy to switch between different languages if needed. Text fields can allow room for long answers so that extra space for notes is not required. In addition, the form can make suggestions, include information that is already known and anticipate the most likely responses. Digital forms can also make use of user profiles so that previously supplied information can be automatically filled in: this creates a more user-friendly environment.

Digital forms can do calculations

Generally, information supplied on paper is evaluated at a later stage and calculations are not done immediately, so it is difficult for users to see the results of the information that they have provided. Digital forms, however, can automatically apply complex mathematical algorithms and check the answers. Instead of being a 'black box' system that is incomprehensible from the outside, digital forms can become tools that show users the results of their input in real time. This can be especially useful if services are being ordered, for example.

Digital forms can be accessible

People with disabilities can often find paper forms to be an obstacle to claiming their own rights and entitlements. Blind or partially sighted users or those with motor impairments find themselves at a particular disadvantage. Digital forms can be adapted to the needs of disabled users, as long as they are designed from the start with this in mind. The options that can make digital forms more accessible include resizing type, changing colours and reading text aloud using a screen reader or converting it into a Braille display. Accessibility is covered by disability discrimination regulations, and as such is often legally required in the public sector and also highly recommended for the private sector. Disabled people make up a significant section of the total population and include a proportionately high number of internet users. Forms designed for maximum accessibility also have the advantage of improved usability on handheld or palmtop devices, or anything else with a limited amount of screenspace.

Digital forms are easier to update

Paper forms are solid and reliable, but when one version of a form becomes outdated for any reason, another one must be created and distributed. Digital forms can be centrally updated, and the user can therefore be certain that only the most up-to-date version of the form can be accessed. However, when a form is taken offline, not only is it no longer accessible from outside, but it can no longer be used for reference or comparison, which may be a disadvantage.

Digital forms are faster

All data can be immediately delivered to as many recipients as required, at any time with no delays. This means written communication that is no longer reliant on the postal service.

Digital disadvantages

Despite all these advantages, digital forms also have their downside. In some circumstances, the familiarity and material nature of paper forms gives them an advantage.

Digital forms are unclear, unwieldy and ephemeral

Users can easily flick through paper forms and see how long they are. They can get an overview and simply move on. The process of filling in the form can be broken off at any time and begun again when convenient. Digital forms are far trickier in this regard. If users don't finish filling it on a single viewing, or want to backtrack and change something, they can sometimes lose all of the responses they've already given and have to begin again from scratch. When the form has been completed and submitted, it vanishes from the screen and there's no proof that it's been sent. There are solutions to this, however, such as printing out a copy or sending an email as confirmation of receipt, but these are not always available. Another major problem with many digital forms is that users cannot look through them to the end without filling them in at the same time, which means that users often don't know enough about what is involved.

Digital forms are not secure

While personal signatures, passports and so on are still widely accepted as proofs of identity, and confidential material sent through the post can be signed for, the security of digital forms, particular on the internet, is not always clear. There are various digital equivalents to providing a signature and showing some ID, such as digital signatures and chip and PIN cards, but as yet there is no single widespread standard. The fact that online data can be passed on quickly and shared with other sources means that many users do not trust that their information will be protected.

Digital forms require technology

Paper forms need to be printed and posted, but this requires relatively little equipment or technology. Digital forms, on the other hand, require the user to possess the right hardware and software, and are therefore an obstacle to anyone who does not have access to the necessary technology. This applies particularly to the socially vulnerable and the elderly, as well as all those whose computers are too old, who are using the wrong operating system or who have a very slow internet connection. If you want to make digital forms as accessible to as many people as possible, you must take technological requirements into account and ensure that compatibility is as high as possible.

Digital forms need to be simplified

There is now a great temptation to handle as many communication processes as possible digitally and online. A lot of money can be saved by speeding up processing and cutting down on staff. However, these advantages are all on the side of the publisher or provider. It is they who have the most to gain by getting rid of paper forms. While you may want to persuade users to communicate with authorities and businesses over the internet, you should not force them to do so unless if you can offer them the genuine advantages of simplicity and convenience. Digital forms need to be simpler, easier to understand and more user-friendly than paper forms if they are to be successful.

Platforms and formats

Digital forms can be used on a range of platforms, from home PCs to bank terminals. Mobile devices are of particular interest because they can be used almost anywhere that paper forms are used. Two of the most important formats for digital forms are PDF and HTML. The PDF format is well suited to distributing forms over the internet, while HTML forms can be built into websites.

Platforms	PCs	Widely used in both home and office environments, most have internet access and are connected to a printer. They have large monitor screens and are generally operated with a keyboard and a mouse. PDF and HTML forms can be used on almost all PCs. Compared to paper forms, they are quite immobile.
	Tablet PCs	Mobile computers with touch-sensitive displays that can be written on directly using a stylus that learns to recognize the user's handwriting. Relatively expensive, but very suitable for forms, which can be filled in the normal way. Because of the large display and the use of standard PC operating systems, PDF and HTML forms can generally be used without any special adaptation.
	PDAs *(Personal Digital Assistants)* and Smartphones	PDAs are small, lightweight mobile computers, generally with wireless internet access. Smartphones combine the functionality of a PDA with a mobile phone. They use special operating systems, but data exchange with PCs is generally problem-free. They have a touchscreen or are used with a stylus and can even recognize handwriting. HTML and PDF forms must be suitable for use on their very small display screens.
	Terminals	This category includes ATM machines and other bank terminals, along with check-in screens at airports and ticket machines. As a means of making automated services available in public spaces, their key requirements are sturdiness, user-friendliness and security. Forms are usually displayed on touch-sensitive screens and are part of an entire interface which includes buttons, keypads and input and output slots.
PDF forms PDFs (standing for *Portable Document Format*) were developed to allow documents to be displayed on all operating systems. They are the standard format for exchanging digital documents and can include interactive functions.	Pros	PDF forms look almost the same whether they are printed out on paper or viewed on a monitor with any operating system. This saves on development costs and allows full control of the design. PDF documents also work offline and can be created with any word-processing or DTP software, so do not require any specialist programming skills.
	Cons	Software is required to view, fill out and print the form. However, PDF readers are free and widely available. It is relatively expensive to make PDF forms fully accessible.
HTML forms HTML is the programming language used by most websites. HTML forms can be used to transfer data between a website and its users.	Pros	HTML is a standard format that can be displayed on any device with a web browser. Interactive functions can be inbuilt. Accessibility is easy to achieve.
	Cons	The design possibilities are limited and the look of the form will change depending on the browser or operating system that is used to display it. Development costs are relatively high.

PDF forms

PDF forms can be created using almost any DTP or word-processing software. To allow the form to be filled in on screen, the interactive elements must be built into the document afterwards. PDF forms are always the first choice if the form is intended to be used both on screen and on paper.

Types of PDF form

There are three types of PDF form, all of which function in different ways. Only interactive PDFs are true digital forms.

Noninteractive PDF forms

These must be printed out first, then filled in and returned. They are a digital version of paper forms, and allow forms to be sent over the internet. They are easier to distribute than paper forms, but they do not make use of the more advanced potential of PDFs.

Interactive PDF forms for printing

These can be filled in on screen but must be printed out to be signed and returned. They include interactive elements that make the form easier to complete. The form can be filled in and printed out using the free Adobe Reader software.

Barcodes are a useful way of allowing the data on a printed form to be read digitally. The PDF form encodes the data entered by the user and turns it into a barcode. The barcode is then printed out along with the form and can be scanned later to read it.

Interactive PDF forms for submitting online

These can often be signed with a digital signature and the input data submitted as an email or in another electronic format. They can be submitted either as a complete PDF form or as a file that contains only the data provided by the user. Form suppliers can then import this information into an empty form or document.

Creating PDF forms

Word, InDesign, Quark XPress, etc. and Adobe Acrobat

The most common way to make a PDF form is by using popular DTP or word-processing software and then saving the file in PDF format. Interactive features can then be added in Adobe Acrobat.

Adobe LiveCycle Designer

This software (for Windows only) allows you to design forms and include interactive elements at the same time. It offers more options than Adobe Acrobat and is particularly suitable for larger projects.

Accessibility

To make a PDF form accessible to users with visual impairments or restricted mobility, it is necessary to add tags. These tags contain information about the structure of the document and descriptions of the individual elements. They allow the form to be read with a screen reader or Braille output device where available, or using the accessibility and zoom settings built into Adobe Acrobat.

Interactive PDF form

This PDF form can be filled in Adobe Reader and is designed in A4 format. This makes it easy to print out, but to see the whole thing on screen, you have to scroll down.

The form elements listed below can be included in a PDF document. The terms are slightly different to those used for HTML forms, but the basic elements are the same.

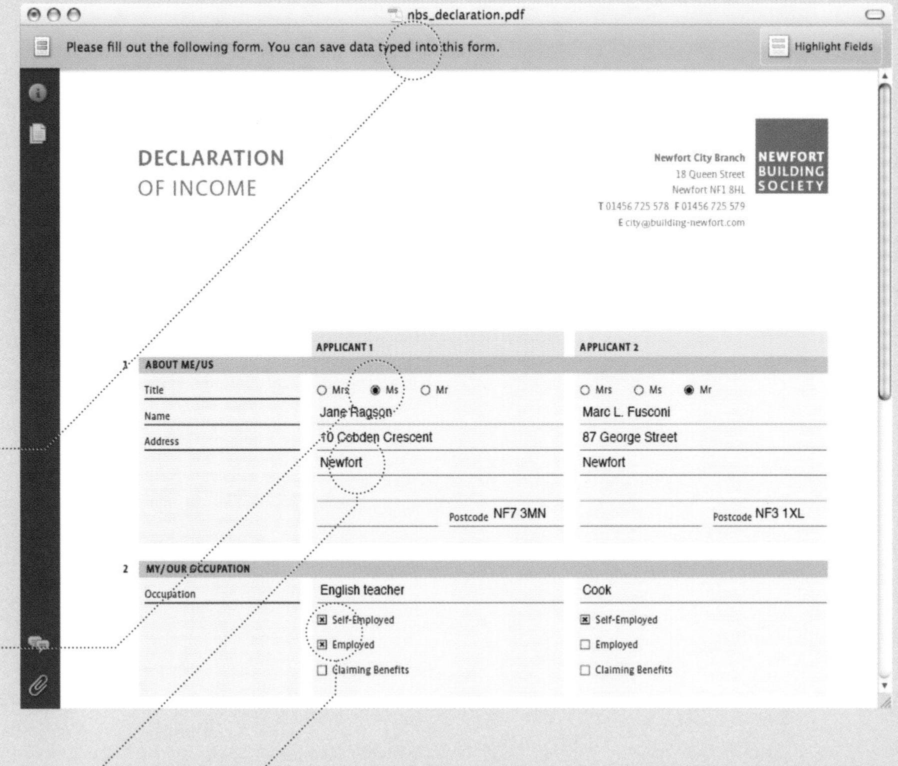

nbs_declaration.pdf

Please fill out the following form. You can save data typed into this form. Highlight Fields

DECLARATION
OF INCOME

Newfort City Branch
18 Queen Street
Newfort NF1 8HL
T 01456 725 578 F 01456 725 579
E city@building-newfort.com

NEWFORT BUILDING SOCIETY

		APPLICANT 1		APPLICANT 2	
1	ABOUT ME/US				
	Title	○ Mrs ◉ Ms ○ Mr		○ Mrs ○ Ms ◉ Mr	
	Name	Jane Ragson		Marc L. Fusconi	
	Address	10 Cobden Crescent		87 George Street	
		Newfort		Newfort	
			Postcode NF7 3MN		Postcode NF3 1XL
2	MY/OUR OCCUPATION				
	Occupation	English teacher		Cook	
		☒ Self-Employed		☒ Self-Employed	
		☒ Employed		☐ Employed	
		☐ Claiming Benefits		☐ Claiming Benefits	

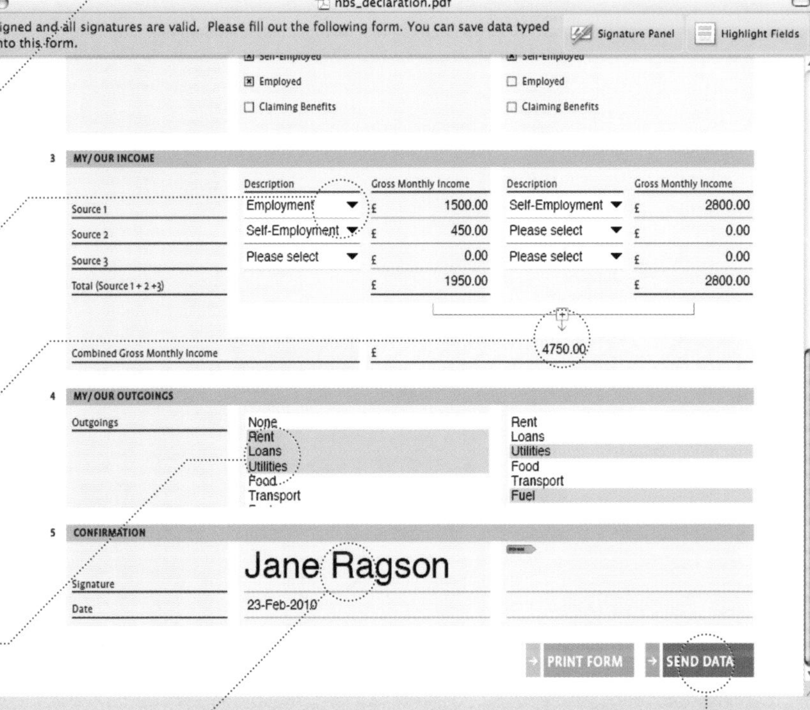

nbs_declaration.pdf

Signed and all signatures are valid. Please fill out the following form. You can save data typed into this form. Signature Panel Highlight Fields

		Description	Gross Monthly Income	Description	Gross Monthly Income
		☒ Employed		☐ Employed	
		☐ Claiming Benefits		☐ Claiming Benefits	
3	MY/OUR INCOME				
	Source 1	Employment	£ 1500.00	Self-Employment	£ 2800.00
	Source 2	Self-Employment	£ 450.00	Please select	£ 0.00
	Source 3	Please select	£ 0.00	Please select	£ 0.00
	Total (Source 1 + 2 + 3)		£ 1950.00		£ 2800.00
	Combined Gross Monthly Income		£ 4750.00		
4	MY/OUR OUTGOINGS				
	Outgoings	None, Rent, Loans, Utilities, Food, Transport		Rent, Loans, Utilities, Food, Transport, Fuel	
5	CONFIRMATION				
	Signature	Jane Ragson			
	Date	23-Feb-2010			

PRINT FORM SEND DATA

Document message bar

This explains that the form is interactive and states whether any rights or security restrictions are imposed on it.

Radio buttons

These present a set of options, from which only one can be chosen. The size and appearance of the buttons and the marks used to fill them can be selected.

Text fields

Fields that allow one or more lines of text to be inserted. Format, alignment, decimal point, currency and other types of input can all be specified.

Checkboxes

For multiple choice responses. The size and appearance of the buttons and the marks used to fill them can be changed.

Combo boxes

These are pop-up menus that let users choose one item from a list of options or input their own text.

Automatic calculations

The value or content of text fields can be automatically calculated. A range of mathematical calculations are available.

List boxes

These display a list of items, allowing one or more of them to be selected. However, checkboxes are clearer and more intuitive for users.

Digital signature

A digital signature can be added to a PDF form. To do this, a digital ID is required: this can either be self-created in Adobe Reader or provided by a third party.

Buttons

Buttons can be used to perform various actions, such as clearing all the text fields or submitting the completed data. They can also be set to open another file or skip over certain fields.

HTML forms

HTML forms are the most widely used tools that allow the interchange of data between websites and their users. They are not only a way of submitting information, but can also include navigational and interactive features such as search tools and log-ins. HTML was not developed specifically for forms, and the standard HTML form elements do not offer a great deal of functionality. Extra functions must be added using other programming tools, such as JavaScript.

Tools

Plain HTML is not enough in itself to create functional and useful web forms. It must be combined with other tools.

HTML *(Hypertext Markup Language)* and CSS *(Cascading Style Sheets)*	An HTML form is a specially standardized section of an HTML document. It includes typical form elements and their labels. The look of the different parts of the form can be altered to some degree by using CSS, a type of style sheet for HTML elements.
JavaScript	JavaScript is a programming language, which can give additional functionality to HTML elements, among other things. For example, it can validate input, carry out calculations, or highlight specific text fields.
XForms	XForms is a new programming format designed specifically for web forms. It includes all the elements of HTML forms with additional standardized functions. It reduces programming costs considerably, and can send and structure data in a user-friendly way. Forms created with XForms will also function on a wider range of user interfaces than HTML forms do. However, XForms is still at the development stage and is not yet compatible with most browsers.

Sending data

For the submitted information to be used, it must be sent to a recipient.

CGI scripts *(Common Gateway Interface)*	HTML forms send data in a very simply structured way: as a simple string of field names and their respective values. This information is passed on to the web server, where a CGI script collects the data and sends or forwards it to a designated recipient.
XML *(Extensible Markup Language)*	XForms can deliver data in the form of an XML file to any number of recipients, without the need for a CGI script. The XML format allows the data to be structured in a complex way; it can also be easily imported into other applications.

Accessibility

To be fully accessible, an HTML form must be set up in a way that users can adapt to fit their own needs and access without using a mouse. It also needs to be compatible with special equipment such as screen readers or Braille output devices.

Basics	All relevant information must be presented as HTML text and not in the form of images. Alternative text must be provided for any images that are used. There should be a clear division between information and layout elements, and CSS, multimedia content and special programming languages such as JavaScript should be avoided, although this can create additional issues with functionality.
Colours	Users should be able to choose alternative colour schemes and understand the form even without the colour information.
Text	It should be possible to display the form in a range of type sizes.
Navigation	Access keys (a form of keyboard shortcut) and a sensible tab order will allow the form to be used without a mouse.
Structure	Every form field must be tagged with its description.

HTML form

Forms rarely fill only a single screen. To avoid the need to scroll down, a form can be divided across several screens. The disadvantage of this is that users cannot get an overview of the whole form and the answers they have already given.

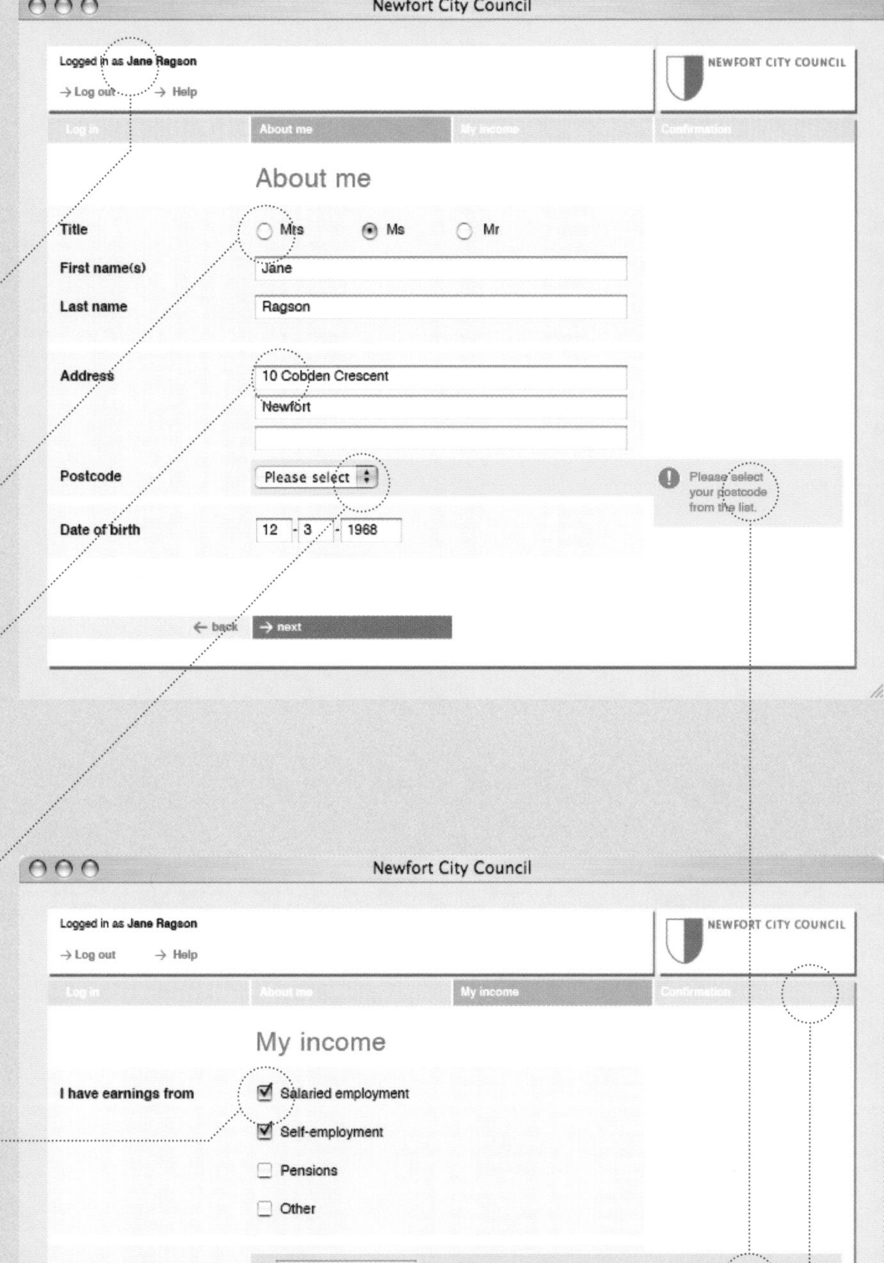

Identity

Creating a user log-in or profile means that previous users can be identified, and saves them time because they don't have to submit the same personal information on every visit to the site.

Radio buttons *(HTML element)*

Single-choice questions are traditionally rendered in HTML as radio buttons.

Text fields *(HTML element)*

These fields allow users to enter one or more lines of text. The length of the field can be set and a sample text can be inserted. The format of the response cannot be specified, so must be checked afterwards, using a script.

Drop-down list *(HTML element)*

A menu that expands when clicked, which allows a single option to be selected.

Checkboxes *(HTML element)*

These are used for multiple choice responses. Unlike with radio buttons, it's possible to select more than one answer.

List box *(HTML element)*

This style of list differs from a drop-down list because it allows more than one answer to be selected. However, many users are not familiar with the way to do this (by holding down the Command or Ctrl key), so it's better to avoid this element and use checkboxes instead.

Buttons

Buttons can be displayed in standard HTML format or using your own customized graphics. To allow the users to move through the form as quickly as possible, it makes sense to create a distinction between primary and secondary actions. This means making important buttons such as 'Next' look darker, brighter or more distinctive, and making others, such as 'Back' or 'More Information', look paler or less important.

Notes and error messages

Notes for users are displayed alongside the next field that needs to be filled. When the 'Next' button is pressed, a script checks the answers. If a response is missing or given in the wrong format, an error message flashes up. This function needs to be programmed in JavaScript. It's best to indicate all mistakes at the same time and add helpful explanations in an appropriate place.

Making progress

For forms that spread across multiple pages, it's important to include a progress bar or orientation system of some kind, so that users can see which stage they've reached and how much of the form they still have to complete.

Good form design

District of Saumur

Certificates

Issued by District Urbain de Saumur, France
Design Intégral Ruedi Baur et Associés, Paris
Identity by Ruedi Baur and Denis Coueignoux, form designs by Eva Kubinyi
Year 1992
Typeface Rotis Semisans

These unusually striking birth and marriage certificates were part of a complete corporate identity for the town of Saumur in western France. The certificates accompany events which are normally a private matter, though inevitably they bring together public institutions and private citizens. These records use suitably dignified typography. The dynamic arrangement of the different elements is strikingly different from conventional forms, but nevertheless extremely functional, as it gives visual shape to the information. Another notable feature is the highlighting of the text fields by using variations in line weight and length.

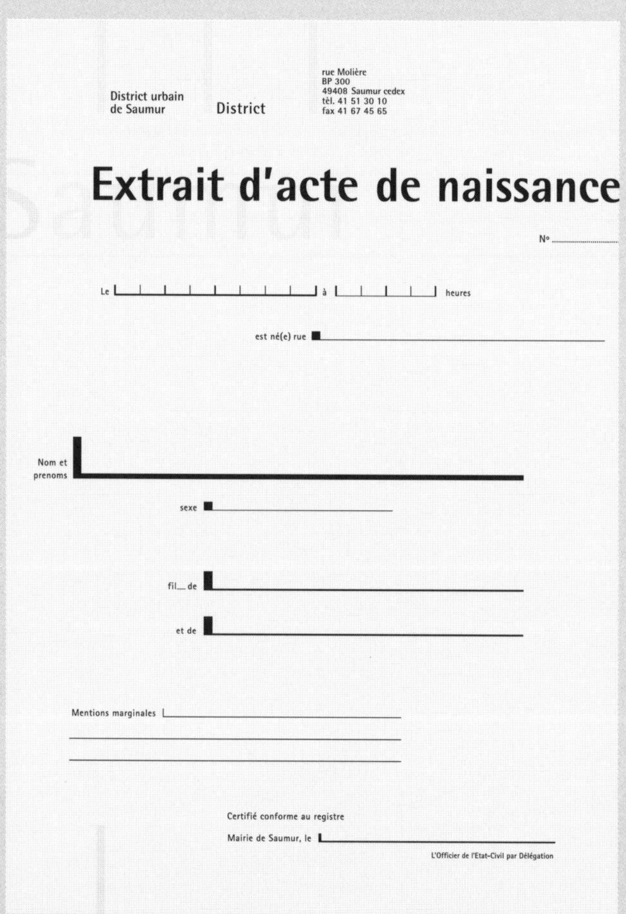

District urbain de Saumur District
rue Molière
BP 300
49408 Saumur cedex
tél. 41 51 30 10
fax 41 67 45 65

Extrait d'acte de naissance

N°

Le à heures

est né(e) rue

Nom et prenoms

sexe

fil__ de

et de

Mentions marginales

Certifié conforme au registre
Mairie de Saumur, le
L'Officier de l'Etat-Civil par Délégation

Birth certificate: A4

District urbain de Saumur District
rue Molière
BP 300
49408 Saumur cedex
tél. 41 51 30 10
fax 41 67 45 65

Déclaration de naissance

N°

Le à heures

Est né(e),

rue

Prénoms de l'enfant

Nom (en majuscules)

Sexe

de

Nom du père

Né à (Commune)

(Département ou pays)

Date de naissance (jou – mois – année)

et de

Nom de jeune fille de la mére (en majuscles)

Prénoms

Né à (Commune)

(Département ou pays)

Date de naissance (jou – mois – année)

Certifié conforme au registre
Mairie de Saumur, le
L'Officier de l'Etat-Civil par Délégation

Birth announcement: A4

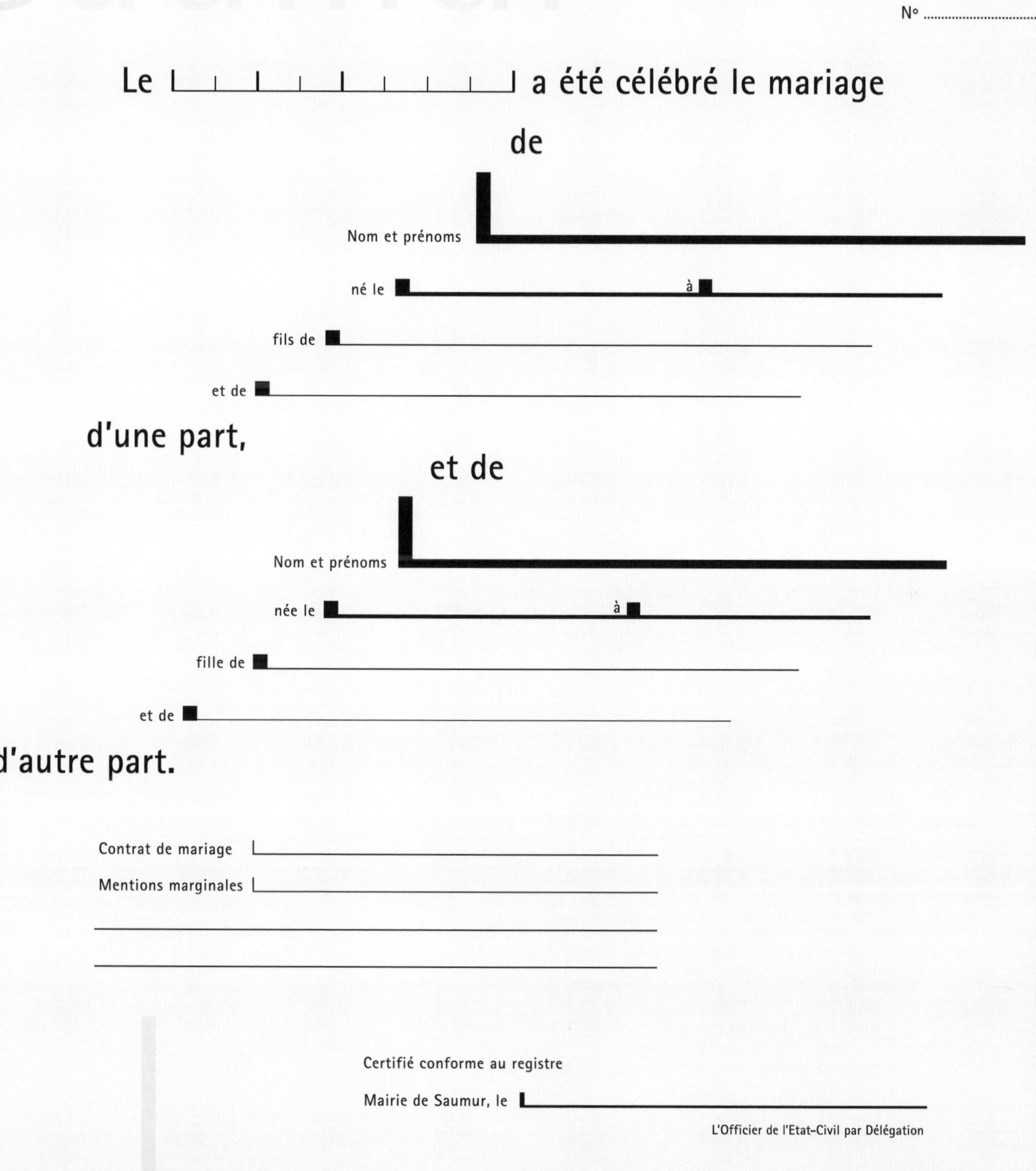

District urbain
de Saumur

District

rue Molière
BP 300
49408 Saumur cedex
tèl. 41 51 30 10
fax 41 67 45 65

Extrait d'acte de mariage

N° ....

Le [ ] a été célébré le mariage

de

Nom et prénoms ______

né le ______ à ______

fils de ______

et de ______

d'une part,

et de

Nom et prénoms ______

née le ______ à ______

fille de ______

et de ______

d'autre part.

Contrat de mariage ______

Mentions marginales ______

______

______

Certifié conforme au registre

Mairie de Saumur, le ______

L'Officier de l'Etat-Civil par Délégation

Marriage certificate: A4

One attractive feature is the way in which the details of bride and groom are laid out in a step-like design.

Amsterdam City Council

Model corporate design forms

Issued by	Gemeente Amsterdam, Netherlands
Design	Edenspiekermann (formerly Eden Design & Communication), Amsterdam
Year	2003–2005
Typeface	Avenir

The city council of Amsterdam recognizes the fact that in a democratic system it is essential that communications should be instantly recognizable, transparent and reliable, as well as accessible to all citizens. Under the motto 'What unites us is greater than what divides us', Eden Design created a clear and simple identity for the city which was used in all council communications, including forms. It was soon apparent that the new forms were filled in more quickly and more accurately, thus proving more efficient and more cost-effective.

User-friendly

Many Dutch forms are designed with a view to the fact that they are meant to serve the applicant and not the administration. The wording on the title page of this application reads: 'In cases of need, the council can give you priority access to rented accommodation. Please use this form.'

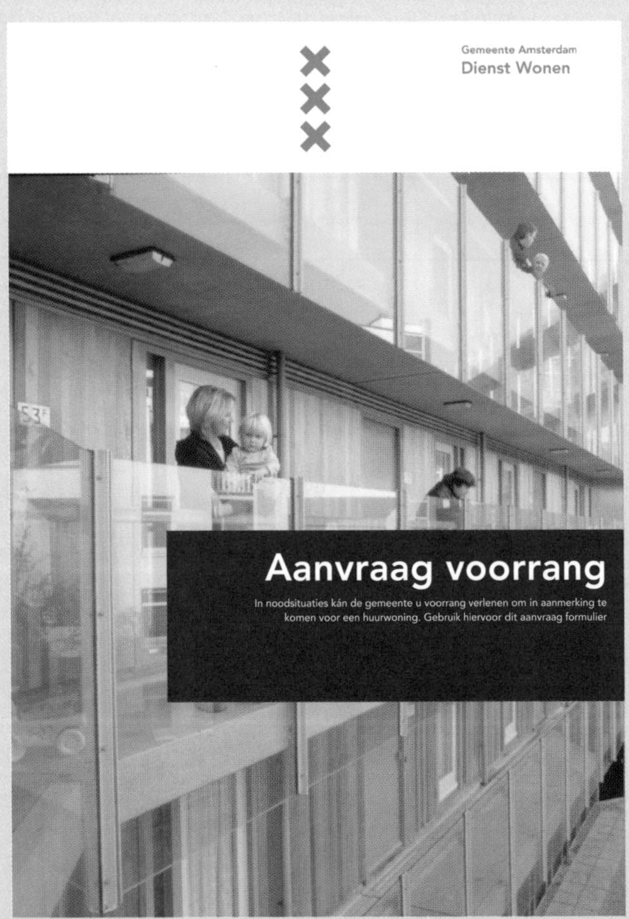

Title page of an application form issued by the Housing Office: A4

4. Kinderen

Alleen invullen als u kinderen heeft die met u meeverhuizen

Geboortedatum en geslacht kinderen ☐ M ☐ V ☐ M ☐ V ☐ M ☐ V ☐ M ☐ V ☐ M ☐ V ☐ M ☐ V

5. Woonsituatie

Woont u zelfstandig? ☐ Ja → **ga naar vraag 5a** ☐ Nee → **ga naar vraag 5e**

5a U woont zelfstandig sinds — Aantal kamers

5b Soort Woning ☐ Koopwoning **[Sluit bij: kopie koopcontract] → ga naar vraag 6**
☐ Huurwoning → Huur per maand

5c Het huurcontract staat op naam van, *zie toelichting* ☐ Uzelf
☐ Iemand anders → Naam

5d Ingangsdatum contract **[Sluit bij: kopie huurcontract] → ga naar vraag 6**

5e U bent inwonend sinds — Aantal kamers

5f U bent inwonend bij

6. Inschrijving bij WoningNet

Staat u ingeschreven bij WoningNet? ☐ Nee
☐ Ja → Inschrijfdatum — Registratienummer

Staat uw partner ingeschreven bij WoningNet? ☐ Nee
☐ Ja → Inschrijfdatum — Registratienummer

7. Inkomen

Uw inkomen, *zie toelichting* €

Inkomen partner

Inkomen kinderen ≥18 € +

Totaal gezamelijk inkomen € **[Sluit bij: kopie loonstroken en/of uitkeringsspecificaties en jaaropgaven]**

8. Ondertekening

Ik verklaar dit formulier volledig en naar waarheid te hebben ingevuld. Ik ga ermee akkoord dat mijn persoonsgegevens (en die van mijn eventuele partner) worden opgenomen in een bestand van de Dienst Wonen. Bovendien kunnen mijn antwoorden worden gecontroleerd bij derden (bijv. andere overheidsinstanties, verhuurder, werkgever).Bij een voorrangsaanvraag ga ik ermee akkoord dat de Dienst Wonen voor meer informatie contact kan opnemen met de genoemde instanties bij vraag 1.
Mijn gegevens worden niet gebruikt voor andere doeleinden.

Heeft u redenen om niet te ondertekenen, dan betekent dit dat uw aanvraag niet in behandeling wordt genomen.

Datum

Handtekening aanvrager — Handtekening partner

Let op! Vergeet niet de gevraagde kopieën bij te sluiten. Ik sluit bij: ☐ Kopie huur- of koopcontract
☐ Kopie recente loonstrook en/of uitkeringsspecificatie en jaaropgave

2

Inside page of application form

The layout has a line-based design. Thinner lines emphasize questions and define text fields. Heavier lines divide the form into sections.

Gemeente Amsterdam
Dienst Wonen

Aanvraag voorrang

1. Reden

Reden aanvraag: ☐ Sociale omstandigheden ☐ Medische omstandigheden

Deze omstandigheden zijn bekend bij
Meerdere antwoorden mogelijk

☐ Maatschappelijk werk	Contactpersoon		Telefoon	
☐ Advocaat	Contactpersoon		Telefoon	
☐ Huisarts	Contactpersoon		Telefoon	
☐ Politie	Contactpersoon		Telefoon	
☐ Verhuurder	Contactpersoon		Telefoon	
☐ Anders	Contactpersoon		Telefoon	

2. Aanvrager

Voorletters en achternaam ☐ M ☐ V

Meisjesnaam

Adres, *zie toelichting*

Postcode en plaats

Postadres, *zie toelichting*

Postcode en plaats

Telefoon privé | Telefoon werk

E-mail adres

Geboortedatum

Woont in Amsterdam sinds

Burgerlijke staat
☐ Alleenstaand ☐ Gehuwd
☐ Samenwonend ☐ Gescheiden
☐ Geregistreerd partnerschap

3. Partner

Alleen invullen als u een partner heeft

Voorletters en achternaam ☐ M ☐ V

Meisjesnaam

Wonen u en uw partner op hetzelfde adres? ☐ Ja → **ga door met vraag 4** ☐ Nee → **vul vraag 3 verder in**

Adres, *zie toelichting*

Postcode en plaats

Telefoon privé | Telefoon werk

E-mail adres

123456789 formuliernummer

1

Inside page of application form

The forms are divided into several columns, with a margin on the left which contains the questions. This stands out and means that questions need to be brief and to the point. Instructions are in italics and are therefore distinct from the rest of the text.

Sample forms for
Amsterdam City Council

Three crosses

The triple cross logo is taken from the three St Andrew's crosses that appear on Amsterdam's 14th-century coat-of-arms. Additional symbols are used to represent different council departments.

Bezoekadres
Bijlmerplantsoen 395
1102 DK Amsterdam

Postbus 23457
1100 DZ Amsterdam
Telefoon 20 652 4800
Fax 020 652 4924

Gemeente Amsterdam
Dienst belastingen
Kwitantie

000265

Let op! *Deze kwitantie is alleen geldig met aangehechte pin-transactiebon*

Ontvangen van: A.S.M. Ruytenbeek van Henegouwen-Rosenthal
Nieuwe Prinsengracht 128
1038 AZ Amsterdam
Subjectnummer: 345678912345667

Ontvangen: 212,23 Eur

Datum ontvangst: 20 juni 2003
Ontvangstnummer: 34567891234
Pinbon/Toelichting: 12345

Soort belasting	Jaar	Vordering	Bedrag	Extra kosten	Rente	Totaalbedrag
OZB-Eigenarenbelasting	1998	212345678903	75,00 Eur	50,00 Eur	6,85 Eur	131,85 Eur
Rioolrecht	2000	456789012345	25,00 Eur	25,00 Eur	0,38 Eur	50,38 Eur
Waterzuivering	2002	567890123456	30,00 Eur			30,00 Eur
						212,23 Eur

Totaal betaald aan vorderingen: 6.345,23 Eur

Invorderingsambtenaar: P.J. van der Horst — Paraaf
Behandelend ambtenaar: R.Pruis — Paraaf

Receipt: 210 mm × 210 mm

This form is filled in and printed digitally. It therefore does not need lines for handwriting, and the line spacing can be reduced.

Gemeente Amsterdam
Bestuursdienst

Op grond van artikel 801 van het Ambtenarenregelement Amsterdam en het besluit Beëdiging Ambtenaren, is besloten de medewerkers van de Bestuursdienst Amsterdam aan te wijzen als ambtenaren waarvoor de verplichting tot het afleggen van een eed of belofte geldt.

Ten overstaan van de Gemeentesecretaris van Amsterdam, Erik Gerritsen,

heeft

op De ambtseed afgelegd:

Ambtseed

"Ik zweer trouw aan de Grondwet en aan de overige wetten des Rijks.
Ik zweer, dat ik om in mijn betrekking te worden benoemd geen geschenken op welke wijze en in welke vorm ook, aan iemand heb gegeven of beloofd.
Ik zweer, dat ik mij in deze betrekking eerlijk, getrouw en nauwgezet zal gedragen en de belangen der Gemeente, zoveel in mijn vermogen is, zal behartigen mij verbindende geheim te houden al hetgeen mij in verband met deze werkzaamheden onder de plicht van geheimhouding is toevertrouwd of waarvan ik het vertrouwelijke karakter moet begrijpen.
Zo waarlijk helpe mij God Almachtig".

Amsterdam

De Gemeentesecretaris De ambtenaar

Oath of office: A4

Even the oath of office signed by city councillors is issued as a form, designed to match the city's corporate identity.

Bezoekadres
Kaspeldreef 8
1011 PN Amsterdam

Postbus 23475
1100 DZ Amsterdam

Gemeente Amsterdam
Dienst belastingen
Kwitantie

B 000265

Naam betaler — Subjectnummer
Straat en huisnummer
Postcode en plaats

Betaling	Belastingbedrag	Bestemd voor belastingmiddel	Jaar	Vorderingsnummer
	€			
	€ +			
Totaal betaald	€			

Datum ontvangst — Betalingsstempel
Ontvangstnummer — Kenmerk kassier — Paraaf

KW 0410

Receipt to be filled in by hand: A5

Gemeente Amsterdam
Dienst Wonen

Functie
Registratienummer
Geldig tot
Handtekening houder Handtekening directeur

Legitimatie

Council worker's pass

Declaration of marital status: multilingual form

The questions in eight different languages are laid out partly in two columns, so that each language is given sufficient space and size to be readable. This enables the council to meet the needs of local people.

Contract: A4

External forms for the different council departments are printed in colour, but internal forms are only in black and white.

Travel and living expenses form: A4

There is a second marginal column on the right for the person processing the form.

Rotterdam City Council

Model corporate design forms

Issued by	Gemeente Rotterdam, Netherlands
Design	Studio Dumbar, Amsterdam
Year	1998
Typeface	Arial

All the departments of Rotterdam City Council use the same striking logo: it symbolizes the living force of the River Maas, flowing right through the heart of the city. The design of the council forms is equally dynamic and self-assured.

Decorative graphics

This unusual background pattern makes the forms instantly recognizable, and perhaps also more appealing to the eye. The disadvantage, however, is that it also makes them less easy to read.

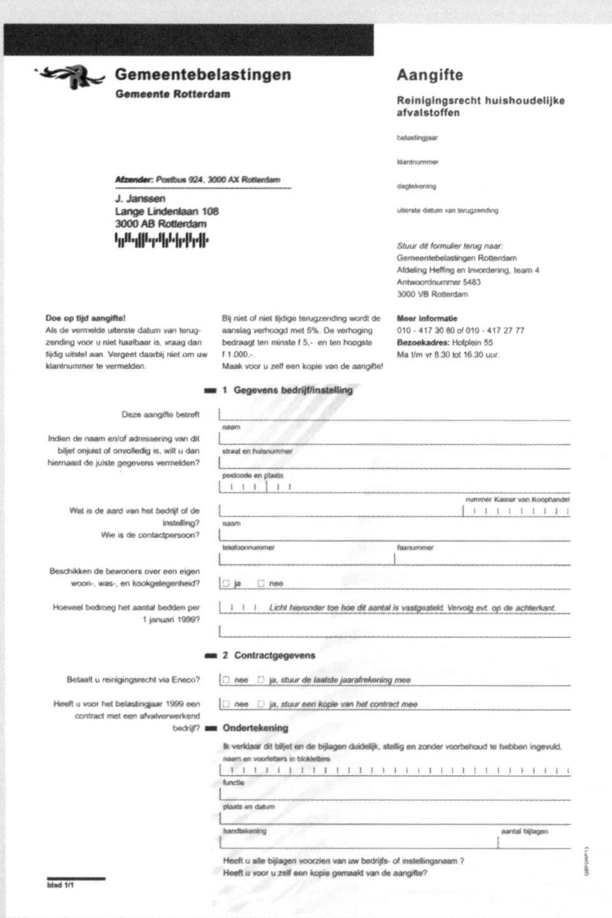

Gemeentebelastingen
Gemeente Rotterdam

Aangifte

Reinigingsrecht huishoudelijke afvalstoffen

belastingjaar

klantnummer

dagtekening

uiterste datum van terugzending

Afzender: Postbus 924, 3000 AX Rotterdam

J. Janssen
Lange Lindenlaan 108
3000 AB Rotterdam

Stuur dit formulier terug naar:
Gemeentebelastingen Rotterdam
Afdeling Heffing en Invordering, team 4
Antwoordnummer 5483
3000 VB Rotterdam

Doe op tijd aangifte!
Als de vermelde uiterste datum van terugzending voor u niet haalbaar is, vraag dan tijdig uitstel aan. Vergeet daarbij niet om uw klantnummer te vermelden.

Bij niet of niet tijdige terugzending wordt de aanslag verhoogd met 5%. De verhoging bedraagt ten minste f 5,- en ten hoogste f 1.000,-.
Maak voor u zelf een kopie van de aangifte!

Meer informatie
010 - 417 30 80 of 010 - 417 27 77
Bezoekadres: Hofplein 55
Ma t/m vr 8.30 tot 16.30 uur.

1 Gegevens bedrijf/instelling

Deze aangifte betreft

Indien de naam en/of adressering van dit biljet onjuist of onvolledig is, wilt u dan hiernaast de juiste gegevens vermelden?

naam
straat en huisnummer
postcode en plaats

Wat is de aard van het bedrijf of de instelling? — nummer Kamer van Koophandel

Wie is de contactpersoon? — naam

telefoonnummer — faxnummer

Beschikken de bewoners over een eigen woon-, was-, en kookgelegenheid? ☐ ja ☐ nee

Hoeveel bedroeg het aantal bedden per 1 januari 1999? *Licht hieronder toe hoe dit aantal is vastgesteld. Vervolg evt. op de achterkant.*

2 Contractgegevens

Betaalt u reinigingsrecht via Eneco? ☐ nee ☐ ja, *stuur de laatste jaarafrekening mee*

Heeft u voor het belastingjaar 1999 een contract met een afvalverwerkend bedrijf? ☐ nee ☐ ja, *stuur een kopie van het contract mee*

Ondertekening

Ik verklaar dit biljet en de bijlagen duidelijk, stellig en zonder voorbehoud te hebben ingevuld.

naam en voorletters in blokletters

functie

plaats en datum

handtekening — aantal bijlagen

Heeft u alle bijlagen voorzien van uw bedrijfs- of instellingsnaam ?
Heeft u voor u zelf een kopie gemaakt van de aangifte?

blad 1/1

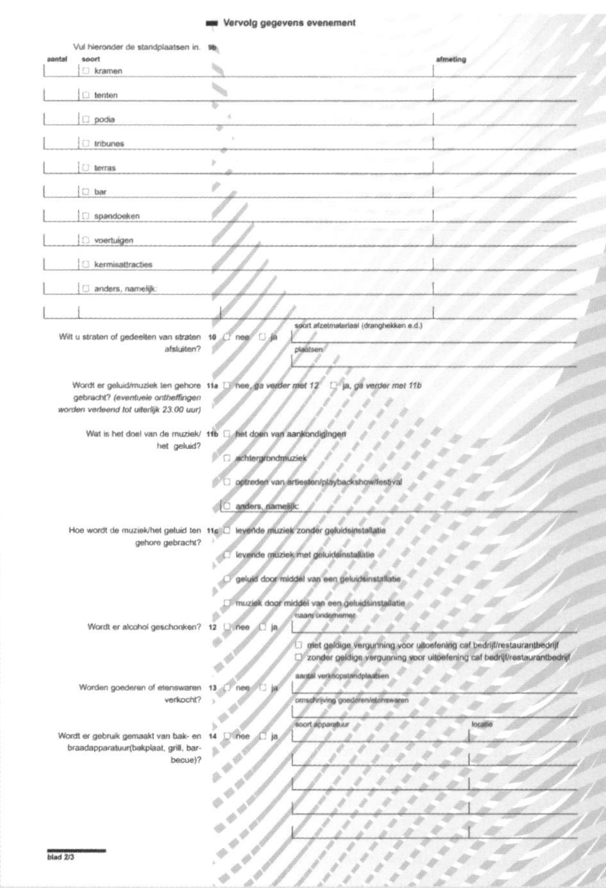

Vervolg gegevens evenement

Vul hieronder de standplaatsen in. **9b**

aantal	soort	afmeting
	☐ kramen	
	☐ tenten	
	☐ podia	
	☐ tribunes	
	☐ terras	
	☐ bar	
	☐ spandoeken	
	☐ voertuigen	
	☐ kermisattracties	
	☐ anders, namelijk:	

Wilt u straten of gedeelten van straten afsluiten? **10** ☐ nee ☐ ja — soort afzetmateriaal (dranghekken e.d.); plaatsen

Wordt er geluid/muziek ten gehore gebracht? *(eventuele ontheffingen worden verleend tot uiterlijk 23.00 uur)* **11a** ☐ nee, *ga verder met 12* ☐ ja, *ga verder met 11b*

Wat is het doel van de muziek/ het geluid? **11b**
☐ het doen van aankondigingen
☐ achtergrondmuziek
☐ optreden van artiesten/playbackshow/festival
☐ anders, namelijk:

Hoe wordt de muziek/het geluid ten gehore gebracht? **11c**
☐ levende muziek zonder geluidsinstallatie
☐ levende muziek met geluidsinstallatie
☐ geluid door middel van een geluidsinstallatie
☐ muziek door middel van een geluidsinstallatie

Wordt er alcohol geschonken? **12** ☐ nee ☐ ja — naam ondernemer
☐ met geldige vergunning voor uitoefening caf bedrijf/restaurantbedrijf
☐ zonder geldige vergunning voor uitoefening caf bedrijf/restaurantbedrijf

Worden goederen of etenswaren verkocht? **13** ☐ nee ☐ ja — aantal verkoopstandplaatsen; omschrijving goederen/etenswaren

Wordt er gebruik gemaakt van bak- en braadapparatuur(bakplaat, grill, barbecue)? **14** ☐ nee ☐ ja — soort apparatuur; locatie

blad 2/3

Two-page application form: A4

The pages have three columns, with the one on the left reserved for questions. If necessary, however, the column division can be ignored, allowing the text fields to span the whole width of the page.

Bibliotheek
Gemeente Rotterdam

Inschrijving

lidmaatschap

Lever dit formulier in aan de balie

Toelichting op dit formulier
In het kader van de Wet Bescherming Persoonsgegevens (WBP) wijzen wij u erop, dat de door u op dit formulier ingevulde gegevens worden vastgelegd in de geautomatiseerde persoonsregistratie Lenersbestand Bibliotheek Rotterdam .

Op deze persoonsregistratie is het Privacyreglement Bibliotheek Rotterdam van toepassing, zoals op 1 februari 1991 door B&W van Rotterdam vastgesteld.
Dit reglement kunt u op aanvraag inzien bij de Uitleenbalie.

Inschrijving

voorletters en achternaam aanvrager — *Gehuwde vrouwen: ook meisjesnaam*

straatnaam en huisnummer

postcode en woonplaats

geboortedatum

soort legitimatiebewijs — *Paspoort, Europese identiteitskaart of rijbewijs*

nummer

telefoonnummer

handtekening — *Bij jeugdleden onder de 12 jaar tekent een van de ouders (of voogd).*

Administratieruimte in te vullen door bibliotheek — *Deze ruimte is bestemd voor de medewerker van de Bibliotheek.*

datum van ingang

contributiecode

lenersnummer

Registration form: A4

Public services do not always need to present a serious and functional image – there is no reason why they should not create a more lighthearted identity for themselves, and forms and logos can be part of this.

Adult Learning Grant

	Application form
Issued by	Adult Learning Grant (ALG)
Design	and/or/if, Towcester
	Richard Bland, Mark Stanton
Year	2007
Typeface	Frutiger

The Adult Learning Grant provides income-assessed support for adult learners in England. The aim of ALG is to support the learners, so the application forms need to have a sense of friendly approachability. At the same time, the forms need to collect very detailed financial and personal information, which is used to assess whether a grant should be awarded.

The task of the forms is further complicated because they need to collect information provided by people other than the applicant. Applicants also need to supply several forms of proof and supporting information along with their completed application.

and/or/if developed a well-written and well-designed suite of application forms that help potential applicants to understand whether they might be eligible or not, and then collect the right information.

Icons

Icons in the margin make it easy to see which sections require the applicant to supply further information or proof. Icons attract the reader's attention, but their use should always be accompanied by explanatory text, as here.

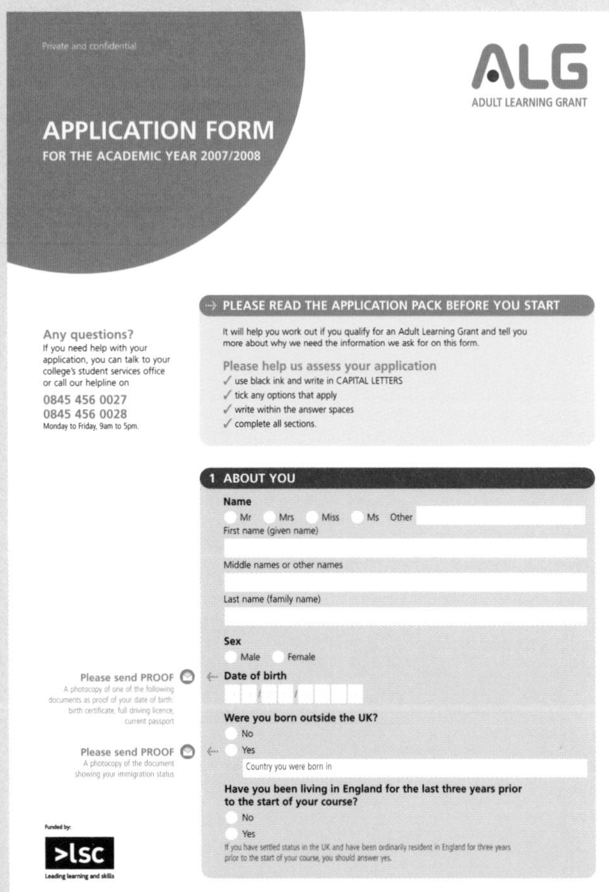

Private and confidential

ALG
ADULT LEARNING GRANT

APPLICATION FORM
FOR THE ACADEMIC YEAR 2007/2008

Any questions?
If you need help with your application, you can talk to your college's student services office or call our helpline on
0845 456 0027
0845 456 0028
Monday to Friday, 9am to 5pm.

PLEASE READ THE APPLICATION PACK BEFORE YOU START

It will help you work out if you qualify for an Adult Learning Grant and tell you more about why we need the information we ask for on this form.

Please help us assess your application
✓ use black ink and write in CAPITAL LETTERS
✓ tick any options that apply
✓ write within the answer spaces
✓ complete all sections.

1 ABOUT YOU

Name
Mr Mrs Miss Ms Other
First name (given name)
Middle names or other names
Last name (family name)

Sex
Male Female

Please send PROOF
A photocopy of one of the following documents as proof of your date of birth: birth certificate, full driving licence, current passport

Date of birth

Were you born outside the UK?
No
Yes
Country you were born in

Please send PROOF
A photocopy of the document showing your immigration status

Have you been living in England for the last three years prior to the start of your course?
No
Yes
If you have settled status in the UK and have been ordinarily resident in England for three years prior to the start of your course, you should answer yes.

Funded by:
>lsc
Leading learning and skills

Application form, page 1: A4
Rounded corners for heading bars and panels reflect the ALG logo and reinforce the sense of approachability.

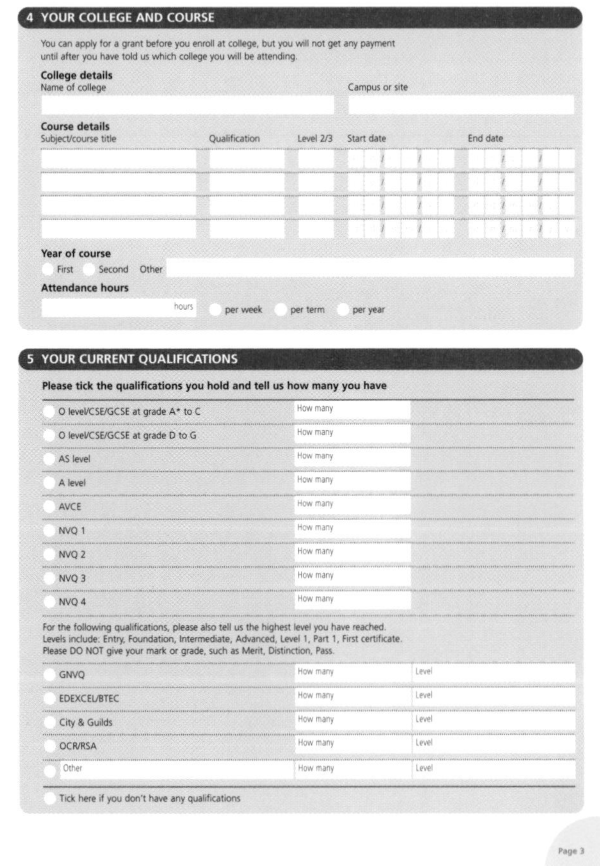

4 YOUR COLLEGE AND COURSE

You can apply for a grant before you enroll at college, but you will not get any payment until after you have told us which college you will be attending.

College details
Name of college | Campus or site

Course details
Subject/course title | Qualification | Level 2/3 | Start date | End date

Year of course
First Second Other

Attendance hours
hours per week per term per year

5 YOUR CURRENT QUALIFICATIONS

Please tick the qualifications you hold and tell us how many you have

O level/CSE/GCSE at grade A* to C	How many
O level/CSE/GCSE at grade D to G	How many
AS level	How many
A level	How many
AVCE	How many
NVQ 1	How many
NVQ 2	How many
NVQ 3	How many
NVQ 4	How many

For the following qualifications, please also tell us the highest level you have reached.
Levels include: Entry, Foundation, Intermediate, Advanced, Level 1, Part 1, First certificate.
Please DO NOT give your mark or grade, such as Merit, Distinction, Pass.

GNVQ	How many	Level
EDEXCEL/BTEC	How many	Level
City & Guilds	How many	Level
OCR/RSA	How many	Level
Other	How many	Level

Tick here if you don't have any qualifications

Page 3

Application form, page 3: A4
The marginal column has been omitted on this page to leave more space for responses, a practical solution to the problem.

Such as: Incapacity Benefit, Industrial Death Benefit, Invalid Care or Carer's Allowance, Jobseeker's Allowance, Retirement Pension, Statutory Sick Pay, Statutory Maternity Pay, Bereavement Allowance and Widowed Parent Allowance

Please also complete
The separate 'Additional information sheet for question 7' – you'll need to ask your Jobcentre Plus Office to complete part of the form for you

7 YOUR TAXABLE BENEFITS BETWEEN 6 APRIL 2006 AND 5 APRIL 2007

Did you receive any taxable benefits between 6 April 2006 and 5 April 2007?
No
Yes

8 YOUR EMPLOYMENT AND BENEFIT DETAILS

Are you currently employed?
No
Yes
Full time
Part time
Employer's address

Postcode

Are you currently claiming any taxable benefits?
No
Yes
If you are currently claiming any taxable benefits, please let us have the address of your Jobcentre Plus office in the box below

Postcode

Please also complete
Your spouse or partner must fill in section 11: Spouse or partner's financial details

9 ABOUT YOUR SPOUSE OR PARTNER

Do any of the following apply to you?
- I'm married and live with my spouse
- I'm in a civil partnership and live with my civil partner
- I live with someone as if we are married

No
Yes

Page 5

Application form, page 4: A4

Some questions require additional forms to be completed. Arrows, icons and text are used to make this clear.

TO BE COMPLETED BY SPOUSE OR PARTNER

Your spouse or partner is applying for an Adult Learning Grant. We need information about your taxable income between 6 April 2006 and 5 April 2007 to help us assess their application.

If you would prefer to give details on a separate form, please photocopy pages 7-8, write your spouse or partner's name and address on the photocopy, and send the completed photocopy to:
FREEPOST
Adult Learning Grant
PO Box 4244
Manchester
M60 3AN

11 TAXABLE INCOME BETWEEN 6 APRIL 2006 AND 5 APRIL 2007

Please tick each type of taxable income you received and tell us how much

Please send PROOF Your P60 for 2006-07, or week 52 or month 12 payslip for 2006-07
Gross taxable salary or wages
This is the amount before any deductions for tax.
£ . Office use area only

Please send PROOF Your P11D for 2006-07
Employee benefits
Such as company car or health insurance – benefits are listed on the P11D, which your employer must give you every year.
£ . Office use area only

Please send PROOF Your completed SA302 Self-assessment tax form for 2006-07, or certified accounts for 2006-07
Income from self employment
£ . Office use area only

Please send PROOF Certified accounts for 2006-07, or a tenancy agreement covering 2006-07
Taxable income from property
£ . Office use area only

Please send PROOF Statements for 2006-07, or tax vouchers for 2006-07
Gross interest from savings, investments and shares.
You only need to give details if this comes to more than £300
£ . Office use area only

Please send PROOF P60 for 2006-07, or statements for 2006-07
Pension, including state, private and employer pensions
£ . Office use area only

Please send PROOF Appropriate official documents – call our helpline if you're not sure
Other taxable income and taxable benefits
£ . Office use area only

I did not receive any taxable income between 6 April 2006 and 5 April 2007

Page 7

Application form, page 7: A4

Colour-coding identifies the sections that need to be completed by people other than the applicant.

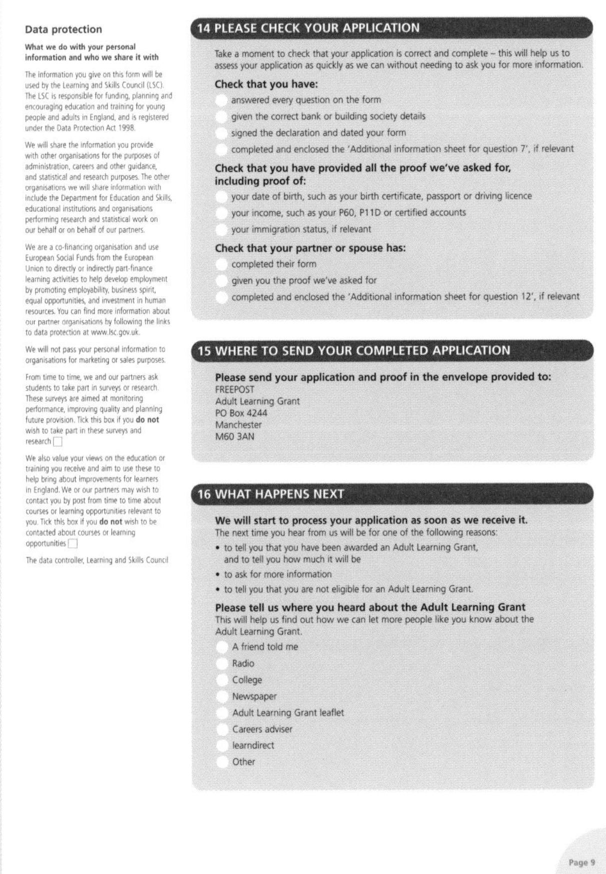

Data protection

What we do with your personal information and who we share it with

The information you give on this form will be used by the Learning and Skills Council (LSC). The LSC is responsible for funding, planning and encouraging education and training for young people and adults in England, and is registered under the Data Protection Act 1998.

We will share the information you provide with other organisations for the purposes of administration, careers and other guidance, and statistical and research purposes. The other organisations we will share information with include the Department for Education and Skills, educational institutions and organisations performing research and statistical work on our behalf or on behalf of our partners.

We are a co-financing organisation and use European Social Funds from the European Union to directly or indirectly part-finance learning activities to help develop employment by promoting employability, business spirit, equal opportunities, and investment in human resources. You can find more information about our partner organisations by following the links to data protection at www.lsc.gov.uk.

We will not pass your personal information to organisations for marketing or sales purposes.

From time to time, we and our partners ask students to take part in surveys or research. These surveys are aimed at monitoring performance, improving quality and planning future provision. Tick this box if you **do not** wish to take part in these surveys and research ☐

We also value your views on the education or training you receive and aim to use these to help bring about improvements for learners in England. We or our partners may wish to contact you by post from time to time about courses or learning opportunities relevant to you. Tick this box if you **do not** wish to be contacted about courses or learning opportunities ☐

The data controller, Learning and Skills Council

14 PLEASE CHECK YOUR APPLICATION

Take a moment to check that your application is correct and complete – this will help us to assess your application as quickly as we can without needing to ask you for more information.

Check that you have:
answered every question on the form
given the correct bank or building society details
signed the declaration and dated your form
completed and enclosed the 'Additional information sheet for question 7', if relevant

Check that you have provided all the proof we've asked for, including proof of:
your date of birth, such as your birth certificate, passport or driving licence
your income, such as your P60, P11D or certified accounts
your immigration status, if relevant

Check that your partner or spouse has:
completed their form
given you the proof we've asked for
completed and enclosed the 'Additional information sheet for question 12', if relevant

15 WHERE TO SEND YOUR COMPLETED APPLICATION

Please send your application and proof in the envelope provided to:
FREEPOST
Adult Learning Grant
PO Box 4244
Manchester
M60 3AN

16 WHAT HAPPENS NEXT

We will start to process your application as soon as we receive it.
The next time you hear from us will be for one of the following reasons:
- to tell you that you have been awarded an Adult Learning Grant, and to tell you how much it will be
- to ask for more information
- to tell you that you are not eligible for an Adult Learning Grant.

Please tell us where you heard about the Adult Learning Grant
This will help us find out how we can let more people like you know about the Adult Learning Grant.
A friend told me
Radio
College
Newspaper
Adult Learning Grant leaflet
Careers adviser
learndirect
Other

Page 9

Application form, last page: A4

The final page contains a checklist, so applicants can make sure that the form is complete. It also provides a return address and information about the next stage of the application process.

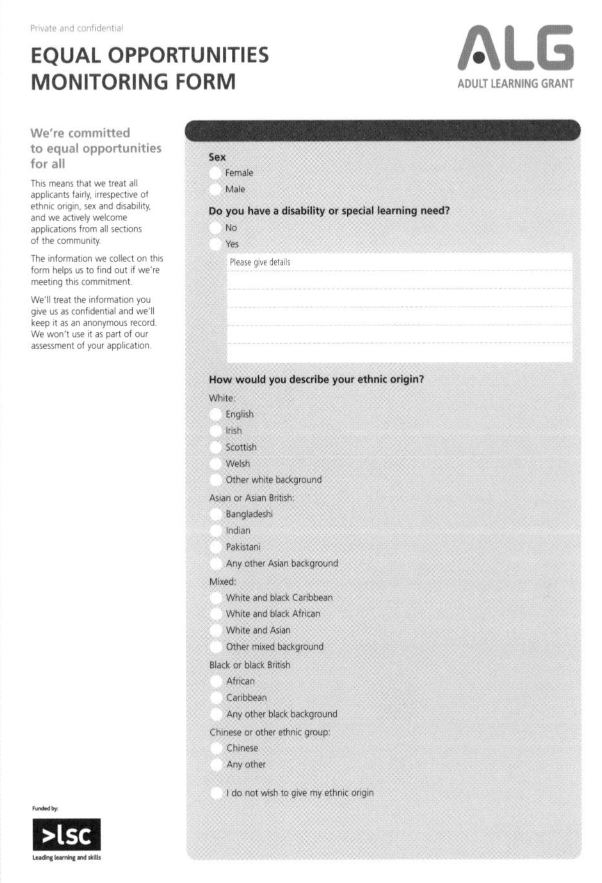

Private and confidential

EQUAL OPPORTUNITIES MONITORING FORM

ALG
ADULT LEARNING GRANT

We're committed to equal opportunities for all

This means that we treat all applicants fairly, irrespective of ethnic origin, sex and disability, and we actively welcome applications from all sections of the community.

The information we collect on this form helps us to find out if we're meeting this commitment.

We'll treat the information you give us as confidential and we'll keep it as an anonymous record. We won't use it as part of our assessment of your application.

Sex
Female
Male

Do you have a disability or special learning need?
No
Yes
Please give details

How would you describe your ethnic origin?
White:
English
Irish
Scottish
Welsh
Other white background
Asian or Asian British:
Bangladeshi
Indian
Pakistani
Any other Asian background
Mixed:
White and black Caribbean
White and black African
White and Asian
Other mixed background
Black or black British
African
Caribbean
Any other black background
Chinese or other ethnic group:
Chinese
Any other

I do not wish to give my ethnic origin

Funded by
>lsc
Leading learning and skills

Equal opportunities monitoring form: A4

One excellent feature is that questions about the applicant's ethnic origin do not appear on the main application form, reassuring the candidates that this will not be a factor in assessing the application.

Dutch Tax Administration

Tax declaration forms

Issued by	Belastingsdienst, Netherlands
Design	Edenspiekermann (formerly Eden Design & Communication), Amsterdam
Year	2006
Typeface	Berthold Imago

Since 1987, Eden Design has been designing Dutch tax declaration forms with a view to doing something unique and innovative in this particular field: the forms are no longer intended solely to provide information needed by the tax authorities, but also set out to make the declaration as simple and comprehensible as possible for the taxpayer. One of the factors in Eden Design's successful solution to this task is the ability always to answer the most important question posed by practically all such forms: What do I gain by filling in this form and providing all these details?

In 2006, Eden Design was faced by new challenges. Since that date, the Dutch tax authorities have not only collected taxes but have also paid out benefits such as healthcare, rent and childcare allowances. This has meant that people who previously had little or no contact with their tax office must now be brought into the fold. The forms and information sheets have therefore been designed in warmer colours, and the standard Dutch tax forms have been brightened up with pictures and text.

Particularly striking are the accompanying information sheets and booklets. The design and content resemble a magazine more than an official document. The texts cater for the expectations and requirements of the applicants without ever appearing condescending.

2

In short

Check the details
If the Tax Authorities has enough details and can make an estimate of the income for 2006, then the income will already be filled in. Check this estimate and fill the form in further.

Who has to sign?
The person who is applying for an allowance signs the form. If you have an allowance partner then they must sign too. The same applies to all co-occupants aged over 18 years.

How and when to return it?
Send the filled in and signed form back in the envelope provided. Don't enclose anything else. Do you want your allowance from the end of December 2005? Then send your application before November 1. You'll be notified within eight weeks. Applications for an allowance for 2006 can be made until April 1 2007.

Advance and payment
You'll receive notice about the calculation of your allowance from the Tax Authorities. This calculation is made on the basis of the estimated details and is an advance. After the year 2006 follows the definitive calculation. If it appears that you have received too much then you pay that amount back. If you've received too little then you get paid the difference as well. Payments are mostly made on a monthly basis.

Pass on any changes
Are your details on the front of the form incorrect? Then still fill the form in and send it back signed. Pass on any changes using a different form. For this call the Tax Telephone: 0800 - 0543

Applying for rent allowance and healthcare allowance

Most of the work is already done

A lot of people don't look forward to it. Yet filling in a form doesn't have to be difficult. Certainly not, if the Tax Authorities have already done most of the work for you. Such as with the application for rent allowance and healthcare allowance. We went onto the street and asked passers-by what they thought.

'That I could get money for my healthcare insurance was new to me'
Hans Schelts (38): I knew that rent allowance was moving from VROM to the Tax Authorities. But that I could also get money for my healthcare insurance was new to me. I'm now in the national health insurance fund. But I'll take out healthcare insurance again soon. I already have a rent allowance and in 2006 I'll certainly apply for a healthcare allowance.

Would you rather apply using a computer? Go to www.toeslagen.nl.

'Our son has to apply for healthcare allowance separately'
Toos Wolters (62): All at once there was a form in the letter-box. At first I didn't understand it. But everyone that now gets rent subsidy has to fill in the application form one more time. Fortunately you apply for healthcare allowance with the same form. That makes a difference. You apply for the allowance for yourself and your partner. My son is over 18 and still lives at home. Therefore I include his details for rent allowance in my form. He has to fill in his own application form for healthcare allowance.'

'Our income for 2006 was already filled in'
Kees Visser (43): 'I have one form for myself and my wife. Our details were pre-printed on the form. So both our incomes for 2006 were estimated. The Tax Authorities use current details as a starting point for this. Of course, I check everything well. Because with our details the Tax Authorities calculate how much rent allowance and healthcare allowance we get in 2006. Therefore it's important that it's right.'

'For the calculation of your allowance for 2006 the Tax Authorities use your income from 2006'

'Send the form back before November 1'
Anneka Schouten (29): 'I help my parents with the filling in. They're scared of anything to do with forms. They're also worried that they won't receive rent allowance any more, now that the Tax Authorities have taken over from VROM. But that's, of course, not how it is. If you now receive rent subsidy and your situation has not changed there's a good chance that you'll get rent allowance in 2006. You've only got to send the form back before November 1 2005. Then the rent allowance appears in your account from the end of December. Together with the healthcare allowance for 2006.'

'I filled it in myself and I'm proud of that'
Wong Chang (62): 'Now, it's in any case better to read the explanation first. Your income for 2006 is often already filled in. But if it's not right you've got to make an estimate yourself. I found that difficult. I saw in the explanation what I had to do. So I managed it myself and I am proud of that. But OK, I wouldn't have been ashamed to ask for help. Because it's not that easy.'

'I put the form in the envelope'
Johan Groenink (67): In fact you get through it quickly. I only had two pages. I checked them well and signed. My wife had to sign as allowance partner. And my two sons are co-occupants. I put both pages in the envelope provided. There's no point enclosing anything extra. I posted the envelope right away.'

Need help with filling in the form?
At www.toeslagen.nl you'll find the nearest point for help and information. Or call the Tax Telephone: 0800 - 0543, on Mondays to Thursdays between 8.00 and 20.00 and on Fridays between 8.00 and 17.00.

3

Please note: the amounts are provisional
At the time of making this explanation the income group borders and the levels of rent and healthcare allowances for the year 2006 were not yet set. When these amounts are definitive you can find them at www.toeslagen.nl.

Conditions for rent allowance
- You are aged 18 or over.
- You independently rent a home.
- The rent is not less than € 189.19 and not more than € 604.72. Or, if you or any allowance partner or co-occupants are younger than 23 years old, not more than € 331.78.
- Your own income, that of any allowance partner or co-occupants determines the level of rent allowance. These income levels are not yet set.
- You and any allowance partner and co-occupants are registered with the local council at the address for which rent allowance is applied for.

If you don't meet these conditions but qualify for an exception (a hardship clause) then call the Tax Telephone: 0800 - 0543.

Conditions for healthcare allowance
- You are aged 18 or older
- You have a healthcare insurance in line with the new Healthcare Insurance Act.
- Your income is not too high. If you don't have an allowance partner it is a maximum of € 25.000. If you do have an allowance partner it is a combined maximum of € 40.000. If the combined income is lower than € 17.500 then you'll probably get the maximum healthcare allowance.

Double page from an information brochure: A4

Here the application procedure is explained in a manner that is very accessible and easy to understand. A special feature of these application forms is that they are frequently filled in by administrators, and only require the applicant's signature.

Applicant's sofi number [applicant's sofi number] | Applicant [initials and surname of interested party] | Page 3

4 **Married or single in 2006** *(Registered partnership counts as married)*

4a Is [initials and surname of spouse/partner], born on [date], sofi number [number], your spouse as at 1 January 2006?

No → *Continue with question* ***5a****. However, if your spouse as at 1 January 2006 is different, complete questions 4b-4f.*

Yes ↓

The Tax Authority estimates this co-occupant's 2006 assessment income to be € [amount]. Is this estimate correct?

No → *Continue with question* ***4d****. Your spouse is your allowance partner.*

Yes ↓

Continue with question ***4e****. Your spouse is your allowance partner.*

4b Initials and surname of your allowance partner

4c Date of birth *(Indicated as dd mm yyyy)* Sofi number

4d Use the calculation aid on pages 6 and 7 of the Notes and estimate your allowance partner's assessment income for 2006. Use the amount from the calculation aid. € , 0 0

4e Does your allowance partner have Dutch healthcare insurance for healthcare expenses as at 1 January 2006? Yes No

4f Allowance partner's signature. *Sign inside the box.*

5 **Co-occupant 1**

5a Is [initials and surname of co-occupant 1], born on [date], sofi number [number], still living with you as at 1 January 2006?

No → *Continue with question* ***6a***

Yes ↓

The Tax Authority estimates this co-occupant's 2006 assessment income to be € [amount]. Is this estimate correct?

Yes → *Continue with question* ***5e***

No ↓

Continue with question ***5d***

5b Initials and surname of this co-occupant

5c Date of birth *(Indicated as dd mm yyyy)* Sofi number

5d Use the calculation aid on pages 6 and 7 of the Notes and estimate this co-occupant's assessment income for 2006. Use the amount from the calculation aid. € , 0 0

5e Review pages 4 and 5 of the Notes. Is this co-occupant your allowance partner as at 1 January 2006? Yes No, *skip question* ***5f***
Note: *There can be only one allowance partner*

5f Does this co-occupant have Dutch healthcare insurance for healthcare expenses as at 1 January 2006? Yes No

5g Co-occupant's signature. *Not required if the co-occupant is less than 18 years old. Sign inside the box.*

11 140 61 03

Inside page of an application form: A4

A typical element of all Dutch tax forms is the fact that they are laid out in a flow-chart style, with yes/no filter questions. These help applicants to find their way through the system and fill in the form correctly.

Belastingdienst

2004 **Refund**
Income tax and
national insurance return

> Antwoordnummer 21310, 6400 TS Heerlen

J.J. Voorbeeld
Voorbeeldlaan 5
1234 AA Voorbeeldstad

Money back from the Tax Authorities

For your healthcare insurance premium, glasses, own contribution for the physiotherapist and other expenses. Or just because you are 65 or older.

Filing a tax return is worth the effort!

According to the details we have you could get money back. It can easily be a couple of hundred euros. Even if you incurred only few costs.

Our staff are pleased to help

The staff from the Tax Telephone are pleased to help you with this form. Call: 0800 - 0543. Or see www.belastingdienst.nl for local help.

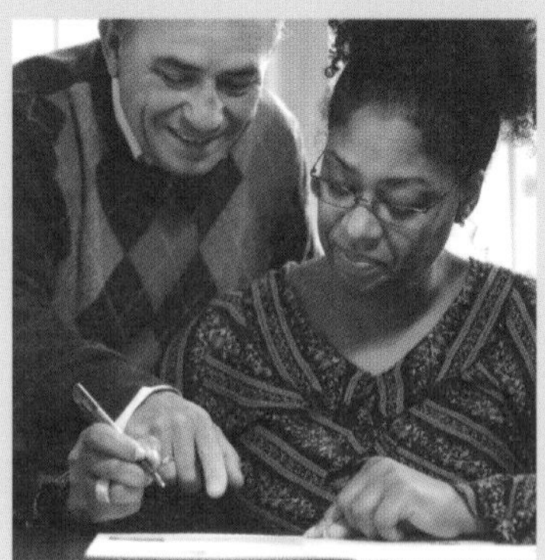

Before you begin

Take your time and read the form through. Look at every question and see if it applies to you. If you have incurred no costs, or the costs have already been reimbursed, then you don't have to fill anything in. In order to avoid extra work the Tax Authorities have already listed some of your details below. You don't have to give these again. If the details are incorrect call the Tax Telephone: 0800 - 0543.

Your sofi-number 2345 63 789
Your date of birth 12 October 1938
Your income such a state pension, private pension or benefit € 9,000

You are entitled to:
General tax credit € 910
Senior citizen's rebate € 776
Fixed rebate for 65 plus € 776

The details of your fiscal partner:
M.P.C. Voorbeeld - Example
Sofi-number 3421 56 876
Date of birth 9 May 1933
Your income such as state pension, private pension or benefit € 9.000

Your fiscal partner is entitled to:
General tax credit € 910
Senior citizen's reduction/rebate € 776
Fixed rebate for 65 plus € 776

Returning the form

Do you want to be considered for a refund from the Tax Authorities? Then send the form back, including this cover page, before July 1 2006. Use the reply envelope.

Payment

After receiving your form the Tax Authorities calculate how much of a refund or compensation you will get. You will be informed of this.

IB 331 - 1Z41CT

Tax return form for the elderly and the chronically ill with low incomes, page 1: A4

These forms were designed in 2005 specifically for people from the above groups, who are entitled to special rebates and benefits, but were formerly obliged to fill in the standard forms.

Copy your sofi-number from the first page and fill it in here.

Tax return sheet 2

7 Cared for in a care or nursing home or at home

Example:
Mrs Berk: 'My husband stayed in a nursing home in 2004. That year we paid a compulsory AWBZ (Exceptional Medical Expenses Act) own contribution of € 8,360. Can we claim this contribution?'

Mark Zomer is an assistant at the senior citizen's union: 'As with most nursing homes, the nursing home where Mr Berk stayed is covered by AWBZ. Mrs Berk may therefore claim 25% of the compulsory own contribution for her husband. That is: 0.25 x € 8,360 = € 2,090.'

In 2004 did you stay in a care or nursing home? And is that home covered by the AWBZ? Then you may claim 25% of the compulsory AWBZ own contribution. Most care or nursing homes and institutions for the physically and mentally handicapped are covered by the AWBZ. Were you cared for at home in 2004 and paid the AWBZ? Then claim your total own contribution AWBZ. Did you have a person-related budget? Then state your total costs minus the net person-related budget.

Costs for care or nursing in 2004 for yourself and your fiscal partner € ,0 0

Tip! *Have the bills from the care provider at hand.*

8 Extra expenses for clothing and bedclothes due to long term illness

Example
Mrs Tamminga: In November 2003 I became very ill. From the spring of 2004 I was in a wheelchair. Through that I had alterations and wear on my clothes that cost € 235. Can I claim these costs?

Anja Tulp from the Tax Telephone:
'Mrs Tamminga was ill for more than a year, of which eight months were in 2004. During that time she had extra expenses. For this set amounts apply. In Mrs Tamminga's situation € 320 for the whole of 2004. So for eight months: 8/12 x € 320 = € 214.

Did you have extra expenses for clothing and bedclothes due to illness or disability in 2004? If this illness or disability lasted at least one year you can claim a set amount, even if you spent less. That amount is € 320. But if the costs incurred by you are more than € 640, then you may claim a set amount of € 800.

Set amount for extra expenses for clothing and bed clothes in 2004 for yourself and your fiscal partner € ,0 0

IB 333 - 1B41PL

Page 2 of the form opposite: A4

Previously only 10% of those entitled to rebates had filled the form in properly. This redesigned form by Eden Design uses a lot of photos and examples and asks comparatively few questions in order to break down existing attitudes of insecurity and distrust towards the tax authorities as well as to reduce sources of error. The result has been an improvement of 70% in the number of returns.

Dutch Ministry of Foreign Affairs

Model corporate design forms

Issued by	Ministerie van Buitenlandse Zaken, Netherlands
Design	Total Identity, Amsterdam
Year	1998
Typefaces	Quadraat, Quadraat Sans Italic

The forms issued by the Dutch Ministry of Foreign Affairs are original and well thought out. However, the kinks in the lines look rather forced and messy. The long feathery logo, which is meant to symbolize the Earth's rotation around the sun, is also impossible to decipher.

an toepassing is.

Goed Redelijk Ma

Tick here

A feature that may irritate applicants is the fact that the lines around the checkboxes seem to form a text field but are not meant to be used for writing. On the positive side, there is an attractive mixture of sans serif italics for questions and serifs for other text.

→ Multiple choice questions: page 178
→ Typefaces and typography: page 130

Travel expenses: A4

The number for section 3 is missing – obviously an oversight in an otherwise exemplary form.

Hours worked: A4

Ministerie van
Buitenlandse Zaken

Aanvraag reservering

De aanvraag zo spoedig mogelijk indienen bij de afdeling FDI / CC.
De uitersterste termijn is één week. Aanvragen die later binnenkomen kunnen niet meer in behandeling worden genomen.
Voor wijziging of annulering kunt u contact op nemen met toestel 4066 / 4811.

Referentienummer

Algemene gegevens

Naam aanvrager

Dienstonderdeel

Telefoonnummer

Voor rekening van ○ budgethouder ○ aanvrager

Gegevens bijeenkomst

Datum bijeenkomst

Tijdstip *Van* uur *Tot* uur

Aantal personen

Gastvrouw / -heer

Reden bijeenkomst

Gewenste bijeenkomstruimte ○ koffiecorner ○ lunchkamer
○ vergaderzaal nr.:
○ lounge c.c. nr.:
○ andere ruimte nl.:

Bijzonderheden

Vergaderhulpmiddelen ○ nee ○ ja nl.:

Bediening ○ nee ○ ja

Restauratieve voorzieningen	*Aantal*	*Tijdstip*
○ koffie		
○ thee		
○ frisdranken		
○ receptiedranken		
○ assortiment garnituren		
○ lunchbon(nen)		
○ lunchbox(en)		
○ broodjes op schaal		
○ broodjes buffet		
○ koffietafel		
○ lunchbuffet		
○ warme lunch (drie gangen)		
○ luxe warme lunch (aperatief + vier gangen)		
○ koud en warm buffet		
○ andere voorzieningen nl.:		

Ondertekening aanvrager

Datum aanvraag

Handtekening

Parafering chef dienstonderdeel

Naam

Datum *Paraaf*

Reservation form: A4

These forms are a fine example of a line-based design. Heavier lines divide the form into sections, and lighter ones denote the areas for writing. As is customary with Dutch forms, the questions stand alongside the blank text fields.

Environment Agency

Application forms and guidance notes

Issued by	Environment Agency, UK
Design	Text Matters, Reading
Years	1997–2007
Typefaces	Stone Sans, Joanna, Swift

Created in 1995 by the bringing together of disparate UK government bodies dealing with the environment, the new Environment Agency wanted to produce clear, standardized documents in a corporate style. A project was devised to establish a design and language approach as well as management strategies within the Agency. Text Matters worked with the Agency for a period of ten years on printed forms and guidance notes and later created interactive PDFs of some forms and early versions of electronic forms. Among other measures, Text Matters conducted customer surveys to find out problems with existing forms. Together with the Agency they set up an internal management procedure to ensure consistency and workshops to raise awareness for Agency staff.

The resulting documents use clear language in a structured sequence to minimize customer resistance to the process of form-filling. The visual design aims to simplify and order information into logical, clearly defined groups. As a result of the work of Text Matters, the number of customer-facing forms used by the Agency was reduced and made consistent with emphasis on usability for both customers and the Agency.

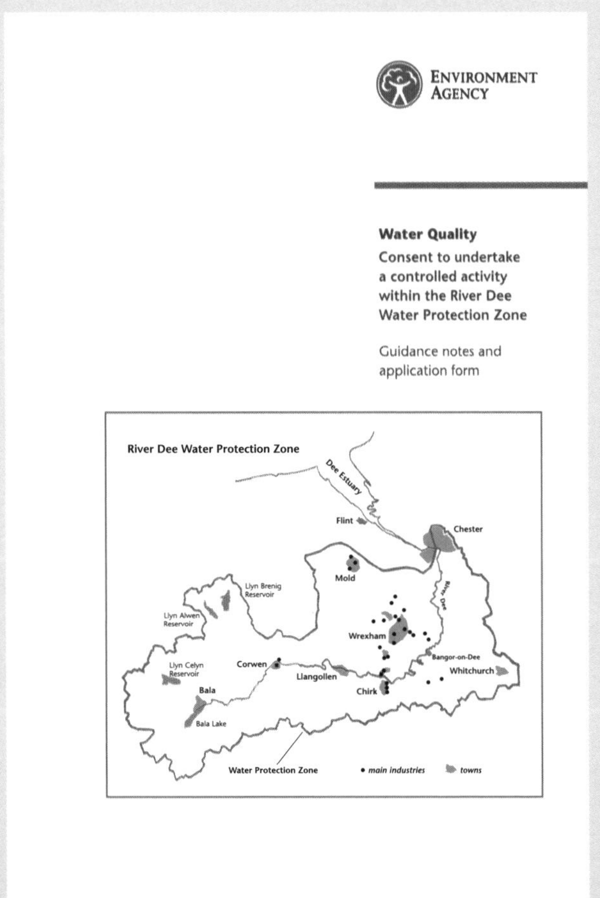

Cover of a folder with guidance notes and application form: 420 × 320 mm

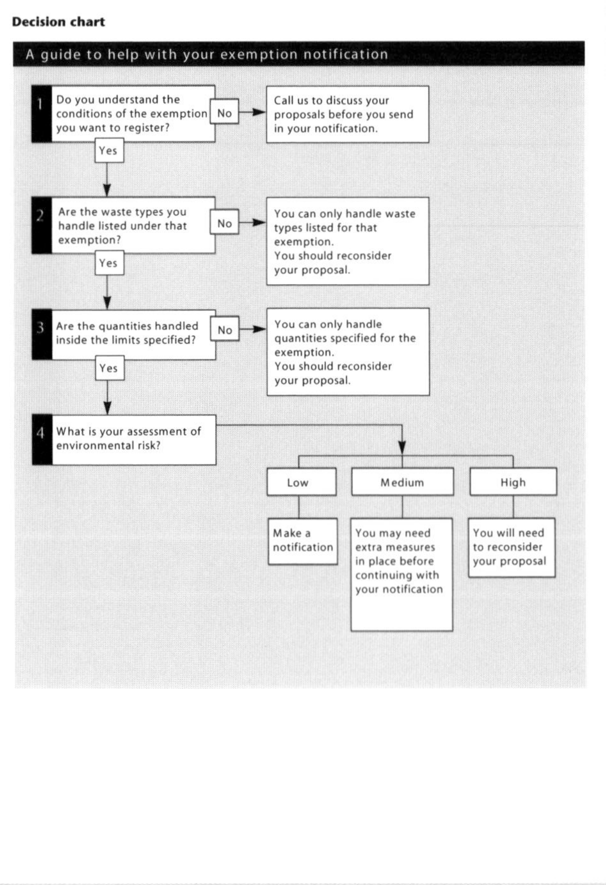

Illustration from the guidance notes

Many application forms are accompanied by text-heavy guidance notes. However, these often include helpful charts and diagrams such as this one.

Form Dee WPZ 1 – Application for consent to undertake a controlled activity within the River Dee Water Protection Zone

For Environment Agency use only	Date received	Fee received: Yes	No	Amount received	Application reference number
		☐	☐		DPZ

ENVIRONMENT AGENCY

Water quality

Application for consent to undertake a controlled activity within the River Dee Water Protection Zone

Water Resources Act 1991, Section 93 and 96, Water Protection Zone (River Dee catchment) (Procedural and Other Provisions) Regulations 1999 and Designation Order 1999

Please read the guidance notes and the form carefully before you complete it.

1 About your application

Type of application

Everyone has to fill in this section of the form.

1.1 Please say what type of application you are making.

☐ A new consent *please go to question 1.4*

☐ An establishment period claim *please go to question 1.4*

☐ Varying the conditions of an existing consent *please go to question 1.2*

☐ Continuing an existing consent in a new name *please go to question 1.2*

1.2 Please give details of the existing consents.

Number of consent

DPZ

Name of consent holder

1.3 Are you applying to vary the conditions of the existing consent?

No ☐

Yes ☐ *we will ask you to give details of the changes you want to make in later sections of the form*

Do you want to change the consent holder?

No ☐

Yes ☐ *please give new name*

1.4 Applicant's name and address

Please read the notes about this question if you are applying on behalf of a partnership or other organisation. If you need to give more than one name and address, you can use a separate sheet for the rest.

Name of person or organisation applying for the consent

Address

Postcode

Phone

Fax

1 About your application *continued*

1.5 Do you want to nominate a separate contact for queries about your application?

A separate contact can be an agent.

No ☐ *we will address all questions and correspondence to the applicant named in question 1.4*

Yes ☐ *we will address all questions and correspondence to the person named here*

Name

Position

Address

Postcode

Phone

Fax

2 Site the application covers

Address and location of site

You must send us a map showing the site the application is for, see guidance notes.

Address

Postcode

Phone

Fax

Type of activity carried out at the site

Please supply a National grid reference.

You can find this on a National Ordnance Survey map.

National grid reference *for example, ST 1234 5678*

Form Dee WPZ 1

Application form: A4

This application form has a practical two-column design that saves space. Black boxes with white text are used to divide the form into sections. If a section runs into a second column, a greyscale box is used to repeat the section title.

CLIC Sargent

Disability Allowance claims form

Issued by	CLIC Sargent, UK
Design	Boag Associates, London
Year	2005
Typeface	Frutiger

For most parents, when their child has been diagnosed with cancer, claiming a benefit will be the last thing on their minds. Although parents face significant costs immediately after diagnosis, claiming Disability Living Allowance (DLA) is a lengthy process and involves filling out a 40-page printed form. In 2005 CLIC Sargent, the UK's leading cancer charity for children, called for a simplification of the claims process and commissioned Boag Associates to identify how the process and form could be streamlined. Boag Associates wrote and designed a 4-page initial claims form, and a significantly shorter main claims form, which will be tailored to the specific case and pre-filled in part.

They also developed recommendations for a new claims process, which makes the whole claim faster and easier. The proposed changes would mean that a weekly payment starts as soon as possible, triggered by the initial payment, with any necessary adjustments made over the course of future payments once the full rate of DLA is assessed. This case study is a good example of how form design is not just about the visual layout of a form but can also mean designing and improving the entire administrative process.

Prepared by Boag Associates for CLIC Sargent – this is a visual for '**Cut the Red Tape**' and not an official document

Disability Living Allowance

Claim for an **initial payment** while a claim for Disability Living Allowance is being assessed for a child under 16 who has cancer

When do I fill this in?
We understand that you must be under a lot of stress right now. Please claim as soon as you can – you can ask a social worker or other adviser to help you.

Is this my claim for DLA?
No. This form is the first step and asks only for the minimum information we need to make an initial payment. This isn't your claim for Disability Living Allowance – we'll send you a separate form based on the information in this form.

It looks complicated
We want to help you get money quickly to cover extra costs such as travel to hospital, clothing and special foods your child might need at this time. If you need help with filling in this form, please call our special helpline on 0000 000 0000.

How much will I get?
We pay a standard rate of £xx a week while your claim for DLA is being assessed. If you're entitled to a higher rate of DLA, you'll get the extra amount due with your first full payment.

How soon will I get some money?
Assuming there are no errors on your form, we'll normally pay the money into your account (or by cheque) within two weeks from when we get your form back. If you don't hear from us within two weeks of the date on this form, please phone our special helpline on 0000 000 0000.

Will I have to pay the money back?
No, not as long as you're entitled to DLA. When we work out how much DLA you're entitled to, we'll take this payment from your first full payment and pay you the balance. If your claim for DLA is turned down you may have to pay the money back.

Cover of 4-page initial payment form: A4

The concept of the initial payment is explained simply and clearly on the first page of the form.

Prepared by Boag Associates for CLIC Sargent – this is a visual for '**Cut the Red Tape**' and not an official document

Doctor's statement

Diagnosis

Date of diagnosis / /

Date treatment started / /

How long treatment is expected to last weeks

Expected recovery period after treatment ends weeks

Any comments relevant to the diagnosis, treatment or recovery

Doctor's declaration

I am the child's ☐ General Practitioner ☐ Hospital consultant ☐ Other (please specify)

I declare that the child named in section 1 of this form is my patient, and that the information I have given in this form is true and complete.

Your name

Daytime phone number

Address or office stamp

Your signature

Date / /

To the doctor: what to do now
Please send this form to us as soon as you can, using the envelope that came with the form – you don't need a stamp. Thank you.

Back cover of 4-page initial payment form: A4

After the applicant's details, the application requests a short statement from a doctor. Colour is used to differentiate this section.

Prepared by Boag Associates for CLIC Sargent – this is a visual for **'Cut the Red Tape'** and not an official document

Statement by a parent or person responsible for the child

1 The first things we need to know

Child's surname or family name

Other names

Date of birth / /

Address

Postcode

Child's illness ☐ Cancer ☐ Leukaemia

Child benefit number You'll find this on letters from the Department for Work and Pensions

2 Getting in touch with you

Your surname or family name

Other names

Your relationship to the child ☐ Parent

☐ Other (please give details

Address if different from the child's

Postcode

Daytime phone number

Mobile phone number We can call or text you to help you complete your Disability Living Allowance claim form

Inside of 4-page initial payment form: A4

The four-page form is designed to encourage a quick-start approach to the claims process. The questions are phrased simply and the person filling in the form is directly addressed.

Design for Democracy

Registration forms and ballots

Issued by AIGA Design for Democracy
Design Studio/lab, Chicago
Marcia Lausen, Gretchen Schulfer, Cheyenne Medina
Year 2006
Typeface Univers

In 2000, the notorious 'butterfly ballot' caused confusion and controversy among the voters in Florida, and sparked a dramatic race for the Presidency. These events made people aware of just how important it is to have well designed and reliable forms if democracy is to function properly. Design for Democracy, an initiative of the designers' association AIGA, took this opportunity to make suggestions for a comprehensive reworking of all election documents. These now form part of the programme officially recommended by the US Election Assistance Commission (EAC), and have actually been implemented in several states.

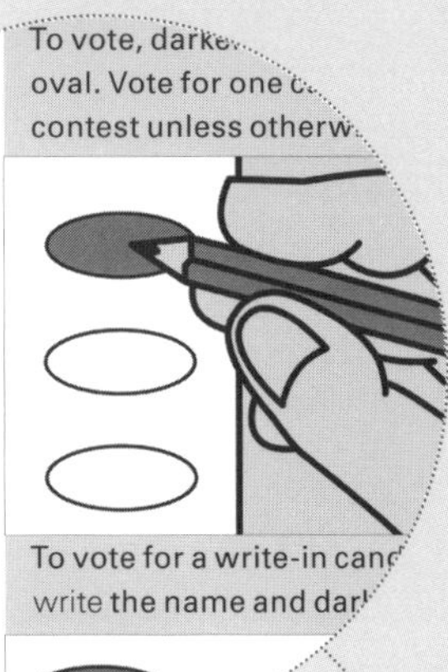

Instructions

Among the different technologies used during US elections, the most widespread and reliable is optical scanning. Many voters are already familiar with it. Nevertheless, simple and clear instructions are essential if the procedure is to be successful.

Voter Registration Application
Before completing this form, review the General, Application, and State specific instructions.

Are you a citizen of the United States of America?
Will you be 18 years old on or before election day?
If you checked "No" in response to either of these questions, do not complete form.
(Please see state-specific instructions for rules regarding eligibility to register prior to age 18.)
This space for office use only.

1 Last Name | First Name | Middle Name(s)
2 Home Address | Apt. or Lot # | City/Town | State | Zip Code
3 Address Where You Get Your Mail If Different From Above | City/Town | State | Zip Code
4 Date of Birth — Month Day Year
5 Telephone Number (optional)
6 ID Number - (See item 6 in the instructions for your state)
7 Choice of Party (see item 7 in the instructions for your State)
8 Race or Ethnic Group (see item 8 in the instructions for your State)
9 I have reviewed my state's instructions and I swear/affirm that:
- I am a United States citizen
- I meet the eligibility requirements of my state and subscribe to any oath required.
- The information I have provided is true to the best of my knowledge under penalty of perjury. If I have provided false information, I may be fined, imprisoned, or (if not a U.S. citizen) deported from or refused entry to the United States.

Please sign full name (or put mark)
Date: Month Day Year

If you are registering to vote for the first time: please refer to the application instructions for information on submitting copies of valid identification documents with this form.

Please fill out the sections below if they apply to you.

If this application is for a **change of name,** what was your name before you changed it?

A Last Name | First Name | Middle Name(s)

If you were **registered before but this is the first time you are registering from the address in Box 2**, what was your address where you were registered before?

B Street (or route and box number) | Apt. or Lot # | City/Town/County | State | Zip Code

If you live in a rural area but do not have a street number, or if you have no address, please show on the map where you live.

C
- Write in the names of the crossroads (or streets) nearest to where you live.
- Draw an **X** to show where you live.
- Use a dot to show any schools, churches, stores, or other landmarks near where you live, and write the name of the landmark.

Example: Route #2, Grocery Store, Woodchuck Road, Public School, X
NORTH

If the applicant is unable to sign, who helped the applicant fill out this application? Give name, address and phone number (phone number optional).

D

Mail this application to the address provided for your State.

Old voter registration form provided by EAC: A4

The national voter registration application is better designed than those for state governments, but there is still room for improvement.

Voter Registration Application

Before completing this form, review the General, Application and State specific instruction. If you are registering to vote for the first time, please refer to the Application instructions for information on submitting copies of valid identification documents with this form.

1 **qualifications** *If you mark "no" in response to either of these questions, do not complete this form.*

Are you a citizen of the United States of America? ☐ yes ☐ no
Will you be 18 years of age on or before election day? ☐ yes ☐ no
Please see state-specific instructions regarding eligibility to register prior to age 18.

2 **personal information** *If you mark no in response to either of these questions, do not complete this form.*

Mr/Mrs/Miss/Ms/Dr last name | first name | middle name(s) | Jr/Sr/I/II/III
home address (include apt. or space number) | city/town | state | zip code
address where you get mail (if different from above) | city/town | state | zip code
date of birth (month/day/year) | phone number (optional) | email address (optional)

3 **political party** *See instructions for your state.*
4 **race/ethnic group** *See instructions for your state.*
5 **ID number** *See instructions for your state.*

6 **signature**

I have reviewed my state's instructions and I swear/affirm that:
→ I am a U.S. citizen
→ I meet the eligibility requirements of my state and subscribe to any oath required

The information I have provided is true to the best of my knowledge under penalty of perjury. If I have provided false information, I may be fined, imprisoned, or (if not a U.S. citizen) deported from or refused entry to the United States.

signature | date today (month/day/year)

Please fill out the sections below if they apply to you.

7 **updating personal information** *If you are using this application to update your voter registration, please provide your previous information.*

Mr/Mrs/Miss/Ms/Dr last name | first name | middle name(s) | Jr/Sr/I/II/III
home address on previous registration | city/town | state | zip code

8 **rural address** *If you live in a rural area and have no street number, or you have no address, please illustrate where you live on the map below.*

→ Write the names of the crossroads (or streets) nearest to where you live.
→ Draw an **X** to show where you live.
→ Use a dot to show any schools, churches, stores or other landmarks near where you live and write the name of the landmark.

example: Route 2, •Grocery Store, Woodchuck Road, Public School•, X
North

9 **registration assistance** *If the applicant is unable to sign, list the name and address of the person who provided assistance.*

name | phone number (optional)
address | city/town | state | zip code

Mail this application to the address provided for your state.

for office use only

Redesigned voter registration form: US Letter

Red is now used only for instructions; there is more space for filling in responses, and black bars divide the form into clear sections.

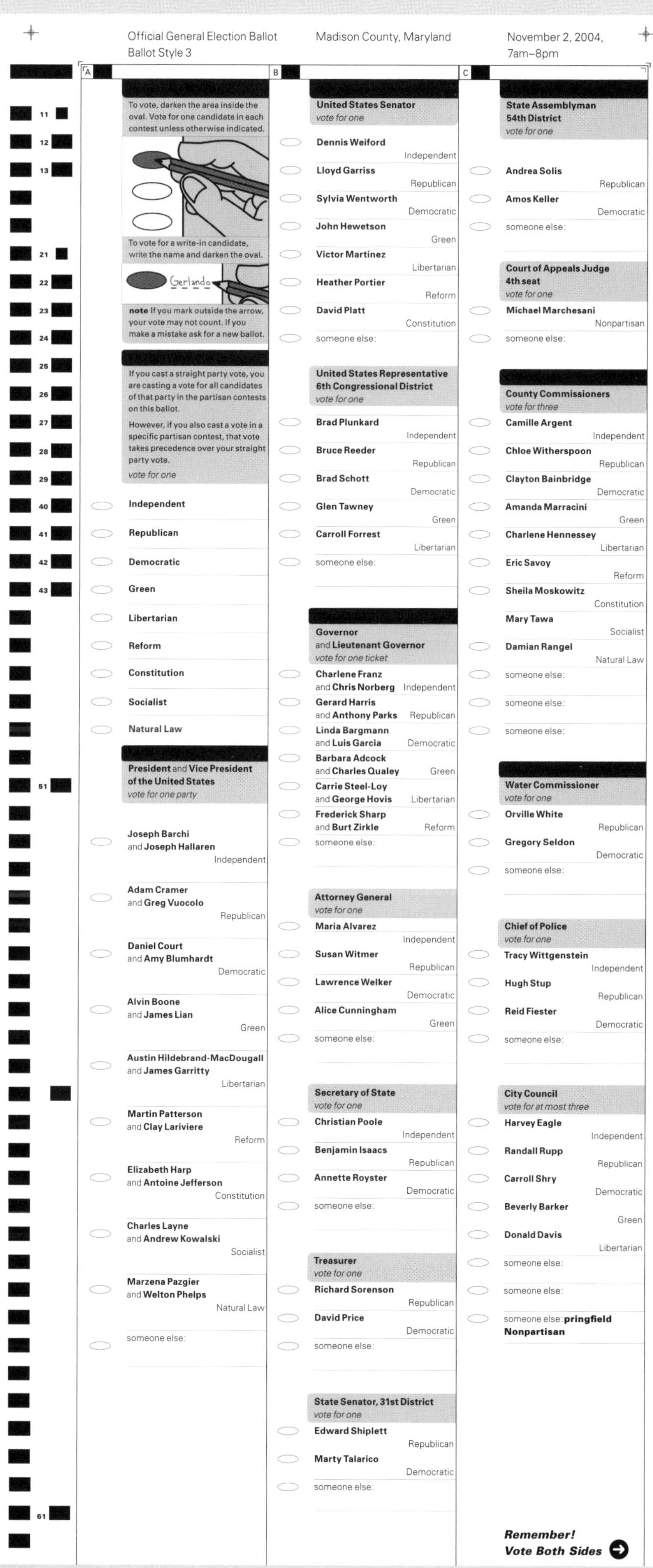

Official General Election Ballot
Ballot Style 3

Madison County, Maryland

November 2, 2004,
7am–8pm

A

To vote, darken the area inside the oval. Vote for one candidate in each contest unless otherwise indicated.

To vote for a write-in candidate, write the name and darken the oval.

Gerlando

note If you mark outside the arrow, your vote may not count. If you make a mistake ask for a new ballot.

If you cast a straight party vote, you are casting a vote for all candidates of that party in the partisan contests on this ballot.

However, if you also cast a vote in a specific partisan contest, that vote takes precedence over your straight party vote.

vote for one

- Independent
- Republican
- Democratic
- Green
- Libertarian
- Reform
- Constitution
- Socialist
- Natural Law

President and **Vice President of the United States**
vote for one party

- **Joseph Barchi** and **Joseph Hallaren** — Independent
- **Adam Cramer** and **Greg Vuocolo** — Republican
- **Daniel Court** and **Amy Blumhardt** — Democratic
- **Alvin Boone** and **James Lian** — Green
- **Austin Hildebrand-MacDougall** and **James Garritty** — Libertarian
- **Martin Patterson** and **Clay Lariviere** — Reform
- **Elizabeth Harp** and **Antoine Jefferson** — Constitution
- **Charles Layne** and **Andrew Kowalski** — Socialist
- **Marzena Pazgier** and **Welton Phelps** — Natural Law
- someone else:

B

United States Senator
vote for one

- **Dennis Weiford** — Independent
- **Lloyd Garriss** — Republican
- **Sylvia Wentworth** — Democratic
- **John Hewetson** — Green
- **Victor Martinez** — Libertarian
- **Heather Portier** — Reform
- **David Platt** — Constitution
- someone else:

United States Representative 6th Congressional District
vote for one

- **Brad Plunkard** — Independent
- **Bruce Reeder** — Republican
- **Brad Schott** — Democratic
- **Glen Tawney** — Green
- **Carroll Forrest** — Libertarian
- someone else:

Governor and **Lieutenant Governor**
vote for one ticket

- **Charlene Franz** and **Chris Norberg** — Independent
- **Gerard Harris** and **Anthony Parks** — Republican
- **Linda Bargmann** and **Luis Garcia** — Democratic
- **Barbara Adcock** and **Charles Qualey** — Green
- **Carrie Steel-Loy** and **George Hovis** — Libertarian
- **Frederick Sharp** and **Burt Zirkle** — Reform
- someone else:

Attorney General
vote for one

- **Maria Alvarez** — Independent
- **Susan Witmer** — Republican
- **Lawrence Welker** — Democratic
- **Alice Cunningham** — Green
- someone else:

Secretary of State
vote for one

- **Christian Poole** — Independent
- **Benjamin Isaacs** — Republican
- **Annette Royster** — Democratic
- someone else:

Treasurer
vote for one

- **Richard Sorenson** — Republican
- **David Price** — Democratic
- someone else:

State Senator, 31st District
vote for one

- **Edward Shiplett** — Republican
- **Marty Talarico** — Democratic
- someone else:

C

State Assemblyman 54th District
vote for one

- **Andrea Solis** — Republican
- **Amos Keller** — Democratic
- someone else:

Court of Appeals Judge 4th seat
vote for one

- **Michael Marchesani** — Nonpartisan
- someone else:

County Commissioners
vote for three

- **Camille Argent** — Independent
- **Chloe Witherspoon** — Republican
- **Clayton Bainbridge** — Democratic
- **Amanda Marracini** — Green
- **Charlene Hennessey** — Libertarian
- **Eric Savoy** — Reform
- **Sheila Moskowitz** — Constitution
- **Mary Tawa** — Socialist
- **Damian Rangel** — Natural Law
- someone else:
- someone else:
- someone else:

Water Commissioner
vote for one

- **Orville White** — Republican
- **Gregory Seldon** — Democratic
- someone else:

Chief of Police
vote for one

- **Tracy Wittgenstein** — Independent
- **Hugh Stup** — Republican
- **Reid Fiester** — Democratic
- someone else:

City Council
vote for at most three

- **Harvey Eagle** — Independent
- **Randall Rupp** — Republican
- **Carroll Shry** — Democratic
- **Beverly Barker** — Green
- **Donald Davis** — Libertarian
- someone else:
- someone else:
- someone else: **pringfield Nonpartisan**

Remember! Vote Both Sides

Optical scan ballot: c. 215 × 480 mm

There are different optical scan technologies in use, and each makes particular demands in relation to paper format, number and length of columns, and the manner in which the voters make their mark. This is a sample ballot paper with oval markings.

In many traditional ballot papers, text and headings are centred, but here the layout is left-justified throughout, making it easier for voters to view the contents at a glance.

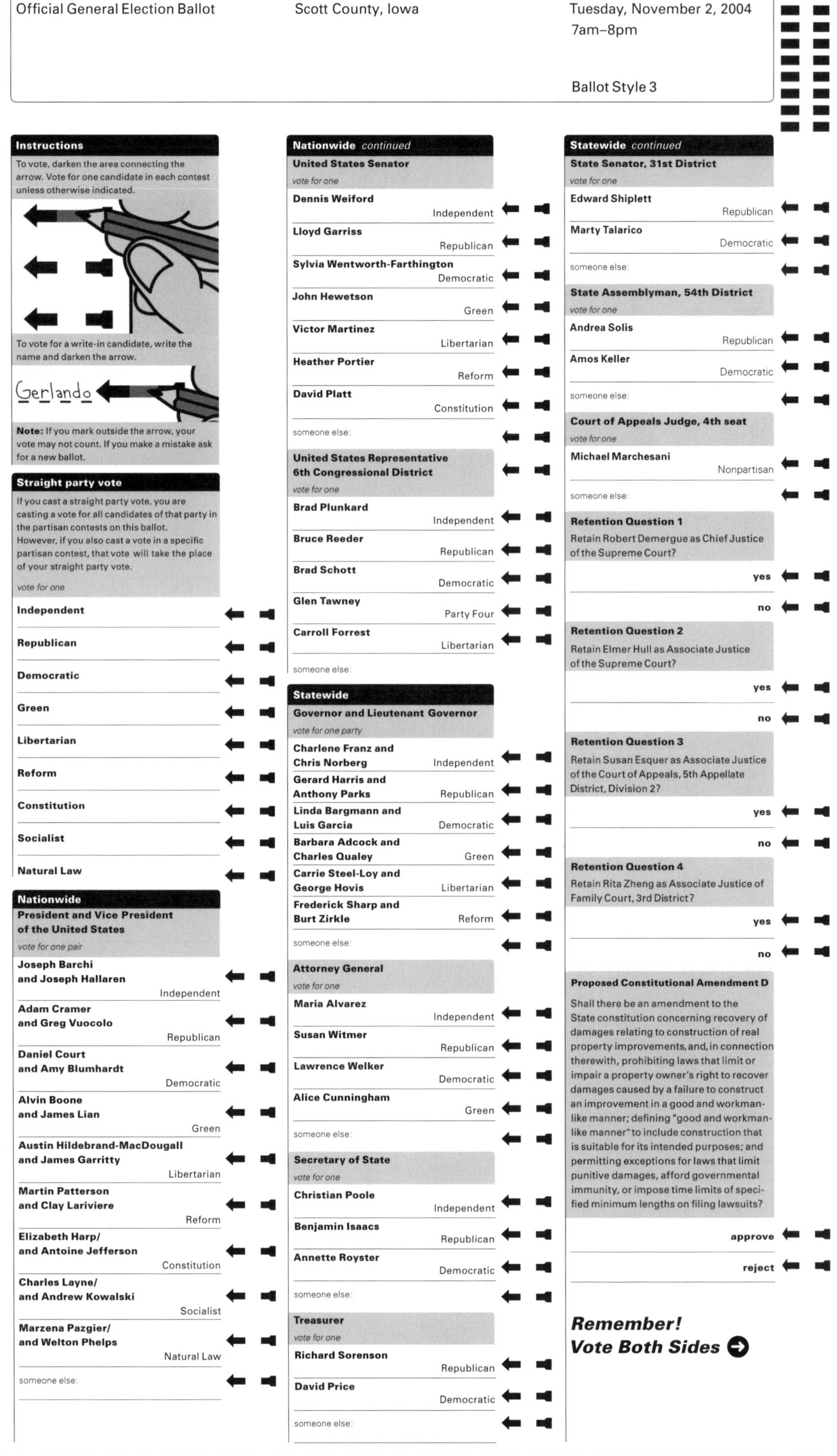

Official General Election Ballot | Scott County, Iowa | Tuesday, November 2, 2004
7am–8pm

Ballot Style 3

Instructions

To vote, darken the area connecting the arrow. Vote for one candidate in each contest unless otherwise indicated.

To vote for a write-in candidate, write the name and darken the arrow.

Gerlando

Note: If you mark outside the arrow, your vote may not count. If you make a mistake ask for a new ballot.

Straight party vote

If you cast a straight party vote, you are casting a vote for all candidates of that party in the partisan contests on this ballot. However, if you also cast a vote in a specific partisan contest, that vote will take the place of your straight party vote.

vote for one

Independent
Republican
Democratic
Green
Libertarian
Reform
Constitution
Socialist
Natural Law

Nationwide

President and Vice President of the United States

vote for one pair

Joseph Barchi and Joseph Hallaren Independent
Adam Cramer and Greg Vuocolo Republican
Daniel Court and Amy Blumhardt Democratic
Alvin Boone and James Lian Green
Austin Hildebrand-MacDougall and James Garritty Libertarian
Martin Patterson and Clay Lariviere Reform
Elizabeth Harp/ and Antoine Jefferson Constitution
Charles Layne/ and Andrew Kowalski Socialist
Marzena Pazgier/ and Welton Phelps Natural Law
someone else:

Nationwide *continued*

United States Senator

vote for one

Dennis Weiford Independent
Lloyd Garriss Republican
Sylvia Wentworth-Farthington Democratic
John Hewetson Green
Victor Martinez Libertarian
Heather Portier Reform
David Platt Constitution
someone else:

United States Representative 6th Congressional District

vote for one

Brad Plunkard Independent
Bruce Reeder Republican
Brad Schott Democratic
Glen Tawney Party Four
Carroll Forrest Libertarian
someone else:

Statewide

Governor and Lieutenant Governor

vote for one party

Charlene Franz and Chris Norberg Independent
Gerard Harris and Anthony Parks Republican
Linda Bargmann and Luis Garcia Democratic
Barbara Adcock and Charles Qualey Green
Carrie Steel-Loy and George Hovis Libertarian
Frederick Sharp and Burt Zirkle Reform
someone else:

Attorney General

vote for one

Maria Alvarez Independent
Susan Witmer Republican
Lawrence Welker Democratic
Alice Cunningham Green
someone else:

Secretary of State

vote for one

Christian Poole Independent
Benjamin Isaacs Republican
Annette Royster Democratic
someone else:

Treasurer

vote for one

Richard Sorenson Republican
David Price Democratic
someone else:

Statewide *continued*

State Senator, 31st District

vote for one

Edward Shiplett Republican
Marty Talarico Democratic
someone else:

State Assemblyman, 54th District

vote for one

Andrea Solis Republican
Amos Keller Democratic
someone else:

Court of Appeals Judge, 4th seat

vote for one

Michael Marchesani Nonpartisan
someone else:

Retention Question 1

Retain Robert Demergue as Chief Justice of the Supreme Court?

yes
no

Retention Question 2

Retain Elmer Hull as Associate Justice of the Supreme Court?

yes
no

Retention Question 3

Retain Susan Esquer as Associate Justice of the Court of Appeals, 5th Appellate District, Division 2?

yes
no

Retention Question 4

Retain Rita Zheng as Associate Justice of Family Court, 3rd District?

yes
no

Proposed Constitutional Amendment D

Shall there be an amendment to the State constitution concerning recovery of damages relating to construction of real property improvements, and, in connection therewith, prohibiting laws that limit or impair a property owner's right to recover damages caused by a failure to construct an improvement in a good and workman-like manner; defining "good and workman-like manner" to include construction that is suitable for its intended purposes; and permitting exceptions for laws that limit punitive damages, afford governmental immunity, or impose time limits of specified minimum lengths on filing lawsuits?

approve
reject

Remember!
Vote Both Sides

Optical scan ballot: 254 × 420 mm

In this example, a vote is marked by connecting the two halves of an arrow. Sections are clearly distinguished by black bars, and the use of upper and lower case for the names of the candidates makes them easier to find and read on the form.

US Bureau of the Census

Questionnaire and information sheets

Issued by	US Bureau of the Census
Design	Two Twelve Associates, Inc., New York
Year	2000
Typefaces	Interstate, Rockwell

Participation in national censuses is compulsory, but they are not very popular. The US holds a national census every ten years, and Two Twelve designed the system for Census 2000. The approach is friendly, the layout is easy to follow, and the explanations are in plain language; as a result, the new questionnaires and information brochures put an end to the downward trend in the number of responses over preceding decades.

Your answers help your community get the services and financial assistance it needs.
boarder, or foster child
roommate

Motivation

Pictograms and short texts explain how the census is carried out for the good of everyone, acting as an encouragement to complete the forms.

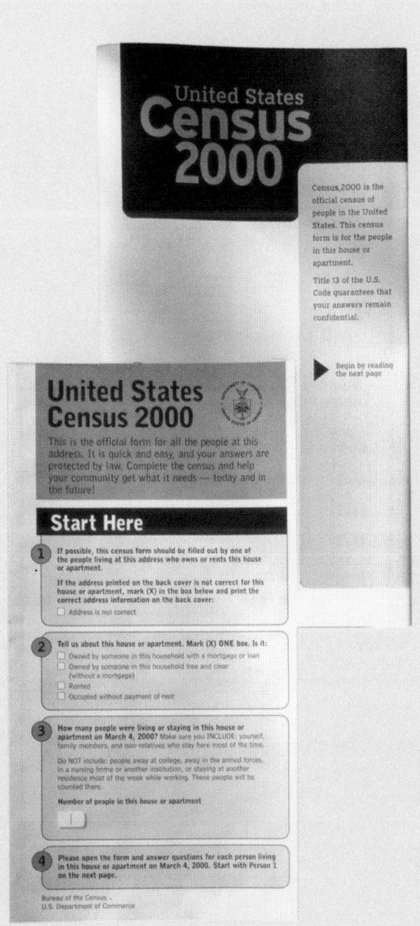

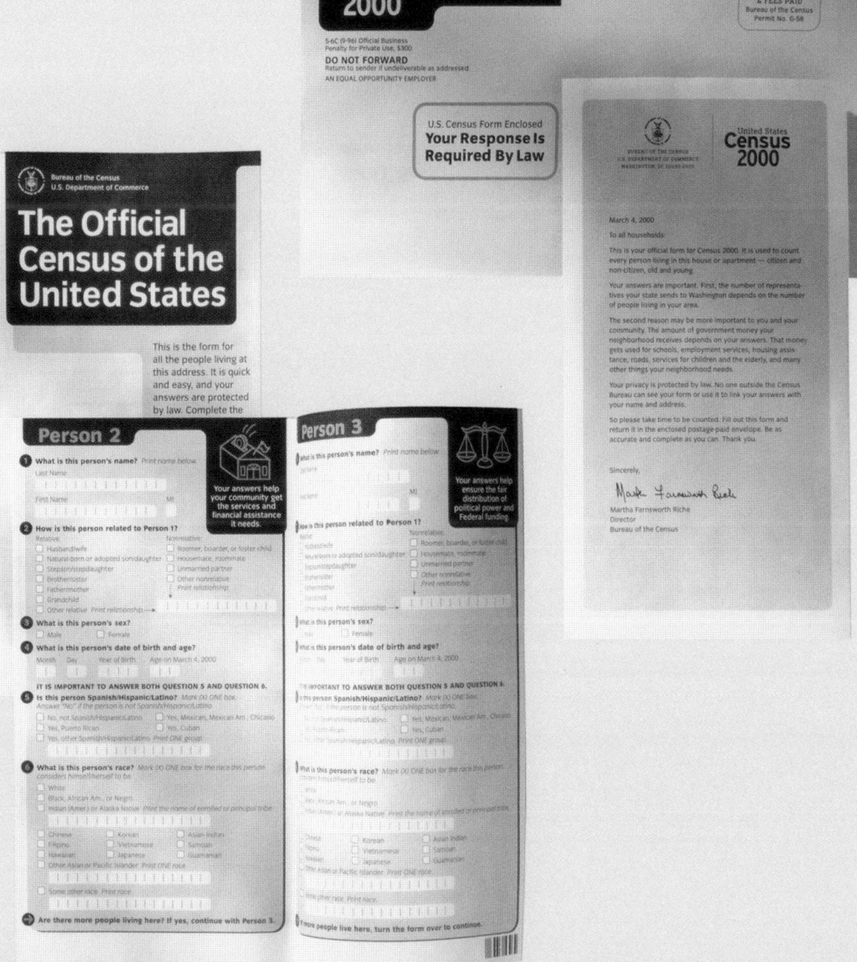

Questionnaires and information sheets

Earth tones and curved shapes give the various elements of the census a friendlier appearance. The straightforward questions and clear instructions make the forms easier to fill in.

The Pensions Regulator

Registration form

Issued by	The Pensions Regulator, UK
Design	The Brand Union, London
	Richard Bland, Mark Stanton
Year	2006
Typeface	InfoText

The Pensions Regulator (TPR) plays a very important role in supervising the pension industry and employers who administer pension schemes. In order to do this, it needs to collect many details from other organizations. The Brand Union was briefed to develop a registration form that was as clear as possible and could also be completed by administrative staff with little detailed technical knowledge. The designers also delivered a set of guidelines that TPR could subsequently apply to other forms.

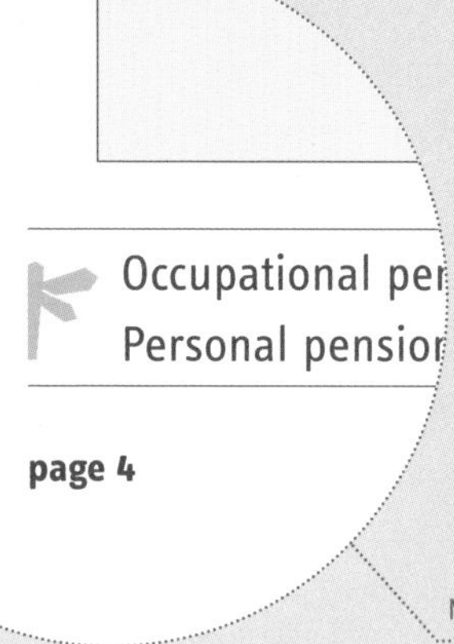

Navigation

Signpost icons help users to understand which sections they need to complete.

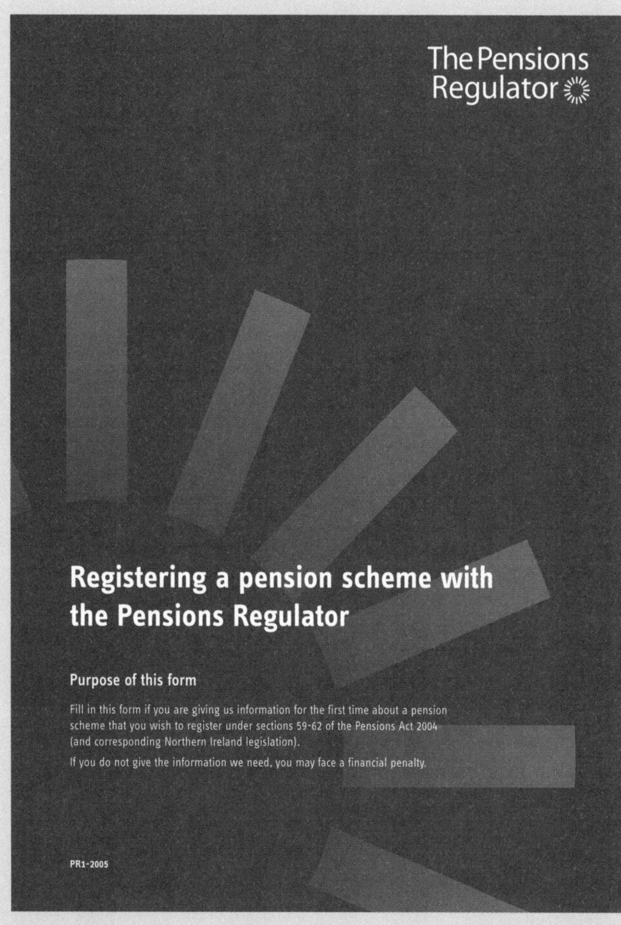

The Pensions Regulator

Registering a pension scheme with the Pensions Regulator

Purpose of this form

Fill in this form if you are giving us information for the first time about a pension scheme that you wish to register under sections 59-62 of the Pensions Act 2004 (and corresponding Northern Ireland legislation).

If you do not give the information we need, you may face a financial penalty.

PR1-2005

Cover: A4

The purpose of the form is briefly described on the cover, helping users to establish quickly whether the form is appropriate for them.

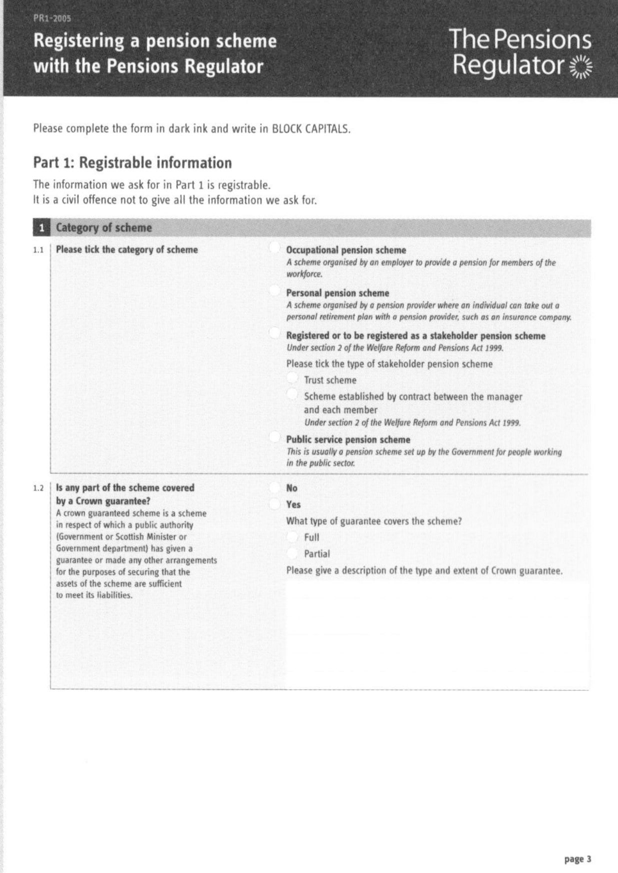

PR1-2005

Registering a pension scheme with the Pensions Regulator

The Pensions Regulator

Please complete the form in dark ink and write in BLOCK CAPITALS.

Part 1: Registrable information

The information we ask for in Part 1 is registrable.
It is a civil offence not to give all the information we ask for.

1 Category of scheme

1.1 **Please tick the category of scheme**

Occupational pension scheme
A scheme organised by an employer to provide a pension for members of the workforce.

Personal pension scheme
A scheme organised by a pension provider where an individual can take out a personal retirement plan with a pension provider, such as an insurance company.

Registered or to be registered as a stakeholder pension scheme
Under section 2 of the Welfare Reform and Pensions Act 1999.

Please tick the type of stakeholder pension scheme

Trust scheme

Scheme established by contract between the manager and each member
Under section 2 of the Welfare Reform and Pensions Act 1999.

Public service pension scheme
This is usually a pension scheme set up by the Government for people working in the public sector.

1.2 **Is any part of the scheme covered by a Crown guarantee?**
A crown guaranteed scheme is a scheme in respect of which a public authority (Government or Scottish Minister or Government department) has given a guarantee or made any other arrangements for the purposes of securing that the assets of the scheme are sufficient to meet its liabilities.

No

Yes

What type of guarantee covers the scheme?

Full

Partial

Please give a description of the type and extent of Crown guarantee.

page 3

First page of form: A4

While general notes are placed at the start of the form, notes referring to specific questions are placed next to the questions themselves.

Part 1: Registrable information continued

2 Scheme name and address

2.1 **Full name of pension scheme to be registered**
As shown on the documentation establishing the scheme or any subsequent amending document.

2.2 **Address of scheme**
This should be an address in the UK where the management of the scheme is carried out. If more than one location is involved, you should give the main address.

Postcode

3 Scheme status

3.1 **Can new members be admitted to the scheme?**
No
Yes

3.2 **Do further benefits accrue to, or in respect of any member of the scheme?**
No
Yes

3.3 **Are further contributions being paid to the scheme?**
No
Yes

3.4 **Are there any active members in the scheme?**
No
Yes

3.5 **Is the scheme a trust scheme that is winding up?**
No
Yes
Give the date the winding up commenced
/ /

4 Insurance details

4.1 **Are any pension scheme benefits provided under any insurance or annuity contract?**
No
Yes
Name of insurance company providing administrative details

Address of the insurance company's pensions department

Postcode

Policy number or insurance company reference number
If there is more than one insurance company, please give details of the other insurance company in section 13.

Occupational pension schemes now complete sections 5 to 8
Personal pension schemes go to section 9

Second page of form: A4
Coloured backgrounds establish very clear sections within the form and keylines mark the start and end of questions.

AssTech

Questionnaire

Issued by	AssTech GmbH
Design	kognito Visuelle Gestaltung, Berlin
Year	2000
Typeface	Univers

A very detailed questionnaire concerning the insurance risks involved in offset printing. Using few graphic devices and a single colour, the design is clear and concise but includes all the points required for insurance purposes. The user is very cleverly and efficiently guided, and despite the high number of questions, the questionnaire remains manageable and does not seem daunting.

y production

ere furnaces?

◯ No info ◯ Yes What fuel

Waste or

◯ No

Nested responses

Questions can be answered with *No*, *No info* or *Yes*. The *Yes* response is highlighted in grey and directs the user to further questions. So that the same principle can be followed through, a clearly nested structure has been used. This basic premise means that the ordering of questions and answers needs to be kept consistent: place the *No* option first, followed by the *Yes*, and position the answers after the checkboxes.

→ Filter questions: page 188

Bayerische
Rück

1
17

Questionnaire on offset printers

This questionnaire is an extract from ELIAS.
Its sole purpose is to capture basic data on the risk.
A comprehensive risk assessment is possible with ELIAS.
ELIAS is a product of AssTech GmbH.
AssTech GmbH also offers on-site inspections.

Risk-data entry offset printers-working

Risk number
Person handling risk
Contact (broker)
Date

Client data

Name of Company
Street
Postal code
Town
Country
Tel./fax
E-mail
Currency
Turnover
No. of staff

Contact — **Do you need reinsurance cover for this risk? If so, please contact our Facultative Liability Department.**

Bayerische Rück
Aktiengesellschaft
80526 München

Tel. +49 89 38 44-0
Fax +49 89 38 44-22 79

E-mail
info.envirocheck@bayerischerueck.com

© 2000 AssTech GmbH

Title page: A4

The introduction gives a short and precise explanation of the purpose of the questionnaire.

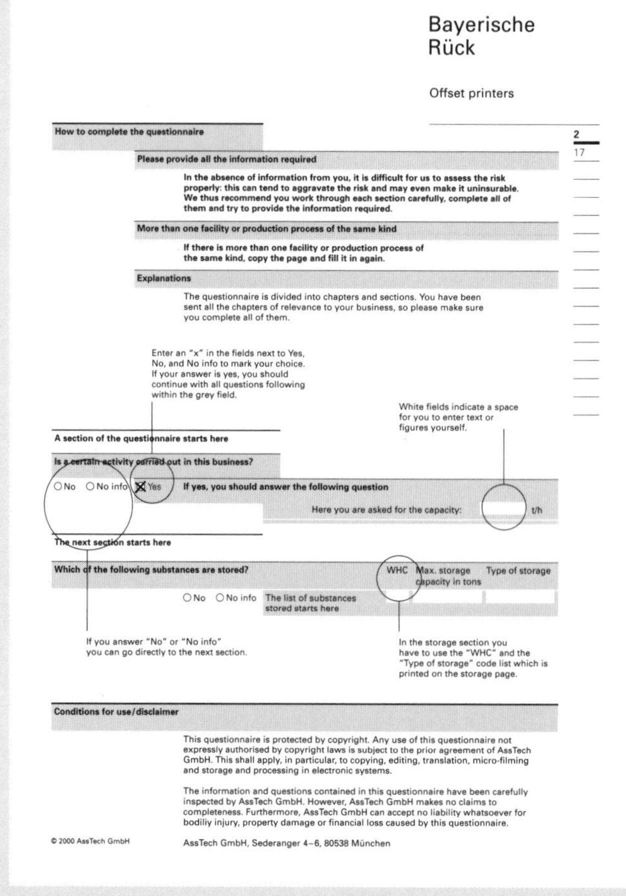

Bayerische
Rück

Offset printers

2
17

How to complete the questionnaire

Please provide all the information required

In the absence of information from you, it is difficult for us to assess the risk properly: this can tend to aggravate the risk and may even make it uninsurable. We thus recommend you work through each section carefully, complete all of them and try to provide the information required.

More than one facility or production process of the same kind

If there is more than one facility or production process of the same kind, copy the page and fill it in again.

Explanations

The questionnaire is divided into chapters and sections. You have been sent all the chapters of relevance to your business, so please make sure you complete all of them.

Enter an "x" in the fields next to Yes, No, and No info to mark your choice. If your answer is yes, you should continue with all questions following within the grey field.

White fields indicate a space for you to enter text or figures yourself.

A section of the questionnaire starts here

Is a certain activity carried out in this business?

◯ No ◯ No info ☒ Yes **If yes, you should answer the following question**

Here you are asked for the capacity: t/h

The next section starts here

Which of the following substances are stored? WHC Max. storage capacity in tons Type of storage

◯ No ◯ No info The list of substances stored starts here

If you answer "No" or "No info" you can go directly to the next section.

In the storage section you have to use the "WHC" and the "Type of storage" code list which is printed on the storage page.

Conditions for use/disclaimer

This questionnaire is protected by copyright. Any use of this questionnaire not expressly authorised by copyright laws is subject to the prior agreement of AssTech GmbH. This shall apply, in particular, to copying, editing, translation, micro-filming and storage and processing in electronic systems.

The information and questions contained in this questionnaire have been carefully inspected by AssTech GmbH. However, AssTech GmbH makes no claims to completeness. Furthermore, AssTech GmbH can accept no liability whatsoever for bodiliy injury, property damage or financial loss caused by this questionnaire.

© 2000 AssTech GmbH AssTech GmbH, Sederanger 4–6, 80538 München

Instruction page

The explanations on the second page are extremely clear and detailed.

Bayerische
Rück

Offset printers

7
17

Energy production

Are there furnaces?

○ No ○ No info ○ Yes **What fuel is used?**

Waste or wood treated with organochlorine compounds

○ No	○ No info	○ Yes	Thermal output		MW
			How old is the facility?		year of construction

Which of the following safety requirements are met when using waste or wood?

○ No	○ No info	○ Yes	Cleaning of flue gas to remove dust (e.g. using electrostatic filters)
○ No	○ No info	○ Yes	Desulphurisation of flue gas
○ No	○ No info	○ Yes	Reduction of nitrogen oxides
○ No	○ No info	○ Yes	Constant monitoring of concentrations of dust, carbon monoxide, sulphur dioxide and nitrogen oxides in exhaust gases
○ No	○ No info	○ Yes	Regular monitoring of concentrations of organic substances, heavy metals and halogen compounds in exhaust gases
○ No	○ No info	○ Yes	Optimum adjustment and maintenance of the furnace
○ No	○ No info	○ Yes	Adequate height of chimney
○ No	○ No info	○ Yes	Other safety measures:

Coal, coke, petrol coke, briquettes

○ No	○ No info	○ Yes	Thermal output		MW
			How old is the facility?		year of construction

Which of the following safety requirements are met when using coal, coke, petrol coke or briquettes?

○ No	○ No info	○ Yes	Cleaning of flue gas to remove dust (e.g. using electrostatic filters)
○ No	○ No info	○ Yes	Desulphurisation of flue gas
○ No	○ No info	○ Yes	Reduction of nitrogen oxides
○ No	○ No info	○ Yes	Constant monitoring of concentrations of dust, carbon monoxide, sulphur dioxide and nitrogen oxides in exhaust gases
○ No	○ No info	○ Yes	Regular monitoring of concentrations of organic substances, heavy metals and halogen compounds in exhaust gases
○ No	○ No info	○ Yes	Optimum adjustment and maintenance of the furnace
○ No	○ No info	○ Yes	Adequate height of chimney
○ No	○ No info	○ Yes	Other safety measures:

Questionnaire page

One excellent detail is the page numbering in the right-hand margin. Users can see at a glance how many sections have been completed and how many are still to come.

Combined Insurance

Multi-product application form

Issued by	Combined Insurance, UK
Design	Boag Associates, London
Year	2007
Typeface	Univers

Combined Insurance agents sell a variety of insurance services within clients' homes. Traditionally this would require the agent to fill out a separate form for every policy and obtain a separate signature for each one. The completed forms would then need to go back to the Combined Insurance offices before the policy could be underwritten.

The company commissioned Boag Associates to write and design a multi-product application form that would contain all policies in a single document, requiring only one signature. As a result, customers only need to fill in their personal information once, instead of repeating it on every form.

Each page of the application form has a carbonless copy. The copies are left with the customer, while the original is taken back to the office for processing. This means that customers are covered as soon as they sign the form.

1.4 Other initials

1.5 Date of birth

D D M M Y Y

1.6 Your age

years

1.7 Are you male or

Male F

Date

Different English-speaking countries have different conventions for writing the date. Adding letters to represent day, month and year avoids the potential for mistakes or confusion.

Fill in the **Health details sections** if you're applying for:
- Income Protection
- Income Protection Plus
- Term Assurance
- Critical Illness
- Family Income Benefit

Combined Insurance · Multi-Product – Application Form · sheet 4 of 8

7 Key questions about your health

Remember that if you miss out any information, or give us misleading information, we may not pay any claim and we may cancel all your cover.

7.1 Have you ever lived outside the UK, Europe, Australia, New Zealand, the USA or Canada?

Yes No

7.2 Are you currently experiencing any symptoms or any medical condition that you haven't seen your doctor about or received treatment for?

Yes No

7.3 What is your height?

7.4 What is your weight?

Have you ever suffered from: *(tick as applicable)*

7.5 Cancer
Hodgkin's disease
lymphoma or leukaemia
brain or spinal tumour (benign or malignant)

7.6 heart disease, including cardiomyopathy
a heart valve disorder
angina
a heart attack

7.7 stroke
transient ischaemic attack (TIA)
brain haemorrhage
any permanent brain injury

7.8 multiple sclerosis
Parkinson's disease
paralysis
Alzheimer's disease
dementia
cerebral palsy

7.9 Have you ever suffered from any disorder of your central nervous system (which includes your brain, spinal cord and nerves) that you haven't already mentioned?

Yes No

7.10 Have you ever suffered from any disease or abnormality of your arteries (including your aorta) or veins, or intermittent claudication?

Yes No

7.11 Have you ever suffered from diabetes or sugar in your urine?

Yes No

7.12 Have you ever suffered from mental illness that meant you needed to be referred to a psychiatrist or needed hospital treatment?

Yes No

8 Your health over the last five years

Within the last five years, have you suffered from: *(tick as applicable)*

8.1 Any mole or freckle that bled, became painful, or changed colour or size, or any cyst, growth, lump or lesion – whether you spoke to a doctor about it or not?

Yes No

8.2 Raised blood pressure or cholesterol levels
a heart murmur
palpitations
chest pain

8.3 Asthma
bronchitis
pneumonia
any other lung condition or disorder

8.4 numbness
a loss of feeling or tingling in the limbs or face
a temporary loss of muscle power

8.5 Any problems with your speech, hearing or balance, or problems with your eyes or vision that could not be corrected by wearing spectacles or contact lenses?

Yes No

8.6 Epilepsy
fits
blackouts
blurred or double vision

8.7 Arthritis, or a disorder of the spine, neck or any joint, including a slipped disc, sciatica, back or neck pain, or gout?

Yes No

Application form, double page: A4

Not all questions need to be answered for all policies. Instructions are given in large type opposite the questions to which they refer.

Combined Insurance · Multi-Product – Application Form · sheet 1 of 8

1 About you

1.1 Your title

Mr   Mrs   Miss   Ms   Other

1.2 Surname

1.3 First name

1.4 Other initials

1.5 Date of birth

D D M M Y Y Y Y

1.6 Your age

years

1.7 Are you male or female?

Male   Female

1.8 Your marital status

1.9 Your home address

Postcode

1.10 Work address

Postcode

1.11 Home phone number

1.12 Mobile phone number

1.13 Email address

1.14 Have you smoked tobacco or used any tobacco product or nicotine replacement products in the last 12 months?

Yes   No

2 Your plans

Plan	Options	✔	Amount you're insured for	Benefit period / term	Deferred period	Your first premium (inc IPT*)	Your subsequent renewal premium	How long before you renew
Accident Income Protection			£	2 years		£	£	
Hospital Cash			£	To age 65		£	£	
Accident Hospital Cash			£	To age 65		£	£	
Personal Accident Plan for your family	Bronze Silver Gold			To age 70		£	£	
Personal Accident Plan for you only	Bronze Silver Gold			To age 70		£	£	
For the following plans, you'll need to fill in the Health details section								
Income Protection			£			£	£	
Income Protection Plus			£			£	£	
Term Assurance (With guaranteed insurability)			£			£	£	
Term Assurance (Without guaranteed insurability)			£			£	£	
Critical Illness	Level Escalating		£	To age 65		£	£	
Family Income Benefit			£			£	£	
					Total	**£**	**£**	

* *Government Insurance Premium Tax*

Application form, first page

Sections are defined using pale blue tinted areas. The white response boxes are visually highlighted. In the section shown here, eleven insurance products are ingeniously encapsulated in one product, option and feature selection table.

ABN AMRO Bank

Application form and agreement

Issued by ABN AMRO Bank, Netherlands
Design Edenspiekermann (formerly Eden Design & Communication), Amsterdam
Year 2008
Typeface Univers

Companies make agreements with this bank to issue corporate credit cards for their employees to use. The forms had to be easy to complete, preventing users from making mistakes. As the forms not only ask for a great deal of data but also give users a lot of information about the credit card's terms and conditions, a very economical layout was needed. The use of colour to distinguish between different types of information helped to make the form as clear as possible.

Character dividers

Character dividers are only given where digits or letters need to be clearly separated from each other, for example for a name that will be printed on the credit card. This means that mistakes can be avoided. Where no character divisions are provided, text fields are filled in more quickly and easily.

ABN AMRO MULTI CORPORATE CARD ABN·AMRO
Agreement

On conclusion of this agreement a Card may be requested for each employee, using the form entitled 'Application for ABN AMRO Multi Corporate Card – Employee Card'

BUSINESS PARTICULARS ICS can only deal with your application if you complete this form **in full**.

Business name
Business address
Postcode Town/city
Country
C. of C. registration number

Only complete if this is different from the business address.

Mail address
Postcode Town/city
Country

Place a cross next to the language in which you wish to receive correspondence.

Preferred language ☐ Dutch ☐ English

PARTICULARS OF CONTACT

A contact is authorised to deal with ICS in respect of Cards, including requesting, taking delivery of and cancelling Cards, notifying changes regarding Cards and Cardholders, taking delivery of and re-requesting PINs, requesting copies of account statements, asking questions about transactions and acting as company administrator in the context of SDOL.

Initials Name
☐ Male ☐ Female Work phone no.
Email address
Identification code, 6 digits
User ID for Smart Data Online

Choose an easy to remember identification code (e.g. your mother's date of birth). You need this for every telephone contact with ABN AMRO Creditcard Services.

Your User ID must contain between 6 and 19 letters or figures and is case-sensitive.

PARTICULARS OF SECOND CONTACT Only complete if applicable.

Initials Name
☐ Male ☐ Female Work phone no.
Email address
Identification code, 6 digits
User ID for Smart Data Online

PARTICULARS OF CONTRACT

This is the maximum amount that can be spent with the Cards.

Company limit €

The amounts due will be collected from this account. See 'List of Charges for Business Payments' for the Card costs.

ABN AMRO account number
Only Dutch Euro bank account

Continue on revers ▶▶

International Card Services B.V. Established in Diemen, C of C no. 33200596

DESIRED COLLECTION Indicate from which account the amounts owed must be collected.

☐ From the business account
☐ From the employee's personal account
☐ From the employee's personal account **with additionally deferred payment**

In the case of additionally deferred payment the amounts are collected not 3 but 28 days after the account statement date.

Day of the month on which your monthly account statement is compiled
Select a day after the 2nd and before the 27th of the month

DESIRED TRANSACTIONS Indicate which transactions the employee can settle with the Card and which *not*

☐ All transactions are permitted

The following transactions are permitted:

Airline and train tickets	☐ Yes	☐ No
Hotels	☐ Yes	☐ No
Car rental	☐ Yes	☐ No
Fuel	☐ Yes	☐ No
Office items	☐ Yes	☐ No
Cash withdrawals	☐ Yes	☐ No
All other transactions	☐ Yes	☐ No

DIVERTED PAYMENT Indicate which transactions have to be diverted, to which account and up to what limit.

In the case of diverted payments the transactions are charged not to the Spending Limit on a Card, but to the Diverted payment limit.

☐ Do not divert any transactions ►► Continue to signature

☐ Airline and train tickets
☐ Hotels
☐ Car rental
☐ Fuel
☐ Office items
☐ Cash withdrawals

If you opt for diverted payment, the transactions will be deducted from this account.

ABN AMRO account number
Only Dutch Euro bank account

Diverted payment limit €

SIGNATURE The agreement becomes effective after approval by ICS.

The authorised signatory states, authorised signatories state:
1 that the above information is correct and complete; **2** that he/she has taken note of and agrees to the General Conditions for the ABN AMRO Multi Corporate Card; **3** International Card Services B.V. ("ICS") to be authorised in that case to collect charges you have made against the given account(s), whereby ICS is authorised to allow a third party to collect on its behalf; **4** to agree that information pertaining to the Company be stored in the ICS and ABN AMRO Bank N.V. administrative systems; **5** to grant ICS permission to forward information to MasterCard Inc. (including in the US) or third parties hired to process transactions; **6** to be aware that information provided by ICS and/or ABN AMRO may not be considered as professional advice; **7** to grant ICS permission to provide all information pertaining to the issuance and use of Cards falling under the terms of this agreement to MasterCard Inc. for use of Smart Data Online.

Date and place

This may only be signed by someone who has been registered as an authorised signatory with the Chamber of Commerce.

Name of authorised signatory Name of authorised signatory
Signature Signature

TO BE COMPLETED BY ABN AMRO

Business contact number
Office and place
PAC-code
Approved by
Handled by
Telephone number of person handling
Signature ABN AMRO and stamp

Agreement, recto and verso: A4

The corporate colours, yellow and green, are used to distinguish the questions from the information boxes.

APPLICATION FOR ABN AMRO MULTI CORPORATE CARD

Employee card

This Card may only be applied for in the context of the ABN AMRO Multi Corporate Card Agreement.

BUSINESS PARTICULARS

ICS can only deal with your application if you complete this form **in full**.

Business name

Corporate account number

PARTICULARS OF CARDHOLDER

Titles | Initials

Prefixes | Surname

☐ Male ☐ Female | Date of birth dd-mm-yyyy

This must not be a PO Box.

Street and number | Postcode

Town/city | Country

Mobile phone | Work phone

Email

Place a cross next to the language in which you wish to receive correspondence.

Choice of language ☐ Dutch ☐ English

SPENDING LIMIT

Spending limit ☐ € 7,000 ☐ Other amount minimum €1,000 €

Choose an easy to remember identification code (e.g. your mother's date of birth). You need this code to activate your Multi Corporate Card. You also need this code for every telephone contact with ABN AMRO Creditcard Services.

ACCOUNT NUMBER AND IDENTIFICATION CODE

Account number of Cardholder. Exclusively Dutch Euro bank account.
Complete only if personal invoicing has been chosen. Check with your manager.

Identification code 8 digits

NAME OF CARDHOLDER ON THE CARD

Name of Cardholder on Card, max. 21 characters

Business name on Card, max. 21 characters

SIGNATURE

The authorised signatory states / authorised signatories state on behalf of the Business: **1** that he/she/they agrees/agree to the provision of a Card to the above-mentioned Cardholder; **2** that the above information is correct and complete; **3** that the Cardholder has signed the form himself/herself; **4** that he/she/they has/have taken note of and agrees/agree to the General Conditions for the ABN AMRO Multi Corporate Card; **5** International Card Services B.V. ("ICS") to be authorised in that case to collect charges you have made against the given account(s), whereby ICS is authorised to allow a third party to collect on its behalf; **6** to agree that information pertaining to the Company be stored in the ICS and ABN AMRO Bank N.V. administrative systems; **7** to be aware that information provided by ICS and/or ABN AMRO cannot be considered as professional advice; **8** to grant ICS permission to forward information to MasterCard Inc. (including in the US) or third parties hired by MasterCard for processing transactions.

The Cardholder states: **1** that he/she has taken note of and agrees to the General Conditions for the ABN AMRO Multi Corporate Card; **2** to agree to allowing personal data to be stored in the administrative systems of International Card Service BV ("ICS") and ABN AMRO Bank N.V.; **3** to grant ICS permission to forward personal data to MasterCard Inc. (including in the US) or third parties hired by MasterCard for processing transactions. **4** to grant ICS permission to provide all information pertaining to the issuance and use of the Card to the Company and to MasterCard Inc. for use of Smart Data Online; **5** (only for private party billing) to authorise ICS to collect monthly the charges incurred from the bank account as named above, whereby ICS is authorised to allow a third party to collect these charges on its behalf.

Date and place | Date and place

Name of authorised signatory/signatories | Name of Cardholder

Signature of authorised signatory/signatories | Signature of Cardholder

TO BE COMPLETED BY ABN AMRO

Office and place | Handled by | Approved by

PAC-code | Telefoonnummer behandelaar | Signature for ABN AMRO and stamp

International Card Services B.V. Established in Diemen, C of C no. 33200596

Application form: A4

The form is given a very distinctive look by the triangular shapes, which echo the logo design and make the section headings stand out.

Legal & General Assurance

Application form

Issued by	Legal & General Assurance
Design	Butcher & Gundersen, London
	Sarah Teasdale
Year	2008
Typeface	Century Gothic

Standard insurance application forms were regarded as off-putting, over-complicated and too time-consuming. Many customers misunderstood the questions and instructions, and the forms did not leave enough space for questions to be answered in full.

This new application form was designed to be clearer and easier to use than its predecessors, more efficient to process, and with greater emphasis on the brand. It also serves as a 'best practice' model for the company's future forms. The design uses a comparatively large amount of white space, and care has been taken to make sure the language is easy to understand. Different colours and icons lead applicants through the form, and help them to see at a glance which sections apply to them.

Reason
for cover
Will this policy re
force/be going a
Do you have any o
to disclose?
If 'Yes', please g
for the other pc
Information) b
Yes N

Icons

Alert icons identify questions where further action may be needed.

CONFIDENTIAL

OLP Connect

Data Application Form and Additional Questionnaires

> Family Protection
> Mortgage Protection
> Business Protection

Welcome to Legal & General.

Please answer all questions in this form to the best of your knowledge and belief, as this will help avoid any delay in processing your application. If you don't answer truthfully and accurately, it will very likely mean that a claim will be declined and your policy may be cancelled.

See overleaf for some brief notes that will help you with your application. Thank you.

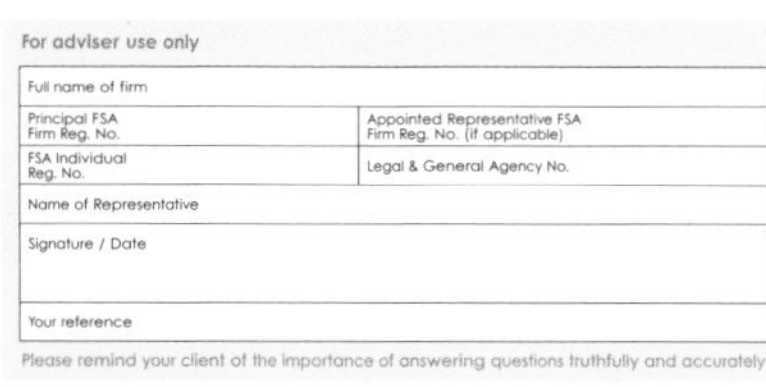

For adviser use only

Full name of firm	
Principal FSA Firm Reg. No.	Appointed Representative FSA Firm Reg. No. (if applicable)
FSA Individual Reg. No.	Legal & General Agency No.
Name of Representative	
Signature / Date	
Your reference	

Please remind your client of the importance of answering questions truthfully and accurately

OLP Connect 1/32

Application form, page 1: A4

The chosen typeface is rather broad, and its letterforms can be hard to read at small sizes.

4 Personal Assurance Questionnaire

This questionnaire only applies if you have answered 'Yes' to question 7 in Part 1 AND you're applying for Family Protection and/or Mortgage Protection.

Client one / Client two

1 Do you have, or are you applying for, any other Life cover with another insurance company? This includes any Life cover provided by your employer. If 'Yes' and you need more space, please use the Additional Information section in Part 9

Yes / No
If 'Yes', please give details:
Company
Start date
Policy type
Term years / Amount of cover £
Reason for cover
Will this policy remain in force/be going ahead? Yes / No
Do you have any other policy(ies) to disclose? Yes / No
If 'Yes', please give the same details as above for the other policy(ies), in Part 9 (Additional Information) before continuing with this section

2 Do you have, or are you applying for, any other Critical Illness cover with another insurance company? If 'Yes' and you need more space, please use the Additional Information section in Part 9

Yes / No
If 'Yes', please give details:
Company
Start date
Policy type
Term years / Amount of cover £
Reason for cover
Will this policy remain in force/be going ahead? Yes / No
Do you have any other policy(ies) to disclose? Yes / No
If 'Yes', please give the same details as above for the other policy(ies), in Part 9 (Additional Information) before continuing with this section

3 Please give details of your gross annual earned income for the last three years. Do not include any unearned income, such as investment income

Current year	Earned income £		**Current year**	Earned income £
Last year	Earned income £		**Last year**	Earned income £
Previous year	Earned income £		**Previous year**	Earned income £

If you are self employed – please give net taxable earnings after deduction of allowable business expenses

If your earned income for the current year is less than £10,000, please continue with question 4. Otherwise, please now go straight to question 5.

4 Please give details of all other household gross annual earned income for the last three years.

Current year	Earned income £		**Current year**	Earned income £
Last year	Earned income £		**Last year**	Earned income £
Previous year	Earned income £		**Previous year**	Earned income £

5 What is the total value of your net assets? £ / £

'Net assets' are your total assets (for example house, car, shares), less your total liabilities (for example mortgage, outstanding debt). **Where examples are shown, they are not intended to be a complete list.**

If you require Family Protection, please continue with question 6. Otherwise, for Mortgage Protection, please now go straight to question 10.

OLP Connect 17/32

Sample page: A4

The three-column layout gives the page a neat and tidy appearance.

3 About your policy

Questions 1 and 2 of this section only apply if you require Mortgage Protection. If you don't require Mortgage Protection, please go straight to question 3.

	Client one	Client two
	For Joint cover, use the 'Client one' column for answers in this Part	
1 What is the name of the mortgage lender, and the amount of the mortgage loan, for the mortgage on which you require Mortgage Protection?	Lender Mortgage loan amount £	Lender Mortgage loan amount £
2 Do you have a new property address?	Yes No **If 'Yes'**, what is the new address, including postcode? Postcode	Yes No **If 'Yes'**, what is the new address, including postcode? Postcode
3 Are any of the policies that you're applying for replacing any existing policies held with Legal & General? If **'Yes'**, please note that your existing policy or policies will be cancelled automatically when this policy(ies) is put in force	Yes No **If 'Yes'**, what is the policy number(s) of your existing Legal & General policy(ies) that will be replaced?	Yes No **If 'Yes'**, what is the policy number(s) of your existing Legal & General policy(ies) that will be replaced?

If you are applying for Mortgage Payment Insurance ONLY, please now go straight to Part 10. Otherwise, please continue with question 4.

4 Are any of the policies that you're applying for, to be issued under Trust?	Yes No **If 'Yes'**, which policy(ies)?	Yes No **If 'Yes'**, which policy(ies)?

If you have answered 'Yes' to question 4, please contact your Financial Adviser about the type of trust most appropriate to you and your circumstances

5 Are any of the policies that you're applying for, to be owned by another individual or company? If you require Business Protection and have selected Key Person Protection and/or Business Loan Protection, you **must answer 'Yes'** to this question	Yes No **If 'Yes'**, which policy(ies)?	Yes No **If 'Yes'**, which policy(ies)?

If you have answered 'Yes' to question 5, please complete a Policy Owner Questionnaire for each policy (Part 8) BEFORE going straight to Part 10.

Sample page: A4

Colours are used to differentiate between instructions and questions.
Background colours and bars divide the form up into sections.

Postbank

Corporate design manual and model forms

Issued by	Deutsche Postbank AG
Design	Team Peter M. Scholz (formerly Agentur Fischer & Scholz, Corporate Communication), Berlin
Year	1997
Typeface	Formata

Many companies that have grown out of former public services need to establish their own identities as independent organizations. The German Postbank recognized the important role played by its forms, especially because these are increasingly taking the place of personal contact with customers. Friendly text and clear design should therefore convey an equal relationship between the bank and its clients.

As a complete contract had to be contained on a single sheet of A4 paper, the original forms required considerable shortening. The new forms therefore drew attention to the most important and most relevant information. It was a design advantage that they did not need to be machine readable. In order to make maximum use of the space available, the page was divided into two columns, with a standardized sequence of repeated modules: title and application, information about the customer, information about the product, conditions and signature.

Postbank Bausparen

Postbank | wüstenrot

Antrag auf Abschluß eines Bausparvertrages mit der **Bausparkasse Wüstenrot**

Bausparkasse Wüstenrot gGmbH, 71630 Ludwigsburg

☐ Neuabschluß eines Bausparvertrages

☐ Erhöhung meines Bausparvertrages mit den Daten:

Bausparnummer: Nummer | Bausparsumme: DM

Meine persönlichen Angaben — **1. Kundin/Kunde**

☐ Frau ☐ Herr ☐ Eheleute

Bitte füllen Sie den Antrag in Druckbuchstaben aus.

Vorname | akademischer Grad

Name

Straße, Hausnummer

Postleitzahl | Ort

Geburtsdatum | Staatsangehörigkeit

Beruf | Familienstand

Telefon tagsüber: Vorwahl | Rufnummer

Meine persönlichen Angaben — **2. Kundin/Kunde**

☐ Frau ☐ Herr

Vorname | akademischer Grad

Name

Straße, Hausnummer

Postleitzahl | Ort

Geburtsdatum | Staatsangehörigkeit

Beruf | Familienstand

Telefon tagsüber: Vorwahl | Rufnummer

Datenschutz, telefonische Beratung Die Bausparkasse GdF Wüstenrot gGmbH, Ludwigsburg und die Deutsche Postbank AG, Bonn arbeiten im Interesse einer umfassenden Beratung und Betreuung ihrer Kunden zusammen. **Damit mich die Postbank sowie deren zuständige Außendienstmitarbeiter in allen Bausparfragen umfassend beraten können, bin ich damit einverstanden, daß die Bausparkasse Wüstenrot der Postbank bzw. deren zuständigen Außendienstmitarbeitern die für die Aufnahme und Durchführung der Beratung erforderlichen Angaben zur dortigen Datenverarbeitung und Nutzung zur persönlichen und telefonischen Beratung übermittelt.**

Übermittelt werden dürfen Personalien (Name, Anschrift, Geburtsdatum, Familienstand, Beruf oder vergleichbare Daten) und Daten über Bausparverträge (Bausparnummer, Tarif, Bausparsumme, vermögenswirksame Leistungen, Saldo des Bausparkontos/Darlehenskontos, Zuteilungsaussichten oder vergleichbare Daten).

Diese Angaben trägt die Postbank/Wüstenrot ein:

Vertragsnummer

Vertriebsschlüssel

Feld für FBB

Meine Bauspardaten ☐ Ich **wähle** folgende **Bausparsumme**: DM

☐ Ich **erhöhe** meine **Bausparsumme** um:

Hinweis

Die Abschluß- bzw. Erhöhungsgebühr beträgt 1 % der Bausparsumme und wird mit den Sparleistungen verrechnet. Der monatliche Regelsparbeitrag beträgt 5 DM je 1000,- DM Bausparsumme.

Mindestsparguthaben: % | Bewertungszahlfaktor: | Zinsbonus: % 80

Zusatzleistung ☐ Ich möchte meinen Bausparvertrag auch zur Anlage vermögenswirksamer Leistungen nutzen.

Einzugsermächtigung zugunsten Wüstenrot – jederzeit widerrufbar – Ziehen Sie meine Sparbeiträge wie folgt ein:

☐ monatlich ☐ vierteljährlich ☐ jährlich

erstmalig am: ☐ 1. ☐ 15. Monat | Jahr

Sparbeitrag: DM

Kontonummer | Bankleitzahl

Geldinstitut

Name der Kontoinhaberin/des Kontoinhabers

Kontoinhaberin/Kontoinhaber: Unterschrift

Hinweis

Unterschrift nur nötig, wenn Kontoinhaberin/Kontoinhaber von Antragstellerin/Antragsteller abweicht.

Hinweise

Diesem Antrag liegen die Allgemeinen Bedingungen für Bausparverträge (ABB 7 PB) zugrunde, die Ihnen ausgehändigt wurden. Sie sind Bestandteil des Vertrages. Die Bausparkasse darf sich vor Zuteilung nicht verpflichten, die Bausparsumme zu einem bestimmten Zeitpunkt auszuzahlen. Die Zuteilungsreihenfolge richtet sich nach den Bausparbedingungen. Sie ist insbesondere von den Spar- und Tilgungsleistungen aller Bausparer abhängig. Die Wartezeit kann dadurch Schwankungen unterworfen sein. Bei Erhöhung eines zugeteilten Vertrages verzichten Sie auf die Rechte der Zuteilung.

Postbank Bausparen ist ein Produkt der Bausparkasse Wüstenrot. Der Bausparvertrag wird mit der Bausparkasse Wüstenrot geschlossen.

Unterschrift 1. Kundin/Kunde, ggf. Minderjährige/r: Unterschrift

2. Kundin/Kunde, ggf. Erziehungsberechtigte/r: Unterschrift

Widerrufsrecht **Ich weiß, daß ich meinen Antrag innerhalb einer Woche nach Vertragsabschluß schriftlich widerrufen kann. Das rechtzeitige Absenden genügt zur Wahrung der Frist. Adresse: Bausparkasse Wüstenrot, Wüstenrot Haus, 71630 Ludwigsburg.**

Datum

Unterschrift 1. Kundin/Kunde, ggf. Minderjährige/r: Unterschrift

2. Kundin/Kunde, ggf. Erziehungsberechtigte/r: Unterschrift

Antrag für die Bausparkasse Wüstenrot

Bausparkasse Gemeinschaft der Freunde Wüstenrot gemeinnützige GmbH, 71630 Ludwigsburg
Aufsichtsratvorsitzender: Dr. Walter Seuferle,
Geschäftsführer: Dr. Gert Haller, Hans Peter Kappes,
Dr. Rolf Kornemann, Hartmut Lechner, Klaus W. Rösch
Amtsgericht Ludwigsburg HRB 143

Request to redeem a mortgage savings plan: A4

A characteristic feature of Postbank forms is the use of red to denote the areas that customers must fill.

Postbank

Darlehens-Jahreskontoauszug

Kontoinhaber	Marta und Willi Pospel
Darlehenskontonummer	06 11 815 192
Abrechnungszeitraum	01.01.1995 – 31.12.1995

Bewilligtes Darlehen	000.000.000,00 DM	Disagio	0.000,00 DM
Darlehensvaluta	000.000,00 DM	Abbuchungskonto	00 00 000 000
Darlehenszinsen	00.000,00 DM	Bankleitzahl	000 000 00
Tilgungsbetrag	000.000,00 DM	Umrechnungsfaktor	1 DM = 0,52 Euro

Buchungsinformation	PN-Nr.	Buchung		DM Umsatz Soll	DM Umsatz Haben
Kontostand 01.01.1995				43.000,00	
Gutschrift	9500	31.01.	31.01.	000,00	000,00
Darlehenszinsen	8035	31.01.	31.01.	000,00	000,00
Valutierung	9500	13.02.	13.02.	000,00	000,00
Gutschrift	9500	28.02.	28.02.	000,00	000,00
Darlehenszinsen	8035	28.02.	28.02.	000,00	000,00
Gutschrift	9500	31.03.	31.03.	000,00	000,00
Darlehenszinsen	8035	31.03.	31.03.	000,00	000,00
Gutschrift	9500	28.04.	28.04.	000,00	000,00
Darlehenszinsen	8035	28.04.	28.04.	000,00	000,00
Gutschrift	9500	31.05.	31.05.	000,00	000,00
Darlehenszinsen	8035	31.05.	31.05.	000,00	000,00
Gutschrift	9500	30.06.	30.06.	000,00	000,00
Darlehenszinsen	8035	30.06.	30.06.	000,00	000,00
Gutschrift	9500	31.07.	31.07.	000,00	000,00
Darlehenszinsen	8035	31.07.	31.07.	000,00	000,00
Gutschrift	9500	31.08.	31.08.	000,00	000,00
Darlehenszinsen	8035	31.08.	31.08.	000,00	000,00
Gutschrift	9500	30.09.	30.09.	000,00	000,00
Darlehenszinsen	8035	30.09.	30.09.	000,00	000,00
Gutschrift	9500	29.10.	29.10.	000,00	000,00
Darlehenszinsen	8035	29.10.	29.10.	000,00	000,00
Gutschrift	9500	30.11.	30.11.	000,00	000,00
Darlehenszinsen	8035	30.11.	30.11.	000,00	000,00
Gutschrift	9500	31.12.	31.12.	000,00	000,00
Darlehenszinsen	8035	31.12.	31.12.	000,00	000,00
Kontostand 31.12.1995				41.762,13	

Bitte beachten Sie die Hinweise auf der Rückseite.

Account statement: A4

Statements are also a type of form, and their design follows the house style.

Postbank Sparkonto

Eröffnen Sie für mich ein Postbank Sparkonto

Meine persönlichen Angaben

Bitte füllen Sie den Auftrag in Druckbuchstaben aus.

1. Kundin/Kunde

☐ Frau ☐ Herr

Vorname | akademischer Grad

Name

Straße, Hausnummer

Postleitzahl | Ort

Geburtsdatum

Staatsangehörigkeit | Land des Hauptwohnsitzes

Telefon privat: Vorwahl | Rufnummer

Telefon geschäftlich: Vorwahl | Rufnummer

Ich bin

☐ selbständig. ☐ nicht selbständig.

☐ in Ausbildung. ☐ im Ruhestand. ☐ Sonstiges.

Meine persönlichen Angaben

2. Kundin/Kunde

☐ Frau ☐ Herr

Vorname | akademischer Grad

Name

Straße, Hausnummer

Postleitzahl | Ort

Geburtsdatum

Staatsangehörigkeit | Land des Hauptwohnsitzes

Telefon privat: Vorwahl | Rufnummer

Telefon geschäftlich: Vorwahl | Rufnummer

Ich bin

☐ selbständig. ☐ nicht selbständig.

☐ in Ausbildung. ☐ im Ruhestand. ☐ Sonstiges.

Meine Sparform

Ich möchte folgendes Postbank Spar-Angebot nutzen:

☐ **Postbank Sparbuch 3000 plus** (3monatige Kündigungsfrist)

☐ **Postbank Sparbuch** mit folgender Kündigungsfrist:

☐ 3 Monate ☐ 1 Jahr ☐ 2½ Jahre ☐ 4 Jahre

☐ **Postbank Sparen mit wachsendem Zins** (3monatige Kündigungsfrist)

Die Vertragssumme beträgt:

DM

☐ **Postbank Sparen mit festem Zins** (3monatige Kündigungsfrist) mit folgender Laufzeit für den festen Zinssatz:

☐ 1 Jahr ☐ 2 Jahre ☐ 4 Jahre

Die Vertragssumme beträgt:

DM

Mein Postbank Sparbuch

Stellen Sie das Postbank Sparbuch wie folgt aus:

☐ für mich ☐ für mich und eine zweite Person (Gemeinschaftskonto)

ggf. zusätzliche Kontobezeichnung

☐ für eine Personenmehrheit (Verein, Gesellschaft o.ä.)

Berechtigungsnachweis

Ich möchte ein Postbank Sparbuch

☐ ohne Berechtigungsnachweis. ☐ mit Berechtigungsnachweis (nicht beim Sparen mit festem Zins).

Erklärung zum Geldwäschegesetz

Ich handle für

☐ eigene Rechnung. ☐ fremde Rechnung.

Information, Werbung

Ich bin damit einverstanden, daß die Postbank mich telefonisch über ihr Leistungsangebot informiert.

☐ ja ☐ nein

Hinweise

Es gelten die veröffentlichten Bedingungen für den Sparverkehr, die besonderen Bedingungen und Leistungsentgelte (Preisverzeichnis) der Deutschen Postbank AG.

Beim Sparen mit festem Zins und bei Spareinlagen mit einer Kündigungsfrist von 1 Jahr und mehr gilt die im Preisaushang und Zinsaushang der Postbank bekanntgegebene Kündigungssperrfrist.

▶ *Bei den im Vorblatt genannten Fällen füllen Sie bitte auch das Postbank Sparkonto Zusatzblatt aus.*

▶ *Beachten Sie bitte die Hinweise auf der Rückseite Ihrer Durchschrift.*

▶ *Trennen Sie bitte Ihre Durchschrift ab, nachdem Sie den Auftrag ausgefüllt haben. Sie ist für Ihre persönlichen Unterlagen bestimmt.*

Datum

Unterschrift

1. Kundin/Kunde: Unterschrift

2. Kundin/Kunde: Unterschrift

Auftrag für die Postbank

Wir bedanken uns für Ihren Auftrag.

08.96 A 926 046 000 100% chlorfrei gebleichter Zellstoff

Form for opening a savings account: A4

The line at the very top of the form reads 'Please open a savings account for me'. In this way, the form becomes an order rather than an application, and customers are given an active role. All Postbank forms begin by stating the customer's wish first.

M&G Investments

Investment statement booklets

Issued by	M&G Investments, UK
Design	Information Engineers (UK) Ltd, Cambridge *Ben Whitmore*
Year	2008
Typeface	FS Albert

M&G wanted to provide customers with up-to-date information relevant to their investment holdings within a single document. This meant replacing a variety of investor documents with individual personalized booklets. Information Engineers used digital colour print technology to devise an entirely new approach to presenting customer investment information.

Fully personalized A4 landscape booklets were produced, each containing the investor's investment statement, graphic performance indicators, and commentaries on the funds held, along with other targeted service and marketing information. In this way, the number of pages could be reduced from a minimum of 58 to an average of 24. A dramatic improvement in client satisfaction was achieved as information is now tailored to their requirements.

Cover: A4
These statements are not pre-printed forms that require information to be filled in. Instead, they are forms in the sense that each statement presents data in the same tabular format and visual style.

5 April to 5 October 2008
Your personalised investment update and statement
Mrs Another Sample

Keeping you in touch with your investments

Contents

Summary page: A4
This page summarizes all the client's investments and allows the values to be easily compared.

Investment update 5 April to 5 October 2008 **Page 6**

Your summary – investment product values

For further details regarding all charges and information relating to your investment, please refer to your Key Features document.

M&G Stocks and Shares ISA

Your M&G client reference: 1234567890

Value on 5 October 2008 £6,828.40
Value on 5 April 2008 £17,179.83

Invested by you this period	£000,000,000.00
Withdrawn by you this period	£9,398.10
Fund income reinvested this period	£53.94
Fund income distributed this period	£0.00

During the statement period the total income paid and income reinvested (including any cash ISA interest and tax reclaims) was £53.94

Transaction details
For details of your transactions please refer to the following page(s):

M&G Corporate Bond Fund	page 10
M&G High Yield Corporate Bond Fund	page 14
M&G Managed Fund	page 18
M&G Managed Growth Fund	page 20

OEIC

Your M&G client reference: 2234567890
Designation: AAAAAAAA

Value on 5 October 2008 £1,727.91
Value on 5 April 2008 £2,003.63

Invested by you this period	£0.00
Withdrawn by you this period	£0.00
Fund income reinvested this period	£7.39
Fund income distributed this period	£0.00

This is a taxable product
Depending on your circumstances, your investments in this OEIC may be taxable. For details of your transactions please refer to the following page(s):

M&G American Fund	page 8

M&G Savings Plan

Your M&G client reference: 1234567890

Value on 5 October 2008 £5,879.11
Value on 5 April 2008 £6,670.39

Invested by you this period	£440.00
Withdrawn by you this period	£0.00

This is a taxable product
Depending on your circumstances, your investments in this Savings Plan may be taxable. For details of your transactions please refer to the following page(s):

M&G European Index Tracker Fund	page 12
M&G Index Tracker Fund	page 16

Important note about your M&G Savings Plan
With effect from 23 January 2009, the shares held within The **M&G Savings Plan** will be registered in the name of 'M&G Nominees Limited (SAV Account)' rather than 'M&G Securities Limited (SAV Account)'. Accordingly, Part 3, Section 9.1 of your Terms and Conditions will be amended as follows:
'We register all Savings Shares we buy on your behalf in the name of "M&G Nominees Limited (SAV Account)" and hold them in trust for you.'
This change has no impact upon the day-to-day administration of your Savings Plan and you can continue to give us instructions to buy and sell shares or update your account details in the usual way.

M&G Global Basics Fund

Fund value **£3,030.5m** Fund manager **Graham French** Overall Morningstar rating ★★★★★ S&P Fund Management rating **AA**

Equity

The Fund's sole aim is long term capital growth through investing wholly or mainly in companies operating in basic industries ('primary' and 'secondary' industries) and also in companies that service these industries. The Fund may also invest in other global equities.

Find out more about this fund at
www.mandg.co.uk/info
or call us on
0800 390 390

Please ensure that you have read and understood the Investment performance information on page 20

Against a backdrop of turmoil in financial markets and deteriorating economic conditions, the fund's performance suffered towards the end of the review period. Following a strong run, the fund's mining and energy-related holdings declined sharply because of fears that the crisis would spread to other parts of the economy, thereby curbing demand for raw materials. Fund manager Graham French had been actively reducing the fund's exposure to these areas but the remaining holdings nevertheless had a detrimental impact on performance. The portfolio retains exposure to a number of attractively valued, well positioned mining and energy companies.

The dominant shift in the portfolio over the past six months has been towards a range of consumer-orientated businesses, such as wine producer Constellation Brands, which Graham believes will benefit from growing incomes in developing countries. More and more people in India, for example, are drinking wine as a sign of their social status and Constellation is set to gain significantly from this trend.

Graham places a strong emphasis on businesses that are well managed and asset-rich, such as Anglo-Dutch consumer goods conglomerate Unilever. The company boasts well-diversified brands and a first-class distribution network. Another attraction is its size – stable, large and well-established firms such as Unilever tend to hold up well in challenging circumstances. And as Graham points out, everybody understands what Unilever does, what deodorants and soaps are and how there will always be demand for such products. He adds: "Investing in such stocks can provide reassurance for the fund's investors in these uncertain times."

We believe that Graham's focus on asset-rich companies, such as Unilever and Constellation Brands, which are benefiting from long-term global themes, should ensure that the fund continues its excellent long-term track record regardless of market conditions.

Performance	last 6 months	last 5 years
M&G Global Basics Fund	–14.1%	125.8%
FTSE Global Basics Composite Index*	–8.4%	70.2%

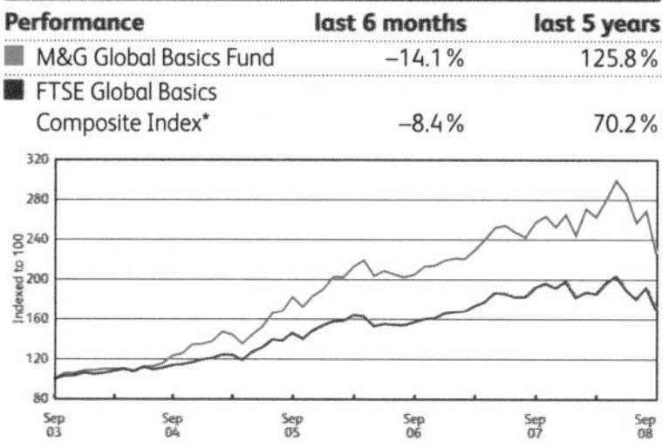

*Comprising FTSE World Index excluding Healthcare, Financials, Technology and Telecommunications sectors.

Single year performance (5 years ending September)

From	30.09.07	30.09.06	30.09.05	30.09.04	30.09.03
To	30.09.08	29.09.07	30.09.06	30.09.05	30.09.04
	–12.4%	25.5%	12.4%	47.7%	23.7%

Distribution yield: 4.66% Underlying yield: 4.5%

Historic yield: 0.17%

Distribution dates

Payment type	XD date	Payment date
Final	01.09.08	31.10.08

Important
Performance information as at 30 September, the nearest measurable point to your statement valuation of 5 October.
Prices may fluctuate and you may not get back your original investment.
Past performance is no guarantee of future performance.
Overseas shares are affected by currency exchange rates.

M&G Global Basics Fund[1]

M&G Savings Plan transactions

Sterling Class A Accumulation Shares **Your M&G client reference: 1234567890**

Number of shares	Share price	Value on 5 October 2008
180.734	**674.75p**	**£1,219.50**

Date	Transaction	Amount	Initial charge (if applicable)	Discount (if applicable)	Amount invested	Share price	Number of shares
Total shares held on 05/04/08							167.375
22/04/08	RSF Sale	£20.00	–£0.80		£19.20	900.62p	2.132
22/05/08	RSF Sale	£20.00	–£0.80		£19.20	950.49p	2.021
23/06/08	RSF Sale	£20.00	–£0.80		£19.20	915.10p	2.099
22/07/08	RSF Sale	£20.00	–£0.80		£19.20	820.01p	2.342
22/08/08	RSF Sale	£20.00	–£0.80		£19.20	822.13p	2.336
22/09/08	RSF Sale	£20.00	–£0.80		£19.20	790.71p[xd]	2.429
Total shares carried forward							**180.734**

Please note
[1]This is a sub-fund of M&G Investment Funds (1), a UK authorised Open-Ended Investment Company.
For further details regarding all charges and information relating to your investment, please refer to your Key Features document.
If the fund you have invested in is quoted as 'xd' please refer to your Key Features document for further details.
The price basis is "forward" which means we buy and sell units using the buying and selling prices calculated at the 12 noon valuation point following receipt of your instruction.

Fund information and transactions: A4

These two pages illustrate and explain the performance of the fund, and list recent share transactions.

Atlantic Electric and Gas

Contract form

Issued by Atlantic Electric and Gas, UK
Design Thomas Manss & Company, London
Year 2002
Typeface DTL Argo

In a market dominated by large energy companies, Atlantic Electric and Gas felt that as newcomers they needed to set themselves apart from their competitors with a friendly and uncomplicated approach. The forms are designed to match this; they have a straightforward look, and are easy to understand and fill in.

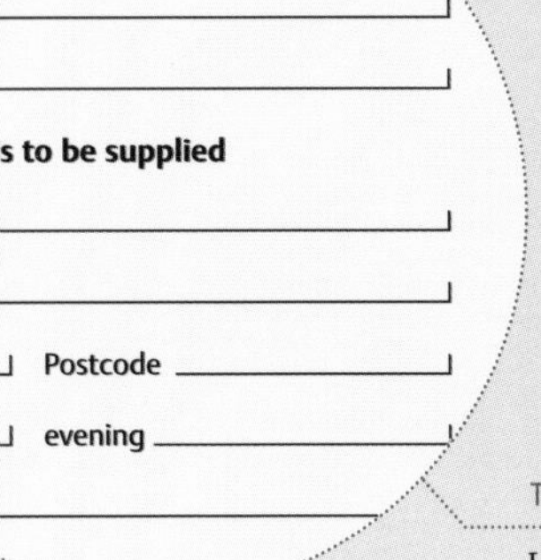

Text fields

Unusually, the text fields are denoted by a line with a right angle at the end. This gives the form a neat look.

Atlantic Electric and Gas Ltd – Change of Supplier Form

Please complete this form to enable us to notify your existing supplier of your intention to switch to Atlantic.

Electricity E

To
Please insert the name of your existing supplier.

Please be advised that I have signed a new electricity supply contract with Atlantic and under the terms of our agreement I wish to cancel my contract with you.

As in our agreement, termination will become effective 28 days from the date given below.

Customer name
Supply address
Postcode

Supply number
S S

Signature
Date

11/00–DESIGNATED

If **you** change your mind

Electricity and Gas E

Atlantic Electric and Gas are pleased that you have chosen us as your supplier. We look forward to giving you first class service and competitive prices for many years to come.

Please be aware that you have signed a supply contract with Atlantic Electric and Gas. If you wish to change your mind, you may cancel the agreement within a seven day 'cooling-off' period. If you wish to terminate after this period of time, your contract will be cancelled 28 days from the date of the termination notice.

If you should wish to transfer, please complete this form and return it to the address below immediately or call the freephone number.

Atlantic Electric and Gas
PO Box 682
Cardiff CF24 0UP
T 0800 052 2081

Customer name
Supply address
Postcode

Supply number
S S

MPR Number
Signature
Date

11/00–DESIGNATED

Atlantic Electric and Gas Ltd – Change Supplier Form

Please complete this form to enable us to notify your existing supplier of your intention to switch to Atlantic.

Gas G

To
Please insert the name of your existing supplier.

Please be advised that I have signed a new gas supply contract with Atlantic and under the terms of our agreement I wish to cancel my contract with you.

As in our agreement, termination will become effective 28 days from the date given below.

Customer name
Supply address
Postcode

MPR Number
Signature
Date

11/00–DESIGNATED

What happens **next**?

1 Telephone check

You may receive a brief call to check that your details were correctly taken and to acknowledge your application.

2 Follow up letter

You may receive a letter to check you were happy with the sales procedure and confirm that your application is being processed.

3 Welcome letter

We will write to you confirming your supply date and ask you to read your meter. Once the process is complete we will send you our welcome letter which includes details of our Standards of Services and emergency numbers. If you have chosen to pay by monthly Direct Debit, Atlantic Electric and Gas will let you know how much your monthly payments will be and on which day of the month we will be collecting payment. These payments will be based on your previous year's electricity and gas consumption.

Further questions

If you have any further questions call us on
0800 052 2081
or e-mail us at
info@atlanticeg.com

Atlantic Electric and Gas Ltd
PO Box 682
Cardiff CF24 0UP

Registered in England and Wales No. 3547417

Additional pages of the contract form: 210 × 330 mm

Atlantic Electric and Gas Ltd – Energy Supply Contract

Contract for the supply of electricity and gas to households

1 Customer

Title ______ First name or initials ______

Surname ______

Address at which electricity and/or gas is to be supplied

______

______

______ Postcode ______

Telephone No. daytime ______ evening ______

E-mail ______

Is the address to be supplied used for commercial or business purposes? Yes ☐ No ☐
If so, is it registered for VAT? Yes ☐ No ☐
Are you a registered charity? Yes ☐ No ☐

2 Correspondence address (if different from supply address)

Address ______

______

______ Postcode ______

3 Supply of electricity

What is your Supply Number? This should be shown on your current bill

S ______ S ______

PRICE SCHEDULE (official use only) ______

What type of electricity meter do you have

Single rate ☐ Two rate Day time and night time (economy 7) ☐ Prepayment ☐

Signature ______ Date ______

4 How would you like to pay for your electricity?

☐ Monthly Direct Debit
☐ Quarterly variable Direct Debit ☐ Quarterly Cash/Cheques

Monthly Direct Debit is based on a budget scheme of equal monthly payments. If you have selected Direct Debit, please complete the Direct Debit Instructions below and indicate here the preferred payment date and amount.

Preferred date ______ Monthly amount £ ______
This should be between the 1st and the 28th of the month. This is a proposed amount, the actual amount will be confirmed.

5 Supply of gas

What is your Meter Point Reference Number? This should be shown on your current bill

MPR Number ______

PRICE SCHEDULE (official use only) ______

What type of gas meter do you have Standard ☐ Prepayment ☐

Signature ______ Date ______

6 How would you like to pay for your gas?

☐ Monthly Direct Debit
☐ Quarterly variable Direct Debit ☐ Quarterly Cash/Cheques

Monthly Direct Debit is based on a budget scheme of equal monthly payments. If you have selected Direct Debit, please complete the Direct Debit Instructions below and indicate here the preferred payment date and amount.

Preferred date ______ Monthly amount £ ______
This should be between the 1st and the 28th of the month. This is a proposed amount, the actual amount will be confirmed.

7 Additional services: special needs

We maintain a register of special needs customers.
Please tick this box if supply is for the elderly, disabled or chronically sick ☐

8 Data protection

Atlantic occasionally allow carefully screened companies to send information to our customers. If you would prefer not to receive such information please tick this box ☐

Atlantic Electric and Gas copy

Agency name ______ Agency ID ______ Agent name ______ Agent No ______

Instruction to your Bank or Building Society to pay Direct Debits

To: The Manager ______ Bank or Building Society

Address ______

______ Postcode ______

Name(s) of Account Holder(s) ______

______

Branch Sort Code (from top right corner of cheque) ______

Bank/Building Society Account No ______
*For Girobank or Alliance and Leicester customers only

Customer Reference No (official use only) ______

11/00–DESIGNATED

Electricity E

Originator Identification No 8 0 9 4 3 4

Instruction to your Bank or Building Society: Please pay Atlantic Electric and Gas Ltd Direct Debits from the account detailed on this instruction subject to the safeguards assured by the Direct Debit Guarantee. I understand that this instruction may remain with Atlantic Electric and Gas or its Agent, and if so details will be passed electronically.

DIRECT Debit

Signature(s) ______

______ Date ______

Instruction to your Bank or Building Society to pay Direct Debits

To: The Manager ______ Bank or Building Society

Address ______

______ Postcode ______

Name(s) of Account Holder(s) ______

______

Branch Sort Code (from top right corner of cheque) ______

Bank/Building Society Account No ______
*For Girobank or Alliance and Leicester customers only

Customer Reference No (official use only) ______

11/00–DESIGNATED

Gas G

Originator Identification No ______

Instruction to your Bank or Building Society: Please pay Atlantic Electric and Gas Ltd Direct Debits from the account detailed on this instruction subject to the safeguards assured by the Direct Debit Guarantee. I understand that this instruction may remain with Atlantic Electric and Gas or its Agent, and if so details will be passed electronically.

DIRECT Debit

Signature(s) ______

______ Date ______

Main page of the contract form: 210 × 330 mm

Yellow and blue grounds clearly differentiate between the sections on gas and electricity. Unfortunately, the position of the checkboxes is not quite consistent. Sometimes they are placed before the answer options and sometimes afterwards.

NS Dutch Railways

Application form

Issued by	NS (Nederlandse Spoorwegen), Netherlands
Design	Edenspiekermann (formerly Eden Design & Communication), Amsterdam
Years	2004/2006
Typeface	Frutiger

The forms issued by the Dutch railway company NS are outstanding as examples of consistent and uncomplicated communication with customers, and this has been reflected by excellent feedback. The top section of each form contains a dialogue offering customers a choice of options, and only then are they asked for the necessary details.

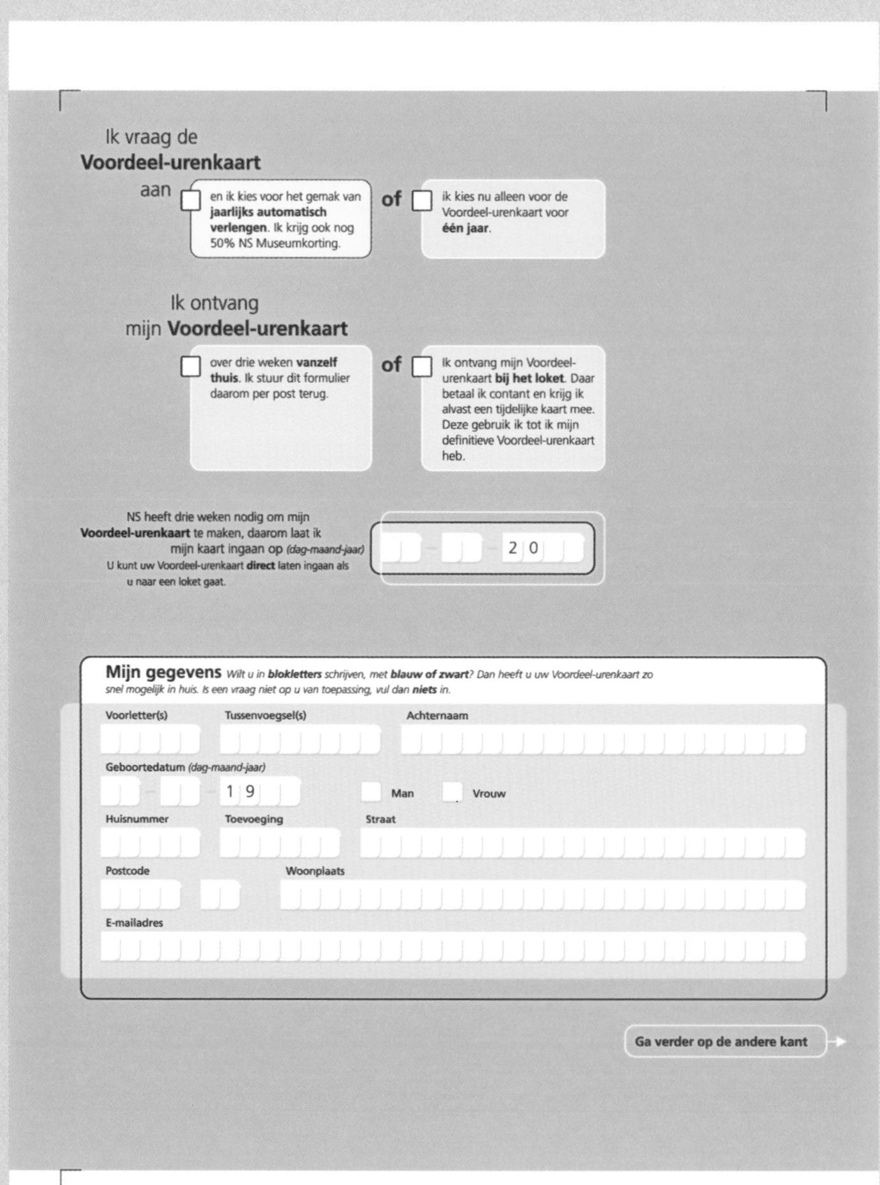

Ik vraag de
Voordeel-urenkaart
aan

☐ en ik kies voor het gemak van **jaarlijks automatisch verlengen**. Ik krijg ook nog 50% NS Museumkorting.

of ☐ ik kies nu alleen voor de Voordeel-urenkaart voor **één jaar**.

Ik ontvang
mijn **Voordeel-urenkaart**

☐ over drie weken **vanzelf thuis**. Ik stuur dit formulier daarom per post terug.

of ☐ Ik ontvang mijn Voordeel-urenkaart **bij het loket**. Daar betaal ik contant en krijg ik alvast een tijdelijke kaart mee. Deze gebruik ik tot ik mijn definitieve Voordeel-urenkaart heb.

NS heeft drie weken nodig om mijn **Voordeel-urenkaart** te maken, daarom laat ik mijn kaart ingaan op *(dag-maand-jaar)*
U kunt uw Voordeel-urenkaart **direct** laten ingaan als u naar een loket gaat.

_ _ - _ _ - 2 0 _ _

Mijn gegevens *Wilt u in **blokletters** schrijven, met **blauw of zwart**? Dan heeft u uw Voordeel-urenkaart zo snel mogelijk in huis. Is een vraag niet op u van toepassing, vul dan **niets** in.*

Voorletter(s) Tussenvoegsel(s) Achternaam

Geboortedatum *(dag-maand-jaar)* _ _ - _ _ - 1 9 _ _ ☐ Man ☐ Vrouw

Huisnummer Toevoeging Straat

Postcode Woonplaats

E-mailadres

Ga verder op de andere kant →

Machine readable application form:
150 mm × 204 mm

This is an application form for one of the most successful NS products: the off-peak discount pass. In the dialogue section, the customer must choose between two simple options: firstly, whether the ticket should be automatically renewed or not, and secondly whether it is to be sent by post or collected direct from the ticket office. The form is not only simple, compact and pleasing to the eye, but also completely machine readable, thus saving the company a great deal of time and money.

Luggage left in **lockers**

Unfortunately, your luggage was left in the locker for longer than permitted. We can send your luggage to your home address. In order for us to be able to do this, we must ask you to complete this form. NS will store your property for up to 3 months. For storage and shipment we will charge you € 70.-.

What **you** have to do

if you still have the locker ticket: Hand in this form, along with the locker ticket and the proof of payment, at an NS service desk or send us the form by post.*

or

if you no longer have the locker ticket: report this to the police. Hand in this form, along with the original police report, at an NS service desk or send us the form by post. An invoice for € 70.- will be sent to you by post.*

What **NS** will do for you

Once NS has received the payment, your luggage will be sent to your home address within 5 to 10 working days.

If it is a non-standard item (longer than 1 metre or heavier than 10 kilograms) or if it has to be sent abroad, this will take at least 10 to 15 working days.

1 Locker contents

Name of the station where the locker was rented

Date of the first day of locker rental

Description of the locker contents. *Fill this in as completely as possible (description of the objects, colour, manufacturer, specific characteristics, etc.)*

2 My details

Initials and name

Male

Female

Address

Postal code

Place

Country

Only to be completed in the event of money left in locker

Bank-/giro account number

If different: state the address to which the luggage left in the locker should be sent.

Address

Postal code

Place

Country

3 My signature

Telephone

Signature

Home telephone number

Date

*****Hand in** this form at an **NS-ticket office**, or send it in a sealed and stamped envelope to NS, Afdeling Kluisvoorwerpen, P.O. Box 2025, 3500 HA Utrecht. Please enclose the following documents; your payment receipt, locker ticket or police report. Enclose **original** documents only, do keep a copy for yourself. Only **fully completed** forms can be dealt with.

We need your data so that we can process your request. We can also use your data to inform you about additional services and products of NS Groep N.V. If you do not want this information, please call us at: 0900 - 202 11 63 (€ 0.10 p.m.).

Valid from January 1, 2006

DX 16039 / 01-06

Form for lost luggage return: A4

The dialogue boxes at the top explain clearly what customers should do if they leave an item of luggage in a locker for too long, and what the company itself will then do. This is completely straightforward and creates a feeling of trust and confidence.

Stadtwerke Bochum

Contract

Issued by	Stadtwerke Bochum GmbH, Germany
Design	Oktober Kommunikationsdesign GmbH, Bochum
Year	2004
Typeface	Frutiger

A well laid-out contract which clearly and concisely defines its subject: energy heating and the systems involved. The grey background conveys seriousness and also provides a good contrast to the orange highlights, which give the promise of warmth and security.

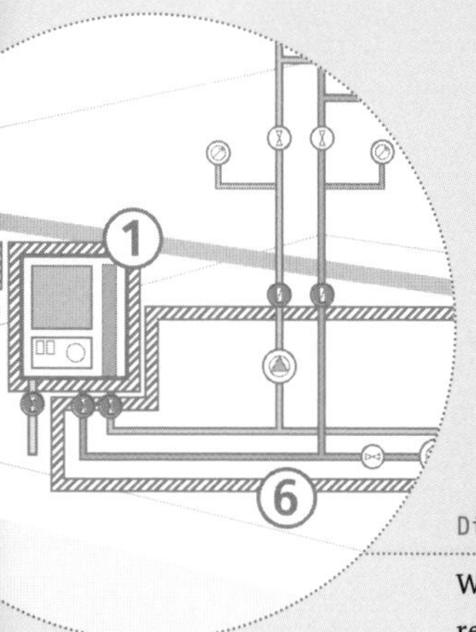

Diagrams

Who supplies what to where, and who is responsible for the different parts of the central heating system? These relationships would be very difficult to describe in words, and so they are portrayed in graphic form.

Cover page of the contract: 190 mm × 297 mm

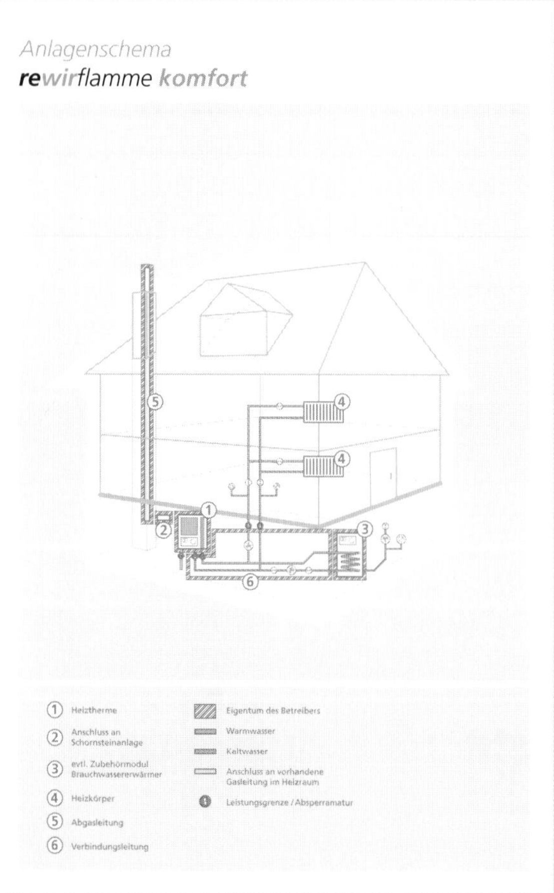

Diagram on an inside page: 190 mm × 297 mm

Wärmeservicevertrag
re*wir**flamme* ***komfort***

zwischen der Stadtwerke Bochum GmbH
Massenbergstraße 15–17, 44787 Bochum

und dem Kunden:

Name/Vorname/Firma

Straße/Hausnummer

Geburtsdatum

PLZ/Ort

E-Mail-Adresse

Telefon/Telefax

für das Objekt:

Straße/Hausnummer

PLZ/Ort

Weitere angeschlossene Objekte

§ 1 Vertragsgegenstand

Die Stadtwerke Bochum liefern dem Kunden Wärme für die Raumbeheizung und ggf. Brauchwassererwärmung in der o. g. Verbrauchsstelle. Zum Zwecke der Wärmelieferung planen, errichten und betreiben die Stadtwerke Bochum für den Kunden in der o. g. Verbrauchsstelle eine Wärmeerzeugungsanlage (WEA) mit folgenden Leistungsbestandteilen:

☐ Heizkessel kW

Fabrikat/Typ

☐ Brauchwassererwärmer Liter

Fabrikat/Typ

☐ Demontage und Entsorgung des vorhandenen Heizkessels/Brauchwassererwärmers

☐

☐ Zusätzliche Heizkreise Stück

☐

Terminwunsch für Einbau der Wärmeerzeugungsanlage

☐

☐ so bald wie möglich

Die Verbrauchsstelle verfügt bereits über einen Gashausanschluss:

☐ Ja

☐ Nein, ich bitte deshalb die Stadtwerke Bochum, mir ein Angebot über die kostenpflichtige Erstellung eines Gashausanschlusses zuzuleiten.

§ 2 Wärmepreis

Für die vom Kunden bezogene Wärme zahlt dieser einen Wärmepreis. Der Wärmepreis setzt sich aus einem ***rewir****flamme* ***komfort*** Preis und einem Erdgaspreissystem zusammen.

I. Der *rewirflamme komfort* Preis

Der ***rewir****flamme* ***komfort*** Preis beträgt

netto = €/Monat

und brutto = €/Monat

Der Netto ***rewir****flamme* ***komfort*** Preis ist gem. § 5 der Allgemeinen Bedingungen zur Wärmelieferung veränderlich und erhöht sich jeweils um die gesetzliche Umsatzsteuer.

Inside page of contract: 190 mm × 297 mm

The division of the page into two columns is good, but despite the wide gutter, it is not clear whether the form should be filled by moving down each column or across the page. The questions in section 1 are very widely spaced and hard for the eye to follow.

Hellmann Executive

Forms for consultancy bonus programme

Issued by Hellmann Worldwide Logistics GmbH & Co. KG, Germany
Design in(corporate communication + design GmbH, Berlin
Year 2001
Typeface Frutiger

Hellmann Executive is a bonus programme for regular customers of this international logistics company. This high-end and expensive system consists of a club card, certificates, benefit book, and forms to match. The consultant uses these forms in discussing with customers how they can achieve their bonuses or optimize service and/or cost-effectiveness.

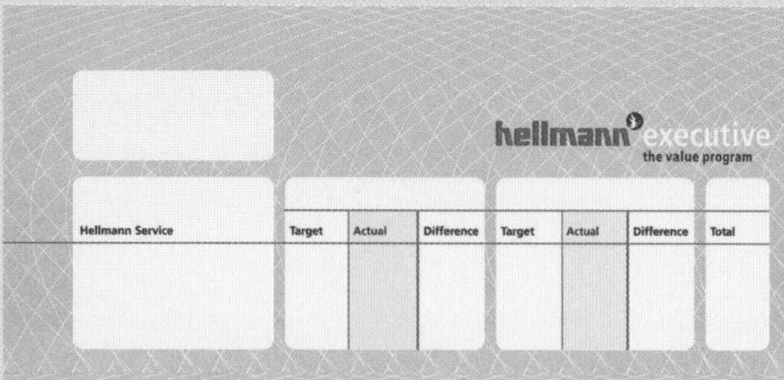

hellmann executive
the value program

Hellmann Service	Target	Actual	Difference	Target	Actual	Difference	Total

Form for costing: DIN Long

A Profile
Period
Company
Hellmann Service
Notice
hellmann executive
the value program
hellmann Worldwide Logistics

Registration form: A4

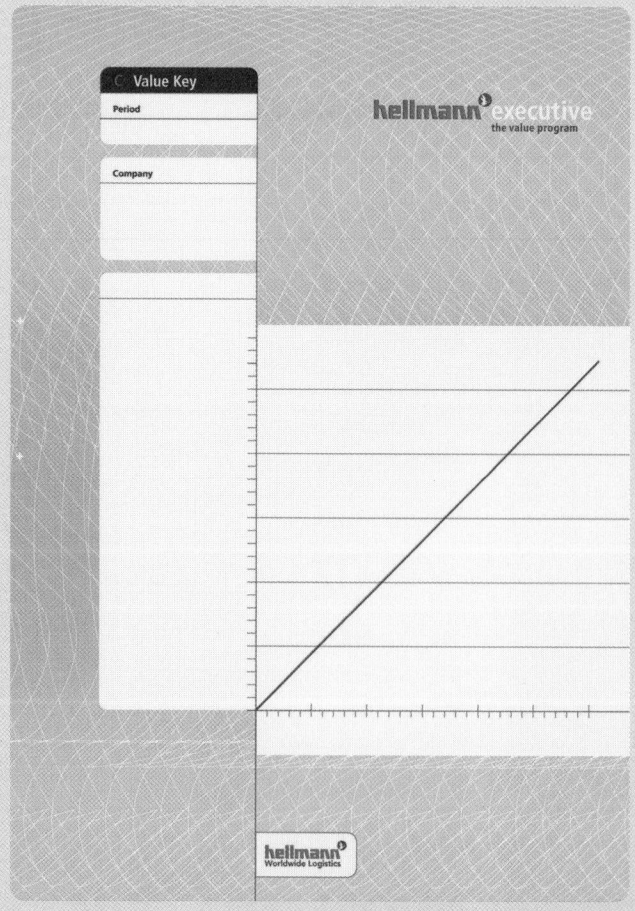

C Value Key
Period
Company
hellmann executive
the value program
hellmann Worldwide Logistics

Consultancy form: A4

B Planning

Period

Company

Hellmann Service

hellmann executive
the value program

Actual	Target	Difference	Bonus

hellmann
Worldwide Logistics

Consultancy form: A4

The silver colour and fine-line patterning are reminiscent of security bonds, and convey a sense of quality and exclusivity.

Royal Mail

Posting dockets

Issued by Royal Mail, UK
Design Information Design Unit, Newport Pagnell
Richard Bland
Year 1998
Typefaces Stempel Garamond, Helvetica

Royal Mail posting dockets are used by mailing houses, mail rooms and other high-volume mail users with Royal Mail accounts. Their primary function is to act as a record of post sent by the customer to the Royal Mail for delivery. A redesign and rewrite of the dockets was commissioned to reduce the high error rate on the forms, and to support changes to the accounting and invoicing system. Known errors included the wrong docket being filled in for the service used, incorrect completion of account details, and mistakes when entering weights and numbers of items.

The solution had to satisfy the needs of different users, including Royal Mail staff and both experienced and inexperienced customers. In the initial stages of the project, an insight into the users' needs and the circumstances in which the dockets are completed and processed was obtained by consulting with both Royal Mail staff and users. Initial designs were shown to users to ensure that these met their needs and expectations.

POSTING DOCKET

for Mailsort, Walksort, Presstream

Your details

Account number

Customer name

Name

Address

Postcode

Poster name

Name

Address

Postcode

Cover of docket pad: A4

After the redesign, the documents looked like they had come from an up-to-date and well-run organization.

Royal Mail

POSTING DOCKET

for Standard letters, Cleanmail, Packetpost, Packetsort

If you have any queries about completing this docket, please phone 0000 000 000.

Docket Number	N
Division Code	

Contact details

This is the person who Royal Mail should contact with any queries about this mailing.

Name

Phone Fax

Customer Job Number

Authorisation

I certify that the details given on this docket are correct.

Signature of the poster Date / /

Name Time :

Customer details

The customer is the person or organisation who has the contract with Royal Mail.

Name

Address

Postcode

Poster details

Name

Address

Postcode

Mailing House Code

Service details – Use one row for each different service and/or item weight

Account Number	Date of posting

Service register numerical code	Service *tick one service box only on each row*: Standard Tariff	Cleanmail OCR	Cleanmail CBC	Packetpost Daily Rate	Packetpost Flat Rate	Packetsort	Special Delivery	Class *tick one for each row*: 1st class	2nd class	Tick if needed: Recorded	Recorded & Advice	Number of items	Average/actual weight per item *(gms)*	Customer notes
	☐1	☐2	☐3	☐4	☐5	☐6	☐7	☐1	☐2	☐1	☐2			
	☐1	☐2	☐3	☐4	☐5	☐6	☐7	☐1	☐2	☐1	☐2			
	☐1	☐2	☐3	☐4	☐5	☐6	☐7	☐1	☐2	☐1	☐2			
	☐1	☐2	☐3	☐4	☐5	☐6	☐7	☐1	☐2	☐1	☐2			
	☐1	☐2	☐3	☐4	☐5	☐6	☐7	☐1	☐2	☐1	☐2			
	☐1	☐2	☐3	☐4	☐5	☐6	☐7	☐1	☐2	☐1	☐2			
	☐1	☐2	☐3	☐4	☐5	☐6	☐7	☐1	☐2	☐1	☐2			
	☐1	☐2	☐3	☐4	☐5	☐6	☐7	☐1	☐2	☐1	☐2			
	☐1	☐2	☐3	☐4	☐5	☐6	☐7	☐1	☐2	☐1	☐2			
	☐1	☐2	☐3	☐4	☐5	☐6	☐7	☐1	☐2	☐1	☐2			

If you require additional rows, please use the next docket in sequence. **Total number of items**

Royal Mail use only

Accepted by

Date / / Time :

Checked by

Date stamp

Top copy Version 1.1 CA80 (E)

Royal Mail

POSTING DOCKET

for Mailsort, Walksort, Presstream

If you have any queries about completing this docket, please phone 0000 000 000.

Docket Number	H
Division Code	

Contact details

This is the person who Royal Mail should contact with any queries about this mailing.

Name

Phone Fax

Customer Job Number

Authorisation

I certify that the details given on this docket are correct.

Signature of the poster Date / /

Name Time :

Customer details

The customer is the person or organisation who has the contract with Royal Mail.

Name

Address

Postcode

Poster details

Name

Address

Postcode

Mailing House Code

Service details – Please use a separate docket for each different service

Account Number	Service register numerical code	Contract number	Date of posting

Please tick the service you need, and fill in the relevant boxes.	☐ Mailsort	☐ Walksort	☐ Presstream	Customer notes
Type of Mailsort service required	☐ 120 ☐ 700 ☐ 1400			
Level of service required *Tick only one box. Please use a separate docket for other services or service levels.*	☐ Mailsort 1 ☐ Mailsort 2 ☐ Mailsort 3	☐ Walksort 1 ☐ Walksort 2	☐ Presstream 1 ☐ Presstream 2 ☐ Profile Price	
Service variant *Tick only one box.*	☐ STD ☐ OCR ☐ CBC			
Magazine details Code or title				
Issue ID				
Number of directs *(items)*				
Number of residues *(items)*				
Total number of items *(items)*				
Actual/average weight per item *(gms)*				
Items for early posting claim *(items)* *Mailsort 1 and Presstream 1 only*				
Consignment reference number *Mailsort 3 only*				

Other details

Main function of this mail

This information will help us understand our customers' needs.

☐ 1 Goods
☐ 2 Magazines
☐ 3 Catalogues
☐ 4 Direct Mail (acquisition)
☐ 5 Direct Mail (loyalty)
☐ 6 Billing
☐ 7 Statements
☐ 8 More than one function
☐ 9 Other *specify below*

Royal Mail use only

Accepted by

Date / / Time :

Checked by

Early posting claim ☐ allowed ☐ disallowed

OCR residue claim ☐ allowed ☐ disallowed

Date stamp

Top copy Version 1.1 CA81 (E)

Dockets for different Royal Mail services: A4

The new design included clearer headings stating the services that the docket can be used for, a prominent helpline and enquiries number, and checkboxes to reduce both the time spent filling in details and the possibility of giving the wrong information.

Royal Mail

Business-to-business invoices

Issued by	Royal Mail, UK
Design	Boag Associates, London
Year	2002
Typeface	Helvetica

The Royal Mail identified a need to improve the layout and appearance of its business-to-business invoices. The research undertaken by Boag Associates then resulted in redefining the brief and establishing key performance indicators. They devised an approach to obtaining customer feedback that allowed them to ensure that the new design met the needs of as many customers as possible. The proposed solutions achieved significant design improvements without recourse to reprogramming the Royal Mail's accounting systems. The success of the new design could be measured in the increased speed of processing and payment by customers, the decreasing volume of invoice-related calls to the helpline, and the improvement of customer satisfaction with the invoicing from around 60% to over 80%.

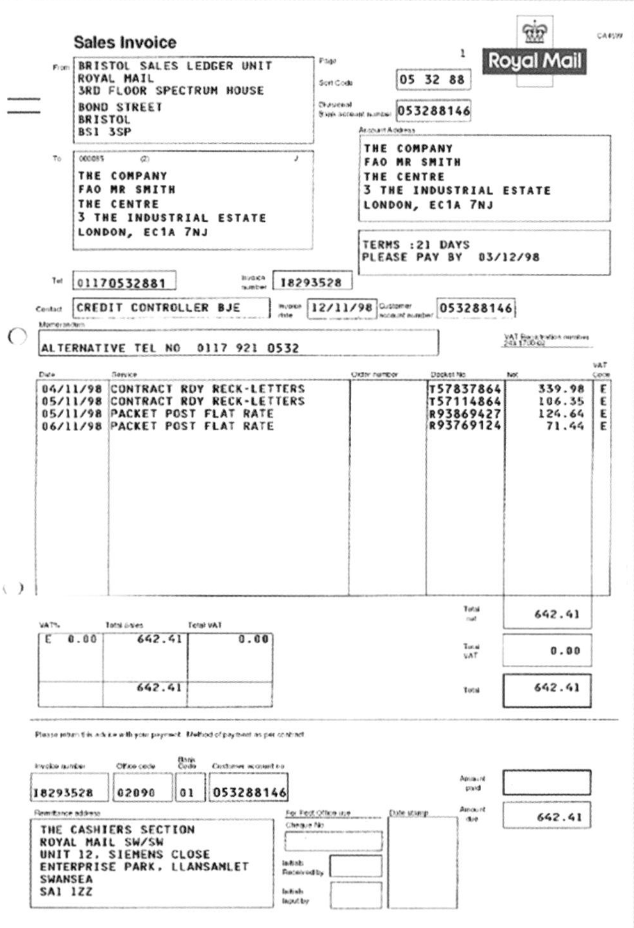

Sales Invoice 1 Royal Mail

From: BRISTOL SALES LEDGER UNIT
ROYAL MAIL
3RD FLOOR SPECTRUM HOUSE
BOND STREET
BRISTOL
BS1 3SP

Page: 1
Sort Code: 05 32 88
Bank account number: 053288146

To: THE COMPANY
FAO MR SMITH
THE CENTRE
3 THE INDUSTRIAL ESTATE
LONDON, EC1A 7NJ

Account Address: THE COMPANY
FAO MR SMITH
THE CENTRE
3 THE INDUSTRIAL ESTATE
LONDON, EC1A 7NJ

TERMS :21 DAYS
PLEASE PAY BY 03/12/98

Tel: 01170532881 Invoice number: 18293528
Contact: CREDIT CONTROLLER BJE Invoice date: 12/11/98 Customer account number: 053288146

Memorandum: ALTERNATIVE TEL NO 0117 921 0532

Date	Service	Order number	Docket No	Net	VAT Code
04/11/98	CONTRACT RDY RECK-LETTERS		T57837864	339.98	E
05/11/98	CONTRACT RDY RECK-LETTERS		T57114864	106.35	E
05/11/98	PACKET POST FLAT RATE		R93869427	124.64	E
06/11/98	PACKET POST FLAT RATE		R93769124	71.44	E

VAT%	Total sales	Total VAT
E 0.00	642.41	0.00
	642.41	

Total net: 642.41
Total VAT: 0.00
Total: 642.41

Please return this advice with your payment. Method of payment as per contract

Invoice number	Office code	Bank Code	Customer account no
18293528	02090	01	053288146

Amount paid:
Amount due: 642.41

Remittance address: THE CASHIERS SECTION
ROYAL MAIL SW/SW
UNIT 12, SIEMENS CLOSE
ENTERPRISE PARK, LLANSAMLET
SWANSEA
SA1 1ZZ

For Post Office use — Cheque No — Initials Received by — Initials Input by — Date stamp

Previous invoice design: A4

Boag Associates identified several key issues that needed to be addressed in the redesign: 1) The listing of the products and services that customers had used did not provide enough detail for accounts departments to process the invoices efficiently. 2) The payment slip details were unclear. 3) There was no clear delineation between different invoice types, credit notes, or statements for different kinds of accounts held by customers. 4) The invoice contained no background information on how to pay and there was no clear helpline or support telephone number.

Finance Service Centre, Royal Mail House,
Stonehill Road, Farnworth, BOLTON BL4 9XX

Royal Mail is a trading name of Consignia plc, registered in England and Wales, Number 4138203, registered office 148 Old Street, LONDON EC1V 9HQ

VAT registration number **243 1700 02**

Invoice enquiries
☎ 0870 606 0882
www.royalmail.com/youraccount
Other enquiries and information
Please see overleaf

Invoice number
IE 123456
Invoice date
12 Jul 2002
Page
1 of 2

Invoice

To
THE COMPANY
FAO MR SMITH
THE CENTRE
3 THE INDUSTRIAL ESTATE
LONDON
EC1A 7NJ

Account held at
THE COMPANY
THE CENTRE
3 THE INDUSTRIAL ESTATE

LONDON
EC1A 7NJ

Customer account number

123456 1AA

New opening times for the Finance Service Centre are 9am to 5pm

Terms
21 days
Please pay by
02 Aug 2002

Docket no.	Posting date Poster	Sender's ref. Contract no.	Service Quantity	Weight (kg)	Unit cost (£)	Net value	VAT
H12345678	29 Jun 02 MK6 1HQ	**12345** 123456M3	MAILSORT 3 26,042	1,562.520		3,731.25	E
H12345678	29 Jun 02	**12345** 123456M3	MAILSORT 3 8,950	537.000		1,281.10	E
H12345678	02 Jul 02 BS3 3NX	**12345** 123456M3	MAILSORT 3 30,000	1,800.000		4,292.10	E
H12345678	03 Jul 02	**12345** 123456M3	MAILSORT 3 29,850	1791.000		4,270.64	E
H12345678	03 Jul 02 MK6 1HQ	**12345** 123456M3	1ST AND 2ND CLASS ACCOUNT MAIL 47	2.820		8.93	E
H12345678	03 Jul 02	**12345** 123456M3	1ST AND 2ND CLASS ACCOUNT MAIL 2,200	173.000		1,762.00	E
H12345678	04 Jul 02 BS3 3NX	**12345** 123456M3	MAILSORT 3 29,850	447.750		4,270.64	E
H12345678	05 Jul 02	**12345** 123456M3	CONTRACT RDY RECK-LETTERS 281	2116.800		5,881.33	E
					Total carried forward to next page	**25,497.99**	

Payment advice

Paying by BACS?

Please instruct your bank to pay the amount due, following the instructions overleaf. Send your payment advice to the address below.

Amount due
£34,322.88

For Royal Mail use only

Office code	Bank code	Rec'd by	Input by
12345	12		

Payment address
THE REMITTANCE CENTRE
ROYAL MAIL
PAPYRUS ROAD
WERRINGTON
PETERBOROUGH
PE4 5PG

Paying by cheque?

Please make your cheque payable to **Royal Mail**, fill in the boxes to the right, then tear off and return this payment advice with your cheque, quoting your account number and invoice number on the reverse of the cheque. If you supply your own payment advice instead, it must include the information listed to the right.

Your cheque number

Amount tendered

Customer account number
123456 1AA

Invoice number
IE 123456

New invoice design: A4

The new invoice provides more detail in its listing of transactions. It has clearer, more visible headings, and provides clear helpline and 'how to pay' information.

Vodafone

Customer bill

Issued by	Vodafone UK
Design	The Brand Union, London
Year	2005
Typefaces	Vodafone (corporate typeface), Helvetica

A mobile phone bill has a hard job to do. Mistrustful customers scrutinize it for the slightest inconsistency, telecom bill managers spend hours analysing it, and all the while it continually plays catch-up to a fast-moving industry that is likely to introduce new products several times a year.

Vodafone's old bill design did not cope well with the new products that it needed to include. A radical restructure was needed that had to be worked through and agreed with people throughout the company – from customer services to product managers to brand managers to credit control. The new bill is designed to match the needs of a new consumer with a single mobile as well as those of a business manager with a thousand mobiles. It is also designed to adapt to both future propositions and future usage patterns, such as increasing text and data usage. As a result, a saving of 35% could be made on production costs and 91% of customers now think the bill is 'clear and easy to understand'.

11:37 01144960423
12:51 01632960463 3
13:04 0151496 0461 2m 49
14:27 09098790980 15m 01s
15:33 07700900452 10m 49s
Fri 2 Jul
10:57 0151496 0467 0m 27s
11:24 07700900234 10m 59s
13:24 07700900468 4m 22s
14:57 01632960483 1m 25s
15:45 Voicemail 121 0m 35s
16:41 01632960464 3m
17:15 01144960427

Dividers

Dotted lines are used to separate entries, while unbroken lines are used to separate days. This creates a subtle yet distinct hierarchy of information which does not overload the form.

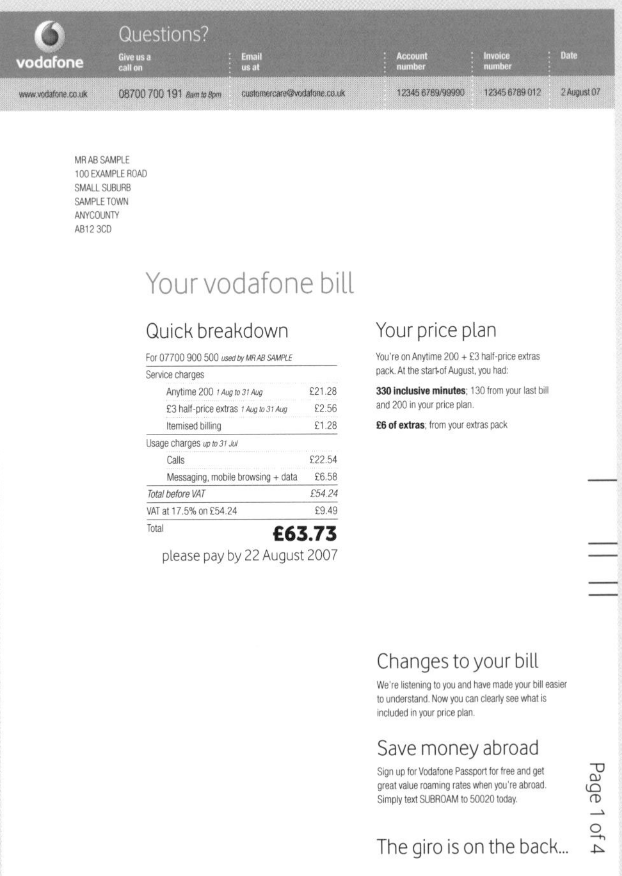

vodafone
Questions?
www.vodafone.co.uk
Give us a call on: 08700 700 191 8am to 8pm
Email us at: customercare@vodafone.co.uk
Account number: 12345 6789/99990
Invoice number: 12345 6789 012
Date: 2 August 07

MR AB SAMPLE
100 EXAMPLE ROAD
SMALL SUBURB
SAMPLE TOWN
ANYCOUNTY
AB12 3CD

Your vodafone bill

Quick breakdown

For 07700 900 500 used by MR AB SAMPLE

Service charges	
Anytime 200 1 Aug to 31 Aug	£21.28
£3 half-price extras 1 Aug to 31 Aug	£2.56
Itemised billing	£1.28
Usage charges up to 31 Jul	
Calls	£22.54
Messaging, mobile browsing + data	£6.58
Total before VAT	£54.24
VAT at 17.5% on £54.24	£9.49
Total	**£63.73**

please pay by 22 August 2007

Your price plan

You're on Anytime 200 + £3 half-price extras pack. At the start of August, you had:

330 inclusive minutes; 130 from your last bill and 200 in your price plan.

£6 of extras; from your extras pack

Changes to your bill

We're listening to you and have made your bill easier to understand. Now you can clearly see what is included in your price plan.

Save money abroad

Sign up for Vodafone Passport for free and get great value roaming rates when you're abroad. Simply text SUBROAM to 50020 today.

The giro is on the back...

Page 1 of 4

New bill, first page: A4

The first page contains a brief summary of the bill. It usefully includes the name of the particular price plan and its key features. These often change and not all customers are aware of what their regular allowances are.

Questions?	Mobile	Account number	Invoice number	Date
Call 08700 700 191 *8am to 8pm*	07700 900 500 *MR AB SAMPLE*	12345 6789	12345 6789 012	2 August 2007

Itemisation

This time you...

- saved £20.73 by using your inclusive minutes
- made 181 minutes of daytime calls
- made 338 minutes of evening + weekend calls
- sent 10 text messages
- sent 0 picture mesages

A new partnership

The National Autistic Society and Vodafone have started a 3 year partnership. With your support we can help those affected and their families. For more details go to www.vodafone.co.uk/autism

Calls

time	*number*	*duration*	*normal cost*	*you pay*	*inc?*
Wed 30 Jun					
09:37	01144960579	0m 28s	0.040	—	✔
09:42	01144960423	0m 03s	0.101	—	✔
10:53	09098790980	2m 10s	0.190	0.190	
Thu 1 Jul					
10:22	Voicemail 121	0m 27s	0.100	—	✔
11:10	09098790980	13m 30s	1.377	1.377	
11:37	01144960423	38m 59s	3.977	—	✔
12:51	01632960463	3m 53s	0.991	—	✔
13:04	0151496 0461	2m 49s	0.240	—	✔
14:27	09098790980	15m 01s	3.184	3.184	
15:33	07700900452	10m 49s	2.759	—	✔
Fri 2 Jul					
10:57	0151496 0467	0m 27s	0.046	—	✔
11:24	07700900234	10m 59s	2.759	2.759	
13:24	07700900468	4m 22s	1.114	—	✔
14:57	01632960483	1m 25s	0.362	—	✔
15:45	Voicemail 121	0m 35s	0.050	—	✔
16:41	01632960464	3m 40s	0.374	—	✔
17:15	01144960427	0m 16s	0.042	—	✔
18:02	01632960481	5m 56s	0.606	—	✔
18:57	07700900452	0m 37s	0.158	0.158	
23:59	Scoot	0m 4s	0.042	0.042	
Sat 3 Jul					
19:21	07700900468	1m 02s	0.264	—	✔
19:47	01632960483	0m 04s	0.042	0.042	
20:50	01144960628	2m 49s	0.240	—	✔
Mon 5 Jul					
11:30	07700900412	4m 22s	1.114	—	✔
13:22	01632960481	3m 53s	0.991	—	✔
17:15	01144960628	0m 16s	0.042	—	✔
17:17	Voicemail 121	0m 35s	0.050	—	✔
17:27	09098790980	15m 01s	3.184	3.184	
18:30	01632960481	3m 40s	0.374	—	✔
18:54	07700900412	0m 37s	0.158	0.158	
Fri 9 Jul					
09:42	01144960628	0m 03s	0.101	—	✔
09:45	07700900434	10m 49s	2.759	—	✔
10:12	07700900387	0m 37s	0.158	0.158	
10:14	01632960481	0m 04s	0.042	0.042	
10:17	01144960346	0m 16s	0.042	—	✔
10:20	01632960480	3m 40s	0.374	—	✔
13:11	0151496 0467	0m 27s	0.046	—	✔
13:20	09098790980	13m 30s	1.377	1.377	
15:45	Voicemail 121	0m 35s	0.050	—	✔
18:25	01144960346	2m 49s	0.240	—	✔
18:40	01632960780	3m 53s	0.991	—	✔
21:33	09098790980	15m 01s	3.184	3.184	
21:54	07700900288	0m 37s	0.158	0.158	

Calls continued

time	*number*	*duration*	*normal cost*	*you pay*	*inc?*
Sat 10 Jul					
13:15	Voicemail 121	0m 27s	0.100	—	✔
14:26	01632960780	1m 25s	0.362	—	✔
18:33	07700900364	0m 37s	0.158	0.158	
Sun 11 Jul					
10:11	0151496 0454	0m 27s	0.046	—	✔
10:17	01144960346	0m 16s	0.042	—	✔
12:02	01632960780	5m 56s	0.606	—	✔
14:27	09098790986	15m 01s	3.184	3.184	
15:22	Voicemail 121	0m 27s	0.100	—	✔
16:20	07700900364	3m 53s	0.991	—	✔
17:27	09098790986	15m 01s	3.184	3.184	
Total of 54 calls		8h 39m 25s	43.27	**22.54**	

Messaging, mobile browsing and data

time	*description*	*details*	*normal cost*	*you pay*	*inc?*
Wed 31 Jun					
08:57	✉ 447700900666	1 text	0.100	—	✔
–	✉ 07700900291	2 texts	0.200	—	✔
20:18	09098790984	1m 30s	1.500	1.500	
Thu 1 Jul					
07:02	✉ 07700900348	1 text	0.100	—	✔
10:18	09098790985	1m 30s	1.500	1.500	
12:37	✉ 07700900728	1 text	0.100	—	✔
–	✉ 07700900381	4 texts	0.400	—	✔
18:50	09098790986	1m 30s	1.500	1.500	
19:50	✉ 07700900329	1 text	0.100	—	✔
22:50	09098790986	1m 30s	1.500	1.500	
Total of messaging, mobile browsing + data				**£6.58**	

Key

- ✔ Included in price plan
- Partly included in price plan
- ✉ Text message
- Multiple texts to the same number
- Picture or multimedia message
- Mobile browsing + data
- Weekend

Page 3 of 4

Itemization page: A4

The listing of all calls made is very clear, legible, and easy to understand.

T-Mobile

	Customer bill
Issued by	T-Mobile, UK
Design	Boag Associates, London
Year	2005
Typeface	Tele-Grotesk

T-Mobile bills lacked clarity and this meant that bill-related queries were the most common cause of customer calls to T-Mobile. Therefore, Boag Associates were commissioned to redesign and maintain a new consumer bill. The ambitious aims were to increase the bill clarity satisfaction score by 10% within 12 months, to reduce the number of unnecessary bill-related helpline calls, to make the bill a key part of the customer's brand experience and to ensure that the design accommodated complex mobile usage and tariff structures. While Boag Associates developed the written bill content, and made recommendations for structure and content across the pages, TMW (Tullo Marshall Warren) carried out the brand design implementation. As result, bill clarity satisfaction did indeed see an increase of 10 percentage points to 55% within a 12-month period, and helpline calls were not only reduced significantly but can also be handled more quickly thanks to the increased clarity of the bills.

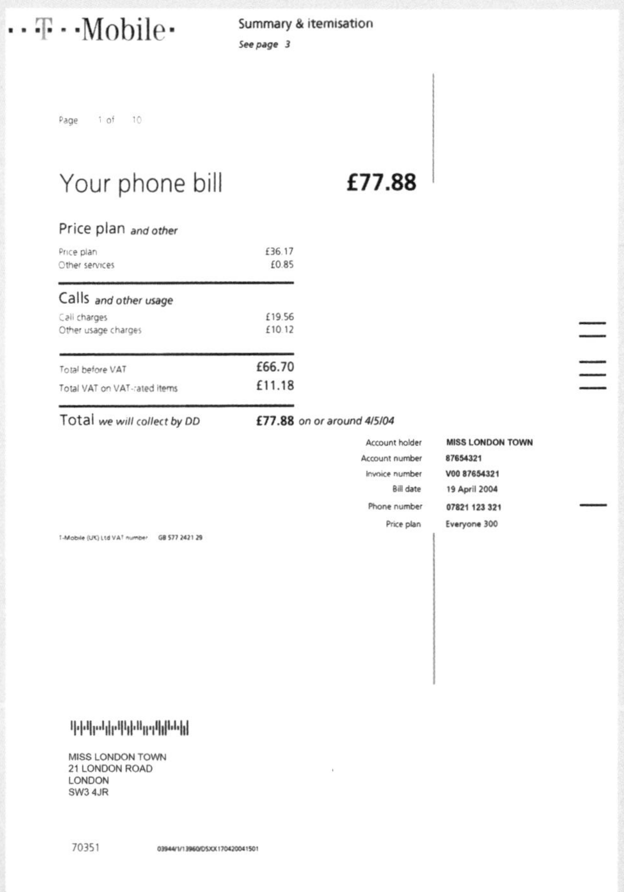

T-Mobile

Summary & itemisation
See page 3

Page 1 of 10

Your phone bill **£77.88**

Price plan *and other*

Price plan	£36.17
Other services	£0.85

Calls *and other usage*

Call charges	£19.56
Other usage charges	£10.12
Total before VAT	£66.70
Total VAT on VAT-rated items	£11.18

Total *we will collect by DD* **£77.88** *on or around 4/5/04*

Account holder	MISS LONDON TOWN
Account number	87654321
Invoice number	V00 87654321
Bill date	19 April 2004
Phone number	07821 123 321
Price plan	Everyone 300

T-Mobile (UK) Ltd VAT number GB 577 2421 29

MISS LONDON TOWN
21 LONDON ROAD
LONDON
SW3 4JR

70351 03944/1/13960/DSXX170420041501

Previous bill, front page: A4

There were no helpline or contact details on the front page of the old bill, and the customer's name, address and details were inconveniently placed.

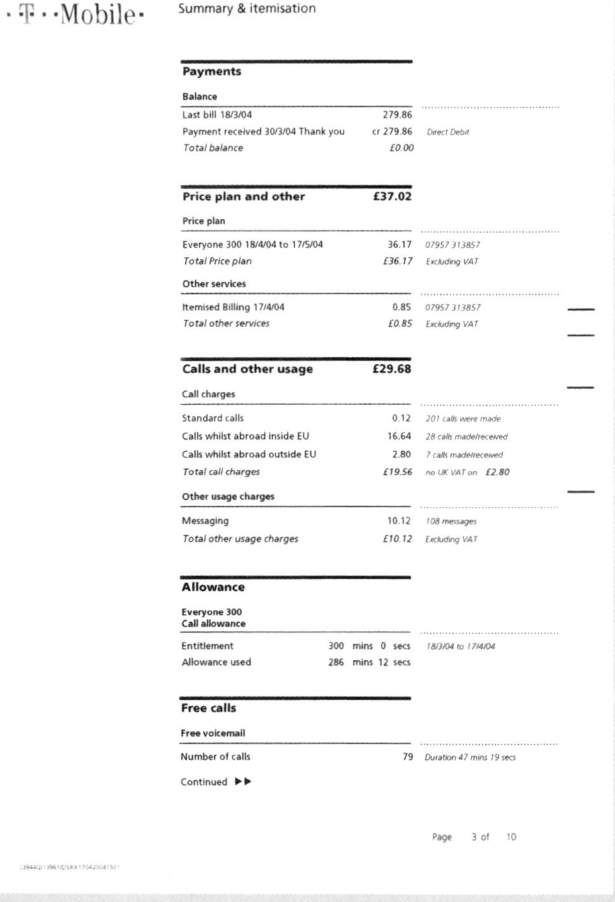

T-Mobile

Summary & itemisation

Payments

Balance		
Last bill 18/3/04	279.86	
Payment received 30/3/04 Thank you	cr 279.86	*Direct Debit*
Total balance	*£0.00*	

Price plan and other	**£37.02**	
Price plan		
Everyone 300 18/4/04 to 17/5/04	36.17	*07957 313857*
Total Price plan	*£36.17*	*Excluding VAT*
Other services		
Itemised Billing 17/4/04	0.85	*07957 313857*
Total other services	*£0.85*	*Excluding VAT*

Calls and other usage	**£29.68**	
Call charges		
Standard calls	0.12	*201 calls were made*
Calls whilst abroad inside EU	16.64	*28 calls made/received*
Calls whilst abroad outside EU	2.80	*7 calls made/received*
Total call charges	*£19.56*	*no UK VAT on £2.80*
Other usage charges		
Messaging	10.12	*108 messages*
Total other usage charges	*£10.12*	*Excluding VAT*

Allowance

Everyone 300 Call allowance		
Entitlement	300 mins 0 secs	*18/3/04 to 17/4/04*
Allowance used	286 mins 12 secs	

Free calls

Free voicemail		
Number of calls	79	*Duration 47 mins 19 secs*

Continued ▶▶

Page 3 of 10

03944/2/13961/DSXX170420041501

Previous bill, page 3: A4

In particular, it was hard for customers to see how they had used their call allowances and what usage was inside or outside the allowance.

Contact us

T-Mobile

150 from your T-Mobile phone
0845 412 5000 from any other phone

To email us please visit
www.t-mobile.co.uk/billenquiry

Bill date: **23 February 2007**
Account holder: **Pc John Smith**
Account number: **12345678**
Invoice number: **V000012345678**
Phone number: **0958 123 456**

PC JOHN SMITH
1 SMITH STREET
SMITHSFIELD
SMITHSHEAD
ABERDEENSHIRE
AB12 3ER

Feb '07

Your last bill

Amount charged	£29.78	
Line rental credit 4/2/07	- £9.78	
Payment received 4/2/07 by Mercury Communica **Thank you**	- £10.00	
Overdue amount	**£10.00**	**Please pay now**

Your latest bill

Outstanding balance	£10.00
Your monthly plan charges	£39.56
New charges this month outside plan	£12.59
Your new balance	**£62.15**

VAT charged at 0% on £52.15

Amount due **£62.15**

Please pay by 9/3/07

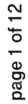

page 1 of 12

New bill, front page: A4

The name and address are now in standard positions. Customer and bill details are at the head of the page, where they are easier to locate, as are the helpline and contact details. Last month's bill total and payment are presented above this month's details, allowing for an immediate comparison.

Contact us

T-Mobile

150 from your T-Mobile phone
0845 412 5000 from any other phone

To email us please visit
www.t-mobile.co.uk/billenquiry

User: **Pc John Smith**

Bill date: **23 February 2007**

For phone number:

07958 123 456

Charges summary

Your monthly plan charges

Relax 30	£25.53	
250 Minutes at any time to Local, National, T-Mobile UK, other UK Mobiles and voicemail (except registered Business Customers with Business Extras). Plus 100 text allowance to T-Mobile & other UK Mobiles		
500 mins for Homezone	£4.25	
500 mins for Homezone	£4.25	
Homezone	£4.25	
Itemised Billing	£1.28	
Fully itemised billing information to allow you to see exactly how you use your phone		
Monthly charge total		**£39.56**

What you used outside of allowance - UK

T-Mobile@home

You made 11:00 mins calls

Calls	
01:00 mins outside of allowance	£0.60
T-Mobile@Home	
00:20 Mins outside of allowance	£0.20
Mobile fax and data	
00:30 mins outside of allowance	£0.30
Texts	
2 texts outside of allowance	£0.30
Picture messages	
3 messages outside of allowance	£0.45
Mobile email	
2 messages outside of allowance	£0.30
Mobile data	
30:15 mins outside of allowance	£2.28
Other T-Mobile services	
Outside of allowance	£0.03

page 3 of 12

continued over >

New bill, page 3: A4

The phone number in large type makes it clear which user the bill relates to, and there is a clear separation of price plan charges and charges outside the allowance.

Contact us

T · · Mobile ·

150 from your T-Mobile phone
0845 412 5000 from any other phone

To email us please visit
www.t-mobile.co.uk/billenquiry

User: **Pc John Smith** Bill date: **23 February 2007** For phone number: **07958 123 456**

How you used your allowance

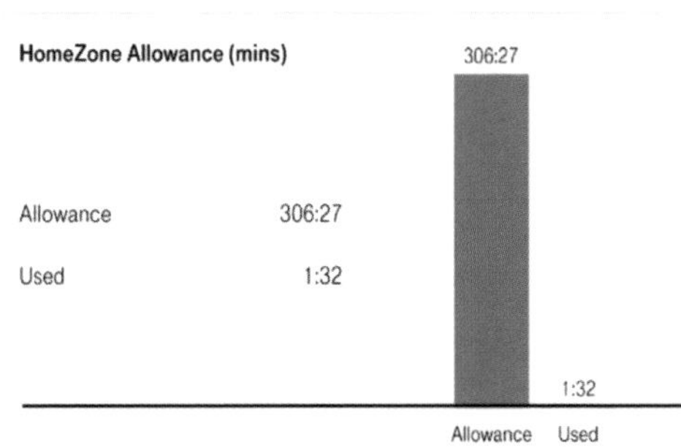

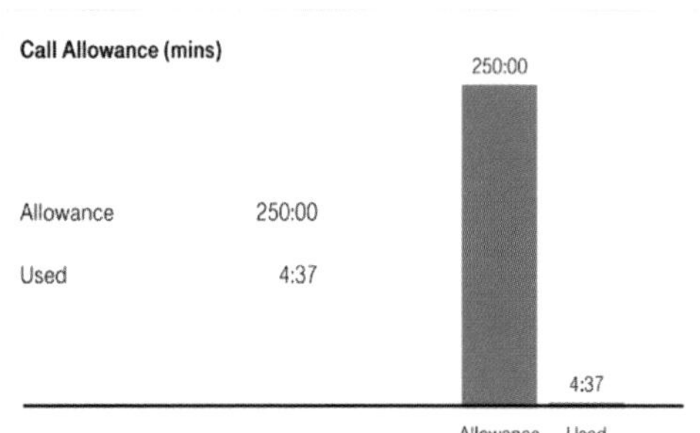

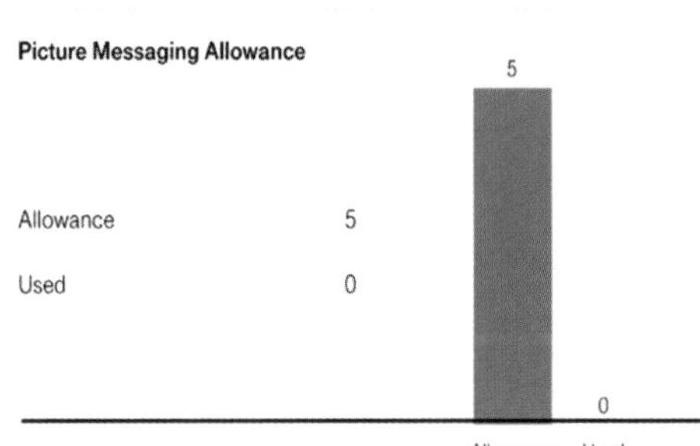

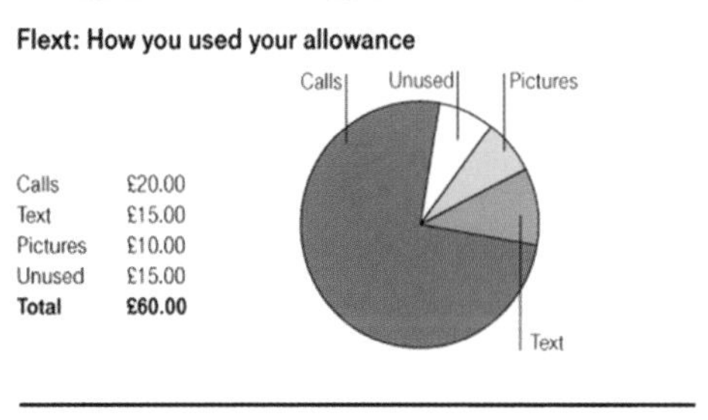

Calls

Within allowance

date	day	time	number	place called	call length hr:min:sec
24 Jan	Wed	20:11	01332 941233	Derby	0:15
3 Feb	SAT	07:39	077332 99133	Other Network	0:15
4 Feb	SUN	04:44	07949 618333	T-Mobile	0:15
11 Feb	SUN	17:05	01332 614933	Derby	0:15
14 Feb	Wed	22:20	020 88330233	London	0:15
17 Feb	SAT	01:10	Voicemail		0:15

Outside allowance £0.600

date	day	time	number	place called	call length hr:min:sec	£
24 Jan	Wed	09:00	0034968487733	Spain	0:15	0.150
1 Feb	Thu	23:05	001780 786633	Canada	0:15	0.150
15 Feb	Thu	00:34	01992 913333	Hoddesdon	0:15	0.150
		02:28	09083490733		0:15	0.150

continued over >

page 5 of 12

New bill, page 5: A4

T-Mobile's new bill set the benchmark as the first major UK mobile telecom to provide visual snapshots of usage in graphical form. Graphs are used to visualize how customers have used their allowances.

Abama Golf & Spa Resort

Order and notice forms

Issued by	Abama Golf & Spa Resort, Tenerife, Spain
Design	Thomas Manss & Company, London
Year	2008
Typefaces	Trajan Pro, Thesis Sans

Hotel forms often need to be bilingual, which generally means the local language plus English. This doubles the quantity of information, which can lead to uncertainty and confusion.

Thomas Manss have found a clear and elegant solution to this problem with their forms for the Abama Resort. The two languages are placed on either side of a central axis, and English is distinguished additionally by being in discreet italics.

Repair assistance form, front and back: 100 × 180 mm

SERVICIO DE REPARACIO

REPAIR ASSISTANCE

Agua	☐	*Water*
Luz	☐	*Light*
Llave	☐	*Key*
Cortina	☐	*Curtain*
Ducha	☐	*Shower*
Baño	☐	*Bath*
Cama	☐	*Bed*
WC	☐	*WC*
Teléfono	☐	*Phone*
Muebles	☐	*Furniture*
Ventana	☐	*Window*

Habitación ____ *Room*

Le rogamos anotar cualquier anomalia para su reparación
Please advise with a mark on the list if you require our immediate assistance

ORDEN DE DESAYUNO

BREAKFAST ORDER

Horario de Desayuno / *Breakfast Time*
Asi con intervalos de 15 minutos hastas las 11h30
Every 15 minutes until 11.30

07h00 - 07h15
07h15 - 07h30
07h30 - 07h45

Horario	______	*Time*
Número de personas	______	*Number of persons*
Habitación	______	*Room*
Firma	______	*Signature*

Por favor, cuelgue esta orden en el exterior de su puerta ante de las 3.00
Please hang this order outside your door knob before 3.00 am

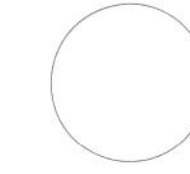

Desayuno Abama / Breakfast Abama

120 €
1/2 Botella de Moët & Chandon – *1/2 Bottle of Moët & Chandon*
Caviar Beluga (30g) acompañado de blinis y crema agria
Beluga Caviar (30gsm) served with blinis and sour cream
Salmón "Balik" – *The "Balik" Salmon*
Cesta de frutas tropicales – *Tropical fruit basket*
Bombones de la casa – *Petits Fours*

Desayuno Americano / American Breakfast

28 €
Cesta de bolleria con croissants y seleccion de panes, mantequilla, mermeladas, miel y crema de quesos
The Baker's basket with croissants and a choice of bread, butter, jam, honey and cream cheese

Zumo de fruta	***Fruit juice***	**Huevos al gusto**	***Eggs of your choice***
Naranja	*Orange*	Revueltos	*Scrambled*
Pomelo	*Grapefruit*	Fritos	*Fried*
Piña	*Pineapple*	Pochados	*Poached*
Tomate	*Tomato*	Cocidos ____ mn	*Boiled ____ mn*
Yogur	***Yoghurt***	Acompañados de:	*Served with:*
Natural	*Natural*	Jamón de York	*Cooked Ham*
de Frutas	*Fruit*	Bacon	*Bacon*
Bio Natural	*Organic*	Salchidas	*Sausages*
Desnatado	*Natural*		
Natural	*low-fat*	**Café**	***Coffee***
		Americano	*American*
Té con	***Tea with***	Expresso	*Expresso*
limón	*lemon*	Descafeinado	*Decaffeinated*
leche fria	*cold milk*	Cappucino	*Capuccino*
leche caliente	*hot milk*	Leche Caliente	*Hot Milk*
		Leche fria	*Cold Milk*

Desayuno a la Carta / À la Carte Breakfast

Zumo de fruta	***Natural fruit juice***	6 €		**Huevos al gusto**	***Eggs of your choice***	10 €
Naranja	*Orange*			Revueltos	*Scrambled*	
Pomelo	*Grapefruit*			Fritos	*Fried*	
Piña	*Pineapple*			Pochados	*Poached*	
Mango	*Mango*			Tortilla francesca	*Omelette*	
Selección de frutas frescas	***Selection of fresh fruits***	10 €		Tortilla de jamón y queso	*Omelette with ham and cheese*	
				Tortilla de jamón	*Ham Omelette*	
Yogur	***Yoghurt***	4 €		Tortilla de queso	*Cheese Omelette*	
Natural	*Natural*			Cocidos mn	*Boiled mn*	
de Frutas	*Fruit*			Acompañados:	*Served with:*	
Bio Natural	*Organic*			Jamón de York	*Cooked Ham*	
Bio Frutas	*Fruit organic*			Bacon	*Bacon*	
Desnatado Natural	*Natural low-fat*			Salchidas	*Sausages*	
Desnatado Frutas	*Fruit low-fat*					
				Otros	***Others***	
Cereales	***Cereals***	5 €		Jamón de York	*Cooked Ham*	6 €
con Miel	*with Honey*			Selección de embutidos	*Mixed Cold cuts*	10 €
Cornflakes	*Cornflakes*			Surtido de quesos	*Assorted cheeses*	10 €
All-Bran	*All-Bran*					
Rice Crispies	*Rice Crispies*			**Cafeteria**	***Cafeteria***	
Special K	*Special K*			Americano	*Americano*	4 €
Coco Pops	*Coco Pops*			Expresso	*Expresso*	4 €
Muesli	*Muesli*			Descafeinado	*Decaffeinated*	4 €
				Cappucino	*Capuccino*	4 €
Pan	***Bread***			Café de Cereales	*Barley coffee*	4 €
Cesta de Bolleria	*Baker's basket*	10 €		Café con leche	*Coffee w/milk*	4 €
Tostadas	*White toasts*	4 €		Chocolate	*Chocolate*	4 €
Tostadas integrales	*Wholewheat toasts*	4 €		Leche Caliente	*Hot Milk*	4 €
				Leche fria	*Cold Milk*	4 €
				Selección de té e infusiones	*Assorted teas and infusions*	6 €

Desayuno Continental / Continental Breakfast

20 €
Cesta de bolleria con croissants y seleccion de panes, mantequilla, mermeladas y miel
The Baker's basket with croissants and a choice of bread, butter, jam and honey

Café	***Coffee***	**Té con**	***Tea with***
Americano	*American*	limón	*lemon*
Decafeinado	*Decaffeinated*	leche fria	*cold milk*
Espresso	*Espresso*	leche caliente	*hot milk*
Capuccino	*Capuccino*		
Cold Milk	*Cold Milk*	**Zumo de fruta**	***Fruit juices***
Hot Milk	*Hot Milk*	Naranja	*Orange*
		Pomelo	*Grapefruit*
		Piña	*Pineapple*

Desayuno Saludable / Healthy Breakfast

22 €
Cesta de bolleria integral con mermelada sin azúcar, matequilla baja en calorías y miel
The Baker's wholemeal basket with a choice of organic low-fat jam, low-fat butter and honey
Surtido de fruta fresca – *Assorted fresh fruits*

Té	*Tea*	**Zumo de fruta**	***Fruit juices***
Decafeinado	*Decaffeinated*	Naranja	*Orange*
Café de Cereales	*Barley's Coffee*	Pomelo	*Grapefruit*
Leche Desnatada	*Skimmed Milk*	Piña	*Pineapple*
Leche de Soja	*Soya Milk*	Zanahoria	*Carrot*

Cuidense, los precios estan en Euros – I.G.I.C no incluido
Please note prices are in Euros – Taxes are not included

Breakfast order, front and back: 120 × 500 mm

H+M Medical Systems

Records and order forms

Issued by	H+M HighTec und Management Systemlösungen GmbH, Germany
Design	Branding Healthcare, Weimar
Years	2004–2006
Typeface	Officina Sans

The H+M group deals in medical equipment and software, for which it provides support and training. The forms are an important aid for customer advisers and also for documenting results and feedback. They have been designed with great attention to detail. The blue background suits the medical context and draws the user's attention to the text fields.

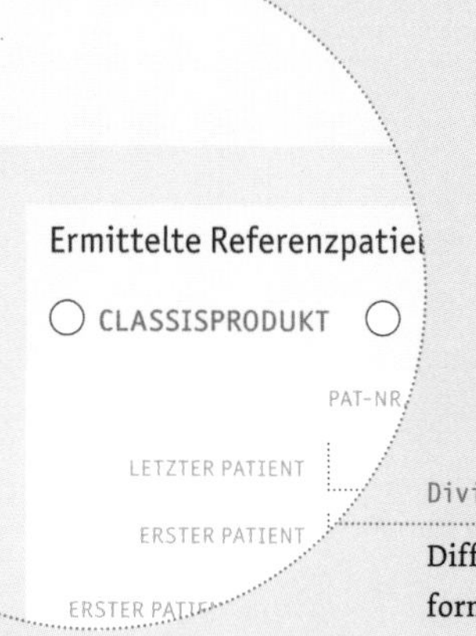

Divisions

Different shades of the basic colour divide the form into sections. Some of the text is also set in paler type. This has a discreet and elegant look, though it does not photocopy well.

→ Graphic divisions: page 190
→ Colour and type: page 138

Qualitätssicherheitsprotokoll

H+M Systeme für Mediziner

H+M HighTec und Management Systemlösungen GmbH & Co. KG
In den Weiden 9, 99099 Erfurt — Telefon 0361 / 442 79 0, Telefax 0361 / 442 79 50
Waldauer Weg 92, 34253 Kassel-Lohfelden — Telefon 0561 / 970 57 0, Telefax 0561 / 970 57 50
Internet http://www.h-m.org — Email info@h-m.org

Ermittelte Referenzpatientendaten
CLASSISPRODUKT NEUPRODUKT CD3 HD ZVG CMD ZI

Ermittelte Referenzliste Leistungen inkl. Historie

Ermittelte KFO-Pläne

Gesamtanzahl KFO-Pläne

Quality and safety record: A4

Auftrag / Bestellung

H+M Systeme für Mediziner

H+M HighTec und Management Systemlösungen GmbH & Co. KG
In den Weiden 9, 99099 Erfurt — Telefon 0361 / 442 79 0, Telefax 0361 / 442 79 50
Waldauer Weg 92, 34253 Kassel-Lohfelden — Telefon 0561 / 970 57 0, Telefax 0561 / 970 57 50
Internet http://www.h-m.org — Email info@h-m.org

hiermit bestelle ich eine H+M-Schulung: Stunden inkl. Anfahrt zu folgenden Nettopreis
hiermit bestelle ich eine H+M-Schulung: Stunden inkl. Anfahrt zu folgenden Nettopreis

Commissions and orders: A4

Arbeitsauftrag

Systeme für Mediziner

A

PRAXISSTEMPEL

H+M HighTec und Management Systemlösungen GmbH & Co. KG

In den Weiden 9 99099 Erfurt	Telefon Telefax	0361 / 442 79 0 0361 / 442 79 50
Waldauer Weg 92 34253 Kassel-Lohfelden	Telefon Telefax	0561 / 970 57 0 0561 / 970 57 50
Internet Email	http://www.h-m.org info@h-m.org	

DATUM	AUSFÜHRENDER	VON	BIS	ARBEITSZEIT	WEGEZEIT	ZONE	KULANZ

GEGENSTAND / FEHLER

DURCHGEFÜHRTE TÄTIGKEIT

B G S

ERSATZTEILE / VERBRAUCHSMATERIAL

- ◯ Arbeit abgeschlossen (Anlage voll funktionsfähig übergeben)
- ◯ Arbeit nicht abgeschlossen
- ◯ Prüfung TG / G
- ◯ Verrechnungsscheck übergeben
- ◯ Einmaleinzugsermächtigung erteilt

DATUM	UNTERSCHRIFT

Es gelten unsere umseitigen Vertragsbedingungen.

Die erledigten Arbeiten wurden abgesprochen und abgenommen.

Commission for work to be done: A4

The layout always separates the head of the form from the content. This is practical when the form has to be folded.

Point Lighting

Order form

Issued by Point Einrichtungssysteme GmbH, Germany
Design Heine Warnecke Design GmbH, Hanover & Münsterland
Year 2006
Typeface BS Mandrax

A simple order form for light bulbs to be used in retail display cases. The prices and options are clearly laid out for the customer and the chosen typeface highlights the technical nature of the product range.

Order form: A4
One striking feature is the size and prominent position of the fax number.

Beschreibung & Artikelnummer	Bezüge je Jahr	Preis je VE	Anzahl VE Bitte eintragen
10 Stück [1 VE] 20 W Kaltlichtspiegel 1.500 Std. Leuchtdauer Ø 35 mm H-20-35-2000	1 x	19,80 €	
	2 x	12,90 €	
	4 x	12,90 €	
	6 x	12,26 €	
	12 x	12,26 €	
10 Stück [1 VE] 20 W Kaltlichtspiegel 1.500 Std. Leuchtdauer Ø 51 mm H-20-51-2000	1 x	19,80 €	
	2 x	12,90 €	
	4 x	12,90 €	
	6 x	12,26 €	
	12 x	12,26 €	
10 Stück [1 VE] 20 W Kaltlichtspiegel 5.000 Std. Leuchtdauer Ø 35 mm 823.39	1 x	19,80 €	
	2 x	12,90 €	
	4 x	12,90 €	
	6 x	12,26 €	
	12 x	12,26 €	
10 Stück [1 VE] 20 W Kaltlichtspiegel 5.000 Std. Leuchtdauer Ø 51 mm 823.59	1 x	19,80 €	
	2 x	12,90 €	
	4 x	12,90 €	
	6 x	12,26 €	
	12 x	12,26 €	
10 Stück [1 VE] 35 W Kaltlichtspiegel Spezialleuchtmittel für Schmuck – keine Farbveränderungen 42887560	1 x	19,80 €	
	2 x	12,90 €	
	4 x	12,90 €	
	6 x	12,26 €	
	12 x	12,26 €	
1 Stück [1 VE] 105 W Transformator 90691411	1 x	19,80 €	
	2 x	12,90 €	
	4 x	12,90 €	
	6 x	12,26 €	
	12 x	12,26 €	

Ich abonniere Licht
und kaufe meine Leuchtmittel so einfach & günstig wie noch nie!

Bitte liefern Sie mir ab sofort die nebenstehend eingetragenen Leuchtmittel bis auf Widerruf frei Haus. Ich akzeptiere die mir bekannten AGB der Point Einrichtungssysteme GmbH. Alle Preise verstehen sich netto zzgl. gesetzlicher Mehrwertsteuer. Die Konditionen gelten nur innerhalb Deutschlands.

Firma

Vorname Name

Straße Nummer

Plz Ort

Telefon

Telefax

E-Mail

Datum Unterschrift

Die Rechnungsbeträge ziehen Sie bitte bis auf Widerruf von folgendem Konto ein [beim Lichtabo ist keine andere Zahlungsweise möglich]:

Institut

Kontonummer

Bankleitzahl

Kontoinhaber

Datum Unterschrift

Point Einrichtungssysteme GmbH ... D-29699 Bomlitz-Uetzingen
Telefon +49. 5161. 9804. 0 ... www.point-pos.de

Fax +49. 5161. 9100. 03

Haberland Drinks Systems

	Order and delivery form
Issued by	Haberland Getränkesysteme GmbH, Germany
Design	Heine Warnecke Design GmbH, Hanover & Münsterland
Year	2005
Typefaces	LinoLetter, Neue Helvetica

This form for a company that sells and installs drinks machines has been designed with great attention to typographical detail, with an attractive mixture of serif and sans serif type.

Tel [040] 6524899 · Fax [040] 6524844
dialog@daslaeuft.com · *www.daslaeuft.com*

Lieferschein
Kundendienstauftrag

HABERLAND

Datum | Kundennr. | Auftrag erteilt durch Frau/Herrn
Automatennr. | Schlüsselnr. | Zählerstand

Haberland Getränkesysteme GmbH
Auf dem Königslande 45 a · D-22041 Hamburg

Artikelnummer | Menge | Bezeichnung

Störungsmeldung | Störungsbehebung

Die Arbeiten wurden ordnungsgemäß durchgeführt und anerkannt. Die Ware bleibt bis zur vollständigen Bezahlung unser Eigentum.

Anfahrtspauschale | gefahrene km | Arbeitszeit in Std. | von | bis
Datum | Unterschrift Monteur | Unterschrift Kunde

Geschäftsführer Martin & Stefan Haberland
HR Hamburg B 32831 · USt.Id-Nr. DE 118689993

Hamburger Sparkasse
Bankleitzahl 20050550 · Konto 1011214333

Customer service and delivery form: A4
The vertically positioned headings look good, save space and emphasize the margin.

Norton & Sons

Fitting sheet

Issued by	Norton & Sons, Savile Row, London
Design	Moving Brands, London
	Ben Wolstenholme, Mat Heinl, Karin Odin
Year	2007
Typeface	British Rail

This fitting sheet is designed to be filled in with the many measurements required for a bespoke suit. The yellow top sheet has two carbonless copies, one blue and one pink. While the original yellow sheet and the blue copy remain intact and go to the client and into the company's archive, the pink copy is divided up into separate 'tickets'. These are stitched to the individual garments of the bespoke suit after cutting, and sent to various trusted tailors in and around London's Savile Row. This ensures that the information is not lost as the piece travels around – some items are passed between several craftsmen. Once the garments are finished, they are sent back to the Norton & Sons shop. There, the tickets are all removed from the items and are then reassembled in their original form, like a jigsaw puzzle. This makes it easy to see that all necessary jobs have been completed and all garments returned.

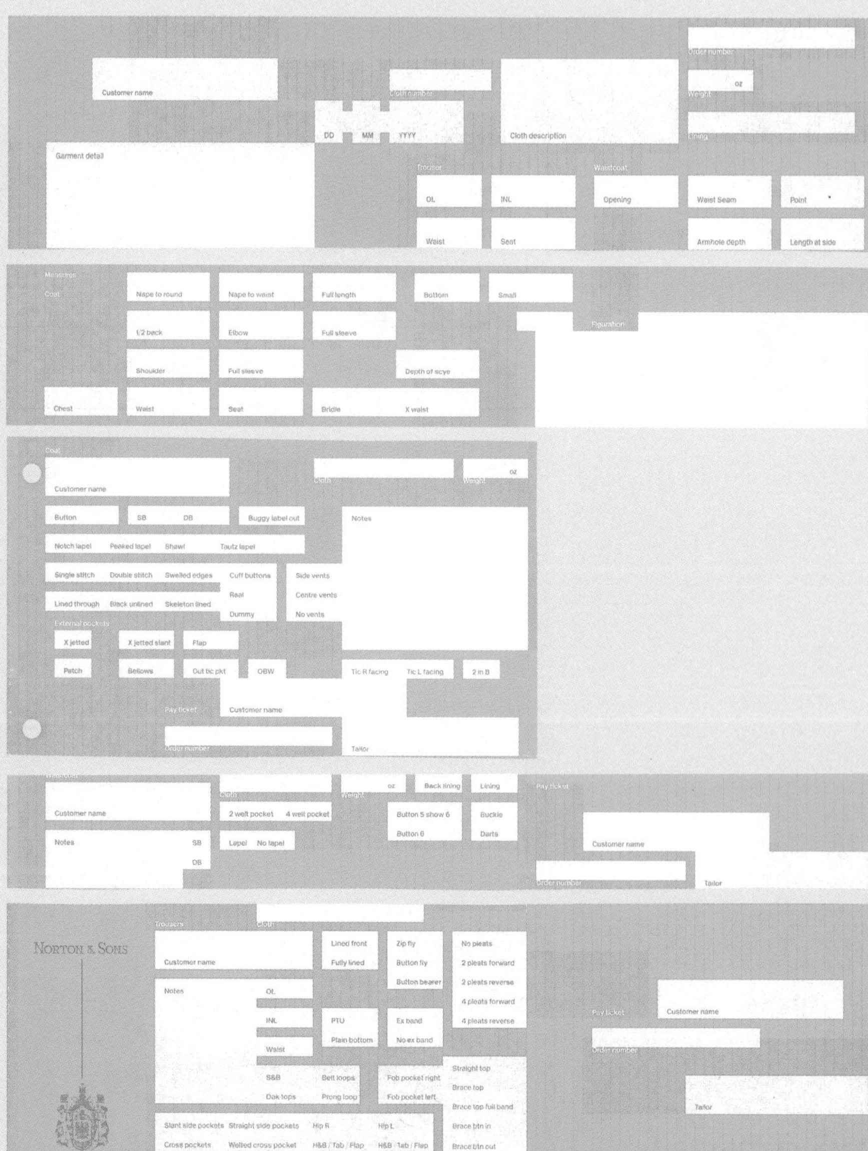
Order number
Customer name
Cloth number
oz
Weight
DD MM YYYY
Cloth description
Garment detail
Trouser
Waistcoat
OL
INL
Opening
Waist Seam
Point
Waist
Seat
Armhole depth
Length at side
Coat
Nape to round
Nape to waist
Full length
Bottom
Small
1/2 back
Elbow
Full sleeve
Figuration
Shoulder
Full sleeve
Depth of scye
Chest
Waist
Seat
Bridle
X waist
Coat
Customer name
Cloth
oz
Weight
Button
SB
DB
Buggy label out
Notes
Notch lapel
Peaked lapel
Shawl
Toutz lapel
Single stitch
Double stitch
Swelled edges
Cuff buttons
Side vents
Real
Centre vents
Lined through
Black unlined
Skeleton lined
Dummy
No vents
External pockets
X jetted
X jetted slant
Flap
Patch
Bellows
Out tic pkt
OBW
Tic R facing
Tic L facing
2 in B
Pay ticket
Customer name
Order number
Tailor
Waistcoat
Customer name
Cloth
2 welt pocket
4 welt pocket
oz
Weight
Back lining
Lining
Pay ticket
Button 5 show 6
Buckle
Button 6
Darts
Notes
SB
DB
Lapel
No lapel
Customer name
Order number
Tailor
Norton & Sons
Trousers
Cloth
Customer name
Lined front
Fully lined
Zip fly
Button fly
Button bearer
No pleats
2 pleats forward
2 pleats reverse
4 pleats forward
4 pleats reverse
Notes
OL
INL
PTU
Plain bottom
Ex band
No ex band
Waist
S&B
Belt loops
Fob pocket right
Straight top
Dok tops
Prong loop
Fob pocket left
Brace top
Brace top full band
Slant side pockets
Straight side pockets
Hip R
Hip L
Brace btn in
Cross pockets
Welted cross pocket
H&B / Tab / Flap
H&B / Tab / Flap
Brace btn out
Brace btn on tab
Pay ticket
Customer name
Order number
Tailor

Fitting sheet divided into 'tickets'
Each ticket represents and refers to a different element of the suit (trousers, jacket, waistcoat). Once the measurements have been taken and the cloth cut, the garments are sent to various tailors and finishers in and around Savile Row in the West End of London.

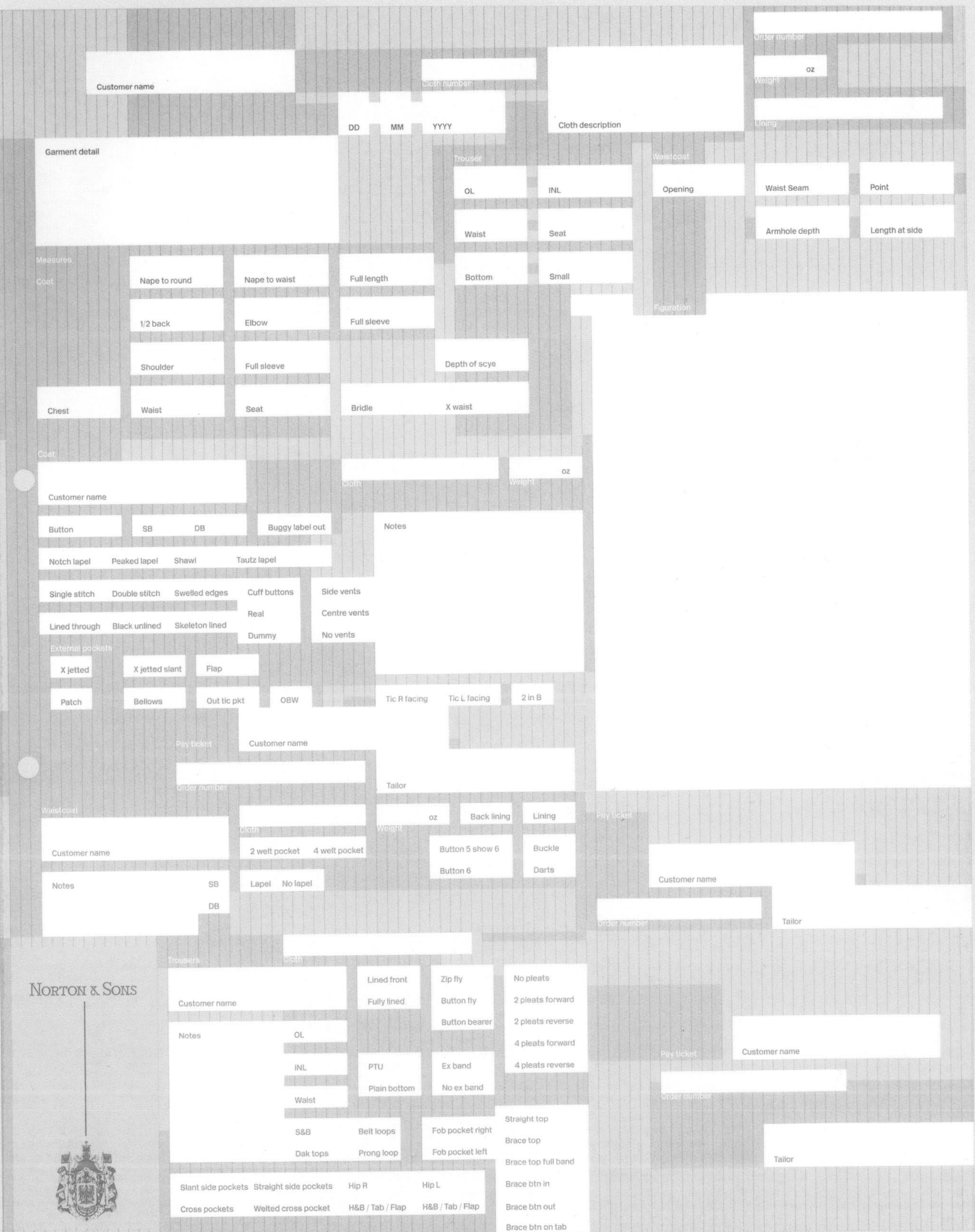
Order number
oz
Weight
Lining
Customer name
Cloth number
DD MM YYYY
Cloth description
Garment detail
Trouser
OL INL
Waist Seat
Bottom Small
Waistcoat
Opening
Waist Seam
Point
Armhole depth
Length at side
Figuration
Measures
Coat
Nape to round
Nape to waist
Full length
1/2 back
Elbow
Full sleeve
Shoulder
Full sleeve
Depth of scye
Chest
Waist
Seat
Bridle
X waist
Coat
Customer name
Cloth
Weight
oz
Button
SB DB
Buggy label out
Notes
Notch lapel Peaked lapel Shawl Tautz lapel
Single stitch Double stitch Swelled edges
Cuff buttons Real Dummy
Side vents Centre vents No vents
Lined through Black unlined Skeleton lined
External pockets
X jetted X jetted slant Flap
Patch Bellows Out tic pkt OBW
Tic R facing Tic L facing 2 in B
Pay ticket
Customer name
Order number
Tailor
Waistcoat
Customer name
Cloth
Weight
oz
Back lining Lining
2 welt pocket 4 welt pocket
Button 5 show 6 Button 6
Buckle Darts
Notes SB DB
Lapel No lapel
Pay ticket
Customer name
Order number
Tailor
NORTON & SONS
Trousers
Cloth
Customer name
Lined front Fully lined
Zip fly Button fly Button bearer
No pleats 2 pleats forward 2 pleats reverse 4 pleats forward 4 pleats reverse
Notes
OL INL Waist
PTU Plain bottom
Ex band No ex band
S&B Dak tops
Belt loops Prong loop
Fob pocket right Fob pocket left
Straight top Brace top Brace top full band Brace btn in Brace btn out Brace btn on tab
Slant side pockets Straight side pockets Hip R Hip L
Cross pockets Welted cross pocket H&B / Tab / Flap H&B / Tab / Flap
Pay ticket
Customer name
Order number
Tailor

Fitting sheet: 280 x 340 mm

The design of the fitting sheet was informed by the process of tailoring itself. This process involves huge amounts of skilled craftsmanship to create complex patterns and structures that lie below the surface of the garments. The various cloths, linings and structural fabrics are reflected in the layered, blocky and multicoloured layout of the fitting sheet.

Heinze Light and Lifestyle

Order form

Issued by	Heinze GmbH, Germany
Design	Hesse Design GmbH, Erkrath
Year	2003
Typeface	Frutiger

This order form for a manufacturer of lighting and home accessories reflects their product range, combining subtle stylishness with efficiency and functionality.

Fax order form: A4

As one of the most important items of information, the fax number is clearly positioned at the top. The oblong form of the checkboxes is the only slight irritant.

Licht und Wohnkultur

heinze

Bestellung
+49 (0)202. 24 25 7-12. Fax

01 Kundenangaben

Kundennummer | Firma | Einkäufer
Straße | Plz. Ort | Fon
Fax | E-Mail | USt.-Identnummer

02 Bestellung

	Artikel	Kurzbezeichnung	Menge	EK per Stück €*	EK gesamt €*
A					
B					
C					
D					
E					
F					
G					
H					
I					
J					

*zzgl. MwSt.

Lieferung ab € 500,00 netto frei Haus darunter zzgl. 4 % für Fracht und Verpackung, mindestens € 6,00 (BRD).

Summe netto*
Fracht netto*
Gesamt netto*

03 Lieferanschrift

Firma | Straße | Plz. Ort

04 Wir bezahlen

☐ **Per Lastschriftverfahren** 10 Tage 3 % Skonto
☐ **Per Lastschriftverfahren** 1 Tag 5 % Skonto

Konto | Blz | Bank | Ort

☐ **Per Rechnung** innerhalb 8 Tagen 2 % Skonto, 30 Tagen netto
☐ **Per Nachnahme** mit 3 % Skonto
☐ **Per Vorkasse** nach Proforma Rechnung mit 3 % Skonto

☐ **Über Einkaufsverband** | Verband | Mitgliedsnummer

Ort. Datum | **Unterschrift**

05 Wird von Heinze ausgefüllt

KGR | VNR

Culture Object

Order and receipt

Issued by	Culture Object, Germany
Design	mikan, Mariko Takagi, Düsseldorf
Year	2006
Typeface	Thesis TheSans

Culture Object is a design gallery in Berlin. Their order form matches the brand identity in its clarity and minimalism, though the little circle motif adds a playful element.

「 」。

order ｡ receipt

date:

total:

tax:

amount:

sign:

culture
object.

owner-manager: prof. holger jahn ｡ linienstraße 127 ｡ 10115 berlin ｡ germany
www.culture-object.com ｡ mail@culture-object.com ｡ t: +49. 30. 53 00 06-30 ｡ f: +49. 30. 53 00 06-33
baden-württembergische bank ｡ blz 600 501 01 ｡ kto 12 66 702 ｡ iban de42 6005 0101 0001 266702
swift-code sola de st ｡ tax number: 14/362/60059 ｡ vat no. de 157 483 716

Order form and receipt: A4
The central table has no heading, because the content can speak for itself.

The Colourhouse

Business forms

Issued by	The Colourhouse, UK
Design	SEA Design, London
Year	2009
Typeface	Akzidenz Grotesk

In keeping with the name of this printing firm, each of its business forms is printed in a different colour. The result is that the forms have a refreshingly bright and friendly appearance. The individual documents are visually linked by a consistent but flexible layout that reflects the shapes of the company logo. The forms shown here are part of a comprehensive rebranding project.

Date
A/C Reference
Page
Statement To

Printed by
The Colourhouse

Date | Reference | Details | Debit | Credit

Current | 30 Day | 60 Day | 90 Day | 120+ Day

The Colourhouse
Arklow Road Trading Estate
Arklow Road
London SE14 6EB

+44 (0)20 8305 8305
sales@thecolourhouse.com
thecolourhouse.com

The Colourhouse Ltd
Registered in England
number 2803142

VAT number 626 4044 56

Amount Due

Date
A/C Reference
Page
Remittance Advice From

Date | Details | Debit | Credit

The Colourhouse
Arklow Road Trading Estate
Arklow Road
London SE14 6EB

+44 (0)20 8305 8305
sales@thecolourhouse.com
thecolourhouse.com

The Colourhouse Ltd
Registered in England
number 2803142

VAT number 626 4044 56

Amount Due

Statement: A4

To

Printed by
The Colourhouse

Date

Job Number

Quantity

Pallet Number

The Colourhouse
Arklow Road Trading Estate
Arklow Road
London SE14 6EB

+44 (0)20 8305 8305
sales@thecolourhouse.com
thecolourhouse.com

The Colourhouse Ltd
Registered in England
number 2803142

Pallet label: A4

Job Number
Order Number
Delivery Note Number
Departure Date
Delivery Contact

Printed by
The Colourhouse

Please Collect

THE COL OUR HOU SE

Arrival Details
Signature
Departure Time
Print
Arrival Time
Driver
Waiting Time
Return to Colourhouse

The Colourhouse
Arklow Road Trading Estate
Arklow Road
London SE14 6EB

+44 (0)20 8305 8305
sales@thecolourhouse.com
thecolourhouse.com

The Colourhouse Ltd
Registered in England
number 2803142

FSC PEFC

Collection note: A4

Delivery Note
Job Number
Order Number
Delivery Note Number
Departure Date
Booking In Reference
Client Contact

Printed by
The Colourhouse

Please Recieve

THE COL OUR HOU SE

Arrival Details – White copy to Client / Blue copy to Despatch / Pink copy to Job
Signature
Departure Time
Print
Arrival Time
Driver
Waiting Time
Return to Colourhouse

The Colourhouse
Arklow Road Trading Estate
Arklow Road
London SE14 6EB

+44 (0)20 8305 8305
sales@thecolourhouse.com
thecolourhouse.com

The Colourhouse Ltd
Registered in England
number 2803142

FSC PEFC

Delivery note: A4

Invoice Number
Invoice Date
Order Number
Reference Number
Sales Contact

Printed by
The Colourhouse

Job Number	Description	Quantity	Cost/(VAT)

THE COL OUR HOU SE

The Colourhouse
Arklow Road Trading Estate
Arklow Road
London SE14 6EB

+44 (0)20 8305 8305
sales@thecolourhouse.com
thecolourhouse.com

The Colourhouse Ltd
Registered in England
number 2803142

VAT number 626 4044 56

Any queries relating to this invoice/job should be notified to The Colourhouse within 7 days of receipt of this invoice.

The Exporter of the Products covered by this document declares that, except where otherwise clearly indicated, this product is of EC preferential origin.

e+oe terms strictly 30 days net.

Goods Total
(VAT Total)
Invoice Total

FSC PEFC

Invoice: A4

Using the same basic layout, each document has its own particular arrangement of the individual elements.

Supply Note
Our Reference
Telephone/Fax
Departure Date

Printed by
The Colourhouse

Quantity	Description	Units	Price	Value

THE COL OUR HOU SE

The Colourhouse
Arklow Road Trading Estate
Arklow Road
London SE14 6EB

+44 (0)20 8305 8305
sales@thecolourhouse.com
thecolourhouse.com

The Colourhouse Ltd
Registered in England
number 2803142

VAT number 626 4044 56

Please note: It is important you have a purchase order for all costs, including any additional incurred costs such as extra out turns, deliveries etc.

If your invoice does not correspond exactly to the value of our purchase order, it will not be posted and will be returned to you.

Total Value (excluding VAT)
Authorised by

FSC PEFC

Purchase order: A4

bueroboss.de

Registration and order forms

Issued by	bueroboss.de
Design	Heine Warnecke Design GmbH, Hanover & Münsterland
Year	2003
Typeface	Officina

bueroboss.de is an association of several office equipment suppliers working under a single brand name and sharing the same customer forms. The carefully designed forms convey an impression of reliability, precision and professionalism, and therefore help to boost customer confidence in the efficiency of the service.

ine Auslieferung des
ine Gebühr in Höhe von €

chriftlich ja nein
elefonisch ja nein
ja nein

Checkboxes

This is probably the most ergonomic design for ticking: two right-angled lines at the top and left, while the bottom right is left open. The angle shows users exactly where to put the pen.

→ Multiple choice questions: page 178

Herzlich Willkommen Free Fax 0 800-92 99-100

bueroboss.de
/kissing-risse

Kissing & Risse Bürocenter GmbH & Co. KG // Iserlohner Landstraße 9 // 58706 Menden
Tel 0 23 73-92 99-0 // Fax 0 23 73-92 99-99 // kissing-risse@bueroboss.de

Kundenkontonr.

Branche

Firma, Rechtsform

Straße

Plz, Ort, Ortsteil

Webadresse

Geschäftsführer/in

Ansprechpartner/in Abteilung

Telefon Fax

E-Mail

Bitte übersenden Sie aktuelle Informationen und Angebote an oben angebene E-Mail-Adresse.

Anzahl Mitarbeiter/innen

Anzahl Büroarbeitsplätze

Bürobedarfsumsatz ca. pro Jahr in €

Lieferung an Firma

Frau/Herr Abteilung

Straße

Plz, Ort

Telefon Fax

E-Mail

Wir freuen uns, Sie in unserem Kundenkreis zu begrüßen. Damit unsere Zusammenarbeit möglichst erfolgreich und unkompliziert für Sie verläuft, bitten wir Sie, nebenstehende Angaben zu machen. Danach richten wir Ihr Kundenkonto ein. So profitieren Sie ab sofort von unseren starken Leistungen:

- Bundesweiter 24-Stunden-Lieferservice
- Komplettlieferung
- Frei-Haus-Lieferungen ab einem Warenwert von € 40,—

- 7.500 Lagerartikel/50.000 Beschaffungsartikel
- Breites Sortiment mit günstigen Markenartikeln und preiswerten Produkt-Alternativen

- Offener Webshop
- Integrative E-Procurement-Lösungen
- Kostenstellengerechte Belieferung und Abrechnung

- Feste Ansprechpartner mit hoher Beratungskompetenz
- Beratungstermine zur Produkt- und Prozessoptimierung in Ihrem Haus
- Einfacher und schneller Warenumtausch

- Technischer Kundendienst für Ihre Bürotechnik
- Büroeinrichtungen per CAD-Planung
- Verschiedene Finanzierungsmöglichkeiten für Investitionsgüter

Ich will Zeit und Geld sparen (2% Skonto). Hiermit ermächtige(n) ich/wir die Kissing & Risse Bürocenter GmbH & Co. KG, bis auf Widerruf alle offenen Rechnungen mittels Lastschriftverfahren einzuziehen.

Bank

Bankleitzahl Kontonummer

Datum, Unterschrift für Einzugsermächtigung

Die AGB der Kissing & Risse Bürocenter GmbH & Co. KG sind mir ausgehändigt worden und Grundlage der beiderseitigen Geschäftsbeziehungen.

Name des Vertragspartners

Datum, Unterschrift, Stempel des Vertragspartners

Client registration form: A4

Ihre Bestellung Free Fax 0 800-07 70-017

bueroboss.de
/giegler

Jean Giegler KG // Friedrich-Gauß-Straße 1 // 97424 Schweinfurt
Tel 0 97 21-77 00-0 // Fax 0 97 21-77 00-17 // giegler@bueroboss.de

Kundennr. Ihre Referenz

Rechnung an Firma

Frau/Herr Abteilung

Straße

Plz, Ort

Telefon Fax

E-Mail

Lieferung an Firma (falls abweichend)

Frau/Herr Abteilung

Straße

Plz, Ort

Telefon Fax

E-Mail

Anzahl	Artikelnummer	Artikelbeschreibung	Einzel €	Gesamt €
		Gesamt netto zzgl. ges. MwSt.		

Geld sparen – im Lastschriftverfahren!

Ich will Zeit und Geld sparen (2% Skonto). Hiermit ermächtige(n) ich/wir die Firma Giegler, bis auf Widerruf alle offenen Rechnungen mittels Lastschriftverfahren einzuziehen.

Bank

Bankleitzahl Kontonummer

Datum, Unterschrift für Einzugsermächtigung

Zahlungsweise

Ab einem Warenwert von € 39,— ist die Lieferung porto- und frachtfrei innerhalb Deutschlands. Alle Preise verstehen sich zuzüglich der gesetzlichen Mehrwertsteuer. Bitte ankreuzen:

Lieferung gegen Rechnung. Schade, Sie verschenken 2% Skonto.

Lieferung gegen Einzugsermächtigung. Sie sparen 2% Skonto! Bitte auch links ausfüllen.

Name des Bestellers

Datum, Unterschrift für Bestellung

Order form: A4

Reparaturauftrag

bueroboss.de
/kassebeer

Wilh. F. Kassebeer GmbH & Co. KG // Matthias-Grünewald-Straße 42 // 37154 Northeim
Tel 0 55 51-963-187 // Fax 0 55 51-963-157 // kassebeer@bueroboss.de

Kundennr. | Ihre Referenz | Abgabeort | Abholort

Rechnung an Firma | Maschine | Nummer

Frau/Herr | Abteilung | Modell | Zählerstand

Straße | Zubehör

Plz, Ort

Telefon | Fax | ☐ Wartung | ☐ Reparatur

E-Mail | ☐

Fehlerbeschreibung

Sie wünschen einen Kostenvoranschlag?
Für die Erstellung berechnen wir eine Pauschale in Höhe von € 15,—. Im Reparaturfall erfolgt keine Berechnung! Reparaturen bis zu einem Betrag von € 25,— werden ohne vorherigen Kostenvoranschlag durchgeführt.

Sie wünschen eine Auslieferung des reparierten/gewarteten Gerätes?
Wir berechnen eine Gebühr in Höhe von € 12,—.

Kostenvoranschlag schriftlich ☐ ja ☐ nein

Kostenvoranschlag telefonisch ☐ ja ☐ nein

Auslieferung ☐ ja ☐ nein

Garantie ☐ ja ☐ nein

Garantiebeleg als Anlage ☐ ja ☐ nein

Anmerkungen

angenommen durch

Name des Vertragspartners

Datum, Unterschrift

Repair form: A4
A two-column layout is used, but where necessary, the text fields extend across both columns.

Foster + Partners

External and internal forms

Issued by Foster + Partners, UK
Design Thomas Manss & Company, London
Year 2006
Typeface Akzidenz Grotesk

When designing an identity for the famous architectural firm of Foster + Partners, Thomas Manss also produced forms for internal and external use. They developed a coherent system that distinguished clearly between the two types. Those for external use are in portrait format, and can be sent out like an ordinary letter, whereas in-house forms are in landscape format, because they are increasingly completed on screen. The design is also very clear-cut, with plenty of white space.

Two internal forms: A4

The landscape format is easier to work with on screen.

Monthly expenses

Foster + Partners

Month

Name

Authoriser's name

Signature

Authoriser's signature

Date	Voucher no.	Description	Job no.	Recoverable Yes	Recoverable No	Total	Net	VAT	N/L account no.	Sub account no.	Cost centre	Sub cost centre
		Total to be reimbursed										

NB: Please refer to company policy on the intranet under the accounts section

Receipts must be pasted flat onto sheets of A4 paper

Cheque no.

Book

Travel request 351

Group no.

Foster + Partners

Please note that all sections are mandatory – the booking will only be processed when all sections are completed and authorised. Please forward this travel request form to your Group Leader, Deputy Leader and Senior PA.

Passenger

Project name

Project no.

Travel type Air Rail

Travel policies Policy A Policy B

Fare type: Business class; Discounted business class; World traveller plus; Economy fully flexible; Economy restr out/flex back; Economy restricted; Cheapest incl. low cost

Request type New Revision

Job no.

Percent of cost %

Flight: Out bound / In bound

Date required

Time (24hrs)

From

To

Hotel

Additional information

Changes to booking affecting travel policy and/or costs

Authoriser's signature Date

Coordinator's signature Date

Remittance Advice

Foster + Partners

AN Other Company
AN Other Payment Centre
Town
AA11 2BB

Date 18/08/06
Supplier XX123
Cheque no. 12345

Invoice date	**Invoice/credit note no.**	**Details**	**Gross amount**
25/07/06	INV VP123456789	123456	000.00

Cheque enclosed 000.00

Foster + Partners Ltd
Riverside, 22 Hester Road
London SW11 4AN
T +44 (0)20 7738 0455
F +44 (0)20 7738 1107

Foster + Partners Ltd

AN Other Bank
00 Road London XX0 0XX

00-00-00
123456: 12345678

Date 18 Aug 2006

Pay British Telecommunications PLC

Millions	Hundreds Thousands	Ten Thousands	Thousands	Hundreds	Tens	Units	Pence
Zero	Zero	Zero	Zero	Zero	Zero	Zero	00

Amount of Pounds in words – Pence in figures

Account payee only

£ ***********000.00

For and on behalf of
Foster + Partners Ltd

123456 123456: 12345678

External remittance form: A4

Clever use of bold and light type, together with two different line weights, gives the page a very clear structure.

Dr Paul F. Showers, Endodontics

Patient communication forms

Issued by	Paul F. Showers DDS MS PC, USA
Design	Studio/lab, Chicago
Year	2001
Typeface	Adobe Garamond

The relationship between doctor and patient is partly influenced by the means of communication employed by the doctor. Letterheads and forms should therefore meet the same standards demanded of the doctor. They should be as friendly, professional, comforting and clear as these forms, designed for a dentist who specializes in endodontics (root canal work).

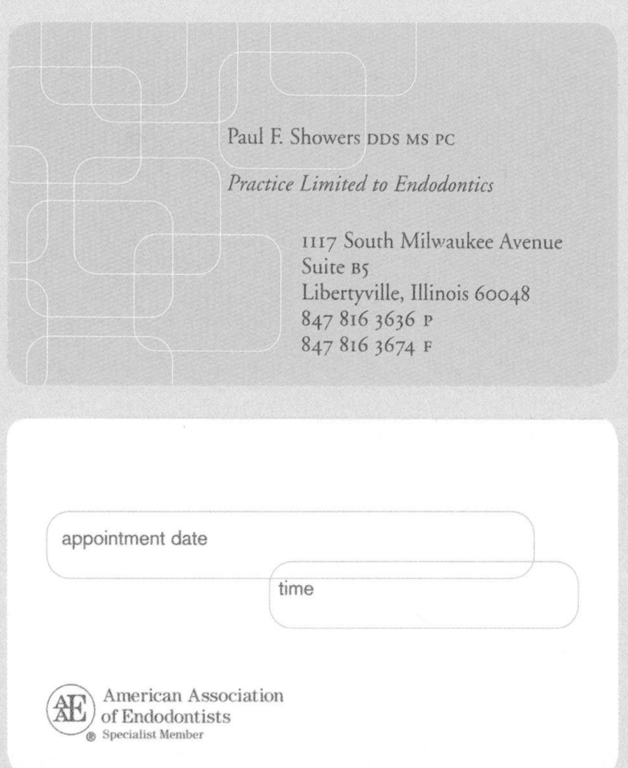

Paul F. Showers DDS MS PC

Practice Limited to Endodontics

1117 South Milwaukee Avenue
Suite B5
Libertyville, Illinois 60048
847 816 3636 P
847 816 3674 F

appointment date

time

American Association of Endodontists
Specialist Member

Front and back of appointment card: 89 × 51 mm

The design discreetly echoes the rounded corners of X-rays, the pink of healthy gums, and the silver of surgical instruments.

Paul F. Showers DDS MS PC

Practice Limited to Endodontics

1117 South Milwaukee Avenue
Suite B5
Libertyville, Illinois 60048
847 816 3636

patient

date

The following treatment plan has been determined:

- ☐ apexification
- ☐ endodontic therapy of tooth number ______
- ☐ retreatment on tooth number ______
- ☐ endodontic surgery on tooth number ______

other considerations

Dear Dr.

I would like to thank you for referring your patient to our office for endodontic care. We strive to serve you and your patient in the best ways we can.

Sincerely,

Paul F. Showers, DDS MS PC

Referral follow-up card: 92 × 184 mm

The documents are in pink and silver, printed on high-quality paper.

Paul F. Showers DDS MS PC

Practice Limited to Endodontics

1117 South Milwaukee Avenue
Suite B5
Libertyville, Illinois 60048
847 816 3636

introducing

date

- [ ] for consultation on
- [ ] for endodontic therapy
- [ ] for retreatment
- [ ] for endodontic surgery

patient's right side								patient's left side							
1	2	3	4	5	6	7	8	9	10	11	12	13	14	15	16
32	31	30	29	28	27	26	25	24	23	22	21	20	19	18	17

comments

Dr.

- [ ] post room
- [ ] please call

Referral form:
A4
Interlocking or overlapping shapes are a subtle but clear way of uniting items that belong together.

Dr Konik, Orthodontist

Medical forms

Issued by	Dr Michael Konik
Design	cyclos design GmbH, Münster, Germany
Year	2006
Typeface	Dax

Instead of using standard, ready-made forms, this orthodontist has opted for individually and attractively designed prescriptions, certificates and appointment cards. They indicate the dentist's speciality, make a friendly impression, and are instantly recognizable.

Dr. med. dent. Michael Konik
Fachzahnarzt für Kieferorthopädie
Tätigkeitsschwerpunkte:
› Ganzheitliche Kieferorthopädie
› Erwachsenen-Kieferorthopädie

Dr. med. dent. Constanze Korz
Dr. med. dent. Ricarda Läuger
Dr. med. dent. Ilana Weisz
Zahnärzte. Tätigkeitsschwerpunkt:
› Kieferorthopädie

Strümpfelbacher Straße 21
71384 Weinstadt-Endersbach
Telefon 07151.969 40-0
Telefon 0700.DIESPANGE
Telefax 07151.969 40-40

Weinstadt, den

Rp.

Prescription: A6

www.konik.de

Dr. med. dent. Michael Konik
Fachzahnarzt für Kieferorthopädie
Tätigkeitsschwerpunkte:
› Ganzheitliche Kieferorthopädie
› Erwachsenen-Kieferorthopädie

und Kollegen

Strümpfelbacher Straße 21
71384 Weinstadt-Endersbach
Telefon 07151.969 40-0
Telefon 0700.DIESPANGE
Telefax 07151.969 40-40

Bescheinigung
über Sprechstundenbesuch

Angaben zum Patienten/zur Patientin

Name ....

Vorname ....

Geb.-Datum ....

Der Patient/Die Patientin befand sich

am ....

von .... bis .... Uhr

in unserer Sprechstunde

Certificate: A6

The telephone number is prominent, since that is the most important piece of contact information.

www.konik.de

Dr. med. dent. Michael Konik
Fachzahnarzt für Kieferorthopädie
Tätigkeitsschwerpunkte:
› Ganzheitliche Kieferorthopädie
› Erwachsenen-Kieferorthopädie

und Kollegen

Strümpfelbacher Straße 21
71384 Weinstadt-Endersbach
Telefon 07151.969 40-0
Telefon 0700.DIESPANGE
Telefax 07151.969 40-40

Wir sehen uns wieder:

Tag: ☐ MO ☐ DI ☐ MI ☐ DO ☐ FR ☐ SA

den: ....

um: ....

Ganzheitliche Zahn- und Kieferregulierungen für Kinder und Erwachsene

Appointment card: A7

Dr Kleinknecht, Dentist

Registration form

Issued by	Dr Peter Kleinknecht
Design	Andi Hemm Design, Filderstadt, Germany
Year	2000
Typeface	Quay Sans

Doctors and dentists are not part of an anonymous service industry – they are people who have personal relationships with their clients. It's therefore only right and proper that their own unmistakable identity should be reflected in personalized forms of communication.

Anmeldebogen

Dr. Peter Kleinknecht
Zahnarzt
Im Beundle 2
71540 Murrhardt
Telefon 0 71 92.90 95 00
Telefax 0 71 92.90 95 02

Patientendaten

Name
Straße
PLZ/Ort
Telefon privat
Geburtsdatum
Krankenkasse
Beruf
Arbeitgeber
Straße
PLZ/Ort
Telefon gesch.

Versicherter

Name
Straße
PLZ/Ort
Geburtsdatum

Bitte beantworten Sie uns folgende Fragen

Ja Nein **Herz-/Kreislauferkrankungen:**
Bluthochdruck
Herzklappenfehler
Herzklappenersatz
Herzschrittmacher
Endokarditis
Herzoperation

Infektiöse Erkrankungen:
AIDS
Hepatitis
Tuberkulose

Allergien bzw. Unverträglichkeiten:
Lokalanästhesie/Spritzen
Schmerzmittel
Metalle:
Sonstige:

Ja Nein **Sonstige Leiden:**
Anfallsleiden (Epilepsie)
Asthma/Lungenerkrankungen
Blutgerinnungsstörungen:
Diabetes/Zuckerkrankheit
Drogenabhängigkeit
Nierenerkrankungen
Ohnmacht
Sonstige Erkrankungen:

Besteht eine Schwangerschaft?
Wenn ja, welcher Monat?

Sind bei Ihnen bereits zahnärztliche Röntgenaufnahmen gemacht worden?
Wenn ja, wann?

Welche Medikamente nehmen Sie regelmäßig bzw. zur Zeit?

Hausarzt

Ich verpflichte mich, alle Änderungen, die während der gesamten Behandlungszeit auftreten, umgehend mitzuteilen. Desweiteren verpflichte ich mich, vereinbarte Termine einzuhalten bzw. mindestens 2 Tage vorher abzusagen. Nicht rechtzeitig abgesagte Termine können in Rechnung gestellt werden. Ich erkläre mich mit der elektronischen Speicherung und Bearbeitung meiner Daten einverstanden.

Ort, Datum

Unterschrift

Bitte beantworten
Ja Nein **Herz-/Kre**
Bluthochdr
Herzklappe
Herzklappe
Herzschritt
Endokardit
Herzoperat

Yes/No

The No boxes could have been omitted, but it's safer to offer both answers. If there are only Yes boxes, a blank might mean *no* but it might also mean *don't know*. Another advantage is that it's immediately apparent if the user has missed out a question. The disadvantage is that it takes a little longer to fill in.

→ Multiple choice questions: page 179

Patient registration form: A4

Schloss Neubeuern

Boarding school admission form

Issued by	Schloss Neubeuern, Germany, boarding school for girls and boys
Design	Team Peter M. Scholz (formerly Agentur Fischer & Scholz, Corporate Communication), Berlin
Year	1998
Typeface	Scala Sans

As only a few forms are needed each year, and in order that the school can make changes to the contract at any time, the form is produced entirely in Microsoft Word. This proves that even using Word alone, it's possible to create well-designed forms.

Contract: A4
First page of a seven-page form, which looks very compact due to its two-column layout. The wide margin prevents it from looking too squashed.

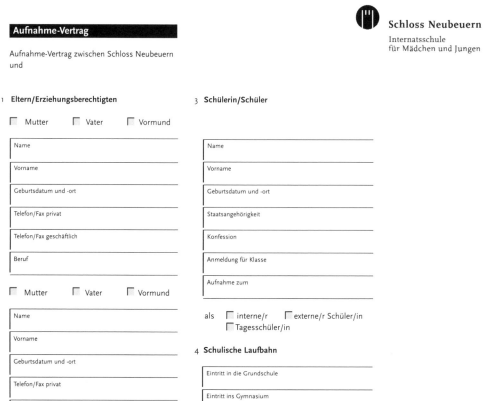

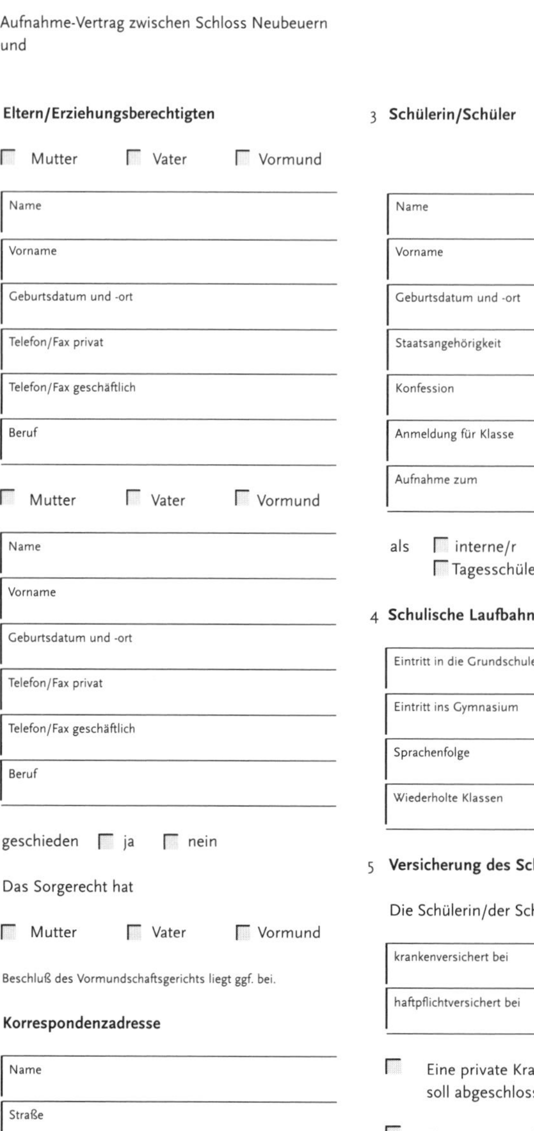

Aufnahme-Vertrag

Aufnahme-Vertrag zwischen Schloss Neubeuern
und

1 **Eltern/Erziehungsberechtigten**

☐ Mutter ☐ Vater ☐ Vormund

Name
Vorname
Geburtsdatum und -ort
Telefon/Fax privat
Telefon/Fax geschäftlich
Beruf

☐ Mutter ☐ Vater ☐ Vormund

Name
Vorname
Geburtsdatum und -ort
Telefon/Fax privat
Telefon/Fax geschäftlich
Beruf

geschieden ☐ ja ☐ nein

Das Sorgerecht hat

☐ Mutter ☐ Vater ☐ Vormund

Beschluß des Vormundschaftsgerichts liegt ggf. bei.

2 **Korrespondenzadresse**

Name
Straße
Ort

3 **Schülerin/Schüler**

Name
Vorname
Geburtsdatum und -ort
Staatsangehörigkeit
Konfession
Anmeldung für Klasse
Aufnahme zum

als ☐ interne/r ☐ externe/r Schüler/in
☐ Tagesschüler/in

4 **Schulische Laufbahn**

Eintritt in die Grundschule
Eintritt ins Gymnasium
Sprachenfolge
Wiederholte Klassen

5 **Versicherung des Schülers**

Die Schülerin/der Schüler ist wie folgt versichert:

krankenversichert bei
haftpflichtversichert bei

☐ Eine private Krankenversicherung soll abgeschlossen werden.

☐ Eine private Haftpflichtversicherung soll abgeschlossen werden.

Original zurück an Absender

Aufnahme-Vertrag 1|7

Centre Pompidou

Annual season ticket

Issued by	Centre Pompidou, Paris, France
Design	Atelier de Création Graphique, Paris
Year	2005
Typefaces	FF DIN, DIN Engschrift

The application form for an annual season ticket to the Centre Pompidou is especially pleasing to the eye because of its unusually bold use of colour.

LE LAISSEZ-PASSER

Pour souscrire 2 possibilités :
• sur place à l'espace Laissez-passer
La présence du titulaire est indispensable. Vous serez pris en photo.
• ou par courrier
Joindre obligatoirement votre photo et votre chèque
à l'ordre de L'Agent comptable du Centre Pompidou.
Centre Pompidou
DAEP - Service des relations avec les publics
75191 Paris cedex 04
Prévoir un délai de 21 jours maximum.

M ○ MME ○ MLLE ○

NOM DATE DE NAISSANCE
PRÉNOM TÉLÉPHONE
ADRESSE **E.MAIL**
(obligatoire pour recevoir les informations)

inscription par courrier Coller ici votre photo découpée aux dimensions du cadre

CODE POSTAL VILLE

Acceptez-vous que votre photo soit conservée sous forme électronique pendant la durée de votre abonnement ? oui ○ non ○
Acceptez-vous de recevoir des offres d'organismes culturels recommandés par le Centre Pompidou ? oui ○ non ○

LE LAISSEZ-PASSER est valable 12 mois (24 pour la formule 2 ans)

Pour tout tarif réduit, un justificatif est indispensable (photocopie pour les demandes par courrier)

INDIVIDUEL	[CI]	44€ ○
INDIVIDUEL 2 ANS	[CX]	70€ ○
DUO «INVITÉ», (**UNE** carte permettant au titulaire de venir accompagné d'une personne)	[CID]	70€ ○
SENIOR (+ de 60 ans, carte d'identité)	[CS]	35€ ○
ARTISTE (Maison des artistes, SACD et Agessa)	[CA]	35€ ○
ENSEIGNANT (certificat d'exercice année en cours)	[CE]	35€ ○
ÉTUDIANT (carte d'étudiant en cours) ou MOINS DE 26 ANS (carte d'identité)	[CJ]	22€ ○
COLLECTIVITÉS	[CG]	35€ ○

nom du CE cachet du CE
nom du contact
adresse complète

RÉABONNEMENT : tarifs appliqués exclusivement avant l'échéance de votre carte

INDIVIDUEL	[CIR]	35€ ○
DUO «INVITÉ» (pour tous les adhérents, quel que soit le type d'adhésion)	[CIRD]	55€ ○

Autres formules : Tarifs inchangés

En cas de perte ou de vol, un duplicata payant sera délivré à l'espace Laissez-passer [CDP] [CDDP] [CDXP] 11€ ○

Tarifs valables du 1er septembre 2005 au 31 août 2006. Aucun changement de formule ne sera accepté après paiement
Conformément à la loi informatique et libertés du 6 janvier 1978, vous disposez d'un droit d'accès et de rectification aux informations vous concernant.

Season ticket order form, back and front: A4

The circular checkboxes come after the options. Although this is relatively unusual, it works here because the spaces between answers are fairly wide.

→ Multiple choice questions: page 180

Corporate Design Award

Posters with registration forms

Issued by	Grafische Cultuurstichting, Netherlands
Design	Samenwerkende Ontwerpers bv, Amsterdam
Years	2003, 2005, 2007
Typefaces	Franklin Gothic (2003), Neuzeit Grotesk (2005), Folio (2007)

Three posters for the Dutch Corporate Design Award, showing how neatly a form can be integrated into a design concept that changes from year to year. The categories on the form always stay the same, making it easy to complete.

2005 poster:
485 mm × 700 mm

In maart 2005 vindt – voor de zesde keer – de tweejaarlijkse jurering plaats voor de Nederlandse Huisstijlprijs. De jurering wordt georganiseerd door de Grafische Cultuurstichting, met medewerking van papiergroothandel ModoVanGelder en Flevodruk Harderwijk en met instemming van de BNO (Beroepsorganisatie Nederlandse Ontwerpers). De Nederlandse Huisstijlprijs is een onderscheiding voor de ontwerper én de opdrachtgever.

Drie categorieën

Ingezonden kunnen worden: merken, 'kleine huisstijlen' (voor kleinere organisaties) en 'grote huisstijlen' (voor grotere/complexe organisaties) die in 2003 of 2004 zijn ontwikkeld.

Inzendingen

Inzending is mogelijk tot 1 maart 2005. Een inzending van een merk dient te bestaan uit een of meer scherpe prints van het merk en een ingevuld deelnameformulier. Meegezonden kunnen worden een korte toelichting en enkele voorbeelden van toepassingen van het merk.

Een inzending van een huisstijl dient in elk geval te bestaan uit een vel briefpapier, ongebruikt én beschreven of 'betypt', een bijbehorende envelop, een visitekaartje en een ingevuld deelnameformulier. Daarnaast kunnen maximaal 10 andere drukwerken worden ingezonden, een korte toelichting op het ontwerp en, indien gewenst, foto's van beletteringen, prints van websites etc. Het werk mag niet groter zijn dan 30 x 40 cm en het drukwerk moet in drievoud worden aangeleverd.

De kosten van deelname zijn 70 euro bij één inzending. Voor elke volgende inzending wordt 35 euro in rekening gebracht. (De bedragen zijn exclusief BTW. Inzenders ontvangen een nota voor het verschuldigde bedrag).

Volledig invullen en voor elke inzending een apart formulier gebruiken, zo nodig een fotokopie.

Inzender	Naam bureau/bedrijf/instelling
	Naam contactpersoon
	Postadres
	Postcode en plaats
	Telefoon
Vormgever	Naam bureau
	Naam ontwerper
	Naam illustrator/fotograaf, indien van toepassing
	Naam contactpersoon
	Postadres
	Postcode en plaats
	Telefoon
Opdrachtgever	Naam bedrijf/instelling
	Naam contactpersoon
	Postadres
	Postcode en plaats
	Telefoon
	Aard bedrijf/instelling (bijvoorbeeld: verzekeringsmaatschappij, onderwijsinstelling, machinefabriek)
Drukker	Naam grafisch bedrijf
	Naam contactpersoon
	Postadres
	Postcode en plaats
	Telefoon
Toegepaste papieren	Soort, type/merk, gewicht
	Papierleverancier
Inzending categorie	O Merken
	O Huisstijlen voor kleinere organisaties
	O Huisstijlen voor grotere/complexe organisaties
Datum	
Handtekening	

Deelnameformulier

Beoordeling

De inzendingen worden beoordeeld in drie categorieën: merken, 'kleine huisstijlen' en 'grote huisstijlen'. De jury maakt per categorie een voorselectie: de nominaties. Vervolgens wordt in elke categorie een winnaar aangewezen.

Criteria

Belangrijke criteria zijn: concept, communicatiekracht, bruikbaarheid en uitvoering.

De jury

De jury bestaat uit:
Jan Brinkman (ontwerper), juryvoorzitter
Ben Bos (ontwerper)
Tirso Francés (partner Dietwee Ontwerpers)
Jaap Kalma (directeur marketing Unilever-Bestfood Italia)
Albertien Jaeger-Kamp (senior consultant SCAN Management Consultants)
Jan Sevenster (partner Samenwerkende Ontwerpers)
Fokko Tamminga (directeur drukkerij Ando Calff & Meischke)
Alwin van Steijn (directeur Grafische Cultuurstichting), secretaris zonder stemrecht

En verder

De jurering vindt plaats in maart 2005. Direct na de jurering ontvangen de inzenders bericht over de nominaties en de prijsuitreiking. Alle inzenders ontvangen een uitnodiging en een uitvoerig juryrapport.

Reglement

1 In het kader van de Nederlandse Huisstijlprijs organiseert de Grafische Cultuurstichting, in samenwerking met het Gerrit Jan Thiemefonds, elke twee jaar een bekroning van de beste merken en huisstijlen.

2 Doel van de Nederlandse Huisstijlprijs is het stimuleren van het gebruik van grafisch werk, zoals drukwerk, beletteringen en webdesigns, om de identiteit van een organisatie (corporate identity) te bevestigen en uit te dragen en het imago van de organisatie in gunstige zin te versterken.

3 Voor mededinging komen uitsluitend in aanmerking merken en huisstijlen van organisaties die in Nederland zijn gevestigd.

4 De aard, inhoud en omvang van de inzendingen, de termijn van inzending, en de door de inzenders te betalen kosten worden door de organisatoren bepaald.
Een inzending is geldig wanneer de door de organisatoren gevraagde stukken, gegevens en betaling tijdig zijn ontvangen.

5 De Nederlandse Huisstijlprijs kent drie categorieën: merken, huisstijlen voor kleinere organisaties en huisstijlen voor grotere/complexe organisaties.

6 De inzendingen worden beoordeeld door een jury van ten minste vijf personen, exclusief de secretaris. Inzendingen van juryleden worden uitgesloten van mededinging.

7 Bij de beoordeling wordt per categorie een voorselectie gemaakt van circa tien inzendingen. Uit deze voorselecties, de nominaties, worden de winnende inzendingen gekozen.

8 De aan de Nederlandse Huisstijlprijs verbonden prijzen – objecten – zijn bestemd voor zowel de ontwerpers en de opdrachtgevers.

9 Een belangrijk criterium is of de huisstijl/het merk – naar de mening van de jury – de identiteit van de desbetreffende organisatie weerspiegelt en een positieve bijdrage levert aan het imago van deze organisatie. Aspecten die beoordeeld worden zijn onder andere: concept, communicatiekracht, bruikbaarheid en uitvoering.

10 Door inzending doet de deelnemer afstand van het eigendom van het ingestuurde/afgeleverde werk en geeft hij/zij de organisatoren toestemming om dit werk, of delen daarvan, op welke wijze dan ook openbaar te maken.

11 Mededelingen over het overleg in de jury worden slechts gedaan door de voorzitter van de jury.

12 In gevallen waarin dit reglement niet voorziet, beslist de jury.

Winnaars

1993 Bloem Zetten en Lithograferen, UNA (Amsterdam) designers
1997 Het Nationale Toneel, Catherine van der Eerden, Studio Dumbar
1999 Hazazah, Koeweiden Postma Associates
2001 Mama Cash, Esther Noyons; Asko Ensemble/Schönberg Ensemble, UNA (Amsterdam) designers
2003 Restaurant Marmouche, ...,staat (i.s.m. Stef Bakker); Nationaal Archief, UNA (Amsterdam) designers; Gemeente Amsterdam, Eden Design & Communicatie/Thonik

Uiterlijk 1 maart 2005 zenden aan: Grafische Cultuurstichting, Jury Nederlandse Huisstijlprijs 2005, Postbus 220, 1180 AE Amstelveen. Afleveradres: Startbaan 10, Amstelveen

Vormgeving Samenwerkende Ontwerpers (Andre Toet m.m.v. Anne Brills), Amsterdam **Fotografie** Getty Images **Drukwerk** Flevodruk Harderwijk **Papier** Euroflash 135 g/m2, ModoVanGelder, Amsterdam © 2002/2003 Grafische Cultuurstichting, Amstelveen

Nee, ik!!!

ModoVanGelder

In maart aanstaande vindt de jurering plaats voor de Nederlandse Huisstijlprijs 2003. Het is de 5e keer dat de Grafische Cultuurstichting de 2-jaarlijkse competitie organiseert: met medewerking van het Gerrit Jan Thiemefonds, papiergroothandel ModoVanGelder en Flevodruk Harderwijk en met instemming van de BNO (Beroepsorganisatie Nederlandse Ontwerpers). De Nederlandse Huisstijlprijs is een onderscheiding voor zowel de ontwerper als de opdrachtgever.

Deelname is mogelijk tot 1 maart 2003!

O.K. **De vorige winnaars:**
1993: Bloem Zetten en Lithograferen **Una**
1997: Het Nationale Toneel **Catherine van der Eerden (Studio Dumbar)**
1999: Hazazah **Koeweiden Postma**
2001: Mama Cash **Esther Noyons;** Asko Ensemble/Schönberg Ensemble **Una (Amsterdam) designers**
2003: ???

Nieuw! **3 categorieën:** Ingezonden kunnen worden merken/kleine huisstijlen/grote huisstijlen die in 2001 of 2002 zijn ontwikkeld.

Inzendingen: Inzending is mogelijk tot 1 maart 2003.

Een inzending van een **merk** dient te bestaan uit een of meer scherpe prints van het merk en een ingevuld deelnameformulier. Meegezonden kunnen worden een korte toelichting en enkele voorbeelden van toepassingen van het merk.

Een inzending van een **huisstijl** dient in elk geval te bestaan uit een vel briefpapier, ongebruikt en beschreven of 'betypt', een bijbehorende envelop, een visitekaartje en een ingevuld deelnameformulier. Daarnaast kunnen maximaal 10 andere drukwerken worden ingezonden, een korte toelichting op het ontwerp en, indien gewenst, foto's van beletteringen, prints van websites etc. Het ingezonden werk mag niet groter zijn dan 30 x 40 cm en het drukwerk moet in 3-voud worden aangeleverd.

De kosten van deelname zijn € 60 bij een inzending. Voor elke volgende inzending wordt € 30 in rekening gebracht. (Deze bedragen zijn exclusief BTW. Inzenders ontvangen een nota voor het verschuldigde bedrag.)

Beoordeling: De inzendingen worden beoordeeld
- in 3 categorieën.
- Merken
- Huisstijlen voor kleinere organisaties
  Huisstijlen voor grotere/complexe organisaties

De jury maakt per categorie een voorselectie: de nominaties. Vervolgens wordt uit elke groep potentiële bekroningen een winnaar gekozen.

Belangrijke criteria zijn:
- Concept
- Communicatiekracht
- Bruikbaarheid
- Uitvoering

De jury bestaat uit:
Ben Bos (ontwerper)
Tirso Francés (partner Dietwee Ontwerpers)
Albertien Jaeger-Kamp (senior consultant SCAN Management Consultants)
David Quay (letterontwerper/typograaf)
Harm Rozie (directielid Communication Concert)
Alwin van Steijn (Grafische Cultuurstichting), secretaris zonder stemrecht
Fokko Tamminga (bestuurslid Gerrit Jan Thiemefonds)
Ronald Widdershoven (directeur Binderij Hexspoor)

En verder: De jurering vindt plaats in maart 2003. Direct na de jurering ontvangen de inzenders bericht over de nominaties. De bekendmaking van de winnaars en de prijsuitreiking vinden plaats in april of begin mei in de Beurs van Berlage te Amsterdam. Alle inzenders ontvangen een uitnodiging en een uitvoerig juryrapport.

Reglement Nederlandse Huisstijlprijs

1: In het kader van de Nederlandse Huisstijlprijs organiseert de Grafische Cultuurstichting, in samenwerking met het Gerrit Jan Thiemefonds, elke 2 jaar een bekroning van de beste merken en huisstijlen.

2: Doel van de Nederlandse Huisstijlprijs is het stimuleren van het gebruik van grafisch werk, zoals drukwerk, beletteringen en webdesigns, om de identiteit van een organisatie (corporate identity) te bevestigen en uit te dragen en het imago van de organisatie in gunstige zin te versterken.

3: Voor mededinging komen uitsluitend in aanmerking merken en huisstijlen van organisaties die in Nederland zijn gevestigd.

4: De aard, inhoud en omvang van de inzendingen, de termijn van inzending, en de door de inzenders te betalen kosten worden door de organisatoren bepaald. Een inzending is geldig wanneer de door de organisatoren gevraagde stukken, gegevens en betaling tijdig zijn ontvangen.

5: De Nederlandse Huisstijlprijs kent 3 categorieën: merken, huisstijlen voor kleinere organisaties en huisstijlen voor grotere/complexe organisaties.

6: De inzendingen worden beoordeeld door een jury van ten minste 5 personen, exclusief de secretaris. Inzendingen van juryleden worden uitgesloten van mededinging.

7: Bij de beoordeling wordt per categorie een voorselectie gemaakt van circa 10 inzendingen. Uit deze voorselecties, de nominaties, worden de winnende inzendingen gekozen.

8: De aan de Nederlandse Huisstijlprijs verbonden prijzen – objecten – zijn bestemd voor zowel de ontwerpers en de opdrachtgevers.

9: Een belangrijk criterium is of de huisstijl/het merk – naar mening van de jury – de identiteit van de desbetreffende organisatie weerspiegelt en een positieve bijdrage levert aan het imago van deze organisatie. Aspecten die beoordeeld worden zijn onder andere: concept, communicatiekracht, bruikbaarheid en uitvoering.

10: Door inzending doet de deelnemer afstand van het eigendom van het ingestuurde/afgeleverde werk en geeft hij/zij de organisatoren toestemming om dit werk, of delen daarvan, op welke wijze dan ook openbaar te maken.

11: Mededelingen over het overleg in de jury worden slechts gedaan door de voorzitter van de jury.

12: In gevallen waarin dit reglement niet voorziet, beslist de jury.

Graag volledig invullen. Voor elke inzending een apart formulier gebruiken, zo nodig een fotokopie.

Inzender: Naam bureau/bedrijf/instelling:
Naam contactpersoon:
Postadres:
Postcode en plaats:
Telefoon:

Vormgever: Naam bureau:
Naam ontwerper:
Naam illustrator/fotograaf, indien van toepassing:
Naam contactpersoon:
Postadres:
Postcode en plaats:
Telefoon:

Opdrachtgever: Naam bedrijf/instelling:
Naam contactpersoon:
Postadres:
Postcode en plaats:
Telefoon:
Aard bedrijf/instelling:
(bijvoorbeeld: verzekeringsmaatschappij, onderwijsinstelling, machinefabriek)

Drukker: Naam grafisch bedrijf:
Naam contactpersoon:
Postadres:
Postcode en plaats:
Telefoon:

Toegepaste papieren: Soort, type/merk, gewicht:
Papierleverancier:

Inzending in categorie: Merken: ○
Huisstijlen voor kleinere organisaties: ○
Huisstijlen voor grotere/complexe organisaties: ○

Datum:
Handtekening:

Uiterlijk **1 maart 2003** zenden aan: **Grafische Cultuurstichting** Jury Nederlandse Huisstijlprijs 2003, postbus 220, 1180 AE Amstelveen. Afleveradres: Startbaan 10, Amstelveen.

2003 poster: 700 mm × 500 mm

In maart 2007 vindt – voor de zevende keer – de twee- jaarlijkse jurering plaats voor de Nederlandse Huisstijlprijs. De jurering wordt georganiseerd door de Grafische Cultuurstichting, met medewerking van papiergroothandel ModoVanGelder en Flevodruk Harderwijk en met instemming van de BNO (Beroepsorganisatie Nederlandse Ontwerpers). De Nederlandse Huisstijlprijs is een onderscheiding voor de ontwerper én de opdrachtgever.

Jury
Jan Brinkman (ontwerper), juryvoorzitter Ben Bos (ontwerper) Tirso Francés (partner Dietwee Ontwerpers) Jaap Kalma (directeur marketing Unilever-Bestfood Italia) Albertien Jaeger-Kamp (senior consultant SCAN Management Consultants) Jan Sevenster (Member Since) Fokko Tamminga (directeur drukkerij Ando Calff & Meischke) Alwin van Steijn (directeur Grafische Cultuur-stichting), secretaris zonder stemrecht

Drie categorieën
Ingezonden kunnen worden: merken, 'kleine huisstijlen' (voor kleinere organisaties) en 'grote huisstijlen' (voor grotere/complexe organisaties) die in 2003 of 2004 zijn ontwikkeld.

Inzendingen
Inzending is mogelijk tot 1 maart 2005. Een inzending van een merk dient te bestaan uit een of meer scherpe prints van het merk en een ingevuld deelnameformulier. Meegezonden kunnen worden een korte toelichting en enkele voorbeelden van toepassingen van het merk.

Een inzending van een huisstijl dient in elk geval te bestaan uit een vel briefpapier, ongebruikt én beschreven of 'betypt', een bijbehorende envelop, een visitekaartje en een ingevuld deelnameformulier. Daarnaast kunnen maximaal 10 andere drukwerken worden ingezonden, een korte toelichting op het ontwerp en, indien gewenst, foto's van beletteringen, prints van websites etc. Het werk mag niet groter zijn dan 30 x 40 cm en het drukwerk moet in drievoud worden aangeleverd.

De kosten van deelname zijn 70 euro bij één inzending. Voor elke volgende inzending wordt 35 euro in rekening gebracht. (De bedragen zijn exclusief BTW. Inzenders ontvangen een nota voor het verschuldigde bedrag)

Beoordeling
De inzendingen worden beoordeeld in drie categorieën: merken, 'kleine huisstijlen' en 'grote huisstijlen'. De jury maakt per categorie een voorselectie: de nominaties. Vervolgens wordt in elke categorie een winnaar aangewezen.

Criteria
Belangrijke criteria zijn: concept, communicatiekracht, bruikbaarheid en uitvoering.

En verder
De jurering vindt plaats in maart 2005. Direct na de jurering ontvangen de inzenders bericht over de nominaties en de prijsuitreiking. Alle inzenders ontvangen een uitnodiging en een uitvoerig juryrapport.

Winnaars
1993 Bloem Zetten en Lithograferen, UNA (Amsterdam) designers **1997** Het Nationale Toneel, Catherine van der Eerden, Studio Dumbar **1999** Hazazah, Koeweiden Postma Associates **2001** Mama Cash, Esther Noyons; Asko Ensemble/Schönberg Ensemble, UNA (Amsterdam) designers **2003** Restaurant Marmouche, ...staat (i.s.m. Stef Bakker); Nationaal Archief, UNA (Amsterdam) designers; Gemeente Amsterdam, Eden Design & Communicatie/Thonik **2005** Döll - Atelier voor bouwkunst, Rotterdam, Dietwee ontwerp en communicatie (Dirkjan Brummelman), Utrecht

2007 poster: 594 mm × 420 mm

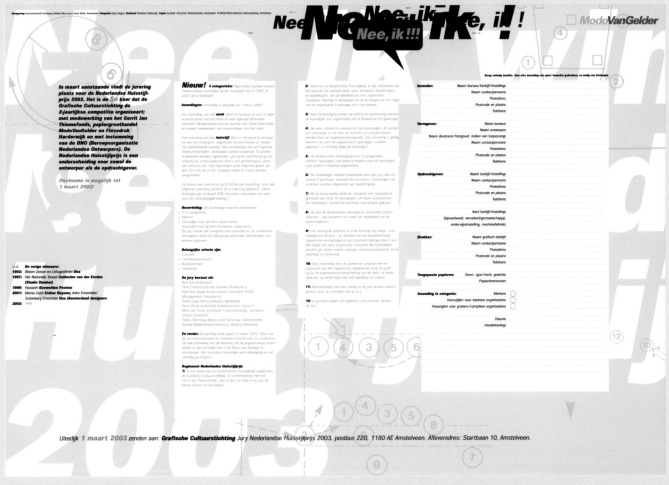

Business Report Competition

Entry forms

Issued by	Grafische Cultuurstichting, Netherlands
Design	Samenwerkende Ontwerpers bv, Amsterdam
Years	2002, 2006
Typefaces	VAG Rounded (2002), Trade Gothic (2006)

Even the entry forms for this Dutch design competition for business reports follow a strong concept. Especially impressive is the way the sequence, layout and alignment of text and lines exploit the aesthetic potential of forms.

Deelnameformulier

de bestverzorgde jaarverslagen

Volledig invullen en voor elke inzending een apart formulier gebruiken, zo nodig een fotokopie.

Inzender Naam bedrijf/instelling/bureau:
Naam contactpersoon:
Postadres:
Postcode en plaats:
Telefoon:

Opdrachtgever Naam bedrijf/instelling:
Naam contactpersoon:
Postadres:
Postcode en plaats:
Telefoon:

Vormgeving Naam bureau:
Naam ontwerper:
(Indien relevant) naam illustrator:
(Indien relevant) naam fotograaf:
Naam contactpersoon:
Postadres:
Postcode en plaats:
Telefoon:

stontwikkeling Naam bureau:
Naam tekstschrijver:
Naam contactpersoon:
Postadres:
Postcode en plaats:
Telefoon:

aarverslag op een
rdt gepresenteerd URL (volledig):

Bedrijfsnaam:
Naam contactpersoon:
Postadres:
Postcode en plaats:

Bedrijfsnaam:
Naam contactpersoon:
Postadres:
Postcode en plaats:

Bindwerk Bedrijfsnaam:
Naam contactpersoon:
Postadres:
Postcode en plaats:

Toegepaste materialen Papier e.d.:

Inzenden vóór 31 augustus 2002, tezamen met 2 exemplaren van het jaarverslag.

Jury De Bestverzorgde Jaarverslagen, Grafische Cultuurstichting, Postbus 220, 1180 AE, Amstelveen

Het verschuldigde bedrag wordt voldaan na ontvangst van de nota.

Datum: Handtekening:

estverzorgde jaarverslagen

2002 poster, front and back: A4

The text is deliberately crooked in relation to the baselines. Rather than being unsightly, this adds visual interest to the form.

_RVERSLAGEN

De Bestverzorgde Jaarverslagen wordt georganiseerd door de Grafische Cultuurstichting, in samenwerking met Uitgeverij Compres (Print Buyer) en Océ-Nederland bv.

INZENDINGEN

Ingezonden kunnen worden jaarverslagen over het jaar 2005. Inzending is mogelijk tot 1 oktober 2006. Elke inzending dient te bestaan uit één exemplaar van het jaarverslag en een ingevuld deelnameformulier. In het geval van een website kan worden volstaan met inzending van het deelnameformulier.

Elke inzending wordt als totaal beoordeeld. Vul meer formulieren in als bijvoorbeeld het financieel jaarverslag en het sociaal jaarverslag afzonderlijk moeten worden beoordeeld.

De kosten van deelname zijn € 60 bij één inzending. Voor elke volgende inzending wordt € 40 in rekening gebracht. (Deze bedragen zijn exclusief BTW. Inzenders ontvangen een nota voor het verschuldigde bedrag.)

BEOORDELING

De jaarverslagen worden in principe in drie categorieën beoordeeld: algemene jaarverslagen, sociale- en milieu-jaarverslagen e.d., jaarverslagen op websites. Desgewenst kan de jury besluiten meer of andere categorieën in te stellen.

✯ Criteria zijn: concept, communicatiekracht en uitvoering.

De selectie van bestverzorgde jaarverslagen zal uit circa 15 jaarverslagen bestaan.

De jury 2006 bestaat uit: Stevijn van Heusden (oud-directeur Kunsten WVC en OCenW en oud-directeur Stedelijk Museum Amsterdam), voorzitter; Marloes Krijnen (directeur Foam_Fotografiemuseum Amsterdam); Freek Kuin (directeur Ando Calff & Meischke); Jan Sevenster (ontwerper/directeur Member Since); Hans Wolbers (ontwerper/directeur Lava grafisch ontwerpers); Alwin van Steijn (Grafische Cultuurstichting), secretaris.

EN VERDER

De presentatie van de bestverzorgde jaarverslagen en het juryrapport aan de inzenders en andere belangstellenden vindt plaats tijdens Papier Hier op 18 november a.s. in het Maagdenhuis in Amsterdam. Print Buyer verzorgt een speciale uitgave over de bestverzorgde jaarverslagen. De selectie wordt uiteindelijk opgenomen in de collectie Zeldzame en Kostbare Werken van de Universiteitsbibliotheek Amsterdam.

Voor publiciteits-, expositie- en archiveringsdoeleinden zullen de organisatoren de inzenders van de bekroonde jaarverslagen vragen twee extra exemplaren in te zenden.

Door inzending doet de deelnemer afstand van het eigendom van het ingezonden werk en geeft hij de organisatoren toestemming om het werk, of delen daarvan, op welke wijze dan ook openbaar te maken.

Grafische Cultuurstichting, postbus 220, 1180 AE Amstelveen
Telefoon 020-5435675, fax 5435568, e-mail info@grafischecultuur.nl

Met dank aan:
Uitgeverij Compres bv (Print Buyer), Grafisch Papier, Océ-Nederland bv, De Longte Dordrecht bv

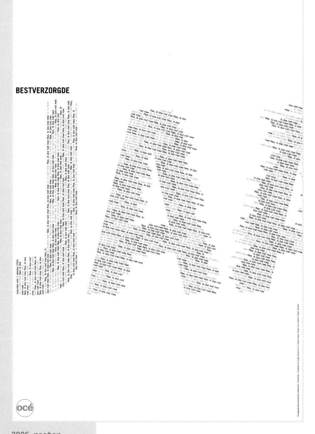

BESTVERZORGDE

DEELNAMEFORMULIER

Inzenden vóór 1 oktober 2006, tezamen met één exemplaar van het jaarverslag.
Jury De Bestverzorgde Jaarverslagen, Grafische Cultuurstichting, postbus 220, 1180 AE Amstelveen
Volledig invullen en voor elke inzending een apart formulier gebruiken, zo nodig een fotokopie.

INZENDER
Naam bedrijf/instelling/bureau____
Naam contactpersoon____
Postadres____
Postcode en plaats____
Telefoon____
E-mail-adres____

OPDRACHTGEVER
Naam bedrijf/instelling____
Naam contactpersoon____
Postadres____
Postcode en plaats____
E-mail-adres____

VORMGEVING
Naam bureau____
Naam ontwerper____
Postadres____
Postcode en plaats____
Telefoon____
E-mail-adres____

(INDIEN RELEVANT) EXTERNE TEKSTONTWIKKELING
Naam bureau____
Naam tekstschrijver____
Postadres____
Postcode en plaats____

(INDIEN RELEVANT) FOTOGRAFIE
Naam bureau____
Naam fotograaf____
Postadres____
Postcode en plaats____

(INDIEN RELEVANT) ILLUSTRATIES
Naam bureau____
Naam illustrator____
Postadres____
Postcode en plaats____

INDIEN DE INZENDING UIT EEN WEBSITE BESTAAT
URL (volledig)____

LITHOGRAFIE
Bedrijfsnaam____
Naam contactpersoon____
Postadres____
Postcode en plaats____

DRUKWERK
Bedrijfsnaam____
Naam contactpersoon____
Postadres____
Postcode en plaats____

BINDWERK
Bedrijfsnaam____
Naam contactpersoon____
Postadres____
Postcode en plaats____

TOEGEPASTE MATERIALEN
(Papier e.d.)____

Het verschuldigde bedrag wordt voldaan na ontvangst van de nota.

Datum____

Handtekening____

2006 poster, front and back: 420 mm × 594 mm

Cambridge International Examinations

Answer book

Issued by	Cambridge International Examinations, UK
Design	Information Design Unit, Newport Pagnell *Richard Bland*
Year	2002
Typeface	Arial

Cambridge International Examinations (CIE) is the world's largest provider of international qualifications for 14 to 19 year olds. Historically, after an examination, candidate answer papers had to be manually sorted, collated and distributed to markers across the country, and possibly overseas. CIE decided to run a pilot to see if the process from examination to result could be improved. The new process would include scanning papers and sending electronic files to markers. The Information Design Unit created an answer booklet that is clean, simple and undaunting to candidates, while still incorporating all the scanning and technical requirements necessary. Arguably the last thing candidates should feel is that working out how to use the answer booklet is part of the examination.

Question number

Remember: write the question number at the beginning of each answer

Do not write anywhere in the margins

page 2

Remember: Always leave a blank line at the end of one answer, before you start the next one

Answer booklet page: A4

As the electronic scanning system would fail if the candidates did not write in a question number with the answer, the left-hand column is highlighted. The character dividers are meant to encourage the candiates to keep their question numbering consistent as they complete the paper. Key instructions at the top and bottom of each page serve as a constant reminder.

Cambridge International Examinations

Answer book

16 pages

Before you start

- **Remember to write in blue or black ink.**
- **Stick one of your personal labels in the blue box.** Use the other label if you use another answer booklet.
- **Answer the question about your details.**

During the examination

- **Write clearly and neatly on both sides of the paper.**
- **Do not tear out any pages, or stick or staple anything in this book. Do not use correcting fluid.**
- **When you answer a question** Write the full question number at the beginning of your answer, in the column on the left. Include the main question number (eg 1, 2) and the subquestion number (eg, c or iii). Do not write anything else in this column.

Question number	Remember: write the question number at th
17 a	This is the answer to the question. This is the a
12 a ii	~~This is the wrong answer. This is the wrong an~~
	~~wrong answer. This is the wrong answer. This~~
	This is the answer to the question. This is the a
5	This is the answer to the question. This is the a

- **If you change your mind about an answer** If you need to start an answer again, or if you decide to do a different question, cross out all the parts that you do not want the examiner to mark. But do not cross out the question number.
- **Always leave a blank line at the end of one answer, before you start the next one.**
- **Rough work** If your question paper tells you to hand in your rough work, do the rough work in this answer book. Then cross it out, but make sure that it can still be read.

At the end of the examination

- **Make sure you have written the numbers of all the questions you have attempted in the column on this page.**
- **Write the total number of answer books you have used in the box on the right.**

Stick your personal label here

▶ Your details

Are all your correct details on the label?

Yes ☐ No ☐ *please fill in your correct details below*

Your full name *given name first, then family name*

Centre number | **Your candidate number**

Syllabus & component number /

▶ Questions you have attempted

Write the main numbers (eg 1, 2) of all the questions you have attempted here, in the order you attempted them.

Question number

▶ Total number of answer books

Front page of answer booklet: A4

The instructions on the front page are broken down into stages, so the candidates can quickly digest the relevant information at the correct stage of the exam. The instructions show how to complete an answer, but equally as important, they explain what to do if candidates want to start a question again.

The Crier

	Subscription form
Issued by	The Crier, USA
Design	This is our work, New York *Riley Hooker*
Year	2007
Typefaces	Civility, Caslon 224 Bl It, Adobe Garamond Pro, Popular, Grotesque MT, Hussy

This subscription form for an independent magazine is notable because the cut-out coupon is not an ugly thing hanging off the bottom of the page, but is placed confidently and strikingly right in the centre. The design is made even more attractive by the playful use of type and background shapes.

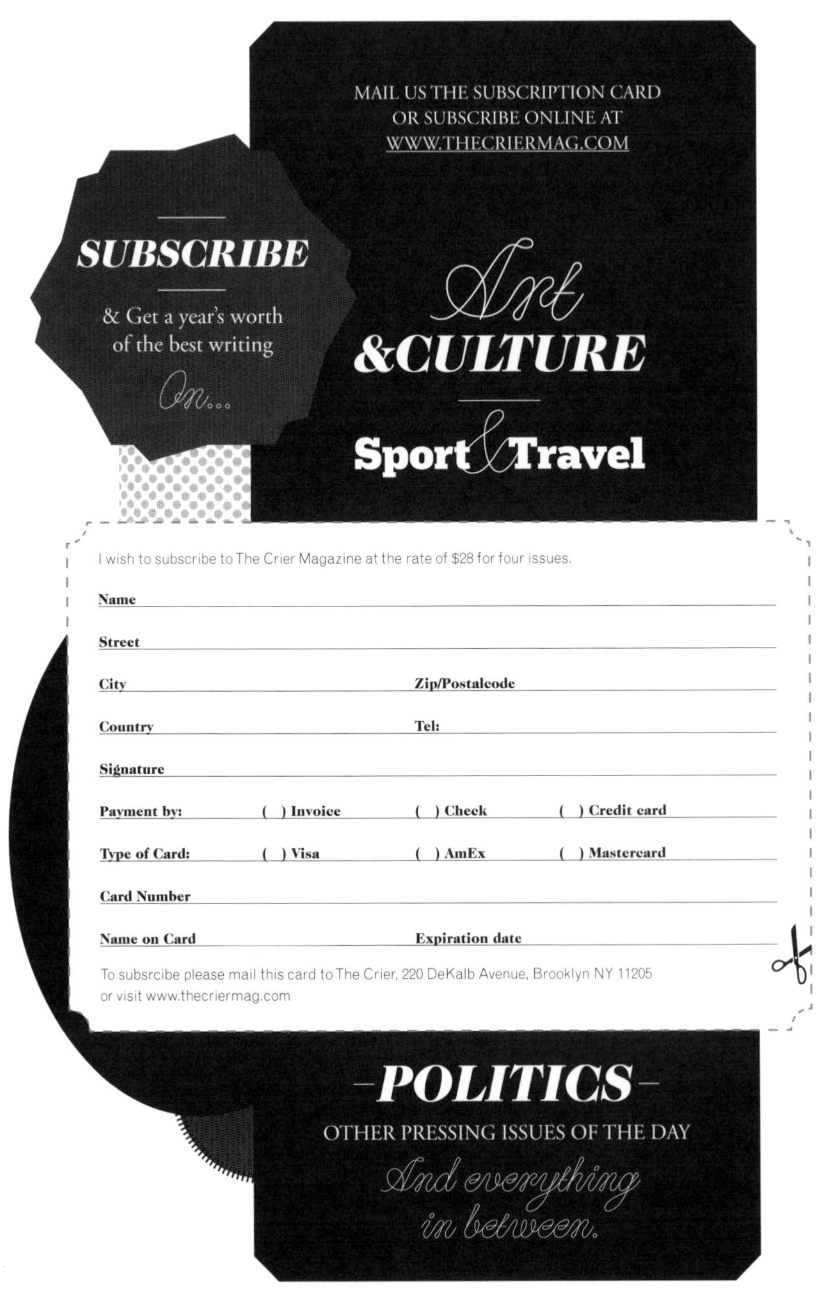
MAIL US THE SUBSCRIPTION CARD
OR SUBSCRIBE ONLINE AT
WWW.THECRIERMAG.COM

SUBSCRIBE
& Get a year's worth of the best writing
On...

Art
&CULTURE
Sport & Travel

I wish to subscribe to The Crier Magazine at the rate of $28 for four issues.

Name

Street

City Zip/Postalcode

Country Tel:

Signature

Payment by: ( ) Invoice ( ) Check ( ) Credit card

Type of Card: ( ) Visa ( ) AmEx ( ) Mastercard

Card Number

Name on Card Expiration date

To subsrcibe please mail this card to The Crier, 220 DeKalb Avenue, Brooklyn NY 11205
or visit www.thecriermag.com

-POLITICS-
OTHER PRESSING ISSUES OF THE DAY
And everything
in between.

Subscription coupon: 152 × 228 mm
A page from *The Crier* magazine, New York, issue 4, vol. 1.

Amnesty International

Charity newsletter

Issued by	Amnesty International, Germany
Design	Fons Hickmann m23, Berlin
	Fons Hickmann, Gesine Grotrian-Steinweg, Franziska Morlok
Year	2006
Typefaces	Neue Helvetica, Rotation

The back of each Amnesty newsletter highlights a campaign that readers can take part in by filling in the postcard and sending it off.

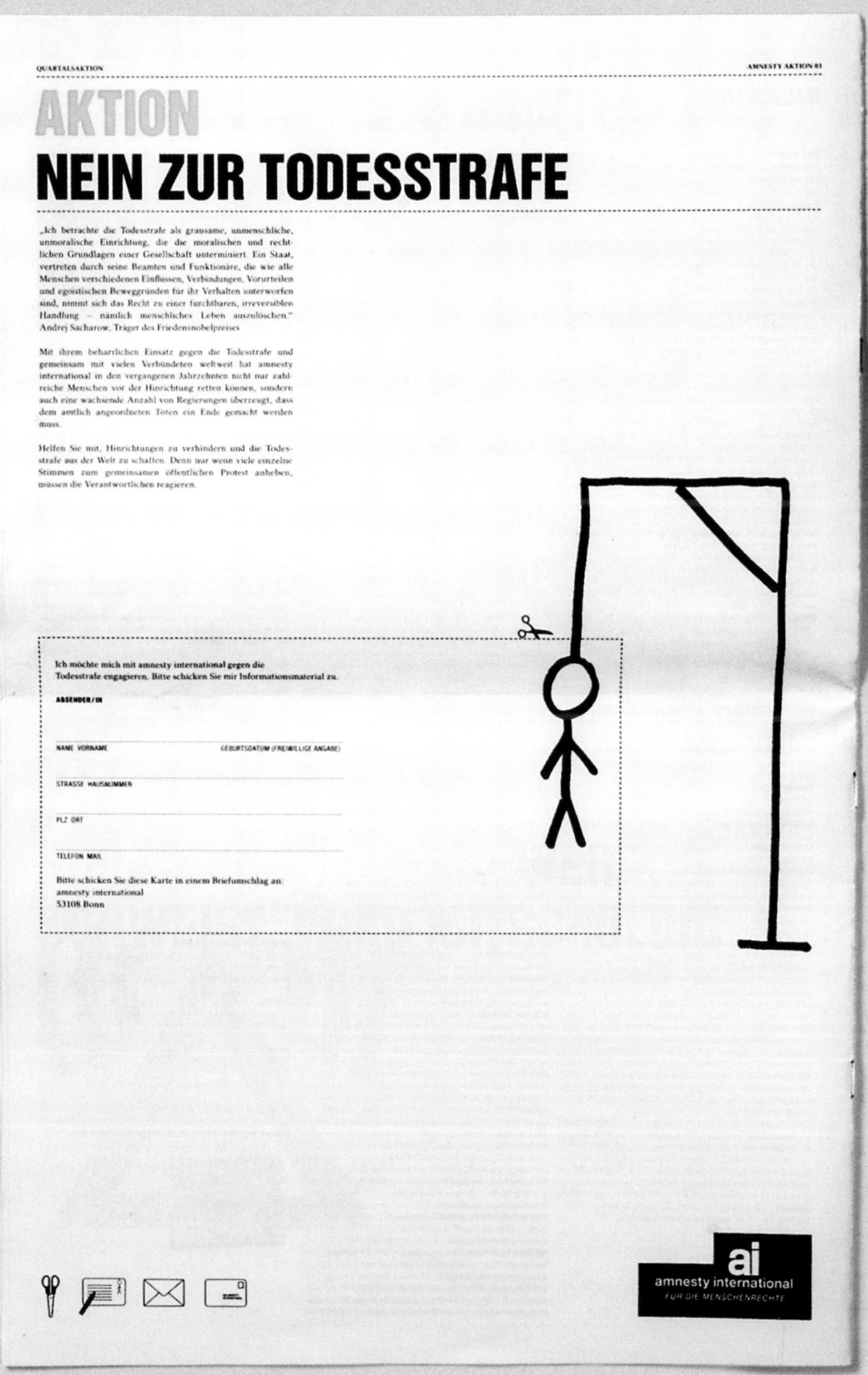

QUARTALSAKTION AMNESTY AKTION 03

AKTION

NEIN ZUR TODESSTRAFE

„Ich betrachte die Todesstrafe als grausame, unmenschliche, unmoralische Einrichtung, die die moralischen und rechtlichen Grundlagen einer Gesellschaft unterminiert. Ein Staat, vertreten durch seine Beamten und Funktionäre, die wie alle Menschen verschiedenen Einflüssen, Verbindungen, Vorurteilen und egoistischen Beweggründen für ihr Verhalten unterworfen sind, nimmt sich das Recht zu einer furchtbaren, irreversiblen Handlung – nämlich menschliches Leben auszulöschen."
Andrej Sacharow, Träger des Friedensnobelpreises

Mit ihrem beharrlichen Einsatz gegen die Todesstrafe und gemeinsam mit vielen Verbündeten weltweit hat amnesty international in den vergangenen Jahrzehnten nicht nur zahlreiche Menschen vor der Hinrichtung retten können, sondern auch eine wachsende Anzahl von Regierungen überzeugt, dass dem amtlich angeordneten Töten ein Ende gemacht werden muss.

Helfen Sie mit, Hinrichtungen zu verhindern und die Todesstrafe aus der Welt zu schaffen. Denn nur wenn viele einzelne Stimmen zum gemeinsamen öffentlichen Protest anheben, müssen die Verantwortlichen reagieren.

Ich möchte mich mit amnesty international gegen die Todesstrafe engagieren. Bitte schicken Sie mir Informationsmaterial zu.

ABSENDER/IN

NAME VORNAME GEBURTSDATUM (FREIWILLIGE ANGABE)

STRASSE HAUSNUMMER

PLZ ORT

TELEFON MAIL

Bitte schicken Sie diese Karte in einem Briefumschlag an:
amnesty international
53108 Bonn

ai
amnesty international

Ad with reply coupon on back page of newsletter: 307 mm × 472 mm

The headline reads: 'Say No to the Death Penalty'. The most striking thing is not so much the form itself as the idea that the act of cutting out the coupon simultaneously communicates the purpose of the protest. This is a fine example of how something that requires effort from the reader can be used playfully to get a message across.

AED Award

Award certificate

Issued by	AED Verein zur Förderung von Architektur, Engineering und Design in Stuttgart e.V., Germany
Design	büro uebele, visuelle kommunikation, Stuttgart
Year	2004
Typeface	Berthold Akzidenz Grotesk Bold

Certificates are a field in which a designer's approach can often be in conflict with the client's expectations. It is therefore very rare to find certificates like this one, which avoids all the clichés and has an almost architectural look.

Pininfarina-Förderpreis
2006

Gefördert von:
pininfarina

Mit freundlicher Unterstützung von:
Virtual Dimension Center, Fellbach

Name

Titel der Arbeit

Kategorie

aed

aed Verein zur Förderung
von Architektur, Engineering
und Design in Stuttgart e.V.

aed Society for the Advancement
of Architecture, Engineering
and Design in Stuttgart

Award certificate for the promotion of architecture, engineering and design: A5

Gerrit Rietveld Academie

Diplomas

Issued by	Gerrit Rietveld Academie, Netherlands
Design	NODE Berlin Oslo, *Anders Hofgard*
Year	2003
Typefaces	Neue Helvetica, Notre Dame

A clever idea for a design academy diploma: the original registration forms filled in by the students themselves are overprinted in gold with the text announcing that the diploma has been awarded. The typical administrative form beneath contrasts strikingly with the new layer above, and also gives each certificate its own touch of individuality.

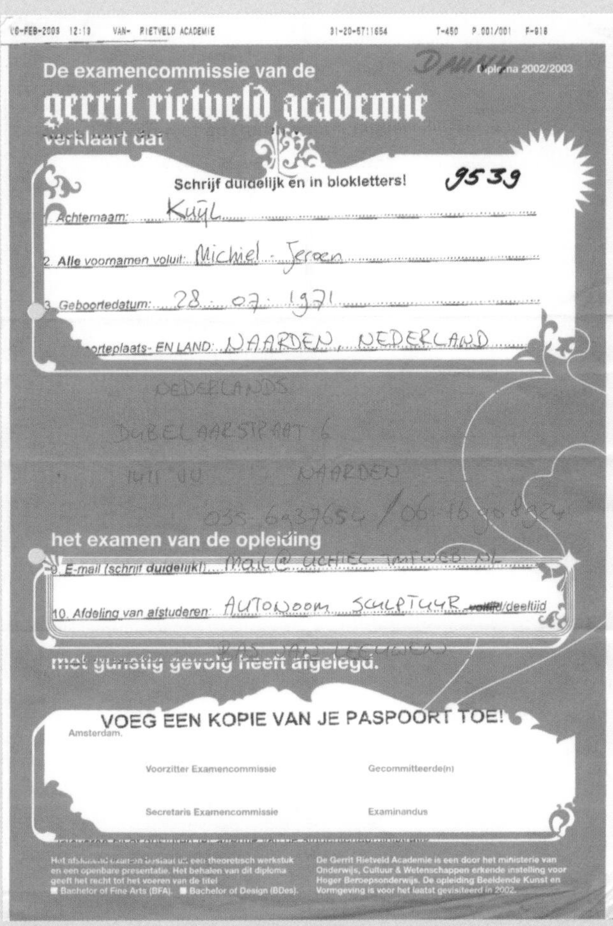

De examencommissie van de
gerrit rietveld academie
verklaart dat
Diploma 2002/2003
Schrijf duidelijk en in blokletters! 9539
Achternaam: Kuijl
2. Alle voornamen voluit: Michiel Jeroen
3. Geboortedatum: 28 07 1971
Geboorteplaats- EN LAND: NAARDEN, NEDERLAND
het examen van de opleiding
9. E-mail (schrijf duidelijk!)
10. Afdeling van afstuderen: AUTONOOM SCULPTUUR voltijd/deeltijd
met gunstig gevolg heeft afgelegd.
VOEG EEN KOPIE VAN JE PASPOORT TOE!
Amsterdam,
Voorzitter Examencommissie
Gecommitteerde(n)
Secretaris Examencommissie
Examinandus

Overprinted application forms: A4

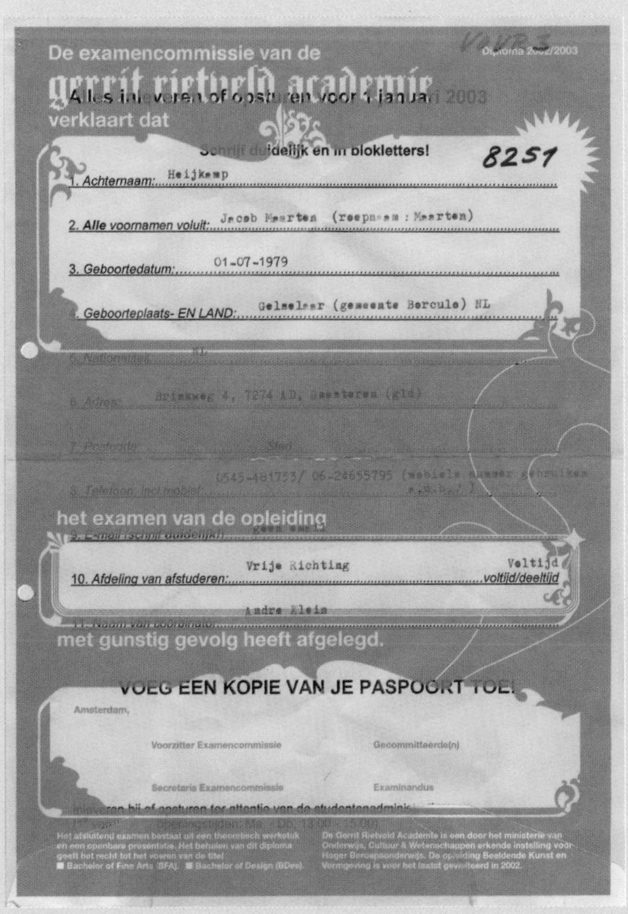

De examencommissie van de
gerrit rietveld academie
verklaart dat
Diploma 2002/2003
Alles inleveren of opsturen voor 1 januari 2003
Schrijf duidelijk en in blokletters! 8251
1. Achternaam: Heijkamp
2. Alle voornamen voluit: Jacob Maarten (roepnaam: Maarten)
3. Geboortedatum: 01-07-1979
4. Geboorteplaats- EN LAND: Gelselaar (gemeente Borculo) NL
het examen van de opleiding
10. Afdeling van afstuderen: Vrije Richting Voltijd voltijd/deeltijd
Andre Klein
met gunstig gevolg heeft afgelegd.
VOEG EEN KOPIE VAN JE PASPOORT TOE!
Amsterdam,
Voorzitter Examencommissie
Gecommitteerde(n)
Secretaris Examencommissie
Examinandus

De examencommissie van de
gerrit rietveld academie
verklaart dat
Diploma 2002/2003
To be send or handed in before January 20 th 2003: You have to write in CAPITAL letters! 11162
1. Surname: HOFGAARD
2. All first names: ANDERS
3. Date of Birth: 06 06 1974
4. Place AND COUNTRY of birth: DRAMMEN, NORWAY
het examen van de opleiding
10. Department of study: GRAPHIC DESIGN Full time/Part time
met gunstig gevolg heeft afgelegd.
INCLUDE A COPY OF YOUR PASSPORT!
Amsterdam
Voorzitter Examencommissie
Gecommitteerde(n)
Secretaris Examencommissie
Examinandus
Hand in at, or send to the attention of: Student Administration (1-st floor, opening hours

Inclusive, Accessible, Archaeology

Online self-assessment toolkit

Issued by	Inclusive, Accessible, Archaeology project, UK
Design	Text Matters, Reading
Year	2007
Typeface	Verdana

The Inclusive, Accessible, Archaeology (IAA) project wants to increase awareness of disability issues in archaeology and improve the integration of disabilities in fieldwork teaching. The project aims to change the emphasis from 'disability' to ability: rather than excluding or categorizing individuals, students should be actively engaged in assessing their own skills. Text Matters designed and produced an online self-evaluation toolkit to assess the physical and psychological abilities of fieldwork students. The toolkit is designed for users with little or no previous experience of archaeological fieldwork. It aims to increase students' awareness of their acquisition of transferable skills and promote career management skills.

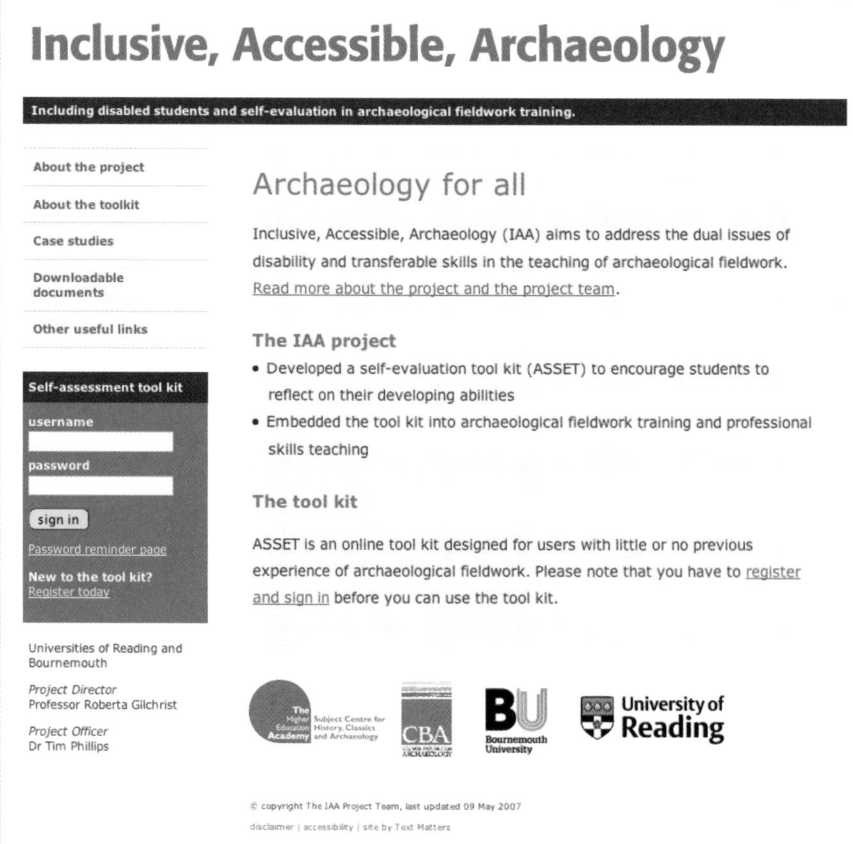

IAA homepage
The website and the toolkit comply with web accessibility standards.

Instruction page
One interesting feature is that the evaluation questions can be answered in any order that the user wishes. The 'question map' serves as a navigation tool and shows which questions have already been answered.

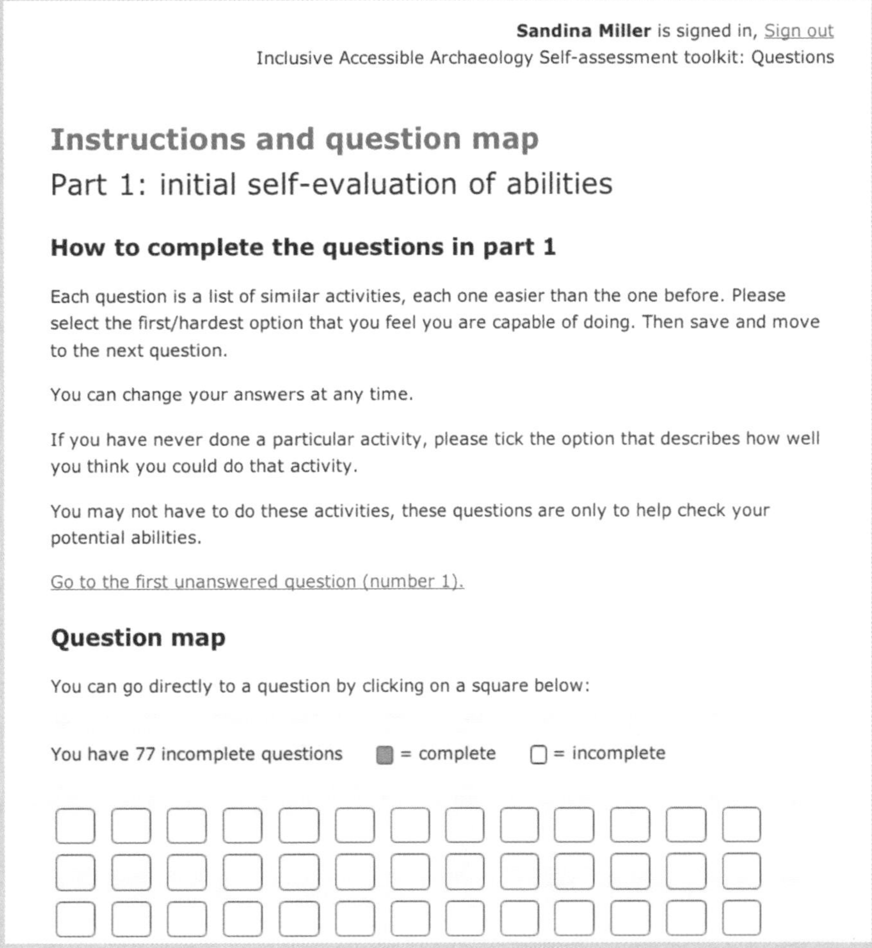

Sandina Miller is signed in, Sign out
Inclusive Accessible Archaeology Self-assessment toolkit: Questions

Instructions and question map

Part 1: initial self-evaluation of abilities

How to complete the questions in part 1

Each question is a list of similar activities, each one easier than the one before. Please select the first/hardest option that you feel you are capable of doing. Then save and move to the next question.

You can change your answers at any time.

If you have never done a particular activity, please tick the option that describes how well you think you could do that activity.

You may not have to do these activities, these questions are only to help check your potential abilities.

Go to the first unanswered question (number 1).

Question map

You can go directly to a question by clicking on a square below:

You have 77 incomplete questions = complete = incomplete

Question page
The multiple choice answers for each question are graded in order of difficulty.

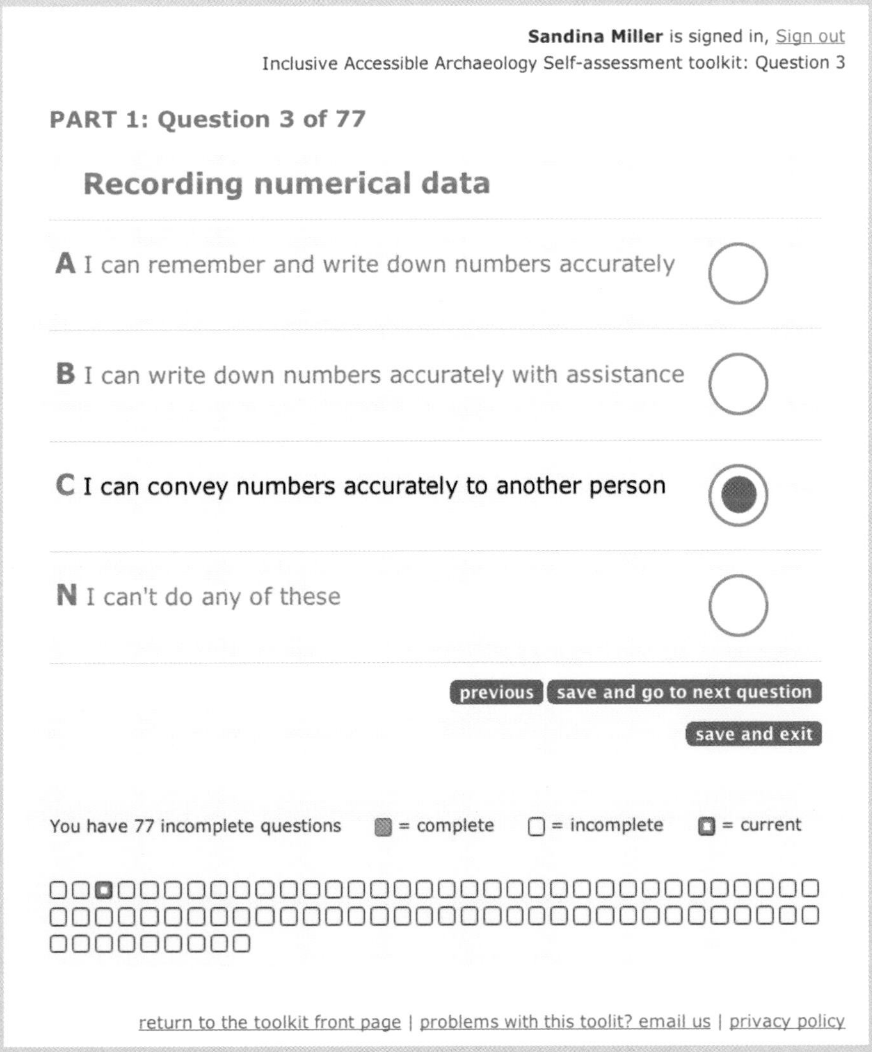

Sandina Miller is signed in, Sign out
Inclusive Accessible Archaeology Self-assessment toolkit: Question 3

PART 1: Question 3 of 77

Recording numerical data

A I can remember and write down numbers accurately

B I can write down numbers accurately with assistance

C I can convey numbers accurately to another person

N I can't do any of these

previous save and go to next question

save and exit

You have 77 incomplete questions = complete = incomplete = current

return to the toolkit front page | problems with this toolit? email us | privacy policy

Question page
The standard entry fields on online forms are often very small and difficult to read. Here the entry fields have sensibly been made much larger than usual.

Sandina Miller is signed in, Sign out
Inclusive Accessible Archaeology Self-assessment toolkit: Question 77

PART 1: Question 77 of 77

Can you identify the numbers in the boxes below?

Each box below has a number. Please typoe this number in the space to the right of the box. If you do not see a number, please write '0'.

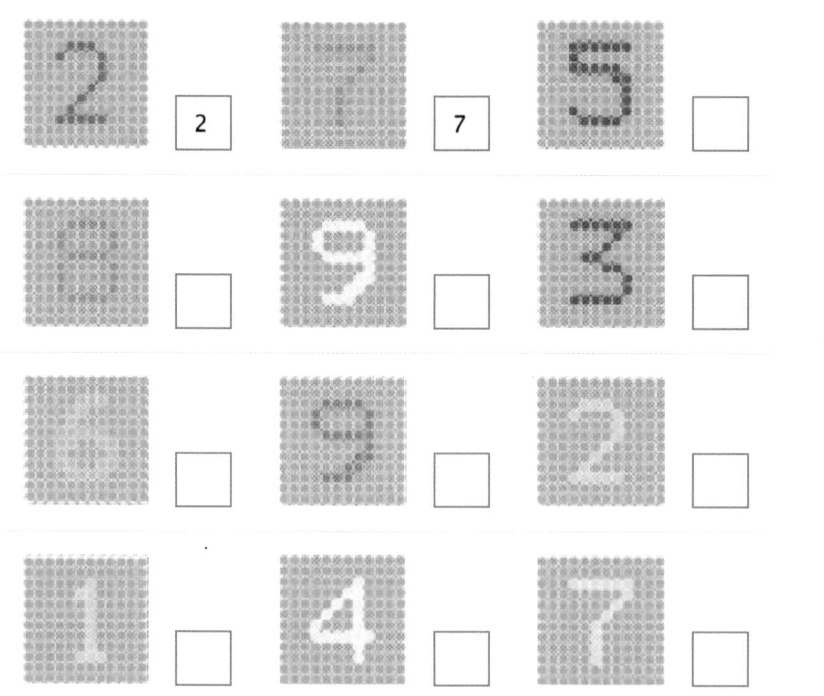

Progress page
The evaluation is made up of several different sections. This page tells the user which sections are already complete and which still need to be finished.

Sandina Miller is signed in, Sign out
Inclusive Accessible Archaeology Self-assessment toolkit: Questions

Your progress: self assessment toolkit

Your current assessment

Part 1: Initial self evaluation of abilities **[complete]**
view and print part 1 report

Part 2 report: abilities and tasks pre-fieldwork checklist **[complete]**
view and print part 2 report

Part 3: abilities and tasks post-fieldwork checklist **[not started]**
start part 3

Part 4: post-fieldwork self-evaluation of skills **[not started]**

exit toolkit

sign out and exit the toolkit

return to the toolkit front page | problems with this toolit? email us | privacy policy

Ambassade Hotel

Reservation form
Issued by Ambassade Hotel B. V., Netherlands
Design Buttgereit und Heidenreich GmbH, Haltern am See
Year 2002

A straightforward, no-obligation hotel reservation form. All the relevant information is laid out very plainly on a single page.

In the centre of Amsterdam

Reservierungen ❧ Reservierungsanfrage

Virtuelle Tour
Allgemeine Informationen
Zimmer
Frühstück Zimmerservice
Tagungs- und Konferenzräume
Reservierungen ❧
Anreise
Aktivitäten
Amsterdam
Ned Eng Fra Deu

Reservation form
Unlike many other online forms, in which compulsory fields are highlighted, the various options here are marked out simply and intelligently.

Ihre Zimmerschlüssel liegen für Sie bereit.

Für eine unverbindliche Reservierungsanfrage füllen Sie bitte das nachfolgende Formular aus. Wir werden uns dann bei Ihnen melden, um die Reservierung verbindlich zu bestätigen.

Ihre Absenderangaben:

Anrede [Herr]
Nachname
Vorname
Firma (optional)
Anschrift
PLZ
Ort
Land

Telefon
Mobiltelefon (optional)
Fax (optional)
eMail

Reservierungsanfrage:

Anreise am tt . mm . jjjj
Abreise am tt . mm . jjjj

Spezial-Angebote:

x Verschiedene Angebote 2006 Das Jahr von Rembrandt (info)

x Angebote 2007 (info)

Bitte tragen Sie eventuelle Optionen des gewählten Angebotes in das Dialogfeld „Bemerkungen oder Hinweise" ein (siehe auch Angebots-Beschreibung).

Anzahl der Zimmer:

Einzelzimmer Junior Suite
Doppelzimmer Senior Suite
Dreibettzimmer Appartement

Anzahl der Personen:

Erwachsene(r) Kind(er) (<12)

Zusätzliche Optionen:

Frühstück

Bemerkungen oder Hinweise:

Zimmertyp	Preis in Euro
Einzelzimmer	185
Doppelzimmer	185 - 225
Dreibettzimmer	225 - 255
Junior Suite	265 - 295
Senior Suite	295 - 335
Appartement	295 - 335

Zusatzleistung	Preis in Euro
Zusatzbett	30
Frühstück	16
Junior Frühstück	8

Preise gütig ab dem 01.03.2006

Preise inklusive Bedienung und MwSt.
Zzgl. 5% Kommunalsteuer.
Alle Preise unter Vorbehalt.

Ambassade Hotel B.V. ****
Herengracht 341
1016 AZ Amsterdam

Telefon: + 31 20 555 0 222
Fax: + 31 20 555 0 277

info@ambassade-hotel.nl

eHotel

Hotel reservations website

Issued by	eHotel AG
Design	Moniteurs Kommunikationsdesign GmbH, Berlin
Year	2006

eHotel is a web portal for over 85,000 hotels worldwide. The new design is effective, offering clear and relevant guidance to the user as well as being fast and secure.

ehotel
my professional choice
about ehotel corporates hotels partner

hotel search groups + meetings cancellation & changes my ehotel help
hotline UK 0871284 1827 (10p/min)

service center
Hotline
UK 0871284 1827 (10p/min)
INT +49 (30) 473 73 245
We call you back for assistance!
Skype us!
Live-chat with our hotel specialists
Email
servicecenter@ehotel.de
Monday - Friday
08:30 - 19:00 Uhr
newsletter
feedback

privacy
The protection of your privacy and your personal data is important to us
Our guarantee
- we follow the strict European legal regulations
- personal data are transmitted SSL-encrypted only
- personal data are not provided to unauthorized 3rd parties

click here for details
privacy
Abgesichert durch thawte
2009-01-31

search result list | booking

Destination | Berlin, Feb 5, 2009 - Feb 6, 2009, 1 Single room
back to search result list

Hilton
Mohrenstr. 30
10117 Berlin

Room: Standard room
Base rate: 400.00 EUR per night, 24.00 EUR Breakfast
Total: 400.00 EUR payable at hotel
Cancel penalty: Reservation may not be cancelled free of charge.

1 your Data | 2 Your reservation | 3 Your confirmation

Traveler
* Input is required for fields marked with a star.
Title - Salutation Mr.
Lastname* First name*

Special service request to the hotel
Your service request will be sent to the hotel without obligation. Additional charges might apply for the requested services.
additional service request max. 120 characters

Booked from:
* Input is required for fields marked with a star.
Company
Title - Salutation Mr.
Lastname* First name*
Phone*
Email*

reservation/guarantee
ehotel AG does not charge your credit card!
FAQ
The reservation is guaranteed for late arrival by credit card. The data is transmitted SSL encrypted.
* Input is required for fields marked with a star.
Credit card institute* Visa
Credit card number*
Credit card holder*
Credit card expiry* (Format: "MM/JJ")

Additional notification:
Email
Fax
+country code area code phone number e.g.: +493047373300
SMS
+country code area code phone number e.g.: +49 151 454545

Reservation form: Step 1
After the hotel has been selected, the room is reserved in three simple steps. Compulsory sections are clearly marked.

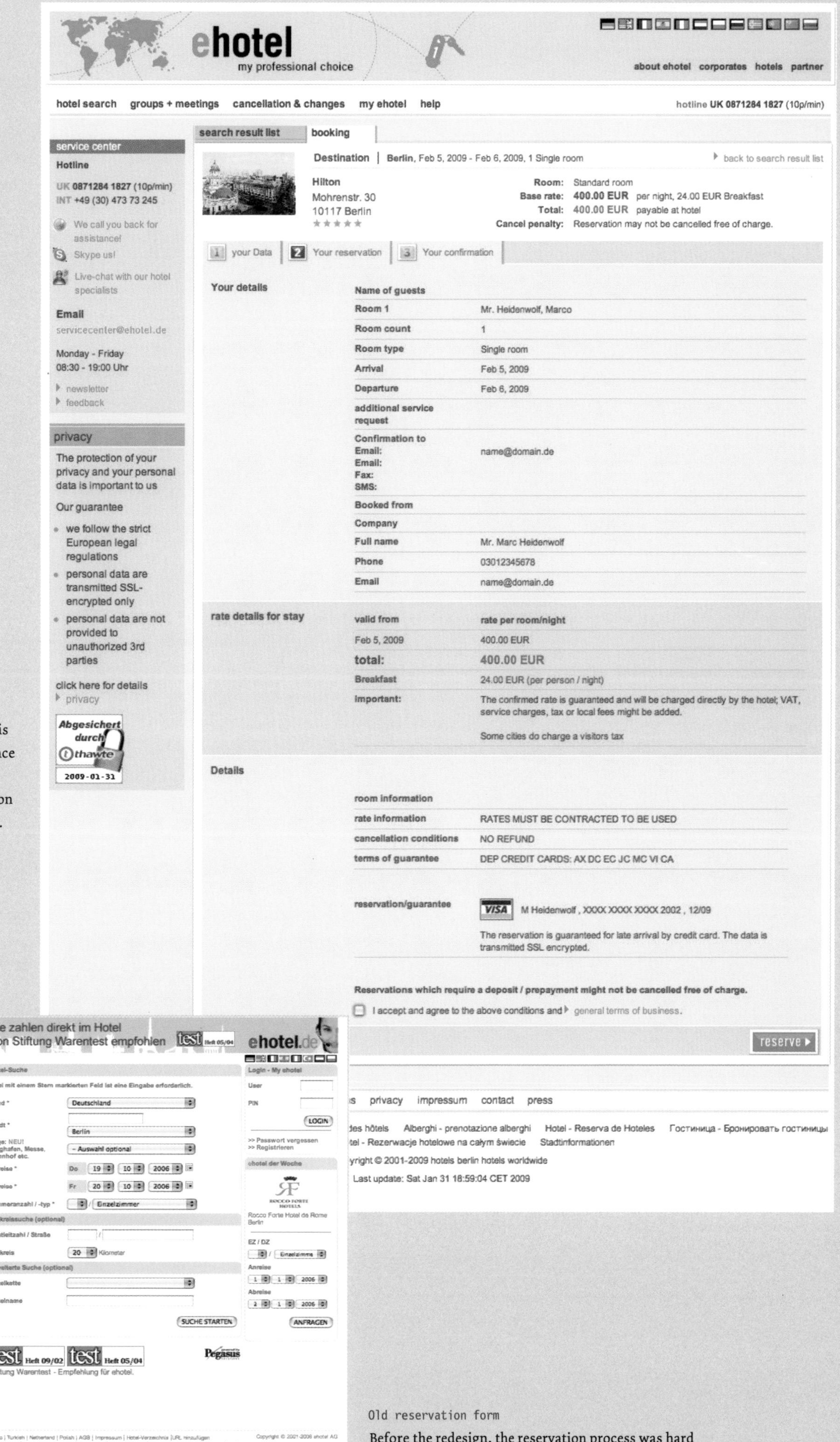

Reservation form: Step 2

In the second step, all the information is clearly presented once again for checking before the reservation is finally confirmed.

Old reservation form

Before the redesign, the reservation process was hard to follow, and the design was untidy and unsystematic.

DA Direkt Insurance

Premium calculator

Issued by DA Direkt, Germany
Design mediaman, Gesellschaft für Kommunikation mbH, Mainz
Year 2005

A very straightforward, clearly laid-out form for calculating car insurance premiums. The first step, illustrated here, provides a no-obligation quote which can then be accepted if desired in the second step.

Insurance quote form
Illustrations provide explanations of technical terms and enable the customer to find the relevant information quickly.

Beitragsrechner Autoversicherung

Mit Stern (*) gekennzeichnete Felder bitte unbedingt ausfüllen.

Autotyp

Mit Fahrzeugschein
Die erforderlichen Daten finden Sie in Ihrem Fahrzeugschein.

29.11.04 0588 775000 NEU
neue Zulassungs-papiere seit 01.10.2005

010262 0588 775000 PKW GESCHLOSSEN EURO 4 ALT

Herstellerschlüsselnummer *
Typschlüsselnummer *

Ohne Fahrzeugschein
Falls Sie den Fahrzeugschein nicht zur Hand haben, können Sie Ihren Autotyp hier suchen.

Autotyp suchen

Daten zum Fahrzeug

Fahrzeugneuwert — unbekannt / bekannt: EUR

Fahrzeugzubehörwert — unbekannt / bekannt: EUR

Kfz-Kennzeichen (zur Berechnung reicht das Ortskennzeichen) * — D F DA 215 — Stadt / Land

Bitte geben Sie an, wann das Fahrzeug zum ersten Mal zugelassen wurde oder bei einem Neufahrzeug voraussichtlich zugelassen wird.

Erstzulassung des Fahrzeuges * — 29.11.04 0588 775000 NEU — neue Zulassungs-papiere seit 1.10.2005 — 76 73 29.11.04 Farbe ZIFF.13:LANG BI ALT — TT MM JJJJ

Datum der Zulassung auf Ihren Namen — TT MM JJJJ

Wegfahrsperre * — ja / nein

Fahrzeug-Ident.-Nr.

Daten zur Fahrzeugnutzung

Hauptsächlicher Fahrzeugnutzer * — Versicherungsnehmer / Partner/in / Kinder / andere

Fahrzeugnutzung * — bitte wählen Sie...

Jahreskilometerleistung * — .000 km

Jahreskilometerleistung * .000 km

Nächtlicher Abstellort des Fahrzeuges * bitte wählen Sie...

Fahrer unter 25 Jahren * ( ) ja (•) nein

Auf wen wird das Fahrzeug zugelassen?
(•) auf mich
( ) meine Anschrift als Versicherungsnehmer ist die gleiche wie meine Anschrift, die ich als Fahrzeughalter habe
( ) meine Anschrift als Versicherungsnehmer ist eine andere als meine Anschrift als Fahrzeughalter
( ) auf eine andere Person

Versicherungsumfang

Versicherungsbeginn * TT MM JJJJ

Es soll nur ein Saisonkennzeichen sein (•) ja, von Monat bis Monat
( ) nein

Wollen Sie dieses Fahrzeug als Zweitfahrzeug versichern? *
( ) ja, ein Schadensfreiheitsrabatt für ein Zweitfahrzeug wurde bereits erworben
( ) ja, ein Schadensfreiheitsrabatt für ein Zweitfahrzeug wurde noch nicht erworben, da zum ersten Mal ein weiteres Fahrzeug auf ihren Namen versichert wird
(•) nein

Kfz-Haftplichtversicherung 50 Mio. EUR Pauschalabdeckung (8 Mio. EUR je Person)

Schadenfreiheitsklasse (SF) / momentaner Beitragssatz * Schadenfreiheitsklasse (SF)

Haftplichtschäden im laufenden Beitragsjahr (Anzahl)

Kfz-Kaskoversicherung

Dazu Teil-/Vollkaskodeckung mit Selbstbeteiligung *
( ) keine Kaskoversicherung
( ) Teilkasko (TK)
Selbstbeteiligung wählen
( ) Vollkasko (VK)
Selbstbeteiligung wählen

Schadenfreiheitsklasse (SF) / momentaner Beitragssatz (Vollkasko) Schadenfreiheitsklasse (SF)

Vollkaskoschäden im laufenden Beitragsjahr (Anzahl)

Zusätzlicher Schutz

Dazu Schutzbrief für 15 EUR/Jahr * ( ) ja (•) nein

Dazu Insassenunfallversicherung keine

Diese Daten benötigen wir noch zur Berechnung Ihres persönlichen Versicherungsangebotes

Ihr Geburtsdatum * TT MM JJJJ

Sie sind ein/e * ( ) Mann ( ) Frau

Sie gehören zur Tarifgruppe *
( ) Öffentlicher Dienst
( ) Bank, Sparkasse, Bausparkasse oder Versicherung
( ) Energieversorgungsunternehmen (Gas, Wasser, Strom)
( ) Bahn, Post, Telekom oder Lufthansa
(•) Normaltarif

Kinder unter 12 Jahren im Haushalt * ( ) ja (•) nein

Wohnen Sie in Ihrem eigenen Haus oder in einer Eigentumswohnung? * ( ) ja (•) nein

Sind Sie bereits DA Direkt-Kunde? * ( ) ja Wie lange schon?
(•) nein

[Berechnen]

Instead of the form being divided over several pages, it is presented on a single, very long page. This does mean that users have to scroll down, but at the same time they can get a swift and simple overview of the whole form.

unreal

Questionnaire

Design unreal, London
Mat Giles, Brian Eagle
Year 2005
Typefaces Helvetica and others

This tongue-in-cheek questionnaire from a London design studio is a shameless spoof of common-or-garden client questionnaires, and is an entertaining way to make a wait in the reception area feel much shorter.

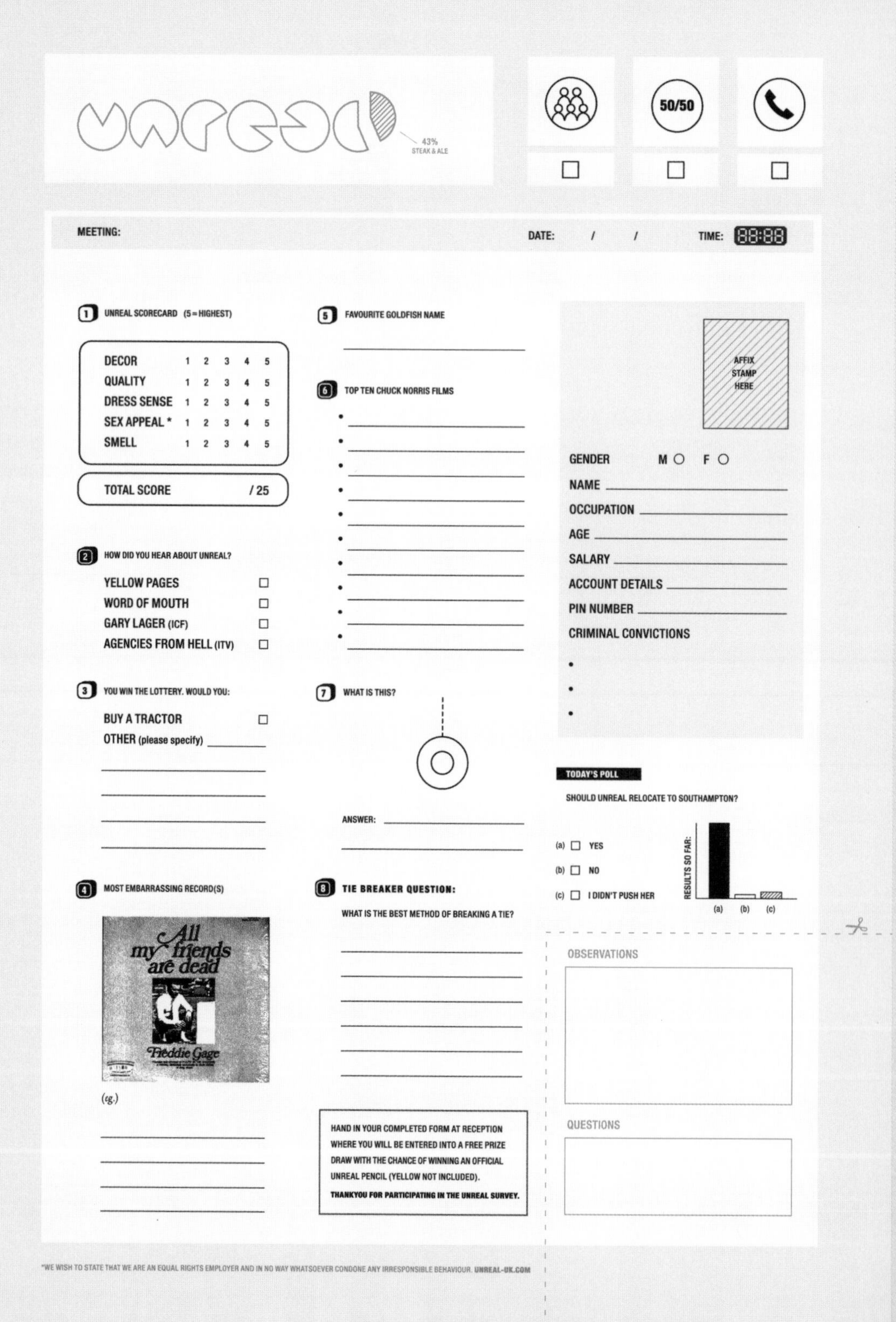

unreal
43% STEAK & ALE

50/50

MEETING:
DATE: / /
TIME: 88:88

1 UNREAL SCORECARD (5 = HIGHEST)

DECOR	1	2	3	4	5
QUALITY	1	2	3	4	5
DRESS SENSE	1	2	3	4	5
SEX APPEAL *	1	2	3	4	5
SMELL	1	2	3	4	5

TOTAL SCORE /25

2 HOW DID YOU HEAR ABOUT UNREAL?

- YELLOW PAGES ☐
- WORD OF MOUTH ☐
- GARY LAGER (ICF) ☐
- AGENCIES FROM HELL (ITV) ☐

3 YOU WIN THE LOTTERY. WOULD YOU:

- BUY A TRACTOR ☐
- OTHER (please specify) ______

4 MOST EMBARRASSING RECORD(S)

(eg.)

5 FAVOURITE GOLDFISH NAME

6 TOP TEN CHUCK NORRIS FILMS

7 WHAT IS THIS?

ANSWER:

8 TIE BREAKER QUESTION:
WHAT IS THE BEST METHOD OF BREAKING A TIE?

HAND IN YOUR COMPLETED FORM AT RECEPTION WHERE YOU WILL BE ENTERED INTO A FREE PRIZE DRAW WITH THE CHANCE OF WINNING AN OFFICIAL UNREAL PENCIL (YELLOW NOT INCLUDED).
THANKYOU FOR PARTICIPATING IN THE UNREAL SURVEY.

AFFIX STAMP HERE

GENDER M ○ F ○
NAME
OCCUPATION
AGE
SALARY
ACCOUNT DETAILS
PIN NUMBER
CRIMINAL CONVICTIONS

TODAY'S POLL
SHOULD UNREAL RELOCATE TO SOUTHAMPTON?
(a) ☐ YES
(b) ☐ NO
(c) ☐ I DIDN'T PUSH HER

RESULTS SO FAR:
(a) (b) (c)

OBSERVATIONS

QUESTIONS

*WE WISH TO STATE THAT WE ARE AN EQUAL RIGHTS EMPLOYER AND IN NO WAY WHATSOEVER CONDONE ANY IRRESPONSIBLE BEHAVIOUR. **UNREAL-UK.COM**

Questionnaire: A4
Even when a form is meant for fun, some questions should provide more food for thought than others, especially if they will be completed and left behind after an interview.

Maksimovic & Partners

Gift vouchers

Design Maksimovic & Partners, Saarbrücken
In-house design

Year 2006

Five stylish pages from a book of gift vouchers sent out by a design bureau to mark the New Year. The design plays with typical features of forms, which are exaggerated and parodied.

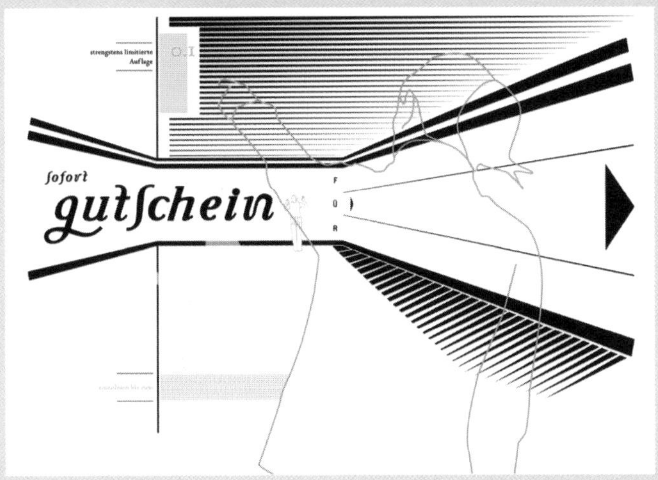

Fine lines

Straight or wavy fine-line patterns are a common design element in forms, bonds and banknotes. They are generally used to make forgery difficult.

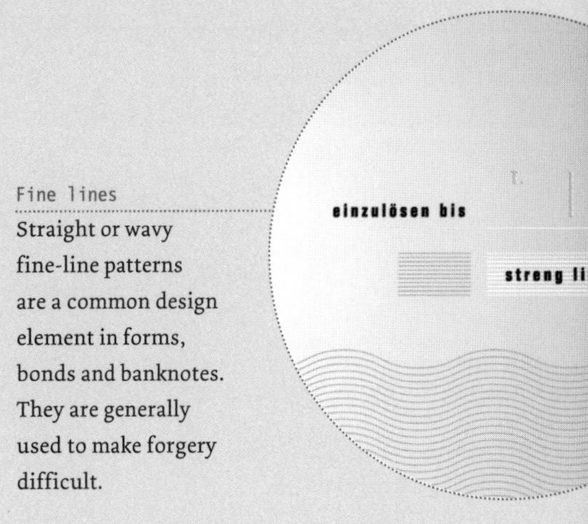

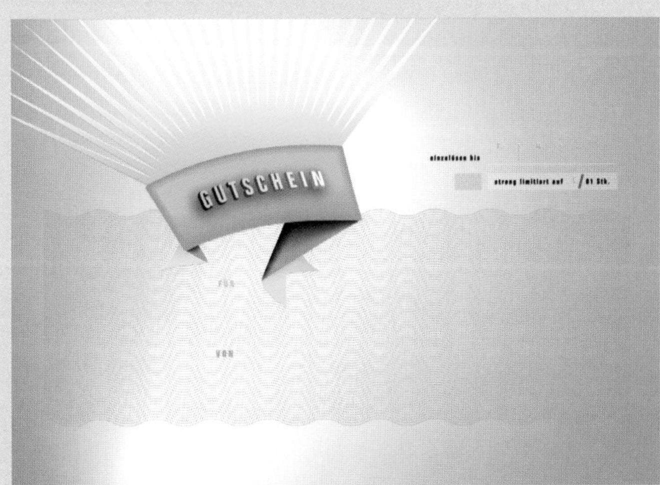

Vouchers: A5

They are printed in black, silver and bright pink.

Directory of designers

Here are contact details for all the designers and agencies whose work is featured in Chapter 3.

Andi Hemm Design
Nürtinger Strasse 41
70794 Filderstadt, Germany
→ 293

and/or/if
Oakridge Barn, Plum Park Estate
Watling Street, Paulerspury
Towcester NN12 6LQ, United Kingdom
www.andorif.co.uk
→ 226, 300

Atelier de Création Graphique
220, rue du Faubourg St.-Martin
75010 Paris, France
www.acgparis.com
→ 295

Boag Associates Ltd
20 Hanover Square
London W1S 1JY
United Kingdom
www.boag.co.uk
→ 236, 246, 266, 270, 277

Branding Healthcare
Eduard-Rosenthal-Strasse 30
99423 Weimar, Germany
www.branding-healthcare.de
→ 276

büro uebele
visuelle kommunikation
Heusteigstrasse 94A
70180 Stuttgart, Germany
www.uebele.com
→ 304

Butcher & Gundersen
3 Castle Row, Horticultural Place
London W4 4JQ
United Kingdom
www.bgundersen.com
→ 250

Buttgereit und Heidenreich GmbH
Turmstrasse 34
45721 Haltern am See, Germany
www.b-und-h.de
→ 309

cyclos design GmbH
Hafenweg 24
48155 Münster, Germany
www.cyclos-design.de
→ 292

edenspiekermann_
amsterdam berlin
Nieuwe Prinsengracht 89
1018 VR Amsterdam
The Netherlands
www.edenspiekermann.com
→ 220, 228, 248, 258

Fons Hickmann m23
Mariannenplatz 23
10997 Berlin, Germany
www.fonshickmann.com
→ 303

Heine Warnecke Design GmbH
Ludger-Hölker-Strasse
48727 Billerbeck, Germany
Gross-Buchholzer Strasse 28
30655 Hanover, Germany
www.heinewarnecke.com
→ 278, 279, 286

Hesse Design GmbH
Düsseldorfer Strasse 16
40699 Erkrath, Germany
www.hesse-design.com
→ 282

in(corporate communication + design GmbH
Rosenthaler Strasse 38
10178 Berlin, Germany
www.incorporate.de
→ 262

Information Engineers (UK) Ltd
York House, 3 Station Court
Great Shelford
Cambridge CB22 5NE
United Kingdom
www.idest.co.uk
→ 254

intégral ruedi baur et associés
5, rue Jules Vallès
75011 Paris, France
www.integral.ruedi-baur.eu
→ 218

Kognito Visuelle Gestaltung
Gesellschaft für Visuelle Gestaltung mbH
Chausseestrasse 35
10115 Berlin, Germany
www.kognito.de
→ 244

Maksimovic & Partners
Johannisstrasse 5
66111 Saarbrücken, Germany
www.maksimovic.de
→ 315

mediaman Gesellschaft
für Kommunikation mbH
Römerpassage 1
55116 Mainz, Germany
www.mediaman.de
→ 312

mikan
Mariko Takagi
Talstrasse 103
40217 Düsseldorf, Germany
www.mikan.de
→ 283

Moniteurs Komunikationsdesign
GmbH
Ackerstrasse 21/22
10115 Berlin, Germany
www.moniteurs.de
→ 310

Moving Brands
7–8 Charlotte Road
London EC2A 3DH
United Kingdom
www.movingbrands.com
→ 280

NODE Berlin Oslo
Anders Hofgaard
Lobeckstrasse 30–35
10969 Berlin, Germany
www.nodeberlin.com
→ 305

Oktober Kommunikationsdesign GmbH
Willy-Brandt-Platz 5–7
44867 Bochum, Germany
www.oktober.de
→ 260

Samenwerkende Ontwerpers bv
Herengracht 160
1016 BN Amsterdam
The Netherlands
www.sodesign.com
→ 296, 298

SEA Design
70 St John Street
London EC1M 4DT
United Kingdom
www.seadesign.co.uk
→ 284

Studio Dumbar
Lloydstraat 21
3024 EA Rotterdam
The Netherlands
www.studiodumbar.com
→ 224

Studio/lab
1 E Wacker Drive, Suite 3030
Chicago, IL 60601
USA
www.studiolab.com
→ 238, 290

Team Peter M. Scholz GmbH
Corporate Communications
Westfälische Strasse 33
10709 Berlin, Germany
www.t-ps.de
→ 252, 294

Text Matters
37 Upper Redands Road
Reading RG1 5JE
United Kingdom
www.textmatters.com
→ 234, 306

The Brand Union
11–33 St John Street
London EC1M 4AA
United Kingdom
www.thebrandunion.com
→ 242, 268

This is our work.
177 Jefferson Street #1
Brooklyn, NY 11206
USA
www.thisisourwork.net
→ 302

Thomas Manss & Company
3 Nile Street
London N1 7LX
United Kingdom
www.manss.com
→ 256, 274, 288

Total Identity
Paalbergweg 42
1105 BV Amsterdam ZO
The Netherlands
www.totalidentity.nl
→ 232

Two Twelve Associates, Inc.
902 Broadway, 20th Floor
New York, NY 10010
USA
www.twotwelve.com
→ 241

unreal
20 Rugby Street
London WC1N 3QZ
United Kingdom
www.unreal-uk.com
→ 314

Bibliography

The following selection of books and articles are useful starting points if you want to study the some of the topics discussed in this book in greater detail.

The function and use of forms

National Audit Office: *Difficult Forms: How Government Agencies Interact with Citizens.* London: The Stationery Office, 2003

Robyn Penman, David Sless (eds.): *Designing Information for People.* Canberra: Communication Research Institute of Australia, 1994

Robert Waller: 'Designing Government Forms: a Case Study', *Information Design Journal*, 1984, vol. 4, pp. 36–57

Robert Waller: *Clearer Communication in Financial Document Design.* London: Royal Mail, 1997

Design history

Werner Heine: 'Futura Without a Future: Kurt Schwitters' Typography for Hanover Town Council, 1929–1934', *Journal of Design History*, vol. 7, no. 2, 1994

Philip B. Meggs: *Meggs' History of Graphic Design*, 4th ed. New York and Chichester: John Wiley, 2006

Günther Roth: *Die Institution der kommunalen Sozialverwaltung.* Berlin: Duncker & Humblot, 1999

Corporate design and corporate identity

Rayan Abdullah, Roger Cziwerny: *Corporate Design. Kosten und Nutzen.* Mainz: Verlag Hermann Schmidt Mainz, 2007

Pat Matson Knapp: *Designing Corporate Identity: Graphic Design as a Business Strategy.* Gloucester, MA: Rockport, 2001

Veronica Napoles: *Corporate Identity Design.* New York and Chichester: John Wiley, 1988

Alina Wheeler: *Designing Brand Identity: A Complete Guide to Creating, Building, and Maintaining Strong Brands.* New York and Chichester: John Wiley, 2003

Form design

Robert Barnett: *Forms for People: Designing Forms that People Can Use.* Electronic & Database Publishing, 2005

Robert Waller: *Designing Forms and Catalogues.* 'Monotype Desktop Solutions' series, Chicago and Redhill: The Monotype Corporation, 1991

Patricia Wright: 'Informed Design for Forms', *Information Design Journal*, vol. 2, pp. 151–178

Principles of design

Jacques Bertin: *Semiology of Graphics. Diagrams, Networks, Maps.* Madison, WI: University of Wisconsin Press, 1984

Lisa Graham: 'Gestalt Laws of Perception: Using Gestalt Theory to Improve Print and Electronic Designs', *Design Principles and Practices: An International Journal*, vol. 3, no. 4, pp. 385–394

Style and language

Martin Cutts: *Oxford Guide to Plain English.* Oxford: Oxford University Press, 2007

Robert D. Eagleson: *Writing in Plain English.* Canberra: Australian Government Publishing Service, 1990

Elizabeth M. Murphy, Shelagh Snell: *Effective Writing: Plain English at Work.* London: Pitman, 1991

Robert Ritter: *The Oxford Style Manual.* Oxford: Oxford University Press, 2003

University of Chicago: *The Chicago Manual of Style*, 15th ed. Chicago: University of Chicago Press, 2003

Accessibility

Adobe Systems, Inc.: *Creating Accessible PDF Forms with Acrobat 9 Pro.* http://www.adobe.com/accessibility/products/acrobat/training.html

Web Accessibility Initiative (WAI): *WAI Resources on Introducing Web Accessibility.* http://www.w3.org/WAI/gettingstarted/Overview.html

Typography

Robert Bringhurst: *The Elements of Typographic Style.* Vancouver: Hartley & Marks Publishers, 2004

Albert Kapr, Walter Schiller: *Gestalt und Funktion der Typografie.* Leipzig: VEB Fachbuchverlag, 1977

Jost Hochuli: *Detail in Typography.* London: Hyphen Press, 2008

Michael Wörgötter: *Type Selector: The User-Friendly Font Swatch.* London: Thames & Hudson, 2006

Questionnaires

Ian Brace: *Questionnaire Design. How to Plan, Structure and Write Survey Material for Effective Market Research.* London: Kogan Page Ltd, 2004

William Foddy: *Constructing Questions for Interviews and Questionnaires.* Cambridge: Cambridge University Press, 1993

Print production

Kaj Johansson, Peter Lundberg, Robert Ryberg: *A Guide to Graphic Print Production*, 2nd ed. Hoboken, NJ: Wiley & Sons, 2007

Helmut Kipphan (ed.): *Handbook of Print Media.* Berlin and New York: Springer, 2001

Digital forms

Ted Padova, Angie Okamoto: *PDF Forms: Using Acrobat and LiveCycle Designer Bible.* London: John Wiley & Sons, 2009

Luke Wroblewski: *Web Form Design: Filling in the Blanks.* Brooklyn, NY: Rosenfeld Media, 2008

Luke Wroblewski: *Technical Communication Summit: Best Practices for Form Design.* http://www.lukew.com/resources/articles/WebForms_LukeW.pdf

Index

Picture credits

10 Visitor's book, German Democratic Republic, 1953: author's collection

12 Declaration of Intention, US Department of Labor, 1953: author's collection

14 Coroner's form, Druckhaus Panzig, Germany, 1999: author's collection

18 Textile store receipt, minä perhonen, 2007: designed by Atsuki Kikuchi (Bluemark Inc.), Japan

20 First aid treatment record, Charité Universitätsmedizin Berlin, 2005*: author's collection

22 Parcel label, Deutsche Postordnung, Germany, 1964: private collection of Prof. Betina Müller

24 Card breakdown record, ADAC e. V., Munich, 2005*: author's collection

26 Memo sheet, Federal Administration of Switzerland, 1995: author's collection

28 Aerial photograph, Aerowest, 2007

57 Letter of indulgence, 1455: Niedersächsische Staats- und Universitätsbibliothek Göttingen, Germany

59 French tax forms, 1790–91: Zurich Central Library, Switzerland

61 Passenger list of the ocean liner *Nevada*, 1892: The Statue of Liberty-Ellis Island Foundation, Inc., New York: www.ellisisland.org

63 Invoice from the Ernst Plange metalware factory, 1924*: author's collection · Bill of exchange, 1926*: author's collection · Receipt, 1924*: author's collection

65 Certificate of cremation, Hanover City Council, 1929, designed by Kurt Schwitters: bpk/Kunstbibliothek, Staatliche Museen zu Berlin · Tax declaration for imported beer, Hanover City Council tax office, 1929, designed by Kurt Schwitters: bpk/Kunstbibliothek, Staatliche Museen zu Berlin · Examination form, City Tuberculosis Hospital, Hanover, 1929, designed by Kurt Schwitters: bpk/Kunstbibliothek, Staatliche Museen zu Berlin · All forms by Schwitters: photos by Dietmar Katz

67 *Ahnenpass* (proof of ancestry), Germany, 1940s: author's collection · Certificate of expatriation, 1943: Brandenburgisches Landeshauptarchiv, Rep. 36A Oberfinanzpräsident Berlin-Brandenburg (II) KK · Certificate of exclusion from the Wehrmacht. 1939: Archiv Gedenk- und Bildungsstätte Haus der Wannsee-Konferenz, Joseph Chotzen Estate

69 Application form, British Telecommunications Prestel, UK, c. 1983: University of Reading, Department of Typography & Graphic Communication

71 Screenshot, *Do it online*, Directgov, UK, 2009: www.direct.gov.uk/en/Dioli/DoItOnline/index.htm · Screenshot, *Apply for a provisional licence*, Directgov, UK, 2009: motoring.direct.gov.uk/service/DvoConsumer.portal?_nfpb=true&_pageLabel=FAP&_nfls=falseg.direct.g · Screenshot, *How to Enrol*, Australian Electoral Commission, Australia, 2009: www.aec.gov.au/Enrolling_to_vote/How_To_Enrol/index.htm · Screenshot, *Electoral Enrolment*, Australian Electoral Commission, Australia, 2009: www.aec.gov.au/enrolment/forms/ER016w_NSW_0208_F.pdf

78 Unemployment benefit form (PDF), Bundesagentur für Arbeit, Nuremberg, Germany, 2006: www.arbeitsagentur.de/nn_26642/Navigation/zentral/Formulare/Buerger/Arbeitslosengeld-II/Arbeitslosengeld-II-Nav.html · State pension claim, The Pension Service, Department for Work and Pensions, UK, 2006*: author's collection · Postal application for a practical driving test appointment (PDF), UK, 2008*: www.direct.gov.uk/cy/Motoring/LearnerAndNewDrivers/PracticalTest/DG_4022539?IdcService=GET_FILE&dID=180650&Rendition=Web · Passenger's charter claim, XC Trains Ltd, UK, 2008*: author's collection · Credit card agreement, MBNA Europe Bank Limited, UK, 2008*: author's collection

79 Naturalization form (PDF), City of Hamburg, Department of the Interior, 2005: http://fhh.hamburg.de · Application form for a Vehicle Registration Certificate V5C, Driver and Vehicle Licensing Agency, Department for Transport, UK, 2007*: author's collection · Application for planning permission (PDF), Cerfa, France, 2004: http://vosdroits.service-public.fr/particuliers/N310.xhtml · Application for planning permission (PDF), Ministry of Housing, Spatial Planning and the Environment, Netherlands, 2003: http://stadsbron.groningen.nl/contents/8063/aanvraag_bouwvergunning_nr7064.pdf · Application for planning permission (PDF), City Department for Urban Planning, Berlin, 2007: http://www.stadtentwicklung.berlin.de/service/formulare/de/bauen.shtml

82 Register of Electors 2009, Oxford City Council, UK, 2008: author's collection · New Jersey Voter Registration form, US: www.squandems.org/SQ_/Images/Forms/Voter%20Registration%20Form_Page_1.jpg · Business registration GewA1, Berlin, 1997: author's collection · TV licence registration, rbb. GEZ, Cologne, Germany, 2004: author's collection · Library registration, Deutsche Bücherei, CIP-Zentrale Leipzig, Germany, 2004*: author's collection

83 Oxfordshire Adult Learning Enrolment Form 2008/2009, Oxfordshire County Council, UK, 2008*: author's collection · Energy transfer request/registration, Southern Electric, UK, 2007: author's collection · City of Weimar marriage registration (PDF), Form-Solutions, Germany, 2005: https://pdf.form-solutions.net/servlet/com.burg.pdf.FillServlet?sid=kq3c1VdRJ5GzP2a9XJJCQZpc7pmTMvJR&j=z.pdf · Victoria & Albert Museum membership form, Friends of the V&A, London, 2008*: author's collection

86 Visa waiver form, US Department of Justice, 2005*: author's collection · Landing card, UK Border Agency, Home Office, UK, 2008*: author's collection · US Individual Income Tax Return, Form 1040, Department of the Treasury – Internal Revenue Service, 2005: http://commons.wikimedia.org/wiki/Image:Form_1040,_2005.jpg · Employment page (PDF), HM Revenue & Customs, UK, 2007*: www.hmrc.gov.uk/forms/sa102.pdf · Income Tax and Benefit Return (PDF), Canada Revenue Agency, 2007*: www.informativetax.ca/forms/5000-r-07e.pdf

87 Voluntary Petition (PDF), United States Bankruptcy Court, Southern District of New York, 2008: http://www.winterhouse.com/designobserver/lehman.pdf · Tax return form for 2006 (PDF). Ministry of Finance, Austria, 2006: www.bmf.gv.at/service/formulare/steuern/auswahl/_start.htm?FNR=E1 · Tax return form 2006 (PDF), Cerfa, France, 2006: http://vosdroits.service-public.fr/particuliers/F358.xhtml · Tax return form Est 1 A 2006 (PDF), Ministry of Finance, Germany, 2007: http://www.bundesfinanzministerium.de/cln_03/nn_3380/DE/Steuern/Ihre__Steuererklaerung/node.html

90 Customer order for Sunrise ADSL and Sunrise Select, TDC Switzerland AG, 2005: author's collection · Order form, The Organic Gardening Catalogue, UK, 2008: author's collection · Order form for a travel pass (PDF), Berliner Verkehrsbetriebe (BVG), Germany, 2007: http://www.bvg.de/index.php/de/Bvg/Index/folder/215 · IsarCard60 Order Form (PDF), Münchner Verkehrsgesellschaft mbH (MVG), Germany, 2009: www.mvg-mobil.de/pdf-dateien/mvv-abo/bestellscheine/mvg_isarcard60_e.pdf · FlexiPass application (PDF), CityRail, NSW Government, Australia, 2009: http://www.cityrail.info/fares/FlexiPass_Application.pdf

91 Royal Mail recorded and special delivery certificates, Royal Mail, UK, 2008*: author's collection · SWISS LOTTO, SWISSLOS, Basel, Switzerland; Blockfabrik AG, Wattwil, 2004: author's collection · Deposit slip, United Overseas Bank (Thai) Public Company Limited, 2006: author's collection · Barclays WellWoman Plan Acceptance Form, Barclays Insurance Health Protection Unit, UK, 2008*: author's collection · Form for opening a company bank account, Deutsche Bank, Privat und Geschäftskunden AG, Germany, 2007*: author's collection · Car rental contract, Robben & Wientjes OHG, Berlin, 2007*: author's collection

94 Invoice, DSGi Business, UK, 2008: author's collection · Council tax bill, Oxford City Council, UK, 2008: author's collection · Bill, Athens, Greece, 2007*: author's collection · Restaurant bill, Taverna L' Antica Grotta, Tropea, Italy, 2005*: author's collection · Receipt, Thailand, 2006*: author's collection · Receipt, USA, 2005*: author's collection

95 Phone bill, British Telecommunications plc, UK, 2008: author's collection · Currency exchange receipt, La Post, Morocco, 2006*: author's collection · Currency exchange receipt, Postbank, Netherlands, 1998*: author's collection · Outpatient receipt, Bandon International Hospital, Bophut Koh Samui, Thailand, 2006*: author's collection

98 Notice of exemption from military service, District Recruitment Office, Berlin, Germany, 1993: author's collection · Parking violation notice, Maryland National Capital Park Police, US, 2004: author's collection · Tax demand for 2004, Finanzamt Mitte/Tiergarten, Berlin, 2005: author's collection · 2005–2006 property tax bill, KCTTC Taxpayer Service Center, Bakersfield, CA, US, 2006: www.kcttc.co.kern.ca.us/projects.cfm · 3rd Quarter Tax 2004, KCTTC Taxpayer Service Center, Bakersfield, CA, US, 2004: www.kcttc.co.kern.ca.us/projects.cfm

99 Gas statement, Southern Electric, UK, 2008: author's collection · Missed delivery notice, DPD, 2008: author's collection · Missed delivery notice, Royal Mail, 2008: author's collection

102 Official Ballot for Brookline, General Election 2004, State of New Hampshire, US, 2004: www.brookline.nh.us/documents/news/Ballot.jpg · Ballot paper, Republic of South Africa, 1994 · Ballot paper for German federal election, 2005: author's collection · Customer feedback questionnaire, Oxford City Council, UK, 2008*: author's collection · Financial Planning questionnaire, Barclays Bank PLC, UK, 2006: author's collection · Questionnaire, Quarantine Station, Japan, 2008: author's collection

103 Renaissance Leipzig Hotel questionnaire, Renaissance Hotels & Resorts, Germany, 2008: author's collection · Census of Jails, US Department of Commerce, Bureau of the Census, US, 1999: www.ojp.usdoj.gov/bjs/pub/pdf/cj-3.pdf · Short form census questionnaire, United Republic of Tanzania, 2002: http://www.tanzania.go.tz/census/short_q.htm

106 Birth certificate, UK, 2005: author's collection · Certificate of death, State of Washington, Department of Health, US, 2007: author's collection · Master's certificate, University of Illinois, 2008: author's collection · Redesigned master's certificate, Fachhochschule Potsdam, Germany, designed by Borries Schwesinger, 2005 · University certificate, Ukraine: www.energomash.spb.ru/new_copy/images/Diplom3-1.jpg

107 Certificate of horse ownership, Verband der Pferdezüchter Mecklenburg/Vorpommern e. V., FN Verlag, Germany, 1999: collection of Dr Gero Kärst · Doctor's registration certificate, German Democratic Republic, 1984*: collection of Dr Gero Kärst · Security pass for Erich Honecker, leader of the GDR, for the Conference on Security and Cooperation in Europe, Helsinki, 1975: Deutsches Historisches Museum, Berlin · Visitor pass, DURABLE, UK, 2008: author's collection · Michigan daily fishing permit, US, 1993: author's collection

110 Eurostar Italia ticket, Trenitalia, Italy, 2005*: author's collection · Amtrak ticket, Magnetic Ticket & Label Corp., US, 2007*: author's collection · Bus ticket, Thailand, 2006*: author's collection · Ticket, San Francisco Municipal Railway (Muni), US, 2007*: author's collection · Airport ticket, Athens, 2007*: author's collection · Train ticket, Schweizer Bundesbahnen, Switzerland, 2007*: author's collection

111 Share certificate, RENUM AG, Germany, 2004: designed by BRANDIT Marketing & Kommunikation, Cologne · Bank cheque, Deutsche Bank AG, Germany, 2004*: author's collection · Theatre ticket, Hans Otto Theater Potsdam, Germany, 2006: designed by formdusche, Berlin · Online ticket, Deutsche Bahn AG, Germany, 2006: author's collection · National Express e-Ticket, National Express Ltd, UK, 2008: author's collection · Online rail ticket, SNCF, France, 2007: author's collection

114 Car repair record, ADAC e. V., Munich, Germany, 2005*: author's collection · Bomb threat checklist (PDF), Homeland Security, US, 2009*: www.dhs.gov/xlibrary/assets/ocso-bomb_threat_samepage-brochure.pdf · Landlord's gas safety record, CORGI, UK, 2008*: author's collection · Office memo, Waser Bürocenter, Buchs, Switzerland, 2005*: author's collection

115 Car rental checklist, Sixt, Portugal, 2007: author's collection · Doctor's certificate, Bandon International Hospital, Bophut Koh Samui, Thailand, 2006*: author's collection · Big Garden Birdwatch (PDF), RSPB, UK, 2009: www.rspb.org.uk/images/bgbw_sheet_2009_tcm9-201495.pdf · Driving test report (PDF), Driving Standards Agency, UK, 2007*: www.dsa.gov.uk/download.asp?path=/Documents/forms/DL2504.07version.pdf

118 Donation form, Water Aid, UK, 2008: author's collection · Direct mail, Deutsche Bahn AG, Germany, 2006: author's collection · Direct mail for gas care plans, British Gas, UK, 2008: author's collection

119 Direct mail with reader questionnaire, *Die Zeit*, Germany, 2007: author's collection · Discount coupons, Sun Store, Saint Sulpice, Switzerland, 2007*: author's collection · Direct mail for collectable postage stamps, Deutsche Post AG, Bonn, Germany, 2006: author's collection

Dates listed without an asterisk refer to the year of printing; dates listed with an asterisk refer to the year of completion. Some forms have been anonymized for data protection reasons. Web addresses provided were correct at the time of printing.

Every effort has been made to trace the copyright holders of the forms contained in this book and we apologize for any unintentional omissions. We would be pleased to insert the appropriate acknowledgment in any subsequent edition of this publication.

Picture credits for Chapter 3 are not listed here, but appear on the pages in question.

Acknowledgments

Many thanks to	all the designers, studios, ad agencies, archives, libraries, businesses, public services, institutions, friends and acquaintances who granted us their kind permission to reproduce forms that they designed or distributed
and	FontShop for kindly providing fonts
and	Corina Höppner, Zurich; Judith Schalansky, Berlin; Prof. Betina Müller, Potsdam; Prof. Mathias Beyrow, Berlin; Peter M. Scholz, Berlin; Prof. Erik Spiekermann, Berlin; Beat Müller, Basel; Francien Malecki, Amsterdam; Margriet Blom, Amsterdam; Uta Oettel, Potsdam; Thekla Siedt, Berlin; Leo H. Schwesinger, Leipzig; formdusche, Berlin; Andrew Boag, London; Rob Waller, Reading; for their support, help, critiques, ideas and corrections.

Fonts: FF Letter Gothic, FF Profile, FF InfoText,
courtesy of FSI FontShop International, www.fontshop.de

Original layout, cover design and illustrations by Borries Schwesinger

Translated from the German *Formulare gestalten* by David H. Wilson

The translation of this work was supported by a grant from the Goethe-Institut which is funded by the German Ministry of Foreign Affairs.

First published in 2010 in hardcover in the United States of America by Thames & Hudson Inc., 500 Fifth Avenue, New York, New York 10110

thamesandhudsonusa.com

Library of Congress Catalog Card Number 2009936403

ISBN 978-0-500-51508-2

Printed and bound in China by Hong Kong Graphics and Printing Ltd.